Why is it so hard to find quality acting work?

Being a trained professional doesn't count for much when the number of actors looking for work is so much greater than the amount of work available. Most actors have a very limited choice when it comes to hearing about quality acting opportunities:

Your Agent

Most agents will submit only one or two clients for each role. Employers who may have preferred to cast you for a role will often never get the opportunity to see your CV and headshot. As a result, many actors find that they receive fewer than 6 casting invitations a year via their agent.

Casting Reports and Casting Websites

Many employers find that publishing a casting breakdown in a casting report or on a casting website will result in them being swamped with hundreds of completely unsuitable CVs and headshots. Many of those suggestions will be from untrained, inexperienced actors who do not meet the requirements of the role. As a result, many employers refuse to publish breakdowns for paid acting work. This is the reason why casting reports are often filled with details of unpaid work or only seeking actors with very unusual physical characteristics or skills.

CastNet

is a casting service with a difference. We are very selective about the actors we allow to join this service. You must have trained at an accredited drama school and have a minimum of three professional acting credits before we will even consider your application.

We do not simply distribute casting information. We carefully check that you only receive details of projects that you want to do containing roles that precisely match your skills, physicality and playing age. We then send your CV and headshot directly to the employer or casting director on your behalf. We take no commission from any work found so this service does not conflict with your agent if you are represented.

Because we are so selective about the actors allowed to join CastNet and only send employers suggestions of actors that precisely meet their requirements, many actors find that they gain more work from CastNet than from any other source.

A subscription to CastNet is only £6.50 per week and is fully tax-deductible. This includes the cost of all submissions, headshots and all of the benefits listed opposite. There is no minimum commitment. You may stop, start or suspend your subscription at any time.

To read more information about this service and to request an application form, please contact us or visit the website at www.castingnetwork.co.uk

The Benefits

• Have submissions made on your behalf for personally selected film, TV, commercials, corporate and theatre work. The cost of all headshots is included in the subscription fee.

• Receive a free text message when new casting information is available and new casting invitations are received.

• Receive free inclusion in the "CastNet Directory" distributed to more than 2,000 employers.

• Have your CV placed on our website with instant messaging facility for casting directors to contact you by e-mail or free text message. We'll also include 4 photographs, your showreel and voice demo at no extra charge.

• Receive a weekly report detailing every production for which you have been submitted.

• Receive free independent assessments of your headshot for character type and playing age.

• Have the chance to be considered for productions exclusively available to CastNet actors.

Plus many other benefits – See website for details

AY2007/AY27/e

web: www.castingnetwork.co.uk - tel: 0800 542 4459 - email: admin@castingnetwork.co.uk

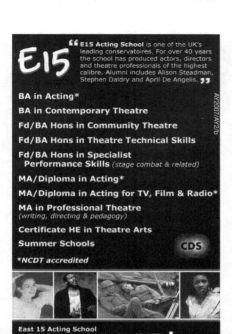

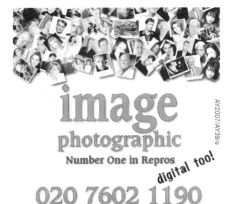

ROSIE STILL
020 8857 6920 or 07767 038658

Sophie Noon

Charlie Clements

Debra Stephenson

Gabrielle Bradshaw

Ed Ward

Liz Fraser

Chris Jarvis

Katie Parker

Ayo Fawole

Jaclyn Bradley

Ian Young

Bella Emberg

www.rosiestillphotography.com

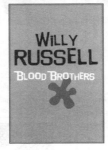
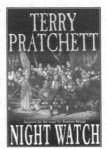
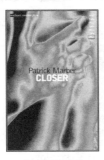

Actors'

YEARBOOK

2007

The essential resource for anyone
wanting to work as an actor

Edited by Simon Dunmore and Andrew Piper

A & C Black • London

Third edition 2006
A & C Black Publishers Limited
38 Soho Square, London W1D 3HB
www.acblack.com

© 2006 A & C Black Publishers Limited

ISBN-10: 0–7136–7385–0
ISBN 13: 978–0–7136–7385–2

A CIP catalogue record for this book is available from the British Library.

The publishers make no representation, express or implied, with regard to the accuracy of
the information contained in this book and cannot accept any legal responsibility for any
errors or omissions that may take place.

This book is produced using paper that is made from wood grown in managed, sustainable forests. It is natural, renewable and recyclable. The logging and manufacturing
processes conform to the environmental regulations of the country of origin.

Typeset by QPM from David Lewis XML Associates Ltd
Printed and bound in Great Britain by William Clowes, Beccles, Suffolk

Contents

Foreword

Other people's words.

There are a lot of them out there. We make our living saying them. Why should you bother with these?

This is a nice fat book, which will take a good amount of time to work through. How can I justify taking more of your time in a foreword? As actor, then as director, and most recently as artistic director (of Sheffield Theatres – there we are under Crucible Theatre, on page 102), I have had to deal with the vagaries of this business for nearly 20 years. In that time, casting directors have become obligatory for plays, where before they largely only did films or telly; the number of agencies and actors in training has gone through the roof; and *Spotlight* has got much fatter – it used to be four volumes, it's now ten. Since I started last year at Sheffield, I've been sent over a thousand CVs, and nearly as many invitations to see people's work. All are read, acknowledged, and filed, and I see those shows that I can. But there are no more jobs than there were 20 years ago. As Tarzan said: "It's a bloody jungle out there." So what will help you distinguish yourself from the multitude?

First of all, talent. There is such a thing. It's deeply unfashionable to say so, but it does exist, and it eventually makes a difference. Let's hope you have it. Second, the talent for having talent, which is just as important. Try to keep your spirits up. If, in the depths of your darkest night, you can still answer with a resounding 'yes', the question 'must I act?', and you suspect that you might be quite good at it, then hi diddle di dee, an actor's life may be for you; look after your mental and physical health and begin to use this book to your advantage. The practicalities of the profession are one thing you can master – they needn't be allowed to master you. That's where this admirable volume comes in.

It's who you love, not who loves you, that makes you the person you are. There are thousands of organisations out there willing to take your money in return for training, representation, taking your photograph, printing your photograph, putting your photograph on a CD Rom … Some of these organisations are better than others. Only detailed study, asking around and getting a feel for the people concerned will tell you which ones you should favour. A judicious use of this book will save you time and money, so the hours you might have spent working in the bar can be spent learning your lines, or practising your dancing or fencing, or just catching up on much-needed sleep.

The field of possible employment for an actor today is actually extraordinarily wide, so try to do a bit of everything (it should mean less time between jobs). Try to be the sort of actor who wants work and not just stardom. Try to go to the theatre occasionally, and try to hang out with real people, not just actors – after all, you will very rarely get to play an actor …

And join our Union. Be a loud, proud, audible member. The contracts that you work on have been negotiated by Equity, and it's right that you should be a member if you intend to use them. The insurance and backstage cover, the pension plan and the protection of your professional name are each worth the subscription by themselves, but there's a better reason to join. Our professional lives (and increasingly, our personal lives) can be fragmented, sometimes lonely. Your Equity card is a sign that you are a valued brother or sister in a proud profession, and your voice matters.

(And if you ever get stuck for inspiration, read David Mamet's introduction to *A Practical Handbook for the Actor* – it's top.)

Good luck.

Samuel West
Artistic Director, Sheffield Theatres
April 2006

Introduction

It is well known that an actor's life is not an easy one. Those who aspire to the 'bright lights' face a seemingly bewildering array of courses, audition processes and funding methods. Drama school graduates confront a bedazzling array of agents, casting directors and production companies (in all media) to whom they could send their precious CVs and photographs. Experienced actors try to become philosophical about how secure-seeming 'contacts' they once had have been superseded by a new generation. ('There's a new bunch of schoolboys running the networks each week.' Joan Collins) The art and crafts of acting are difficult enough – the prospect of navigating through 'bald' lists of services and potential employers can overwhelm all but the most determined. Those with time and money can simply blitz every agent (for instance) that they can find, in the hope that some may respond with offers of representation – this will cost several hundred pounds, let alone the time spent stuffing envelopes. And the chances of success, with this kind of unfocused approach, will be extremely limited. Judicious targeting, using the information in this book and your own research (especially on the Internet), can save a considerable amount of money and will give you a greater chance of satisfaction and success.

The aim of this book is also to make some more detailed sense of the ever-diversifying world of professional acting – from training to the wide range of companies offering work in all media, via the 'brokers' (agents and casting directors) of much of that work. In addition, you will find more details of the available services (photographers, showreel companies, and so on) so that you can make detailed comparisons before committing your precious funds. In order to help you cut your way through the 'jungle' of performing arts information, the listings are restricted to those directly relevant to aspiring and work-seeking actors. (For instance, agents who only represent directors, designers, and so forth, are not included.) Careful study of the section(s) appropriate to you at a particular moment could save you time and money through more accurate 'targeting' of your intentions – whether looking for appropriate training, whom to send your CV and photograph to, where to get your showreel made, and so forth.

This book contains details of those organisations and individuals from whom we were able to glean more full information, beyond the basic contact details. Some were prepared to provide helpful information but requested that their telephone numbers, for instance, should not be included. You'll find more organisations listed in *Contacts* (published an-nually by The Spotlight). Some individuals and organisations declined to contribute to this book, apparently fearful of attracting even more actor-submissions. Some simply did not respond. Some information will go out of date – new companies will start up and others go out of business – and personnel will change; this profession has a highly mobile population. However, the listings will help focus your research and enable you to 'target' more accurately and efficiently.

Actors' Yearbook is designed to work in harmony with my *An Actor's Guide to Getting Work* (4th edition, A&C Black, 2004), in which you will find much more detailed advice on how to market yourself and enhance your chances as a professional actor.

Simon Dunmore
Consultant Editor
www.simon.dunmore.btinternet.co.uk

Training
Introduction

This section is largely devoted to those who are 18 and older. This is not to dismiss the fact that there is training (of varying kinds) for those under that age. However, the field is so wide that the confines of this book limit listings to the major organisations only.

In spite of the fact that a minority of well-known actors did not formally train, it is very important for today's aspirant to do so. An ever-increasing number of people want to become actors, so those with 'casting clout' (agents, casting directors and directors) have more and more people to choose from. Doesn't it make more sense to select from those who've undergone the rigours of a respected training process? It is an essential fact that the acting industry works on very tight time-scales and budgets – trained actors should be quicker, more reliable and, usually, more inventive than their untrained counterparts. For instance, an untrained voice that cracks up after a few days of live performance is time-consuming and costly for a management – only the larger productions can afford under-studies. An untrained actor, who may look good on camera, will take time to learn how to work on a television set, where time spent keeping technicians waiting is very, very expensive. A fight (in a theatre or on camera) has to be staged so that it (a) looks real, (b) is safe for the participants and (c) can be seen properly by camera and/or audience – actors who've been trained in the essentials of combat will make this staging process much, much quicker. Moving correctly in period costumes, performing all kinds of formal dance and using microphones properly are just a few of the other time-saving skills that the trained actor can bring to a production. It is only an exceptional few who, nowadays, have the opportunity to 'learn on the job'.

For today's aspiring actor, it is important to train on a professionally recognised course. The established drama schools are the focus of such training. There are acting-related university degree courses which have a reasonable proportion of vocational training (as well as academic work) and there are numerous part-time, short-term and 'foundation' courses which will give you basic insights into the many crafts involved in acting. However, because of the intense competition, a full-time drama school course of at least a year is essential for most people.

For those who have already trained, there are opportunities to learn new skills and refine those already acquired, or simply to keep them in trim when the acting work is not coming in. The latter is very important, as you can be asked to demonstrate your skills at very short notice. Being an actor is a bit like being a fireman – without the regular salary. Also, the more you can legitimately add to the 'Skills' section of your CV, the more you can enhance your chances of finding work.

Training for the under-18s

It is a fact that many child stars do not succeed as adult actors. There are notable exceptions – Nicholas Lyndhurst, Dennis Waterman and Jenny Agutter, for instance – but they are the exceptions that prove the rule. I also wonder whether a childhood largely devoted to performing is entirely healthy: what about learning about life? And what about learning other essential skills in order to earn one's living when the acting work is not coming in? Generally speaking, the best thing for the stage-struck child is to send him or her to one of the numerous youth theatre groups and drama workshops that exist in almost every town and city. These are often listed in *Yellow Pages*, and many are members of the National Association of Youth Theatres – see below. Public productions are often the last priority of such groups – especially for the younger ages – but a terrific amount can be learnt by the young from what seem like simple make-believe games. Children in such groups won't learn many of the technical skills necessary to acting, but they will learn a lot of important social skills and the fundamental business of 'interacting' that is so important to an acting ensemble: that it's not just what you can create that matters, it's what you can create with other people. Some youth theatres are allied to agencies who will promote their members for professional work, but it is important to note that employment of the under-16s is very strictly regulated.

National Association for Youth Drama in Ireland (NAYD)

34 Upper Gardiner Street, Dublin 1, Ireland
tel 00353 1878 1301 *fax* 00353 1878 1302
email info@nayd.ie
website www.youthdrama.ie

The National Association for Youth Drama is the umbrella organisation for youth drama and youth theatre in Ireland, providing support for more than 70 youth theatre groups in both Northern and Southern Ireland. Every 4-5 years it organises the National Youth Theatre – an event which brings together young people from all over the country, who work with a youth theatre director and a professional crew to produce a theatre production.

National Youth Theatre shows are produced to a professional standard, and are performed for an audience consisting of members of the general public and representatives from the theatre world. Previous productions have included: *The Young Europeans* (1986), written and directed by Gerry Stembridge; *Our Town* (1984) and *The Crucible* (1987), both directed by the Abbey Theatre's current Artistic Director, Ben Barnes; and *Strawberries in December* (1996), written by Antoine O'Flatharta and directed by Brian Brady. The 2001 National Youth Theatre production entitled *The Old Lady Says 'No!'*, by Denis Johnston, was directed by John White and featured a cast of 35 from 19 youth theatres throughout the country.

In addition, NAYD organises a National Festival of Youth Theatres, Regional Youth Drama Festivals, a National Youth Theatre Festival of the Deaf, Irish participation in the European Youth Theatre Encounter, and training for drama practitioners, youth leaders and young people. The National Youth Theatre has also launched the acting careers of a host of young performers, including Cathy Belton, Jasmine Russell, Anthony Brophy, Noelle Brown, Eunice McMenamin and Tom Murphy.

National Association of Youth Theatres (NAYT)

Arts Centre, Vane Terrace, Darlington DL3 7AX
tel (01325) 363330 *fax* (01325) 363313
email nayt@btconnect.com
website www.nayt.org.uk

Founded in 1982, the National Association of Youth Theatres is the leading development organisation for youth theatre practice in England and Wales. On behalf of registered groups it works with the Department for Education and Skills (DfES), Arts Council England, Regional Arts Councils and local authorities to achieve greater recognition and improved funding for the sector. Registration is open to any group or individual using theatre techniques in their work with young people, outside of formal education.

The NAYT provides a variety of resources, information and support for registered groups including training programmes, advice on a wide range of policy and strategy issues, an archive with project reports, surveys and case studies, and a monthly *Bulletin* containing the latest news on funding, training, performances and vacancies. With online information and contact details for more than 700 registered groups, the organisation also enables young people to contact youth theatres directly.

National Youth Arts Wales (NYAW)

245 Western Avenue, Cardiff CF5 2YX
tel 029-2026 5060 *fax* 029-2026 5014
email nyaw@nyaw.co.uk
website www.nyaw.co.uk/nytw.html
Artistic Director Greg Cullen

NYAW represents the National Youth Brass Band of Wales, National Youth Choir of Wales, National Youth Chamber Ensemble of Wales, National Youth Dance Wales, National Youth Orchestra of Wales, and National Youth Theatre of Wales (NYTW).

The National Youth Theatre of Wales was founded in 1976 and has since provided opportunities for hundreds of young people, many of whom are now actively involved with the theatre as professional actors, directors, writers, designers and stage managers. The NYTW is aimed at young people aged 16-21 who are drawn from all over Wales. With guidance from its Artistic Director, the youth theatre prepares and rehearses during the summer of each year for a series of high-profile public performances.

In addition, the NYTW spearheads a development programme of workshops and education activities, designed to increase interest and participation in youth theatre.

The NYTW recently produced the play *Frida and Diego*, a love story with a Welsh-language twist provided by Ian Staples. The play was a multimedia spectacle incorporating the paintings of the Mexican artists Frida Kahlo and Diego Rivera.

National Youth Music Theatre (NYMT)

email enquiries@nymt.org.uk,
auditions@nymt.org.uk (Auditions);
sheena.clark@nymt.org.uk (Sponsorship & Support)
website www.nymt.org.uk

The National Youth Music Theatre exists to produce challenging music theatre work (both major productions and workshops) for young people of all backgrounds as participants; and, in helping them to explore new and existing works, to inspire themselves and each other – giving them the opportunity to achieve their highest aspirations and realise their talent, imagination and creativity.

In 2006 they are producing 7 exciting new music theatre projects around the UK; 2 of these are adaptations of novels and 5 are completely new projects or developments of new musicals created in 2005.

National Youth Theatre (NYT)

443-45 Holloway Road, London N7 6LW
tel 020-7281 3863

website www.nyt.org.uk
Membership, Auditions & Courses Stephen Daly

Founded in 1956, the NYT is one of the UK's premier youth arts organisations. It provides young people aged 13-21 with the opportunity for creative participation through theatre arts. Offers courses in Acting, Stage Management, Lighting and Sound, Costume, Scenery and Prop Building at a professional standard which culminate in a season of productions in professional venues in London, across the country and abroad.

Many leading names in the entertainment industry started out with the company, including Sir Ben Kingsley, Sir Derek Jacobi, Dame Helen Mirren, Daniel Craig, Timothy Dalton, Daniel Day-Lewis, Chiwetel Ejiofor, Gina McKee, Timothy Spall, Liza Tarbuck, Alex Kingston and Orlando Bloom.

The NYT auditions roughly 3000 applicants every year at one of 13 audition centres across the UK. Approximately 500 new members are recruited annually from all over the country. Successful applicants are offered a place on one of the courses at either the NYT Headquarters in London or across the UK. Having completed a course, members are entitled to audition for NYT productions. A major production is mounted in August/September with other tours and seasons occurring throughout the year. Recent productions include: *Watch Over Me*, *Murder in the Cathedral*, *Kes* and *Immaculate Conceit*.

Also runs an Outreach programme which aims to include many young people who would not otherwise have the opportunity of becoming involved in drama.

Scottish Youth Theatre

3rd Floor, Forsyth House, 111 Union Street, Glasgow G1 3TA
tel 0141-221 5127 *fax* 0141-221 9123
email info@scottishyouththeatre.org
website www.scottishyouththeatre.org
Artistic Director Mary McCluskey *Key contact* Julie Austin

Founded in 1977, Scottish Youth Theatre is Scotland's national theatre for and by young people. Runs weekly drama classes for young people aged 3-25, in addition to a variety of training courses, festivals, educational workshops, youth theatre projects and productions throughout the year. There is no audition process to attend the drama classes, but participants in the annual summer festival are asked to prepare a 2-minute speech and a song. In 2003 almost 2000 applications were received and 1000 places offered. Stages at least 5 productions each year, which in recent years have included: *Mary Queen of Scots* and *Dying for It*. Staff are happy to help applicants with any enquiries.

Youth Music Theatre: UK

London Office Unit 10, Bridge Wharf, 156 Caledonian Road, London N1 9UU

4 Training

tel 0870-240 5057
Northern Ireland Office Ballyvoy Lodge, 56 Ballybracken Road, Doagh, Ballyclare, County Antrim BT39 0TG
tel 028-9334 0871
website www.youth-music-theatre.org.uk

Established in 2003, Youth Music Theatre: UK is a new organisation which involves young people in all aspects of music theatre. It is open to all young people aged 11-21 and runs projects in the countries of the British Isles and occasionally abroad. Many of these projects involve young people creating and devising the work themselves, supported by professional directors, choreographers and musical directors. The company will be providing a full range of residential workshops during the school holidays, offering young people the chance to improve their skills in a number of areas – from audition techniques to martial arts.

All auditions take the form of 'taster' workshops with about 25 young people taking part at the same time.

Working together, the group learns songs, dances and short scenes; individuals may be asked to perform a short extract on their own. Productions will normally be based at a regional theatre and will rehearse there for a period of 2-3 weeks before playing for a further 1-2 weeks.

Projects cost somewhere between £500 and £1000, which will help to cover the costs of food, accommodation and pastoral care. The exact fee for each project depends on its duration and where it is taking place.

Three new pieces of musical theatre were developed in 2004: *Over the Edge* was rehearsed in Belfast for 12 days and presented at the Belfast Festival; *Amy's Wedding* rehearsed for 3 weeks with performances at the Garage in Norwich; and *Red Hunter* rehearsed for 9 days in Newcastle and was presented at Gateshead College. In 2006 they are producing 7 exciting new music theatre projects around the UK: 2 of these are adaptations of novels, and 5 are completely new projects or developments of new musicals created in 2005. As all work is residential, applications are welcome from all parts of the UK.

Drama schools

Currently there is a core of established drama schools which belong to an organisation called the Conference of Drama Schools (CDS – **www.drama.ac.uk**). Most of these run courses that are 'accredited' by the National Council for Drama Training (NCDT – **www.ncdt.co.uk**) – for more details, see the article on the NCDT and accreditation. There are schools outside the CDS which have courses with 'accreditation'; there are courses in CDS schools that are not 'accredited'; and there are a few well-respected courses that are neither. The reasons for these variations are too complex to explain here. However, if you get a place on a three-year accredited course, you stand a higher than 'evens' chance of getting funding in the same way as those accepted on conventional university courses.

It is important to check the current funding arrangements for each course you intend applying for. Don't simply rely on what arrangements were in place last year, as things have a habit of changing. Many three-year accredited courses have 'degree' status – in spite of the fact that there is little or no written component to the courses, let alone formal, written exams. (Historically, the schools took the 'degree' route to help students get funding on the same basis as those following conventional academic courses.) Degree status actually means very little in the acting profession, and courses with degree status are not necessarily better than those without it. Some schools have been quite vociferous about not wishing to become embroiled in the whole philosophy and bureaucracy that is fundamental to degree education – believing that joining with a university would compromise the purely vocational character of their courses. One such adds: 'Universities are academic institutions, and the intelligence required of an academic is different from that required of an actor. While some are blessed with both kinds, many talented and intelligent actors are of indifferent academic ability. We would not wish to exclude them.' Degree status will enable you to go on to a higher degree and enhance your employment prospects outside the profession – but not within it.

Funding for some accredited one- and two-year courses is available, but not with the same frequency as for three-year courses. However, there is advice on finding funds from private sources on both the NCDT and the CDS websites, and some schools have scholarships and/or are good at helping students with this task.

It is worth spending time checking through all the courses listed below – also, read through the CDS's *Guide to Professional Training in Drama and Technical Theatre* which is available from their website. (Additionally, if possible seek the opinion of those with recent knowledge of drama schools.) Then get prospectuses for any school that you feel could be viable for you – and read each one thoroughly. Important considerations include whether you could be eligible for funding for your fees (and a maintenance loan), and potential living costs – central London is significantly more expensive to live in than Manchester, for example. (Bear in mind, too, whether a degree qualification at the end of the course is important to you.) Above all, it's important to try to assess which courses you feel would suit you best, and to apply – some require application via UCAS **www.ucas.ac.uk** – to as many as you can afford the audition fees and travel costs for. Don't forget to factor in the cost of overnight accommodation, if necessary. The plain truth is that competition for places is so intense (especially for women) that you need to audition for as many places as possible. Every time you do another audition you will learn more about the techniques of auditioning than any book or class can teach you – particularly if it's your first time. It is important to take on board the fact that many people take two or three years of auditioning, and sometimes more, before they get places. If you are determined to become a professional actor, you have to take rejection in your stride – learn from it and keep on trying until you succeed.

Finally, carefully check the application deadlines, funding details and audition specifications of each school you intend applying to – there are some considerable variations. You may find it useful to read *An Applicant's Guide to Auditioning and Interviewing at Dance and Drama Schools*, which is available from the NCDT's website. Andrew Piper's website **www.andrew-piper.com** contains useful advice on auditioning and fundraising for drama school, as well as an account of his own first year.

Notes

● For general information on funding for fees and maintenance loans, see **www.dfes.gov.uk/studentsupport**.

● Places on some accredited courses are currently funded through Dance and Drama Awards (DaDAs). These were introduced in the late 1990s and provide funding for about two-thirds of successful applicants. For more details check each relevant school's prospectus and website – also look at **www.direct.gov.uk/danceanddrama**.

* denotes membership of the Conference of Drama Schools

Academy Drama School

189 Whitechapel Road, London E1 1DN
tel 020-7377 8735
email ask@the-academy.info
website www.the-academy.info
Key contact Judith Reynolds

Full-time acting courses

2 scholarships are available for the courses listed below and are offered at specific auditions in April, May and June. Public funding, however, is not available for any of the courses.
• Evening Acting Course (2 years). Applicants must be over the age of 20. Course fee is £4050 p.a. Received approximately 200 applications in 2003 and offered 30 places. *Audition requirements*: 1 modern and 1 classical speech for solo audition. *Audition fee*: £25
• Postgraduate Acting Course (1 year). Applicants must be over the age of 21 and hold a relevant degree. Course fee is £6450. Received approximately 180 applications in 2003 and offered 12 places. *Audition requirements/fee*: as above
• Medallion Acting Course (1 year). Applicants are normally aged 17-20. Course fee is £3150. Received approximately 200 applications in 2003 and offered 30 places. *Audition requirements*: either 1 classical or 1 modern speech. *Audition fee*: £25

The Academy of Live and Recorded Arts (ALRA)*

The Royal Victoria Building, Fitzhugh Grove, Trinity Road, London SW18 3SX

tel 020-8870 6475 *fax* 020-8875 0789
website www.alra.co.uk
Principal Pat Trueman

Accredited acting courses

• National Diploma in Professional Acting (3 years). Applicants must be aged 18 or over, preferably with A levels. Course fee is £10,340 p.a.; public funding is available for some students. Applications should be made direct to the school by April. The school received 392 applications in 2004 for 33 places. *Audition requirements*: 1 modern speech and 1 Shakespeare for solo audition. *Audition fee*: £30 (As we go to print, the school hopes that this course will become a BA (Hons) in Professional Acting from September 2006.)
• National Advanced Certificate in Professional Acting (1 year). Applicants must be aged 21 or over, preferably graduates. Course fee is £11,100 with public funding available for some students. Applications should be made direct to the school by April. The school received approximately 290 applications in 2004 for 22 places. *Audition requirements/fee*: as above

The Arden Theatre School

The Arden, City Campus, City College, Whitworth Street, Manchester M1 3HB
tel 0161-279 7257 *fax* 0161-279 7218
email AMurray@ccm.co.uk
website www.thearden.ac.uk (School) or www.ccm.ac.uk (College)

Head of School David O'Shea *Administrator* Angela Murray

The Arden was established over 15 years ago, in a unique collaboration between Manchester University, City College and The Royal Exchange Theatre. The School now offers 3 BA (Hons) programmes and a postgraduate Diploma in Writing for the Stage.

Full-time courses

• BA (Hons) Acting Studies (3 years full-time). Applicants must be aged 18 or over at the start of the course with a minimum of 12 UCAS tariff points. "Entry to the School is, however, by audition only and therefore we are willing to consider mature students with relevant experience in place of qualifications." Applications must be made through UCAS and auditions run from December to June.

• BA (Hons) Musical Theatre Studies (3 years full-time). Applicants must be aged 18 or over at the start of the course with a minimum of 12 UCAS tariff points. "Entry to the School is, however, by audition only and therefore we are willing to consider mature students with relevant experience in place of qualifications." Applications must be made through UCAS and auditions run from December to June. This course accepted its first intake of students in September 2006.

Arts Ed London*

Cone Ripman House, 14 Bath Road, London W4 1LY
tel 020-8987 6666 *fax* 020-8987 6699
email drama@artsed.co.uk
website www.artsed.co.uk
Director of the School of Acting Jane Harrison *Director of the School of Musical Theatre* Ian Watt-Smith *Key contacts* Nicola Ramsbottom (Acting), Vivienne Hobbs (Musical Theatre)

Part of the Dance and Drama Awards scheme. Applications for courses and awards should be made direct to the school. All courses are accredited by the National Council for Drama Training or the Council for Dance Education and Training, and validated by City University.

Accredited acting courses

• BA (Hons) Acting (3 years). Applicants must be aged 18 or over. Course fee is £8790 p.a.; public funding is available for some students. In 2004 the school received 500 applications for 35 places. *Audition requirements*: 1 modern and 1 Shakespeare speech for solo audition. *Audition fee*: £30
• BA (Hons) Musical Theatre Programme (3 years). Applicants must be aged 18 or over. Course fee is £9294 p.a.; public funding is available for some students. In addition, the school has a limited number of bursaries. Applications will be accepted until the end of February but the academy recommends early applications. *Audition requirements*: first round consists of a movement audition and a song from a musical; second round

involves an acting audition, a further singing audition, an interview and an Orthopaedic Assessment. Course is accredited by the Council for Dance Education and Training (CDET – **www.cdet.org.uk**). *Audition fee*: £30
• MA Acting (1 year postgraduate). Applicants must be aged 21 or over. Course fee is £9297; public funding is available for some students. In 2004 the school received 300 applications for 30 places. *Audition requirements/fee*: as for 3-year course

Birmingham School of Acting* (formerly Birmingham School of Speech and Drama)

The Link Building, Paradise Place, Birmingham B3 3HJ
tel 0121-262 6800 *fax* 0121-262 6801
email bssd@bssd.ac.uk
website www.bssd.ac.uk
Principal Stephen Simms *Admissions Manager* Roger Franke

Accredited acting courses

• BA (Hons) Acting (3 years). Applicants must be aged 18 or over with 2 A levels (grade E or above) or equivalent. Course fee is £3000 p.a. Applications should be made direct to the school by 31st March. In 2003 the school received 450 applications for 42 places. *Audition requirements*: 1 modern and 1 other speech for solo audition; 2nd audition requires 1 modern and 1 classical speech and 1 song. *Audition fee*: £20 for first round, £10 for second
• Graduate Diploma in Acting (1 year). Applicants must be aged 21 or over with a university degree or relevant professional experience. Course fee is £3000. In 2003 the school received 110 applications for 16 places. Applications should be made directly to the school by 31st March. *Audition requirements/fee*: as above

The Birmingham Theatre School

The Old Rep Theatre, Station Street, Birmingham B5 4DY
tel 0121-643 3300 *fax* 0121-643 3300
email info@birminghamtheatreschool.co.uk
website www.birminghamtheatreschool.co.uk
Principal Chris Rozanski *Key contact* Sarah Watts (Arts Admin Manager)

Full-time acting courses

• HND Performing Arts/Theatre Acting (2 years). Applicants must be aged 18 or over with 12 points at A level or BTEC. 60 applications were received in 2003 and 20 places offered. *Audition requirements*: 1 modern and 1 classical speech for solo audition. *Audition fee*: no charge
• BTEC National Diploma in Performing Arts. Applicants must be aged 16 or over.
• Advanced Acting Diploma (1 year). Applicants must be aged 17 or over. Course fee is £6900 for which no

public funding is available. More than 35 applications were received in 2003 and 25 places offered. *Audition requirements/fee*: as above
• Open Access Foundation in Acting (1 year). Applicants must be aged 16 or over.

The Bridge Theatre Training Company

Cecil Sharp House, 2 Regent's Park Road, London NW1 7AY
tel 020-7424 0860 *fax* 020-7424 9118
email admin@thebridge-ttc.org
website www.thebridge-ttc.org
Joint Artistic Directors Mark Akrill, Judith Pollard
Company Administrator Rebecca Smedley

The Bridge is a non-profit-making organisation which provides intensive training for a career in professional acting. Courses include comprehensive career guidance, and a graduating season of public productions in London theatres with a West End showcase at the Criterion Theatre in front of agents, directors and casting directors.

Full-time acting courses

• Professional Acting Course (2 years). Applicants must be aged 18 or over. Course fee is £3825 p.a. for which some funding is available.
• Acting Course (1 year postgraduate). Applicants must be aged 21 or over with a university degree or significant relevant experience. Course fee is £3825 p.a. for which some funding is available. *Audition fee*: £25

Bristol Old Vic Theatre School*

2 Downside Road, Clifton, Bristol BS8 2XF
tel 0117-973 3535 *fax* 0117-923 9371
email enquiries@oldvic.ac.uk
website www.oldvic.ac.uk
Principal Christopher Denys

An affiliate of the Conservatoire for Dance and Drama. All courses are entirely vocational and are validated by the University of West England.

Accredited acting courses

Fees for the courses listed below are expected to be £3000 p.a. for 2006/7. The official age for entry is 18-30 but the school frequently makes exceptions in the case of older applicants. Applications should be made direct to the school.
• BA (Hons) Professional Acting (3 years). *Audition requirements*: 1 classical verse speech (preferably Shakespeare), 1 modern prose piece – each lasting no longer than 2 minutes for solo audition. Candidates should also prepare a short song. Recalls take the form of a weekend audition in Bristol. *Audition fee*: £30 for first audition; no charge for the weekend-school recall
• Diploma of Professional Acting (2 years). *Audition requirements/fee*: as above

Other full-time acting courses

• Certificate of Higher Education in Professional Acting (1 year). *Audition requirements/fee*: as above

Central School of Speech and Drama*

64 Eton Avenue, London NW3 3HY
tel 020-7722 8183 *fax* 020-7722 4132
email enquiries@cssd.ac.uk
website www.cssd.ac.uk
Principal Professor Gary Crossley

Scholarships/Bursaries Diana Wade Memorial Award, Gary Bond Memorial Award, Robert Tunstall Memorial Award

Accredited acting courses

• BA (Hons) Acting (Acting for Stage) – 3 years. Applicants must be aged 18 or over. For 2007 start, normal entry requirements are a minimum of 2 Cs at A level, a minimum of 3 Cs at GCSE, and selection by audition. Exceptionally, applicants who do not meet this requirement but demonstrate appropriate academic potential may be accepted. Applications should be made through UCAS by January 2007. For 2006 start, course fees were: £3000 p.a. for home/EU students, for which some public funding is available; £9000 p.a. for overseas students. In 2005 the school received 3058 applications for a maximum of 66 places for its BA (Hons) Acting course. *Audition fee*: £30

Other full-time acting courses

• BA (Hons) Acting (Music Theatre) – 3 years. Applicants must be aged 18 or over. For 2007 start, normal entry requirements are a minimum of 2 Cs at A level, a minimum of 3 Cs at GCSE, and selection by audition. Exceptionally, applicants who do not meet this requirement but demonstrate appropriate academic potential may be accepted.
• BA (Hons) Acting (Physical and Visual Theatre) – 3 years. Applicants must be aged 18 or over. For 2007 start, normal entry requirements are a minimum of 2 Cs at A level, a minimum of 3 Cs at GCSE, and selection by audition. Exceptionally, applicants who do not meet this requirement but demonstrate appropriate academic potential may be accepted. Applications should be made through UCAS by January 2007. For 2006 start, course fees were: £3000 p.a. for home/EU students, for which some public funding is available; £9000 p.a. for overseas students. In 2005 the school received 3058 applications for a maximum of 66 places for its BA (Hons) Acting course. *Audition fee*: £30
• Alternative Theatre and New Performance Practices (qualification, BA (Hons) Theatre Practice). For 2007 start, normal entry requirements are a minimum of 2 passes at A level plus 3 GCSEs at grade C or above. Applications should be made through UCAS by January or March 2007. For 2006 start, course fees were: £3000 p.a. for home/EU students, for which some public funding is available; £9000 p.a. for overseas students. In 2005 the school received 587 applications for a maximum of 131 places for its BA (Hons) Theatre Practice course.

All the 1-year courses listed below are for postgraduates or actors (aged 21 or over) with significant professional experience. Applications for all postgraduate courses should be made direct to the school. For 2006 start, course fees were £5200 or £5500 (dependent on course) for home/EU students, and £10,200 or £10,500 (dependent on course) for overseas students.

• Acting Musical Theatre. In 2005 the school received 116 applications for a maximum of 31 places.
• Classical Acting. In 2005 the school received 195 applications for a maximum of 33 places.
• Advanced Theatre Practice – Performing. In 2005 the school received 211 applications for a maximum of 57 places.
• Movement Studies. In 2005 the school received 17 applications for a maximum of 6 places.
• Actor Training & Coaching. In 2005 the school received 11 applications for a maximum of 6 places.
• Acting for Screen. In 2005 the school received 76 applications for a maximum of 20 places.

The Cygnet Training Theatre*

New Theatre, Friars Gate, Exeter EX2 4AZ
tel (01392) 277189 fax (01392) 277189
email CygnetArts@btinternet.com
website www.drama.ac.uk
Principal Monica Shallis Key contact Mary G Evans

A member of the Conference of Drama Schools, Cygnet offers a 3-year, full-time training course based in its own studio theatre. Functions as a small touring company, drawing its members from all over the UK and abroad. The small number of applicants selected each year (6-8) are chosen for their flexibility, maturity, awareness and self-discipline. They are expected to work with professional commitment from the first day in this ensemble training. Financial assistance is occasionally available to third-year students.

Full-time acting courses

• Professional Acting Certificate (3 years). Applicants must be aged 18 or over. Course fee is £6000 p.a. for which no public funding is available. More than 200 applications were received in 2003 and 8 places were offered. Audition requirements: 1 modern and 1 classical speech lasting 1-3 minutes each, and 1 unaccompanied song. Applicants are auditioned on their own and in a group. Audition fee: £25

Other options include: Acting with Music, Acting with Directing, and Acting with Stage Management. People may come to train straight from school, after a university degree, or as a career change. All need stamina, commitment and an ability to put the work of the ensemble before their personal feelings. This training, regardless of the option, requires serious commitment.

Drama Centre*

Central Saint Martins College of Art and Design, Saffron House, 10 Back Hill, London EC1R 54Q
tel 020-7514 8778 fax 020-7514 8777
email drama@arts.ac.uk
website www.csm.arts.ac.uk/drama
Principal Dr Vladimir Mirodan Key contact Maggie Wilkinson

Trains students (18+) to become professional actors and directors. Established 40 years ago, it is now part of the University of the Arts London, and is a member of the Conference of Drama Schools. The school awards 3 UK/EU scholarships each year and 1 international Leverhulme scholarship to second-year students.

Accredited acting courses

• BA (Hons) Acting (3 years). Applicants must be aged 18 or over with 2 A levels. Course fee is £3000 p.a.; public funding is available for some students. Applications should be made through UCAS. In 2005 the school received 1353 applications for 32 places. Audition requirements: 1 modern speech (post-1830) and 1 classical verse speech (Shakespeare or other Renaissance playwright) for solo audition. Ear test will be required at recalls. Audition fee: £35

Other full-time acting courses

• MA in European Classical Acting (1 year). 24 places are available.
• MA in Performance (60 weeks over 2 years). 16 places are available.
• Applicants for both MA courses must be aged 21 or over with a related degree, a diploma in dance or drama, an honours degree in another discipline supported by performance-related experience (professional, amateur or student), or significant professional experience. Audition fee: £35
• Diploma in Foundation Studies – Performance (1 year), subject to validation. Applicants must be aged 18 or over by or during their first term, and have 1 A level, a BTEC National Diploma in Performing Arts or equivalent. 40 places are available. Audition fee: £35

Drama Studio London (DSL)

1 Grange Road, London W5 5QN
tel 020-8579 3897 fax 020-8566 2035
email registrar@dramastudiolondon.co.uk
website www.dramastudiolondon.co.uk
Director Peter Craze Registrar Sue Quelch-Woolls

Drama Studio London (DSL) provides training for mature and postgraduate students in acting and directing, and both courses are full-time and intensive. A maximum of 60 acting and 2 directing places are offered each year. Acting auditions are held throughout the year: applicants will be contacted by the course director to arrange auditions. Contact the registrar (**registrar@dramastudiolondon.co.uk**) for a prospectus, an application form or information about Open Days and course fees. This information is also available on the website.

Some scholarship funding is available according to need. All successful candidates will be offered the chance to apply.

Accredited acting courses
• DSL Diploma in Acting (1 year postgraduate).
Applicants are usually aged 21 or over. *Audition
requirements*: 1 speech of any genre of a maximum of
2 minutes, and a group-based workshop. *Audition fee*:
£30

East 15 Acting School*
Hatfields, Rectory Lane, Loughton IG10 3RY
tel 020-8508 5983 *fax* 020-8508 7521
email east15@essex.ac.uk
website www.east15.ac.uk
Director John Baraldi *Key contact* Linda Humphreys

Accredited acting courses
• BA Acting (3 years). 40 places were offered in 2004.
Deadline for applications is June. Applicants must be
aged 18 or over with A level grades EE, AVCE grades
EE or BTEC National overall pass or equivalent. (If
an applicant does not meet the specific criteria, he or
she may discuss the application with East 15
admissions.) Students over the age of 21 are not
required to fullfil the same A-level grade criteria.
There is no upper age limit, although it is unusual to
admit students over 40 years. Deadline for
applications is June. Course fee is £3000 p.a. for
qualifying UK and EU students (£8500 for overseas
students). *Audition requirements*: In the first instance,
all students must apply using the application forms
available through the school or on the school's
website. Students must also register through the
UCAS system. Auditions are required of all acting
students. Students are offered 2 alternative dates for
UK auditions, which are held on Saturdays from
October to June. These sessions start at 11am and are
usually completed by 6pm. In the UK, all auditions
are held at East 15's campus. The audition consists of
a series of workshops (movement and singing), as
well as the presentation of audition speeches and a
prepared song, during which helpful suggestions and
feedback are often given. East 15 Acting School's
audition procedures have been praised for being a
thorough experience, through which students are
encouraged to do their best. While many drama
schools give students 3 minutes, East 15 Acting
School gives its auditionees up to 6 hours – including
the opportunity to ask questions. Overseas students
may apply via video or through personal interview in
certain countries. For audition purposes each
candidate must perform 3 contrasting, short speeches
as follows: 1 speech from a Shakespeare or Jacobean
play of 10 lines only; 1 'serious' speech from a 20th-
century play; 1 contrasting speech from a
contemporary play (post-1950). Speeches should not
exceed 2 minutes each. Each applicant should also
prepare a short song, and bring sheet music (in the
correct key) for use by the accompanist. *Audition fee*:
£35 (non-refundable) for UK auditions and for video
applicants; £50 for overseas auditions (held in the
spring – contact the school for details)

• MA/PG Acting (1 year). Selection for this course is
based upon experience and potential. All applicants
must be over the age of 21; there is no upper age
limit. Applicants must hold a BA degree (normally at
least a 2:1) or have suitable previous life professional
or academic experience. Course fee is £8700 for UK/
EU students (£10,200 for overseas); public funding is
available for some students. 28 places were offered in
2004. Deadline for applications is June. *Audition
requirements/fee*: as above
• MA/PG Acting for TV, Film and Radio (1 year).
Selection for this course is based upon experience and
potential. All applicants must be over the age of 21;
there is no upper age limit. Applicants must hold a
BA degree (normally at least a 2:1) or have suitable
previous life professional or academic experience.
Course fee is £8900 for UK/EU students (£10,700 for
overseas); public funding is available for some
students. 16 places were offered in 2004. *Audition
requirements/fee*: as above

Other full-time acting courses
• BA in Contemporary Theatre (3 years). All
applicants must be aged 18 or over at time of
enrolment. There is no upper age limit, although it is
unusual to admit students over 40 years. Applicants
must hold A-level grades EE, AVCE grades EE or
BTEC National overall pass or equivalent. (If an
applicant does not meet the specific criteria, he or she
may discuss the application with East 15 admissions.)
Students over the age of 21 have no minimum
educational requirements. Deadline for applications
is June. Course fee is £3000 p.a. for UK/EU students
(£8500 p.a. for overseas). 14 places were offered in
2004. *Audition requirements/fee*: as above. This course
is pending NCDT Accreditation.
• Foundation in Acting (1 year). Applicants must be
aged 18 or over with 2 A levels or equivalent. Course
fee is £3000 for UK/EU students (£8500 for overseas).
50 places were offered in 2004. *Audition requirements/
fee*: as above
• MA in Professional Theatre (see website for details)
• Certificate of Higher Education in Theatre Arts (see
website for details)
• Foundation Degree/BA Degree in Community
Theatre (see website for details)
• Foundation Degree/BA Degree in Specialist
Performance Skills (Stage Combat) (see website for
details)

GSA Conservatoire* (formerly Guildford School of Acting)
Millmead Terrace, Guildford GU2 4YT
tel (01483) 560701 *fax* (01483) 535431
email enquiries@conservatoire.org
website www.conservatoire.org
Director Peter Barlow

GSA was founded in 1935 and from 1964 onwards
has concentrated on the vocational training of actors
and stage managers. Since 1987 the Musical Theatre

Course has held a strong position in the world of actor training.

Accredited acting courses

Applications for the courses listed below should by made direct to the Conservatoire by March.
• BA (Hons) Acting (3 years). Applicants must be aged 18 or over with 2 A levels. Course fee is £9310 p.a. for which some public funding is available. 35 places were offered in 2004. *Audition requirements*: 1 modern and 1 classical speech, each lasting 2 minutes for solo audition. *Audition fee*: £30
• BA (Hons) Theatre, Musical Theatre (3 years). Applicants must be aged 18 or over with 2 A levels. Course fee is £10,192 p.a. for which some public funding is available. 47 places were offered in 2004. *Audition requirements*: any 2-minute speech and a 2-minute musical theatre repertoire for solo audition. *Audition fee*: £30
• Diploma in Acting (1 year postgraduate). Applicants must be aged 21 or over. Course fee is £9310. 15 places were offered in 2004. *Audition requirements/ fee*: as above

Full-time acting courses
• MA in Musical Theatre (4 terms postgraduate) – subject to validation. Applicants must be aged 21 or over. Course fee is £10,192. *Audition requirements/fee*: as above

Guildhall School of Music & Drama*

Silk Street, Barbican, London EC2Y 8DT
tel 020-7628 2571 *fax* 020-7256 9438
email registry@gsmd.ac.uk
website www.gsmd.ac.uk
Director of Drama Wyn Jones

Accredited acting courses
• BA (Hons) Acting (3 years). Applicants must be aged 18 or over with 1 A-level pass and 2 AS-level passes or equivalent. Applicants over the age of 21 will be assessed on their own merits only. Applications should be made direct to the school as early as possible, and by the end of January at the latest. Course fees are covered by mandatory awards (except for graduates and non-EU citizens). *Audition requirements*: 1 Shakespeare or Jacobean speech, 1 modern and 1 other contrasting speech, each lasting no longer than 2 minutes. A short unaccompanied song is also required. Recall auditions include voice, movement and improvisation work (some of this in small groups), more detailed work on audition pieces, and a short interview. *Audition fee*: £39

In the final year of training, clear guidance is given on starting in the acting profession. There are regular talks and visits by regional theatre directors, agents, casting directors, income tax advisers and representatives from Equity.

Hertfordshire Theatre School

40 Queen Street, Hitchin SG4 9TS
Principals Kirk Foster, John Gardiner *Bursar & key contact* Annie Wilkinson

Has been providing training for actors for 17 years. Current total of 50 students. Graduation showcase takes place at a West End theatre.

Full-time acting courses
• Acting and Musical Theatre Course (3 years). Applicants must be aged 18 or over with a good level of education, either at A level or at BTEC. Course fee is £6500 p.a.; no public funding is available, but the school has a charitable trust offering reduced fees to students paying privately. A maximum of 20 places are available. *Audition requirements*: 1 modern, 1 classical and 1 comedy speech and 1 song. *Audition fee*: £25
• Advanced Acting and Musical Theatre (1 year postgraduate). Applicants must be aged 21 or over with a university degree or relevant professional experience. Course fee is £6500 for which no public funding or bursaries are available. A maximum of 6 places are available. *Audition requirements/fee*: as above

Interact Training Scheme

c/o NTC Touring Theatre, The Playhouse, Bondgate Without, Alnwick, Northumberland NE66 1PQ
tel (01665) 602586 *fax* (01665) 605837
email admin@ntc-touringtheatre.co.uk
website www.ntc-touringtheatre.co.uk
Artistic Mentor Gillian Hambleton *General Manager* Anna Flood

Not a formal drama-school training, but a 1-year scheme to provide a bridge between education or training and the profession, with the aim of encouraging and retaining talent within the North of England. The training consists of a series of workshops, masterclasses and placements within professional companies. There are no fees. Trainees are awarded bursaries of £8000; this is based on Equity's average wage for a professional actor. Accommodation, travel and theatre tickets are also provided. *Audition requirements*: 1 modern speech and 1 classical speech (2 minutes each), and an unaccompanied song. At least 1 of the speeches should demonstrate an awareness of physical theatre. In 2005 there were 67 applications for 7 places. Minimum age is 18, although most applicants will have a degree. "All applicants *must* either originate from Northumberland, Tyne & Wear, Cumbria, Durham or Cleveland, or have trained or studied in those regions within the past 5 years. We endeavour to provide facilities and access to accommodate all disabilities."

Italia Conti Academy of Theatre Arts Ltd*

'Avondale', 72 Landor Road, London SW9 9PH
tel 020-7733 3210 *fax* 020-7737 2728
email acting@lsbu.ac.uk
website www.italiaconti-acting.co.uk
Course Director (Acting) Nick Moseley

A member of the Conference of Drama Schools, the Academy offers a 3-year BA (Hons) Acting Degree, validated by London South Bank University and accredited by the National Council for Drama Training. This course takes a unique approach to actor training. Based loosely on the teachings of Sanford Meisner, whose work now dominates in the United States, it trains actors to be open, responsive and spontaneous.

Accredited acting courses
• BA (Hons) Acting (3 years). Applicants must be aged 18 or over with 5 GCSEs (grade C or above), including English, and 2 A levels (grade E or above) or equivalent. Course fee for 2004 for UK/EU students is £3000 p.a. with public funding available for some students. *Audition fee*: £30

The Liverpool Institute for Performing Arts (LIPA)*
Mount Street, Liverpool L1 9HF
tel 0151-330 3232/3116/3084/3022 *fax* 0151-330 3131
email admissions@lipa.ac.uk
website www.lipa.ac.uk

LIPA is dedicated to providing the best teaching for people who want to pursue a lasting career in the arts and entertainment economy, and offers a variety of styles of courses aimed at different age groups. It looks for more than acting talent in its students, and applicants should show evidence of versatility and trainable ability in other performance-related skills.

Full-time acting courses
• BA (Hons) Performing Arts – Acting (3 years). Applicants must be aged 18 or over; there is no upper age limit. Educational attainment, relevant experience and interdisciplinary interest and ability will be taken into account when applying. Applications should be made through UCAS initially. If invited to audition, further information will be required. Course fee is £3000 p.a. with some public funding available.
• Postgraduate Diploma in Acting (1 year). Applicants are usually aged 21 or over, and educated to degree-level standard with some acting experience. Mature students without degree qualifications but with considerable related professional experience are welcome to apply. Course fee is £8250. This is a new, intensive year-long programme enabling students to become flexible, multi-skilled practitioners.

London Academy of Music and Dramatic Art (LAMDA)*
155 Talgarth Road, London W14 9DA
tel 020-8834 0500 *fax* 020-8834 0501
email enquiries@lamda.org.uk
website www.lamda.org.uk
Principal Peter James

The London Academy of Music and Dramatic Art traces its antecedents back to 1861, making it the oldest institution of its kind in the UK. In June 2004, LAMDA became an affiliate of the UK's prestigious Conservatoire for Dance and Drama (CDD). LAMDA trains approximately 250 students each year on a variety of acting and stage management courses. There are a number of bursaries and scholarships available to LAMDA students, which are awarded at the Academy's discretion and for which there is no prior application procedure. However, eligible UK/EU students awarded places on the 3- and 2-year Acting courses may apply for a Government-funded place as at other higher education institutions. Eligible UK students can also apply for student loans.

Accredited acting courses
• BA (Hons) Professional Acting (3 years). This is LAMDA's flagship acting course, providing comprehensive practical training for actors of exceptional talent. It is accredited by the NCDT and validated by the University of Kent. Applicants must be aged 18 or over. Applications should be made directly to the school by May. *Audition requirements*: 1 20th- or 21st-century speech and 1 Elizabethan or Jacobean speech, each lasting no longer than 3 minutes. Solo audition. *Audition fee*: £30
• BA (Hons) Professional Acting (2 years). This intensive course for students with experience concentrates on progress and development. *Audition requirements/fee*: as above. Accredited by NCDT and validated by the University of Kent.

Other full-time acting courses
• Classical Acting Courses (1 year/double semester or single semester). These courses offer a concentrated period of classical training for modern actors. Visit the website for information on how to apply.
• Foundation Course (1 year). Aimed at students with little or no experience, this is a broad-based introduction to different aspects of theatre including acting, stage management, writing and design. Admission to the course is by audition or interview, dependent on experience and career intent.

London Academy of Performing Arts
St Matthews Church, St Petersburgh Place, London W2 4LA
tel 020-7727 0220 *fax* 020-7727 0330
email admin@lapadrama.com
website www.lapadrama.com
Principal Cecilia Hocking *Key contact* Administrator

Conservatory-style drama school founded in 1981 by Cecilia Hocking to provide postgraduate training in classical acting.

Full-time acting courses
• Classical Acting with options in Musical Theatre and Directing (1 year postgraduate). Most students are aged 21 with a university degree. Also takes older students looking for a career change, and other students without a university degree, who have

considerable performance experience and personal maturity. Course fee is £7260 for which no public funding is available. 80 applications were received in 2004 and 20 places were offered. *Audition requirements*: 1 modern and 1 classical speech for solo audition. A song is required for the musical option only. *Audition fee*: £25

London Academy of Radio, Film & TV
1 Lancing Street, London NW1 1NA
tel 0870 850 4994
website www.media-courses.com
Principal Eric Deacon *Key contact* Estelle Burton

The academy has more than 30 teaching staff; around 1200 students take one or more of its 100+ courses. It is situated opposite Euston Station.

Full-time acting courses
• Diploma in Screen Acting. In 2005 there were 24 applicants for 24 places. Application deadline is June. Age range: 16+. Entry is by audition: 1 modern and 1 classical speech. There is no audition fee. Course fee: £6000

London Drama School
30 Brondesbury Park, London NW6 7DN
tel 020-8830 0074 *fax* 020-8830 4992
email enquiries@startek-uk.com
website www.startek-uk.com
Key contact Sarah Mann

Established 1996. All teachers are actors, directors, writers or producers currently working in the industry. 2 bursaries are available to talented students with financial difficulties; these bursaries cover half the tuition fees.

Full-time acting courses
• One Year Advanced Acting Course. Course fee is £7500 for which some public funding is available. More than 80 applications were received in 2004 and 21 places were offered. *Audition requirements*: 1 modern speech (from a play or film) lasting 3-5 minutes for solo audition. An unaccompanied song is optional. Advises applicants to choose a character close to own age and experience. *Audition fee*: £25
• One Year Foundation Acting Course. Prepares students to audition for either the course above or for other Drama Schools. Course fee is £6500. *Audition requirements*: 1 speech or poem lasting 1 minute. *Audition fee*: £25

London School of Musical Theatre
83 Borough Road, London SE1 1DN
tel 020-7407 4455 *fax* 020-7407 4455
email info@lsmt.co.uk
website www.lsmt.co.uk
Course Director Fenton Gray *Course Producer* Glenn Lee *Key contact* Nikki Rose

Full-time acting courses
• Musical Theatre Diploma Course (1 year). Age range for entry is 18-35. Course fee is £11,000 with

public funding available for some students. 350 applications were received in 2004 and 40 places were offered. *Audition requirements*: 1 speech of applicant's choice lasting 2-3 minutes, and 2 contrasting musical theatre songs (i.e. 1 ballad and 1 up-tempo) for solo audition. *Audition fee*: £20

London Studio Centre (LSC)
42-50 York Way, London N1 9AB
tel 020-7837 7741 *fax* 020-7837 3248
email suzanne.wright@london-studio-centre.co.uk
website www.london-studio-centre.co.uk
Director Nic Espinosa *Audition Enquiries* Suzanne Wright *Head of Studies* Robert Penman

Primarily a dance college offering a BA Hons in Theatre Dance, accredited by the Council for Dance Education and Training and validated by the University of the Arts, London. The LSC also offers a 1-year full-time diploma in Musical Theatre, for those students who have completed a performing arts course elsewhere and who wish to further their training in this specialist area. Public funding is not available for this 1-year course. More details are available from the website.

Manchester Metropolitan University School of Theatre*
School of Theatre, Mabel Tylecote Building, All Saints, Manchester M15 6BH
tel 0161-247 1305 *fax* 0161-247 6875
email k.daly@mmu.ac.uk
website www.theatre.mmu.ac.uk
Course Director Niamh Dowling *Key contact* Kath Daly

See entry under *University acting-oriented courses* on page 19 for further details.

Accredited acting courses
BA (Hons) Theatre Arts/Acting (3 years). Applicants must be aged 18 or over with 2 A levels or equivalent. Course fee is £3000 p.a. for which some public funding is available. Applications should be made through UCAS by January. Receives more than 1000 applications for around 28 places each year. *Audition requirements*: 1 modern, 1 classical and 1 other speech for both group and solo auditions. *Audition fee*: £30

Mountview Academy of Theatre Arts*
Ralph Richardson Memorial Studios, Clarendon Road, London N22 6XF
tel 020-8881 2201 *fax* 020-8829 0034
email enquiries@mountview.ac.uk
website www.mountview.ac.uk
Principal Paul Clements

Scholarships/Bursaries Sir John Mills Scholarship, Dame Judi Dench Scholarship, Margaret Rutherford Scholarship, Peter Coxhead Scholarship (all for postgraduate performance courses)

Accredited acting courses
Applications for the courses listed below should be made direct to the school, by March for the BA (Hons) and by July for the postgraduate diploma.

• BA (Hons) Acting (3 years). Applicants must be aged 18 or over, usually with A levels but these are not essential. Course fee is £9402 p.a.; Dance and Drama Awards are available for a significant number of students. The school received more than 700 applications in 2004 and offered 32 places. *Audition requirements*: 1 modern speech (post-1945) and 1 Shakespeare for both group and solo auditions. *Audition fee*: £30
• BA (Hons) Musical Theatre (3 years). Applicants must be aged 18 or over, usually with A levels but these are not essential. Course fee is £10,077 p.a.; Dance and Drama Awards are available for a significant number of students. The school received more than 700 applications in 2004 and offered 32 places. *Audition requirements*: 1 modern speech (post-1945), 1 contrasting speech and 2 contrasting songs for both group and solo auditions. *Audition fee*: £30
• PG Dip in Acting/MA in Performance (1 year). Applicants must be aged 21 or over, usually with a university degree. Course fee is £12,368. The school received 300 applications in 2004 for 30 places. *Audition requirements/fee*: as above
• PG Dip in Musical Theatre/MA in Performance (1 year). Applicants must be aged 21 or over, usually with a university degree. Course fee is £12,220. The school received 300 applications in 2004 for 30 places. *Audition requirements/fee*: as above

Other full-time acting courses
• PG Dip in Acting – Screen and Radio (1 year). Applicants must be aged 21 or over, usually with a university degree. Course fee is £12,368. *Audition requirements/fee*: as above

Oxford School of Drama*
Sansomes Farm Studios, Woodstock, Oxford OX20 1ER
tel (01993) 812883 *fax* (01993) 811220
email info@oxforddrama.ac.uk
website www.oxforddrama.ac.uk
Principal George Peck *Key contact* Stephen Minay

Provides a significant number of Dance and Drama Awards for its 1- and 3-year courses. Also offers its own Hardship fund which is distributed each year to students on full-time courses at the school. Students not in receipt of a DaDA are prioritised for funding. The Lionel Bart Foundation and the Sir John Gielgud Charitable Trust currently support the school; in addition, students have also won the Henry Cotton Memorial Fund Award and the *Evening Standard/Patricia Rothermere Award*.

Accredited acting courses
Applications for the courses listed below should be made direct to the school by April. The fees for both courses were set at £10,290 p.a for 2005/6.
• Diploma in Acting (3 years). Applicants must be aged 18 or over. 18 places were offered in 2004. *Audition requirements*: 1 modern and 1 classical

speech, each lasting no longer than 90 seconds for solo audition, and 1 group movement/improvisation session. *Audition fee*: £30
• One Year Acting Course. Applicants must be aged 21 or over. 14 places were offered in 2004. *Audition requirements/fee*: as above

Poor School
242 Pentonville Road, London N1 9JY
tel 020-7837 6030 *fax* 020-7837 5330
email acting@thepoorschool.com
website www.thepoorschool.com
Principal Paul Caister

The school was created in 1986 with the aim of providing high-quality acting training that is financially within the reach of all, or almost all. Training lasts 2 years and operates in the evenings and at weekends until the final 2 terms, when daytime work is involved. Since March 1993 the Poor School has owned its own theatre, the Workhouse. This is a flexible studio theatre seating 50-80.

Full-time acting courses
• Two Year Acting Course (6 terms). Most students are in their early 20s but the school offers many places to older and younger people. Course fees are £1350 per term. Accepts 39 students each October. *Audition requirements*: 2 dramatic speeches (1 from Shakespeare) each lasting between 90 seconds and 2 minutes. *Audition fee*: £20

Queen Margaret University College*
School of Drama and Creative Industries, Gateway Theatre, Elm Row, Edinburgh EH7 4AH
tel 0131-317 3900 *fax* 0131-317 3902
email cowen@qmuc.ac.uk
website www.qmuc.ac.uk
Key contact Catherine Owen

See entry under *University acting-oriented courses* on page 19 for further details.

Accredited acting courses
• BA (Hons) Acting and Performance (3-4 years). Applicants must be aged 18 or over with Scottish Higher CCC, A level at grade E, BTEC or HNC/NC. Applications should be made through UCAS by March. Course fee is £1700 p.a. with public funding available to some students. In 2004 the college received 900 applications for this course and offered 22 places. *Audition requirements*: 1 modern and 1 classical speech for first audition; may also be asked to sing. Recall involves improvisation and movement workshops, sight-reading, singing, 2 additional pieces and an interview. *Audition fee*: £30 for first audition and £10 for recall. Initially the core subjects of acting, voice, text and movement are taught separately; as the course progresses, they combine and focus on performance through a wide variety of productions and projects. In the past few years, highly successful collaborations with students on other courses (stage

managers, directors, playwrights, etc.) have become a feature of the course. Close collaborations with professional theatre companies provide another dimension to the training.

Other full-time acting courses
• BA (Hons) Drama and Theatre Arts (4 years). This course is designed to develop understanding and practical experience in the broad canvas of drama. In years 1 and 2, students have classes in drama and performance and study the texts and contexts of theatre crossing between theory and practice. In years 3 and 4, students complement their studies with intensive work in a specialist area of study, including playwriting, directing, contemporary performance, producing, dramaturgy, community theatre and arts journalism.

The REP College
17 St Mary's Avenue, Purley on Thames, Berks RG8 8BJ
Key contact David Tudor

Provides acting students with 1 year of practical education, including 14 public performances. Course includes classes on audition techniques and planning. 4-8 scholarships of £1187-2375 are awarded annually.

Full-time acting courses
• Acting Course (1 year). Applicants must be aged 18 or over. Course fee is £9500 with public funding available for some students. 289 applications were received in 2003 and 20 places were offered. *Audition requirements*: group full-day workshop. *Audition fee*: £25

Richmond Drama School
Richmond Adult Community College, Parkshot, Richmond, Surrey TW9 2RE
tel 020-8891 5907
email david.whitworth@racc.ac.uk or mark.woolgar@racc.ac.uk
Key contact David Whitworth (1-year course), Mark Woolgar (2-year course)

Full-time acting courses
• Access Course (1 year, daytimes). Applicants must be aged 18 or over, preferably with A levels. *Course fee*: approx £3000 for which no public funding is available. 80 applications were received in 2005 and 16 places were offered. *Audition requirements*: 1 modern and 1 classical speech for solo audition. *Audition fee*: £20
• Foundation degree (2 years, evenings and weekends). Vocational acting course, incorporating a foundation degree. Contact Mark Woolgar for details of course fee. *Audition requirements & fee*: as above

Rose Bruford College*
Lamorbey Park, Burnt Oak Lane, Sidcup DA15 9DF
tel 020-8308 2600 *fax* 020-8308 0542

email enquiries@bruford.ac.uk
website www.bruford.ac.uk
Principal Professor Alastair Pearce

Accredited acting courses
Applicants for the BA degree courses listed below must be over the age of 18 with the equivalent of a minimum of 2 A levels at grade C or above. Course fees for 2006/7 were £3000 p.a. with some public funding and loans available. Applications should be made through UCAS.
• BA (Hons) Acting (3 years). *Audition requirements*: 1 modern and 1 classical speech each lasting no longer than 90 seconds. 1 song from musical theatre repertoire for recall audition. *Audition fee*: £30

Other full-time acting courses
• BA (Hons) American Theatre Arts (3 years). *Audition requirements*: 1 modern speech (post-1945) lasting no longer than 2 minutes
• BA (Hons) European Theatre Arts (3 years). *Audition requirements*: 1 speech from a European (incl. UK) play, lasting no longer than 3 minutes
• BA (Hons) Actor Musicianship (3 years). *Audition requirements/fee*: as above (but with an additional instrument audition at recall stage)
• MA Theatre Practices (1 year). Contact the college for more details.

Royal Academy of Dramatic Art (RADA)*
62-64 Gower Street, London WC1E 6ED
tel 020-7636 7076 *fax* 020-7323 3865
email enquiries@rada.ac.uk
website www.rada.org
Principal Nicholas Barter *Key contact* Sally Power

Founded in 1904 by Sir Herbert Beerbohm Tree at His Majesty's Theatre, the Academy moved to its present premises a year later. In 1996 the Academy received a Lottery Grant from the Arts Council and embarked on a £32 million rebuilding programme, opening its new premises in 2000. The final stage of the estate's strategy was completed at the end of 2004. Some maintenance bursaries are available for students to supplement their own fundraising efforts. Applications should be made direct to the school by March.

Accredited acting courses
• BA (Hons) Acting (3 years). Normal age-range for entry is 18-30. Course fee is £3000 p.a. for which some public funding is available. Receives approximately 2000 applications each year for a maximum of 32 places. *Audition requirements*: 1 Shakespeare or Jacobean speech and 1 contrasting speech, each lasting no longer than 3 minutes for solo audition. Recalls may take the form of second audition, group workshop or individual working session; an unaccompanied song is also required. The

auditions are 'lengthy and rigorous' and the process may span several months. *Audition fee*: £33

The course is for students who wish to earn a living working not only in the more traditional outlets, but also in the many alternative areas of theatre, film, television and radio. It is intensive, with a minimum working day of 10.00am – 6.00pm and individual classes in the evening. When public performances take place, the working day can be from 10.00am until 11.00pm.

Royal Academy of Music

Music Theatre Department, Marylebone Road, London NW1 5HT
tel 020-7873 7483 *fax* 020-7873 7484
email mth@ram.ac.uk
website www.ram.ac.uk/mth
Head of Music Theatre Mary Hammond F.R.A.M, L.R.A.M *Course Leader* Karen Rabinowitz

Students are enrolled at the Royal Academy of Music, one of Europe's leading conservatories and a full member of the University of London. Fellow students include instrumentalists, pianists, concert and opera singers, composers, jazz and commercial musicians.

Full-time Acting Courses

• One Year Music Theatre Course. Aimed at graduates, mature students and professionals wishing to refocus their careers. The aim of the course is to give a thorough professional musical and drmatic training to students of postgraduate (or equivalent) level to equip them for performance in contemporary musical theatre, through the integration of singing, acting and movement. It aims to bridge the gap between the acting singer and the singing actor. Course fee for 2006/07 was set at £9800. Audition fee is £60. Audition requirements, along with a full prospectus, can be found on the website. No public funding is available for this course.

Royal Scottish Academy of Music and Drama*

100 Renfrew Street, Glasgow G2 3DB
tel 0141-332 4101 *fax* 0141-332 8901
email registry@rsamd.ac.uk
website www.rsamd.ac.uk
Principal John Wallace

Accredited acting courses

Applications for the courses listed below should be made direct to the school by March. Public funding is available for some students.
• BA (Hons) Acting (3 years). Applicants are normally aged 18-21 but this is flexible. Course fee is £1700 p.a. Received 584 applications for 20 places in 2004. *Audition requirements*: 1 Shakespeare speech and 1 other for solo audition. *Audition fee*: £35

Other full-time acting courses

• Master of Performance in Musical Theatre (1 year). Course fee is £7500. 12 places will be available.

Audition requirements: contact the Academy. *Audition fee*: £35
• BA (Hons) Contemporary Theatre Practice (4 years). Applicants must hold 3 highers, 2 advanced highers or 2 A levels. Course fee is £1700 p.a. In 2004 the Academy received 63 applications for 12 places. *Audition requirements*: group workshop and written exercise. *Audition fee*: £35

Royal Welsh College of Music and Drama*

Castle Grounds, Cathays Park, Cardiff CF10 3ER
tel 029-2039 1327
email drama.admissions@rwcmd.ac.uk
website www.rwcmd.ac.uk
Principal Edmond Fivet *Drama Admissions Officer* Luise Moggridge

Accredited acting courses

• BA (Hons) Acting (3 years). Applicants should be aged 18 or over. Course fee is £3000 p.a. for which some public funding is available. Applications should be made through UCAS. Normally offers 20 places each year.
• Graduate Diploma in Acting (1 year). Applicants should be aged 21 or over. Course fee is £3835 (2005 figure), with no public funding available. Applications should be made direct to the college. Normally offers 10 places.

The School of the Science of Acting

Dept E, 67-83 Seven Sisters Road, London N7 6BU
tel 020-7272 0027 *fax* 020-7272 0026
email find@scienceofacting.org.uk
website www.scienceofacting.org.uk
Key contact Jack Curzon

Full-time acting courses

No public funding is available for the courses listed below, but students may apply for a limited number of scholarships.
• Three Year Acting Course. Applicants must be aged 18 or over. Course fee is £9990 p.a. Offers 14 places each year. *Audition requirements*: 1 modern, 1 classical and 1 other speech, and 1 song for solo audition. *Audition fee*: £25
• One Year Acting Course. Applicants must be aged 18 or over. Course fee is £9990. Offers 14 places each year. *Audition requirements/fee*: as above
• Two Year Evening Acting Course. Applicants must be aged 16 or over. Course fee is £4160 p.a. Offers 14 places each year. *Audition requirements/fee*: as above

Webber Douglas Academy of Dramatic Art*

website www.webber-douglas-academy.co.uk

All courses are now based at Central School of Speech and Drama. See entry on page 8.

The NCDT and accreditation
Ian Kellgren

If you were going to buy electrical goods and wanted some reassurance about the quality of a particular product – making it fit for purpose, and safe – you might well look to see if it had an industrial kitemark. If you wanted reassurance about a particular vocational drama course, you would be wise to look and see if it was accredited by the National Council for Drama Training (NCDT).

This accreditation aims to give students confidence that the courses they choose are recognised by the drama profession as being relevant to the purposes of their employment. In its turn, the profession can have confidence that any people they employ who have completed these courses will possess the skills and attributes required for the continued well-being of the industry.

NCDT was formed in 1976, after a Gulbenkian Foundation report, 'Going on the Stage', recommended its establishment. There were fears then that a recent severe increase in unemployment in the profession, coupled with a multiplication of training establishments, was leading to a critical situation for vocational drama training. NCDT was created to provide some way of judging which courses were truly vocational – realistically leading to a career. Local authorities were the major funders of drama students, and they wanted some way of distinguishing those courses that the profession would recognise as being of value.

At that time, there were only seven universities offering drama degrees: there are now more than 2000 degrees with 'drama' in the title. The need for potential students and the current funders to have some way of knowing which are vocational is stronger than ever – not least because of the changes that have taken place since 1976.
- Equity is no longer a closed shop (although there are 37,000 members, and extensive use of Equity contracts is made by employers); the profession has undergone massive change.
- Few, if any, reps exist in the way that they did in the early 70s.
- Musical theatre is a much more dominant force, demanding a supply of 'triple threat' performers – that is, those who can act, sing and dance, all to a high standard.
- Technological advances have revolutionised the ways in which the recorded media operate, and this area provides many more first-employment opportunities.
- Local Education Authority student grants have given way to the Dance and Drama Awards and core funding from the three national funding councils, in England, Scotland and Wales, at various rates.
- In Further and Higher Education, the Conference of Drama Schools (CDS) schools are now subject to the relevant Quality Assurance requirements.

NCDT accredits courses, not drama schools. Currently, there are about 50 courses in 20 drama schools that are accredited by NCDT: in acting, stage management and technical and musical theatre. Some courses that are not currently accredited may well apply to be so in the near future, and these would have to pass stringent tests as to their 'vocationality'. If they became accredited, they would have to apply for re-accreditation after six years.

The accreditation process
The application process for both accreditation and re-accreditation is similar. This involves the school submitting documentation about the course, which is examined in detail by

specialists. The course is then visited by a panel, which talks to the staff who deliver the course and to the students who are on it, as well as attending classes. Panel members are looking all the time at the professional relevance of the programme of training.

For this, they really need to have their finger on the pulse – so that everyone contributing to the accreditation process has to have at least five years' professional experience; a good general knowledge of current practice relevant to the course, with some being subject specialists as well; and a keen interest in the development of drama training in this country. Panel members are all well trained for their tasks.

At the end of a re-accreditation visit, the panel decides if the course should be re-accredited or not. They may decide to re-accredit but with recommendations or conditions. The Chair of the panel submits a recommendation in a report to the Review Committee; this is a group of 14 people who are current practitioners with demonstrable knowledge in at least one of the following skill areas: acting, casting, dance & movement, directing, knowledge of funding and statutory inspectorate regimes, film, musical theatre, production management, radio, representation, stage management, technical, television, vocational drama school training, and voice. The Review Committee decides on this recommendation and passes its judgement to the Council of NCDT for formal approval.

In addition to the accreditation visits, schools are required to submit annual reports, and there is a system of show reporting. This is where professionals visit the shows or showcases of a course and complete a report for NCDT. Each year, NCDT is therefore able to decide if a particular course is still fulfilling the aim of accreditation.

Embracing change

Recently, NCDT recognised that it needed to check its operation in the light of the host of changes since its inception. A period of intense research produced a programme of reform that is now being implemented.

NCDT is a unique partnership of employers in the theatre, broadcast and media industry, employee representatives and training providers. When it began, it had three 'wings': the industry, Equity and CDS. Now, under its new Chair, Sir Brian Fender, it has a more widely composed membership which, as well as Equity and CDS, includes the BBC, Channel 4, ITV, the Theatre Managers Association and up to five independent members.

Their brief is to not only to work to safeguard the highest standards, and to provide a credible process of quality assurance through accreditation for vocational drama courses in the UK; it is also to ensure that NCDT exists to act as a champion for the industry, by working to optimise support for professional drama training and education, and embracing change and development.

The discerning shopper will want the electrical goods they buy to be not only fit for purpose and safe, but also to have benefited from development and innovation. NCDT offers such 'shoppers' a means of identifying those vocational drama courses which are based on the best practices of more than a hundred years of drama training, but which also recognise and embrace all the benefits of development and innovation.

Ian Kellgren is an award-winning theatre director. He started out as an assistant director at the Royal Court in London, rising to Literary Manager, before becoming Artistic Director of Durham Theatre Company and the longest-serving Artistic Director of the Liverpool Playhouse. Currently, alongside his theatre and media work, he is NCDT Review Committee Chair.

University acting-oriented courses

On the positive side, on one of these courses you'll have much more free time to 'do your own thing' than your drama school counterpart; on the negative side, most don't provide nearly enough vocational acting training for today's professional. However, one of these courses can be a viable option for those who simply wish to pursue drama as a career, but are not yet convinced that an actor's life is for them. Those who don't get drama school places (or funding) could also consider such a course. If, at the end, you decide that you want to be a professional actor, it is very important to get at least one year's vocational training on a recognised, 'postgraduate' acting course – some of which now offer the chance of also adding 'MA' after your name.

If you are determined to be a professional and choose the university route, it's also worth considering other subjects that might better enhance your earning-power when not in acting work. While one of these might not enhance your knowledge of dramatic literature, you will embark upon your postgraduate acting course uncluttered by the intellectual 'baggage' that can inhibit a complete connection with a vocational acting training. Instinctive impulses are probably more important than intellect in acting – and some people find it difficult to properly readjust the 'brain/gut balance' in the short space of a single year.

The following is a selected sample of university acting-oriented courses; more can be found from UCAS **www.ucas.ac.uk** and the Standing Conference of University Drama Departments **www.art.ntu.ac.uk/scudd**.

Brunel University

Department of Performing Arts, Brunel University, Uxbridge, Middlesex UB8 3PH
tel (01895) 274000 ext. 4486 *fax* (01895) 816224
email barry.edwards@brunel.ac.uk
website www.brunel.ac.uk/depts/pfa

Courses offered: BA (Hons) in Modern Drama Studies. Course has strong practical emphasis covering the key skill areas of performing, devising, critical analysis, performance analysis, directing and writing for performance.

De Montfort University, Leicester

Faculty of Humanities, Clephan Building, De Montfort University, Leicester LE1 9BH
tel 0116-250 6199 *fax* 0116-257 7199
email huadmiss@dmu.ac.uk
website www.dmu.ac.uk/faculties/humanities/pa

Courses offered: BA (Hons) Drama Studies. Focuses on the study of theory through practice. Teaching staff are engaged in ongoing professional practice, devising and directing theatre at a national and international level; in addition, and in keeping with the university's professional and vocational ethos, the course includes contributions by well-known visiting professional practitioners.

There are also active links between Drama at De Montfort University and regional theatres and art centres. Students have opportunities to take part in full public productions in professional theatre spaces and at theatre festivals in Britain, including Cultural Exchanges, the faculty's own annual week of events.

Students are offered the chance to collaborate on productions with Drama departments across Europe and to show their own work in professional spaces abroad.

Goldsmiths College, University of London

Drama Department, Goldsmiths College, University of London, New Cross, London SE14 6NW
tel 020-7919 7414 *fax* 020-7919 7413
email drama@gold.ac.uk
website www.goldsmiths.ac.uk/departments/drama

Courses offered:
• BA (Hons) Drama and Theatre Arts, Certificate in Performance Skills and Theatre Studies. Explores the theory and practice of performance across a range of media, with a strong focus on performance and production work.
• MA in Performance Making. Creative research is developed through classes and workshops in performance, focusing on physical training methodologies drawn from a range of cultural forms. Work will address questions of performer-spectator relationships and the specific environments –

community, cultural and architectural – for which they are created.

Liverpool Hope University College

Department of Drama and Theatre Studies, Liverpool Hope, University College, Hope Park, Liverpool L16 9JD
tel 0151-291 3000
website www.hope.ac.uk

Courses offered: Drama & Theatre Studies is offered as part of the BA Combined Honours programme and should be studied with another subject such as Fine Art or English.

Manchester Metropolitan University

All Saints Building, All Saints, Manchester M15 6BH
tel 0161-247 2000 *fax* 0161-247 6390
email enquiries@mmu.ac.uk
website www.mmu.ac.uk

Courses offered: BA (Hons) Contemporary Theatre and Performance, BA (Hons) Theatre Arts (Acting). Contemporary Theatre and Performance offers a broad experience of practical work in both devised and scripted theatre and covers a variety of performing traditions. The Acting course develops the range of skills and abilities required for a career in acting, including voice, movement, acting, textual analysis and research. This programme is accredited by the National Council for Drama Training and students receive full Equity Cards upon graduation.

See entry under *Drama schools* for further information.

Queen Mary, University of London

School of English and Drama, Queen Mary, University of London, Mile End Road, London E1 4NS
tel 020-7882 3172 *fax* 020-7882 3357
email sedadmissions@qmul.ac.uk
website www.english.qmul.ac.uk

Courses offered: BA (Hons) Drama. Examines the theory and practice of performance across a range of social and historical contexts.

Roehampton University

Erasmus House, Roehampton Lane, London SW15 5PU
tel 020-8392 3232
website www.roehampton.ac.uk

Courses offered: BA/BSc Drama, Theatre & Performance Studies. Focuses on analysing the art of performance through integrated practical and theoretical study. Offers a wide range of emphases but is not designed for those wishing to pursue vocational actor training.

St Mary's University College, University of Surrey

School of Communication, Culture and Creative Arts, St Mary's College, Waldegrave Road, Twickenham TW1 4SX
tel 020-8240 4008
website www.smuc.ac.uk

Courses offered: BA (Hons) Drama. Building on its programme of practical theatre-making and theoretical investigation, the course has expanded in 3 new directions from 2004: Drama and Performance Studies; Physical Theatre; and Drama in the Community.

University College Chichester

School of Performing Arts, University College Chichester, Bishop Otter Campus, College Lane, Chichester, West Sussex PO19 6PE
tel (01243) 816253
email c.ferguson@ucc.ac.uk
website www.ucc.ac.uk/arts/performing_arts

Courses offered: Performing Arts (Contemporary Performance Practice). The primary focus is on devised theatre with an emphasis on group and teamwork. This is developed within a vocational context that prepares students for graduate careers in the creative arts industries.

University College Northampton

Avenue Campus, St George's Avenue, Northampton, Northamptonshire NN2 6JD
tel (01604) 735500
website www.northampton.ac.uk

Courses offered: BA (Hons) Drama. Students develop skills in improvisation, adaptation, physical and vocal technique, and critical analysis.

University College Worcester

Department of Arts, Humanities and Social Science, University College Worcester, Henwick Grove, Worcester WR2 6AJ
tel (01905) 855000
website www.worc.ac.uk

Courses offered: BA (Hons) Drama and Performance Studies. Explores drama and performance through a variety of contexts and media, and develops practical performance skills.

University of Birmingham

Department of Drama and Theatre Arts, University of Birmingham, Edgbaston, Birmingham B15 2TT
website www.bham.ac.uk/drama

Courses offered: Drama and Theatre Arts as a Single, Joint or Minor Honours degree. Undergraduate degree programme integrates theoretical and practical approaches to theatre.

University of Bristol

Department of Drama, University of Bristol, Cantocks Close, Woodland Road, Bristol BS8 1UP
tel 0117-928 7833 *fax* 0117-928 7832
website www.bristol.ac.uk/drama

Courses offered: BA (Hons) Drama or Joint Honours with English or a modern language. Plays are studied in the light of their historical background as well as for their own interest as dramatic texts. Opportunities are provided for students to develop practical skills within areas such as acting and directing, design, lighting and stage management through workshop sessions and productions.

University of Chester

Department of Performing Arts, Parkgate Road, Chester, Cheshire CH1 4BJ
tel (01244) 511000 ext. 3138 fax (01244) 392890
email performingarts@chester.ac.uk
website www.chester.ac.uk/performingarts

Courses offered: BA (Hons) Drama and Theatre Studies. Focus is on the study and practice of performance, with practical workshops, performances, lectures, seminars and research.

University of East Anglia

University of East Anglia, Norwich NR4 7TJ
tel (01603) 592280 fax (01603) 507728
email wwweas@uea.ac.uk
website www.uea.ac.uk/eas/sectors/drama

Courses offered: BA (Hons) Drama, BA (Hons) English Literature and Drama, and BA (Hons) Scriptwriting and Performance. UEA's programme in Drama has a strong practical emphasis on all aspects of dramatic production, and combines this with the study of the theory, history and social significance of drama. Students on all Drama programmes also study in other schools (for example, in Film & Television, and in American Studies).

University of Exeter

Department of Drama, Thornlea, New North Road, Exeter EX4 4LA
tel (01392) 264580 fax (01392) 264594
email drama@exeter.ac.uk
website www.ex.ac.uk/drama

Courses offered: BA (Hons) Drama. Composed of a series of modules, all of which place emphasis on the social nature of theatre. The relationship between theory and practice is key. All drama students get equal opportunities to act, direct and write.

University of Huddersfield

School of Music and Humanities, St Peter's Building, St Peter's Street, Huddersfield HD1 1RA
tel (01484) 478455 fax (01484) 478428
website www.hud.ac.uk/theatre

Courses offered: BA (Hons) Theatre Studies. A diverse range of modules is on offer, all of which combine studio-based practical work with theoretical study. Joint Honours with Media and Music also offered.

University of Hull

Drama Department, University of Hull, Hull HU6 7RX
tel (01482) 466210

website www.drama.hull.ac.uk

Courses offered: BA (Hons) Drama. Introduces and develops key practical and theoretical approaches to the study of drama. Allows students to tailor the course to suit their specific academic and practical interests at a later stage.

University of Kent

School of Drama, Film & Visual Arts, Rutherford College, University of Kent, Canterbury CT2 7NY
tel (01227) 764000 fax (01227) 827850
email DramaSecs@kent.ac.uk
website www.kent.ac.uk/sdfva

Courses offered: MDrama. The BA (Hons) Drama and Theatre Studies has recently become a Masters degree due to its additional fourth year. A range of approaches to performance in practice and theory are studied in the first 3 years, while the last year allows students to pursue a specialism in depth. There are also limited opportunities to spend the third year at a European University or in America.

University of Lancaster

Lancaster Institute for Contemporary Arts, Lancaster University, Lancaster LA1 4YW
tel (01524) 594156 fax (01524) 39021
email k.beale@lancaster.ac.uk
website www.theatre-studies.lancs.ac.uk

Courses offered: BA (Hons) Theatre Studies. Department has extensive links with professional performance, theatre and drama groups, and with individual practitioners, through its work in the Nuffield Theatre and other projects. Also: MA by Research in Theatre Studies; MPhil/PhD by Research.

University of Leeds

School of Performance and Cultural Industries, University of Leeds, Bretton Hall Campus, West Bretton, Wakefield, West Yorkshire WF4 4LG
tel 0113-343 9109
email enquiries-pci@leeds.ac.uk
website www.leeds.ac.uk/paci

Courses offered: BA (Hons) Acting. Combines technical work in voice, movement, singing and dancing with performance theory. Allows students to specialise in defined aspects of theatre, and to represent their talents in a number of professional contexts. Note: This course will be relocated to the main campus of the University of Leeds in the summer of 2007.

University of Lincoln

University of Lincoln, Brayford Pool, Lincoln LN6 7TS
tel (01522) 882000
email enquiries@lincoln.ac.uk
website www.lincoln.ac.uk/courses/drama/index

Courses offered: BA (Hons) Drama. Provides sufficient time and space to explore and experiment with performance and the making of plays. The course offers lots of contact with faculty and guest artists to hone and direct students' creative instincts and skills.

University of Loughborough

Department of English and Drama, Loughborough University, Loughborough, Leicestershire LE11 3TU
tel (01509) 222951
email p.higgs@lboro.ac.uk
website www.lboro.ac.uk/departments/ea

Courses offered: BA (Hons) Drama, BA (Hons) Drama with English. Examines the history and theory of performance, and develops students' practical and technical skills.

University of Manchester

Department of Drama, School of Music and Drama, University of Manchester, Oxford Road, Manchester M13 9PL
tel 0161-275 3347 *fax* 0161-275 3349
email drama@man.ac.uk
website www.art.man.ac.uk/DRAMA

Courses offered: BA (Hons) Drama, BA (Hons) Drama and Screen Studies, BA (Hons) Drama with English. Founded in 1961 following a gift from Granada Television, the Drama department aims to provide an academic study of theatre and drama based on history, theory and practical performance.

University of Middlesex

School of Arts, Middlesex University, Cat Hill, Barnet, Hertfordshire EN4 8HT
tel 020-8411 5000
website www.mdx.ac.uk/arts

Courses offered: BA (Hons) Drama and Theatre Studies, BA (Hons) Drama and Theatre Arts, BA (Hons) Drama and Theatre Arts with Performing Arts, BA (Hons) Drama and Technical Theatre Arts. A study of modern drama and theatre allowing extensive practical exploration of a wide range of material.

University of Salford

Faculty of Arts, Media and Social Sciences, University of Salford, Salford, Greater Manchester M5 4WT
tel 0161-295 5000 *fax* 0161-295 4704
website www.famss.salford.ac.uk

Courses offered: BA (Hons) Performing Arts, BA (Hons) Media and Performance. Performing Arts focuses on the development of creative performance skills to a professional level. Media and Performance allows students to combine key aspects of performance activity with practical media production and performance.

University of Staffordshire

School of Humanities and Social Sciences, Staffordshire University, College Road, Stoke-on-Trent ST4 2XW
tel (01782) 294415 ext. 4869
email a.dinnivan@staffs.ac.uk
website www.staffs.ac.uk/dta

Courses offered: BA (Hons) Drama and Theatre Arts. Develops knowledge and understanding of performance skills, theory, texts and contexts.

University of Sunderland

School of Arts, Design, Media & Culture, University of Sunderland, Priestman Building, Green Terrace, Sunderland SR1 3PZ
tel 0191-515 2182
email admcenquiry@sunderland.ac.uk
website www.sunderland.ac.uk

Courses offered: BA (Hons) Drama. Offers a programme of practical and theoretical work focusing on the development of collaborative work in a contemporary context.

University of the West of England, Bristol

St Matthias Campus, Oldbury Court Road, Fishponds, Bristol BS16 2JP
tel 0117-965 6261
website www.uwe.ac.uk/humanities

Courses offered: BA (Hons) Drama, BA (Hons) Drama and Education, BA (Hons) Drama and English, BA (Hons) Film Studies and Drama. The Drama programme is not intended to provide a vocational training for work in the theatre; rather, it offers a balance between practical, contextual and theoretical approaches to the study of theatre and has close links with the Bristol Old Vic.

University of Ulster at Coleraine

School of Media and Performing Arts, University of Ulster, Northland Road, Londonderry, Co. Londonderry BT48 7JL
tel 0870-040 0700
website www.ulst.ac.uk/faculty/humanities/mpa

Courses offered: BA (Hons) Drama. Develops skills and knowledge associated with the various disciplines of drama, with particular emphasis on collaborative work.

University of Wales, Aberystwyth

Department of Theatre, Film & Television Studies, Parry-Williams Building, University of Wales, Aberystwyth, Penglais Campus, Aberystwyth, Ceredigion SY23 3AJ
tel (01970) 622828 *fax* (01970) 622831
website www.aber.ac.uk/tfts

Courses offered: BA (Hons) Drama, BA (Hons) Drama and Performance Studies, BA (Hons) Drama and Film & Television Studies, BA (Hons) Drama and English. Focuses attention on a variety of different aspects of theatre as an artform and as a social phenomenon.

University of Warwick

School of Theatre Studies, University of Warwick, Coventry CV4 7AL

tel 024-7652 3020 *fax* 024-7652 4446
email tsraj@warwick.ac.uk
website www.warwick.ac.uk/fac/arts

Courses offered: BA (Hons) Theatre and Performance Studies.

University of Winchester (formerly King Alfred's College)

Faculty of Arts, West Hill, Winchester, Hants SO22 4NR

tel (01962) 841515 *fax* (01962) 842280
email course.enquiries@winchester.ac.uk
website www.winchester.ac.uk

Courses offered: BA (Hons) Drama Studies, BA (Hons) Performing Arts, BA (Hons) Drama, Community Theatre & Media.

The Drama Studies programme is designed to offer an experience of drama in its social, theoretical and practical contexts as well as a critical analysis of the relationships between practice and theory.

Performing Arts is an interdisciplinary programme looking to the role of performance in communities of the future. Work in theatre, dance and music is combined with approaches to live and virtual art, comedy, and innovation in performance technology and design.

Drama, Community Theatre & Media is split between the study of theatre and documentary.

Encourages students to combine the mediums in innovative and creative ways. The emphasis of the drama element is on community/alternative forms of theatre, while the media part of the course focuses on researching and producing documentaries.

University of Wolverhampton

Humanities, Languages and Social Sciences, Wolverhampton City Campus, Wulfruna Street, Wolverhampton WV1 1SB

tel (01902) 321056 *fax* (01902) 323379
website www.asp.wlv.ac.uk

Courses offered: BA (Hons) Drama, HND Performing Arts. The Drama programme covers practical, creative and critical skills, allowing students to develop performance skills and learn from visiting professionals. HND Performing Arts focuses on acting techniques and performance theory. It also offers practical and theoretical knowledge in a wide range of related areas.

York St John College

York St John College, Lord Mayor's Walk, York YO31 7EX

tel (01904) 624624 *fax* (01904) 612512
email admissions@yorksj.ac.uk
website www.yorksj.ac.uk

Courses offered: BA (Hons) Performance: Theatre. Theory is integrated with practice at all points throughout the degree programme, and there are many opportunities to become involved in work placements, independent performance projects and the International Exchange Programme (IEP).

Short-term and part-time courses

This section lists both 'taster' opportunities for drama school aspirants and further training for professional actors. In *Contacts*, you will also find many individual teachers. If you are thinking of approaching one of these, try to get some advice on his/her current knowledge of the profession and abilities as a teacher before spending your money.

Pre-drama-school courses

Competition for drama school places seems to be growing even more ferocious, and many applicants will enhance their chances if they go on a pre-drama-school course. You may for example have done A-level Drama, but the actual acting training on such courses is often limited – generally geared more towards the exam-passing university entrant than auditioning for drama school. Whatever your acting background, a 'taster' course (for just a week, for instance) can give you a good idea of what further help/training you need in order to prepare you properly for drama school auditions.

Additional skills

As well as the organisations listed below, there are periodic 'one-off' workshops around the country. These are usually 'trailed', and sometimes advertised, in *The Stage*. Equity occasionally subsidises such enterprises (some, away from the major cities), so it is worth checking with your local Branch/Organiser. Actors Centres are not just places to sharpen up your existing skills and develop new ones, but also great meeting places for actors to exchange ideas and information.

Academy Drama School

189 Whitechapel Road, London E1 1DN
tel 020-7377 8735
email ask@the-academy.info
website www.the-academy.info
Key contact Judith Reynolds

Courses offered

• Part-time Evening Acting Course (1 year). Course fee is £1350 with 6 hours of classes per week. Entry is by audition
• Saturday Foundation Acting (overall duration of course is flexible). Fee for 4 weeks with 2.5 hours of classes per week is £65. No audition required
• Audition Course (1 week). Course fee is £200 for 26 hours' tuition. Entry is by audition
• Summer Evening Acting Course (2 weeks). Overall fee is £300 for 46 hours of tuition; no audition required

Actors Centre (London)

1A Tower Street, Covent Garden, London WC2H 9NP
tel 020-7240 3940
email act@actorscentre.co.uk
website www.actorscentre.co.uk

Full membership is open to Equity members, registered graduates from the Conference of Drama Schools in their first year of registration (must hold a student Equity card), and foreign actors holding an Equity letter of exemption. Members are entitled to a wide range of subsidised classes and workshops led by experienced directors and tutors who are active in the industry, plus full use of the centre, café facilities when available and a quarterly schedule. Membership fees are £50 per year or £32.50 for 6 months. Associate membership is also available for £25 per year; associates are entitled to observe designated workshops but not to participate in them. Provisional membership is open to applicants whose training/ experience is not as substantial as that of the majority of members; this is available on the basis of an audition and is reviewed after a 6-month period.

Regular classes and workshops include Acting, Tool Box, TV and Film, Auditions, Advice, Labwork, Voice, Shakespeare, Stage Combat, Directing, Musical Theatre and Writing. In addition, members can book individual sessions to work on singing, acting, sight-reading, Alexander Technique, dialect, voice and movement. Contact the centre for a membership form or a current brochure.

Actors Centre North East

2nd Floor, 1 Black Swan Court, Westgate Road, Newcastle upon Tyne NE1 1SG

tel 0191-221 0158 *fax* 0191-221 0158
email enquiries@actorscentrene.co.uk
website www.actorscentrene.co.uk

Actors Centre North East is threatened with closure following recent funding problems. At the time of writing, the play library, IT facilities and Green Room have been closed, but the centre remains open so far for courses. See the website or telephone for latest information.

Arts Ed London

Cone Ripman House, 14 Bath Road, London W4 1LY
tel 020-8987 6666 *fax* 020-8987 6699
email receptionist@artsed.co.uk
website www.artsed.co.uk

Courses offered

• Foundation in Performance (1 year part-time). Course fee is £1000-1250 with 7.5 hours of classes per week. Entry is by audition
• Various short courses (10 weeks). Course fee is £150-250 with 2-3 hours of classes per week. Entry is in January, April, July and October. No audition required
• Intensive courses (1-2 weeks at Easter or in the summer). Course fee is £150-350 with 25-30 hours of classes per week. No audition required

Contact the school by telephone or email **ncussons@artsed.co.uk** for further details of the courses listed above.
• Post-Diploma BA (Hons) in performance, validated by City University. Course director is Terrie Fender (020-8987 6659, **fender@artsed.co.uk**). This is a 1-year part-time course to enable those with a diploma from NCDT- or CDET-accredited courses from 1995 onwards, or those who have undertaken vocational training of 3 years and can offer appropriate professional experience, to upgrade to a degree qualification.

Birkbeck College Faculty of Continuing Education

26 Russell Square, London WC1B 5DQ
tel 020-7631 6633 *fax* 020-7631 6688
email performance@bbk.ac.uk
website www.bbk.ac.uk

The faculty is a leading provider of part-time Higher Education courses in London. Their Performance Studies programme offers Foundation and Diploma courses in Acting, Dance, Opera, and Concert Singing. It does not offer scholarships or bursaries. The college is committed to doing everything it can to support students with disabilities.

Acting courses offered

• Performance Studies: Foundation in Acting. The course lasts 96 hours (3 hours per week) and entry is by audition. Contact the college for details of fees
• Performance Studies: Diploma in Acting. The course lasts 192 hours (6 hours per week) and entry is by audition. Contact the college for details of fees

Birmingham School of Acting

The Link Building, Paradise Place, Birmingham B3 3HJ
tel 0121-262 6800 *fax* 0121-262 6801
email bssd@bssd.ac.uk
website www.bssd.ac.uk
Principal Stephen Simms *Admissions Manager* Roger Franke

Courses offered

• Creative Drama (30 weeks part-time). Course fee is £306 with 3 hours of classes per week
• Acting Summer School. Course fee is £510 for 2 weeks in August
• Shakespeare Summer School. Course fee is £299 for 4 days in August
• Musical Theatre Week. Course fee is £350 for 6 days in August
• Musical Theatre Weekend. Course fee is £185 for 2 days in August

The Birmingham Theatre School

The Old Rep Theatre, Station Street, Birmingham B5 4DY
tel 0121-643 3300 *fax* 0121-643 3300
email info@birminghamtheatreschool.co.uk
website www.birminghamtheatreschool.co.uk
Principal Chris Rozanski *Key contact* Sarah Watts (Arts Admin Manager)

Courses offered

• Professional Diploma (Evenings & Weekends). Applicants must be aged 18 years or over
• Acting for Beginners (11 weeks). Covers the basics of character creation, voice, improvisation and performance discipline for acting beginners. Students participate in all aspects of the creative process from basic exercises to final presentations. Course fee is £79 per term; classes take place in the evening
• Creating Performance (11 weeks). Each term, students will create and perform using a variety of techniques and using both texts and devised work. All aspects of character creation and working with an audience will be explored. Suitable for people with previous experience in acting. Course fee is £79 per term; classes take place in the evening
• Pub Theatre (11 weeks). Provides students with the chance of experiencing exactly what working in a fringe theatre company is all about. Course fee is £89 per term; classes take place in the evening

The Bloomsbury Alexander Centre

Bristol House, 80A Southampton Row, London WC1B 4BB
tel 020-7404 5348 or 020-8374 3184
email bloomsbury.alexandercentre@btinternet.com
Directors Stephen Cooper, Natacha Osorio

The centre specialises in teaching the Alexander Technique. Teachers are available for private lessons, with discounts available for students and actors.

There are ongoing introductory workshops and courses, as well as drop-in vocal work for actors with experience of the AT. The introductory course runs for 4 weeks (1.5 hours a week) and costs £80. The drop-in AT vocal work classes are £15 per session. *Note for actors with disabilities*: "Our premises are on the ground floor with one step up onto the main entrance and one other just inside."

British Academy of Dramatic Combat

3 Castle View, Helmsley, North Yorkshire Y062 5AU
email enquiries@badc.co.uk
website www.badc.co.uk

Offers a Performance Certificate in Stage Combat at Foundation, Basic, Basic Level 2, Recommended and Advanced levels. Training is available in the following methods: Broadsword & Shield, Double Handed Broadsword, Quarterstaff, Rapier & Dagger, Rapier & Cloak, Rapier & Buckler, Smallsword, Unarmed Combat. Programmes of workshops are arranged throughout the country, and anyone with suitable venue spaces or wanting to be added to the workshop mailing list should email **workshops@badc.co.uk**.

Central School of Speech and Drama

64 Eton Avenue, London NW3 3HY
tel 020-7722 8183 *fax* 020-7722 4132
email enquiries@cssd.ac.uk
website www.cssd.ac.uk
Principal Professor Gary Crossley

Courses offered (a selection of courses offered in 2005/06)

• Saturday Drama Classes (1 term). Course fee is £145, entry is possible throughout the year. For ages 6-17
• Winter Introduction to Audition Speeches (3 days, January). Course fee is £275. Separate classes for ages 18+ and 16+
• Easter Scenes Workshop (9 days, April). Course fee is £380
• Introduction to Acting (2 evenings p.w., termly). Course fee is £385, entry is possible throughout the year. For ages 18+
• Introduction to Text (2 evenings p.w., termly). Course fee is £385, entry is possible throughout the year. For ages 18+
• Working Text (2 evenings p.w., termly). Course fee is £385, entry is possible throughout the year. For ages 18+
• Working Shakespeare (2 evenings p.w., termly). Course fee is £385, entry is possible throughout the year. For ages 18+
• Classical Theatre – Level 2 (2 evenings p.w., termly). Course fee is £385, entry is possible throughout the year. For ages 18+
• Introduction to Movement for Performance (2 evenings p.w., termly). Course fee is £385, entry is possible throughout the year. For ages 18+
• Movement for Perfomers – Level 2 (2 evenings p.w., termly). Course fee is £385, entry is possible throughout the year. For ages 18+

• Introduction to Voice for Performance (2 evenings p.w., termly). Course fee is £385, entry is possible throughout the year. For ages 18+
• Introduction to Acting for Camera (2 evenings p.w., termly). Course fee is £385, entry is possible throughout the year. For ages 18+
• Directed Scenes (Saturdays, termly). Course fee is £460
• Puppetry (2 evenings p.w., termly). Course fee is £385, entry is possible throughout the year. For ages 18+
• Singing (1 evening p.w., termly). Course fee is £165, entry is possible throughout the year. For ages 18+
• Central Theatre Group (1 evening p.w., termly). Course fee is £230, entry is possible throughout the year. For ages 18+

Summer School Courses

• Combat and Stage Fighting (1 week, July). Course fee is £440. For ages 17+
• Mask (1 week, July). Course fee is £440. For ages 17+
• Devising (1 week, July). Course fee is £740. For ages 17+
• Musical Theatre (1 week, July). Course fee is £870. For ages 17+
• Summer Shakespeare (1 week, July). Course fee is £870. For ages 17+
• Directed Scenes (1 week, August). Course fee is £740. For ages 17+
• Voice and Text (1 week, July). Course fee is £440. For ages 18+
• Actors' Auditions Pieces (1 week, July-August). Course fee is £550. For ages 17+
• Youth Theatre For Actors – 1 week (1 week, July). Course fee is £380. For ages 5-17
• Youth Theatre For Actors – 3 weeks (3 weeks, July-August). Course fee is £1140. For ages 5-17

The City Lit

16 Stukeley Street, London WC2B 5LJ
tel 020-7430 0544 *fax* 020-7405 3347
email v.rochester@citylit.ac.uk
website www.citylit.ac.uk
Head of Drama, Dance & Speech Vivienne Rochester

The college offers an eclectic mix of activities – such as acting, movement, voice, mime, circus, stage fighting, magic, comedy, dance, self-presentation, accents, sight-reading and pronunciation – which develop vocational, social and personal skills. The John James Bursary is open to Access Course students and there are various other small access grants that might cover travel, books or child-care. Students may ring or come into the office for an interview between 12.30 and 1.30pm (Monday and Wednesday) or 5.30 and 6.30pm (Monday, Tuesday and Thursday).

The Rep Company was set up to train a company of actors to produce work of the highest professional standard, providing a platform for its members to hone their skills and display their talents. Directors, teachers and practitioners are invited and engaged to facilitate.

Its members are made up of a combination of graduates from the Access course, or from the advanced/professional provision in the Drama, Dance & Speech department's programme, and experienced practitioners who wish to further their experience with the college. Auditions are held annually.

The college has awarded associate status to a number of actors who have produced an excellent body of work with the company. All company members are eligible for the 3 productions staged each year, and are invited if appropriate to professional castings that are occasionally held at the Lit.

Courses offered

• Foundation course (1 year part-time). Applicants must be aged 19 or over. Entry is by audition
• Access course (1 year part-time). Applicants must be aged 19 or over. Entry is by audition
• Musical Theatre Diploma (1 year part-time). Applicants must be aged 19 or over. Entry is by audition
• Cacchetti Ballet School (1 year part-time). Applicants must be aged 19 or over. Entry is by interview
• Stage Fighting (1 year part-time). Applicants must be aged 19 or over. Entry is by interview

A range of acting, voice, movement and self-presentation classes is also available. Courses run for 12 weeks with entry at various points throughout the year.

Drama Studio London (DSL)

1 Grange Road, London W5 5QN
tel 020-8579 3897 *fax* 020-8566 2035
email admin@dramastudiolondon.co.uk
website www.dramastudiolondon.co.uk
Director Peter Craze *Key contact* Amanda Carrara

Courses offered

• Summer Acting Course (4 weeks). Course fee is £950, entry is in August

East 15 Acting School

Hatfields, Rectory Lane, Loughton IG10 3RY
tel 020-8508 5983 *fax* 020-8508 7521
email east15@essex.ac.uk
website www.east15.ac.uk
Director John Baraldi *Key contact* Linda Humphreys

Courses offered

All courses listed below take place in July:
• Introduction to Acting (1 week), fee is £220
• Approaches to Shakespeare and Jacobean Theatre (2 weeks), fee is £350
• Devised Theatre (3 weeks), fee is £500
• Audition Technique (1 week), fee is £220
• Physical Theatre (1 week), fee is £220

• Stage Combat (1 week), fee is £250 (includes BADC examination fee)

All of the above courses carry University of Essex credits. Applicants must be aged 17 years or over.

Equity (Wales and South West England Office)

Transport House, 1 Cathedral Road, Cardiff CF11 9SD
tel 029-2039 7971 *fax* 029-2023 0754
email info@cardiff-equity.org.uk
website www.equity.org.uk

In 2005, Equity ran 2 series of new workshops in Devon and Cornwall: a Creative Partnership Training Scheme based in Plymouth, and an Audition Skills Workshop in collaboration with the BBC. Workshops in the past have included improvisation, movement, working with text, puppetry, fooling, and taking direction; these have been offered at various points throughout the year. Contact the office to find out if and when more workshops are scheduled.

Exeter Dance Consultancy

Holly Tree Cottage, Clyst St George, Exeter EX3 0RB
tel (01392) 873683
email info@exedance.demon.co.uk

Offers 1:1 tuition in dance movement therapy for performing artists, specialist movement coaching for actors, and dance coaching for auditions. A 10% discount is available for Equity members, Spotlight members and students. To arrange an appointment, contact Jeanette Macdonald.

GSA Conservatoire (formerly Guildford School of Acting)

Millmead Terrace, Guildford GU2 4YT
tel (01483) 560701 *fax* (01483) 535431
email enquiries@conservatoire.org
website www.conservatoire.org
Director Peter Barlow

Courses offered

• Singing in the Theatre (1 week). A summer course designed for students over the age of 17 who wish to improve their singing. Other disciplines relating to the voice will also be explored. Entry is in July and the fee is £299
• Musical Theatre (2 weeks). Culminating in a performance in the Bellairs Playhouse, this course is open to students aged 17 or over and takes place in July/August. Course fee is £499
• Audition Techniques (1 week). Course takes place in August and is geared towards students aged 17 or over. Course fee is £198

Guildhall School of Music & Drama

Silk Street, Barbican, London EC2Y 8DT
tel 020-7628 2571 *fax* 020-7256 9438
email registry@gsmd.ac.uk

website www.gsmd.ac.uk
Director of Drama Wyn Jones

Founded in 1880, the Guildhall School is acknowledged internationally as a leading conservatoire for both music and drama.

Courses Offered

• Shakespeare and Contemporary Theatre. 3 weeks of intensive Shakespeare and Contemporary Theatre workshops, tuition and rehearsals. The course is designed to appeal to various levels of experience, including beginners and those who wish to pursue full-time drama training. Students have group classes for half the day, and work on scenes in small groups with a director for the other half. The rehearsed scenes are presented at the end of the course before an audience of students and staff. The course aims to demystify Shakespeare and provide a challenging insight into modern drama. Includes class work with many of the school's core staff and masterclasses with Director of Drama, Wyn Jones; Head of Acting, Christian Burgess; Head of Voice, Patsy Rodenburg; and Head of Movement, Wendy Allnutt. Starts summer 2006
• Musical Theatre. This 3-week course has been devised for beginners, for those wishing to refresh their skills, and for prospective full-time musical theatre students. It is also designed to benefit acting students and actors who wish to improve their singing and dancing skills within the context of musical theatre. Students are divided into 2 groups, with each group working as an ensemble. Each group has classes for half the day and works with a director, a choreographer and a musical director for the other half. The course concludes with a presentation to students and staff. Starts summer 2006

At least 2 visits to attend performances in London theatres are included in the fees of both courses, which are set at £1200; there is a £150 non-refundable deposit. Applicants must be at least 18 years old by the start of the course; there is no upper age limit. A good standard of English is essential. Accommodation is available. Please consult the website or telephone 020-7382 7183 for details of the application process. Email enquiries to **dramasummerschool@gsmd.ac.uk**.

"There is no application deadline but, in view of the limited number of places, applicants are strongly advised to book early. If the summer school is full, you will be placed on a waiting list."

Hope Street Ltd

13a Hope Street, Liverpool L1 9BQ
tel 0151-708 8007 *fax* 0151-709 3242
email peter@hopestreet.org
website www.hope-street.org
Principal Peter Ward *Key contact* Alan Richardson

Provides actors with training for physical theatre and young people's theatre. Places are also available for trainee directors and workshop leaders. Courses culminate in 4 public performances directed by professionals. Fees stated below cover the 6-month course period and are applicable only to non-Merseyside residents. Merseyside residents may apply for an £80 weekly allowance.

Courses offered

• Physical Theatre (26 weeks full-time). Applicants must be aged 18 or over. Course fee is £2800. 8 places are offered each year
• Young People's Theatre (26 weeks full-time). Applicants must be aged 18 or over. Course fee is £2800. 4 places are offered each year

Desmond Jones – Mime and Physical Theatre

20 Thornton Avenue, London W4 1QG
tel 020-8747 3537 *fax* 020-8742 3537
email enquiries@desmondjones.co.uk
website www.desmondjones.co.uk
Key contact Desmond Jones

Provides tuition in mime and physical theatre. Desmond Jones is a teacher, choreographer, director, performer and consultant and has worked on Hollywood films, in the West End and with the Royal Ballet.

London Academy of Music and Dramatic Arts (LAMDA)

155 Talgarth Road, London W14 9DA
tel 020-8834 0500 *fax* 020-8834 0501
email enquiries@lamda.org.uk
website www.lamda.org.uk
Principal Peter James

Courses offered

Housing is available for short courses in London; contact the Admissions office for details.
• Shakespeare Summer Workshop (4 weeks). The aim of the course is to demystify Shakespeare – to prevent poetic drama from seeming an unscalable mountain. Disciplines include textual analysis, history seminars, practical voice classes, movement, dance, physical theatre, singing (choral and solo), scene study, Alexander technique and stage combat. Course culminates in a non-public open rehearsal and includes visits to the Royal Shakespeare Company in Stratford-upon-Avon and performances at London theatres. Entry is by application and references. Course takes place from July to August
• Shakespeare and His Contemporaries Workshop (8 weeks). An intensive classical acting course for students with some performance experience. Featured playwrights include Shakespeare, Marlowe, Jonson and the Jacobeans. Disciplines covered as for 4-week workshops (see above). Includes visits to the Royal Shakespeare Company in Stratford-upon-Avon and performances at London theatres. Entry is by

application and references. Course takes place from June to August
• Physical Theatre Summer School (2 weeks). Comprising work on Le Jeu, Neutral Mask, Musicality of Movement, Clown and the Bouffon, this is an intensive training course for the professional or student actor. Entry is by application and references. Course takes place in August

For more information, visit the website.

London Academy of Performing Arts
St Matthew's Church, St Petersburgh Place, London W2 4LA
tel 020-7727 0220 *fax* 020-7727 0330
email admin@lapadrama.com
website www.lapadrama.com
Principal Cecilia Hocking *Key contact* Administrator

Courses offered
• Classical Acting Course (1 semester full-time). An intensive course for professional performers, directors, drama students and teachers who want practical work on Shakespearean texts. Classes are timetabled between 9.00am and 6.00pm, 5 days a week. Students must also be available for occasional extra evening and weekend rehearsals, if required. Course fee is £2420. *Audition requirements*: 2 Shakespeare monologues. *Audition fee*: £25
• Summer School Shakespearean Acting (1 month). Course takes place in July and August and is intended for professional performers, drama students (aged 17 and over) and other interested people who wish to explore the English Classical Theatre tradition. Course fee is £850. No audition is required

London Academy of Radio, Film & TV
1 Lancing Street, London NW1 1NA
tel 0870-850 4994
website www.media-courses.com
Principal Eric Deacon *Key contact* Estelle Burton

The academy has more than 30 teaching staff; around 1200 students take one or more of its 100+ courses. It is situated opposite Euston Station.

Courses offered
• Acting Masterclass (1 week – 30 hours). Course fee is £695. No audition required.
• Acting for Film & TV (9-week course – 9 x 3 hours). Course fee is £395. No audition required. (*Note*: 2 versions of this course exist – 1 on a weekday evening; 1 on a Saturday)

London Drama School
30 Brondesbury Park, London NW6 7DN
tel 020-8830 0074 *fax* 020-8830 4992
email enquiries@startek-uk.com
website www.startek-uk.com
Key contact Sarah Mann

Courses offered
• Saturday Drama Workshop (10 weeks). Course fee is £450 plus VAT for 6 hours of classes per week, or £250 plus VAT for 3 hours of classes per week

• Thursday Evening Workshop (10 weeks). Course fee is £180 plus VAT for 2 hours of classes per week
• Summer Beginners (4 weeks). Course fee is £1100 (including VAT). Entry is by audition
• Summer Advanced (5 weeks). Course fee is £1350 or £2150 (including VAT) for beginners and advanced. Entry is by audition
• Advanced Drama Workshop (10 weeks). The course runs on Tuesday evenings for 2 hours and costs £190 plus VAT

Morley College Theatre School
61 Westminster Bridge Road, London SE1 7HT
tel 020-7450 1832
email keith-brazil@morleycollege.ac.uk
website www.morleycollege.ac.uk
Key contacts Jane Carr, Dominic Grant

Offers part-time acting classes which lead to London Open College Network accreditation. Classes are led by specialist acting tutors with extensive professional experience. An Access Hardship Fund and concessionary fees are available to some students.

Courses offered
• A range of evening and part-time acting skills courses are available, including: Actors' Voice Workshop, The Acting Business, Singing for Actors and Dancers, Absolute Beginners Drama Workshop, Developing Acting Skills, Introduction to Physical Theatre, and many different styles of Dance
• Intermediate Foundation Theatre Arts (1 year part-time). Covers Acting Techniques (including voice, improvisation, text work and scenes) and Dance Techniques (Jazz and Contemporary) leading to performances in term 3. Course fee is approximately £650 p.a. for EU students, with concessions and hardship grants available. Entry is by audition
• Acting Studies (1-year evening school). Develops improvisation, characterisation, voice and movement skills through a series of workshops and rehearsals. Course fee is approximately £400, with concessions and hardship grants available. Entry is by audition
• Morley Theatre School (1-year evening school). For those with ability and confidence as actors who want to consolidate their skills. Workshops explore different techniques and approaches, and lead towards performance at the end of the course. Entry is by audition

Mountview Academy of Theatre Arts
Ralph Richardson Memorial Studios, Clarendon Road, London N22 6XF
tel 020-8881 2201 *fax* 020-8829 0034
email enquiries@mountview.ac.uk
website www.mountview.ac.uk
Principal Paul Clements

Courses offered
• Foundation Acting (1 year). Course fee is £1100 with 9 hours of classes per week. Entry is by audition

• Foundation Musical Theatre (1 year). Course fee is £1300 with 9 hours of classes per week. Entry is by audition
• Acting for Screen (2 terms). Course fee is £800 with 3 hours of classes per week. Entry is by audition
• Professional Masterclass, available from 1 day to 1 week during spring and autumn. Fees vary. No audition required
• Summer School Acting (2 weeks). Courses take place in July/August, fee is £550. No audition required
• Summer School Musical Theatre (2 weeks). Courses take place in July/August, fee is £550. No audition required
• Audition Technique (4-6 weeks). Courses take place in spring and autumn, fee is £180. No audition required
• Perform: Acting (2 terms). Course fee is £700 with 6 hours of classes per week. Entry is by audition
• Perform: Musical Theatre (2 terms). Course fee is £700 with 6 hours of classes per week. Entry is by audition

Northern Actors Centre

21-31 Oldham Street, Manchester M1 1JG
tel 0161-819 2513 *fax* 0161-819 2513
email info@northernactorscentre.co.uk
website www.northernactorscentre.co.uk

Core provision of ongoing professional development for trained actors. Provide workshops for all Equity members, covering every aspect of an actor's toolbox and led by leading industry professionals. Equity members or professional actors with sufficient experience are eligible for membership. Membership fees are £25 per year or £18 for 6 months. Graduates in the first year following graduation from an NCDT-accredited course are entitled to a reduced membership fee and to receive a current brochure.

Regular workshops include Acting for Screen, Auditioning for TV & Theatre, Beginners' Meisner Technique, Tools for Learning an Accent, Shakespeare Surgery, Advice, Voice, Stage Combat, and Directing. Members can book individual sessions to work on any chosen area.

Oxford School of Drama

Sansomes Farm Studios, Woodstock, Oxford OX20 1ER
tel (01993) 812883 *fax* (01993) 811220
email info@oxforddrama.ac.uk
website www.oxforddrama.ac.uk
Principal George Peck *Key contact* Stephen Minay

Courses offered

• 6-month Foundation course which runs from September to March. Aimed at students aged 17 and over (most are 18-19 years old), the course covers acting methods and technique, movement, voice, singing, film and television, stage fighting, stage management and history of theatre. Course fee is

£4200 with 32 hours of classes per week. Entry is by audition

Pineapple Dance Studios

7 Langley Street, London WC2H 9JA
tel 020-7836 4004 *fax* 020-7836 0803
email studios@pineapple.uk.com
website www.pineapple.uk.com

Pineapple offers more classes than any other studio throughout Europe, and the widest variety of dance styles. The philosophy behind the creation of the Pineapple Dance Studios was to break down the elitist barriers surrounding dance, making it available to everyone – from the absolute beginner to the advanced and the professional dancer. All classes are open, so you do not need to book; you can just come along at any time and take a class. Everybody is welcome: Pineapple offers classes for all levels and all ages (from dancers who are 4 years of age to those in their 90s – its oldest member is currently 93!). Around 40 different varieties of dance styles are taught, at approx. 200 classes per week, ranging from classical ballet to street jazz, hip hop to Salsa, Egyptian dance to Bollywood grooves plus many more. *Opening hours*: Mon to Fri: 9am – 9pm; Sat: 9am – 6.30pm; Sun: 10am – 6pm.

The Questors Theatre Ealing

12 Mattock Lane, London W5 5BQ
tel 020-8567 0011 *fax* 020-8567 8736
email enquiries@questors.org.uk
website www.questors.org.uk
Principal David Emmet *Key contact* Administrator

Provides part-time training for actors in the context of a working theatre. Financial support is available from a private trust fund for a limited number of students.

Courses offered

• Acting: Foundation and Performance (2 years). Course fee is £220 with 15 hours of classes per week. Entry is by audition
• Introduction to Acting (1 year). Age range for entry is 17-20. Course fee is £120 with 5 hours of classes per week. Entry is by audition

Richmond Drama School

Parkshot Centre, Parkshot, Richmond TW9 2RE
tel 020-8843 7921
email Mark.Woolgar@racc.ac.uk
Key contact Mark Woolgar

Courses offered

The school offers many new courses, including Lecoq Physical Theatre, Stand Up Comedy, Radio, TV, Acting – Comedy/Shakespeare/Chekhov, Audition and Interview Skills, Actor and Text, Circus Skills, Stage Fighting, Effective Communication, AS Level Performing Arts, Acting Skills, and Directing. There are also a number of proposed longer, full-time courses: for details, contact Mark Woolgar.

Rose Bruford College

Lamorbey Park, Burnt Oak Lane, Sidcup DA15 9DF
tel 020-8308 2600 *fax* 020-8308 0542
email enquiries@bruford.ac.uk
website www.bruford.ac.uk
Principal Professor Alastair Pearce

Courses offered

• Acting Summer School (2 weeks). Designed for participants over the age of 18 (16+ for non-residential), this programme includes classes, rehearsals and workshops on voice, movement, acting and improvisation.

Royal Academy of Dramatic Art (RADA)

62-64 Gower Street, London WC1E 6ED
tel 020-7636 7076 *fax* 020-7323 3865
email enquiries@rada.ac.uk
website www.rada.org
Principal Nicholas Barter

Courses offered

• Acting Shakespeare (8 weeks). Designed for experienced actors, this course offers an opportunity to expand, explore and deepen awareness of Shakespeare's texts. Covers all aspects of vocal technique, with classes to develop the resonance and range of each student's voice. The last 2 weeks of the course are spent in full-time rehearsal for a workshop production culminating in 3 performances in a RADA theatre. Entry is deliberately restricted and places are awarded by competitive audition. Students below the age of 18 are not normally accepted; most students are in their 20s. Course fee is £4500 which includes breakfast, lunch and refreshments Monday-Friday. Course takes place in June and July. *Audition requirements*: 1 speech from Shakespeare and 1 from a modern play, each lasting no longer than 3 minutes. *Audition fee*: £33
• The RADA Summer School (4 weeks). Based on exploring Shakespeare from an actor's point of view, this course mixes rehearsing scenes and speeches with intensive classes in essential acting skills. Students below the age of 18 are not normally accepted; most students are in their 20s. Course fee is £2560 which includes breakfast, lunch and refreshments Monday-Friday. Course takes place in July and August. No audition required.
• Skill Development through Classical Acting (3 weeks). This course explores the acting skills required to handle the complex texts of the English Classical Theatre. Each week a director works on a different era in classical theatre: week 1 – Shakespeare; week 2 – Jacobean/Caroline tragedy; week 3 – Restoration comedy. Students also attend classes in voice and speech, movement, sword fighting and period dance.

Students below the age of 18 are not normally accepted; there is no upper age limit. Course fee is £1750 which includes a light continental-style breakfast and lunch
• Musical Theatre (5 days). This course is designed for intermediate and advanced singer-actors who have already received some formal vocal training and are intending to pursue a career in musical theatre. During the course, guidance on casting and help with audition repertoire is given. Students work with a singing tutor, director, choreographer and musical director, both in groups and individually, to develop the necessary skills required by the successful singer-actor in today's musical theatre. At the end of the course there is an informal presentation of selected pieces for an invited audience, followed by individual feedback. Course fee is £725
• RADA Directing Course – How to Rehearse (2 weeks). This is an intensive course for 6 selected directors, focusing on the rehearsal period – what to do in it, how to shape rehearsals, and how to work with actors to discover the meaning and structure of the play. There is also the opportunity to work with designers and writers. Students study how to develop a method of work, and work on scenes with actors, with a presentation at the end of the course. Students below the age of 18 are not normally accepted; there is no upper age limit. Course fee is £1400 which includes a light continental-style breakfast and lunch
• The RADA Contemporary Drama Summer School (10 days). This course provides the opportunity to work on modern or contemporary texts. Students work in groups led by a director, with support from a voice and a movement instructor. Other playwrights talk about their work during special evening sessions, describing their experience of working with actors and what they expect from them, following presentations of excerpts from their plays by RADA graduates. Students present rehearsed material and receive feedback from the director and the voice and movement teachers on the last day of the course. Students below the age of 18 are not normally accepted; there is no upper age limit. Course fee is £1250 which includes a light continental-style breakfast and lunch

The School of the Science of Acting

Dept E, 67-83 Seven Sisters Road, London N7 6BU
tel 020-7272 0027 *fax* 020-7272 0026
email find@scienceofacting.org.uk
website www.scienceofacting.org.uk
Key contact Jack Curzon

Courses offered

• Intensive Acting Course (33 weeks). Course fee is £1440 with 6 hours of classes per week. No audition required
• Spring Workshop (2 weeks). Course takes place in March and the fee is £500. No audition required
• Summer Workshop (2 weeks). Course takes place in July and the fee is £400. No audition required

• Autumn Workshop (2 weeks). Course takes place in March and the fee is £500. No audition required

Youngblood

The Rag Factory, 16-18 Heneage St, London E1 5LJ
tel 020-7193 3207
email info@youngblood.co.uk
website www.youngblood.co.uk

A company of fight directors and stage-combat teachers. Runs ongoing classes for professional actors in various locations around London. Also provides fight directors and trainers for film, television and theatre projects, including low-budget productions.

Agents and casting directors
Introduction

Actors have probably existed since before the invention of writing; actors' agents have only been around since the invention of the telephone, just over a century ago. Prior to this, work-seeking actors had to make themselves known in person to potential employers – for instance, certain hostelries in the Covent Garden area of central London were well-known 'talent-spotting' haunts. Actors would also 'catch a ride' with one of the touring companies in the hope of proving themselves to the manager – and then being put on the payroll. Others would pay managers to let them play small parts in the hope of being noticed. All this meant a lot of hard work and/or expense (let alone the time needed to earn his/her living by other means) for the pre-electronic-age actor. The invention of actors' agents seemed to fill a vital gap.

In the 1970s, a number of actors dissatisfied with the (by then) traditional agent system formed the first co-operative agencies (see page 68). This apparently simple idea – with all members taking turns to 'man' the office – took a while to become established. Like many 'simple ideas', the pioneers found that there were more complications involved than they'd initially envisaged, and employers were slow to accept the idea. Thirty years later, the best 'co-ops' have as much professional credibility as their conventional counterparts.

It used to be the case that only the biggest companies used casting directors. The administrative burden inherent in running such a company (let alone directing productions) meant that assistance in the casting process became essential. The 1990s saw a rise in the use of casting directors and in the number of freelancers working on short-term contracts: most of the latter work in a wide variety of fields.

The simple fact is that a significant proportion of properly paid acting work is 'brokered' by casting directors and agents.

Being an agent
Brian Taylor

The image of an agent – Woody Allen in *Broadway Danny Rose*, on the phone at a desk piled chaotically high in a crowded office, ringing around and touting for business, responding to rumours of possible castings and going out to lunch an awful lot! – still holds fast in many minds. But much has changed: the electronic age has arrived; agents now work in a sophisticated way, making great use of the Internet, faxes, emails, etc.

Brian Taylor Associates is an established, middle-sized agency with two full-time members of staff and two part-time, and about 80 clients. As such, we are typical of most actors' agencies. Over many years we have established strong, friendly and important contacts with the major television companies – providers of a great deal of work; with theatre producers and directors; with theatre companies in London, theatres around the country, the RNT and the RSC; and with casting directors, both commercial and non-commercial, across all aspects of the business. As a result our suggestions have become respected and are taken seriously: we do not suggest actors inappropriately, simply because they are not working. This is essential to the successful running of the business.

On a busy day the agency can be kept occupied simply responding to the casting breakdowns that are fed to us from all directions: by phone, email, fax and post. We respond with our suggestions, sending out letters with photographs and CVs; sometimes by fax, with names and Spotlight numbers only; by email, attaching jpeg photos and CVs; and most frequently now, by the Spotlight Link. So it's important that actors go into Spotlight, even impoverished students just out of drama school, if they are not to miss out on casting.

When not putting up suggestions, talking to casting directors, giving appointments to clients, listening to their worries and concerns, etc., time has to be found to interview actors looking for representation. Actors writing in, please think carefully about how you address us. 'Dear Sir/Madam' gets nowhere; 'To Whom It May Concern' receives even less consideration! Do not be over-familiar. Be brief and concise. Do not try to be witty and facetious. Always include an sae if you want a reply. Do not 'slag off' your old agent.

Time must also be found to go and see clients in performance. This is always a priority, sometimes involving long journeys, and it's not always possible. Requests are received to go and see other actors, again involving long journeys ... and all this at the end of a hard day in the office. Actors often forget that. In touch with the major drama schools, we try to see their student productions, and eventually their showcases, in our search for new and exciting talent. In fact there is a period, starting even before Easter, when if one chose (or was able to) one could be out at a showcase almost every day of the week, such is the proliferation of drama schools today.

So a typical agent's day, in and out of the office, will involve most of the above plus the administrative, book-keeping and accounting work involved in running any busy concern. Hopefully this will go some way towards rectifying some actors' image of their agent as a wining, dining, do-nothing layabout. Not true!

Brian Taylor read History at Leeds University, was Head of Department at a large London comprehensive school, and then worked as a Producer/Director for ILEA Television where he was responsible for a variety of programmes, including history documentaries, drama series and art programmes. He left to set up his own video production company, which produced a widely marketed video, 'Discovering London', presented by Sir Ian McKellen. He also taught at LAMDA, and eventually came to work with agent Nina Quick. In 1995 he bought out the business, now renamed Brian Taylor Associates. Brian lives and works in Kensington, but escapes each weekend to his cottage in the Cotswolds, to escape the rigours and stresses of being an agent.

Agents

A good agent understands contracts, knows the current rates in every field of work and – most importantly – has plenty of professional contacts and access to far more casting information than most individuals can ever possess. Directors and casting directors rely on the agents they know and trust to help with the filtering process of whom to interview. A good agent will work hard at promoting each of his/her clients; in return, it is not unreasonable that they charge commission on every contract they negotiate for you – generally, 10-20 per cent (plus VAT, if appropriate). A good agent will also (a) have only as many clients as they can reasonably handle, and (b) ensure that they have a good range of ages and types of actors to cover as many casting opportunities as possible.

When you are seeking representation, it is advisable to contact agents by post in the first instance – unless specifically informed otherwise. It is a good idea to include a separate 10x8in (25x20cm) photograph, and it is important that all your enclosures give your name and the best way to contact you (not a long list of confusing alternatives). Agents receive many requests for representation, and photographs can become separated from their accompanying letters and CVs, so proper labelling is essential.

Use the listings that follow to (a) target your submission as accurately as possible (by writing to a specific, named person, for example), (b) check for any details that could inform the content of your letter, and (c) find out whether each would be interested in any extras, like a showreel. Time spent checking details can save money and enhance your chances of being noticed more than the next person. Unless you have a good collection of professional credits, it is generally best to write to agents when there's an opportunity for them to see you in something.

If you are invited to meet an agent, that is often a good sign. You should approach the occasion in much the same way as you would an interview for a production. The major difference is that you should be prepared to ask (reasonable) questions – rates of commission, for instance.

When seeking representation, it can be a good idea to target only those agencies that you think might suit you. For instance, might you feel lost in a large agency, but feel more comfortable with a smaller one? On the other hand, some larger agencies have huge 'clout' and can be the first 'port of call' for the casting of prestigious productions.

When you've been taken on by an agent, it is important to establish how your working relationship will function. Be clear about any areas of work that you don't want to be suggested for, discuss your availability for auditions and interviews, agree how much promotion you should do for yourself, and so on.

These listings only contain agents who represent adult actors – there are many others who represent children, models, extras and so on.

21st Century Vaux Casting

The Corn Exchange, Fenwick Street, Liverpool L2 7QS
tel 0151-258 1679 *fax* 0151-231 1067
email 21stcenturyvaux@beeb.net
Key personnel David Williamson

Established in 1991, the agency represents 20 actors. Areas of work include theatre, television, film, commercials, corporate and voice-overs.

Will consider attending performances at venues in Greater London and the North West with at least 1 week's notice. Accepts submissions (with CVs and photographs) from actors previously unknown to the company sent by post or email. Will also accept showreels, voice tapes, and invitations to view individual actors' websites. *Commission*: 7.5%

41 Management

3rd Floor, 74 Rose Street, North Lane, Edinburgh EH2 3DX
tel 0131-225 3585 *fax* 0131-225 4535
email mhunwick@41man.co.uk
Key personnel Maryam Hunwick

A personal management established in 1999. 1 agent represents actors. Areas of work include theatre, musicals, television, film, commercials and voice-overs. Also represents vocal coaches for theatre, musicals, television and film industries.

Will consider attending performances at venues within Greater London and in Scotland given 4 weeks' notice. Accepts submissions (with CVs and photographs) from actors previously unknown to the company if sent by post. Will also accept showreels. *Commission*: Theatre 10%; TV and Broadcast Media 12.5%; Commercials 15%

A&J Management

242A The Ridgeway, Botany Bay, Enfield EN2 8AP
tel 020-8342 0542 *fax* 020-8342 0842
email info@ajmanagement.co.uk
website www.ajmanagement.co.uk
Managing Director Jackie Michael *Key personnel* Joanne Michael, Hannah Liebeskind

Established in 1984. 3 agents represent actors. Areas of work include theatre, musicals, television, film, commercials, corporate and voice-overs.

Will consider attending performances at venues within Greater London with a minimum of 2 weeks' notice. Accepts submissions (with CVs and photographs) from actors previously unknown to the company if sent by post. Invitations to view individual actors' websites are also accepted. *Commission*: 15% plus VAT

June Abbott Associates

The Courtyard, 10 York Way, London N1 9AA
tel 020-7837 7826 *fax* 020-7833 0870
email jaa@thecourtyard.org.uk
website www.thecourtyard.org.uk
Agent June Abbott *Assistant Agent* Tanya Parkin

Established in 1994. 2 agents represent 50 actors. Areas of work include theatre, musicals, television, film, commercials, corporate and voice-overs.

Attendance at performances is dependent on potential client submissions/interviews. Accepts submissions (with CVs and photographs) from actors previously unknown to the company if sent by post. Enclose an sae if a reply is required and for the return of CVs and photographs. Showreels and voice tapes should only be sent on request. Actors should only apply if they have training, and will only be contacted if the agency is interested. Recommends the photographer Peter Simpkin (see entry under *Photographers and repro companies* on page 282 for further details). *Commission*: Theatre 10%; Voice-Over and Radio 12%; Film and TV 15%

Acting Associates

71 Hartham Road, London N7 9JJ
tel 020-7607 3562 *fax* 020-7607 3562
email Fiona@actingassociates.co.uk
website www.actingassociates.co.uk
Agent Fiona Farley

Established in 1988. 1 agent represents 45-50 actors.

Will consider attending performances with 1 week's notice. Accepts submissions (with CVs and photographs) from actors previously unknown to the company if sent by post. Recommends the photographer Catherine Shakespeare Lane (see entry under *Photographers and repro companies* on page 275 for further details). *Commission*: Theatre 10%; Other 15%

Actors Ireland

Crescent Arts Centre, 2-4 University Road, Belfast BT7 1NH
tel 028-9024 8861 *fax* 028-9024 8861
email Geraldine@actorsireland.com
website www.actorsireland.com

Established in 2001. 2 agents represent 90 actors. Areas of work include theatre, musicals, television, film, commercials, corporate and voice-overs.

Will consider attending performances at venues in Northern Ireland. Accepts submissions (with CVs and photographs) from actors previously unknown to the company if sent by post. Will also accept invitations to view individual actors' websites. *Commission*: Theatre 5%; TV 10%

Actual Management

The Studio, 63a Ladbroke Road, London W11 3PD
tel 020-7243 1166 *fax* 0870-874 1149
email agents@actualmanagement.co.uk
website www.actualmanagement.co.uk

Established in 2002. 2 agents represent 50 actors. Areas of work include theatre, television, film and commercials.

Will consider attending performances at venues in Greater London with at least 2 weeks' notice. Accepts submissions (with CVs and photographs) from actors previously unknown to the company sent by post or email. Will also accept showreels, voice tapes, and invitations to view individual actors' websites.

Anita Alraun Representation

5th Floor, 28 Charing Cross Road, London WC2H 0DB
tel 020-7379 6840 *fax* 020-7379 6865
Sole Proprietor/Agent Anita Alraun

1 agent represents a varying number of actors. Areas of work include theatre, musicals, film, television, commercials, radio drama, corporate and some voice-overs.

Attendance at performances is dependent on potential client submissions/interviews. Accepts submissions (with CV, photograph and sae – essential for reply) by post only from trained/experienced actors previously unknown to the company. Emailed submissions will not be considered. Showreels and voice tapes should be sent only if requested, following interview. *Commission*: Radio 10%; Theatre 10-12.5%; Film and TV 12.5%; Commercials 15%

Alvarez Management

86 Muswell Road, London N10 2BE
tel 020-8883 2206 *fax* 020-8444 2646

Established in 1990. 2 agents represent 55 actors. Areas of work include theatre, musicals, television, film, commercials, corporate and voice-overs.

Will consider attending performances at venues within Greater London with 3-4 weeks' notice. Accepts submissions (with CVs, photographs and sae) from actors previously unknown to the company if sent by post. "When you are on the phone, please introduce yourself." "Have a really decent photograph taken." *Commission*: Theatre and Radio 10%; Film and TV 12.5%; Commercials 15%

ALW Associates

1 Grafton Chambers, Grafton Place, London NW1 1LN
tel 020-7388 7018 *fax* 020-7813 1398
email alweurope@onetel.com

Established in 1977 as Vernon Conway Ltd. Sole representation of 35 actors. Areas of work include theatre, musicals, television, film and commercials.

Will consider attending performances at venues within Greater London and occasionally elsewhere with 1 week's notice. Accepts submissions (with CVs and photographs) from actors previously unknown to the company sent by post or email. Also accepts invitations to view individual actors' websites. Showreels and voice tapes should only be sent on request. *Commission*: Theatre and Radio 10-12.5%; Film and TV 12.5%; Commercials 15%

Amber Personal Management Ltd

189 Wardour Street, London W1F 8ZD
tel 020-7734 7887 *fax* 020-7734 9883
email info@amberltd.co.uk
website www.amberltd.co.uk

Established in 1986. 3 agents represent around 80 actors. Areas of work include theatre, musicals, television, film, commercials, corporate and voice-overs. Also represents directors and presenters (normally as an additional skill of actors already represented by the agency). Management has agents based in London as well as in Manchester.

Will consider attending performances at venues within Greater London and elsewhere with 3-4 weeks' notice. Accepts submissions (with CVs, photographs and sae) from actors previously unknown to the company if sent by post. *Commission*: Theatre and Radio 6.5-8.5%; Film, TV and Commercials 15%; Live Presentation 10%

The American Agency

14 Bonny Street, London NW1 9PG
tel 020-7485 8883 *fax* 020-7482 4666
email americanagency@btconnect.com
Agent Ed Cobb

Areas of work include theatre, musicals, television, film, commercials, corporate and voice-overs. 2 agents represent 80 actors. Will consider attending performances within the Greater London area. Accepts submissions (with CVs and photographs) from actors previously unknown to the agency if sent by post, but not by email. Invitations to view individual actors' websites, showreels and voice tapes are also accepted. Welcomes enquiries from actors with disabilities. *Commission*: Theatre 10%; Other 15%

Susan Angel & Kevin Francis Ltd

1st Floor, 12 D'Arblay Street, London W1F 8DU
tel 020-7439 3086 *fax* 020-7437 1712
email angelpair@freeuk.com
Director Kevin Francis

Established in 1976. 3 agents represent 70 actors. Areas of work include theatre, television, film, and commercials.

Will consider attending performances at venues within Greater London and occasionally elsewhere (e.g. Leeds, Bristol, Manchester) with 2 weeks' notice. Accepts brief postal submissions (with CVs and photographs) from actors previously unknown to the company. Emailed applications are not considered due to the volume of mail. *Commission*: 10-12.5%

APM Associates

PO Box 834, Hemel Hempstead, Hertfordshire HP3 9ZP
tel (01442) 252907 *fax* (01442) 241099
email apm@apmassociates.net

website www.apmassociates.net
Managing Director Linda French *Agent* Claire Brenner

Established in 1989. 2 agents represent around 65 actors. Areas of work include theatre, musicals, television, film, commercials, corporate and voice-overs. Also represents actor-writers, presenters and directors.

Will consider attending performances at venues within Greater London with 2 weeks' notice. Accepts submissions (with CVs and photographs) from actors previously unknown to the company if sent by post with sae. Will also accept showreels and voice tapes. Will consider looking at websites only if actor's CV is of interest. Welcomes applications from disabled actors. *Commission*: Brochure available upon offer of interview

Argyle Associates

St John's Buildings, 43 Clerkenwell Road, London EC1M 5RS
tel 020-7608 2095 *fax* 020-7608 1642
email argyle.associates@virgin.net
Director Richard Linford *Key personnel* Geraldine Pryor

Established in 1995. 2 agents represent 30 actors. Areas of work include theatre, musicals, television, film, commercials and corporate.

Will consider attending performances at venues in Sussex and Surrey (e.g. Eastbourne, Brighton, Guildford, Dorking, Windsor) with 2 weeks' notice. Accepts submissions (with CVs and photographs) from actors previously unknown to the company if sent by post. Invitations to view individual actors' websites are also accepted. "Be clear about what you think you have to offer the agency – your type and roles. Your photograph should look like you and be a high-grade holiday snap." *Commission*: Theatre and Radio 10%; TV 12.5%; Commercials, Film, Corporate and CD Rom 15%

Ash Personal Management

3 Spencer Road, Mitcham Common, Surrey CR4 15G
tel/fax 020-8646 0050
email ash-personal-mgmt@yahoo.co.uk
Agent Anthony Hyland

Established in 1986. 1 agent represents 15 actors working in theatre, musicals, television, film and commercials.

Will consider attending performances within Greater London and beyond, given 1-2 weeks' notice. Accepts submissions (with CVs and photographs) from actors previously unknown to the agency sent by post or email. Will also accept showreels, voice tapes and invitations to view an actor's website; follow-up telephone calls, however, are not welcomed. *Commission*: Stage 10%; Screen 15%

Asquith & Horner

The Studio, 14 College Road, Bromley BR1 3NS
tel 020-8466 5580 *fax* 020-8313 0443
website www.spotlightagent.info (view PIN 9858-0919-0728)
Senior Partner Anthony Vander Elst *Partner* Helen Melville

Established 1989. 2 agents represent 70 actors. Also represented are directors, choreographers, presenters, singers, dancers and commercial models. Areas of work include theatre, musicals, television, film, commercials, corporate and voice-overs. Will consider attending performances at venues within Greater London and elsewhere but requests as much notice as possible. Accepts submissions (CVs and photographs) from actors previously unknown to the company; also accepts showreels and voice tapes, and invitations to view actors' websites. "Unsolicited enquiries should always be accompanied by an appropriately stamped and addressed envelope for return of answer, photo, tape, etc."

Associated International Management (AIM)

Sanctuary House, 45-53 Sinclair Road, London W14 0NS
tel 020-7300 6506 *fax* 020-7300 6656
email info@aimagents.com
website www.aimagents.com
Key personnel Derek Webster, Stephen Gittins, Lisa-Marie Assenheim

An international management established in 1984. 3 agents represent 70 actors. Areas of work include theatre, television, film and commercials. Also represents directors.

Will consider attending performances within the Greater London area with at least 3 weeks' notice. Accepts submissions (with CVs and photographs) from actors previously unknown to the agency if sent by post, but not by email. *Commission*: 12-15%

BAM Associates

Benets Cottage, Dolberrow, Churchill, Bristol BS25 5NT
tel (01934) 852942
email bam@louisealexander.plus.com
website www.ebam.tv

2 agents represent 45 actors. Areas of work include theatre, musicals, television, film, commercials, corporate and voice-overs.

Will consider attending performances at venues within Greater London and the South West, but requests as much notice as possible. Accepts submissions (with CVs and 10x8in black and white photographs) from actors previously unknown to the company if sent by post. Welcomes enquiries from disabled actors. *Commission*: Theatre 10%; Mechanical Media 15%

Gavin Barker Associates Ltd

2D Wimpole Street, London W1G 0EB
tel 020-7499 4777 *fax* 020-7499 3777
email amanda@gavinbarkerassociates.co.uk
website www.gavinbarkerassociates.co.uk
Managing Director Gavin Barker *Associate
Director* Michelle Burke

Established in 1998. 2 agents represent 55 actors and
a handful of creatives. Areas of work include theatre,
musicals, television, film, commercials, corporate and
voice-overs. Also represents directors and
choreographers.

Will consider attending performances at venues in
Greater London given at least 3 weeks' notice.
Accepts submissions (with CVs and photographs)
from actors previously unknown to the company if
sent by post. Follow-up calls are not welcome. Happy
to receive showreels and voice tapes. Does not
encourage representation enquiries from disabled
actors. *Commission*: 10-12.5%

Olivia Bell Ltd

189 Wardour Street, London W1F 8ZD
tel 020-7439 3270 *fax* 020-7439 3485
email info@olivia-bell.co.uk
Managing Director Xania Segal

Established in 2001. 2 agents represent 90 actors.
Areas of work include theatre, musicals, television,
film and commercials.

Will consider attending performances at venues
within Greater London with a minimum of 1 week's
notice. Accepts submissions (with CVs and
photographs) from actors previously unknown to the
company if sent by post. Invitations to view
individual actors' websites and showreels or voice
tapes are also accepted. *Commission*: 12.5-20%

Jorg Betts Associates

Gainsborough House, 81 Oxford Street, London
W1D 2EU
tel 020-7903 5300 *fax* 020-7903 5301
email jorg@jorgbetts.com

Established in 2001. Areas of work include theatre,
musicals, television, film, commercials and corporate.
Also represents directors and presenters.

Accepts submissions (with CVs and photographs)
from actors previously unknown to the company if
sent by post.

Billboard Personal Management

Unit 5, 11 Mowll Street, London SW9 6BG
tel 020-7735 9956 *fax* 020-7793 0426
email billboardpm@btconnect.com
website www.billboardpm.com
Agent Daniel Tasker

Established in 1985. 1 agent represents 55 actors.
Areas of work include theatre, musicals, television,
film, commercials, corporate and voice-overs.

Will consider attending performances at venues in
Greater London given a minimum of 2 weeks' notice.
Accepts submissions (with CVs and photographs)
from actors previously unknown to the company if
they are currently performing. *Commission*:
Commercials 16%; Film and TV 13.5%; Other 11%

Bishop Burnett Agency & Management

47 Dean Street, London W1P 5BE
tel 020-7734 9995 *fax* 020-7734 9996
email lara@mcslondon.com
Key personnel Keith Bishop, Lara James

Areas of work include theatre, musicals, television,
film, commercials, corporate and voice-overs. 3
agents represent 35 actors. Also represents models,
presenters, reporters, celebrities and celebrity
hairdressers. Will consider attending performances
within the Greater London area with at least 1
month's notice. Accepts submissions (with CVs and
photographs) from actors previously unknown to the
company (include an sae). Invitations to view
individual actors' websites, showreels and voice tapes
are also accepted. Welcomes enquiries from actors
with disabilities. *Commission*: Theatre 10-15%

Bloomfields Management

34 South Molton Street, London W1K 5BP
tel 020-7493 4448 *fax* 020-7493 4449
email emma@bloomfieldsmanagement.com
website www.bloomfieldsmanagement.com
Director Emma Bloomfield

Established in 2004. Areas of work include theatre,
musicals, television, film, commercials and corporate.
2 agents represent 40 actors. Will consider attending
performances anywhere, given at least 2 weeks'
notice. Accepts submissions (with CVs and
photographs) from actors previously unknown to the
company if sent by post, but not by email. Invitations
to view individual actors' websites, showreels and
voice tapes are also accepted. Welcomes enquiries
from actors with disabilities.

Sandra Boyce Management

1 Kingsway House, Albion Road, London N16 0TA
tel 020-7923 0606 *fax* 020-7241 2713
email info@sandraboyce.com
Agents Sandra Boyce (MD), Paul Cullen

2 agents represent 70 actors in all areas of acting
work; directors also represented. Welcomes
performance notices if given at least 2 weeks in
advance, and is prepared to travel within the Greater
London area. Happy to accept letters (by post, not
email) with CV and photograph from individuals
previously unknown to the company, but does not
welcome follow-up calls. Encourages approaches
from actors with disabilities. Also welcomes showreels
and voice tapes. Advises those approaching the
agency to "always include a stamped, addressed
envelope (of correct size) for return of photos/
showreels".

The Bridge Agency Ltd
PO Box 261, Loughton IG10 2WS
tel 0870-116 1388 *fax* 0870-116 1389
email the_bridge_agency@yahoo.co.uk
Agent Robert Stokvis

Established in 2002. 1 agent represents 10 actors.
Areas of work include theatre, musicals, television,
film, commercials, corporate and voice-overs.

Will consider attending performances at East 15
Acting School only, and with 2 weeks' notice. Accepts
showreels and voice tapes from East 15 graduates.
"Our agency is open to graduates of East 15 Acting
School only. We aim to see all productions at East 15
and to intensify this cooperation." *Commission*: 8-
18%

BROOD
3 Queen's Garth, Taymount Rise, London SE23 3UF
tel 020-8699 1071 *mobile* (07932) 022635
email broodmanagement@aol.com
website www.broodmanagement.com
Director Brian Parsonage Kelly

Established in 2003. 1 agent represents 40 actors.
Areas of work include theatre, musicals, television,
film, commercials and corporate. Also represents
models.

Accepts submissions (with CVs and photographs)
from actors previously unknown to the company if
sent by post. Recommends the photographer Janie
Airey (**www.janie-airey.com**). *Commission*: Theatre
10%; Other 15%

Valerie Brook Agency
10 Sandringham Road, Cheadle Hulme, Cheshire
SK8 5NH
tel 0161-486 1631 *fax* 0161-488 4206
email colinbrook@freenetname.co.uk

2 agents represent 75 actors. Areas of work include
theatre, musicals, television, film, commercials and
corporate role-play.

Will consider attending performances at venues
outside Greater London with 2 weeks' notice. Accepts
postal submissions (with CVs and photographs) from
actors previously unknown to the company.
Invitations to view individual actors' websites are also
accepted. *Commission*: Negotiated with clients
individually

Brown & Simcocks
1 Bridgehouse Court, 109 Blackfriars Road, London
SE1 8HW
tel 020-7928 1229 *fax* 020-7928 1909
email mail@brownandsimcocks.co.uk
website www.brownandsimcocks.co.uk
Partners Carrie Simcocks, Peter Walmsley

Established in the 1970s; 2 agents represent 65-70
actors. Areas of work include theatre, musicals,
television, film, commercials and corporate.

Will consider attending performances within the
Greater London area given 2-4 weeks' notice. Accepts
submissions (with CVs and photographs) from actors
previously unknown to the company if sent by post.
Follow-up telephone calls, showreels, voice tapes and
emails are not welcome. *Commission*: 10-15%

Brunskill Management Ltd
Suite 8A, 169 Queen's Gate, London SW7 5HE

Agency represents more than 100 actors. Areas of
work include theatre, musicals, television, film,
commercials, corporate and voice-overs. Also
represents producers, directors and musical directors.

Will consider attending performances at venues in
Greater London and occasionally elsewhere, but
requests as much notice as possible. Accepts
submissions (with CVs and photographs) from actors
previously unknown to the company if sent by post.
Enclose an sae of an appropriate size for the return of
CVs and photographs. Emails are not encouraged,
particularly if they include large attachments.

Bronia Buchanan Associates Ltd
Nederlander House, 7 Great Russell Street, London
WC1B 3NH
tel 020-7631 2004 *fax* 020-7631 2034
email info@buchanan-associates.co.uk
website www.buchanan-associates.co.uk
Agents Bronia Buchanan, Phil Belfield, Mark Ward

Sole representation of approximately 25 creatives and
150 actors. Areas of work include theatre, musicals,
television, film and commercials.

Will consider attending performances at venues
within Greater London and elsewhere, but requests as
much notice as possible. Accepts submissions by post
or email (with CVs and photographs) from actors
previously unknown to the company. Showreels and
voice tapes are also encouraged. Recommends the
photographer Chris Baker (020-8441 3851).
Commission: 10% plus VAT

Burnett Granger Associates Ltd
3 Clifford Street, London W1S 2LF
tel 020-7437 8008 *fax* 020-7287 3239
email associates@burnettgranger.co.uk
Agents Barry Burnett, Lindsay Granger, Lizanne
Crowther

Established in 1965. 3 agents represent 140 actors.

Will consider attending performances at venues
within Greater London, with 3 weeks' notice. Accepts
submissions (with CVs, photographs and sae) from
actors previously unknown to the company if sent by
post. *Commission*: 10-12%

CADS Management
209 Abbey Road, Bearwood, Birmingham B67 5NG
tel 0121-420 1996 *fax* 0121-434 4909
email info@cadsmanagement.co.uk

website www.cadsmanagement.co.uk
Manager T Smith *Coordinator/Key contact* Rosina
Chaudry *IT/Administration* Ben Steel

Established in 1990. Sole representation of 60-70
actors. Areas of work include theatre, musicals,
television, film, commercials, corporate, voice-overs
and role-play. Also represents directors and
presenters.

Will consider attending performances at venues
within Greater London and elsewhere with 3 weeks'
notice. Accepts submissions (with CVs and
photographs) from actors previously unknown to the
company sent by post or email. Showreels and voice
tapes are also accepted. Workshops are run in August
each year, and contracts renewed in September.
Commission: 20%

Jessica Carney Associates

4th Floor, 23 Golden Square, London W1F 9JP
tel 020-7434 4143 *fax* 020-7434 4175
email info@jcarneyassociates.co.uk

Established in 1950. Areas of work include theatre,
television, films, commercials and musicals. Also
represents technicians and directors.

Will consider attending performances at venues
within Greater London with 2-3 weeks' notice.
Accepts submissions (with CVs and photographs)
from actors previously unknown to the company if
sent by post. Actors should only write if they are
performing in a London show. An sae must be
included if a reply is required. Emails should only be
sent with a sensible-sized photo pasted into the body
of the email; attachments will not be opened.
Commission: 10%; Commercials 15%

Casting Couch Productions Ltd

213 Trowbridge Road, Bradford-On-Avon, Wiltshire
BA15 1EU
tel (01225) 869212 *fax* (01225) 869029 *mobile* (07932)
785807
email moiratownsend@yahoo.co.uk
Key personnel Moira Townsend

Established in 1991. Sole representation of 25 actors.
Areas of work include theatre, musicals, television,
film, commercials, corporate and voice-overs.

Will consider attending performances at venues
within Greater London and elsewhere, with 2-3
weeks' notice. Accepts submissions (with CVs and
photographs, clearly stating age and nationality) from
actors previously unknown to the company,
preferably by email. An sae should be included for
the return of hard-copy CVs and photographs. Actors
will only be contacted if the agent would like to meet
them. *Commission*: 15% across the board

See entry under *Casting directors* on page 82 for
further details.

The Casting Department

Unit 15, Elysium Gate, 126-128 Kings Road, London
SW6 4LZ
tel 020-7384 0388 *fax* 020-7736 2221
email jillscastingdpt@aol.com
Key personnel Jill Searle

1 agent represents 200 actors. Areas of work include
television and commercials.

Accepts submissions (with CVs and photographs)
from actors previously unknown to the company if
sent by post.

CFA Management

22 Church Street, Briston, Melton Constable, Norfolk
NR24 2LE
tel (01263) 860650 *fax* (01263) 860650
email frances@cfamanagement.fsnet.co.uk
Key personnel Frances Ross

Established in 2000. 1 agent represents 30 actors.
Areas of work include theatre, television, film and
commercials.

Will consider attending performances in London and
East Anglia with 2-3 weeks' notice. Accepts
submissions (with CVs and photographs) from actors
previously unknown to the company if sent by post.
An invitation to telephone for further discussion and
possible appointment will be offered if suitable. Items
will be returned if an sae has been provided.
Commission: Theatre 12.5%; Film and Television
15%; Commercials 20%

Peter Charlesworth Associates

2nd Floor, 68 Old Brompton Road, London SW7
3LQ
tel 020-7581 2478 *fax* 020-7589 2922
email petercharlesworth@tiscali.co.uk
Director Peter Charlesworth *Associate* Sharry Clarke

Does not welcome unsolicited contact – including
performance notices – from actors previously
unknown to the company.

Cinel Gabran Management

Ty Cefn, 14-16 Rectory Road, Canton, Cardiff CF5
1QL
tel 029-2066 6600 *fax* 029-2066 6601
email info@cinelgabran.co.uk
website www.cinelgabran.co.uk
Managing Director/Agent David Chance *Agent* Sioned
James

Established in 1988. 2 agents represent 65 actors. Also
represents presenters, singers who act, and actors who
write. The company has a London client list,
although 60% of clients are Wales-based. It works in
both English- and Welsh-language production.

Will consider attending performances at venues in
Wales and Central London with 2 weeks' notice.
Accepts submissions (with CVs and photographs)

from actors previously unknown to the company if sent by post. An sae should be included with CVs and photographs. *Commission*: Varies according to type of work

Cloud Nine Agency
96 Tiber Gardens, Treaty Street, London N1 0XE
tel/fax 020-7278 0029
email cloudnineagency@blueyonder.co.uk
website www.cloudnineagency.co.uk

Established in 1995; 2 agents represent around 80 actors working in theatre, musicals, television, film, commercials and corporate role-play.

Will consider attending performances in North London and the West End given 2 weeks' notice. Accepts submissions (with CVs, showreels, photographs and sae) from actors previously unknown to the agency if sent by post. Will also accept invitations to view an actor's website. Follow-up telephone calls and emails, however, are not welcomed. *Commission*: 20%

Elspeth Cochrane Personal Management
16 Old Town, Clapham, London SW4 0JY
tel 020-7819 6256 *fax* 020-7819 4297
email elspeth@elspethcochrane.co.uk

One agent represents 40+ actors in theatre, musicals, TV, film, commercials and corporate work. Welcomes performance notices as far in advance as possible, and is prepared to travel to most venues in Greater London. Welcomes letters (by post or email) with CV and photograph from individuals (including disabled actors) previously unknown to the company. Also welcomes showreels. *Commission*: 12.5%

Cole Kitchenn Ltd
Vaudeville Theatre Offices, 404 Strand, London WC2R 0NH
tel 020-7580 2772 *fax* 020-7580 2992
email info@colekitchenn.com
website www.colekitchenn.com
Directors Guy Kitchenn, David Cole *Personal Manager* Stuart Piper

2 agents represent 15-20 actors. The agency works in theatre, musicals, television, film, commercials and voice-overs; it also represents directors, choreographers, musical directors and designers. Recommends LB Photography – see separate entry under *Photographers and repro companies*.

Welcomes performance notices within Greater London given 2-3 weeks' notice. Happy to receive letters and emails (with CVs, photographs and showreels) from new actors, but prefers not to receive follow-up telephone calls.

Shane Collins Associates
11-15 Betterton Street, Covent Garden, London WC2H 9BP

tel 020-7470 8864 *fax* 0870-460 1983
website www.shanecollins.co.uk
Agents Shane Collins, Polly Andrews, Paul Martin

Established in 1986, the agency represents around 85 actors working in all areas of the industry.

Will consider attending performances within Greater London given as much notice as possible. Accepts submissions (with CVs and photographs) from actors previously unknown to the company; however, follow-up telephone calls, emails, showreels, voice tapes and invitations to view an actor's website are not welcomed. Photos, CVs and showreels will only be returned if the actor includes a stamped, addressed envelope.

Collis Management
182 Trevelyan Road, London SW17 9LW
tel 020-8767 0196 *fax* 020-8682 0973
email marilyn@collismanagement.co.uk
Agent Marilyn Collis

Established in 1992. 1 agent represents 60 actors working in theatre, musicals, television, film, commercial and corporate work. Will consider attending performances within the Greater London area with 3 weeks' notice. Welcomes letters, showreels and invitations to view websites from actors previously unknown to the company, but not emailed CVs or follow-up calls. *Commission*: 10-15%

Conway van Gelder Ltd
18-21 Jermyn Street, London SW1Y 6HP
tel 020-7287 0077 *fax* 020-7287 1940
Agents Jeremy Conway, Nicola van Gelder, John Grant, Liz Nelson

4 agents represent actors working in all areas of the industry.

Will consider attending performances within Greater London and occasionally elsewhere, given 3-4 weeks' notice. Accepts postal submissions (with CVs, photographs and sae to ensure reply) from actors previously unknown to the agency, along with invitations to view an actor's website. Showreels and voice tapes should only be sent if requested after initial contact has been made. Follow-up telephone calls and emails are not welcomed. *Commission*: Varies according to contract

Howard Cooke Associates (HCA)
19 Coulson Street, London SW3 3NA
tel 020-7591 0144
Managing Director/Senior Agent Howard Cooke
Junior Agent Bronwyn Sanders

2 agents represent 40 actors. Areas of work include theatre, musicals, television, film, commercials and corporate.

Will consider attending performances at venues within Greater London and elsewhere (if within easy travelling distance) with 3 weeks' notice. Hard-copy applications (with CVs, photographs and sae) from actors previously unknown to the company are welcome, but email submissions are not accepted. "Having trained as an agent at Frazer-Skemp Management, former actor Howard Cooke formed HCA in 1993. The company specialises in a very personal style of representation over a wide range of media, and is committed to handling a selective number of clients." *Commission*: 10-20% depending on type of engagement

Clive Corner Associates

73 Gloucester Road, Hampton, Middlesex TW12 2UQ
tel 020-8287 2726 *fax* 020-8979 4983
email cornerassociates@aol.com
website www.cornerassociates.cwc.net
Key personnel Clive Corner, Duncan Stratton, Bill Upton

Established in 1988. 3 agents represent 75 actors. Areas of work include theatre, musicals, television, film, commercials and corporate.

Will consider attending performances at venues within Greater London with 3 weeks' notice. Rarely prepared to travel elsewhere. Accepts submissions (with CVs and photographs) from actors previously unknown to the company if sent by post. Showreels, voice tapes and invitations to view individual actors' websites are not accepted unless requested following receipt of CV/photograph. *Commission*: Theatre and Radio 10%; TV, Film and Corporate 15%; Commercials 20%

Coulter Management Agency

333 Woodlands Road, Glasgow G3 6NG
tel 0141-357 6666 *fax* 0141-357 6676
email cmaglasgow@btconnect.com
Agent Anne Coulter *Assistant* S Bartram

2 agents represent 80 actors. Areas of work include theatre, television, film, commercials, corporate and voice-overs.

Will consider attending performances at venues in Scotland with 3 weeks' notice. Accepts submissions (with CVs and photographs) from actors previously unknown to the company if sent by post. Showreels and voice tapes are also accepted. *Commission*: 7.5-15% (sliding scale)

Covent Garden Management

5 Denmark Street, London WC2H 8LP
tel 020-7240 8400 *fax* 020-7240 8409
email agents@coventgardenmanagement.com

Established in 2002. The agency represents around 30 actors. Areas of work include theatre, musicals, television, film, commercials, corporate and voice-overs. Also represents directors.

Will consider attending performances at venues within Greater London with 2 weeks' notice. Accepts

submissions (with CVs and photographs) from actors previously unknown to the company if sent by post. *Commission*: 10-15%

CSM Artists

Honeysuckle Cottage, 93 Telford Way, Yeading, Middlesex UB4 9TH
tel 020-8839 8747
email csmartists@aol.com
Proprietor Angela Radford *Agent* Carole Deamer
Personal Assistant Anthea Francis

Personal management established in 1984. Sole representation of 40-50 actors. Areas of work include theatre, musicals, television, film, commercials and corporate.

Will consider attending performances at venues within Greater London with 3 weeks' notice. Accepts submissions (with CVs and photographs) from actors previously unknown to the company if sent by post. An sae must be included. *Commission*: 15%

Curtis Brown Ltd

Haymarket House, 28-29 Haymarket, London SW1Y 4SP
tel 020-7393 4400 *fax* 020-7393 4401
email info@curtisbrown.co.uk
website www.curtisbrown.co.uk
Agents Jacquie Drewe, Maxine Hoffman, Sarah MacCormick, Sarah Spear, Kate Staddon

One of Europe's oldest and largest independent literary and media agencies. Established over 100 years ago, there are now more than 20 agents within the Book, Media, Actors and Presenters Divisions, 5 of whom represent actors. Also represents writers, directors, playwrights and celebrities.

Submissions should be sent by post and addressed to 'Actors Agents'. They should include a covering letter with email address, CV, photograph, showreel on VHS (if actor has one) and sae for the return of the showreel. Tries to respond within 4-6 weeks. Does not meet potential clients before viewing their work. Does not accept email or faxed submissions. *Commission*: 12.5-15%

Lisa D Management Ltd

PO Box 4050, Bracknell RG12 9BZ
tel (01344) 643568
email agents@lisad.co.uk
website www.lisad.co.uk
Agent Lisa Dennis

2 agents represent 40-50 actors. Areas of work include theatre, musicals, television, film, commercials and corporate.

Will consider attending performances at venues within Greater London and sometimes elsewhere, given as much notice as possible. Accepts submissions (CV with photograph embedded is acceptable) from actors previously unknown to the company if sent by post. Applicants sending emails should ring first to let the agent know to expect them. Welcomes enquiries from disabled actors.

Caroline Dawson Associates
125 Gloucester Road, London SW7 4TE
tel 020-7373 3323 *fax* 020-7373 1110
email cda@cdalondon.com

3 agents represent 60 actors.

Will consider attending performances at venues within Greater London with 3 weeks' notice. Accepts submissions (with CVs and photographs) from actors previously unknown to the company if sent by post. Showreels, voice tapes and invitations to view individual actors' websites are also accepted. *Commission*: Variable

Felix de Wolfe
Kingsway House, 103 Kingsway, London WC2B 6QX
tel 020-7242 5066 *fax* 020-7242 8119

3 agents represent 100 actors. Areas of work include theatre, musicals, television, film, commercials, corporate and voice-overs. Also represents directors and producers.

Will consider attending performances at venues within Greater London and elsewhere, given 10 days' notice. Accepts submissions (with CVs and photographs) from actors previously unknown to the company if sent by post. *Commission*: Variable

DP Management
1 Euston Road, London NW1 2SA
tel 020-7843 4331 *fax* 020-7278 3466
email danny@dpmanagement.org
Agent Danny Pellerini

Founded in 2005. 1 agent represents 30 actors for all forms of acting work. Welcomes performance notices with as much notice as possible, and is prepared to travel to performances in the Greater London area. Welcomes letters and emails (with CVs and photographs) from individuals previously unknown to the company, including actors with disabilities, and welcomes follow-up calls. Also welcomes both showreels and invitations to view individuals' websites. *Commission*: 10-15%

DQ Management
Suite 2, Kingsway House, 134–140 Church Road, Hove, East Sussex BN3 2DL
tel (01273) 721221 *fax* (01273) 779065
email info@dqmanagement.com
website www.dqmanagement.com
Senior Partners Peter Davis, Kate Davis

Established in 2003. Areas of work include theatre, musicals, television, film, commercials and corporate. 2 agents represent 40 actors. Will consider attending performances within the Greater London area and elsewhere with at least 2 weeks' notice. Accepts

submissions (with CVs and photographs) from actors previously unknown to the company if sent by post. Invitations to view individuals' websites, showreels or voice tapes are also accepted. Welcomes enquiries from actors with disabilities. *Commission*: Theatre 10%; West End 12.5%; TV/Film/Commercials 15%

Bryan Drew Ltd
Mezzanine, Quadrant House, 80-82 Regent Street, London W1B 5AU
tel 020-7437 2293 *fax* 020-7437 0561
email bryan@bryandrewltd.com
Managing Director Bryan Drew *Personal Assistant* Mina Parmar

Established in 1963. 2 agents represent 40 actors. Areas of work include theatre, musicals, television, film, commercials, corporate and voice-overs. Also represents writers.

Will consider attending performances at venues within Greater London with a minimum of 2 weeks' notice. *Commission*: 12.5-15%

Kenneth Earle Personal Management
214 Brixton Road, London SW9 6AP
tel 020-7274 1219 *fax* 020-7274 9529
email kennethearle@agents-uk.com
website entertainment-kennethearle.co.uk

Established in 2000. 1 agent represents 10-15 actors. Areas of work include theatre, musicals, television, film, commercials, corporate and voice-overs.

Will consider attending performances at venues in Greater London and elsewhere with 1 week's notice. Accepts submissions (with CVs and photographs) from actors previously unknown to the company if sent by post. Follow-up telephone calls and invitations to view individual actors' websites are also accepted. Showreels and voice tapes should only be sent on request. *Commission*: 10-15%

Susi Earnshaw Management
5 Brook Place, Barnet, Hertfordshire EN5 2DL
tel 020-8441 5010 *fax* 020-8364 9618
email casting@susiearnshaw.co.uk
website www.susiearnshaw.co.uk
Agents Christine Jacquemin, Susi Earnshaw

Established in 1989. 2 agents represent 50 actors. Areas of work include theatre, musicals, television, film, commercials and corporate role-play.

Will consider attending performances at venues within Greater London with 2-3 weeks' notice. Accepts postal submissions (with CVs and photographs) from actors previously unknown to the company. *Commission*: Theatre 10%; TV, Film and Commercials 15%

East 15 Management
East 15 Acting School, Hatfields, Rectory Lane, Loughton, Essex IG10 3RY

tel 020-8508 3746 *fax* 020-8508 3746
email e15management@yahoo.com

1 agent represents around 60 East 15 graduates. The agency works in all fields of the acting industry.

Does not welcome performance notices or submission enquiries from actors unknown to the agency.

Annie Elliott Management
Top Floor, 19 Camden Passage, London N1 8ED
tel 020-7226 4863
email annieelliottmgmt@aol.com
Agent Clare Allen

Established in 2002. 1 agent represents 15 actors. Areas of work include theatre, musicals, television, film, commercials and corporate.

Will consider attending performances at venues within Greater London and occasionally elsewhere, given as much notice as possible. Accepts submissions (with CVs and photographs) from actors previously unknown to the company sent by post or email. Follow-up telephone calls, showreels, voice tapes and invitations to view individual actors' websites are also accepted. *Commission*: Theatre 5%; Technical 15%

June Epstein Associates
62 Compayne Gardens, London NW6 3RY
tel 020-7328 0864 (main number) or 020-7372 1928 *fax* 020-7328 0684
email june@june-epstein-associates.co.uk

Established in 1973; 1 agent represents 50-60 actors working in theatre, musicals, television, film commercials and corporate role-play. Recommends the photographers Jonathan Dockar-Drysdale (**fact-d@lineone.net**) and Peter Simpkin (**petersimpkin@aol.com**).

Will consider attending performances within Greater London given 2-3 weeks' notice. Accepts postal submissions (with CVs and photographs) from actors previously unknown to the agency, and voice tapes from singers. Follow-up telephone calls, emails and showreels are not welcomed. *Commission*: 10%; Commercials 15%

Et-Nik-A Prime Management and Castings Ltd
3rd Floor, Balfour House, 46-54 Great Titchfield Street, London W1W 7QA
tel 020-7299 3555 *fax* 020-7299 3558
email info@et-nik-a.co.uk
website www.et-nik-a.co.uk
Managing Director Aldo Arcilla

Established in 2000. 3 agents represent 80 actors. Areas of work include theatre, musicals, television, film, commercials, corporate and voice-overs.

Will consider attending performances at venues within Greater London and occasionally elsewhere

with 1-2 weeks' notice. Accepts submissions (with CVs and photographs) from actors previously unknown to the company if sent by post. Invitations to view individual actors' websites are also accepted. Showreels and voice tapes should only be sent on request. *Commission*: Theatre 10%; TV and Films 15%; Commercials 20%

Ethnics Artiste Agency
86 Elphinstone Road, Walthamstow, London E17 5EX
tel 020-8523 4242 *fax* 020-8523 4523
email info@ethnicsaa.co.uk
website www.ethnicsartisteagency.com
Managing Director Pauline Oni

Founded in 1997. 2 agents represent 60 actors in all areas of acting work. The company represents multicultural and international performers and artistes from across the globe, including actors, singers, dancers, musicians and martial artists from Asia, Africa and Europe, and performers of ethnic-minority British origin. Specialises in representation of performers of colour and those with fluent foreign-language skills. Welcomes performance notices 2-3 weeks in advance; will consider travelling to shows within Greater London. Welcomes letters (with CVs and photographs) from individuals previously unknown to the company if sent by post but not by email. Welcomes showreels, but not invitations to view individuals' websites. Welcomes representation enquiries from disabled actors.

– see entry under WIS Celtic Management on page 65

Evolution Management
Studio 21, The Truman Brewery Building, 91 Brick Lane, London E1 6QB
tel 020-7053 2128 *fax* 020-7375 2752
email info@evolutionmngt.com
website www.evolutionmngt.com
Development Directors Loftus Burton, Henrik Bjork

Founded in 1999; 3 agents represent around 30 actors working in theatre, musicals, television, film and commercials. The agency also represents directors, make-up artists and presenters.

Welcomes performance notices within Greater London and occasionally further afield, given a minimum of 2 weeks' notice. Also accepts letters and emails with CVs and photographs, showreels and voice tapes. Always provide an sae if you wish your material to be returned. Advises actors to have monologues prepared when coming to see the agency – especially if agents have not had the opportunity to see your work beforehand. *Commission*: Theatre 10-15%; Commercials 20%

Colette Fenlon Personal Management
26 Hope Street, Liverpool LL1 9BX
tel 0151-707 7703 *fax* 0151-706 0838

email collettefenlon@hotmail.com
Director Colette Fenlon

Established in 1989, the agency represents 10 actors working in theatre, musicals, television, film and commercials.

Will consider attending performances within Greater London and beyond, given as much notice as possible. In general, does not welcome representation enquiries from actors unknown to the agency. *Commission*: 15-20%

First Act Personal Management

2 St Michaels, New Arley, Coventry CV7 8PY
tel (01676) 540285 *fax* (01676) 542777
email firstactpm@aol.com
website www.spotlightagent.info/firstact
Agent John Burton

Established in 2003. 1 agent represents 25 actors. Areas of work include theatre, musicals, television, film, commercials, corporate and voice-overs.

Will consider attending performances in England and Wales with at least 2 weeks' notice. Accepts submissions (with CVs and photographs) from actors previously unknown to the company if sent by post. Invitations to view individual actors' websites, showreels or voice tapes are also accepted. Welcomes enquiries from actors with disabilities. "Always enclose an sae." *Commission*: 10-15%

Sharon Foster

310 Greenhorse, Custard Factory, Digbeth, Birmingham B9 4AA
tel 0121-224 7676 *fax* 0121-224 7677
email enquiries@magnetmanagement.co.uk
website www.magnetmanagement.co.uk

1 agent represents around 40 actors working in theatre, musicals, television, radio, film, commercials and corporate role-play.

Will consider attending performances given sufficient notice. Accepts submissions (with CVs and photographs) from actors previously unknown to the agency sent by post or email. Follow-up telephone calls, showreels, voice tapes and invitations to view an actor's website are also accepted. *Commission*: 10-15%

Fushion

27 Old Gloucester Street, London WC1N 3XX
tel (08700) 111100 *fax* (08700) 111020
email info@fushion-uk.com
website www.fushion-uk.com
Key personnel Lee Dennison CDA

Established in 1998, Fushion is now based in London and New York with 4 agents representing 40 professional artists worldwide, including recording artists PHATS, Lee Kaay, IGNORANTS and Lisa B. Areas of work include theatre, music, television and film.

Will consider attending performances at venues worldwide, given a minimum of 4-6 weeks' notice. Please email the office before submitting any details. If interested, the agency will contact actors for interview at either the London or the New York office. *Commission*: 15%; Recording 20%

Galloways One

15 Lexham Mews, London W8 6JW
tel 020-7376 2288 *fax* 020-7376 2416
email hugh@gallowaysone.com
website www.gallowaysone.com
Directors Hugh Galloway, Jill Moore *Personal Assistant* Isabelle Desrochers

Established in 1971. Agency represents 150 actors. Areas of work include television, commercials, corporate and voice-overs, with the primary focus on commercials.

Will consider attending performances at venues within Greater London and occasionally elsewhere, given as much notice as possible. Accepts submissions (with CVs and photographs) from actors previously unknown to the company if sent by post. Enclose an appropriately sized sae for the return of personal details. *Commission*: TV 10%; Other 18%

Gardner Herrity Management

Douglas House, London SW1P 4PB
tel 020-7828 7748 *fax* 020-7828 7758
email info@gardnerherrity.co.uk

Areas of work include theatre, musicals, television and film. Will consider attending performances within the Greater London area with at least 3 weeks' notice. Accepts submissions (with CV and photograph) from actors previously unknown to the company if sent by post, but not by email. Also accepts showreels, voice tapes, and invitations to view individual actors' websites. Welcomes enquiries from actors with disabilities. *Commission*: 10%

Michael Garrett Associates

23 Haymarket, London SW1Y 4DG
tel 020-7839 4888 *fax* 020-7839 4555
email enquiries@michaelgarrett.co.uk
website www.michaelgarrett.co.uk

A personal management representing professional actors and actresses. Areas of work include theatre, musical theatre, television, film, commercials and corporate. Also represents a limited number of theatre designers, choreographers, directors and musical directors.

Accepts submissions from actors previously unknown to the company if sent by post. Does not welcome email submissions or telephone enquiries.

Garricks

5 The Old School House, The Lanterns, London SW11 3AD

tel 020-7738 1600 *fax* 020-7738 1881
email megan@garricks.net
Key personnel Megan Willis

Established in 1981. Areas of work include theatre, television, film, commercials and corporate. Also represents directors and presenters.

Will consider attending performances at venues within Greater London and elsewhere with 2 weeks' notice. Accepts submissions (with CVs and photographs) from actors previously unknown to the company sent by post or email. Invitations to view individual actors' websites are also accepted. *Commission*: TV, Film and Theatre 10%; Commercials 15%

Gilbert & Payne Personal Management

Room 236, 2nd Floor, Linen Hall, 162-168 Regent Street, London W1B 5TB
tel 020-7734 7505 *fax* 020-7494 3787
email ee@gilbertandpayne.
Director Elena Gilbert *Key personnel* Elaine Payne

Established in 1996. 2 agents represent 50 actors. Areas of work include theatre, musicals, television, film, commercials and corporate, with a particular emphasis on musical theatre. Also represents choreographers.

Will consider attending performances at venues in Greater London with a minimum of 1 week's notice. Accepts submissions (with CVs and photographs) from actors previously unknown to the company if sent by post. Follow-up telephone calls are also accepted. *Commission*: Theatre 10%

Grantham-Hazeldine

Suite 605, The Linen Hall, 162-168 Regent St, London W1B 5TG
tel 020-7038 3737/8 *fax* 020-7038 3739
email agents@granthamhazeldine.com
website www.granthamhazeldine.com
Partners John Grantham, Caroline Hazeldine

Established in 1984. 2 agents represent 75 actors. Areas of work include theatre, musicals, television, film, commercials, corporate and voice-overs. Also represents writers and stunt co-ordinators.

Will consider attending performances at venues in Greater London and elsewhere with 1 month's notice. Accepts submissions (with CVs and photographs) from actors previously unknown to the company if sent by post. Will not accept showreels and voice tapes at the initial stage of contact. *Commission*: Theatre and Radio 10% plus VAT; TV and Film 15% plus VAT

Darren Gray Management

2 Marston Lane, Portsmouth, Hampshire PO3 5TW
tel 023-9269 9973 *fax* 023-9267 7227
email darren.gray1@virgin.net
website www.darrengraymanagement.co.uk

Managing Director Darren Gray

Established in 1994. 2 agents represent 60 actors in both England and Australia. Agency mainly represents Australian actors, the majority of whom come from Australian soap operas. Areas of work include theatre, musicals, television, film, commercials, corporate and voice-overs. Also represents directors, producers, writers and presenters.

Will consider attending performances at venues within Greater London and elsewhere at whatever notice possible. Accepts submissions (with CVs and photographs) from actors previously unknown to the company sent by post or email. Showreels, voice tapes and invitations to view individual actors' websites are also accepted. Welcomes enquiries from disabled actors. *Commission*: 10%

Joan Gray Personal Management

29 Sudbury Court Island, Sunbury-on-Thames, Middlesex TW16 5PP

1 agent represents a small number of actors. Areas of work include theatre, musicals, television, film, commercials, corporate and voice-overs. Not looking to take on any new actors at the moment. *Commission*: 10%

Grays Management Ltd

Panther House, 38 Mount Pleasant, London WC1X 0AP
tel 020-7278 1054 *fax* 020-7278 1091
email e-mail@graysmanagement.idps.co.uk
website www.graysman.com
Agent Mary Nelson

2 agents represent approximately 90 actors working in theatre, musicals, television, film, commercials and corporate role-play.

Will consider attending performances within Greater London given 1 week's notice. Advises actors to contact the agency only when currently appearing in a production, as the agency does not welcome general representation enquiries. *Commission*: Theatre 10%; Screen 15%

Sandra Griffin Management Ltd

6 Ryde Place, Richmond Road, East Twickenham TW1 2EH
tel 020-8881 5676 *fax* 020-8744 1812
email office@sandragriffin.com
Key personnel Sandra Griffin, Howard Roberts

Established in 1989. Represents actors in theatre, musicals, television, film, commercial and corporate work.

Welcomes written enquiries from actors seeking representation (with CV, photograph and sae to ensure reply), but does not accept unsolicited demo tapes, DVDs or showreels. Will consider seeing potential clients in current theatre productions, if in easily accessible locations. *Commission*: Varies according to contract

Harris Personal Management Ltd
64-66 Millman Street, London WC1N 3EF
tel 020-7430 9890 *fax* 020-7430 9229
email agent@harrispersonalmanagement.co.uk
website www.harrispersonalmanagement.co.uk
Managing Director/Senior Agent Melanie Harris
Agents Georgina Coombs, Rosie Nimmo

Established in 2001; 2 agents represent up to 50 actors. Areas of work include theatre, television, film, commercials and corporate.

Will consider attending performances at venues within Greater London given as much notice as possible. Accepts submissions (with CVs, photographs and showreels if possible) from actors previously unknown to the company if sent by post. Enclosing an sae will ensure a reply. *Commission*: 12.5-15% depending on the type of work

Harrispearson Management Ltd
See entry under Harris Personal Management Ltd

Hatton McEwan
PO Box 37385, London N1 7XF
tel 020-7253 4770 *fax* 020-7251 9081
email info@thetalent.biz
website www.thetalent.biz

Established in 1988, the agency represents actors working in theatre, musicals, television, film, commercials and corporate. Other clients include directors, composers and designers.

Will consider attending performances within Greater London (but rarely elsewhere) given 4 weeks' notice. Accepts submissions (with CVs and photographs) from actors previously unknown to the company sent by post or email. Showreels, voice tapes and invitations to view an actor's website are also accepted, but follow-up telephone calls are not welcomed.

Henry's Agency
53 Westbury, Rochford, Essex SS4 1UL
tel (01702) 541413 *fax* (01702) 541413
email info@henrysagency.co.uk
website www.henrysagency.co.uk

Established in 1995; 1 agent represents 35 actors. Areas of work include theatre, musicals, television, film, commercials and corporate.

Will consider attending performances at venues within Greater London with 2 weeks' notice. Accepts submissions (with CVs and photographs) from actors

previously unknown to the company if sent by post. Emails are accepted if attachments consist of Word documents or small jpeg files. Follow-up telephone calls, showreels and voice tapes are also accepted. Recommends the photographer Ash (**ash@ashphotomedia.com**). *Commission*: Variable

Edward Hill Management
Teddington Film and Television Studios, Broom Road, Teddington, Middlesex TW11 9NT
tel 020-8614 2678 *fax* 020-8614 2694
email hill@management.freeserve.co.uk

1 agent represents 40 actors. Will accept submissions (with CVs and photographs) from actors previously unknown to the company if sent by post. *Commission*: 10-15%

Elinor Hilton Associates
BAC, Lavender Hill, London SW11 5TF
tel 020-7738 9574 *fax* 020-7924 4636
email agent@elinorhilton.co.uk
website www.elinorhilton.com

Established in 2003. Areas of work include theatre, musicals, television, film, commercials, corporate and voice-overs. 1 agent represents 80 actors; also represents writers and directors.

Will consider attending performances in the Greater London area with at least 2 weeks' notice. Accepts submissions (with CVs and photographs) from actors previously unknown to the company if sent by post. Invitations to view individual actors' websites, showreels and voice tapes are also accepted. Welcomes enquiries from actors with disabilities. "Always enclose an sae." *Commission*: 12.5%

Dee Hindin Associates
9B Brunswick Mews, Great Cumberland Place, London W1H 7FB
tel 020-7723 3706 *fax* 020-7258 0651

Established in 1991. Represents 15-20 actors. Areas of work include theatre, musicals, television, film, commercials, corporate and voice-overs.

Recommends the photographer Chris Baker (020-8441 3851). *Commission*: 12.5-15% depending on the type of work

Liz Hobbs Group Ltd
65 London Road, Newark, Notts NG24 1RZ
tel 0870-070 2702 *fax* 0870-333 7009
email casting@lizhobbsgroup.com
website www.lizhobbsgroup.com
Managing Director Liz Hobbs MBE *Agent* Katie Eckersley

2 agents represent 50-60 actors. Areas of work include theatre, musicals, television, film, commercials, corporate and voice-overs.

Will consider attending performances at venues in Greater London and elsewhere with 1-2 months' notice. Accepts submissions (with CVs and photographs) from actors previously unknown to the company sent by post or email. Will also accept showreels, voice tapes and invitations to view individual actors' websites. *Commission*: 10-15% depending on the type of work

Hobson's Actors

62 Chiswick High Road, Chiswick, London W4 1SY
tel 020-8995 3628 *fax* 020-8996 5350
website www.hobsons-international.com
Drama Agent Christina Beyer *Commercial Agent* Linda Sacks

Areas of work include theatre, musicals, television, film, commercials and corporate.

Will consider attending performances at venues within Greater London given 2 weeks' notice. Accepts submissions (with CVs and photographs) from actors previously unknown to the company if sent by post. Showreels and voice tapes are also accepted.

Hamilton Hodell Ltd

Fifth Floor, 66-69 Margaret Street, London W1W 8SR
tel 020-7636 1221 *fax* 020-7636 1226
email info@hamiltonhodell.co.uk
website www.hamiltonhodell.co.uk

3 agents represent 80 actors, working in leading roles in film, television, theatre and radio productions.

Jane Hollowood Associates Ltd

Apartment 17, 113 Newton Street, Manchester M1 1AE
tel 0161-237 9141 *fax* 0161-237 9142
email janehollowood@ukonline.co.uk
Agents Jane Hollowood, Charlotte Reeve

Established in 1998; 2 agents represent approx. 75 actors working in many areas of the industry.

Will consider attending performances within Greater London and potentially elsewhere, depending on diary commitments and provided that 2-3 weeks' notice is given. Accepts postal submissions (with CVs and photographs) from actors previously unknown to the agency. Showreels and voice tapes should only be sent on request, and follow-up telephone calls and emails are unwelcome. *Commission*: Theatre 10%; Radio, Role-play and Voice-overs 12%; Television, Film and Commercials 15%

Amanda Howard Associates

21 Berwick Street, London W1F 0PZ
tel 020-7287 9277 *fax* 020-7287 7785
email mail@amandahowardassociates.co.uk
website www.amandahowardassociates.co.uk
Agents Amanda Fitzalan Howard, Mark Price, Darren Rugg, Kirsten Wright *Voice-over Agent* Annette Parnell

5 agents represent around 100 actors working in theatre, musicals, television, radio, film, commercials,

corporate role-play and voice-overs. Other clients include writers, broadcasters, designers, directors and composers.

Will consider attending performances within Greater London given 2-3 weeks' notice. Welcomes submissions (with CVs, photographs, showreels, voice tapes and sae) from actors previously unknown to the agency if sent by post. Does not accept email applications or invitations to view an actor's website. *Commission*: 10-15% depending on the medium

ICM

Oxford House, 76 Oxford Street, London W1D 1BS

11 agents represent actors. Areas of work include theatre, musicals, television, film, commercials, corporate and voice-overs. Also represents directors, writers, technicians and presenters.

Will consider attending performances at venues within Greater London. Accepts submissions (with CVs and photographs) from actors previously unknown to the company if sent by post. 10x8in photographs are preferred. *Commission*: 10%

Icon Actors Management

Tanzaro House, Ardwick Green North, Manchester M12 6FZ
tel 0161-273 3344 *fax* 0161-273 4567
email info@iconactors.net
website www.iconactors.net
Agent Philip Hammond

Established in 2000. 1 agent represents 50 actors. Areas of work include theatre, musicals, television, film, commercials, corporate and voice-overs.

Will consider attending performances at venues in the North West/Yorkshire. Accepts submissions with CVs, photographs and showreels (if applicable) from actors previously unknown to the company – please send by post.

Inter-City Casting

Portland Tower, Portland Street, Manchester M1 3LF
tel 0161-226 0103 *fax* 0161-226 0103
email intercity@bigfoot.com
website www.iccast.co.uk
Agent Caroline Joynt

Established in 1983. 2 agents represent approximately 60 actors. Areas of work include theatre, musicals, television, film, commercials and corporate.

Will consider attending performances at venues in Manchester and Liverpool. Accepts submissions (with CVs and photographs) from actors previously unknown to the company if sent by post. Showreels, voice tapes and invitations to view individual actors' websites also accepted. Recommends the photographer Michael Pollard (see entry under *Photographers and repro companies* on page 275 for further details). *Commission*: 10-12.5% plus VAT

International Artistes Ltd
4th Floor, Holborn Hall, 193-197 High Holborn,
London WC1V 7BD
website www.intart.co.uk

7 agents represent approx. 220 actors. Also represents producers, directors, casting directors, presenters, light-entertainment artists and comedians. The company has a separate voice-over department. (Artists are represented by a total of 11 agents.)

Will consider attending performances at venues within Greater London and occasionally elsewhere, given 4 weeks' notice. Accepts submissions (with CVs and photographs) from actors previously unknown to the company if sent by post. Showreels, voice tapes and invitations to view individual actors' websites are also accepted. *Commission*: 10-12.5% plus VAT

International Theatre & Music Ltd
54 Haymarket, London SW1Y 4RP
tel 020-7968 4994 *fax* 020-7968 4995
email info@internationaltheatreandmusic.com
website www.internationaltheatreandmusic.com
Managing Director Piers Chater-Robinson *Personal Assistant* Claire Lloyd *Assistant* Emma Brown

2-3 agents represent 35 actors. Areas of work include musicals, television and commercials.

Will consider attending performances at venues in Greater London and occasionally elsewhere, given as much notice as possible. Accepts submissions (with CVs and photographs) from actors previously unknown to the company if sent by post. Will also accept voice tapes/CDs of singing voices. "It is likely that all prospective clients will be auditioned, unless their work is established in the industry." *Commission*: Theatre 10%; Film and TV 12.5%

Alex Jay Personal Management
8 Higher Newmarket Road, Newmarket GL6 0RP
tel (01453) 834783 *fax* (01453) 834783
email alexjay@alex-jay-pm.freeserve.co.uk
Director Alex Jay

Established in 1992. 2 agents represent 30 actors. Areas of work include theatre, musicals, television, film, commercials, corporate and voice-overs.

Will consider attending performances in Greater London and elsewhere with 2 weeks' notice. Accepts submissions (CVs and photographs) from actors previously unknown to the agency. Encourages enquiries from actors with disabilities. Welcomes showreels and invitations to view actors' websites. *Commission*: 12-20%

JB Associates
1st Floor, 3 Stevenson Square, Manchester M1 1DN
tel 0161-237 1808 *fax* 0161-237 1809
email info@j-b-a.net
website www.j-b-a.net
Proprietor John Basham

Established in 1996. 2 agents represent 60 actors. Areas of work include theatre, musicals, television, film, commercials, corporate and voice-overs.

Will consider attending performances at venues in the North and occasionally within Greater London, given 3-4 weeks' notice. Accepts submissions (with CVs and photographs) from actors previously unknown to the company if sent by post. Will also accept showreels, voice tapes, and invitations to view individual actors' websites. *Commission*: Theatre 10%; TV 15%

Jeffrey & White Management
9-15 Neal Street, London WC2H 9PW
tel 020-7240 7000 *fax* 020-7240 0007
Partners Judith Jeffrey, Jeremy White *Key personnel* Laura Elgar

Established in 1986. 3 agents represent 85 actors. Areas of work include theatre, musicals, television, film, commercials and corporate.

Will consider attending performances given as much notice as possible. Accepts submissions (with CVs and photographs) from actors previously unknown to the company if sent by post. *Commission*: Theatre, Film and TV 12.5%; Commercials 15%

JGM
15 Lexham Mews, London W8 6JW
tel 020-7376 2414 *fax* 020-7376 2416
email mail@jgmtalent.com
website www.jgmtalent.com
Director Jilly Moore

Established in 1997. 3 agents represent 100-150 actors. Areas of work include theatre, musicals, television, corporate and voice-overs. Also represents directors, musical directors and choreographers.

Will consider attending performances within Greater London with at least 3 weeks' notice. Accepts submissions (with CVs and photographs) from actors previously unknown to the agency (please include sae). Invitations to view individual actors' websites are accepted, as are showreels and voice tapes. Welcomes enquiries from actors with disabilities.

JLM Personal Management
259 Acton Lane, London W4 5DG
tel 020-8747 8223 *fax* 020-8747 8286
email jlm.pm@btconnect.com
Agents Janet Malone, Sharon Henry

Established in 1978. 2 agents represent 80 actors. Areas of work include theatre, musicals, television, film, commercials, corporate and voice-overs.

Will consider attending performances at venues within Greater London given 2 weeks' notice. Showreels and voice tapes should only be sent on request. Welcomes letters (with CVs and photographs) from actors previously unknown to the company, including disabled actors. Does not welcome approaches via email. *Commission*: Theatre 10%; TV 15%

Johnston & Mathers Associates Ltd

PO Box 3167, Barnet, London EN5 2WA
tel 020-8449 4968 *fax* 020-8449 2386
email JohnstonMathers@aol.com
website www.johnstonandmathers.com
Key personnel Dawn Mathers, Suzanne Johnston

Established in 2001. Areas of work include theatre, musicals, television, film, commercials and corporate. 2 agents represent 65 actors.

Will consider attending performances within the Greater London area with at least 1 month's notice. Accepts submissions (with CVs and photographs) from actors previously unknown to the company if sent by post or email. Invitations to view individual actors' websites are accepted, as are showreels and voice tapes. Welcomes enquiries from actors with disabilities.

KAL Management

95 Gloucester Road, Hampton, Middlesex TW12 2UW
tel 020-8783 0039 *fax* 020-8979 6487
email kaplan222@aol.com
website www.kaplan-kaye.co.uk
Key personnel Kaplan Kaye

Established in 1982. Sole representation of approximately 25 actors. Areas of work include theatre, musicals, television, film, commercials, corporate and voice-overs.

Will consider attending performances at venues within Greater London given as much notice as possible. Accepts submissions (with CVs and photographs) from actors previously unknown to the company if sent by post. Showreels and voice tapes should only be sent on request. *Commission*: Theatre 10%; TV 15%

Roberta Kanal Agency

82 Constance Road, Twickenham, Middlesex TW2 7JA
tel 020-8894 2277 *fax* 020-8894 7952
email roberta.kanal@dsl.pipex.com
Director Roberta Kanal

Established in 1972; 1 agent represents approximately 30 actors working in all areas of the industry.

Will consider attending performances within Greater London and occasionally elsewhere, given sufficient notice. Accepts submissions from actors (able-bodied or disabled) who have already checked that it is appropriate to do so. Follow-up telephone calls, emails, showreels, voice tapes and invitations to view an actor's website are not welcomed. "Courtesy is still important! Don't waste postage; ask first – and please do not expect items to be returned when postage has not been included. Take a simple approach: phone

first; send a CV if requested, with a clear letter and 1 photograph along with an sae for their return. As with casting directors, only use email if requested. Unsolicited items will be ignored due to the growing number of applications becoming impossible to handle."

Steve Kenis & Co

Royalty House, 72-74 Dean Street, London W1D 3SG
tel 020-7434 9055 *fax* 020-7287 6328
email sk@sknco.com
Agents Steve Kenis, Sharon Thomas

Founded in 2000. 2 agents represent 14 actors, as well as directors and technicians. Does not welcome any unsolicited contact from individuals unknown to the company. "As we are such a small agency, specialising in older, established actors, we will not take on any new clients." *Commission*: 10%

Adrian King Associates

33 Marlborough Mansions, Cannon Hill, London NW6 1JS
tel 020-7435 4600/ 4700 *fax* 020-7435 4100
email akassocs@aol.com
Agent Adrian King *Assistant* Caroline Funnell

Established in 1989. 1 agent represents 48 actors. Areas of work include theatre, musicals, television, film, commercials, corporate and voice-overs. Also represents presenters and directors.

Welcomes showreels and letters from actors, as well as invitations to view individual actors' websites. May attend performances within the Greater London area, given 2 weeks' notice. *Commission*: 10%

Richard Kort Associates

2-4 Clasketgate, Lincoln LN2 1JS
tel (01522) 526888 *fax* (01522) 511116
email richardkort@dial.pipex.com
website www.richardkortassociates.com

Established in 2005. 1 agent represents 50 actors. Areas of work include theatre, musicals, television, film, commercials, corporate and voice-overs. Also represents presenters.

Will consider attending performances within Greater London and elsewhere, with at least 2 months' notice. Accepts submissions (with CVs and photographs) from actors previously unknown to the agency; showreels, voice tapes and invitations to view individual actors' websites are also accepted. Welcomes enquiries from actors with disabilities. *Commission*: 15%

Laine Management

131 Victoria Road, Salford M6 8LF
tel 0161-789 7775 *fax* 0161-787 7572
email info@lainemanagement.co.uk
website www.lainemanagement.co.uk
Company Director Samantha Greeley

Areas of work include theatre, television, film, commercials and corporate. Will consider attending performances at venues in Manchester and the surrounding area with 2-4 weeks' notice. Accepts CVs and photographs from individuals previously unknown to the agency, but emails, showreels and invitations to view individuals actors' websites are not welcomed. *Commission*: 15%

Langford Associates Ltd

17 Westfields Avenue, Barnes, London SW13 0AT
tel 020-8878 7148
Key personnel Barry Langford

Established in 1987. 1 agent represents 40-45 actors. Areas of work include theatre, television, film, commercials, corporate and voice-overs.

Will consider attending performances at mainstream venues within Greater London given 2 weeks' notice. Accepts submissions (with CVs and photographs) from actors previously unknown to the company if sent by post, but does not accept submissions by email or fax. "I am always happy to receive details by post, and I regularly meet with new actors. When writing, please include an sae if you would like your details to be returned. Please do not send unsolicited showreels. I prefer to receive 10x8in photographs, and would suggest that you use a good photographer and update your photo at least every 18 months. Make sure you are listed in Spotlight, as this is a prerequisite for all professional actors."

L'Brooke Personal Management

7 Malt House Place, High Street, Romford RM1 1AR
tel (01708) 723883 *fax* (01708) 723883
email lbrooke@btopenworld.com
Director Nancy Walker

Established in 2002. 1 agent represents 20 actors. Areas of work include theatre, musicals, television, film, commercials and corporate.

Will consider attending performances at venues within Greater London and elsewhere, given 2 weeks' notice. Accepts submissions (with CVs and photographs) from actors previously unknown to the company sent by post or email. Showreels, voice tapes and invitations to view individual actors' websites are also accepted.

Jane Lehrer Associates

100a Chalk Farm Road, London NW1 8EH
tel 020-7482 4898 *fax* 020-7482 4899
email janelehrer@aol.com
Sole Proprietor Jane Lehrer *Agent* Caz Swinfield

Established in 1986. 2 agents represent 80 actors. Areas of work include theatre, musicals, television, film, commercials and voice-overs. Also represents presenters.

Will consider attending performances at venues in Greater London with 2-3 weeks' notice. Accepts submissions (with CVs and photographs) from actors previously unknown to the company if sent by post. An sae must always be included with CVs and photographs. Showreels and voice tapes should only be sent on request.

Leigh Management

14 St David's Drive, Edgware HA8 6JH
tel 020-8951 4449 *fax* 020-8951 4449
email leighmanagement@aol.com

Established in 1989. 2 agents represent 75 actors. Areas of work include theatre, musicals, television, film, commercials and corporate. Also represents presenters.

Will consider attending performances at venues within Greater London given a minimum of 1 week's notice. Accepts submissions (with CVs and photographs) from actors previously unknown to the company if sent by post. Follow-up telephone calls and invitations to view individual actors' websites are also accepted. *Commission*: 10-15%

Lime Actors Agency & Management Ltd

First Floor, Alexandra Buildings, 28 Queen Street, Lincoln Square, Manchester M2 5LF
tel 0161-835 3550 *fax* 0161-835 2550
email Debbie.pine@limemanagement.co.uk
Director Debbie Pine

Established in 1999. 1 agent represents 40 actors. Areas of work include theatre, musicals, television, film, commercials, corporate and voice-overs. Also represents musical directors.

Will consider attending performances at venues within Greater London and elsewhere, given 4 weeks' notice. Accepts submissions (with CVs and photographs) from actors previously unknown to the company sent by post or email. Follow-up telephone calls, showreels, voice tapes and invitations to view individual actors' websites are also accepted. Recommends the photographer Michael Pollard (see entry under *Photographers and repro companies* on page 275 for further details). *Commission*: Theatre 5%; TV 15%

Linkside Agency

21 Poplar Road, Leatherhead KT22 8SF
tel (01372) 802374 or (01372) 378398 *fax* (01372) 801972

Established in 1986. 2 agents represent 40 actors. Areas of work include theatre, musicals, television, film, commercials, corporate and voice-overs.

Will consider attending performances at venues within Greater London given a minimum of 2 weeks' notice. Accepts submissions (with CVs and photographs) from actors previously unknown to the company if sent by post. An sae should be included for the return of CVs and photographs. Showreels and voice tapes are also accepted.

Eva Long Agents

107 Station Road, Earls Barton, Northants NN6 0NX
mobile (07736) 700849
fax (01604) 811921
email EvaLongAgents@yahoo.co.uk
Key personnel Eva Long

Established in 2003. 1 agent represents 50 actors.
Areas of work include theatre, musicals, television,
film, commercials, corporate and voice-overs.

Will consider attending performances within the
Greater London, Midlands and East Anglia areas,
with at least 1 month's notice. Accepts submissions
(with CVs and photographs) from actors previously
unknown to the agency if sent by post, but not by
email. Showreels, voice tapes and invitations to view
individual actors' websites are also accepted.
Welcomes enquiries from actors with disabilities.
Commission 15%

Pat Lovett Associates

43 Chandos Place, London WC2N 4HS
tel 020-7379 8111 *fax* 020-7379 9111
email London@pla-uk.com
Scottish office: 5 Union Street, Edinburgh EH1 3LT
tel 0131-478 7878 *fax* 0131-478 7070
website www.pla-uk.com
Key personnel Dolina Logan

Established in 1981. Areas of work include theatre,
musicals, television, film, commercials, corporate and
voice-overs.

Will consider attending performances at venues in
Greater London and Scotland (handled by Scottish
office) with 2-3 weeks' notice. Accepts submissions
(with CVs and photographs) from actors previously
unknown to the company if sent by post. Invitations
to view individual actors' websites are also accepted.

LSW Promotions

181a Faunce House, Doddington Grove, London
SE17 3TB
tel 020-7793 9755 *fax* 020-7793 9755
email lswpromos@hotmail.com
website www.londonshakespeare.org.uk
Executive Director Bruce Wall *Development
Associate* James Croft

Established in 1998. 2 agents represent 20 actors.
Areas of work include theatre, musicals, television
and film.

Will consider attending performances at venues
within Greater London and elsewhere, given 2 weeks'
notice. Accepts submissions (with CVs and
photographs) from actors previously unknown to the
company sent by post or email. Invitations to view
individual actors' websites are also accepted.
Commission: 10% donation to charity (LSW Prison
Project)

Dennis Lyne Agency

108 Leonard Street, London EC2A 4RH
tel 020-7739 6200 *fax* 020-7739 4101
email info@dennislyne.com
Agent Dennis Lyne *Assistant Agent* Clare Ewing

Established in 1995. 1 agent represents 50 actors.
Areas of work include theatre, musicals, television,
corporate.

Will selectively consider attending performances
within Central London, given at least 2 weeks' notice.
Does not welcome submissions from actors
previously unknown to the agency – unless they are
appearing in something. *Commission* 10%;
Commercials 15%

Magnolia Management

136 Hicks Avenue, Greenford, Middlesex UB6 8HB
tel 020-8578 2899 *fax* 020-8575 0369
email jaffreymag@aol.com
Proprietor Jennifer Jaffrey

Established in 1982. 2 agents represent 55-60 actors.
Areas of work include theatre, musicals, television,
film, commercials, corporate and voice-overs.

Will consider attending performances at venues
within Greater London and occasionally elsewhere,
given as much notice as possible. Accepts submissions
(with CVs and photographs) from actors previously
unknown to the company if sent by post.
Photographs should have the actor's name written on
the back, and sae(s) enclosed for the return of
personal details. Follow-up telephone calls should
only be made if the agency has shown an interest in
the actor. Showreels, voice tapes and invitations to
view individual actors' websites should only be sent
on request. *Commission:* 10-15%

Management 2000

23 Alexandra Road, Mold, Flintshire CH7 1HJ
tel (01352) 771231 *fax* (01352) 771231
email jackey@management-2000.co.uk
website www.management-2000.co.uk

Established in 2000. 1 agent represents 40 actors.
Areas of work include theatre, musicals, television,
film, commercials, corporate and voice-overs.

Will consider attending performances at venues
within Greater London and elsewhere, given at least 1
week's notice. Accepts submissions (with CVs and
photographs) from actors previously unknown to the
company if sent by post. Follow-up telephone calls,
showreels and voice tapes are also accepted.
Commission: 10-15%

Andrew Manson Personal Management

288 Munster Road, London SW6 6BQ
tel 020-7386 9158
email post@andrewmanson.com
website www.andrewmanson.com

Established in 1988.

Will consider attending performances at venues within Greater London given as much notice as possible. Industry referrals are preferred. Follow-up telephone calls, showreels, voice tapes and invitations to view individual actors' websites are accepted. Advises actors to visit the Talent Room website (**www.talentroom.com**).

Markham & Marsden

405 Strand, London WC2R 0NE
tel 020-7836 4111 *fax* 020-7836 4222
email info@markham-marsden.com
website www.markham-marsden.com
Agents John Markham, David Marsden

Areas of work include theatre, musicals, television, film, commercials, corporate and voice-overs. Consult the website for information about how to approach the agency with representation enquiries.

Ronnie Marshall Agency

66 Ollerton Road, London N11 2LA
tel 020-8368 4958

Established in 1980. 1 agent represents 25 actors. Areas of work include theatre, musicals, television, film, commercials, corporate and voice-overs.

Will consider attending performances at venues within Greater London with 2 weeks' notice. Accepts business-like submissions (with CVs and photographs) from actors previously unknown to the company if sent by post. Photographs should be a good likeness. Enclose an sae for return of personal details. Follow-up telephone calls and invitations to view individual actors' websites are also accepted. *Commission*: If instigated by client, 10%; otherwise 20%

Scott Marshall Partners

2nd Floor, 15 Little Portland Street, London W1W 8BW
tel 020-7637 4623 *fax* 020-7636 9728
email smpm@scottmarshall.co.uk
Agents/Company Directors Amanda Evans, Suzy Kenway, Manon Palmer

Areas of work include theatre, musicals, television, film, commercials, corporate and voice-overs. Also represents directors (theatre and TV) and sound designers.

Will consider attending performances at venues within Greater London if given as much notice as possible. Accepts submissions (with CVs and photographs) from actors previously unknown to the company if sent by post. *Commission*: Commercials 15%; Other 10%

Cassie Mayer Ltd

5 Old Garden House, The Lanterns, Bridge Lane, London SW11 3AD
tel 020-7350 0880 *fax* 020-7350 0890

Agents Cassie Mayer, Jayne Billington, Rachel Dyson, Karen Beesley

Established in 1985. 4 agents represent 50-60 actors. Areas of work include theatre, musicals, television, film, commercials and corporate. Also represents directors, presenters and designers.

Will consider attending performances at Equity venues within Greater London if given 3 weeks' notice. Accepts submissions (with CVs and photographs) from actors previously unknown to the company sent by post or email. All artists' applications will receive an answer. *Commission*: PMA-recommended rates

MBA

Concorde House, 18 Margaret Street, Brighton BN2 1TS
tel (01273) 685970 *fax* (01273) 685971
email mba.concorde@virgin.net
website mbagency.fsnet.co.uk
Key personnel Bo Keller, Andrea Todd, Peter Stanford

Established in 1964. Sole representation of 85-90 actors. Areas of work include theatre, musicals, television, film, commercials and corporate.

Will consider attending performances at venues within Greater London and on the South Coast with 1 month's notice. Accepts submissions (with clearly written CVs and photographs) from actors previously unknown to the company if sent by post. Photographs should be of a good quality. Enclose an sae for return of personal details. Showreels, voice tapes and invitations to view individual actors' websites are also accepted. *Commission*: 10-17% depending on the type of work

Alexandra McLean-Williams

212 Piccadilly, London W1J 9HG
tel 020-7917 2806 *fax* 020-7917 2805
email alex@mclean-williams.com

Established in 2002; 1 agent represents approximately 40 clients working in theatre, musicals, television, film, commercials and corporate role-play.

Will consider attending performances within Greater London given 2 weeks' notice. Welcomes submissions (with CVs, photographs, showreels and voice tapes) from actors previously unknown to the agency. Will also accept follow-up telephone calls, emails and invitations to view an actor's website.

Bill McLean Personal Management Ltd

23b Deodar Road, London SW15 2NP
tel 020-8789 8191 *fax* 020-8789 8192

Established in 1972.

Will consider attending performances in Greater London with sufficient notice. Accepts submissions (with CVs and photographs) from actors previously unknown to the company if sent by post. Follow-up telephone calls are also accepted. *Commission*: Theatre 10%; TV 12.5%; Commercials 15%

Ken McReddie Ltd

21 Barratt Street, London W1U 1BD
tel 020-7499 7448 *fax* 020-7408 0886
email ken@kenmcreddie.com
website www.kenmcreddie.com
Directors Ken McRreddie, Roger Charteries

5 agents represent actors for theatre, television, film, commercials and voice-overs. Also represents directors.

MCS Agency

47 Dean Street, London W1D 5BE
tel 020-7734 9995 *fax* 020-7734 9996
email info@mcs-group.freeserve.co.uk
Agent Keith Bishop

Established in 1994. 2 agents represent actors. Areas of work include theatre, musicals, television, film, commercials and voice-overs. Also represents presenters.

Will consider attending performances at venues within Greater London with 2 weeks' notice. Accepts submissions (with CVs and photographs) from actors previously unknown to the company if sent by post. Showreels, voice tapes and invitations to view individual actors' websites are also accepted. *Commission*: 15-20%

MKA

11 Russell Kerr Close, London W4 3HF
tel 020-8994 1619 *fax* 020-8994 2992
email mka.agency@virgin.net
Key personnel Malcolm Knight

Founded under a different name in 1955, MKA was established under its present name in 1995. 2 agents represent 70 actors. Areas of work include theatre, musicals, television, film, commercials, corporate and voice-overs.

Will consider attending performances at venues within Greater London with 2 weeks' notice. Accepts submissions (with CVs and photographs) from actors previously unknown to the company if sent by post. *Commission*: 10-20% depending on the job

Morgan & Goodman

Mezzanine, Quadrant House, 80-82 Regent Street, London W1B 5RP
tel 020-7437 1383 *fax* 020-7437 5293
email mgl@btinternet.com
Proprietor Lyndall Goodman *Key personnel* Tanya Greep, Natalie Elliott

Established in 1981. 2 agents and 1 assistant represent 70-80 actors. Areas of work include theatre, musicals, television, film, commercials, corporate and voice-overs.

Will consider attending performances at venues within Greater London with 2 weeks' notice if an actor is playing a substantial role. Accepts submissions (with CVs and photographs) from experienced actors if sent by post. An sae must always be included for the return of CVs and photographs. Showreels and voice tapes should only be sent on request. *Commission*: 12.5%

Elaine Murphy Associates

Suite 1, 50 High Street, London E11 2RJ
tel 020-8989 4122 *fax* 020-8989 1400
email elaine@elainemurphy.co.uk
Director Elaine Murphy

Established in 1990. 2 agents represent 50 actors. Areas of work include theatre, musicals, television, commercials, corporate and voice-overs. Will consider attending performances within Greater London with plenty of notice. Accepts submissions (with CVs and photographs) from actors previously unknown to the agency; showreels, voice tapes and invitations to view individual actors' websites are also accepted.

The Narrow Road Company

22 Poland Street, London W1F 8QH
tel 020-7434 0406 *fax* 020-7439 1237
email agents@narrowroad.co.uk
Agents Jeanette Hunter, Amy Ireson, Annie Curthoys, Sandra Chalmers, Michael Cronin

Established in 1986, the agency has 3 offices with each agent representing approximately 40 actors. Areas of work include theatre, musicals, television, film, commercials, corporate and voice-overs. The Surrey Office also represents writers, directors, lighting designers, fight directors and choreographers.

Will consider attending performances within the Greater London given 1-2 weeks' notice. Accepts submissions (with CVs and photographs) from actors previously unknown to the company if sent by post, but does not welcome email submissions. Showreels and voice tapes should be sent only if requested. "We always try to be helpful and informative, but callers should be aware of how busy we often are." *Commission*: 10-15%

Surrey office

182 Brighton Road, Coulsdon, Surrey CR5 2NF
tel 020-8763 9895 *fax* 020-8763 2558
email coulsdon@narrowroad.co.uk
Agents Richard Ireson, Frazer Ashford

Manchester office

Grampian House, 4th Floor, 144 Deansgate, Manchester M3 3EE
tel 0161-833 1605 *fax* 0161-833 1605
email manchester@narrowroad.co.uk
Agent Elizabeth Stocking

Northern Lights Management

Dean Clough Mills, Halifax, Yorkshire HX3 5AX
tel (01422) 330101
Agents Maureen Magee, Angie Cowton

Established in 1998. 2 agents represent 40 Northern and Northern-based actors. Areas of work include theatre, musicals, television, film, commercials, corporate and voice-overs.

Will consider attending performances at venues within Greater London and elsewhere, given 2 weeks' notice. Accepts submissions (with CVs and photographs) from actors previously unknown to the company if sent by post. Showreels and voice tapes are also accepted. Enclose an sae for the return of items sent. Telephone calls and emails with attachments are not accepted. Advises actors that the agency is small and rarely takes on new clients.

Norwell Lapley Associates

Lapley Hall, Lapley ST19 9JR
tel (01785) 841991 *fax* (01785) 841992
email norwellapley@freeuk.com
website www.norwellapley.co.uk
Director Chris Davis *Artist Managers* Claire Sibley, Kerry Foley

Sole representation of more than 50 actors. Areas of work include theatre, musicals, television, film, commercials, corporate and voice-overs. Also represents directors, presenters, technicians and musical directors.

Will consider attending performances at venues within Greater London and elsewhere, given as much notice as possible. Accepts submissions (with CVs and photographs) from actors previously unknown to the company sent by post or email. Follow-up telephone calls, showreels, voice tapes and invitations to view individual actors' websites are also accepted. *Commission*: Various rates

NS Artistes' Management

25 Claverdon House, Hollybank Road, Billesley, Birmingham B13 0QY
tel 0121-684 5607 *mobile* (07870) 969577
email nsmanagement@fsmail.net
website www.nsmanagement.co.uk
Managing Director Neale Stephen McGrath *Director* Arali Niamh McGrath

Founded in 2004, and representing 75 actors in all areas of acting work including role-play, presenting and training, the company also represents individuals for writing, consultancy, design, stage management, presenting, drama tutoring and fight arranging. "If you have a talent in the business, even if I have not mentioned it, then I am interested – no matter what age, creed or colour you are, or whether you are disabled or able-bodied."

Welcomes performance notices a fortnight in advance; will consider attending performances around the UK. Welcomes letters (with CVs and photographs) from actors previously unknown to the company if sent by post, but not by email. Does not welcome unsolicited showreels or invitations to view individual actors' websites. *Commission*: Theatre 12.5%; Stage Management 10%; Other 15%

Nyland Management Ltd

20 School Lane, Heaton Chapel, Stockport SK4 5DG

2 agents represent 60 actors. Areas of work include theatre, musicals, television, film, commercials, corporate and voice-overs.

Will consider attending performances at venues within Greater Manchester and the North West given at least 1 week's notice. Accepts submissions (with CVs, photographs and sae) from actors previously unknown to the company if sent by post. *Commission*: 15%

The Offstage Agency

No. 199, 2 Lansdowne Row, Mayfair, London W1J 6HL
tel 020-7543 7780 *fax* 020-7493 4935
email info@theoffstageagency.com
website www.offstageagency.com
Managing Director Dean Salvara

Established in 2004. 2 agents represent 40 actors. Areas of work include television, film, commercials, corporate and voice-overs. Also represents presenters.

Accepts submissions (with CVs and photographs) from actors previously unknown to the company if sent by post. Also accepts showreels, voice tapes and invitations to view individual actors' websites. Welcomes enquiries from actors with disabilities.

David Padbury Associates

44 Summerlee Avenue, Finchley, London N2 9QP
tel 020-8883 1277 *fax* 020-8883 1277
email info@davidpadburyassociates.com
website www.davidpadburyassociates.com
Director David Padbury

2 agents represent 50-60 actors. Areas of work include theatre, musicals, television, film, commercials and corporate. Also represents presenters.

Will consider attending performances within Greater London with at least 1 week's notice. Accepts submissions (with CVs and photographs) from actors previously unknown to the agency. Invitations to view individual actors' websites are also accepted. Welcomes enquiries from actors with disabilities. Recommends the photographer Mark Davis, **mad.photo@onetel.net**. *Commission*: 15–20%

Parr & Bond

The Tom Thumb Theatre, Eastern Esplanade, Cliftonville, Kent CT9 2LB
tel (01843) 221791 *fax* (01843) 221791

Established in 1969. Sole representation of 12-20 actors. Areas of work include theatre, musicals, television, film, commercials, corporate and voice-overs.

Will consider attending performances at venues within Greater London and elsewhere, given 2 weeks' notice. Accepts submissions (with CVs and photographs) from actors previously unknown to the company if sent by post. *Commission*: Theatre 10%; TV and Film 20%

Pelham Associates

The Media Centre, 9-12 Middle Street, Brighton BN1 1AL
tel (01273) 323010 *fax* (01273) 202492
email petercleall@pelhamassociates.co.uk
website www.pelhamassociates.co.uk
Agent Peter Cleall

Established in 1993. Areas of work include theatre, musicals, television, film, commercials, corporate and voice-overs.

Will consider attending performances at venues within Greater London and elsewhere, given at least 2 weeks' notice. Accepts submissions (with CVs and photographs) from actors previously unknown to the company if sent by post. *Commission*: 8-12.5%

Pemberton Associates Ltd

Express Networks, 1 George Leigh Street, Manchester M4 5DL
tel 0161-235 8440 *fax* 0161-235 8442

Established in 1989. 4 agents represent 100 actors. Areas of work include theatre, musicals, television, film, commercials, corporate and voice-overs.

Will consider attending performances at venues in the North West with 2-3 weeks' notice if looking for new clients. Accepts submissions (with CVs and photographs) from actors previously unknown to the company if sent by post.

Performers Directory

PO Box 29942, London SW6 1FL
tel 020-7610 6699 *fax* 020-7736 6088
email admin@performersdirectory.co.uk
website www.performersdirectory.co.uk
Directors Antonia Stratton, Clive Stevens

Established in 1995. 5 agents represent the actors. Areas of work include theatre, musicals, television, film, commercials and corporate.

Will consider attending performances at venues within Greater London with 7-10 days' notice. Accepts submissions (with CVs and photographs) from actors previously unknown to the company if sent by post. Also accepts follow-up telephone calls, showreels, voice tapes and invitations to view individual actors' websites. "We do not welcome emails; however, feel free to enter your details on our website, and call us to let us know they are there. We also encourage companies to post audition or casting information free of charge on the website." *Commission*: 10-20%

See also entry under *The Spotlight, casting directories and information services* on page 267.

PFD

Drury House, 34-43 Russell Street, London WC2B 5HA
tel 020-7344 1010 *fax* 020-7836 9544
website www.pfd.co.uk
Agents Lucy Brazier, Duncan Hayes, Thea Martin, Maureen Vincent, Kathryn Fleming, Lindy King, Dallas Smith, Ruth Young *Head of Commercials Department* Ruth Cooper *Associate Agents* Olivia Hanan, Duncan Millership

In 1924, A D Peters established what has now become 'PFD'. Previously known as Peters, Fraser and Dunlop, it is one of Europe's leading literary and talent agencies in terms of both turnover and breadth of representation. PFD became part of the CSS Stellar group in 2001. The PFD Actors Department represents a diverse portfolio of clients working in leading roles in film, television, theatre and radio productions. 8 agents represent approximately 500 actors. The agency also represents writers, presenters, directors, producers, technicians, composers, editors, sportsmen and women, and make-up artists.

Accepts submissions (with CVs and photographs) from actors previously unknown to the company if sent by post; tries to respond within 8 weeks, although the company cannot guarantee a response. Does not welcome email enquiries or follow-up telephone calls. The Commercials Department works in the areas of voice-overs, corporate and commercial work, but only considers existing clients – it does not take on any artists from outside the agency.

Frances Phillips

Elstree Film & TV Studios, Borehamwood, Hertfordshire WD6 1JG
tel 020-8324 2296 *fax* 020-8324 2353
email derekphillips@talk21.com

Established in 1983. 2 agents represent more than 40 actors. Areas of work include theatre, musicals, television, film, commercials, corporate and voice-overs.

Will consider attending performances at mainstream theatre venues within Greater London, with 4 weeks' notice. The agency does not cover fringe work, however. Accepts submissions (with CVs, photographs and sae) from actors previously unknown to the company if sent by post. Showreels and voice tapes are also accepted. "Particularly interested in artists with good CVs." *Commission*: 10-15%

PHPM

184 Bradway Road, Sheffield S17 4QX
tel 0114-235 3663

email philippa@phpm.co.uk
Key personnel Philippa Howell

Established in 1996. 1 agent represents 80 actors.
Areas of work include theatre, musicals, television,
film, commercials, corporate and voice-overs.

Will consider attending performances at venues
outside Greater London if given as much notice as
possible. Accepts submissions (with CVs and
photographs) from actors previously unknown to the
company if sent by post. Enclose an sae bearing the
correct postage. Showreels and voice tapes are also
accepted. Recommends the photographer Andrew
Chapman (see entry under *Photographers and repro
companies* on page 275 for further details).
Commission: Theatre, Radio and Voice-over 10%;
Film, TV and Commercials 15%

Janet Plater Management Ltd

Floor D, Milburn House, Dean Street, Newcastle
upon Tyne NE1 1LF
tel 0191-221 2490 *fax* 0191-221 2491
email magpie@tynebridge.demon.co.uk

Established in 1997. 1 agent represents approximately
50 actors. Areas of work include theatre, musicals,
television, film, commercials, corporate and voice-
overs.

Will consider attending performances at venues in
North East England with 1-2 weeks' notice. Accepts
submissions (with CVs and photographs) from actors
previously unknown to the company if sent by post.
Showreels and voice tapes should only be sent on
request. *Commission*: Maximum of 15%

Poplar Management

22 Knightswood, Woking, Surrey GU21 3PY
tel/fax (01483) 828056
email karenfoley@poplarmanagement.co.uk
website www.poplarmanagement.co.uk
Key personnel Karen Foley

Established in 2003. 1 agent represents 20 actors.
Areas of work include theatre, musicals, television,
film and commercials.

Will consider attending performances within Greater
London with at least 2 weeks' notice. Accepts
submissions (with CVs and photographs) from actors
previously unknown to the agency if sent by post, but
not by email. Showreels, voice tapes and invitations
to view individual actors' websites are also accepted.

PPM

73 Leonard Street, Shoreditch, London EC2A 4QS
tel 020-7739 7552 *fax* 020-7739 7552
Managing Director Polo Piatti

Established in 1996. Agency represents 3 actors and
works mainly in musicals/music videos.

Will consider attending performances at venues
within Greater London with 3-4 weeks' notice, if

complimentary tickets are provided. Accepts
submissions (with CVs and photographs) from actors
previously unknown to the company sent by post or
email. Showreels and voice tapes are also accepted.
"We will always consider actors wishing to expand
into music work, including pop music." *Commission*:
15-20%

Price Gardner Management

85 Sherrolds Road, London SW6 7TU
Contact Sarah Barnfield

1 agent represents 35 actors. Areas of work include
theatre, musicals, television, film, commercials,
corporate and voice-overs. Accepts submissions (with
CVs and photographs) from actors previously
unknown to the company if sent by post, but not by
email. Showreels, voice tapes and invitations to view
individual actors' websites are also accepted.

Principal Artistes

4 Paddington Street, London W1U 5QE
tel 020-7224 3414 *fax* 020-7486 4668
email principalartistes@hotmail.com

Established in 1993. 2 agents represent 60 actors.
Areas of work include theatre, musicals, television,
film, commercials and corporate.

Will consider attending performances at venues in
Greater London with at least 1 week's notice. Accepts
submissions (with CVs and photographs) from actors
previously unknown to the company if sent by post.
Always enclose an sae bearing the correct postage for
the return of photographs and CVs, and if a response
is required. *Commission*: Theatre 10%; Other 15%

Profile Management

The Old Chapel, 9 West End, Ashwell, Herts SG7
5TH
tel (01462) 743843 *fax* (01462) 742967
Agent George Perry

Agency represents 35 actors. Areas of work include
theatre, television, film and commercials. Also
represents physical theatre artists.

Will consider attending performances (particularly of
physical theatre) at venues within Greater London
and Hertfordshire, Cambridgeshire and Bedfordshire,
given 3 weeks' notice. Accepts submissions (with CVs
and photographs) from actors previously unknown
to the company if sent by post. Showreels and voice
tapes are also accepted. Does not welcome telephone
calls.

Pure Actors Agency & Management Ltd

39 Urmston Lane, Manchester M32 9BG
tel 0161-864 1902 *fax* 0161-866 9700
email enquiries@pure-management.co.uk
website www.pure-management.co.uk
Director Debbie Pine

Established in 2005. 1 agent represents 25 actors. Areas of work include theatre, musicals, television, film, commercials, corporate and voice-overs.

Will consider attending performances within the Manchester area, given at least 6 weeks' notice. Recommends the photographer Michael Pollard, **info@michaelpollard.co.uk**. Accepts submissions (with CVs and photographs) from actors previously unknown to the agency – but be sure to include an sae. Showreels, voice tapes and invitations to view individual actors' websites are also accepted. Welcomes enquiries from actors with disabilities. *Commission*: 15%

Randall Richardson Actors

2nd Floor, 145-157 St John Street, London EC1V 4PY
tel 020-7060 1645 *fax* 0870-762 3212
email mail@randallrichardson.co.uk
website www.randallrichardson.co.uk
Agent Juliet Fergus

Established in 2001. 2 agents represent 40 actors. Areas of work include theatre, musicals, television, film, commercials, corporate and voice overs.

Will consider attending performances within 1 hour's journey time from London, given at least 1 week's notice. Accepts submissions (with CVs and photographs) from actors previously unknown to the agency; also welcomes enquiries from actors with disabilities. *Commission*: 10%

RDF Management

The Gloucester Building, Kensington Village, Avonmore Road, London W14 8RF
tel 020-7013 4103 *fax* 020-7013 4101
website www.rdfmanagement.com
Agent/Head of Agency Debi Allen

Established in 2002. 4 agents represent 40-50 actors. Areas of work include theatre, musicals, television, film, commercials, corporate and voice-overs. Also represents writers, directors and presenters.

Will consider attending performances at venues within Greater London, but requests as much notice as possible. Accepts submissions (with CVs and photographs) from actors previously unknown to the company sent by post or email. Follow-up telephone calls, showreels, voice tapes and invitations to view individual actors' websites are also accepted. *Commission*: 15%

Redroofs Associates

160/1 The Admin Building, Pinewood Studios, Pinewood Road, Iver Heath, Bucks SL10 0NH
tel (01753) 785444 *fax* (01753) 785443
email agency@redroofs.co.uk
website www.redroofs.co.uk

Established in 1947, the agency only represents Redroofs graduates and current students. It does not, therefore, welcome performance notices or representation enquiries from actors unknown to the school. Areas of work include theatre, musicals, television, film, commercials, corporate and voice-overs. *Commission*: 15%

Rhino Management

Oak Porch House, 5 Western Road, Nazeing, Essex EN9 2ON
tel/fax (01992) 893259
email info@rhinomanagement.co.uk
website www.rhinomanagement.co.uk
Owner/Head Booker J K Sands *Assistant Booker* Steve Day

Represents 72 actors (as well as 14 presenters and 10 voice-over artists) in all areas of acting work.

Welcomes performance notices if given at least 1 week ("the longer the better") in advance. Prepared to travel within Greater London and elsewhere. Welcomes letters (with CVs and photographs) from individuals previously unknown to the company sent by post or email. Happy to receive follow-up calls. Welcomes showreels, voice tapes and invitations to view individual actors' websites. Welcomes approaches from disabled actors. *Commission*: Up to 20%

Lisa Richards Agency

46 Upper Baggot Street, Dublin 4 Eire
tel 0035-316 603534 *fax* 0035-316 603545
email info@lisarichards.ie
website www.lisarichards.ie
Managing Director Lisa Cook *Agents (Actors)* Lisa Cook, Richard Cook, Jonathan Shankey
Administrator Lorraine Cummins

The Lisa Richards Agency was founded in 1989 by Lisa and Richard Cook. Originally established as a theatrical agency, Lisa Richards now provides representation for actors, comedians, voice-over artists, authors, playwrights, directors and designers. The company employs a staff of 9 people across the different departments. 3 agents represent the 90-100 actors, and there is 1 voice-over agent, 1 comedy agent, and 1 literary agent.

Welcomes performance notices if sent 3 weeks in advance, and prepared to travel around Ireland. Welcomes letters (with CVs and photographs) from actors previously unknown to the company if sent by post, but not by email; does not welcome follow-up calls. Happy to receive showreels and invitations to view individual actors' websites. Welcomes enquiries from disabled actors.

Rossmore Personal Management

70-76 Bell Street, London NW1 6SP
tel 020-7258 1953 *fax* 020-7258 0124
email agents@rossmoremanagement.com

Established in 1993. 4 agents represent 120 actors. Areas of work include theatre, musicals, television, film, commercials, corporate and voice-overs.

Will consider attending performances at venues within Greater London. Accepts submissions (with CVs and photographs) from actors previously unknown to the company if sent by post. *Commission*: Theatre and Radio 10%; Film, TV and Commercials 15% plus VAT

Royce Management

29 Trenholme Road, London SE20 8PP
tel/fax 020-8778 6861
email office@roycemanagement.co.uk

Established in 1980. 1 agent represents 45 actors. Areas of work include theatre, musicals, television, film, commercials, corporate and voice-overs.

Will consider attending performances at venues within Greater London with a minimum of 1 week's notice. Accepts submissions (with CVs and photographs) from actors previously unknown to the company if sent by post. Include an sae if a reply is required. *Commission*: Commercials 15%; All other work 10%

RWM Management

The Aberdeen Centre, 22-24 Highbury Grove, London N5 2EA
tel 020-7226 3311 *fax* 020-7226 3371
email rwm.mario-kate@virgin.net
Joint Partners Mario Renzullo, Kate Whaley

Established in 2000; 2 agents represent 40-50 actors working in all areas of the industry. The agency also looks after presenters.

Welcomes postal submissions (with CVs and photographs) from actors previously unknown to the agency, but does not accept emails or follow-up telephone calls. Showreels and voice tapes are accepted. *Commission*: 12.5%

St James's Management

19 Lodge Close, Stoke D'Abernon, Cobham, Surrey KT11 2SG
tel (01932) 860666 *fax* (01932) 860444
Managing Director Jacqueline Leggo

Established in 1965. 1 agent represents approximately 50 actors. Areas of work include theatre, musicals, television, film, commercials, corporate and voice-overs.

Actors should approach the company by letter and should enclose an sae.

Saraband Associates

265 Liverpool Road, London N1 1LX

2 agents represent actors. Areas of work include theatre, musicals, television, film and commercials.

Will occasionally consider attending performances at venues in Greater London, given 1 month's notice. Accepts submissions (with CVs and photographs) from actors previously unknown to the company if

sent by post. An sae should be included with CVs and photographs. *Commission*: Varies

SCA Management

77 Oxford Street, London W1D 2ES
tel 020-7659 2027 *fax* 020-7659 2116
email agency@sca-management.co.uk

Established in 1980. 2 agents represent 50 actors. Areas of work include theatre, musicals, television, film, commercials and corporate.

Will consider attending performances within Greater London given sufficient notice. Accepts submissions (with CVs and photographs) from actors previously unknown to the company if sent by post. Showreels and voice tapes are also accepted. *Commission*: 15%

Tim Scott

284 Grays Inn Road, London WC1X 8EB
tel 020-7833 5733 *fax* 020-7278 9175
email timscott@btinternet.com

Established in 1988. Areas of work include theatre, television, film, and commercials.

Accepts postal submissions (with CVs and photographs) from actors previously unknown to the company.

Dawn Sedgwick Management

3 Goodwins Court, London WC2N 4LL
tel 020-7240 0404 *fax* 020-7240 0415
email dawn@dawnsedgwickmanagement.com
website www.dawnsedgwickmanagment.com
Key personnel Dawn Sedgwick, Laura Quartarone

Established in 1992. 2 agents represent 30 actors. Areas of work include theatre, television, film, commercials, corporate and voice-overs. Also represents presenters, comedians and writers.

Accepts submissions (with CVs and photographs) from actors previously unknown to the agency if sent by post, but not by email. Showreels, voice tapes and invitations to view individual actors' websites are also accepted. Welcomes enquiries from actors with disabilities. *Commission*: 10-15%

Vincent Shaw Associates

186 Shaftesbury Avenue, London WC2H 8JB
tel 020-7240 2927 *fax* 020-7240 2930
email info@vincentshaw.com
website www.vincentshaw.com

Sole representation of 100 actors. Areas of work include theatre, musicals, television, film, commercials and corporate.

Will consider attending performances at venues within Greater London given sufficient notice. Accepts submissions (with CVs and photographs) from actors previously unknown to the company if sent by post. Include an sae if a reply is required. Showreels should only be sent on request. *Commission*: 10-15%

Shepherd Management Ltd

13 Radnor Walk, London SW3 4BP
tel 020-7352 2200 *fax* 020-7352 2277
email info@shepherdmanagement.co.uk
Agent Christina Shepherd

2 agents and 1 junior agent represent 120 actors, 1 director and 1 designer. Areas of work include theatre, musicals (occasionally), television, film, corporate and voice-overs.

Will consider attending performances within Greater London given as much notice as possible. Accepts postal submissions (with CVs, photographs and sae) from actors previously unknown to the agency. Showreels and voice tapes will also be accepted. Emails and follow-up telephone calls are not welcomed.

Silvey Associates

11-15 Betterton Street, London WC2H 9BP
tel 020-7470 8812 *fax* 020-7379 0801
email denise@silveyassociates.co.uk
Agents Denise Silvey, Dean Harper

Founded in 2005. 2 agents represent 35 actors in theatre, musicals, television, film, commercials and corporate work. Also represents directors, MDs, presenters, lighting designers and production managers.

Welcomes performance notices and is prepared to travel within the Greater London area with at least 1 week's notice. Welcomes representation enquiries (with CVs and photographs) from individuals, whether submitted by post or by email, but does not encourage follow-up calls or enquiries from disabled actors. Does not welcome unsolicited showreels or invitations to view actors' websites. *Commission*: 12.5% to 15%

Also runs a production company called Cahoots Theatre Company from the same address. See entry on page 132.

Sandra Singer Associates

21 Cotswold Road, Westcliff-on-Sea, Essex SSO 8AA
tel (01702) 331616 *fax* (01702) 339393
email sandrasinger@btconnect.com
website www.sandrasinger.com
Key personnel Sandra Singer (MIEAM)

Main areas of work are feature films, film, TV, commercials and musical theatre. Also represents singers.

Will consider attending performances when looking for new clients to join the management. Accepts postal applications only with sae. No zip files, jpegs, or emails with large files unless requested. Showreels should only be sent on request. Enclose an sae for the return of material.

Helen Stafford Management

14 Park Avenue, Bush Hill Park, Enfield EN1 2HP
tel 020-8360 6329 *fax* 020-8482 0371

email Helen.Stafford@blueyonder.co.uk
Agent Helen Stafford

Established in 1991. Sole representation of 20 actors. Areas of work include theatre, musicals, television, film, commercials, corporate and voice-overs.

Will consider attending performances at venues within Greater London with 2 weeks' notice. Accepts submissions (with CVs and photographs) from actors previously unknown to the company if sent by post. Showreels and voice tapes should only be sent on request. "Hard work pays off – don't ever give up!" Recommends the photographer Mark Davis, MAD Photography (200 Gladbeck Way, Enfield Chase, Enfield EN2 7HS; *tel* 020-8363 4182). *Commission*: Commercials 15%; Other 10%

Stage & Screen Personal Management Ltd

20b Kidbrooke Grove, Blackheath, London SE3 0LF
tel (07958) 648740 *fax* 020-8297 4290
email stageandscreen1@yahoo.co.uk
Agents Orit Sutton, Natasha Jones

Established in 2005. 2 agents represent 20 actors. Areas of work include theatre, musicals, film, commercials and corporate.

Will consider attending performances at venues in the Greater London area with 2 weeks' notice. Accepts CVs and photographs from actors previously unknown to the agency, including disabled actors, but please do not send by email. Welcomes invitations to view individual actors' websites, but not unsolicited showreels or voice tapes. *Commission*: 12.5%

Natasha Stevenson Management Ltd (NSM)

85 Shorrolds Road, London SW6 7TU
tel 020-7386 5333 *fax* 020-7385 3014
email nsm@netcomuk.co.uk
Agents Natasha Stevenson, Jennifer Withers, Pippa Godfrey

3 agents represent 85 actors. Areas of work include theatre, musicals, television, film, commercials, corporate and voice-overs.

Will consider attending performances at venues within Greater London with 2 weeks' notice. Actors should approach the company by post enclosing an sae. Showreels should only be sent on request.

Stiven Christie Management

1 Glen Street, Tollcross, Edinburgh EH3 9JD
tel 0131-228 4040 *fax* 0131-228 4645
email info@stivenchristie.co.uk
website www.stivenchristie.co.uk
Proprietor Douglas Stiven

Founded in 1983 (and incorporating The Actors Agency of Edinburgh); 1 agent represents actors for theatre, musicals, television, film, commercials, corporate and voice-overs.

Welcomes performance notices for shows around the UK, given 2-3 weeks' notice. Happy to receive letters (with CVs and photographs), emails, showreels and voice tapes from actors previously unknown to the company, and welcomes follow-up calls.

Take Flight Management

22 Streatham Close, Leigham Court Road, London SW16 2NQ
email info@takeflightmanagement.com

1 agent represents 35 actors for theatre, musicals, TV, film, commercials and corporate. Also represents some presenters and choreographers.

Welcomes performance notices 2 weeks' in advance, and is prepared to travel within the Greater London area. Welcomes letters (by post or email) from individuals previously unknown to the company. Does not welcome follow-up calls, and does not encourage applications from disabled actors. Welcomes showreels and invitations to view individual actors' websites. *Commission*: 12.5%

Talent Artists Ltd

59 Sydner Road, London N16 7UF
tel 020-7923 1119 *fax* 020-7923 2009
Director Jane Wynn Owen

Talent Artists Ltd represents actors working in all fields of the industry. Agents will consider seeing potential clients perform within Greater London, given a minimum of 2 weeks' notice. Actors are welcome to write to the agency with their CVs and photographs, but are asked not to follow-up their submissions by telephone or email.

Brian Taylor Associates

50 Pembroke Road, London W8 6NX
tel 020-7602 6141 *fax* 020-7602 6301
email briantaylor@nqassoc.freeserve.co.uk
Director Brian Taylor

Formerly known as Brian Taylor–Nina Quick Associates, the agency was established in 1975 with 3 agents representing approximately 80 actors. Areas of work include theatre, musicals, television, film, commercials, corporate and voice-overs.

Will consider attending performances at venues within Greater London given 2 weeks' notice. Accepts submissions (with CVs and photographs) from actors previously unknown to the company, and will respond if an sae is enclosed. Showreels and voice tapes should only be sent if requested; email submissions are not welcomed. *Commission*: 10% and 15%

TCG Artist Management

4th Floor, 6 Langley Street, London WC2H 9JA
tel 020-7240 3600 *fax* 020-7240 3606

email info@tcgam.co.uk
website www.spotlightagent.info/tcgam

Established in 1998. 3 agents represent 60 actors. Areas of work include theatre, musicals, television, film, commercials and corporate role-play.

Will consider attending performances at venues within Greater London given as much notice as possible. Accepts submissions (with CVs and photographs) from actors previously unknown to the company if sent by post. Follow-up telephone calls, showreels and voice samples are also accepted. *Commission*: 10-15% depending on the job

Paul Telford Management

23 Noel Street, London W1F 8GT
tel 020-7434 1100 *fax* 020-7434 1200
email info@telford-mgt.com
Partner Paul Telford

Established in 1994. 2 agents represent 75 actors. Areas of work include theatre, musicals, television, film, commercials and corporate.

Will consider attending performances at venues within Central London given at least 2 weeks' notice. Accepts submissions (with CVs and photographs) from actors previously unknown to the company if sent by post. Showreels and voice tapes are also accepted. Include sae for return of material. *Commission*: Variable

Katie Threlfall Associates

2a Gladstone Road, Wimbledon, London SW19 1QT
tel 020-8543 4344 *fax* 020-8543 7545
email katie@ktthrelfall.co.uk
Agent Katie Threlfall

Founded in 1996 as Hillman Threlfall; in 2006 changed its name to Katie Threlfall Associates. 1 agent represents 90 actors in theatre, musicals, TV, film, commercials and corporate.

Will attend performances at venues within Greater London if given 1 month's notice. Accepts submissions from actors (CV and photographs) previously unknown to the company. Welcomes showreels and invitations to view individual actors' websites. "Address letters correctly to the agent. Only write in if you have a showreel, or with an invitation to a show: we do not take on or meet people whose work we do not know." *Commission*: Commercials 15%; Other 12.5%

Janice Tildsley Associates

8a Addison Road, London E17 9LT
tel 020-8521 1888 *fax* 020-8521 1174
email info@janicetildsleyassociates.co.uk
website www.janicetildsley.co.uk
Agents Janice Tildsley, Kathryn Kirton

Established in 2003. 2 agents represent 60-70 actors. Areas of work include theatre, musicals, television, film and commercials.

Will consider attending performances within the Greater London area with at least 1 month's notice. Accepts submissions (with CVs and photographs) from actors previously unknown to the agency if sent by post, but not by email. Welcomes enquiries from actors with disabilities. *Commission*: 10-15%

Total Vanity Ltd

35 Wyvenhoe Road, South Harrow, Middlesex HA2 FLR
tel 020-8426 4327
email teresa.hellen@totalvanityltd
website www.totalvanity.com
Agent Teresa Hellen

Established in 2000. 1 agent represents 50 actors. Areas of work include theatre, musicals, television, film, commercials, corporate and voice-overs. Also represents presenters.

Will consider attending performances within the Greater London area with at least 1 week's notice. Accepts submissions (with CVs and photographs) from actors previously unknown to the company if sent by post. Showreels, voice tapes and invitations to view individual actors' websites are also accepted. Welcomes enquiries from actors with disabilities. *Commission*: 20%

Two's Company

244 Upland Road, London SE22 0DN
tel 020-8299 4593 *fax* 020-8299 3714
email 2scompany@britishlibrary.net
Agent Graham Crowley

Founded in 2002; 1 agent represents 6 actors in all areas of acting work.

Recommends the photographer Philip Gammon (**pgammon@dsl.pipex.com**). Does not welcome performance notices or any other unsolicited approach from actors. The company "doesn't anticipate taking any more actors on." *Commission*: 10%; Commercials 12.5%

Urban Talent

1st Floor, Alexandra Buildings, 28 Queen Street, Lincoln Square, Manchester M2 5LF
tel 0161-834 0990 *fax* 0161-834 0014
email liz@nmsmanagement.co.uk
Key personnel Liz Beeley

Urban Talent represents 30-50 actors. Areas of work include theatre, television, film, commercials, corporate and voice-overs. Also represents presenters.

Will consider attending performances at venues in the North West with 2 weeks' notice. Accepts submissions (with CVs and photographs) from actors previously unknown to the company sent by post or email. Also accepts invitations to view individual actors' websites. *Commission*: 15%

VisABLE People

PO Box 80, Droitwich WR9 0ZE
tel (01905) 776631
email louise@visablepeople.com
website www.visablepeople.com
Agent Louise Dyson

Founded in 1996, VisABLE is the UK's first agency representing only people with disabilities for professional engagements. It represents artistes with a wide range of impairments and in every age group, including children. 1 agent represents around 50 artistes in all areas of acting, including presenting.

Does not welcome performance notices: "Sorry, no time to get out and see them usually; existing clients only." Happy to receive other enquiries (with CVs and photographs) from disabled actors via email only. Showreels should always be accompanied by an sae for return. Also happy to receive invitations to view individual actors' websites. Recommends the photographer Derek Lee. *Commission*: 10-17%

Vocalworks International

Rivington House, 82 Great Eastern Street, London EC2A 3JF
tel 0870-609 2629 *fax* 0870-609 2629
email vocalworks@btinternet.com
website www.vocalworks-international.com
Director Stephanie Evans

Established in 2003. 1 agent represents 60 actors. Areas of work include theatre, musicals, television, film, commercials and corporate.

Will consider attending performances in England and Wales with at least 1 month's notice. Accepts submissions (with CVs and photographs) from actors previously unknown to the company if sent by post, but not by email. Invitations to view individual actors' websites are also accepted. Welcomes enquiries from actors with disabilities. *Commission*: 10%

Waring & McKenna Ltd

31 Sackville St, Mayfair, London W1S 3DZ
tel 020-7734 7555 *fax* 020-7734 5050
email dj@waringandmckenna.com
Agents Daphne Waring, John Summerfield

Established in 1993. 2 agents represent approx. 80 actors. Areas of work include theatre, musicals, television, film, commercials, corporate and voice-overs.

Will consider attending performances at venues within Greater London and occasionally elsewhere, given at least 1 month's notice. Accepts postal submissions (with CVs and photographs) from actors previously unknown to the company. Follow-up telephone calls are also accepted. Showreels and voice tapes should only be sent on request. *Commission*: Theatre 10%; TV and Low-Budget Films 12.5%; Commercials and Feature Films over £4 million 15%

Janet Welch Personal Management

11 Sunbury Court Island, Lower Hampton Road,
Sunbury-on-Thames TW16 5PP
tel (01932) 766190 *fax* (01932) 766191
email info@janetwelcg.pm.co.uk

Established in 1990. 1 agent represents 60-70 actors.
Areas of work include theatre, musicals, television,
film, commercials, corporate and voice-overs.

Will consider attending performances at venues
within Greater London and sometimes elsewhere,
given sufficient notice. Accepts submissions (with
CVs and photographs) from actors previously
unknown to the company if sent by post.

West End Management

188 St Vincent St, Glasgow G2 5SG
tel 0141-226 8941 *fax* 0141-226 8983
email info@west-endmgt.com
website www.west-endmgt.com
Agents Maureen Cairns, Martin Bristow

Established in 1996. 2 agents represent 50 actors.

Will consider attending performances at venues in
Scotland with 3-4 weeks' notice. Accepts submissions
(with CVs and photographs) from actors previously
unknown to the agency, including disabled actors –
but please do not submit by email. Showreels, voice
tapes and invitations to view individual actors'
websites are also accepted. *Commission*: 15%

Williamson & Holmes (formerly Campbell Associates)

9 Hop Gardens, St Martin's Lane, London WC2N
4EN
tel 020-7627 0859 *fax* 020-7627 6231
email info@williamsonandholmes.co.uk
Agents Jackie Williamson, Michelle Holmes *Voice-
over Agent* Jack Mytton

Established in 1996, the agency represents 70 actors
and 30 voice-over artists. Areas of work include
theatre, musicals, television, film, commercials,
corporate and voice-overs.

Will consider attending performances at venues
within Greater London with 2 weeks' notice. Accepts
submissions (with CVs and photographs) from actors
previously unknown to the company if sent by post.
Showreels and voice tapes are also accepted with sae
for their return. Emails with attachments will not be
opened. *Commission*: Theatre 10%; TV, Film,
Commercials and Radio 15%

Willow Personal Management

151 Main Street, Yaxley, Peterborough PE7 3LD
tel (01733) 240392 *fax* (01733) 240392
email email@willowmanagement.co.uk
website www.willowmanagement.co.uk
Director Peter Burroughs

Established in 1995. 1 agent represents 150 actors.
Specialises in the representation of short actors

(under 5 foot). Areas of work include theatre,
musicals, television, film, commercials, corporate and
voice-overs.

Accepts submissions (with CVs and photographs)
from actors previously unknown to the company if
sent by post, but not by email. Showreels, voice tapes
and invitations to view individual actors' websites are
also accepted. Welcomes enquiries from actors with
disabilities. *Commission*: 10-15%

Newton Wills Management

The Studio, 29 Springvale Avenue, Brentford,
Middlesex TW8 9QT
tel (07989) 398381
email newtoncttg@aol.com
Managing Director Newton Wills
International Christopher Socci *Talent* Julia Hunt
Office Administrator Helene Barber

Established in 1963. 4 agents represent 70 actors.
Areas of work include theatre, musicals, television,
film and commercials. Also represents TV presenters,
cameramen (film) and location-finders (Europe).

Will consider attending performances at venues
within Greater London and elsewhere, but requests as
much notice as possible. Accepts submissions (with
CVs and photographs) from actors previously
unknown to the company sent by post or email.
Showreels and voice tapes are also accepted. "Find
out as soon as possible what an agent does. The
relationship between actor and agent should be a
partnership – work with your agent to develop your
talents and add new ones to your repertoire."
Commission: Theatre 10%; Film 15%

WIS Celtic Management

86 Elphinstone Road, London E17 5EX
tel 020-8523 4234 *fax* 020-8523 4523
email wis.celtic@ethnicsaa.co.uk
Managing Director Pauline Oni

Established in 2004, specialising in Welsh, Irish and
Scottish actors. Areas of work include theatre,
musicals, television, film, commercials, corporate and
voice-overs. One agent represents 12 actors.

Will consider attending performances within Greater
London with at least 3 weeks' notice. Accepts
submissions (with CVs and photographs) from actors
previously unknown to the agency if sent by post, but
not by email. Welcomes showreels and voice tapes,
and enquiries from actors with disabilities.
Commission: Varies

Edward Wyman Agency

67 Llanon Road, Llanishen, Cardiff CF14 5AH
tel 029-2075 2351 *fax* 029-2075 2444
email edward.wyman@btconnect.com
website www.wymancasting.co.uk
Managing Director Edward Wyman *Casting/
Accounts* Judith Gay *Casting* Audrey Williams

Established in 1969, the agency represents more than 200 actors. Areas of work include television, film, commercials, corporate and voice-overs. Also represents directors, singers, dancers, circus performers, models, look-alikes, extras and promotions people.

Accepts submissions from actors previously unknown to the company. Actors should send an sae or download an application form from the website. All submissions should be sent by post only, and should include CVs, photographs and sae. "The large majority of our work is in the Welsh language and is filmed in the South Wales area, so Welsh actors are particularly welcome." Recommends the photographer Brian Tarr (6 Bangor Street, Cardiff CF24 3LR). *Commission*: OAPs 12.5%; Others 15%

Yellow Balloon Productions Ltd

Freshwater House, Outdowns, Effingham KT24 5QR
tel (01483) 281500 or (01483) 281501 *fax* (01483) 281502
email yellowbal@aol.com

Managing Director Mike Smith *Producer* Daryl Smith *Consultant* Sally James

A management company established in 1974 and covering all aspects of clients' career and long-term development; represents around 10 actors. Areas of work include television, film, commercials, corporate and voice-overs. Also represents radio and TV presenters and sports stars.

Will consider attending performances at venues in Greater London and elsewhere, given 2-3 weeks' notice. Accepts submissions (with CVs and photographs) from actors previously unknown to the company sent by post or email. Also accepts showreels and voice tapes. Invitations to view individual actors' websites are only accepted if sent via email. Submitted CVs should be as complete as possible, and clearly separate professional experience from student productions. Applicants should always state if they have yet to acquire a professional role. *Commission*: 15-20% according to press, accountancy, and PR agreements

The co-operative agency

Kim Gillespie

One of the standard questions we ask applicants seeking to join the agency is, "Why do you want to join a co-operative personal management?" We get various replies depending on age, experience and level of honesty, but tucked away somewhere in most of them is the word 'control'.

Most people working in our industry will at some point admit to feeling a lack of control over the direction and/or purpose of their career. At such moments they may feel they are having little active input into their own professional lives. If they have an agent, they may describe sitting at home waiting for the phone to ring. They may feel frustrated because they have no knowledge of what parts, if any, they are being submitted for; they may even feel part of a large, anonymous and cynically commercial outfit where the promise of getting personal attention is noticeably absent. If they don't have an agent, then the lack of control and focus becomes even more acute since there is no-one – even nominally – working on their behalf.

So, either to get their first agent or to change from an existing conventional one, people come to co-ops for more control – as well as for more knowledge of the industry, more contact with other actors, more advice and help from colleagues and more camaraderie. And, of course, more work.

The most common question that people ask *us* at audition is, "What kind of work comes into the agency?" Most co-ops I know, and certainly my own, will deal with a very wide range of work opportunities. In common with conventional agents and personal managers, co-ops will receive daily casting breakdowns for theatre, TV, film and commercials. Unlike most conventional agents they will also seek corporate training work, role-play, voice-overs, new writing development work and educational workshops. Because most co-ops are small and because they are active and entrepreneurial, they are busy and they try to keep their actors busy too.

I'm biased, but I've never really seen the disadvantages of being in a co-op. There are some, let's be honest; some casting directors still have prejudices and some people find the decision-making process boring. For most, though, this democratic control and participation is the whole point. As for casting directors, the Co-operative Personal Management Association works hard to dispel any myths there might be about co-ops not being completely efficient or not having a commercial attitude. The Association is also seeking to establish high standards of professionalism through its code of conduct and training events.

All co-ops will have different entry requirements, procedures for running the office, and ways of making decisions and forming policy; but they all give members – often after a probationary period – an equal share, an equal voice and equal responsibility. This is not for everyone, but for many actors – especially those new to the industry – co-ops provide the kind of supportive structure they seek. In turn, this reduces the trials and tribulations of an already pressurised job.

Kim Gillespie is a freelance director and actor. He runs an arts education consultancy and is a teacher, examiner, certified life coach, and role-player/facilitator for corporate training companies. He has been a member of the Central Line co-op for five years and is Secretary of the Co-operative Personal Management Association.

Co-operative agencies

Before making an approach, it is important to understand what being a member of one of these entails, and to be clear about your reason(s) for wanting to join.

21st Century Actors Management

E10 Panther House, 38 Mount Pleasant, London WC1X 0AP
tel 020-7278 3438 *fax* 020-7833 1158
email twentyfirstcenturyactors@yahoo.co.uk

Co-operative management established in 1992. Represents 21 actors. Areas of work include theatre, musicals, television, film, commercials, corporate and voice-overs. Members are expected to work 3 days in the office per month.

Will consider attending performances at venues in Greater London. Accepts submissions (with CVs and photographs) from actors previously unknown to the company if sent by post. Actors requesting representation should write stating why they wish to join a co-operative and outlining their casting type and skills. *Commission*: Theatre 10%; TV, Advertisements and Film 12%

1984 Personal Management Ltd

Suite 508, Davina House, 137 Goswell Road, London EC1V 7ET

Co-operative management representing 22 actors. Areas of work include theatre, musicals, television, film, commercials, and corporate. Members are expected to work 4 days in the office per month unless paying commission.

Will consider attending performances at venues in Greater London with 1 month's notice. Accepts letters (with CVs and photographs) from actors previously unknown to the company following an initial telephone call. Actors should always enquire whether the agency is recruiting before sending CVs. Will also accept showreels and follow-up telephone calls. *Commission*: 10%

Actors Alliance

Disney Place House, 14 Marshalsea Road, London SE1 1HL
tel 020-7407 6028 *fax* 020-7407 6028
email actors@actorsalliance.fsnet.co.uk

A co-operative group of actors established in 1976 to advance one another's careers. Currently there are 18 members, who are all in *Spotlight* and belong to Equity. Areas of work include theatre, musicals, television, film, commercials, corporates and voice-overs. Members are expected to work in the office at least 1 day a week.

When interested, and given a minimum of 2 weeks' notice, will attend an applicant's performance in Greater London. Apply (with CV and photograph) by post only, enclosing an sae for reply. Do not send a showreel unless requested to do so. Actors Alliance is not funded from commission.

Actors' Creative Team

Albany House, 82-84 South End, Croydon CR0 1DQ
tel 020-8239 8892 *fax* 020-8239 8818
email office@actorscreativeteam.co.uk
website www.actorscreativeteam.co.uk

Founded in 2001, the agency has 20 members working in theatre, musicals, television, film, commercials and corporate projects. Members are expected to work 4 days in the office each month.

Welcomes performance notices for events within Greater London (inside the M25), given 1 month's notice. Will also accept letters (with CVs and photographs) and follow-up telephone calls from actors previously unknown to the agency. Does not welcome emails, showreels or voice tapes. Is unlikely to look at an actor's website unless the agency has already shown interest. "Understand what a co-op is, and the financial/time commitment it involves, before you write to us. Make sure that this is the direction you want to pursue, and include your reasons in a covering letter." *Commission*: Theatre 10%; Media 12.5%

Actors Direct Ltd

Gainsborough House, 109 Portland Street, Manchester M1 6DN
tel 0161-237 1904 *fax* 0161-237 1904
email actorsdirect@aol.com
Administrators Eilis Hetherington, Jonathan Byrne

Established in 1994. Co-operative management. Sole representative of approximately 25 actors. Areas of work include theatre, musicals, television, film, commercials, corporate and voice-overs. Members are expected to work 2-3 days in the office each month.

Will consider attending performances at venues in the North (Manchester, Leeds, and Liverpool areas) if given 2 weeks' notice. Accepts submissions (with CVs and photographs) from actors previously unknown to the company if sent by post. Also accepts showreels and voice tapes. Will consider applications from trained professional actors with excellent IT and communications skills and the ability to perform office duties to a high standard. "Actors Direct is constantly striving to maintain a high professional image and to provide a first-class service to casting directors." *Commission*: 10% for members

Actors Exchange Management (AXM)
206 Great Guildford Business Square, 30 Great Guildford Street, London SE1 0HS
tel 020-7261 0400 *fax* 020-7261 0408
email info@axmgt.com
website www.axmgt.com

Established in 1983. Co-operative management representing 20 actors. Areas of work include theatre, musicals, television, film, commercials, corporate and voice-overs. Members are expected to work 4 days in the office per month.

Will consider attending performances at venues in Greater London, given 1 month's notice. Accepts submissions (with CVs and photographs) from actors previously unknown to the company if sent by post. Showreels and voice tapes should only be sent on request following an interview. *Commission*: 10%

The Actors File
Spitfire Studios, 63-71 Collier Street, London N1 9BE
tel 020-7278 0364 *fax* 020-7278 0364
email mail@theactorsfile.co.uk
website www.theactorsfile.co.uk

Established in 1983. Co-operative management representing 20-25 actors. Areas of work include theatre, musicals, television, film, commercials, corporate and voice-overs. Members are expected to work 4 days in the office per month and to attend business meetings.

Will consider attending performances at venues in Greater London and occasionally elsewhere, if given a minimum of 3 weeks' notice. Accepts submissions (with CVs and photographs) from actors previously unknown to the company if sent by post. Will also accept showreels. *Commission*: 12% (negotiable on low fees)

The Actors' Group
21-31 Oldham Street, Manchester M1 1JG
tel/fax 0161-834 4466
mobile (07963) 832060
email enquiries@theactorsgroup.co.uk
website www.theactorsgroup.co.uk

Co-operative management representing 20 actors. Areas of work include theatre, musicals, television, film, commercials, corporate and voice-overs. Members are expected to carry out various office duties.

Will consider attending performances at venues in the North West with 2-4 weeks' notice. Accepts submissions (with CVs and photographs) from actors previously unknown to the company if sent by post. Will also accept follow-up telephone calls, showreels,

voice tapes and invitations to view individual actors' websites.

Actors Network Agency
55 Lambeth Walk, London SE11 6DX
tel 020-7735 0999 *fax* 020-7735 8177
email info@ana-actors.co.uk
website www.ana-actors.co.uk
Coordinator and Administrator Sandie Bakker

Established in 1985. Co-operative management representing 20-30 actors. Areas of work include theatre, musicals, television, film, commercials and corporate. Also represents role-play. Members are expected to work 4 days in the office per month.

Will consider attending performances at venues in Greater London and occasionally elsewhere, given as much notice as possible. Accepts submissions (with CVs and photographs) from actors previously unknown to the company if sent by post. Will also accept showreels. "An interest in, and commitment to, this type of agency is essential." *Commission*: 10%; Commercials 12.5%

Actorum Ltd
3rd Floor, 21 Foley Street, London W1W 6DR
tel 020-7636 6978 *fax* 020-7636 6975
email actorum2@ukonline.co.uk
website www.actorum.com

Co-operative management representing 30 actors. Members are expected to work 4 days in the office per month.

Will consider attending performances at venues in Greater London and elsewhere, given 4 weeks' notice. Accepts submissions (with CVs and photographs) if sent by post. "No applications by email, please." Will also accept showreels, voice tapes and invitations to view individual actors' websites. *Commission*: Theatre 10%; TV, Commercials and Film 15%

Alpha Personal Management
Studio B4, 3 Bradbury Street, London N16 8JN
tel 020-7241 0077 *fax* 020-7241 2410
email alpha@alphaactors.com
website www.alphaactors.com

Established in 1983, the agency represents 25 actors in theatre, musicals, television, film, commercials and corporate work. Members are expected to work 4 days in the office each month, and pay 10% commission on all acting work (with concessions for less-well-paid work).

Will consider attending performances within Greater London given as much as notice as possible. Welcomes submissions (with CVs and photographs) from actors previously unknown to the company sent by post or email. Will also accept invitations to view an actor's website. Follow-up telephone calls, however, are not appreciated.

Arena Personal Management Ltd

E11 Panther House, 38 Mount Pleasant, London
WC1X 0AP
tel 020-7278 1661 *fax* 020-7278 1661
email arenapmltd@aol.com
website www.arenapmltd.co.uk

Co-operative management representing 20 actors.
Areas of work include theatre, musicals, television,
film, commercials, corporate and voice-overs.
Members are expected to work 1 day in the office per
week.

Will consider attending performances at venues in
Greater London given 3-4 weeks' notice. Accepts
submissions (with CVs and photographs) from actors
previously unknown to the company if sent by post.
Will also accept follow-up telephone calls, showreels,
voice tapes and invitations to view individual actors'
websites. *Commission*: Theatre 10%; Commercials
12.5%

Cardiff Casting

Chapter Arts Centre, Market Road, Cardiff CF5 1QE
tel 029-2023 3321 *fax* 029-2023 3380
email admin@cardiffcasting.co.uk
website www.cardiffcasting.co.uk
Key personnel Co-operative Administrator

Established in 1981. Co-operative management
representing 20-25 actors. Areas of work include
theatre, musicals, television, film, commercials,
corporate and voice-overs. Members are expected to
work 2-3 days in the office per month.

Will consider attending performances at venues in
Greater London, Cardiff, South West England and
Wales given 2 weeks' notice. Accepts submissions
(with CVs and photographs) from actors previously
unknown to the company if sent by post. Will also
accept follow-up telephone calls, showreels, voice
tapes and invitations to view individual actors'
websites. Applicants are asked to state clearly why
they have approached a co-operative. *Commission*:
Theatre 8%; Mechanical Media 10%

CCM

Panther House, 38 Mount Pleasant, London WC1X
0AP
tel 020-7278 0507 *fax* 020-7813 3103
email casting@ccmactours.com
Key contacts Hayley Williams (Secretary), Lee Moore

Established in 1993. Co-operative management
representing 22 actors. Areas of work include theatre,
musicals, television, film, commercials and corporate
role-play. Members are expected to work 3 days in
the office per month.

Will consider attending performances at venues in
Greater London given 1 month's notice. Accepts
letters and emails (with CVs and photographs) from
actors previously unknown to the company. Will also
accept invitations to view individual actors' websites.

"Actors must be aware of how co-operatives work,
and their role within them. Information is available
from Equity and Spotlight." *Commission*: Theatre
12%; TV, Advertisements and Film 15%

Central Line

11 East Circus Street, Nottingham NG1 5AF
tel 0115-941 2937 *fax* 0115-950 8087
email centralline@btconnect.com

Established in 1984. Co-operative management
representing 15-25 actors. Areas of work include
theatre, musicals, television, film, commercials,
corporate and voice-overs. Also represents directors.
Members are expected to work in the office as and
when appropriate.

Will consider attending performances at venues in
Greater London and elsewhere. Accepts submissions
(with CVs and photographs) from actors previously
unknown to the company sent by post or email. Will
also accept follow-up telephone calls, showreels, voice
tapes and invitations to view individual actors'
websites. *Commission*: 10%

Circuit Personal Management Ltd

Suite 71 SEC, Bedford Street, Stoke-on-Trent ST1
4PZ
tel (01782) 285388 *fax* (01782) 206821
email mail@circuitpm.co.uk
website www.circuitpm.co.uk

Established in 1988. Co-operative management
representing 18-20 actors, with 1 full-time
coordinator. Areas of work include theatre, musicals,
television, film, commercials, corporate and voice-
overs. Members are expected to work 1 day in the
office every 6 weeks.

Will consider attending performances at venues in
Greater London, the West Midlands, North West and
West Yorkshire, given 3-4 weeks' notice. Accepts
submissions (with CVs and photographs) from actors
previously unknown to the company sent by post or
email. Will also accept follow-up telephone calls.

City Actors' Management

Oval House, 52-54 Kennington Oval, London SE11
5SW
tel 020-7793 9888 *fax* 020-7793 8282
email info@city-actors.freeserve.co.uk
website www.city-actors.freeserve.co.uk

Co-operative management representing 21 actors.
Areas of work include theatre, musicals, television,
film, commercials and corporate. Members are
expected to work 4 days in the office per month.

Will consider attending performances at venues in
Greater London with a minimum of 2 weeks' notice.
Submissions (with CVs and photographs) should be
sent by post and not by email. Advises actors to
contact the agency when appearing in a show, or with
a showreel, as new members will not be admitted

without their work being seen. Will also accept follow-up telephone calls. *Commission*: Theatre 10%; Mechanical Media 12.5%

Crescent Management
10 Barley Mow Passage, Chiswick, London W4 4PH
tel 020-8987 0191
email mail@crescentmanagement.co.uk
website www.crescentmanagement.co.uk

Established in 1991, the agency has 24 members working in theatre, musicals, television, film, commercials and corporate drama. Members are expected to work 4 days in the office each month.

Will consider attending performances within Greater London given 2 weeks' notice. Accepts submissions (with CVs and photographs) from actors previously unknown to the agency if sent by post. Email applications are unwelcome. Will also accept follow-up telephone calls, showreels, voice tapes and invitations to view an actor's website. *Commission*: Theatre 10%; Television 12.5%; Film 15%

Denmark Street Management
Packington Bridge Workspace, Unit 11, 1B Packington Square, London N1 7UA
tel 020-7354 8555 *fax* 020-7354 8558
email mail@denmarkstreet.net

Established in 1985. Co-operative management representing 15-25 actors. Areas of work include theatre, musicals, television, film, commercials, corporate and voice-overs. Members are expected to work 4 days in the office per month.

Will consider attending performances at venues in Greater London and elsewhere, given 1 month's notice. Accepts submissions (with CVs and photographs) from actors previously unknown to the company if sent by post. Showreels and voice tapes should only be sent on request. Applicants should state why they would like to join a co-operative. Ethnic-minority and older actors are particularly welcome. *Commission*: Theatre 10%; TV and Film 12.5%; Commercials 15%

Direct Personal Management
Park House, 62 Lidgett Lane, Leeds LS8 1PL
tel/fax 0113-266 4036
email daphne.franks@dline.org.uk
website www.dline.org.uk

Established in 1984 (formerly Direct Line Personal Management). Co-operative management representing 35 actors. Areas of work include theatre, musicals, television, film, commercials, corporate, role-play and voice-overs. Members are expected to work 2 days in the office each month.

Will consider attending performances at venues within Greater London and elsewhere, with 1 month's notice. Accepts submissions (with CVs and photographs) from actors previously unknown to the

company sent by post or email. Follow-up telephone calls, showreels, voice tapes and invitations to view individual actors' websites are also accepted. "Every applicant's enquiry is discussed at a monthly meeting. We do reply, but would appreciate it if actors enclosed an sae to help reduce our costs."
Commission: 5-15%

Frontline Management
Colombo Centre, 34-68 Colombo Street, London SE1 8DP
tel 020-7261 9466 *fax* 020-7261 9466
email frontlineactor@freeuk.com
Key personnel Holly Richardson

Established in 1984. Co-operative management representing 18-22 actors. Areas of work include theatre, musicals, television, film, commercials and corporate. Members are expected to work 3 days in the office per month.

Will consider attending performances at venues in Greater London given 3-7 days' notice. Accepts letters or emails (with CVs and photographs) from actors previously unknown to the company. Follow-up telephone calls, showreels, voice tapes and invitations to view individual actors' websites are also accepted. *Commission*: 10-12.5% depending on amount of earnings

IML
Oval House, 52-54 Kennington Oval, London SE11 5SW
tel 020-7587 1080 *fax* 020-7587 1080
email iml.London@btconnect.com
website www.iml.org.uk
Key contact All members

Co-operative management established in 1980. Represents 22 actors. 2 members work in the office each day on a rotational basis. Areas of work include theatre, musicals, television, film and commercials. Members are expected to work 4 days in the office per month.

Will consider attending performances at venues in Greater London given 3 weeks' notice. Accepts submissions (with CVs and photographs) from actors previously unknown to the company if sent by post. Will also accept follow-up telephone calls. Showreels and voice tapes should only be sent on request. *Commission*: 5-15% depending on the job

Inspiration Management
Room 227, The Aberdeen Centre, 22-24 Highbury Grove, London N5 2EA
tel 020-7704 0440 *fax* 020-7704 8497
email applications@inspirationmanagement.org.uk
website www.inspirationmanagement.org.uk
Key contact Applications Team

Established in 1986, Inspiration is a co-operative management representing 20-25 actors. Principal areas of work include theatre, television, film and commercials; occasionally corporate, audio and role-play. Members work 3 days in the office per month, when not engaged in professional acting work, and attend regular meetings.

Actors should apply by post only, including a CV, 10x8in headshot and covering letter with land-line number and email address if available; do not send demos or showreels initially. Members are consulted on all applications and will interview candidates wherever possible. Actors are advised to consult the website to check for casting overlaps. As at least 2 members will need to see an applicant's work; a minimum of 3 weeks' notice is required for any forthcoming appearances. *Commission*: 10%

Links Management

34-68 Colombo Street, London SE1 8DP
tel 020-7928 0806 *fax* 020-7928 0806
email links@eidosnet.co.uk
website www.links-management.co.uk
Office Manager Louise North

Established in 1984. Co-operative management representing 25 actors. Areas of work include theatre, musicals, television, film, commercials and voice-overs. Members are expected to work 1 day in the office per week.

Will consider attending performances at venues within Greater London given 2 weeks' notice. Accepts submissions (with CVs and photographs) from actors previously unknown to the company if sent by post. Also accepts follow-up telephone calls, showreels and voice tapes. *Commission*: Theatre 10%; TV and Film 12.5%

Longtime Management

36 Lord Street, Radcliffe, Manchester M26 3BA
tel 0161-724 6625 *fax* 0161-724 6625
email longtime_mgt@btopenworld.com
Coordinator Nigel Adams

Established in 1994, the agency has 10 members working in theatre, television, film, commercials and corporate role-play.

"We are a small actors' co-operative agency and a production co-operative. While we don't welcome details regarding representation, we are happy to receive CVs and photographs from Northern-based actors (particularly Manchester) in respect of future theatre productions."

North of Watford Actors Agency

Bridge Mill, Hebden Bridge, West Yorks HX7 8EX
tel (01422) 845361 *fax* (01422) 846503
email northofwatford@btconnect.com
website www.northofwatford.com
New Applications Coordinator Chris Orton

Established in 1992. Co-operative management representing 25-30 actors. Areas of work include theatre, musicals, television, film, commercials, corporate and voice-overs. Members are expected to work 3-4 days in the office per month.

Will consider attending performances at venues in Northern locations (Leeds, Manchester, etc.) but requests as much notice as possible. Accepts submissions (with CVs and photographs) from actors previously unknown to the company if sent by post. Will also accept follow-up telephone calls, showreels, voice tapes and invitations to view individual actors' websites. *Commission*: Varies depending on the work

North One Management

HG08 Aberdeen Studios, Highbury Grove, London N5 2EA
tel 020-7359 9666 *fax* 020-7359 9449
email actors@northone.co.uk
website www.northone.co.uk

Established in 1987. Co-operative management representing 25 actors. Areas of work include theatre, television, film, commercials and corporate. Members are expected to work 3 days in the office per month.

Will consider attending performances at venues within Greater London given at least 1 week's notice. Accepts submissions (with CVs and black-and-white 10x8in photographs) from actors previously unknown to the company if sent by post. Will also accept follow-up telephone calls, showreels and voice tapes. Prefers to hear from actors when currently performing. Administration and technical skills are advantageous. Applications from non-European performers are particularly welcome. *Commission*: 10%

Otto Personal Management Ltd

The Printer's Loft, 111 Arundel Lane, Sheffield S1 4RF
tel 0114-275 2592 *fax* 0114-275 0550
email admin@ottopm.co.uk
website www.ottopm.co.uk

Established in 1985. Co-operative management representing 30-35 actors. Areas of work include theatre, musicals, television, film, commercials, corporate and voice-overs. Also represents directors and presenters. Members are expected to work an average of 3 weeks per year in the office.

Will consider attending performances at venues in Yorkshire, the North Midlands, Manchester and the surrounding areas with approximately 1 month's notice. Accepts submissions (with CVs and photographs) from actors previously unknown to the company sent by post or email. Will also accept follow-up telephone calls, showreels, voice tapes and invitations to view individual actors' websites. "We mainly recruit actors living within a viable distance of Sheffield – Leeds to the North, Mansfield to Manchester." *Commission*: 10-15% depending on kind of work

Park Management Ltd

Unit C3, 62 Beechwood Road, London E8 3DY
tel 020-7923 1498 *fax* 020-7923 1422
email park_management@hotmail.com
Coordinator Stephen Leslie

Established in 1977. Co-operative management representing 20 actors. Areas of work include theatre, musicals, television, film, commercials and corporate. Members are expected to work 3-4 days in the office per month.

Will consider attending performances at venues within Greater London with 3 weeks' notice. Accepts submissions (with CVs and photographs) from actors previously unknown to the company if sent by post. Will also accept showreels, voice tapes and invitations to view individual actors' websites. "Only write if you are performing in something." *Commission*: Theatre 11%; TV and Film 13.5%

Performance Actors Agency

137 Goswell Road, London EC1V 7ET
tel 020-7251 5716 *fax* 020-7251 3974
email performance@p-a-a.co.uk
website www.p-a-a.co.uk
Key personnel Lionel Guyett

Established in 1984. Co-operative management representing 30+ actors. Areas of work include theatre, musicals, television, film, commercials, corporate and voice-overs. Members are expected to work 4 days a month in the office.

Will consider attending performances at venues within Greater London and occasionally elsewhere, given as much notice as possible. Accepts submissions (with CVs and photographs) from actors previously unknown to the company if sent by post and enclosing sae. Will also accept showreels and voice tapes. " We only recruit new members when specific categories are required. Call first." *Commission*: 10%

Rattlebag Actors Agency Ltd

Everyman Theatre Annexe, 13-15 Hope Street, Liverpool L1 9BH
tel 0151-708 7273 *fax* 0151-709 0773
email actors@rattlebag.co.uk
website www.rattlebag.co.uk

Established in 1995. Co-operative management representing more than 25 actors. Areas of work include theatre, musicals, television, film, radio, commercials, corporate and voice-overs. Many of the actors have other, additional skills. Members are expected to work a minimum of 4 full weeks within a 12-month period.

Will consider attending performances at venues in the North West (Manchester, Liverpool, North Wales) and nationally with 3-4 weeks' notice. Accepts brief, straightforward submissions (with CVs and photographs) from actors previously unknown to the company if sent by post. Photographs should ideally be current black-and-white head-shots. Showreels, voice tapes and invitations to view individual actors' websites are also accepted. "If invited to an audition or interview, it is always best to call in with a response – whether you wish to accept or not." *Commission*: 12.5%

Rogues & Vagabonds Management

The Print House, 18 Ashwin Street, London E8 3DL
tel 020-7254 8130
email rogues@vagabondsmanagement.com
website www.vagabondsmanagement.com

Co-operative management representing 28-30 actors. Areas of work include theatre, musicals, television, film, commercials and corporate. Members are expected to work in the office 3 days per month.

Will consider attending performances anywhere, if given at least 3-4 weeks' notice. Accepts submissions (with CVs and photographs) from actors previously unknown to the company if sent by post or email. Showreels, voice tapes and invitations to view individual actors' websites are also accepted. Welcomes enquiries from actors with disabilities. *Commission*: TV/Film 10% on first £200, 15% thereafter; Theatre 10%

Rosebery RM Management Ltd

Hoxton Hall, 130 Hoxton Street, London N1 6SH
tel 020-7684 0187 *fax* 020-7684 0197
email roseberymgt@aol.com

Established in 1984. Represents 27 actors in theatre, musicals, television, film, commercials, corporate work and voice-overs. Rosebery has a full-time administrator who has seen auditions triple and revenue quadruple. Members are expected to work 2 days in the office per month, and pay 10% commission on all acting work.

Will consider attending performances at all venues within Central London. Only accepts submissions from actors seeking representation if sent by post. Submissions must include a 10x8in black-and-white photograph, a current CV and a covering letter explaining why Rosebery is the right choice. Showreels, voice tapes and singing reels are also welcomed.

Stage Centre Management Ltd

41 North Road, London N7 9DP
tel 020-7607 0872 *fax* 020-7609 0213
email stagecentre@aol.com

Established in 1984. Co-operative management representing 18-26 actors. Areas of work include theatre, musicals, television, film, commercials and corporate. Members are expected to work 1 day in the office per week.

Will consider attending performances at venues within Greater London and elsewhere, given at least 2 weeks' notice. Accepts submissions (with CVs and photographs) from actors previously unknown to the company sent by post or email. All applicants are advised to call asking for a specific contact name before applying. Will also accept follow-up telephone calls, showreels, voice tapes and invitations to view individual actors' websites. Applicants should not apply if they are unable to provide visible evidence of their work (e.g. performance notice, showcase or showreel). *Commission:* 10%

West Central Management

E4 Panther House, 38 Mount Pleasant, London WC1X 0AP
tel 020-7833 8134 *fax* 020-7833 8134
email mail@westcentralmanagement.co.uk

website www.westcentralmanagement.co.uk

Established in 1984. Co-operative management representing 15-20 actors. Areas of work include theatre, musicals, television, film, commercials and corporate. Members are expected to work 4 days in the office per month.

Will consider attending performances at venues within Greater London with 2 weeks' notice. Accepts submissions (with CVs and photographs) from actors previously unknown to the company sent by post or email. Will also accept invitations to view individual actors' websites. "We would need to see an applicant's live performance or showreel, but only after an initial meeting/audition." *Commission:* 10%

Voice-over agents

This section lists agencies that specialise in voice-overs. Check the details of how each wishes to be approached, and refer to the 'Showreel & Voice-Demo Companies' section for more about getting a voice demo made. Some of the larger conventional agencies have their own voice-over departments – generally, for their existing clients only.

AD Voice
Oxford House, 76 Oxford Street, London W1D 1BS
tel 020-7323 2345 *fax* 020-7323 0101
email info@advoice.co.uk
website www.advoice.co.uk
Key personnel Susan Bartlett

1 agent represents more than 100 clients working in television and radio commercials, documentaries, corporate, animations and audiobook recordings.

Welcomes letters with CVs and voice samples from new actors, but strongly recommends that an sae is included for their return. Prefers not to be contacted by email.

Calypso Voices
25-26 Poland Street, London W1F 8QN
tel 020-7734 6415 *fax* 020-7437 0410
email calypso@calypsovoices.com
website www.calypsovoices.com
Manager Jane Savage

2 agents represent 80 clients for voice-over work. Areas of work include television and radio commercials, documentaries, animation, corporate, audiobooks and on-air promotions.

Foreign Versions
60 Blandford Street, London W1U 7JD
tel 020-7935 0993 *fax* 020-7935 0507
email info@foreignversions.co.uk
website www.foreignversions.com
Directors Margaret Davies, Anne Geary *Project Manager* Bérangère Capelle

Works with advertising agencies for foreign markets, corporate clients, companies producing audioguides, and film and television companies.

As the agency specialises in foreign languages, all voices must be mother-tongue speakers. Voice samples should be sent on MP3 via email or on a CD, together with a CV.

Hobson's Voices
62 Chiswick High Road, London W4 1SY
tel 020-8995 3628 *fax* 020-8996 5350
email voices@hobsons-international.com
website www.hobsons-international.com
Company Manager David Hodge *Agents* Tania Edwards, Maggie Kruger, Linda Spinetti, Sarah Vlatas, Janet Ferguson-Lees

5 agents represent 160 clients. Welcomes CVs (with voice showreels) from individuals unknown to the company, but please do not approach by email. Does not welcome follow up calls: "We always reply."

Lip Service
60-66 Wardour Street, London W1F 0TA
tel 020-7734 3393 *fax* 020-7734 3373
email bookings@lipservice.co.uk
Key personnel Susan Mactavish

4 agents represent 75 clients. Areas of work include television, film, commercials and audiobooks.

Accepts submissions (with CVs and voice CDs) from individual actors previously unknown to the company sent by email or post. Please enclose an sae for their return.

Rabbit Vocal Management
2nd Floor, 18 Broadwick Street, London W1F 8HS
tel 020-7287 6466 *fax* 020-7287 6566
email info@rabbit.uk.net
website www.rabbit.uk.net
Founder Melanie Bourne *Managing Director* Rebecca Fuller *Agent* Lexi Cantacuzene-Speransky

3 agents represent 120 clients. Areas of work include television, film, commercials, audiobooks and radio.

Accepts submissions (with CVs) from actors previously unknown to the agency if sent by post, but not by email – and please always enclose an sae. Invitations to view individual actors' websites are also accepted. Represents actors with disabilities.

Rhubarb Voice-Overs
First Floor, 1a Devonshire Road, Chiswick, London W4 2EU
tel 020-8742 8683 *fax* 020-8742 8693
email enquiries@rhubarb.co.uk
website www.rhubarb.co.uk
Key personnel Johnny Garcia

The agency works in every major platform of the spoken word, from commercial and corporate pieces, to film dubbing, animation and multimedia projects, with 3 agents representing around 70 artists.

Actors seeking representation should send a cover letter or email with CV (including relevant voice work), headshot and CD showreel, together with an sae. The agency prefers not to receive follow-up telephone calls.

Shining Management Ltd

12 D'Arblay Street, London W1F 8DU
tel 020-7734 1981 *fax* 020-7734 2528
Director Clair Daintree *Key personnel* Jennifer Taylor

2 agents represent 55 clients. Areas of work include voice-overs for television, film, commercials and audiobooks.

Accepts submissions (with CVs and voice CDs) from individual actors previously unknown to the company if sent by post. Include an sae for the return of submissions. Also accepts voice tapes – although CDs are preferred. "Please do not ring with submission enquiries." *Commission*: 15%

Speak Ltd

59 Lionel Road North, Brentford, Middlesex TW8 9QZ
tel 020-8758 0666 *fax* 020-8758 0333
email info@speak.ltd.uk
website www.speak.ltd.uk
Key personnel Mou Mukherjee *Director* Abigail Wells-Hardy

Established in 1992. 3 agents represent more than 100 clients working in television and radio, commercials and channel idents, corporate, documentaries, IVRs, animation and CD Rom games.

Submissions should be sent by post only, with CD, photo and CV; they must also enclose an sae. Does not welcome calls or emails and will only look at professionally recorded showreels. Advises actors to look at the 'Careers Advice' page on the website for information on how to proceed.

Recommends USP (24 Newman Street, London W1; 020-7927 6600) for production.

Speak-Easy Ltd

1 Dairy Yard, High Street, Market Harborough, Leicestershire LE16 7NL
Voice-Overs & Corporate Agent Sarah Pickering
Television Agent Kate Moon (Director)

2 agents represent 80 clients. Areas of work include television, commercials and audiobooks.

Accepts submissions (with CVs and voice CDs) from individual actors previously unknown to the company if sent by post. Enclose an sae for reply.

Talking Heads

2-4 Noel Street, London W1F 8GB
tel 020-7292 7575 *fax* 020-7292 7576
email voices@talkingheadsvoices.com
website www.talkingheadsvoices.com
Key personnel John Sachs

4 agents represent 150 clients, including foreign-language voice-over clients. Areas of work include commercials, television, film, animation, corporate videos and audiobooks.

Accepts submissions (with CVs and voice CDs) from individual actors previously unknown to the company if sent by post. Invitations to view websites are also accepted. *Commission*: 15%

Sue Terry Voices Ltd

18 Broadwick Street (3rd Floor), London W1F 8HS
tel 020-7434 2040 *fax* 020-7434 2042
email sue@sueterryvoices.co.uk
website www.sueterryvoices.co.uk

15 agents represent 100 clients. Areas of work include commercials and radio.

Accepts submissions (with CVs) from actors previously unknown to the company if sent by post, but not by email. Welcomes unsolicited voice tapes. Always enclose a voice reel with your CV. *Commission*: 15%

Tongue & Groove

3 Stevenson Square, Manchester M1 1DN
tel 0161-228 2469 *fax* 0161-237 1809
email info@tongueandgroove.co.uk
website www.tongueandgroove.co.uk
Producers Beverley Ashworth, John Basham

3 agents represent 47 clients. Areas of work include voice-overs for television, commercials and audiobooks.

Accepts submissions (with CVs and voice CDs) from individual actors previously unknown to the company if sent by post. Also accepts voice tapes and invitations to view individual actors' websites.

Voice & Script International

Aradco House, 132 Cleveland Street, London W1T 6AB
tel 020-7692 7700 *fax* 020-7692 7711
email info@vsi.tv
website www.vsi.tv
Voice-Over Coordinator Jenny Morris *Voice-Over Project Managers* Bea Potashnik, Isobel George *Key contacts* Maja Ludford-Thomas, Anna Jury

5 voice-over agents represent approx. 750-1000 foreign-language voice-over clients. Areas of work include voice-overs for television, film and commercials.

Accepts submissions (with CVs) from individual actors previously unknown to the company sent by post or email. Also accepts voice tapes and invitations to view individual actors' websites. "We only use mother-tongue foreign-language speakers."

Voice Box Agency Ltd

Laser House, Waterfront Quay, Salford Quays, Manchester M50 3XW
tel 0161-874 5741
Manager Elinor Stanton

1 agent represents 40 clients. Areas of work include voice-overs for television, film, commercials and audiobooks.

Accepts voice tapes from individual actors previously unknown to the company. *Commission*: 15%

Voice Shop
First Floor, 1a Devonshire Road, London W4 2EU
tel 020-8742 7077 *fax* 020-8742 7011
email info@voice-shop
website www.voice-shop.co.uk
Key contact Maxine Wiltshire

3 agents represent 44 clients working in television, film, commercials and audiobook recording.

Welcomes letters or emails with CD/MP3 audio samples from new actors, but prefers not to receive follow-up telephone calls or tapes. All submissions should include an sae with sufficient postage, and all audio samples should contain appropriate material and be professionally produced. *Commission*: 15%

Voice Squad
62 Blenheim Gardens, London NW2 4NT
tel 020-8450 4451 *fax* 020-8452 7944
email voices@voicesquad.com
website www.voicesquad.com
Director Neil Conrich

2 agents represent 45 clients. Areas of work include television, film, commercials and audiobooks.

Accepts submissions (with CVs and voice CDs) from individual actors previously unknown to the

company if sent by post. Also accepts voice tapes. *Commission*: 15%

Suzy Wooton Voices
75 Shelley Street, Kingsley, Northampton NN2 7HZ
tel 0870-765 9660 *fax* 0870-765 9668
email suzy@suzywoottonvoices.com
website www.suzywoottonvoices.com

1 agent represents 38 clients. Areas of work include television, film, commercials and audiobooks.

Accepts submissions (with CVs) from individual actors previously unknown to the company sent by post or email. Also accepts follow-up telephone calls, voice tapes, showreels and invitations to view individual actors' websites. *Commission*: 15%

Yakety Yak All Mouth Ltd
8 Bloomsbury Square, London WC1A 2NE
tel 020-7430 2600 *fax* 020-7404 6109
email info@yaketyyak.co.uk
website www.yaketyyak.co.uk
Proprietor Jolie Williams

4 agents represent 155 clients. Areas of work include voice-overs for television, film, commercials, animation and audiobooks.

Accepts submissions (with CVs and voice CDs) from individual actors previously unknown to the company if sent by post. Include an sae for the return of submissions. Also accepts voice tapes – although CDs are preferred. "Please do not ring with submission enquiries." *Commission*: 15%

The working life of a theatre casting director

Sophie Marshall

Twenty-something years ago, when I became the first Casting Director for the Royal Exchange Theatre in Manchester, I inherited a four-drawer filing cabinet, stuffed with letters from actors who were keen to be seen by the directors. I had no idea how long the letters had been there, but soon found out that many actors had moved, others had become TV regulars, and one or two had even died. I realised then that casting is, and has to be, an 'in the moment' activity – circumstances change too much, too often.

The title Casting Director is perhaps a misnomer; s/he is more a facilitator, coordinator and encyclopaedia of information, rather than the final decision-maker – that has to be the director, at least in theatre. In television and film the process is much the same, in terms of selection for interview, although the readings and screen tests may often need to be more 'spot on'.

The process starts with a discussion between myself and the director about the play, from which can come a casting breakdown (which may be made accessible to actors and agents, or may be kept for us to work on in private). The director will generally have some actors in mind, or the project may be based on an element of 'lead' casting, and I will then add my own lists of ideas. About ten weeks before rehearsals begin I will then start on all the clerical back-up work – checking availabilities, sifting through the agents' and actors' submissions, setting up interviews. This is followed by the hands-on part: being at the auditions and probably reading-in, discussing the outcomes with the director, arranging recalls, offering and negotiating contracts.

Actors and agents sometimes assume that a casting breakdown is written in stone, and will not change, but this is very often only a starting point; in the ensuing weeks the ideas will develop throughout the audition process. When I was casting *A Midsummer Night's Dream*, we decided not to put out a breakdown; however, agents knew the production was happening, and submitted around 1000 CVs, and actors wrote too – probably about another 1000 letters. Everyone had an idea of how Oberon ought to look, how small Hermia should be, what regional accent Bottom could use. It can take literally hours to open all the envelopes, unfold the contents and read them, and it is even more time-consuming when the letters are badly typed or vague, the CVs uninformative, and the photos so bleached you can't distinguish any features.

In theatre it is by no means essential to have an agent, and even if you do, a letter from an actor is always interesting and the CV invariably more detailed. (In fact, it's a good idea to ask your agent for a copy of your CV, so you can see how they are promoting you. They are, after all, your representative and business partner.) When you write in for a particular production, by all means mention which role attracts you, and show a little of your personality in the letter; but your attached CV should tell all the truthful facts about your experience and skills, and your photo should look like you! The CV, photo and letter are a package, but one which should be altered according to the recipient. The CV and photo would most likely be fixed, but the letter would refer to the particular company or project. Don't repeat your whole CV in the text of the letter, but do refer to any specifically useful points. If you no longer look like your photo, get a new one! There may be instances where you are selected for interview because you resemble another member of the cast, for instance (lots of twins in Shakespeare!) – and if you turn up on the day and look nothing like the photo, the director's reaction could be very demoralising. It's harder to write for specific screen jobs, but the process of sending details to the casting director should be the same.

Silver pen on black paper, letters in rhyme, photos of you in a school production, camomile teabags ("to soothe you as you read my letter") ... all of these make you look a little desperate. Firm facts are better, and an approach such as, "I haven't had the opportunity to be in a Shakespeare play since I was at college, but I hope my music and movement skills will be of interest to you for the role of First Fairy," is much more positive and pertinent. It would show your interest, the fact that you've read the play, and make us look immediately at your CV to see which plays you covered at college, and what special skills you have – Result!

Some of the hardest auditions to deal with are those where we know the actor is terrific, but is so well-behaved in the interview – only speaking when spoken to, reading cautiously before getting some director input, and so on – that there is absolutely no personality and no sense of this being a two-way process. When we offer you an audition, it is not a charitable act – it's because we think you are worth it. So interact, be a part of it, ask questions, say what works for you. It's not an exam, so if you weren't happy with your speech or reading, for example, say so: that way, the director knows you are aware of what you are doing. It's worth remembering that if you get the job, you will be in a rehearsal room for a number of weeks with this person, so see what you can find out about him/her, the production, the way of working.

Obviously a large part of our job is to watch shows, showcases, TV, films, even commercials. Sometimes the first half is enough – we're there for work, not fun, and may have five more nights out that same week. We sometimes hold general meetings with actors we know a little about, to discover more – especially for screen work, where you need to find out more about the actor's personality, their ability to cope without much rehearsal, and so on. Our knowledge of any actor is like a jigsaw puzzle, and putting another piece in it to complete the picture is helpful.

Of course, I remember some actors for the wrong reasons, such as the one who offered to knee-cap me if I didn't give him an interview, and the one who, in the course of doing a speech of adoration to a car engine, stripped down to a black leather jock-strap! I've had to cast cartoon characters, deadly sins, a statue, a pack of dogs, and the Marx Brothers, never mind all the run-of-the-mill roles. So really, there are jobs out there for all of you, if you just keep your cool and use your common sense. Good luck!

Sophie Marshall was born in Cheshire and joined the Royal Exchange Theatre Company in Manchester in 1973. She began as Secretary to the Project Manager for the building of the new theatre, and was able to see the company grow from a small part-time organisation (producing around three productions per year) to the nationally renowned company it is today, producing work on the main stage and in The Studio. Having seen the theatre built, bombed, and rebuilt, she left in 2004 to work freelance.

Casting for musical theatre

David Grindrod

The process of producing/casting a musical can be a very long and costly affair. Everyone is looking for the next *Phantom of the Opera* or *Mamma Mia!*; years of work can go into the production you see on stage today. Workshops have now become a necessity to see if a show 'has legs' without spending too much money. In consultation with the producer and creative team, I will assemble a group of actors who may not be totally right for the roles but who work well in a workshop situation. If the green light is given after the workshop presentation, the casting process – in conjunction with everything else – begins.

A casting breakdown is drawn up: this consists of all the details required by gents and artists about the characters, vocal ranges, etc. plus the proposed dates of the production. Open calls are sometimes organised for specific roles, but normally the breakdown gets sent to agents via The Spotlight Link, which reaches 500 agents/representatives at the touch of a button.

There is always a 'wish list' of actors whom producers would like in their production, but the bulk of submissions will come through agents in the form of photos and CVs. Unsolicited mail is also received; sometimes it is difficult to keep all this on file due to sheer number of submissions. Either I or my associates will also attend college shows and presentations to look for specific talent.

When preparing your photos and CVs, always remember that these are the calling cards with which you promote yourself! A good photograph is not 'artistic' (i.e. showing a face half in shadow); rather, it should always present a good full face that really does look like you. Your CV should ideally be just one page stapled to the back of your photograph. It should include all relevant details (*not* forgetting contact details) to show your skills. Make the information clear and precise. If you feel that you are suitable for musical casting, be very accurate and truthful about your vocal range: don't make it complicated – basically, tenor or soprano, with the top of your range noted. We can normally tell your style by the shows you have appeared in.

The audition process normally begins with artists performing two contrasting songs that show range and personality. Make an effort to pick a song that is suitable for the show – not pop, for example, when you are up for Rogers & Hammerstein. Nerves will take over; therefore, don't sing the song you learnt yesterday, but perform something tried and tested (something you would be happy singing naked in Trafalgar Square!). When we ask, "Have you got something else?" we don't want the answer, "My agent said you only wanted two songs,"; have your book of audition pieces with you and give us the chance to choose an alternative. Actors often ask whether I have favourite songs that I like to hear – or songs that I don't: I only really mind when they come in with completely the wrong song for the production.

If an actor is successful, they will receive a call-back for a dance/movement call. This normally causes concerns, but actually it is not usually that specific; we only want to see whether a person is happy with his/her body. If the audition is for a major dance show, hopefully you will know your limitations and either not audition at all, or be ready to throw yourself into the routine. Again, be honest: then you won't upset the creative team.

Further recalls take place with music and script from the show: the musical supervisor or associate director normally takes these calls. If you come in for the musical supervisor, come back with music prepared and your own song. *Always* bring your own song, it's a good reminder for the team. In addition to any script you are asked to read, you may get asked for a speech: have a couple of acting pieces prepared and again, nerves will take over, so make sure you know them properly. Remember that these speeches are also to allow the director to assess how well you can respond to direction, and how readily you can take a note.

The culmination of the casting process: 'the finals' – the most nerve-wracking experience even for a highly experienced artist. Bring everything with you that you have been given. You may not get *asked* for everything, but have it just in case. You may have been asked to dress in a certain way; always put some thought into that, as directors can be blinkered at times ... I have known artists to arrive with a couple of outfits and ask me to pick one! The panel will consist of the whole creative team and the producers. At this stage I can't do any more for you – though hopefully I can keep the atmosphere in the room happy and 'up'. Stay calm, don't change anything that you have been told, and audition to the best of your abilities.

Now the wait to see if you have the role. Always remember that you have got this far in the process because you can sing and act far better than anyone else. In the end, the decision could come down to height, look, hair colour; funnily enough it may not have anything to do with your singing/acting skills at this point. And you may not get an instant answer, you may have to wait until other meetings have taken place. You may get put on 'hold': normally that means you are not first on the list, but if somebody above you declines the offer you may move up. If you are lucky, the phone call will come with a straight offer. How exciting is that ... Contractual details are then advised and if all that is agreed, your date for first rehearsal is given. Always remember that you are a small part of the bigger picture – a small part of the jigsaw puzzle that goes together to form: The Musical.

David Grindrod founded David Grindrod Associates (DGA) with Stephen Crockett in January 1998, after 20 years' experience in the theatre in various roles ranging from assistant stage manager to general manager. Current West End casting includes *Chicago*, *Evita*, *The Lord of the Rings*, *Mamma Mia!* (worldwide), *Spamalot*, *The Sound of Music*. Films include *The Phantom of The Opera*. DGA are also casting consultants for *On The Town* and *Kismet* at the English National Opera, and belong to the Casting Directors Guild of Great Britain.

Casting directors

Essentially, casting directors take on the 'nitty-gritty' work involved in the casting process – it is usually the director, and sometimes the producer, who actually 'directs' the casting decisions. The crucial thing to remember is that each one is employed – by someone else. Some casting directors are employed on a full-time basis; a significant number work freelance and can be as concerned about where their next job is coming from as you are. Therefore, if one gets you to meet their director-employer, it is important that you live up to that casting director's expectations: carefully absorb any brief that s/he gives you. If you suddenly decide to take a radically different approach, s/he will be put into a difficult position with that director-employer.

Fundamental to the job of being a casting director is a wide knowledge of all kinds of actors. Therefore a good one is seeing as many productions as possible. Like squirrels storing nuts for the winter, they keep extensive notes and are continually adding to their collections of actor-profiles. An empathetic, intuitive and imaginative casting director has immeasurable value to both actors and director.

You should approach casting directors in much the same way as you would agents: however, it's even more important that there's something they can see you in. You can keep reasonably up to date with the activities of some casting directors by looking at the website of the Casting Directors Guild (CDG) – **www.thecdg.co.uk**.

Joanne Adamson Casting

4 Hillthorpe Square, Leeds LS28 8NQ
tel (07787) 311270
email watts07@hotmail.com

Main areas of work are theatre, musicals, television, film and commercials. Casting credits include: *Flesh and Blood* and *Nice Guy Eddie* (BBC), and *Fat Friends II* (Rollem, Tiger Aspect and Yorkshire Television).

Will consider attending performances at venues in Greater London and elsewhere given 1-2 weeks' notice. Accepts submissions (with CVs and photographs) from actors previously unknown to the casting director if sent by post, but does not welcome email enquiries. Will also accept showreels. "I am eager to arrange general meetings with actors."

Pippa Ailion

3 Towton Road, London SE22 9EE

Main areas of work are theatre, musicals, television and commercials. Casting credits include: West End productions of *The Lion King, We Will Rock You, Billy Elliot – The Musical, Blue Man Group, Tonight's The Night, Simply Heavenly, The Postman Always Rings Twice, Acorn Antiques – The Musical, Jerry Springer – The Opera* (the tour), and *Tonight's The Night* (the tour).

Dorothy Andrew Casting

Mersey TV, Campus Manor, Childwall Abbey Road, Childwall, Liverpool L16 OJP

tel 0151-737 4044 *fax* 0151-722 9079
email casting@merseytv.com

Casts mainly for television, film and commercials. Recent credits include: *Hollyoaks, Grange Hill* and *Court Room.*

Will accept postal submissions (with CVs and photographs) from actors previously unknown to the company, but unsolicited emails and showreels are not welcomed. "When writing, make your letter short and to the point. Always include a photograph (10x8in, black and white) and a CV. Only send in a showreel if requested."

Sarah Bird CDG

PO Box 32658, London W14 0XA
tel 020-7371 3248 *fax* 020-7602 8601

Casts for film, television, theatre and commercials. Casting credits include: *You Don't Have To Say You Love Me*, directed by Simon Shore (Samuelson Productions); *Ladies in Lavender*, directed by Charles Dance (Scala Productions); *Fortysomething* (Carlton TV); and *Calico*, directed by Edward Hall (Sonia Friedman Productions).

Lucy Boulting CDG

22 Montreal Road, Brighton BN2 9UY
email lucy@boultingcasting.wanadoo.co.uk

Casts mainly for film. Casting credits include: *Besieged* (Bernardo Bertolucci); *Shadowlands*

(Richard Attenborough); and *Sexy Beast* (Jonathan Glazer).

Siobhan Bracke CDG

Basement Flat, 22a The Barons, St Margaret's, Middlesex TW1 2AP

Main areas of work are theatre, television and film. Casting credits include: *Sex, Chips and Rock n' Roll* (BBC). and seasons at Shakespeare's Globe.

Will consider attending performances at venues in Greater London and occasionally elsewhere, given as much notice as possible (preferably 4-5 weeks). Accepts submissions (with CVs and photographs) from actors previously unknown to the casting director if sent by post. Does not welcome email enquiries.

Susie Bruffin CDG

133 Hartwood Road, London W12 9NG
tel 020-8740 9895 *fax* 020-8749 4571

Casts mainly for television and television films. Casting credits include: 16 Catherine Cookson adaptations (drama serials), *Dinner Ladies* (comedy series), and *Complicity* (film).

Candid Casting

2nd Floor, 111-113 Great Titchfield Street, London W1W 6RY
tel 020-7636 6644 *fax* 020-7636 5522
email mail@candidcasting.co.uk
Casting Director Amanda Tabak CDG *Assistant Casting Director* Brendan McNamara

Main areas of work are television, film and commercials. Casting credits include: *The Low Down* (film) and *Is Harry on the Boat?* (television film), *WASP* (Oscar-winning short film), *Kidulthood*, and *Mr Harvey Lights a Candle* (TV).

Will consider attending performances at venues in Greater London given at least 2 weeks' notice. Accepts submissions (with CVs and photographs) from actors previously unknown to the casting director if sent by post. Does not welcome email enquiries, unsolicited showreels or invitations to view individual actors' websites.

Cannon Dudley & Associates

43a Belsize Square, London NW3 4HN
tel 020-7433 3393 *fax* 020-7433 3599
email cdacasting@blueyonder.co.uk
Casting Director Carol Dudley CDG, CSA *Casting Associate* Helena Palmer

Main areas of work are theatre, television and film. Casting credits include: *Sunday Father* (Hampstead theatre), and *Nine Lives* and *The Card Player* (feature films).

Will consider attending performances at venues in Greater London given as much notice as possible.

Accepts submissions (with CVs and photographs) from actors previously unknown to the casting director if sent by post. Does not welcome email enquiries. CVs which are not submitted for specific projects or with reference to current shows or television performances cannot be kept for future reference. Telephone enquiries about current casting projects or progress of mailed submissions are not welcomed.

John Cannon

PO Box 53807, London SE27 0YD
email john@johncannon.co.uk
BBC Elstree, Room N202 Neptune House, Clarendon Road, Borehamwood WD6 1JF
tel 020-8228 7122 *fax* 020-8228 8311
email john.cannon@bbc.co.uk

Former Resident Casting Director for the Royal Shakespeare Company, now working for BBC Drama. Recent credits include: *The Bill* (ITV); *Presence* by Doug Lucie (Plymouth Drum); *See How They Run* (No. 1 Tour); *Hedda Gabler* (West Yorkshire Playhouse/Liverpool Playhouse); and *Yellowman* (tour for Liverpool Everyman).

Welcomes performance notices with at least 2 weeks' notice. Also happy to receive letters and emails (with CVs and photographs) from actors, as well as invitations to view individual actors' websites. Does not welcome unsolicited showreels.

Anji Carroll CDG

4 Nesfield Drive, Winterley, Cheshire CW11 4NT
tel (01270) 250240 *fax* (01270) 250240

Main areas of work are film, television and commercials. Casting credits include: *London's Burning* (LWT), *This Life* (BBC), and *Out of Depth* (feature film directed by Simon Marshall).

The Casting Angels (London and Paris)

Suite 4, 14 College Road, Bromley BR1 3NS
fax 020-8313 0443
Key personnel Michael *(Big Decisions)*, Gabriel *(Announcements)*, Raphael, Uriel *(The Daily Grind)*, Lucifer *(Special Consultant)*

Main areas of work are television, musicals, film and commercials with "casting across the board". Casts for the UK and other countries within Europe.

Will consider attending performances at venues in Greater London and elsewhere, given as much notice as possible. Accepts showreels.

Casting Couch Productions Ltd

213 Trowbridge Road, Bradford-on-Avon, Wiltshire BA15 1EU
mobile (07932) 785807
email moiratownsend@yahoo.co.uk
Casting Director Moira Townsend

Main areas of work are television, film and commercials. Casting credits include: *Who Killed*

Tutankhamen? (documentary), and advertisements for DVLA and Lunn Poly.

Will consider attending performances at venues in Greater London and elsewhere (especially Bath/Bristol area), given 2-3 weeks' notice. Accepts submissions from actors previously unknown to the casting director if sent by email. Actors will only receive a response if the casting director is able to attend a performance.

See entry under *Agents* on page 36 for further details of the company's work.

Casting UK

88-90 Grays Inn Road, London WC1X 8AA
tel 020-7430 1122 *fax* 020-7430 1155
email drew@castinguk.com
Casting Director Andrew Mann

Casts mainly for film and commercials. Casting credits include: commercials for Bacardi, Acuview, DFS, ASDA and Maltesers; and pop videos for Placebo, Sugarbabes and Busted.

Will consider attending performances at venues in Greater London given 2 weeks' notice. Accepts submissions (with CVs and photographs) from actors previously unknown to the casting director if sent by post. Does not welcome email enquiries.

Suzy Catliff CDG

PO Box 39492, London N10 3YX
tel 020-8442 0749
email soose@soose.co.uk

Casts mainly for film, television and theatre. Most recent credits include: *Stormbreaker* (feature film), *Silent Witness* (Series IX & X – BBC), *Blitz* (Channel 4), *D-Day* (BBC), *Sir Gadabout* (ITV), and *Life x 3* (No. 1 Tour). Worked as an assistant on François Ozon's *Swimming Pool.*

Urvashi Chand

115a Kilburn Lane, London W10 4AN
tel 020-8968 7016
email urvashi@cinecraft.biz

Main area of work is film. Recent credits include: *What We Did in Our Holidays* (directed by Scott Peake), and *Red Mercury* (directed by Roy Battersby).

Will consider attending performances within the Greater London area and elsewhere with at least 2 weeks' notice. Accepts submissions (with CVs and photographs) from actors previously unknown to the agency if sent by post, but not by email. Showreels, voice tapes and invitations to view individual actors' websites are also accepted.

Alison Chard CDG

23 Groveside Court, 4 Lombard Road, London SW11 3RQ
tel 020-7223 9125 *fax* 020-7223 9125
email alisonchard@castingdirector.freeserve.co.uk

website www.thecdg.co.uk

Main areas of work are theatre, television, film and commercials. Casting credits include: *M.I.T.* and *The Bill* (television). Casts for the Royal National Theatre; formerly Head of Casting for the Royal Shakespeare Company.

Will consider attending performances at venues in Greater London given 1 month's notice. Accepts submissions (with CVs and photographs) from actors previously unknown to the casting director if sent by post. Only CVs may also be emailed. Showreels are accepted if they are on DVD, accompanied by an sae of good quality (does not welcome filmed stage pieces). Invitations to view individual actors' websites are unnecessary; ensuring that Spotlight entries are up-to-date is more useful. Advises actors to: "Target performance notices in accordance with the location of the recipient. Guard against unnecessary expense and disappointment by doing your research; find out what they are working on, who they are working with and if they are familiar with your work."

Charkham Casting

97 Mortimer Street, London W1W 7SU
tel 020-7927 8335 *fax* 020-7927 8336
email info@charkhamcasting.co.uk
Casting Directors Beth Charkham, Gary Ford

Areas of work include theatre, musicals, television, film and commercials. Recent credits include: *Charlie and the Chocolate Factory*, *Silent Witness* and *The Bill.*

Jayne Collins

38 Commercial Street, London E1 6LP
tel 020-7422 0014 *fax* 020-7422 0015
email info@jaynecollinscasting.com
website www.jaynecollinscastin.com

Areas of work include theatre, musicals, television, film and commercials. Will consider attending performances within the Greater London area and elsewhere, given at least 1 week's notice. Accepts submissions (with CVs and photographs) from actors previously unknown to the company if sent by post, but not by email. Welcomes showreels.

John Connor CDG

See entry for Jane Davies Casting Ltd

Lin Cordoray

66 Cardross Street, London W6 0DR

Main areas of work are television and commercials.

Will consider attending performances at venues in Greater London. Accepts submissions (with CVs and photographs) from actors previously unknown to the casting director if sent by post. Does not welcome email enquiries.

Irene Cotton Casting

25 Druce Road, Dulwich Village, London SE21 7DW
tel 020-8299 1595 *fax* 020-8299 2787

email irenecotton@btinternet.com
Director Irene Cotton CDG

Recent credits include: *The Bill* (ITV), *The Countess* (Criterion Theatre, London), *Panorama* (BBC), and *Caffe Latte* commercial (Home Productions). Welcomes performance notices as far in advance as possible, and is prepared to travel to performances within Greater London. Does not welcome any other unsolicited form of approach, including CVs, photographs, showreels or invitations to view individual actors' websites. Advises actors to make contact only to inform the casting director "when [she] can see their work – TV, film or stage".

Irene Cotton CDG

25 Druce Road, London SE21 7DW

Main areas of work are theatre, musicals, television, film and commercials. Casting credits include: *Hutton Report* (for BBC *Panorama*) and *The Bill* (television); *Being Dead* (feature film); and an advertisement for Thorntons chocolates.

Will consider attending performances at venues in Greater London given as much notice as possible. Accepts invitations to view individual actors' websites. "Always write and ask if a showreel can be sent. I welcome fliers for fringe productions."

Margaret Crawford

92 Castelnau, London SW13 9EU

Casts mainly for television. Casting credits include: *Bad Girls* (Series 2-8), *Footballers' Wives* (Series 1-5), *Footballers' Wives Extra Time* (Series 1 & 2), *Waterloo Road* (Series 1) and *Bombshell* (Series 1).

Will consider attending performances at venues in Greater London and occasionally elsewhere, given as much notice as possible. Accepts submissions (with CVs and photographs) from actors previously unknown to the casting director if sent by post. Does not welcome email enquiries. Also accepts showreels, voice tapes and invitations to view individual actors' websites.

Crocodile Casting

9 Ashley Close, Hendon, London NW4 1PH
tel 020-8203 7009 *fax* 020-8203 7711
website www.crocodilecasting.com
Casting Directors Tracie Saban, Claire Toeman

Established in 1996 with the aim of constantly accessing new faces and fresh talent. The company casts mainly for commercials, pop videos and corporate work; sometimes holds general auditions to meet new actors and models.

Jane Davies Casting Ltd

PO Box 680, Sutton, Surrey SM1 3ZG
tel 020-8715 1036 *fax* 020-8644 9746
email info@janedaviescasting.co.uk

Casting Directors Jane Davies CDG, John Connor CDG

Casts mainly for television. Casting credits include: *My Family*, *The Green Green Grass*, and *Black Books*.

Will consider attending performances of light drama, and particularly of comedies, at venues in Greater London.

Gary Davy CDG

1st Floor, 55-59 Shaftesbury Avenue, London W1D 6LD

Casts mainly for film, theatre and television. Casting credits include: *Band of Brothers* (mini-series directed by Tom Hanks); *Revengers Tragedy* (Alex Cox); *Babyfather Two* and *Sweeney Todd* (starring Ray Winstone – BBC); Nick Cave's *The Proposition* (John Hillcoat); and *The Business* (Nick Love). Also cast BAFTA-winning film, *Kiss of Life* (Emily Young). Welcomes enquiries by email or phone, and will consider short film projects.

Stephanie Dawes

Casting Department, London Weekend Television, Upper Ground, London SE1 9LT
tel 020-7261 3509 *fax* 020-7737 8541

Works mainly for television. Recent credits include: casting for *Crime Monthly* and *Most Wanted* (LWT); and children and extras casting for *Spaced* (LWT/Paramount Comedy Channel for Channel 4) and *Johnny and the Dead* (LWT).

See entry for Granada under *Independent television* on page 221 for further details.

Kate Day CDG

Pound Cottage, 27 The Green South, Warborough, Oxfordshire OX10 7DR

Main areas of work are television, film and commercials.

Will consider attending performances at venues in Greater London and occasionally elsewhere, given as much notice as possible. Accepts submissions (with CVs and photographs) from actors previously unknown to the casting director if sent by post. Does not welcome email enquiries.

The Denman Casting Agency

Burgess House, Main Street, Farnsfield, Notts NG22 8EF
Key Personnel Jack Denman

Main areas of work are theatre, musicals, television, film and commercials. Casting credits include: *Peak Practice*, *Doctors*, and *Crimewatch* (television); videos for PC World and Boots. Awarded Preferred Agents status by the BBC for supporting artists and walk-ons.

Will consider attending performances at venues in the Midlands with as much notice as possible.

Accepts submissions (with CVs and photographs) from actors previously unknown to the casting director if sent by post. Does not welcome email enquiries. No short film enquiries.

Lee Dennison CDA

Fushion, 27 Old Gloucester Street, London WC1N 3XX
tel 0870-011 1100 *fax* 0870-011 1020
email leedennison@fushion-uk.com
Casting London/New York Lee Dennison *Assistant* Dean Saunder *Casting New York* Ram Tucker

Casts mainly for television, film and music promos. Recent credits include: *Buffalo Girls* (Fluid Films); *Wonderbread and Ecstasy, Life and Death of Joey Stefano* (Universal/Chuck Films); *The Bourne Ultimatum* (UK Casting); *Ciao Baby* (Seasons 1-4 – Salute); and *Reps* (Season 1 – Sky 1).

Will consider seeing performances in the UK, Europe and New York given 4 weeks' notice. Accepts submissions (with CVs and photographs) from actors previously unknown to the company sent by post or email. Showreels should only be sent on request. Also runs an agency; see entry for Fushion under *Agents* on page 36 for further details.

Malcom Drury CDG

34 Tabor Road, London W6 0BW
tel 020-8748 9232

Casts mainly for television. Casting credits include: *The Bill, Heartbeat, The Beiderbecke Affair* and Laurence Olivier's *King Lear*.

Carol Dudley CDG, CSA

See entry for Cannon Dudley & Associates.

Julia Duff CDG

73 Wells Street, London W1T 3QG
tel 020-7436 8860 *fax* 020-7436 8859

Casts mainly for film, television and commercials. Casting credits include: *Hamish Macbeth, Hotel Babylon* and *Lorna Doone* (for television), and UK casting for *The House of Mirth* (Terence Davies). Welcomes enquiries via email from filmmakers with a synopsis, and will consider short film projects.

Irene East Casting CDG

40 Brookwood Avenue, Barnes, London SW13 0LR
tel 020-8876 5686 *fax* 020-8876 5686
email IrnEast@aol.com

Main areas of work are theatre and film. Casting credits include: *Jealousy, Love Bites, Big Claus, Little Claus*, and UK casting for *Scandinavian Features* (film); *Twelfth Night, Wuthering Heights, Two Into War, Murder in Paris*, and *Picasso's Women* (theatre).

Will consider attending performances at venues in Greater London and occasionally elsewhere, given a couple of days' notice. Showreels should only be sent on request.

EJ Casting

Lower Ground Floor, 86 Vassall Road, London SW9 6JA
tel 020-7564 2688
email info@EJCasting.com
Director Edward James

Casts for theatre, musicals, film, commercials and corporate work. Casting credits include: *Into the Woods* and *Sweet Charity* (theatre); commercials for AOL, Lloyds Bank, Sony BMG, Universal Music, and Cadbury's Fingers, AOL; and *Air on a G String* (film).

Will consider attending performances at venues in Greater London and occasionally elsewhere. Accepts showreels containing work which has been broadcast. Photographs and CVs should be sent by post; email applications will not be considered. All enquiries should be sent with cast breakdown, synopsis, and production details. Will consider short film work.

Richard Evans CDG

10 Shirley Road, London W4 1DD
tel 020-8994 6304
email info@evanscasting.co.uk
website www.evanscasting.co.uk
Key personnel Richard Evans CDG

Main areas of work are theatre, musicals, television, film and commercials. Casting credits include: *The Rat Pack – Live From Las Vegas* (theatre).

Welcomes enquiries from new filmmakers, but short-film/low-budget work only considered if not on deferred or no-payment fee basis. Make contact by email or post (please, no large attachments by email). Include information on project, shoot dates and details of cast requirements.

Bunny Fildes Casting CDG

56-60 Wigmore Street, London W1U 2RZ
tel 020-7935 1254 *fax* 020-7298 1871

Casts mainly for theatre, television, film and commercials.

Will consider attending performances within Greater London given 2 weeks' notice. Accepts postal submissions (with CVs and photographs) from actors previously unknown to the company. Unsolicited emails and showreels, however, are not welcomed.

Janie Frazer CDG

LWT, London Television Centre, Upper Ground, London SE1 9LT
tel 020-7261 3848 *fax* 020-7737 8541

Casts mainly for television (drama and comedy, serials and one-offs); currently Resident Casting Director at ITV (Granada) and LWT. Casting credits include: *Coronation Street, Vincent, Murder in Suburbia, Blue Murder, Island at War*, and *Spaced*.

See entry for ITV under *Independent television* on page 221 for further details. Also see See Janie's article on page 217 for advice on television casting.

Caroline Funnell

25 Rattray Road, London SW2 1AZ
tel 020-7326 4417

Areas of work include theatre and musicals. Will consider attending performances within the Greater London area with at least 2 weeks' notice.

Nina Gold CDG

117 Chevening Road, London NW6 6DU
tel 020-8960 6099 *fax* 020-8968 6777

Main areas of work are film, television and commercials. Casting credits include: *Vera Drake*, directed by Mike Leigh (Thin Man Films); *The Life and Death of Peter Sellers*, directed by Stephen Hopkins; *The Jacket*, directed by John Maybury (Warner Bros); *Daniel Deronda*, directed by Tom Hooper (BBC TV); *Amazing Grace* and *Rome* both directed by Michael Apted; *Starter for Ten* directed by Tom Vaughan; *The Illusionist* directed by Neil Burger; and *Brothers of the Head* directed by Keith Fulton & Louis Pepe.

Miranda Gooch

102 Leighton Gardens, London NW10 3RP

Casts mainly for feature films. Recent credits have included: *True Story* and *Tooth*.

Will consider attending performances within Greater London given as much notice as possible. Accepts submissions (with CVs and photographs) from actors previously unknown to the company sent by post or email. Showreels are also accepted.

Jill Green CDG

Cambridge Theatre, Earlham Street, Seven Dials, Covent Garden, London WC2H 9HV
tel 020-7379 4795 *fax* 020-7379 4796

Casts for theatre, musicals and film. Casting credits include: *The Producers* (Drury Lane Theatre); *Thoroughly Modern Millie* (Shaftesbury Theatre); *Contact* (Queens Theatre); and *Beyond the Sea* (film directed by Kevin Spacey).

Will consider attending performances within Greater London and occasionally elsewhere, given a minimum of 2 weeks' notice. Accepts postal submissions (with CVs and photographs) from actors who are currently appearing in a production, but does not welcome blanket mailings, unsolicited emails or showreels (unless an sae is enclosed for their return).

Marcia Gresham CDG

3 Langthorne Street, London SW6 6JT
tel 020-7381 2876 *fax* 020-7381 4496
email marcia@greshamcast.com

Main area of work is television. Casting credits include: *The Debt, Walk Away and I Stumble, The Project* and *Innocents* (television).

Will consider attending performances at venues in Greater London given 1 month's notice. Accepts submissions (with CVs and photographs) from actors previously unknown to the casting director if sent by post, but does not welcome email enquiries. Showreels and voice tapes (with sae for return) are also accepted.

David Grindrod CDG

4th Floor, Palace theatre, Shaftesbury Avenue, London W1D 5AY
tel 020-7437 2506 *fax* 020-7437 2507
email dga@grindrodcasting.co.uk

Casts for musicals and film. Casting credits include: *The Phantom of the Opera* (film directed by Joel Schumacher); *The Woman in White, Brighton Rock, Jerry Springer the Opera* and *Chicago* (all West End musicals).

Will consider attending performances within Greater London and possibly elsewhere, given as much notice as possible. Does not welcome unsolicited submissions from actors. Casting breakdowns are released via Cast Web, *SBS* and *PCR*, and therefore actors should only write in with reference to specific productions. See also David's article *Casting for musical theatre* on page 80.

Janet Hall

69 Buckstones Road, Shaw, Oldham OL2 8DW

Main areas of work include television, film and commercials. Casting credits include: AXA commercial, and *The Sound of Music* (theatre).

Will consider attending performances at venues in Greater London and in Manchester, Liverpool and Leeds, given 1 week's notice. Accepts submissions (with CVs and photographs) from actors previously unknown to the casting director sent by post or email. Also accepts showreels, voice tapes and invitations to view individual actors' websites.

Louis Hammond

30-31 Peter Street, London W1F 0AR
tel 020-7734 0626 *fax* 020-7439 2522

Main areas of work are theatre, television, film and commercials. Casting credits include: *Mirrormask* and *Arsene Lupin* (films).

Will consider attending performances. Accepts submissions (with CVs and photographs) from actors previously unknown to the casting director. "When sending submissions, I suggest a photograph built into the CV. 10x8in photographs may not be retained by the casting director."

Gemma Hancock CDG

The Rosary, Broad Street, Cuckfield, West Sussex RH17 5DL

tel (01444) 441398 *fax* (01444) 441398

Main areas of work are theatre, television and film. Casting credits include: *The Bill* (Talkback Thames); Peter Ackroyd's *London* (BBC 2); *Blithe Spirit* (West End and tour); and *The Dresser* (Bath Theatre Royal and tour).

Judi Hayfield CDG

Granada Television, Quay Street, Manchester M60 9EA
tel 0161-832 7211 *fax* 0161-827 2853

Resident Casting Director for Granada. See entry under *Independent television* on page 221 for further details.

Polly Hootkins CDG

PO Box 25191, London SW1V 2WN
tel 020-7233 8724 *fax* 020-7828 5051
email phootkins@clara.net
website www.thecdg.co.uk
Key personnel Polly Hootkins

Main areas of work are theatre, television and film. Casting credits include: *A New Day in Old Sana'a* and *Captain Jack*.

Will consider attending performances at venues in Greater London and occasionally elsewhere, given as much notice as possible. Accepts submissions (with CVs and photographs) from actors previously unknown to the casting director if sent by post. Does not welcome email enquiries. Showreels, voice tapes and invitations to view individual actors' websites are also accepted.

Dan Hubbard CDG

Hubbard Casting, 2nd Floor, 19 Charlotte Street, London W1T 1RL
tel 020-7636 9991 *fax* 020-7636 7117

Casts mainly for film, television, theatre and commercials. Casting credits include: *Murder Squad* (Granada television); *Paradise Heights* (BBC); *The Murder of Stephen Lawrence* (Granada); *Tomb Raider 1* and *2* (films for Paramount); and *Dracula 2000* (Miramax/Dimensions films).

Sarah Hughes

Stephen Joseph Theatre, Westborough, Scarborough YO11 1JW

Resident Casting Director for the Stephen Joseph Theatre. See entry under *Producing theatres* on page 99 for further details.

International Collective

Harrow Exchange, 2 Grayton Road, Harrow HA1 2XU
tel 020-8901 4010 *fax* 020-8901 4001
email chris@internationalcollective.co.uk
website www.internationalcollective.co.uk

Key personnel Christopher Mange

Areas of work include theatre, musicals and commercials. Recent work includes: *What a Feeling* (UK tour) and *Noah's Ark* (Manhattan Theatre Club).

Will consider attending performances within the Greater London area and elsewhere, given at least 1 week's notice. Welcomes invitations to view actors' showreels and websites.

Sue Jackson

Resident Casting Director for Yorkshire TV Ltd. See entry under *Independent television* on page 221 for further details.

Trevor Jackson CDG

1 Bedford Square, London WC1B 3RA
tel 020-7637 8866 *fax* 020-7436 2683

Casts mainly for musicals produced by Cameron Mackintosh Ltd. Casting credits include: *My Fair Lady*, *Les Miserables*, *Miss Saigon*, *Phantom of the Opera*, *Mary Poppins* and *Avenue Q*.

Will consider attending performances at venues in Greater London given as much notice as possible. Accepts submissions (with CVs and photographs) from actors previously unknown to the casting director if sent by post, but does not welcome email enquiries. Showreels, voice tapes and invitations to view individual actors' websites are also accepted.

Jennifer Jaffrey

136 Hicks Avenue, Greenford, Middlesex UB6 8HB
tel 020-8578 2899 *fax* 020-8575 0369
Key personnel Jennifer Jaffrey *(Proprietor)*

Main areas of work are theatre, musicals, television, film and commercials. Casting credits include: *Cross My Heart*, *Ten Minutes Older* and *Such a Long Journey*.

Will consider attending performances at venues in Greater London given as much notice as possible. Accepts submissions (with CVs and photographs) from actors previously unknown to the casting director if sent by post, but does not welcome email enquiries. Photographs should have the actor's name written on the back and an sae must be included for the return of material. Showreels should only be sent on request.

Lucy Jenkins CDG

74 High Street, Hampton Wick, Kingston-upon-Thames KT1 4DQ
tel 020-8943 5328 *fax* 020-8977 0466

Casts mainly for film, television, theatre and commercials. Casting credits include: *Babyfather* (BBC), *The Bill* (television), *Top Dog* (short film) and *Emma* (theatre).

Doreen Jones
PO Box 22478, London W6 0WJ
tel 020-8746 3782 *fax* 020-8748 8533

Casts mainly for television and film. Recent credits include: *Fingersmith*, *Lawless* and *Prime Suspect*.

Will consider attending performances within Greater London and occasionally elsewhere, given as much notice as possible. Unsolicited submissions and enquiries from actors are not welcomed.

Sam Jones CDG
Head of Casting for the Royal Shakespeare Company (see entry on page 111 for contact details). Other credits include: *Journey's End* (West End and tour); *After Mrs Rochester* (for Shared Experience); *Abigail's Party* (Hampstead Theatre/West End); *Trial & Retribution* (for La Plante Productions/ITV); and *Human Cargo* (for CBC/Force Four – nominated for 17 Gemini Awards).

Sue Jones CDG
24 Nicoll Road, London NW10 9AB
tel 020-8838 5153 *fax* 020-8838 1130

Main areas of work are film, television, theatre and commercials. Casting credits include: *The Virgin of Liverpool*, starring Ricky Tomlinson and Imelda Staunton (MOB Films); *The Sound of Thunder*, with Ed Burns, Ben Kingsley and Catherine McCormack; *The Origins of Evil* (CBS/Alliance Atlantis); *Messiah* and *Coriolanus* (both plays directed by Stephen Berkoff); *The Vicar* (BBC television); and *The Politician's Wife* (Channel 4).

Anna Kennedy Casting
86 Hydethorpe Road, London SW12 0JB

Welcomes performance notices, for productions within the Greater London area, with 2 weeks' notice. Will accept letters, but not emails, with CVs and photographs from individuals previously unknown to the casting director; also welcomes showreels and invitations to view actors' websites.

Beverley Keogh
29 Ardwick Green North, Ardwick, Manchester M12 6DL
tel 0161-273 4400 *fax* 0161-273 4401
email Beverley@beverlykeogh.tv

Main areas of work are television, film and commercials. Casting credits include: *Fat Friends*, *Clocking Off* and *Second Coming*.

Accepts submissions (with CVs and photographs) from actors previously unknown to the casting director sent by post or email.

Suzy Korel CDG
20 Blenheim Road, St John's Wood, London NW8 0LX

Will consider attending performances at venues in Greater London given as much notice as possible. Accepts submissions (with CVs and photographs) from actors previously unknown to the casting director if sent by post, but does not welcome email enquiries. Invitations to view individual actors' websites are also accepted.

Matthew Lessall
Relocated to LA and does not therefore welcome any contact from UK-based actors.

Sharon Levinson
30 Stratford Villas, London NW1 9SG

Main areas of work are television, film and commercials. Casting credits include: *Two Thousand Acres of Sky* and *A Christmas Carol* (television).

Will consider attending performances at venues in Greater London and occasionally elsewhere, given 2 weeks' notice. Not currently casting.

Karen Lindsay-Stewart CDG
PO Box 2301, London W1A 1PT

Main areas of work are television and film. Casting credits include: *Sylvia*, *Harry Potter and the Chamber of Secrets* and *Cambridge Spies*.

Will consider attending performances at venues in Greater London with sufficient notice. Accepts submissions (with CVs and photographs) from actors previously unknown to the casting director if sent by post, but does not welcome email enquiries. Do not send sae(s) for replies.

Maggie Lunn
Resident Casting Director for the Almeida and Chichester Festival theatres. See entries for respective theatres under *Producing theatres* on page 99.

Kay Magson Casting
PO Box 175, Pudsey, Leeds LS28 7LN
tel 0113-236 0251 *fax* 0113-236 0251
email kay.magson@btinternet.com
Casting Director Kay Magson

Recent credits include *Alice in Wonderland* (West Yorkshire Playhouse); *Billy Liar*, *Seasons Greetings* (Liverpool Playhouse); *One Last Card Trick*, *Cinderella* (Watford); *Macbeth* (Derby); *Twelfth Night* (West Yorkshire Playhouse); *Tempest* (Liverpool); *Much Ado About Nothing* (Manchester Library); *East is East* (York); *Singin' in the Rain*, *Round the Horne Revisited*, *Dracula* (National tours).

Will consider attending performances within the Greater London area and elsewhere, with at least 4 weeks' notice. Accepts submissions (with CVs and photographs) from actors previously unknown to the casting director if sent by post, but not by email.

Lisa Makin

Resident Casting Director for the Royal Court Theatre. See entry under *Producing theatres* on page 99 for further details.

Andrew Mann

See entry for Casting UK.

Carolyn McLeod

PO Box 26495, London SE10 0WO
tel 020-7400 1720
email actors@cmcasting.eclipse.co.uk

Main areas of work are film, television and promos. Casting director credits include: *The Bill*, *Pumpkinhead 3: Ashes to Ashes*, *Pumpkinhead 4: Dark Hell*. Casting associate credits include: *Basic Instinct 2: Risk Addiction*, *Rottweiler*, *Im Auftrag Des Vatikans*.

Will consider attending performances at venues in Greater London and occasionally elsewhere, given 2-3 weeks' notice. Accepts submissions (with CVs and photographs) from actors previously unknown to the casting director sent by post or email. Showreels, voice tapes and invitations to view individual actors' websites are also accepted. Applicants should only submit their details once. Advises actors that: "As most casting directors have little capacity for storing CVs, it may be worth telephoning to check whether they are accepting submissions – though do be warned that some people may not appreciate the phone call. If you already have an agent, ask them to contact us on your behalf."

Chrissie McMurrich

16 Spring Vale Avenue, Brentford, Middlesex TW8 9QH

Main areas of work are theatre and television. Casting credits include: *The Hobbit*, *A Christmas Carol* and *The Commander*.

Will consider attending performances at venues in Greater London given 2 weeks' notice. Accepts submissions with performance notices (containing CVs and photographs) from actors previously unknown to the casting director if sent by post. No unsolicited emails are accepted.

Anne McNulty

Resident Casting Director for Donmar Warehouse. See separate entry under *Producing theatres* on page 99.

Sooki McShane CDG

8a Piermont Road, East Dulwich, London SE22 0LN
tel 020-8693 7411 *fax* 020-8693 7411

Works mainly in theatre, film and television. Casting credits include: *Rainbow Room* (Granada television); *My Brother Rob* (feature film); and casting for the Warehouse Theatre Croydon.

Currently Resident Casting Director for the Nottingham Playhouse. See entry under *Producing theatres* on page 99 for further details.

Hannah Miller

Birmingham Repertory Theatre, Centenary Square, Broad Street, Birmingham B1 2EP
tel 0121-245 2000
website www.birmingham-rep.co.uk
Casting Director Hannah Miller *Casting Coordinator* Alison Soloman

Resident Casting Director for Birmingham Repertory Theatre (see page 100 for more details). Recently cast: *Three Sisters*, *Wizard of Oz* and *Romeo & Juliet*.

Welcomes performance notices 2-6 weeks in advance, and is prepared to travel around the UK dependent on workload. Welcomes letters (with CVs and photographs) and showreels if sent by post but not by email. Does not welcome invitations to view individual actors' websites.

Carl Proctor CDG

15b Bury Place, London WC1A 2JB
tel 020-7681 0034 *fax* 020-7916 2533
website www.carlproctor.com

Casts mainly for film, television, theatre and commercials. Casting credits include: *Mrs Palfrey at the Claremont*, *Something Borrowed* and *Dead Cool*.

Performance notices, submissions, showreels and unsolicited emails are not welcomed. Advises that CVs and photographs are no longer kept on file as these details are available on Spotlight Interactive.

Andy Pryor CDG

7 Garrick Street, London WC2E 9AR
tel 020-7386 8298 *fax* 020-7836 8299

Casts mainly for film, television and commercials. Casting credits include: *Perfect Strangers* and *The Lost Prince* (both directed by Stephen Poliakoff for BBC television); and *Long Time Dead* (film directed by Marcus Adams).

Gennie Radcliffe

Casting Director for *Coronation Street*. See entry for Granada under *Independent television* on page 221 for further details.

Francesca Raftery CDG

Studio 4, 33 Chatsworth Road, London CR0 1HE
tel 020-8667 0527 *fax* 020-8667 0527
email info@francescaraftery.com
website www.francescaraftery.com
Casting Director Francesca Raftery CDG

Casts mainly for commercials. Casting credits include: commercials for Grolsch, Knorr, Coca Cola, Volkswagon and Visa.

Will consider attending performances at venues in Greater London given sufficient notice. Accepts submissions (with CVs and photographs) from actors previously unknown to the casting director if sent by post, but does not welcome email enquiries.

Simone Reynolds CDG

60 Hebdon Road, London SW17 7NN

Main areas of work are film, television, theatre and commercials. Casting credits include: *Honeymoon Suite* (theatre); *The Vicar of Dibley*; *Quicksand* (film); and *Turning Points: Emma's Story* (both for BBC television); *Jack and Sarah* (film for Granada); and *Shining Through* (film for Twentieth Century Fox).

Will consider attending performances at venues in Greater London and elsewhere, given as much notice as possible. Accepts postal submissions (with CVs and photographs) from actors previously unknown to the casting director, but does not welcome email enquiries. Advises actors to: "Keep CVs clear (separate out the part from the director and venue) and keep covering submissions brief."

Danielle Roffe Casting

71 Mornington Street, London NW1 7QE

Works in film and television. Recent credits include: *The Upside of Anger, She's Gone,* and *Holy Cross.*

Welcomes performance notices and is prepared to travel within Greater London. Does not welcome unsolicited CVs, photographs or showreels, but is happy to receive invitations to view individual actors' websites.

Laura Scott CDG

56 Rowena Crescent, London SW11 2PT
tel 020-7978 6336 *fax* 020-7924 1907

Main areas of work are film, television, theatre and commercials. Casting credits include: *Berkeley Square* (costume drama for BBC television); *The Railway Children* (Carlton); and *Where There's Smoke* (Talisman films).

The Searchers

70 Sylvia Court, Cavendish Street, London N1 7PG
Directors Wayne Waterson, Ian Sheppard

Casts mainly for television, film and commercials. Recent credits include: commercials for Pepsi, Nike, Kellogg's and Royal Mail. Has worked for directors including Terry Gillingham, Tarsem and Earl Morris.

Will consider attending performances within Greater London given 1 week's notice. Accepts submissions (with CVs, showreels and photographs) from actors previously unknown to the company, but does not welcome unsolicited emails or invitations to view an actor's website.

Phil Shaw

Suite 476, 2 Old Brompton Road, London SW7 3DQ
tel 020-8715 8943 *mobile* (07702) 124935

fax 020-8408 1193
email shawcastlond@aol.com

Main areas of work are theatre, television, film and commercials. Casting credits include: *The Turn of the Screw* (theatre); *The Last Post* (film – BAFTA nominated); *When Harry Tries to Marry* (film); *La Mere Sauvage* (film); *The Alchymist's Cat* (film); *The House of Bernarda Alba* (film); *Body Story* (TV documentary); *Days in the Trees* (radio).

Will consider attending performances at venues in Central London given a minimum of 2 weeks' notice. Accepts postal submissions (with CVs and photographs) from actors previously unknown to the casting director, but does not welcome unsolicited showreels or email enquiries.

Michelle Smith CDG

220 Church Lane, Woodford, Stockport SK7 1PQ
tel 0161-439 6825 *fax* 0161-439 0622

Main areas of work are film, television and commercials. Casting credits include: *Steel River Blues* (ITV); *Max and Paddy* (Channel 4); *Phoenix Nights* (Channel 4); and *Cold Feet* (Series 1-5 – Granada).

Suzanne Smith CDG

33 Fitzroy Street, London W1T 6DU
tel 020-7436 9255 *fax* 020-7436 9690

Main areas of work are film, television, theatre and musicals. Casting credits include: UK casting for *Alien vs Predator* (directed by Paul Anderson for 20th Century Fox); *The Dark* (directed by John Fawcett for Impact Pictures); UK casting for *Black Hawk Down* (directed by Ridley Scott); and *Band of Brothers* (for television – HBO/Dreamworks).

Wendy Spon CDG

c/o National Theatre, South Bank, London SE1 9PX

Main areas of work are film, television, theatre and musicals. Until recently, Head of Casting at Talkback Thames (*The Bill*), and now Head of Casting at the National Theatre (see entry under *Producing theatres* on page 107). Casting credits include: *The Graduate* (theatre, directed by Terry Johnson); *Oklahoma* and *Oh What a Lovely War* (both for the National Theatre); and *Shadow Man* (short film).

Gail Stevens Casting CDG

2 Sutton Lane, 54A Clerkenwell Road, London EC1M 5PS

Main areas of work are television, film and commercials. Casting credits include: *Twenty-Eight Days Later, Calendar Girls* and *Spooks.*

Sam Stevenson CDG

PO Box 50225, London EC1Y 8WD
tel 020-7256 5727 *fax* 020-7920 0852

Main areas of work are television, theatre and film. Casting credits include: UK casting for *The Life*

Aquatic (film directed by Wes Anderson); *Happy Days* (for theatre, directed by Sir Peter Hall); *The Bill* (Talkback Thames); *Eastenders*, *Holby City* and *Doctors* (for BBC television).

Employed as the Casting Coordinator for the Royal Shakespeare Company for two seasons.

Liz Stoll

BBC Elstree, Room N223 Neptune House, Clarendon Road, Borehamwood WD6 1JF
tel 020-8228 8285 *fax* 020-8228 8311
email liz.stoll@bbc.co.uk

Has worked in all areas of actor casting, but currently working for BBC TV. Recent credits include: *Holby City*, *A View from a Hill* (BBC4, 2005), *Waking The Dead*, *Dalziel & Pascoe*, *Magnificent Seven* (BBC2, 2005), *Judge John Deed*, *Down To Earth*, and a series of six *Afternoon Plays* for BBC Drama.

Happy to receive performance notices at least 2 weeks in advance, and is prepared to travel within Greater London (sometimes further, work permitting) to see shows. Welcomes letters (but not emails) with CVs and photographs from actors previously unknown to the casting director; does not welcome unsolicited showreels, but is happy to receive invitations to view individuals' websites.

Lucinda Syson CDG

1st Floor, 33 Old Compton Street, London W1D 5JT
tel 020-7287 5327 *fax* 020-7287 3629

Recent feature films include: *The Intimidation Game – Batman Begins*, directed by Chris Nolan; *Alexander*, directed by Oliver Stone; *Troy*, directed by Wolfgang Petersen; *League of Extraordinary Gentlemen*, directed by Steve Norrington; and *Spygame*, directed by Tony Scott.

Amanda Tabak CDG

See entry for Candid Casting.

Moira Townsend

See entry for Casting Couch Productions Ltd.

Jill Trevellick CDG

123 Rathcoole Gardens, London N8 9PH
tel 020-8340 2734 *fax* 020-8348 7400

Main areas of work are film, television, theatre and commercials. Casting credits include: *North and South* (BBC 1 serial); *The Canterbury Tales* (series of 6 films for BBC television); *Sons and Lovers* (television film for Company television/ITV); *Me Without You* (feature film for Dakota, directed by Sandra Goldbacher); and *Piccadilly Jim* (film directed by John McKay).

Sarah Trevis CDG

c/o Twickenham Studios, St Margaret's, Twickenham TW1 2AW

tel 020-8607 8888 *fax* 020-8607 8766

Main areas of work are television and film. Recent casting credits include: work for Granada television, the BBC and Twentieth Century Fox.

Will consider attending performances given 2 weeks' notice. Accepts submissions (with CVs and photographs) from actors previously unknown to the casting director if sent by post. Does not welcome email enquiries.

Vital Productions

PO Box 26441, London SE10 9GZ
tel 020-8316 4497 *fax* 020-8316 4497
email mail@vital-productions.co.uk
Key personnel Melissa Waudby

Main areas of work are theatre and television. Casting credits include: *BBC Crimewatch* and *The Great Dome Robbery* (television).

Will consider attending performances at venues in Greater London and elsewhere, given 1 month's notice. Accepts submissions (with CVs and photographs) from actors previously unknown to the casting director if sent by post. Does not welcome email enquiries. "Because of time pressure, we tend to use *Spotlight* and specific agents or individual suggestions rather than CVs and photographs submitted to us."

Anne Vosser CDG

Nederlander House, 7 Great Russell Street, London WC1B 3NH
tel 020-7079 0272 *fax* 020-7631 2034
email anne@vosser-casting.co.uk

Main areas of work are theatre and musicals. Casting credits include: *Romeo and Juliet* and *Taboo* (both in the West End); *Fame* and *Saturday Night Fever* (West End and tour).

June West

Resident Casting Director at Granada. See entry under *Independent television* on page 221 for further details.

Matt Western

59-61 Brewer Street, London W1F 9UN
tel 020-7434 1230 *fax* 020-7439 1941

Main areas of work are film, television, theatre and commercials. Casting credits include: *The Other Boleyn Girl* (film for BBC television); *The Night Detective* (series for Zenith/BBC); and *Essential Poems* (for Talkback Productions).

Toby Whale CDG

80 Shakespeare Road, London W3 6SN
tel 020-8993 2821 *fax* 020-8993 8096
website www.whalecasting.com

Until recently, Head of Casting at the National Theatre. Main areas of work are film, television and theatre. Casting credits include: *East is East* (Assassin Films/FilmFour); *Spoonface Steinberg* (BBC film); *Wire in the Blood* (Series 1 & 2 – Coastal/ITV); and more than 40 theatre productions for the Royal Court Theatre, Out of Joint, the Almeida Theatre, English Touring Theatre and Sheffield Crucible, among others.

Keith Whitall Casting
10 Woodlands Avenue, West Byfleet, Surrey KT14 6AT
tel (01932) 343655
Director Keith Whitall

Areas of work include theatre, musicals and revues. Recent credits include: *Bush Bar to Open*, *The Pleasure of your Company* and *An Evening with Sheila Mathews*.

Will consider attending performances within the Greater London area with at least 6 weeks' notice. Accepts submissions (with CVs and photographs) from actors previously unknown to the casting director if sent by post, but not by email. Welcomes invitations to view individual actors' websites. Particularly interested in actors who can tap.

Tara Woodward
Top Flat, 93 Gloucester Avenue, Primrose Hill, London NW1 8LB

tel 020-7586 3487 *fax* 020-7681 8574

Main areas of work are film, television, theatre and commercials. Casting credits include: *The Early Days*, *Post* and *Hello Friend* (all for Shine/Film Four Lab); *Chasing Heaven* (for Venice Film Festival); *The Browning Version* and *Romeo and Juliet* (theatre); and commercials for Parmalat Aqua and Royal Danish Post. Has worked as Casting Assistant to Nina Gold on films including *All Or Nothing* (directed by Mike Leigh) and *Love's Labours Lost* (directed by Kenneth Branagh).

Jeremy Zimmermann Casting
36 Marshall Street, London W1F 7EY
tel 020-7478 5161 *fax* 020-7437 4747

Main areas of work are film and television. Recent casting work includes: the films *Keeping Mum*, *The Contract*, *Van Wilder 2*, *Dog Soldiers* and *Blood And Chocolate*.

Will consider attending performances at venues in Greater London and elsewhere. Accepts postal submissions (with CVs and photographs) from actors previously unknown to the casting director, but does not welcome email enquiries. Invitations to view individual actors' websites are also accepted.

Theatre
Introduction

Theatres and theatre companies/managements abound in all kinds of different forms, and paid opportunities for live performance are not restricted to putting on productions. The days of the permanent repertory company are almost gone, but there is a much wider diversity of work available. The larger companies/managements often use casting directors (see page 82), who should usually be your first port of call with your letter, CV and photograph. However, it can be worth exploiting any personal contacts that you may have.

For reasons of space, this section does not include the numerous theatres (often subsidised by a local authority) and arts centres which largely present touring and (sometimes) amateur productions. However, a number of these do mount their own professional pantomimes and it can be useful to look through the 'Theatres – Provincial/Touring' section of *Contacts* to check which. Many have websites. Another way of finding out is to check through the reviews in *The Stage* every Christmas. (Also look at **www.its-behind-you.com** which lists forthcoming pantomimes.) Pantomimes in such theatres will often be directed by the resident director and usually cannot afford the services of a casting director.

For all approaches, it is important to send your submissions to the person named – unless you have a personal contact.

Some organisations have regular casting patterns – see The Casting Calendar on page 194 for details.

A director's life

Jeremy Raison

So I've just finished directing *Therese Raquin*, my first show as Artistic Director of the Citizens' Theatre. Well, 'finished' is a misnomer. There's still work to be done, but we've had the press night and any work now can only be minimal, as all the stage management and some of the cast have moved on to the next show. And an actor asks the inevitable question: "What do you do now the show's opened?"

Well, what I'd really like is to take a nice long holiday somewhere hot. But I won't. Not yet ...

First I have 188 emails waiting for me on my computer. I also have a pile of letters three-and-a-half inches high. Then there's work to do on a major capital development for an innovative new creative learning centre at the Citizens'. A vision, a business plan and architectural plans all need to be formulated within an incredibly short period of time. I have to attend meetings at the Scottish Arts Council, with the City Council, with the architects, and with the consultants. The deadline is looming fast.

The Citizens' also has to make a submission to the Cultural Commission, which is looking at all cultural provision in Scotland in order to come up with a blueprint for the future, and could prove incredibly important to the future of the Arts here. Set up by the Scottish Executive, the Citizens' Theatre's response needs serious and considered thought.

I have three workshops to do on the show I've just directed, as well as a post-show discussion. I try to attend as many performances of the show as possible, and to make sure I'm here to meet the many people who come to see it.

I need to work on the design for the Christmas show which I am directing. Study the script. Make cuts. Find an assistant director – my original one having just pulled out. Finalise casting and also find three Acting ASMs, all of whom will go on, so must be of a high standard. Casting has mainly taken place in June, when we held a week of auditions in Glasgow and in London. The Citizens' has long worked with a pool of actors: in the early days of the Havergal/Prowse/Macdonald regime, open auditions were held at the Roundhouse in London and 600 people would turn up before nine o'clock in the morning. All would be seen for five minutes, and interesting ones brought back later. Gradually this built up a group of inspiring actors who have worked regularly at the Citizens'; this pool is added to each year. So I am seeing some regulars whom I don't yet know; some new people I have seen in other shows, or been told about, or had some connection with; some actors I've worked with before; and, very occasionally, some I've just seen a picture of.

Deciding whom to audition from a huge pile of CVs is an impossible process. If a particular skill is required – such as the ability to play a particular musical instrument – well, it is much easier to whittle actors down to a number that can be seen. However, if the part is open to interpretation, it is much more difficult. You can't see everyone. Pictures are misleading. I do look to see which directors an actor has worked with; but the best way to get work is to work, undoubtedly. To be seen in shows, to put on shows, anything to get your face noticed. And suppose you get that audition, what then?

As a director, you are desperate to find the right person, and always hope that the next actor will be 'the one'. But they look wrong, or can't speak well enough, or don't move well, or can't sing, or they're the wrong age, or a couple wouldn't pair well together, or they're late without reason, or simply unprepared ... You must know the play you're coming to audition for; ideally, know the director's work; know the Theatre's work; be curious, and *be pleasant*. Some actors I simply won't cast, no matter how good they seem, because they are unpleasant and will cause havoc.

I often ask people to read. As far as is possible, pages will be sent to actors beforehand – but sometimes I may ask them to read different pages. At this stage, if you can't read for any reason (particularly dyslexia), just say. It won't go against you, but if you read badly you can look unintelligent, and I always looks for intelligence in actors, even if it is an instinctive intelligence rather than an academic one. I always look for people who have lots of ideas, who are sparky, who think in different ways. I want to have a buzzy rehearsal period with fascinating people, all of whom challenge each other to go that bit further.

The Citizens' often asks people to do speeches. It is a test, but it is curiously revealing: it shows up laziness and lack of technique very quickly. All trained actors should be able to speak Shakespearean verse well. Nowadays, many actors can't: basic technique is lacking, and it affects not just Shakespeare but every part they will play, particularly on a main stage, and even in a house as acoustically good as the Citizens' Main Theatre.

I cast the final actors in the Christmas show. So what next? I need to programme the spring, and have meetings with designers, directors and actors I am chasing. Book children's shows – a new regular Saturday afternoon slot. And book the other visiting shows. Liaise with Celtic Connections and the Comedy Festival about possible slots. Organise workshops for the spring.

I need to see someone else's shows for a change, to get a perspective on what else is happening outside my own brick walls. There is a list of shows opening that I would like to see. And I need to see the Citizens' own shows: as well as my production in the main house, we have a season of five plays performed by six actors, four of whom are directing in our circle studio. A unique but extremely rewarding experiment which produces incredibly polished results, but ideally I should attend at least one dress rehearsal and also the press night of each. And I need to touch base with our Education and Outreach department, in order to catch up and also discuss future plans at a time when the department's three-year funding is running out.

I have another meeting at Glasgow City Council about our capital plans; am asked to attend the Deacon Convenor's Dinner at the Trades Hall of Glasgow – White Tie, and Carriages at 10.20pm; and the Chancellor's dinner at the University of Glasgow. I'm also asked to be a judge for the short film category of the Scottish BAFTAs.

I need to prepare a speech for a Corporate Citizens' night.

And ... view tapes people have sent me; talk to staff, and deal with any problems; oversee the director coming in to direct the next show. Talk to the cast of my show most days, tell my artistic collaborators how the show has gone and thank them for their work. Do interviews for the newspapers. Organise trips to London and Dublin to see work.

And ... get a haircut. Bank some cheques. Answer my personal mail. Buy birthday presents for my sister, my niece, my brother. Book flights for Christmas. Do my tax return. Send flowers to a friend. Lead a 'normal' life. See my wife and children. Go to a movie. Have a day off without thinking about the Theatre at all.

I love my job. I love its variety. I love the way it plugs you into a culture, shows a side of this city I wouldn't otherwise see. I love the privilege of putting on shows. Expressing a vision. Developing this great theatre and its audience. The challenge of engaging with an increasingly multi-cultural Glasgow. It's a job that's never finished. Things always move on. One project completed always means there's something else to do. It's easy to see why artistic directors tend to burn out.

I only have 34 emails to answer now. My letters are down to a thin pile. I have read 15 plays in the past month. The spring season is just about taking shape. The last visiting show will soon be in place. The copy needs checking, proofing. The look of the publicity will need discussing: what are we trying to sell, and how? But already I'm back in rehearsal and the whole cycle is starting again.

Sooner or later another actor will ask: "And what do you do now the show's opened?" Oh. And I still need that nice long holiday somewhere hot.

Jeremy Raison is Artistic Director of the Citizens' Theatre in Glasgow. He was previously Artistic Director of Chester Gateway Theatre, for which he won a TMA Award for Special Achievement in Regional Theatre. He has worked in many regional theatres, and at the National, with actors such as Sir Dirk Bogarde, Ralph Fiennes and Robert Carlyle. He has also worked in television and film. Awards and nominations include: Best Young Playwright Radio 4; Plays and Players Best Children's Play; and Manchester Evening News/Liverpool Post Best Production (twice).

Producing theatres

Included in this section are the national and regional building-based companies that mount their own productions – sometimes in co-operation with others, and sometimes sending out tours. (Almost all also receive touring productions.) The majority are subsidised by the national and regional Arts Councils (and use Equity's regional theatre contract), but a few are not (and use Equity's commercial theatre contract), and a few have their own contractual arrangements. Almost all have websites which can be very useful for keeping track of their activities. A little extra insight – beyond that listed on the following pages – into a theatre might just tip the balance in your favour.

In real terms, rates of pay are better than they were a decade and more ago, but they are still only 'adequate' – especially if you are incurring the extra costs of living away from home. However, rehearsing and performing a production in such a theatre can be an exhilarating experience. A well-run theatre has a wonderful 'family' atmosphere, and in the close-knit working environment you can often make friendships which sustain for many years afterwards – as well as contacts who might be useful in years to come. It is well worth checking each theatre's 'casting procedures' very carefully as there are significant variations between them. It is also worth familiarising yourself with their programmes of productions via *The Stage* and/or their websites.

Almeida Theatre

Almeida Street, London N1 1TA
tel 020-7288 4900 *fax* 020-7288 4901
email info@almeida.co.uk
website www.almeida.co.uk
Artistic Director Michael Attenborough *Associate Director* Howard Davies *Artistic Associate* Jenny Worton *Executive Director* Neil Constable *General Manager* Ros Brooke-Taylor

Production details

The Almeida is committed to staging British and international drama presented to the highest possible standards, and productions which reveal classic plays in a new light. Embraces international classics, foreign classics in newly commissioned versions, and new plays – in addition to an annual Opera season of specially commissioned operas, music theatre pieces and concerts of contemporary music. Stages approximately 6 productions each year. Recent productions include: *Macbeth, Hedda Gabler, Blood Wedding, Romance* by David Mamet, *The Hypochondriac*, and *The Late Henry Moss* by Sam Shepard.

Casting procedures

Actors may write at any time requesting inclusion. Welcomes submissions (with CVs and photographs) sent by post or email. Also accepts showreels and invitations to view individual actors' websites. Uses the TMA/Equity Subsidised Rep contract. Will consider casting disabled actors to play characters with disabilities.

Yvonne Arnaud Theatre

Millbrook, Guildford, Surrey GU1 3UX
tel (01483) 440077 *fax* (01483) 564071
website www.yvonne-arnaud.co.uk
Artistic Director James Barber

Production details

The Yvonne Arnaud Theatre is a busy producing and receiving house, creating shows in Guildford and touring nationally, with many transferring to the West End. On both the main stage and in the Mill Studio an eclectic mix of classical and contemporary work is staged by new, lesser-known and established writers.

The Youth and Education facility offers an exciting mix of activities for young people and adults all year round. The Yvonne Arnaud opened the 80-seat Mill Studio in 1993 to provide a venue for work that would not otherwise be seen in Guildford. It also forms the base for the Youth Theatre's activities. Recent productions include: *Aladdin, Drowning on Dry Land* and *Telstar*.

Belgrade Theatre

Belgrade Square, Coventry CV1 1GS
tel 024-7625 6431
email admin@belgrade.co.uk

website www.belgrade.co.uk
Theatre Director & Chief Executive Hamish Glen

The theatre is closed for refurbishment during 2006, although it staged a production of *The Mysteries* in the bombed-out shell of Coventry Cathedral in the summer. The first production after that will be the 2006 pantomime.

Birmingham Repertory Theatre

Centenary Square, Broad Street, Birmingham B1 2EP
tel 0121-245 2000
website www.birmingham-rep.co.uk
Artistic Director Rachel Kavanaugh *Literary Manager* Ben Payne *Executive Director* Stuart Rogers *Head of Education* Steve Ball *Casting Director* Hannah Miller *Casting Co-ordinator* Alison Solomon

Production details

Stages 15 productions in the main house each year and 6 in the studio. Also runs Outreach, Community and Education programmes. Jonathan Church, the former Artistic Director, has now moved to Chichester Festival Theatre.

Casting procedures

Sometimes uses freelance casting directors. Welcomes submissions (with CVs and photographs) sent by post or email, preferably in relation to specific productions. Also accepts invitations to view individual actors' websites. Particularly interested to hear from performers in the West Midlands region.

Birmingham Stage Company (BSC)

Suite 228, 162 Regent Street, London W1B 5TG
tel 020-7437 3391 *fax* 020-7437 3395
email info@birminghamstage.net
website www.birminghamstage.net
Actor-Manager Neal Foster *Producing Assistant* Louise Eltringham *Education* Ellen Mills *Administrator* Philip Compton

Production details

Founded in 1992, the BSC stages 5 shows each year, 4 of which tour nationally. Produces a range of plays with particular emphasis on new writing, and is recognised for its children's shows which visit 60 venues around the UK. Recent productions include: *The Return* at the Old Red Lion, and *The Jungle Book*.

Casting procedures

Uses freelance casting directors and sometimes holds general auditions. Casting breakdowns are available by postal application (with sae), in *PCR* and on Castweb (see entry under *The Spotlight, casting directories and information services* on page 267). Welcomes submissions (with CVs and photographs) sent by post or email, preferably in response to postings in *PCR*. Also accepts showreels, voice tapes

and invitations to view individual actors' websites. "Do as much research as you can before submitting." Offers TMA/Equity approved contracts. Will consider applications from disabled actors to play characters with disabilities.

Bristol Old Vic

King Street, Bristol BS1 4ED
tel 0117-949 3993 *fax* 0117-949 3993
email sreade@bristol-old-vic.co.uk
website www.bristol-old-vic.co.uk
Artistic Director Simon Reade *Assistant to the Artistic Director* Kate Yedigaroff *Director of Education* Charlotte Summerford

Production details

Classical theatre company producing its own repertoire throughout the year. Stages 8 shows in the main house each year and 4 in the studio. Also runs Education programmes. Recent productions include: *Paradise Lost, Beasts and Beauties,* and *The Rivals.*

Casting procedures

Uses freelance casting directors. Actors may send letters (with CVs and photographs) which will be forwarded to the casting director. Does not welcome email submissions, showreels or requests for meetings. Actors are welcome to call Kate Yedigaroff to find out about the forthcoming season towards the end of the previous one; where possible they will be told which casting directors are being used. A file of local actors is held at the theatre.

The Bush Theatre

Shepherds Bush Green, London W12 8QD
tel 020-7602 3703 *fax* 020-7602 7614
email info@bushtheatre.co.uk
website www.bushtheatre.co.uk
Artistic Director Mike Bradwell *Executive Producer* Fiona Clark

Production Details

Founded in 1972, The Bush specialises in developing and producing new writing to the highest professional standard. It stages 5-8 productions a year, totalling around 280 performances. Also tours productions to up to 8 venues, although the bulk of performances are at The Bush itself. Up to 6 actors are employed on each production, and the company offers TMA/Equity approved contracts. Recent productions include: *Monsieur Ibrahim & The Flowers of The Qur-an* and *When You Cure Me* (Bush Theatre); *Mammals* (national No. 1 tour); and a number of rehearsed readings.

Casting procedures

Casts in-house and does not hold general auditions or issue public casting breakdowns. Welcomes letters (not emails) from actors previously unknown to the company. Does not welcome showreels or invitations to view individual actors' websites. Actively encourages applications from disabled actors and promotes the use of inclusive casting.

Byre Theatre

Abbey Street, St Andrews KY16 9LA
tel (01334) 476288 *fax* (01334) 475370
email enquiries@byretheatre.com
website www.byretheatre.com
Artistic Director Stephen Wrentmore *Associate Director* Rita Henderson *Managing Director* Tom Gardner

Production details

Founded in 1933, the Byre moved into a new state-of-the-art theatre in 2001. Presenting a mixed programme of in-house and guest productions, the theatre stages 6-8 shows each year in its main auditorium and studio theatres. Also runs TIE, Outreach and Community programmes. Recent productions include: *Vincent in Brixton*, *The BFG* and *Private Lives*.

Casting procedures

Holds general auditions. Actors may write at any time requesting inclusion. Welcomes submissions (with CVs and photographs) sent by post or email. Also accepts invitations to view individual actors' websites. Happy to meet actors by appointment.

Chichester Festival Theatre

Oaklands Park, Chichester PO19 6AP
Artistic Director Jonathan Church *Casting Director* Maggie Lunn *Executive Director* Maggie Saxon

Production details

Consists of the main house set in parkland, the Minerva Studio, and a multipurpose auditorium. In-house plays and musicals are produced in the main house during the festival season (April-September), and family shows at Christmas. The Minerva Studio places emphasis on new and experimental work during the festival and also stages an in-house Christmas production. 4 productions are staged both in the main house and the Minerva Studio each year. Also runs TIE, Outreach and Community programmes (contact Alison Roden). Recent productions include: *The Merchant of Venice*, *Pinocchio*, *The Seagull* and Gilbert & Sullivan's *The Gondoliers*.

Casting procedures

Occasionally holds general auditions. Actors should write in December or January requesting inclusion. Welcomes submissions (with CVs and photographs) sent by post or email.

The Theatre, Chipping Norton

2 Spring Street, Chipping Norton, Oxfordshire OX7 5NL
tel (01608) 642345 *fax* (01608) 642324
email admin@chippingnortontheatre.co.uk
website www.chippingnortontheatre.co.uk
Artistic Director Caroline Sharman *General Manager* Christopher C Durham *Community & Education Officer* Ellen Mainwood

Production details

The Theatre is a pivotal part of the artistic life of the area, and takes care to programme as diverse a range of performances – theatre, film, dance, comedy and opera – as possible. Its Community & Education programme takes film and opera out to village halls.

An intimate space, it seats 217 (including 4 wheelchair spaces) in either proscenium (end-on) or in-the-round configurations. While predominantly a receiving house, The Theatre produces an annual pantomime which runs for around 80 performances over the Christmas period, as well as occasional smaller ventures. Recent productions include: *Puss in Boots*, a new pantomime by Simon Brett; and *Taste*, a new play which toured Normandy.

Casting procedures

Does not use casting directors. Welcomes unsolicited CVs and photographs from actors unknown to the company, as well as invitations to view actors' websites. Showreels, and CVs and photographs sent by email are not, however, welcome. Casting breakdowns for the pantomime are available from mid-summer – via the website, postal application (with sae), the Equity Job Information Service, and occasionally *The Stage*; this is the best time to write to request inclusion. The Theatre offers TMA/Equity approved contracts. It actively encourages applications from disabled actors, and promotes the use of inclusive casting.

Citizens Theatre

Gorbals, Glasgow G5 9DS
tel 0141-429 5561 *fax* 0141-429 7374
website www.citz.co.uk
Artistic Director Jeremy Raison *Company Manager* Lyn Pullen

Production details

Internationally renowned producing theatre. Also has annual guest seasons, and hosts the Scottish Youth Theatre Summer Festival. Stages 4-5 shows in the main auditorium and 1-2 in the studio theatre each year. Also runs Education and Outreach programmes (contact Lyn Pullen).

Casting procedures

Does not use freelance casting directors. Sometimes holds general auditions. Actors should write in April requesting inclusion. Welcomes letters (with CVs and photographs) but not email submissions. Offers TMA/Equity approved contracts.

Clwyd Theatr Cymru

Mold, Flintshire CH7 1YA
tel (01352) 756331 *fax* (01352) 701558
email mail@clwyd-theatr-cymru.co.uk
website www.clwyd-theatr-cymru.co.uk
Artistic Director Terry Hands *Associate Director* Tim Baker *Casting Director* Kate Crowther (freelancing)

Production details

The major drama-producing company in Wales. Although most work is presented in English, some pieces are performed in Welsh. Stages 5-6 shows in the main house and 5-6 in the studio each year, with some mid/large-scale productions touring Wales and England. Also runs TIE programmes. Recent productions include: *Troilus and Cressida*, *Brassed Off* and *Hobson's Choice*.

Casting procedures

Welcomes enquiries from actors: these should be sent to Kate Crowther at the above address. Offers TMA/Equity approved contracts. Will consider applications from disabled actors to play characters with disabilities.

Coliseum Theatre

Fairbottom Street, Oldham OL1 3SW
tel 0161-624 1731 *fax* 0161-624 5318
email mail@coliseum.org.uk
website www.coliseum.org.uk
Artistic Director Kevin Shaw *Administrative Director* Liz Wilson *Administrator* Joanne Moss

Production details

A traditional repertory theatre producing 8 shows each year, with additional incoming tours and one-off special events. Also runs TIE, Outreach and Community programmes (contact Justine Potter Williams). Recent productions include: *Home*, *Be My Baby*, *Wizard of Oz*, and *Neville's Island.*

Casting procedures

Does not use freelance casting directors. Sometimes holds general auditions. Casting breakdowns are available through postal application (with sae). Welcomes letters and email submissions (with CVs and photographs). Also accepts invitations to view individual actors' websites. Offers TMA/Equity approved contracts. Will consider applications from disabled actors to play characters with disabilities.

Contact Theatre

Oxford Road, Manchester M15 6JA
tel 0161-274 3434 *fax* 0161-274 0640
website www.contact-theatre.org
Artistic Director John McGrath *Executive Producer* Jon Morgan *Associate Director* Cheryl Martin *Administrative Officer* Katie Taylor (casting enquiries) *Head of Creative Development* Ekua Bayunu

Production details

Since re-opening in 1999, Contact has emphasised its work with young adults (aged 13-30), putting participation at the heart of its ethos and activities. Contact is also one of the most culturally diverse theatres in the country; it was awarded the inaugural ECLIPSE award for cultural diversity, as well as the Arts Council's ART04 Award Northwest for 'outstanding achievement in the arts'.

Contact has striven to rewrite the rulebook on what 'theatre' can be. A wide range of touring theatre, music, dance and mixed-media work complements the theatre's in-house productions. The huge variety of participatory work with young people is integrated as closely as possible with the company's 'professional' programme. High quality and innovation are key to Contact's participatory work; leading companies working with young people at Contact have included: Frantic Assembly, RJC Dance, Quarantine, and Nitro – as well as a huge range of artists from hip hop to forum theatre and from verse drama to contemporary dance. Recent productions include: *Perfect* (Kaite O'Reilly and Paul Clay); *Slamdunk* (Felix Cross, Benji Reid with Nitro); *Dancing within Walls* (by Rani Moorthy with Rasa); *Dreaming of Bones* (with Red Ladder).

Casting procedures

Uses freelance casting directors and does not advertise casting breakdowns publicly. Welcomes letters (with CVs and photographs) from actors but warns that it is unable to reply to unsolicited submissions. The theatre prefers not to receive showreels, emails and invitations to view actors' websites. Offers TMA/Equity approved contracts. Actively encourages applications from disabled actors and promotes the use of inclusive casting.

Crucible Theatre

55 Norfolk Street, Sheffield S1 1DA
tel 0114-249 5999 *fax* 0114-249 6003
email info@sheffieldtheatres.co.uk
website www.sheffieldtheatres.co.uk
Artistic Director Samuel West *Associate Director* Josie Rowke *Chief Executive* Angela Galvin *Creative Development Director* Karen Simpson

Production details

Comprises 2 theatres: the Crucible Theatre (thrust stage, 960 capacity) and the Studio Theatre (200-400 capacity). Stages 5-6 shows each year in the main house and 3-4 in the studio. Also runs TIE programmes. Recent productions include: *Lear* by Edward Bond; Schiller's *Don Carlos*; and *The Romans in Britain* by Howard Brenton.

Casting procedures

Uses freelance casting directors. Casting breakdowns are available twice yearly (June and October), by postal application (with sae) to theatre. Welcomes letters (with CVs and photographs) but suggests that realistically, this may not be the most productive use of actors' resources. If writing: "Take the trouble to find out whom to write to!" Offers TMA/Equity approved contracts. Will consider applications from disabled actors to play characters with disabilities.

Derby Playhouse

Theatre Walk, Eagle Centre, Derby DE1 2NF
tel (01332) 363271 *fax* (01332) 547200
website www.derbyplayhouse.co.uk
Co-Artistic Leaders Karen Hebden, Stephen Edwards
Casting Director Samantha Relph

Production details

Stages 8 shows in the main house each year. Also runs Outreach and Community programmes (contact Kim Miller). Recent productions include: *Company, Arsenic & Old Lace, Macbeth*.

Casting procedures

Welcomes letters (with CVs and photographs) but not email submissions. Casting breakdowns are available on the website. Showreels and invitations to view individual actors' websites are also accepted. Offers TMA/Equity approved contacts. Actively encourages applications from disabled actors and promotes the use of inclusive casting where possible.

Donmar Warehouse

41 Earlham Street, London WC2H 9LX
tel 020-7240 4882
website www.donmarwarehouse.com
Artistic Director Michael Grandage *Executive Producer* Nick Frankfort *General Manager* Tobias Round *Development Director* Kate Mitchell *Casting Director* Anne McNulty

Production details

Independent producing house located in Covent Garden. The building originally served as a vat room and hop warehouse for the local brewery. In 1961 it was purchased by Donald Albery and converted into a rehearsal studio for the London Festival Ballet, which he formed with ballerina Margot Fonteyn. The theatre takes its name from them.
In the 1990s the Donmar was redesigned. The current theatre space retains the characteristics of the former warehouse while incorporating a new thrust stage. Recent productions include: *The Cut, The Wild Duck, Mary Stuart, The Philanthropist*, and *The God of Hell*.

Casting procedures

Casting breakdowns are not publicly available. Offers TMA/SOLT/Equity approved contracts. Rarely has the opportunity to cast disabled actors.

The Dukes

Moor Lane, Lancaster LA1 1QE
tel (01524) 598505 *fax* (01524) 598579
website www.dukes-lancaster.org
Artistic Director Ian Hastings *Theatre Secretary and PA to Artistic Director* Jacqui Wilson

Production details

A producing theatre with an independent cinema. Stages 5 shows each year in the main house (313 seats) and 1 in the studio (178 seats), with a focus on contemporary drama and outdoor site-specific productions. Also runs a Youth Arts programme. Recent productions include: *Blue Remembered Hills, Betrayal, Under Milk Wood, The Accrington Pals*, and *Tom Thumb and Other Giant Stories* (outdoor production).

Casting procedures

Does not use freelance casting directors. Casting breakdowns are obtainable through the website, postal application (with sae), Equity Job Information Service and *PCR*. Welcomes letters (with CVs and photographs) but not email submissions. Showreels and invitations to view individual actors' websites are also accepted. Offers TMA/Equity approved contracts. Actively encourages applications from disabled actors and promotes the use of inclusive casting.

Dundee Repertory Theatre

Tay Square, Dundee DD1 1PB
tel (01382) 227684 *fax* (01382) 228609
website www.dundeerep.co.uk
Artistic Director Dominic Hill *Chief Executive* James Brining

Production details

Producing theatre housing Dundee Repertory Ensemble – Scotland's only permanent acting company. Stages 6 shows each year in the main house. Also runs TIE, Outreach and Community programmes (contact James Brining/Dominic Hill). Recent productions include: *Peter Pan* and *Twelfth Night*.

Casting procedures

Does not use freelance casting directors. Welcomes letters (with CVs and photographs) but not email submissions. Actors should write in the spring.

Gate Theatre

Above Prince Albert Pub, 11 Pembridge Road, London W11 3HQ

tel 020-7229 0906 *fax* 020-7221 6055
email gate@gatetheatre.freeserve.co.uk
website www.gatetheatre.co.uk
Artistic Director Thea Sharrock *Associate Artistic Director* Tali Pelman *Education Officer* Lynne Gagliano *Associate Directors* Daniel Kramer, Anna Mackmin

Production details

Presents new writing and undiscovered classics from around the world in original and visually imaginative productions. Stages 7-9 shows each year in the main house. Also runs a Community programme. Recent productions include: *Electra* by Jean Giraudoux; *The Riot Act* by Tom Paulin; and *Angels of the Universe* by Icelandic Take-Away Theatre.

Casting procedures

Does not use freelance casting directors. Welcomes letters (with CVs and photographs) but not email submissions. "Individual directors tend to cast from their own lists – contact with the director is the best way to ensure that your application is considered."

Greenwich Theatre

Crooms Hill, Greenwich, London SE10 8ES
tel 020-8858 4447 *fax* 020-8858 8042
email info@greenwichtheatre.org.uk
website www.greenwichtheatre.org.uk
Executive Director Hilary Strong *Associate Director* Fiona Laird

Production details

Currently mainly receiving touring productions, but occasionally produces shows in-house. Specialises in musical theatre and produces showcases, semi-staged readings and cabarets at different points of the year which often involve professional performers. Recent productions include: *Longitude* (play with music), and *Aladdin* (pantomime). The theatre also runs a year-round programme of training for 14-19 year-olds (the Greenwich Musical Theatre Academy) including a full-time course.

Casting procedures

Generally uses freelance casting directors. "Please don't send unsolicited applications, as we can't maintain a sensible filing system. Please do look at the casting section on the website, as we aim to provide advance information on our future productions and answer standard questions. We are keen to hear from locally based musical performers and especially anyone that has experience of working with young people." Offers TMA/Equity approved contracts. Does not have a specific policy on casting disabled actors, as the stage is not wheelchair-accessible: "It depends on the actor's particular needs."

Hampstead Theatre

Eton Avenue, London NW3 3EU
tel 020-7449 4200 *fax* 020-7449 4201
email info@hampsteadtheatre.com
website www.hampsteadtheatre.com
Artistic Director Anthony Clark *Literary Director* Frances Stirk *Education Director* Jonathan Siddall

Production details

Hampstead Theatre identifies and produces important new writers. It aims to challenge established writers and seek out the best international work to bring to London. Plays are sometimes provocative, always intelligent and often full of laughter. The auditorium has been built for writers who understand actors, and The Space will provide a dedicated arena for a rich and varied education and workshop programme. Presents 7 shows in the main house each year and a varying number in the studio. Recent productions include: *When the Night Begins* by Hanif Kureishi; *Follow my Leader* by Alastair Beaton; *Yellow Man* by Dael Orlander Smith; *Love Me Tonight* by Nick Stafford; and *Darwin in Malibu* by Crispin Whittell.

Casting procedures

Uses freelance casting directors; suggests that actors write 2 months before each season starts. Casting breakdowns are sometimes available by postal application (with sae) or email, depending on the director. Welcomes letters and emails (with CVs and photographs) from actors but prefers not to receive showreels.

Haymarket Theatre

Wote Street, Basingstoke RG21 7NW
tel (01256) 323073
email barbaralilley@haymarket.org.uk
website www.haymarket.org.uk
Artistic Director John Adams *PA to Artistic Director* Barbara Lilley *Executive Director* Zöe Curnow

Production details

Regional producing theatre since the 1970s; now presenting a mixed programme of touring and in-house work, with emphasis on new writing. Currently stages 5-6 shows each year, including a Christmas show and the occasional musical – but this may reduce in 2007 and beyond. Recent productions include: *Hamlet*, *Gasping*, *Private Lives*, *Blue on Blue*, and *Return to the Forbidden Planet*.

Casting procedures

Casts some productions in-house, mainly through Spotlight Interactive; casts others through freelance casting directors. Write or (preferably) send an email to Barbara Lilley for details. Keeps records of actors with instrumental skills (to a professional standard) and local actors. Offers TMA/Equity approved contracts. Actively encourages applications from disabled actors and promotes the use of inclusive casting.

Hull Truck Theatre

Spring Street, Hull HU2 8RW
tel (01482) 224800 *fax* (01482) 581182
email admin@hulltruck.co.uk
website www.hulltruck.co.uk
Artistic Director John Godber *Associate Director* Gareth Tudor Price *Executive Director* Joanne Gower *Casting Assistant* Jennifer Marshall

Production details

In operation since 1971, Hull Truck has established a national/international reputation for excellence. It presents a mix of new writing, classic adaptations and one-night comedy/music events. The theatre also works on TIE, Outreach and Community projects for which Gavin Coles is the lead contact. Stages 13 productions per year, touring to 74 venues including theatres, educational and community venues. Roughly 2-6 actors used in each production. Recent productions include: *Under the Whaleback* by Richard Bean; *Up N Under* written and directed by John Godber; and *Confessions of a City Supporter* by Alan Plater. Offers TMA & ITC Equity approved contracts.

Casting procedures

Casting is done in-house. Casting breakdowns are advertised on the website, in *PCR* and *The Stage*, and are also available by postal application (with sae). Welcomes letters (with CVs and photographs) from actors, but prefers not to receive emails or showreels.

Key Theatre

Embankment Road, Peterborough, Cambridgeshire PE1 1EF
tel (01733) 552437 *fax* (01733) 567025
email michael.cross@peterborough.gov.uk
website www.peterboroughkeytheatre.co.uk
Artistic Director Michael Cross *Youth Theatre/TIE Officer* Paul Collings

Production details

Mainly a receiving house with occasional in-house productions including an annual pantomime and TIE tours. Stages 4 shows each year. Recent productions include: *A Christmas Carol*, *A New Year's West End Nights*, and *Sleeping Beauty*.

Casting procedures

Does not use freelance casting directors. Occasional general auditions. Unsolicited communications are not advised. Casting requirements are sometimes available through the website, but usually through professional casting services, *PCR* and *The Stage*.

"Actors working in the area (and especially touring to the Key) are always encouraged to make contact with the Artistic Director and introduce themselves. Invitations to see artists working in productions are always welcome – and wherever possible accepted!" Offers TMA/Equity contracts. Rarely (or never) has the opportunity to employ disabled actors.

Library Theatre Company

St Peter's Square, Manchester M2 5PD
tel 0161-234 1913 *fax* 0161-228 6481
email ltcadmin@manchester.gov.uk
website www.librarytheatre.com
Artistic Director Chris Honer *Associate Director* Roger Haines

Production details

Regional producer of contemporary drama; also produces a play for families and children at Christmas. Produces 5-6 shows each year, and runs an Education programme (contact Liz Postlethwaite). Recent productions include: *The Price*, *Dancing at Lughnasa*, *Larkin with Women*, *The Safari Party*, *Oliver Twist*, and *The Real Thing*.

Casting procedures

Uses freelance casting directors. "Read the plays in our programme and submit yourself for a specific part about 12 weeks before the first performance." Also holds general auditions in the summer; write to request inclusion in these in March or April. Offers TMA/Equity approved contracts. Actively encourages applications from disabled actors and promotes the use of inclusive casting.

Live Theatre

27 Broad Chare, Quayside, Newcastle upon Tyne NE1 3DQ
tel 0191-261 2694 *fax* 0191-232 2224
email info@live.org.uk
website www.live.org.uk
Artistic Director Max Roberts *Associate Directors* Jeremy Herrin, Paul James

Production details

New writing theatre established in 1973. Produces 8-10 shows each year in the main house. Also runs TIE, Outreach and Community programmes (contact Paul James).

Casting procedures

Does not use freelance casting directors. Welcomes submissions (with CVs and photographs) sent by post or email. Actors may write at any time. Showreels and invitations to view individual actors' websites are also accepted. Offers ITC/Equity approved contracts. Actively encourages applications from disabled actors and promotes the use of inclusive casting.

Liverpool Everyman and Playhouse Theatres

13 Hope Street, Liverpool L1 9BH
tel 0151-708 3700 *fax* 0151-708 3701
email info@everymanplayhouse.com
website www.everymanplayhouse.com
Artistic Director Gemma Bodinetz

Production details

Since January 2004 the Playhouse, like the Everyman, has been predominantly a producing theatre placing emphasis on creative interpretations of great plays. The Playhouse is Liverpool's home of classic drama, from ancient to modern, while new writing forms the core of the programme at the Everyman. The theatre also hosts touring companies from around the country; runs a busy Literary Department, working to nurture the next generation of Liverpool playwrights; and has an active Community Department which takes work to all corners of the city and surrounding areas. Recent productions include: *The Morris*, *Dr Faustus* and *The Odd Couple*.

Lyric Theatre

55 Ridgeway Street, Belfast BT9 5FB
email clare@lyrictheatre.co.uk
website www.lyrictheatre.co.uk
Artistic Director Paula McFetridge *General Manager* Mike Blair *Education Officer* Una Nic Eoin *Admin Manager* Clare Gault *Production Manager* Marianne Crossle

Production details

Northern Ireland's only full-time producer of professional theatre. Presents a distinctive, challenging and entertaining programme of new writing as well as contemporary and classic plays by Irish, European and American writers. Stages 6 shows each year in the main house. Also runs an Education programme. Recent productions include: *1974 … The End of the Year Show* (World Premiere); *Merry Christmas Betty Ford*; *Snow Queen*; *Hamlet* (co-produced with the Abbey Theatre); and *The Lonesome West* (produced in association with An Grianan).

Casting procedures

Does not use freelance casting directors. Welcomes submissions (with CVs and photographs) sent by post or email – actors may write in at any time. Advises actors to check the website for its future programme. Offers TMA/Equity approved contracts. Will consider applications from disabled actors to play characters with disabilities.

Lyric Theatre Hammersmith

King Street, London W6 0QL
tel (08700) 500511 *fax* 020-8741 5965
email enquiries@lyric.co.uk
website www.lyric.co.uk
Artistic Director David Farr

Production details

Produces and co-produces original theatre for a wide audience. Recently completed work which redeveloped the theatre, creating 2 new spaces – a purpose-built rehearsal studio, and an education/training room. The theatre runs an extensive Education programme and focuses on working with disadvantaged communities and young people in the local area. For further information, contact the Education Administrator, Herta Queirazza. Recent productions include: *Don Juan* and *The Firework-Maker's Daughter.*

Casting procedures

Different directors cast their own productions using freelance casting directors.

Manor Pavilion Theatre

Manor Road, Sidmouth, Devon EX10 8RP
tel 020-7636 4343 *fax* 020-7636 2323
email cvtheatre@aol.com
Artistic Director Charles Vance *Associate Director* Imogen Vance

Production details

Summer repertory theatre with a 3-month season (July-September). Now in its 19th year of operation of weekly repertory theatre. Stages 12 shows each year in the main house.

Casting procedures

Welcomes letters (with CVs and photographs) but not email submissions. Actors should write in February sending application to Head Office, Hampden House, 2 Weymouth Street, W1W 5BT.

Mercury Theatre

Balkerne Gate, Colchester, Essex CO1 1PT
tel (01206) 577006 *fax* (01206) 769607
email info@mercurytheatre.co.uk
website www.mercurytheatre.co.uk
Chief Executive Dee Evans *Associate Directors* Janice Dunn, Adrian Stokes, David Hunt, Nix Rosewarne

Production details

A regional repertory theatre which opened in 1972, producing 3 ensemble shows each season. Stages 6 shows each year in the main house and 1-2 in the studio. Also runs a Community programme (contact Adrian Stokes). Recent productions include: *Macbeth*, *The Triumph of Love*, *Ion* and *To Kill a Mockingbird.*

Casting procedures

Each show is cast by the director from within an ensemble company which has evolved over the past 6 years. It is preferred for actors to build up a relationship with the artistic team rather than to approach by letter or email. A knowledge of the Mercury's work is essential.

The Mill at Sonning Theatre

Sonning Eye, Reading RG4 6TY
tel 0118-969 6039
email admin@millatsonning.com
website www.millatsonning.com
Artistic Director Sally Hughes

Production details

Popular 'dinner theatre' venue, producing a range of plays for audiences to watch while eating a meal. Recent productions include: *French Without Tears, Time to Kill, It Runs in the Family*.

Casting procedures

Forthcoming productions are listed on the website. Actors should send their details, along with specific casting suggestions, to the Artistic Director 2 months before each show.

National Theatre

South Bank, London SE1 9PX
tel 020-7452 3335 *fax* 020-7452 3340
email info@nationaltheatre.org.uk
website www.nationaltheatre.org.uk
Artistic Director Nicolas Hytner *Head of Casting* Wendy Spon CDG

Production details

A National Theatre was first proposed in 1848. In 1951 a foundation stone was laid by the Royal Festival Hall, and in 1962 Sir Laurence Olivier was appointed the National's first director, based at London's Old Vic Theatre. Finally, in 1976, the new NT officially opened with a production of *Hamlet*. Today, the National stages a range of classics, musicals, new plays and entertainment "for all the family". It comprises 3 theatres: the Olivier (open-stage, capacity 1120 people); the Lyttleton (proscenium arch, capacity 890); and the Cottesloe (studio theatre on 3 levels with flexible staging, capacity 300). Recent productions include: *The Life of Galileo, Southwark Fair, Royal Hunt of the Sun, Coram Boy* and *The Voysey Inheritance*.

Casting details

The National Theatre's casting team works with approximately 10 directors a year casting NT shows. Actors known to the theatre may be approached directly, but casting is predominantly carried out through agents. The NT will first approach agents to check actors' availability, then audition a shortlist. New talent is actively sought out and the casting team sees several performances a week within London and (less frequently) outside. It also attends drama schools' showcases and will sometimes approach other casting directors known to the NT.

National Theatre of Scotland (NTS)

Atlantic Chambers, 45 Hope Street, Glasgow G2 6AE
tel 0141-221 0970 *fax* 0141-248 7241
email info@nationaltheatrescotland.com
website www.nationaltheatrescotland.com
Artistic Director & Chief Executive Vicky Featherstone
Director-in-Residence Davey Anderson *Administrator* Kate Cattell

Inaugurated in February 2006, the National Theatre of Scotland (NTS) is highly unusual – as national theatres go – in that is has no physical building or permanant theatre space. Instead, its remit is to produce its own work and collaborate with others to tour the length and breadth of Scotland, from the largest theatres in the major cities to the smallest island communities. As well as the large-scale projects that one might associate with the term 'national theatre' – some of which tour internationally – 2 small, touring companies have been established. One of these is comprised of recently graduated actors, directors, technicians and producers, mentored by the NTS artistic team; the other, of more experienced performers. Both tour a wide range of arts, community and school venues across Scotland. The NTS makes a virtue of its lack of building by supporting artists concerned with creating site-specific work, or with collaborating with other artists to "challenge existing models of theatre-making".

New Vic Theatre

Etruria Road, Newcastle-under-Lyme ST5 OJG
tel (01782) 717954 *fax* (01782) 712885
email admin@newvictheatre.org.uk
website www.newvictheatre.org.uk
Artistic Director Gwenda Hughes *General Manager* Nick Jones

Production details

Purpose-built theatre-in-the-round with a full programme of in-house drama, concerts and occasional touring productions. Stages 10 shows each year in the main house. Also very active with Outreach and Education programmes (contact Sue Moffat and Jill Rezzano respectively). Recent productions include: *Sweeney Todd, My Night with Reg, The Duchess of Malfi, Kes* and *The Marriage of Figaro*. Gwenda Hughes is stepping down as Artistic Director from Christmas 2006. She will be succeded by Theresa Heskins.

Casting procedures

Does not use freelance casting directors. Casting breakdowns are obtainable by postal application (with sae), and up-to-date casting information is posted on the casting section of the website.

Welcomes letters (with CVs and photographs), but not email submissions. Submissions should be specific and referenced to a particular role. Also accepts invitations to view individual actors' websites.

Northcott Theatre

Northcott Theatre, Stocker Road, Exeter EX4 4QB
tel (01392) 223999
website www.northcott-theatre.co.uk
Artistic Director Ben Crocker

Production details

The Northcott produces or co-produces a varied programme of 10-11 shows each year, with runs of between 10 days and 3.5 weeks (the Christmas show being the only one that runs for approximately 6 weeks). Over the last 2 years the theatre has been developing links with other theatre companies, and hopes to build on this – leading to more joint ventures with repertory companies across the country.

In addition the theatre runs active Community and Education departments, giving people of all ages a chance to be involved in shows, workshops, masterclasses and trips. Recent productions include: *Humble Boy*, *Dancing at Lughnasa*, *Jack and the Beanstalk* and *Harry in the Moonlight*.

Northern Stage (formerly Newcastle Playhouse)

Barras Bridge, Newcastle NE1 7RH
tel 0871-7000 124 *fax* 0191-261 8093
email directors@northernstage.co.uk
website www.northernstage.co.uk
Chief Executive/Artistic Director Erica Whyman
Associate Director Neil Murray

Production details

Northern Stage is the largest producing theatre company in the North East of England. Following a £9m redevelopment programme, the company's new home – formerly Newcastle Playhouse and Gulbenkian Studio – re-opened in summer 2006 as Northern Stage. The new building has 3 stages and presents and produces a wide repertoire of UK and international theatre. Staging 6 shows a year, the company also works on participator projects, with Kylie Lloyd as the lead contact. Recent productions include: *Blaze!*, *Homage to Catalonia*, *Great Expectations* and *1001 Nights Now*.

Casting procedures

Casting breakdowns are available on the website twice a year.

Nottingham Playhouse

Wellington Circus, Nottingham NG1 5AF
Artistic Director Giles Croft *Associate Director* Richard Baron *Casting Director* Sooki McShane *Director of Roundabout & Education* Andrew Breakwell

Production details

Nottingham Theatre Trust was founded in 1946 and moved to its current location in 1963. Stages 8 shows each year in the main house and 5 Roundabout productions. Also runs TIE, Outreach and Community programmes. Recent productions include: *Rat Pack Confidential*, *Ethel and Ernest* and *Polygraph* (main house); *Walking the Tightrope* and *Mohammed* (Roundabout).

Casting procedures

Does not use freelance casting directors. Casting breakdowns are available from the casting director, Sooki McShane. Welcomes letters (with CVs and photographs) but not email submissions. Showreels and invitations to view individual actors' websites are also accepted.

Nuffield Theatre

University Road, Southampton SO17 1TR
tel 023-8031 5500 *fax* 023-8031 5511
email info@nuffieldtheatre.co.uk
website www.nuffieldtheatre.co.uk
Artistic Director Patrick Sandford *Associate Director* Russ Tunney *Administrative Director* Kate Anderson

Production details

A regional theatre performing a range of classic plays and new writing. Stages 5-7 shows each year in the main house, and 3-4 in the studio. Also runs TIE, Outreach and Community programmes. Recent productions include: *Hamlet*; *Nelson* (new play by Pam Gems); *Wizzil* (touring primary schools).

Casting procedures

Uses freelance casting directors. Holds local auditions for actors in the Southampton area. Actors may write at any time requesting inclusion. Casting breakdowns are sometimes available through *PCR* or Equity Job Information Service. Offers ITC and TMA/Equity approved contracts. "We consider applications from disabled actors in exectly the same way as applications from able-bodied actors."

Octagon Theatre

Howell Croft South, Bolton BL1 1SB
tel (01204) 529407 *fax* (01204) 556502
email info@octagonbolton.co.uk
website www.octagonbolton.co.uk
Artistic Director Mark Babych *Executive Director* John Blackmore *Head of Production* Lesley Chenery

Production details

Stages 8-9 shows each year in the main house and 18 in the studio. Also runs TIE, Outreach and Community programmes (contact Activ8 Department). Recent productions include: *Score* (TIE tour), *Boston Marriage*, *Carmen*, *Cooking with Elvis* and *The Weir*.

Casting procedures

Does not use freelance casting directors. Actors may write requesting inclusion in the company at any time and should enclose an sae. Accepts invitations to view individual actors' websites.

The Old Vic

The Cut, London SE1 8NB
tel 020-7928 2651 *fax* 020-7261 9161
email ovtcadmin@oldvictheatre.com
website www.oldvictheatre.com
Artistic Director Kevin Spacey

Production details

After a number of years as a receiving house, The Old Vic's Chief Executive (Sally Greene), Artistic Director (Kevin Spacey) and Producer (David Liddiment) launched The Old Vic Theatre Company in 2004, with the aim of revitalising the theatre and making it a destination as a producing house once again. Recent productions have included: *Aladdin*, with Ian McKellen as Widow Twankey; *The Philadelphia Story* with Jennifer Ehle; and *Richard II*, for which Trevor Nunn directed Kevin Spacey in the title role.

Casting procedures

"We're not able to accept CVs or speculative applications for employment."

Open Air Theatre

Inner Circle, Regent's Park, London NW1 4NR
website www.openairtheatre.org
Artistic Director Ian Talbot *Office Manager* Shona McCarthy *Casting Director* Jane Salberg

Production details

Stages 4 shows each year in the main house and 1 in the studio theatre. Recent productions include: *A Midsummer Night's Dream*, *Taming of the Shrew* and *The Boyfriend*.

Casting procedures

Sometimes uses freelance casting directors and occasionally holds general auditions. Actors should write in January or February requesting inclusion. Welcomes submissions (with CVs and photographs) sent by post or email. Also accepts showreels and invitations to view individual actors' websites.

Orange Tree Theatre

1 Clarence Street, Richmond TW9 2SA
tel 020-8940 0141 *fax* 020-8332 0369
email admin@orange-tree.demon.co.uk
website www.orangetreetheatre.co.uk
Artistic Director Sam Walters

Production details

"The Orange Tree Theatre is wholly concerned with the performance of quality live theatre, and with reaching as wide an audience as possible with its work. Over the 30 years of its existence it has established a reputation for being the leader in its field and is the only permanent theatre-in-the-round in London." Presents a mixture of new writing, classic plays, comedies and musicals. Education and Community work forms a major area of activity. Stages 7 shows each year.

Casting procedures

Does not use freelance casting directors. Casting breakdowns are obtainable by postal application (with sae). Welcomes letters (with CVs and photographs) but not email submissions. Write in June for the new season. Also accepts invitations to view individual actors' websites. Offers TMA/Equity approved contracts. Actively encourages applications from disabled actors and promotes the use of inclusive casting.

Perth Theatre at Horsecross

185 High Street, Perth PH1 5UW
tel (01738) 472700 *fax* (01738) 624576
email info@horsecross.co.uk
website www.horsecross.co.uk
Creative Directors Graham McLaren, Ian Grieve
Secretary Elaine White *Education Officer* Jennifer McGregor

Production details

Scotland's oldest theatre company with a mixed programme of in-house and guest productions throughout the year, including drama, musical theatre and pantomime. Produces 6-7 shows each year. Also runs Outreach and Community programmes. Recent productions include: *Oliver!*, *Communicating Doors*, *The Yellow on the Broom*, *Good Things* and *Aladdin and the Enchanted Lamp*.

Casting procedures

Does not use freelance casting directors. Welcomes submissions (with CVs and photographs) sent by post or email. Actors should write in the spring. Also accepts invitations to view individual actors' websites.

Pitlochry Festival Theatre

Port-Na-Craig, Pitlochry PH16 5DR
tel (01796) 484600 *fax* (01796) 484616
email admin@pitlochry.org.uk
website www.pitlochry.org.uk
Artistic Director John Durnin *Chief Executive* Nikki Axford *Community and Education Director* Drew Scott

Production details

Founded in 1951, Pitlochry Festival Theatre is a producing and presenting theatre located in the Perthshire Highlands. Comprises the main house (capacity 544), an extensive production facility, and Explorers: The Scottish Plant Hunters Garden, containing a number of open-air performance spaces. Between April and October each year a 20-strong acting ensemble presents a season of 6 major productions performed in day-change repertoire. Visiting theatre, music, dance, opera and other activities are presented during the winter months. Also runs TIE and Community programmes. Recent productions include: *A Man for All Seasons*, *Things We Do for Love*, *Kind Hearts And Coronets*, *To Kill A Mockingbird*, *Treasure Island* and *Dolly West's Kitchen*.

Casting procedures

Does not use freelance casting directors. Recruits new members of the acting ensemble each autumn and winter, with a detailed casting breakdown published each September. The closing date for applications is usually in mid-November; auditions are then held in London and Edinburgh in November, December and January. Casting breakdowns are obtainable by postal application (with sae) from September. Submissions at any other time – or not in response to the casting breakdown – will not be considered. TMA/Equity contracts are offered. The theatre actively encourages applications from disabled actors and promotes the use of inclusive casting.

Queen's Theatre

Billet Lane, Hornchurch, Essex RM11 1QT
website www.queens-theatre.co.uk
Artistic Director Bob Carlton *Associate Director* Matt Devitt *Education Manager* Samantha Lane *Administrator* Henrietta Duckworth

Production details

Has been a producing theatre since it was first established in 1953. Currently works with actor-musicians in a permanent repertory company model. Stages 9 shows each year in the main house. Also runs TIE, Outreach and Community programmes. Recent productions include: *A Midsummer Night's Dream*, *Jane Eyre* and *Return to the Forbidden Planet*.

Casting procedures

Does not use freelance casting directors. Holds general auditions; actors should write in April or May requesting inclusion. Welcomes letters (with CVs and photographs) from actor-musicians only.

Rose Theatre

24-26 High Street, Kingston-upon-Thames, Surrey KT1 1HL
tel 020-8546 6983
email admin@kingstontheatre.org
website www.kingstontheatre.org
Artistic Director Sir Peter Hall *Executive Director* Sue Higginson OBE

At the time of going to press The Rose is still under construction, with completion not anticipated until late 2006/early 2007. When open, the theatre will have a resident company, under the direction of Peter Hall, presenting a range of modern and classical work. The company will comprise an ensemble of professional actors together with actors, directors and writers drawn from the new Postgraduate Theatre Course at Kingston University, where Sir Peter is Chancellor. There will be 8 plays a season in the main auditorium; at any one time, at least 3 different plays will be performed on different evenings or as matinees, including Sunday afternoons, to encourage families to visit and enjoy the theatre. Approaches from actors are discouraged until the theatre is nearer completion. Refer to the website for up-to-date information.

Royal & Derngate Theatres

Guildhall Road, Northampton NN1 1DP
tel (01604) 626222 (Admin) or (01604) 627566 (TIE)
website www.royalandderngate.com
Artistic Director Laurie Sansom *Associate Director* Dani Parr *Chief Executive* Donna Munday

The theatre is closed during 2006, with re-opening scheduled for later in the year. The 2006 pantomime at the Derngate is *Peter Pan* (produced by Qdos).

Royal Court Theatre

Sloane Square, London SW1W 8AS
tel 020-7565 5050 *fax* 020-7565 5001
email info@royalcourttheatre.com
website www.royalcourttheatre.com
Artistic Director Dominic Cooke *Associate Director* Ramin Gray *Casting Directors* Lisa Makin, Amy Ball

Production details

Since 1956 the English Stage Company at the Royal Court has focused on developing, funding and producing new writing. Productions frequently transfer to the West End and Broadway. Stages 6 productions each year in the Jerwood Theatre downstairs and 8 upstairs. Also presents programmes of rehearsed readings (contact Lisa Makin). Recent productions include: *Hitchcock Blonde* by Terry Johnson; *A Number* by Caryl Churchill; and *Harvest* by Richard Bean.

Casting procedures

Welcomes submissions (with CVs and photographs) by post or email. Also accepts showreels and invitations to view individual actors' websites. Offers SOLT/TMA/ Equity approved contracts.

Royal Exchange Theatre

St Ann's Square, Manchester M2 7DH
tel 0161-833 9833
website www.royalexchange.co.uk
Artistic Directors Greg Hersov, Braham Murray
Casting Director Jerry Knight-Smith *Casting Associate*
Katherine Lawson *Education Director* Amanda Dalton

Production details

Manchester's leading producing theatre company,
comprising a main theatre and studio space. Presents
7-8 productions, on average, in the main theatre and
5-6 in the studio each year. Also runs Education and
Community programmes involving schools, young
people, community groups and theatre enthusiasts of
all ages. Work is based around the theatre's repertoire
and its unique building. Where possible the
department leads sessions in the theatre and
frequently works with other departments around the
building to give participants an insight into how
theatre, and particularly the Royal Exchange, works.
Recent productions include: *Great Expectations*,
Major Barbara, *The Importance of Being Earnest* and
Six Degrees of Separation.

Casting procedures

Has a casting department of 2 who coordinate casting
for each show. Actors are contracted for individual
plays rather than for a season of work. Occasionally
holds general auditions, but this depends on the
director. Releases advance production information to
around 200 agents, on the website, and to the Actors
Centres for their noticeboards. Detailed casting
breakdowns are only available for some shows.

Will consider attending performances at venues in
the North West and London with sufficient notice.
Accepts submissions (with CVs and photographs),
but actors should bear in mind that the department
expects to receive more than 2000 CVs and photos
each season – and more in the summer months
following graduation at the drama schools. All
submissions are considered while a season is being
cast (a period of 4-6 months) but they are not kept
on file indefinitely.

Also operates a 'cover' system which has been agreed
with Equity. Employs 1 actor and 1 actress on each
production who read-in for some, or all, of the male
and female roles should they be indisposed. These
actors are contracted on Equity minimum payment
to be at the theatre throughout each show for this
purpose, and must therefore be based in Manchester.

Royal Lyceum Edinburgh

Grindlay Street, Edinburgh EH3 9AX
tel 0131-248 4800 *fax* 0131-228 3955
email info@lyceum.org.uk
website www.lyceum.org.uk
Artistic Director Mark Thomson

Production details

The Royal Lyceum is one of Scotland's largest
producing theatre companies with a season of in-
house drama productions running from September
to May. In addition the theatre stages a children's
show every Christmas, tours in Scotland and abroad,
hosts touring companies, and runs an ambitious and
acclaimed Education department. Recent productions
include: *Othello*; John Osborne's *Look Back in Anger*
with David Tennant; a new play, *The Girl with Red
Hair* by Sharman Macdonald; John Clifford's brand
new adaptation of Tolstoy's *Anna Karenina*; and a
revival of Tom McGrath's comic biography of Laurel
& Hardy.

Casting procedures

General auditions are held at the Lyceum throughout
the year by the Artistic Director and invited directors.
These are not auditions for a specific play or part, but
to give actors a chance to be seen and put on file with
a view to possibly being considered for a part in the
future. This type of audition is useful for a young
actor trying to establish him/herself in the field. To
apply for an open audition, send a letter with a CV
and photo to Casting at the address above; be
prepared to perform 2 contrasting pieces – 1
contemporary and 1 classic. The readings should last
1-2 minutes, although the whole audition can take
around 15 minutes. Bear in mind that the directors
can see up to 20 or 30 people a day during open
auditions. Any actor called to audition for a specific
part should have read the script and be familiar with
the role for which they are auditioning. Initial
auditions usually last about 30 minutes and recalls
can last about an hour.

Royal Shakespeare Company (Casting Department)

1 Earlham Street, London WC2H 9LL
tel 020-7845 0500 *fax* 020-7845 0505
email casting.coordinator@rsc.org.uk
website www.rsc.org.uk
Artistic Director Michael Boyd *Casting Director* Sam
Jones *Casting Assistant* Lucy Jenkins

Production details

One of the best-known theatre companies in the
world, the RSC has been operating under its present
name since 1961, a year after Peter Hall was
appointed director. The repertoire was widened at
this time to include modern writing and classics other
than Shakespeare. Over the next 30 years the
company continued to expand under the artistic
directorships of Peter Hall, Trevor Nunn, Terry
Hands and Adrian Noble. Michael Boyd succeeded
Adrian Noble as Artistic Director in 2003. The RSC is
formed around an ensemble of actors and core of

associate actors who are committed to a "distinctive and unmissable approach to theatre". Stages approximately 15 productions each year. Recent productions include: *Hamlet*, *Beauty and the Beast*, *Macbeth* and *Romeo and Juliet*.

Casting procedures

Welcomes letters (with CVs and photographs) but not email submissions. More information about Sam Jones can be found with her entry in *Casting directors* on page 82.

Salisbury Playhouse

Malthouse Lane, Salisbury SP2 7RA
Artistic Director Joanna Read *Casting Coordinator* Nicholas Gall

Production details

Stages 9 productions each year in the main house, alongside a studio programme. Also runs an Outreach programme.

Casting procedures

Casting breakdowns are available by postal application (with sae). Welcomes submissions (with CVs and photographs) by post only. Actors should write in May or October. Also accepts invitations to view individual actors' websites. Offers TMA/Equity approved contracts. Actively encourages applications from disabled actors and promotes the use of inclusive casting.

Shakespeare's Globe

21 New Globe Walk, Bankside, London SE1 9DT
tel 020-7902 1400 *fax* 020-7902 1401
email info@shakespearesglobe.com
website www.shakespeares-globe.org
Artistic Director Dominic Dromgoole *General Manager* Rowan Walker-Brown *Company Administrator* Sid Charlton *Casting Director* Jasmine Lawrence

Production details

A reconstruction of Shakespeare's Globe, the theatre has a repertoire which includes the work of Shakespeare, his contemporaries and new writing. The season runs from May to October with up to 6 productions staged each year. Also runs Outreach and Community programmes (contact Deborah Callan on 020-7902 1430). Recent productions include: *Coriolanus*, *Titus Andronicus*, *Antony and Cleopatra*, *The Comedy of Errors*, *Under the Black Flag* (by Simon Bent) and *In Extremis* (by Howard Brenton).

Casting procedures

Welcomes letters (with CVs and photographs) but not email submissions. Actors should write to the Casting Director in December and early January. Offers actors Equity approved contracts through an in-house agreement. Actively encourages applications from disabled actors and promotes the use of inclusive casting. The website has more information about casting procedures.

Sheringham Summer Theatre

75 Byron Avenue, Colchester CO3 4HQ
tel (01206) 768765
Artistic Director Seymour Matthews

Production details

Founded in the early 1980s and formerly known as Frinton Summer Theatre, the company has now moved on to Sheringham Summer Theatre. Hires out the Little Theatre and presents a 12-week repertory theatre season (comprising 8 productions) from July to September. Recent productions include: *Star Spangled Girl*, *Make Me A Widow*, *Run for your Wife* and *Bedside Manners*.

Casting procedures

Holds general auditions. Actors should write between January and April to request inclusion. Casting breakdowns are only occasionally made available via Equity Job Information Service. Welcomes letters (with CVs and photographs) but not email submissions. "In general, we don't issue casting breakdowns because we nearly always use actors known to us. However, we do look out for extremely versatile actors."

Sherman Theatre

Senghennydd Road, Cardiff CF24 4YE
tel 029-2064 6901 *fax* 029-2064 6902
website www.shermantheatre.co.uk
Artistic Director Phil Clark

Production details

Stages 4 shows each year and specialises in work for young audiences. Often uses actor-musicians.

Casting procedures

Does not use freelance casting directors. Sometimes holds general auditions. Welcomes letters (with CVs and photographs) but not email submissions. Also accepts invitations to view individual actors' websites.

Soho Theatre

21 Dean Street, London W1D 3NE
tel 020-7478 0117 *fax* 020-7287 5061
website www.sohotheatre.com
Artistic Director Lisa Goldman *Associate Director* Jonathan Lloyd *Casting Director* Ginny Schiller *Administrative Producer* Mark Godfrey

Production details

The Soho Theatre is a new writing venue, staging 8 productions each year. Also runs Outreach and

Community programmes (contact Jonathan Lloyd), and presents some guest productions and rehearsed readings. See entry under *Fringe theatres* (on page 175) for more detailed information.

Casting procedures

Uses freelance casting directors. Welcomes submissions (with CVs and photographs) by post or email. Actors may write at any time.

Southwold & Aldeburgh Summer Theatre

14 York House, Upper Montagu Street, London W1H 1FR
tel 020-7724 5432 *fax* 020-7724 3210
Artistic Director Jill Freud *Associate Director* Anthony Falkingham *Company Coordinator* Carol Carey

Production details

Summer theatre with an extensive programme. Stages 5 productions each year . Recent productions include: *Charley's Aunt, The Browning Version, Dames at Sea, Hobsons's Choice* and 6 guest children's shows.

Casting procedures

Does not use freelance casting directors. Holds general auditions; actors should write in November requesting inclusion. Casting breakdowns are available by phone. Welcomes letters (with CVs and photographs) but not email submissions, and advises that it is not possible to see everyone who writes in. Offers non-Equity contracts. Rarely (or never) has the opportunity to cast disabled actors.

Stephen Joseph Theatre

Westborough, Scarborough YO11 1JW
tel (01273) 370540 *fax* (01273) 360506
email sarah.hughes@sjt.uk.com
website www.sjt.uk.com
Artistic Director Alan Ayckbourn *Casting Director* Sarah Hughes *Executive Director* Stephen Wood

Production details

Stages 6-7 productions each year with lunchtime shows, late nights, rural and national touring. Most work is new writing. Recent productions include: *Improbable Fiction, Playing God,* and *Villette.*

Casting procedures

Does not use freelance casting directors. Sometimes holds general auditions; actors may write at any time requesting inclusion. Welcomes submissions (with CVs and photographs) by post or email. Also accepts showreels and invitations to view individual actors' websites. Offers TMA/Equity approved contracts. Will consider applications from disabled actors to play characters with disabilities.

Theatre By The Lake

Lakeside, Keswick, Cumbria CA12 5DJ
Artistic Director Ian Forrest *Associate Director* Stefan Escreet *Artistic Coordinator* Sophie Curtis

Production details

Produces a summer season of 6 plays, an Easter production and a Christmas production each year. Also promotes a touring programme of visiting professional work across all artforms, and runs an Outreach programme. Recent productions include: *Dead Funny, Dick Barton: Special Agent,* and *On Golden Pond.*

Casting procedures

Does not use freelance casting directors. Auditions 3 times per year, for which casting breakdowns are obtainable by postal application (with sae). Prefers not to receive general submissions from actors. Offers TMA/Equity approved contracts. Will consider applications from disabled actors to play characters with disabilities.

Theatre Royal & Drum Theatre Plymouth

Royal Parade, Plymouth PL1 2TR
tel (01752) 230340 *fax* (01752) 230499
website www.theatreroyal.com
Chief Executive Adrian Vinken, *Artistic Director* Simon Stokes

Predominantly a receiving house, but produces some shows (especially musicals) which transfer to the West End.

Theatre Royal Stratford East

Gerry Raffles Square, London E15 1BN
tel 020-8534 7374 *fax* 020-8534 8381
email theatreroyal@stratfordeast.com
website www.stratfordeast.com
Artistic Director Kerry Michael *Resident Director* Dawn Reid *Head of Education* Caroline Barth

Production details

Committed to work which portrays the experiences of different social and ethnic communities, the theatre is constantly striving to present shows which resonate with its diverse local audiences. Stages 8 shows each year. Also runs TIE, Outreach and Community programmes. Recent productions include: *Urban Afro Saxons, People Next Door, Funny Black Women on the Edge* and *Da Boyz.*

Casting procedures

Casting breakdowns are advertised on the website. Welcomes submissions (with CVs and photographs) sent by post or email. Advises actors to research the theatre's work before writing, and to think carefully about their own suitability. Invitations to view individual actors' websites also accepted.

Theatre Royal Windsor

Thames Street, Windsor SL4 1PS
tel (01753) 863444 *fax* (01753) 831673
website www.theatreroyalwindsor.co.uk
Artistic Director Mark Piper

Production details

A long-standing, non-subsidised producing theatre.
Shows run for 2-3 weeks. Stages 15 productions each
year with some going on to tour. Recent productions
include: *Stepping Out*, *Lord Arthur Saville's Crime* and
A Man for All Seasons.

Casting procedures

Does not use freelance casting directors. Welcomes
letters (with CVs and photographs) but not email
submissions. Offers TMA/Equity approved contracts.
Will consider applications from disabled actors to
play characters with disabilities.

The Tobacco Factory

Raleigh Road, Southville, Bristol BS3 1TF
tel 0117-902 0345 *fax* 0117-902 0162
email theatre@tobaccofactory.com
website www.tobaccofactory.com
Artistic Director Dan Danson *Theatre Manager* David
Dewhurst

Production details

Stages 2 productions a year in the theatre space, and
also works with the local community. Does not offer
Equity approved contracts.

Casting procedures

Casts in-house and does not hold general auditions.
Casting breakdowns are available from the website,
via postal application (with sae), and via *SBS*.
Welcomes letters (by post and email) from actors
previously unknown to the company, but does not
welcome showreels or invitations to view individual
actors' websites. Actively encourages applications
from disabled actors and promotes the use of
inclusive casting.

Torch Theatre

St Peter's Road, Milford Haven SA73 2BU
tel (01646) 694192 *fax* (01646) 698919
email info@torchtheatre.co.uk
website www.torchtheatre.co.uk
Artistic Director Peter Doran *PA to Artistic
Director* Lynn Muir *Casting Director* Christine
O'Reilly

Production details

Stages 4-5 productions each year. Recent productions
include: *Macbeth*, *One Flew Over the Cuckoo's Nest*
and *Blue Remembered Hills.*

Casting procedures

Sometimes holds general auditions; actors should
write in June requesting inclusion. Casting
breakdowns are available by postal application (with
sae) and Equity Job Information Service. Welcomes
submissions (with CVs and photographs) sent by
post or email. Showreels and invitations to view
individual actors' websites are also accepted. Advises
actors to join the mailing list so they know what is
being planned 6 months in advance. Offers TMA/
Equity approved contracts. Actively encourages
applications from disabled actors and promotes the
use of inclusive casting.

Traverse Theatre

Cambridge Street, Edinburgh EH1 2ED
tel 0131-228 3223 *fax* 0131-229 8443
email philip@traverse.co.uk
website www.traverse.co.uk
Artistic Director Philip Howard *Associate
Director* Lorne Campbell

Production details

Scotland's only theatre committed to new writing.
Presents a mixed programme of in-house and guest
productions. Stages 4 shows each year in the main
house and 2 in the studio. Also runs Outreach and
Script Development programmes (contact Neil
Coull). Recent productions include: *People Next Door*
by Henry Adam; *Dark Earth* by David Harrower; *Iron*
by Rona Munro; and *Outlying Islands* by David
Greig.

Casting procedures

Does not use freelance casting directors. Welcomes
letters (with CVs and photographs) but not email
submissions. Actors should write in January, June or
September. Particularly interested to hear from
Scottish actors. Invitations to view individual actors'
websites are also accepted.

Tricycle Theatre

269 Kilburn High Road, London NW6 7JR
tel 020-7372 6611 *fax* 020-7328 0795
email admin@tricycle.co.uk
website www.tricycle.co.uk
Artistic Director Nicolas Kent *General Manager* Mary
Lauder

Production details

Since opening in 1980, the Tricycle has striven to
produce a challenging and innovative programme of
theatre, cinema and visual arts reflecting the cultural
diversity of its neighbourhood – and in particular
plays by Irish, African-Caribbean, Jewish and Asian
writers – as well as responding to contemporary
issues and events with its ground-breaking 'tribunal'
plays. The new Tricycle now comprises a 230-seat

theatre, a 300-seat cinema, a large rehearsal studio, a visual arts studio for educational use, a smaller theatre/workshop space, an Art Gallery, and a new room called the Creative Space for educational/social exclusion workshops. The Tricycle maintains a comprehensive Youth and Education programme in Brent schools, and a thriving youth theatre reaching more than 20,000 children and young people each year through access schemes and community work. The theatre stages 5 plays each year. Recent productions have included: the premières of Harold Pinter's *The Dwarfs* and Athol Fugard's *Sorrow and Rejoicings*; 2 plays about the political situation of Northern Ireland – *As the Beast Sleeps* by Gary Mitchell, and *10 Rounds* by Carlo Gebler; and a collaboration with the Royal National Theatre of Zinnie Harris's *Further than the Furthest Thing*.

Casting procedures

Uses freelance casting directors but also occasionally posts casting breakdowns on the noticeboard section of the website. Does not welcome casting enquiries and submissions from actors unknown to the company. The Tricycle does however keep files on Black/Asian actors for its own information and as a resource for others; in these cases a photograph and CV are welcome.

Warehouse Theatre

Dingwall Road, Croydon CR20 2NF
tel 020-8681 1257 *fax* 020-8688 6699
email info@warehousetheatre.co.uk
website www.warehousetheatre.co.uk
Artistic Director Ted Craig *Administrative Director* Evita Bier *Education Manager* Rose-Marie Vernon

Production details

New-playwriting producing theatre for South London, presenting a mixed programme of in-house and guest productions. Recent productions include: the *Dick Barton* series; *Femme Fatale*; *Blowing Whistles*; and *Woody Allen's Murder Mysteries*.

Casting procedures

Uses freelance casting directors. Welcomes postal submissions at any time (with CVs and photographs) with sae for reply, but not email submissions. Offers ITC/Equity approved contracts. Encourages applications from disabled actors, although the building is not wheelchair-accessible.

Watermill Theatre

Bagnor, Nr Newbury RG20 8AE
tel (01635) 45834 *fax* (01635) 523726
website www.watermill.org.uk
Artistic Director James Sargent *Associate Directors* John Doyle, Edward Hall *Outreach Director* Ade Morris

Production details

A producing theatre where actors live onsite. Stages 6 shows each year with runs of 6-8 weeks, and 2 Outreach tours. Recent productions have included: Shakespeare, Music Theatre, New Writing and Classics. Following the untimely death of Artistic Director Jill Fraser in February 2006, James Sargent has taken up the post until October 2007.

Casting procedures

Does not use freelance casting directors. Casting breakdowns are available by postal application (with sae), but actors should call first. Welcomes letters (with CVs and photographs) with reference to specific castings only. Offers TMA/Equity approved contracts. Will consider applications from disabled actors to play characters with disabilities.

Watford Palace Theatre

20 Clarendon Road, Watford WD17 1J2
tel (01923) 235455 *fax* (01923) 819664
email enquiries@watfordtheatre.co.uk
website www.watfordtheatre.co.uk
Artistic Director Brigid Larmour *Literary Director* Joyce Branagh *Executive Producer* Mary Caws

Production details

Producing theatre built in 1908 and recently refurbished, it currently stages 9 shows each year. The theatre presents a varied programme but with an emphasis on new plays and adaptations. Also involved in Community theatre for which Kirstie Davis is the lead contact.

Casting procedures

Uses freelance casting directors. Casting breakdowns are available by postal application (with sae) and on Spotlight Interactive. Welcomes letters (with CVs and photographs) and invitations to view websites from actors, but prefers not to receive emails or showreels.

West Yorkshire Playhouse

Playhouse Square, Quarry Hill, Leeds LS2 7UP
tel 0113-213 7800 *fax* 0113-213 7250
website www.wyp.org.uk
Artistic Director Ian Brown *Producer* Paul Crewes

Production details

Founded in 1990, the West Yorkshire Playhouse has 2 auditoria – the Quarry (750 seats), and the Courtyard (350 seats). Works include new writing, classics, Shakespeare and musicals, as well as guest productions from incoming touring companies. Also runs TIE, Outreach and Community programmes (contact Gail McIntyre): the schools company tours 3 times a year. Stages 15-17 productions each year across both theatre spaces. Recent productions include: *Hamlet, Singin' in the Rain, The Wind in the Willows* and *Off Camera.*

Casting procedures

Currently the West Yorkshire Playhouse casts through agents' submissions, and works with casting directors on productions on a show-by-show basis. Replies to individual actors can only be sent on receipt of sae. Casting breakdowns are only available to agents. Offers TMA/Equity contracts. "The West Yorkshire Playhouse is an equal opportunities employer in relation to casting."

The New Wolsey Theatre

Civic Drive, Ipswich IP1 2AS
tel (01473) 295911 *fax* (01473) 295910
email info@wolseytheatre.co.uk
website www.wolseytheatre.co.uk
Artistic Director Peter Rowe

Production details

Mixed producing/receiving house, staging 4-5 productions a year in the main house and 2 in the studio. Also works in TIE and Community Outreach; the contact for this is Lynn Whitehead. Recent productions include: *Sugar, Sleeping Beauty, The Tempest, The Day of the Triffids,* and *Company.*

Casting procedures

Uses freelance casting directors and does not hold general auditions. Casting breakdowns are available via postal application (with sae). Does not welcome unsolicited approaches from actors, unless in response to a casting breakdown. Offers TMA/Equity approved contracts. Actively encourages applications from disabled actors and promotes the use of inclusive casting.

York Theatre Royal

St Leonard's Place, York YO1 7HD
tel (01904) 658162 *fax* (01904) 611534
website www.yorktheatreroyal.co.uk
Artistic Director Damian Cruden *Chief Executive* Daniel Bates

Production details

One of the oldest theatres in the country, seats 867 in the main theatre and 106 in the studio. Productions include classics, new writing and the famous York pantomime every Christmas. Also hosts touring companies, premières and has a partnership with Pilot Theatre Company who are resident at the theatre. Stages 7-8 shows each year in the main theatre and 6-7 in the studio. Also runs Outreach and Community programmes (contact Gill Adamson). Recent productions include: *Old Mother Goose, Brassed Off, The Beauty Queen of Leenane, Single Spies* by Alan Bennett, and Bryony Lavery's *Behind the Scenes at the Museum.*

Casting procedures

Does not use freelance casting directors and does not welcome submissions from actors.

Young Vic

66 The Cut, London SE1 8LZ
email info@youngvic.org
website www.youngvic.org
Artistic Director David Lan *Associate Artistic Director* Sue Emmas

Production details

During 2005/6 the Young Vic was on Walkabout, producing its shows at other theatres in London and on tour while its home in The Cut was redeveloped. From the new building, the Young Vic now runs TIE, Outreach and Community programmes (contact Sue Emmas). Recent productions include: *Skellig* by David Almond (directed by Trevor Nunn); *Hobson's Choice* adapted by Tanika Gupta (directed by Richard Jones); *Simply Heavenly* by Langston Hughes (directed by Josette Bushell-Mingo); and *Cruel and Tender* by Martin Crimp (directed by Luc Bondy).

Casting procedures

Uses freelance casting directors. Does not welcome direct submissions from actors. Offers TMA/Equity approved contracts. Actively encourages applications from disabled actors and promotes the use of inclusive casting.

Independent managements/theatre producers

This section mostly lists commercial organisations that mount West End and touring productions to larger-scale venues – some of which originate in the subsidised sector. Most such productions will be led by well-known actors, but they will usually need supporting actors who can also understudy those leads. (In long-running West End productions, the understudies get a chance to do their own performance – a useful opportunity to 'showcase' for agents and casting directors.) Sometimes, such a production will tour to try it out before (hopefully) coming into the West End; at others, a management will tour to 'milk' further profits from a West End success.

On tour, apart from 'Acting ASMs' (assistant stage managers who also understudy), you shouldn't be asked to do any of the graft of get-ins and get-outs – unlike on smaller-scale touring. However, if you are also understudying, you will be expected to do an understudy rehearsal every week until the last stages of the tour. This rehearsal will probably be taken by the company manager (rarely, the director) and the whole ambience will feel very unsympathetic to good acting. Despite this, it is very important to be as fully prepared as possible for the chance that the 'name' you are understudying will be unavoidably delayed one night. Touring is fraught with potential delays, and a reputation for being able to 'deliver the goods' at very short notice will enhance future employment prospects. The downside of playing small parts and understudying is that you can become stuck doing this – a good agent will be able to advise in this area.

Touring is not for everyone: long periods away from home, wide variations in the quality of digs (often costing more in holiday resorts during the 'season'), and the fact that you could miss opportunities to be seen for other work are some of the potential disadvantages. On the plus side, contracts for large-scale tours are usually at least three months with a minimum of a week in each venue, and you should have time to see some of the most beautiful sights in the UK (if not Europe and further afield).

Although not as expensive as major films, such productions do cost a lot of money to mount, and productions have been known to collapse suddenly without any warning. When accepting work in this area it is important to have a proper Equity contract.

Ambassador Theatre Group (ATG)

Duke of York's Theatre, 104 St Martin's Lane, London WC2N 4BG
Head of Production Meryl Faiers *Production Associate (Casting)* Neil Rutherford

Production details

ATG is the second-largest theatre owner and operator in the UK, with 22 venues (11 in the West End and 11 regionally). It produces across the UK, Japan, Europe and New York. Anywhere between 3 and 30 actors work on each production. Recent productions include: *Guys and Dolls*, *Sweeney Todd*, Matthew Bourne's *Nutcracker* and *Highland Fling*, and *The Rocky Horror Show*.

Casting procedures

Uses freelance casting directors. Welcomes letters (with CVs and photographs), but not email submissions. Actors may write at any time, but prefers contact to be made via an agent and preferably during pre-production. Advises actors against sending expensive photos 'on spec', especially if unaccompanied by a letter. Offers Equity approved contracts. Actively encourages applications from disabled actors and promotes the use of inclusive casting.

Anthony Vander Elst Productions

The Studio, 14 College Road, Bromley BR1 3NS
tel 020-8466 5580
Director Anthony Vander Elst

Established in 1977. Produces 1-2 productions per year touring the UK. Recent productions include: *Appearances* (Mayfair Theatre, London); *The Teddy Bears Picnic* (Chester Gateway Theatre); and *Last of the Red Hot Lovers* (London). Unsolicited approaches from actors are discouraged. Offers TMA/Equity approved contracts.

British Stage Productions

Victoria Buildings, 1B Sherwood Street, Scarborough YO11 1SR
tel (01723) 507186 *fax* (01723) 501328
email britstage@aol.com
Partners Gareth Stewart, Michael Conradd

Production details

Founded in 1994, the company specialises in summer seasons, pantomime, music hall, variety touring and residencies, staging an average of 10-12 productions each year. In general the company tours to 70 arts centres, theatres and community venues across the UK with an annual total of 300-350 performances. Recent productions include: *The Good Old Days of Music Hall, We'll Meet Again, Fabulous 40s and 50s* and *Snow White*.

Casting procedures

Casting breakdowns are advertised on Equity Job Information Service and in *The Stage*. Welcomes letters (with CVs and photographs) from actors previously unknown to the company but will not accept emails or showreels. Offers non-Equity contracts. Rarely (or never) has the opportunity to cast disabled actors.

Nick Brooke Ltd

The Penthouse, 7 Leicester Place, London WC2H 7RJ
tel 020-7851 0393 *fax* 020-7734 7185
email info@nickbrooke.com
Directors Nick Brooke, Philip Noel

Production details

Founded in 2002 as an independent theatre production company, Nick Brooke Ltd stages 2 productions each year, averaging an annual total of about 280 performances. Tours to approximately 30 theatres throughout England and Wales annually. In general 6-10 actors work on each production. Recent productions include: *Corpse* and *The Shell Seekers*.

Casting procedures

Occasionally employs freelance casting directors. Also holds general auditions; actors should write in

January and in the early summer to request inclusion. Casting breakdowns are publicly available via the website and postal application. Welcomes submissions (with CVs and photographs) from actors previously unknown to the company if sent by post, but does not welcome email enquiries. Also accepts invitations to view individual actors' websites.

Cole Kitchenn Ltd

Vaudeville Theatre Offices, 404 Strand, London WC2R ONH
tel 020-7836 2502 *fax* 020-7240 8477
website www.colekitchenn.com
Key personnel Stuart Piper, David Cole, Guy Kitchenn

Production details

Production company established in 1970; personal management established in 2005. Has produced more than 60 productions in the West End over the past 35 years. Offers Equity approved contracts.

Casting procedures

Casting breakdowns available from *SBS*, Spotlight and Castweb. Welcomes letters (with CVs and photographs) from actors previously unknown to the company sent by post or email. Invitations to view individual actors' websites and showreels are accepted. Rarely has the opportunity to cast disabled actors.

Ray Cooney Plays

Everglades, 29 Salmons Road, Chessington KT9 2JE
Director Ray Cooney *General Manager* Alan Osman

Production details

Occasionally directs, but no longer produces, plays.

Casting procedures

Sometimes holds general auditions. Welcomes letters (with CVs and photographs) from actors previously unknown to the company, but not email submissions.

CV Productions Ltd

Hampden House, 2 Weymouth Street, London W1W 5BT
tel 020-7636 4343 *fax* 020-7636 2323
email cvtheatre@aol.com
Director Charles Vance

Production details

Regional touring theatre company.

Casting procedures

Does not use freelance casting directors. Sometimes holds general auditions. Casting breakdowns are not publicly available. Welcomes submissions (with CVs and photographs) sent by post or email. Invitations to view individual actors' websites are also accepted.

Paul Elliot Ltd

1st Floor, 18 Exeter Street, London WC2E 7DU
tel 020-7379 4870 fax 020-7379 4860
email info@paulelliot.ltd.uk
Director Paul Elliot General Manager David Bownes

Production details

Large-scale theatre producers, touring no. 1 venues across the UK with plays and musicals. Stages 2-4 productions a year, touring from between 6 weeks to 2 years or more. May use from 3 to 30 actors in each production. Offers ITC/Equity approved contracts. Recent credits include: Stones in his Pockets.

Casting procedures

Casts in-house and also uses freelance casting directors. Actors may write at any time requesting inclusion in auditions. Casting breakdowns are published in The Stage, PCR and SBS, and included in Spotlight Link. Happy to receive CVs and photographs, by post or email, from actors previously unknown to the company. Also happy to receive showreels and invitations to view individual actors' websites. Will consider applications from disabled actors to play characters with disabilities.

Andrew Fell Ltd

4 Ching Court, 49-51 Monmouth Street, London WC2H 9EY
tel 020-7240 2420 fax 020-7240 2499
email hq@andrewfell.co.uk
Directors Andrew Fell, Sally Hoskins

Production details

Theatre production company and general management. Recent productions include: The Producers – the new Mel Brooks musical; Romeo and Juliet; The Lieutenant of Innishmore; and Taboo.

Casting procedures

Uses freelance casting directors.

Vanessa Ford Productions Ltd

Upper House Farm, Upper House Lane, Shamley Green GU5 0SX
tel (01483) 278203 fax (01483) 271509
email Vanessa@vfpltd.fsnet.co.uk
website www.vfpltd.com
Managing Director Vanessa Ford Director Glyn Robbins

Production details

Founded in 1979. Tours to approximately 30 theatres throughout the UK each year. On average, 14 actors work on each production. Recent productions

include: The Hobbit, A Christmas Carol and Shirley Valentine.

Casting procedures

Occasionally uses freelance casting directors, and sometimes holds general auditions. Casting breakdowns are available on the website and through Spotlight. Welcomes submissions (with CVs and photographs) by post and email. Invitations to view individual actors' websites are also accepted.

Robert Fox Ltd

6 Beauchamp Place, London SW3 1NG
tel 020-7584 6855 fax 020-7225 1638
email info@robertfoxltd.com
website www.robertfoxltd.com
Director Robert Fox

Production details

Founded in 1980. Theatre and film production company specialising in large-scale theatre productions and musicals as well as feature films. Performances are staged in the West End and on Broadway. Recent theatre productions include: The Breath of Life, The Boy from Oz and Gypsy. Also recently produced the feature films The Hours and Iris.

Casting procedures

Employs casting directors for specific projects and does not welcome unsolicited submissions from actors. Casting breakdowns are available on the website, and details of casting directors are sometimes posted there as well.

Gareth Johnson Ltd

Plas Hafren, Eglwysrw, Crymych, Pembrokeshire SA41 3UL
tel (01234) 891368 mobile (07779) 007845
email gjltd@mac.com
Director Gareth Johnson

Production details

Founded in 2000, this general management company produces (for a client) up to 6 shows a year, including West End, UK and European tours. Recent productions have included: The Far Pavilions (Shaftesbury Theatre); Jus' Like That! (Garrick Theatre and tour); Songs My Mother Taught Me (Lorna Luft at the Savoy Theatre); and a UK tour of The Merchant of Venice. Offers Equity contracts.

Casting procedures

Uses freelance casting directors and does not welcome unsolicited contact of any kind from actors. Policy on actors with disabilities "depends on the client".

David Graham Entertainment Ltd

72 New Bond Street, London W1S 1RR
tel 0870-321 1600 *fax* 0870-321 1700
email info@david graham.co.uk
website www.davidgrahamentertainment.com
Director David Graham

Production details

Theatre producer and concert promoter. Stages around 8 productions in 70-80 theatres and concert halls on an annual basis, with more than 300 performances per year. Countries covered include Britain, Holland, Germany, Canada, Spain, Norway and Ireland. In general, 12 performers work on each production. Recent productions include: *The Real Monty*, *The Wonderful West End* and *Hold Tight, It's 60s Night*.

Casting procedures

Does not use freelance casting directors or hold general auditions. Casting breakdowns are available via the website, *PCR* and advertisements in *The Stage*.

Hiss & Boo Company Ltd

1 Nyes Hill, Wineham Lane, Bolney, West Sussex RH17 5SD
tel (01444) 881707 *fax* (01444) 882057
email email@hissboo.co.uk
website www.hissboo.co.uk
Artistic Director Ian Liston

Production details

Established in 1977. Pantomime producers also specialising in touring plays and revues in the UK and overseas.

Casting procedures

Works with a known pool of performers. Casting and auditions are only available via Spotlight Interactive Casting. Does not welcome unsolicited CVs. Offers actors TMA/Equity approved contracts.

Paul Holman Associates Ltd

20 Deane Avenue, South Ruislip, Middlesex HA4 6SR
tel 020-8845 9408 *fax* 020-8582 2557
email enquiries@paulholmanassociates.co.uk
website www.paulholmanassociates.co.uk
Director Paul Holman *Associate Producers* Adrian Jeckells, John Ogle

Production details

Founded approximately 15 years ago. Produces pantomimes, summer shows and one-night attractions. Stages 10 productions annually at 10 or more theatre venues. On average, at least 10 actors work on each production. Recent productions include: *Peter Pan* and a *Summer Spectacular*.

Casting procedures

Casting breakdowns are released to agents and are available on Castweb (see entry under *The Spotlight, casting directories and information services* on page 267). Welcomes submissions (with CVs and photographs) sent by post and email. Showreels and invitations to view individual actors' websites are also accepted.

Thelma Holt Ltd

Waldorf Chambers, 11 Aldwych, London WC2B 4DG
tel 020-7379 0438 *fax* 020-7836 9832
email Thelma@dircon.co.uk
website www.thelmaholt.co.uk
Managing Director Thelma Holt *Executive Director* Malcolm Taylor

Production details

Founded in 1990. Theatre producer of classic plays in the West End, on tour and internationally (particularly Japan). Stages 4-5 productions annually with a total of 250 performances. Tours 6 theatres across the UK each year. On average, 18 actors work on each production. Recent productions include: *Hamlet*, *The Taming of the Shrew*, *All's Well that Ends Well*, *Othello* and *Pericles*.

Casting procedures

Offers Equity/TMA/SOLT approved contracts. Uses freelance casting directors. Does not hold general auditions. Advises that the company does not encourage unsolicited approaches with letters or photographs, as they will be ignored if not in production. When casting, requirements are made well known via casting directors. "I have employed disabled actors and will continue to do so – not necessarily to play characters with disabilities. When an actor's good, it's horses for courses."

Hull Truck Theatre

See entry under *Producing theatres*.

Bruce James Productions

68 St George's Park Avenue, Westcliff-on-Sea, Essex SS0 9UD
tel/fax (01702) 335970
email info@brucejamesproductions.co.uk
website www.brucejamesproductions.co.uk
Artistic Director Bruce James

Production details

Produces dramas, comedies, thrillers, pantomimes, children's shows and 'summer schools' for many theatres all over the UK. Stages around 12 productions a year. Between 2 and 14 actors are involved in each production. Does not offer Equity-approved contracts. Recent productions include

Mother Goose (Pomegranate Theatre, Chesterfield); *Babes in the Wood* (Tyneside Theatre); and UK tours of *Dry Rot* (farce) and *The Case of the Frightened Lady* (thriller).

Casting procedures

Casts in-house and holds general auditions. Actors should write in January, May and September to request inclusion. Casting breakdowns are published via *SBS*, Castcall and Castweb. Welcomes letters (by post, not by email) with CVs and photographs from individuals previously unknown to the company. "Do not, under any circumstances, send unsolicited emails containing large [file-sized] photographs." Does not welcome showreels, but is happy to receive invitations to view individuals' websites. Will consider applications from disabled actors to play characters with disabilities. Advises actors: "Never give up or stop trying to get seen!"

Andy Jordan Productions Ltd

5 Underwood Cottages, The Coombe, Streatley-on-Thames, Berkshire RG8 9RA
tel (01491) 871411 *fax* (01491) 871411
email andyjordan@aol.com
Director Andy Jordan

Production details

Founded in 2000. Commercial production company, largely producing new plays of all genres. Stages 2-4 productions annually and gives 50-100 performances per year. Performs annually in 4-10 theatres across the UK, including Northern Ireland and Eire. Also tours overseas. On average, 3-7 actors work on each production. Recent productions include: *Last Song of the Nightingale*, *Kings of the Road*, *Three on a Couch*, *Calculus* and *Talk About the Passion*.

Casting procedures

Uses freelance casting directors. Actors may write at any time requesting inclusion. Casting breakdowns are publicly available via Spotlight Link. Welcomes submissions (with CVs and photographs) sent by post and email.

Richard Jordan Productions Ltd

Mews Studios, 16 Vernon Yard, London W11 2DX
tel 020-7243 9001 *fax* 020-7213 9667
email Richard.Jordan@virgin.net
Director Richard Jordan

Production details

Founded in 1998. Produces theatre in the West End, throughout the UK and internationally. Main area of work is new writing and revivals of plays; occasionally produces musicals. Company also works as general managers and consultants for a wide range of producers and theatres in the UK and abroad. Stages

5-10 productions annually and gives 300 performances during the course of the year. Recent productions include: *The Twits*, *Single Spies* and *The Lady in the Van*.

Casting procedures

Uses freelance casting directors. Sometimes holds general auditions. Casting breakdowns are sometimes publicly available in *PCR*. Welcomes letters (with CVs and photographs) but not email submissions. Applications are particularly welcome if actors are currently in a production that the company can go and see. Advises that applicants should have an awareness of the type of work produced by the company before sending CVs.

Bill Kenwright Ltd

BKL House, 106 Harrow Road, London W2 1RR
tel 020-7446 6200 *fax* 020-7446 6222
email info@kenwright.com
website www.kenwright.com

Production details

Commercial producing management presenting revivals and new works for the West End and for touring theatres. Recent (or current) productions include: in the West End – *Blood Brothers*, *Hay Fever*, *Whistle Down the Wind*, *The Crucible*, and *A Man for All Seasons*; on tour – *Blood Brothers*, *Festen*, *Joseph & The Amazing Technicolor Dreamcoat*, *The Hollow*, and *This Is Elvis*.

Casting procedures

Uses freelance casting directors, but does some casting in-house. Welcomes letters (with CVs and photographs) sent to Tom Siracusa or David Bingham.

Limelight Entertainments

Unit 4, The Gateway, 2a Rathmore Road, London SE7 7QW
tel 020-8858 6141 *fax* 020-8805 2684
email enquiries@limelightents.co.uk
website www.limelightents.co.uk
Artistic Director Richard Lewis *Executive Producer* Martin Ronan

Production details

Established in 1996. Stages 2-3 productions annually, touring to 50 theatres and arenas. Roughly 4-6 actors used in each production. Recent productions include: *Sing-A-Long-A-ABBA*, *The Fimbles*, *Love Shack* and *Fully Committed*. Equity approved contracts.

Casting procedures

General auditions are usually held in September. Encourages applications from disabled actors and promotes the use of inclusive casting.

Cameron Mackintosh Ltd

1 Bedford Square, London WC1B 3RB
tel 020-7637 8866 *fax* 020-7436 2683
Chairman Cameron Mackintosh *Managing Director* Nicholas Allot *Casting Director/Associate Producer* Trevor Jackson

Production details

Stages musical theatre productions worldwide. Recent productions include: *Les Miserables, Miss Saigon* and *The Phantom of the Opera*.

Casting procedures

In-house casting. Does not hold general auditions. Welcomes letters (with CVs and photographs) but not email submissions. Also accepts showreels and invitations to view individual actors' websites.

Christopher Malcolm Ltd

1 Calton Road, Bath BA2 4PP
tel (01225) 445459 *fax* (01225) 427778
email cm@christophermalcolm.co.uk
Director Christopher Malcolm *Other key personnel* Judith Lloyd

Production details

Founded in 1980, the company works in both licensing and production. Theatre producer for the West End, UK touring and European touring. Stages 2-3 productions annually with 200-300 performances during the course of the year. Tours on average 30-40 UK venues, and 100-150 European venues annually. 13-25 actors are involved in each production. Recent productions include: *The Rocky Horror Show* and *Footloose*.

Casting procedures

Uses freelance casting director, Debbie O'Brien. Sometimes holds general auditions. Actors should write to the casting director only, requesting inclusion. Advises actors to use their agents as a means of contact with the casting director. Unsolicited letters and photographs are not considered.

Johnny Mans Productions Ltd

PO Box 196, Hoddesdon, Herts EN10 7WG
tel (01992) 470907 *fax* (01992) 470516
email real@legend.co.uk
Managing Director Johnny Mans *Company Secretary* Philip Crowe

Production details

Founded in 1989. Activities include producing one-night stands, celebrity concerts and touring shows, casting for TV and pantomime, artist management and personal management of Sir Norman Wisdom OBE. Stages about 38 productions annually, totalling 350 performances during the course of the year. Tours to 300 different arts centres and theatres across the UK and Ireland each year. Recent productions include: *Norman Wisdom and Friends, Max Bygraves and the Beverley Sisters* and *Thoughts of Chairman Alf* with Warren Mitchell.

Casting procedures

Sometimes holds general auditions. Actors requesting inclusion should write at New Year and in mid-summer. Welcomes letters (with CVs and photographs) and email submissions. Showreels should only be sent on request. Offers Equity approved contracts. Will consider applications from disabled actors to play characters with disabilities.

Morning Vicar Productions Ltd

43B Camberwell New Road, London SE5 ORZ
tel/fax 020-7582 2242
email info@morningvicar.co.uk
website www.morningvicar.co.uk
Directors Stuart Piper, Stephen Carlile

Production details

Founded in 2003, the company produces theatre in the West End and on tour, staging 1-2 productions each year. Recent productions include: *Snoopy* (West End/UK tour).

Casting procedures

Uses freelance casting directors and also holds general auditions. Casting breakdowns are available on their website, by postal application (with sae), and from Equity Job Information Service, *PCR* and *The Stage*. Welcomes letters and emails (with CVs and photographs) from actors previously unknown to the company. Will also accept showreels and invitations to view actors' websites.

Norwell Lapley Associates

Lapley Hall, Lapley, Staffs ST19 9JR
tel (01785) 841991 *fax* (01785) 841992
email norwelllapley@freeserve.com
website www.norewelllapley.co.uk
Director Chris Davis *Artiste Managers* Claire Sibley, Kerry Foley

Production details

Produces theatre in the West End and touring productions. Stages 4-5 productions annually and gives 40-50 performances during the course of the year at theatres nationwide. Recent productions include: *Zipp*.

Casting procedures

Uses freelance casting directors and does not deal directly with actors. See entry under *Agents* on page 36 for further details about the company's work.

David Pugh Ltd

Canaletto Yard, 41-45 Beak Street, London W1F 9SB
tel 020-7434 9757 *fax* 020-7287 8856
Director David Pugh

Production details

Theatre production company staging 2-3 productions annually in the West End and Broadway, and touring to theatres throughout the UK. Recent productions include: *Art*, *The Play What I Wrote* and *Blues Brothers*.

Casting procedures

Sometimes holds general auditions. Actors should address requests for inclusion to Sarah Bird CDG (see entry under *Casting directors* on page 82), who is responsible for all casting.

Michael Redington

10 Maunsel Street, London SW1P 2QL
tel 020-7834 5119
Director Michael Redington

Production details

Founded in 1979. Produces new and original plays. Stages 1 theatre production annually. Recent productions include: *Japes*.

Casting procedures

Uses freelance casting directors. Sometimes holds general auditions.

Rho Delta Ltd

52 Tottenham Street, London W1T 4RN
tel 020-7436 1392 *fax* 020-7436 1395
email info@ripleyduggan.com
Director Greg Ripley-Duggan

Production details

Founded in 1991. Produces West End and touring commercial theatre. Stages 1 production annually which tours to 6 theatres. Recent productions include: *The Old Masters*, *Life x 3* and *The Memory of Water*.

Casting procedures

Uses freelance casting directors and does not deal directly with actors.

Suzanna Rosenthal Ltd

PO Box 40001, London N6 4YA
tel 020-8340 4421 *fax* 020-8340 4421
email admin@suzannarosenthal.com
website www.suzannarosenthal.com

Production details

Founded in 2001, the company produces Off-West End shows. Stages 3-5 productions annually with 100 performances over the year in theatres and outdoor venues across London. In general 5-15 actors are involved in each production. Recent productions include: *Henry VIII* and *The Resistible Rise of Arturo Ui*, *Victor/Victoria* and London's Free Open-Air season at The Scoop.

Casting procedures

Uses freelance casting directors. Sometimes holds general auditions. Actors should only write requesting inclusion in response to advertisements. Casting breakdowns are available via the website, *PCR* and advertisements in *The Stage*.

Marc Sinden Productions

3 Grand Union Walk, Camden Town, London NW1 9LP
tel 020-8455 3278
website www.sindenproductions.com
Director Marc Sinden

Production details

A West End and touring theatre producer, reaching theatres and arts centres across the UK and Europe. For details of recent productions, please consult the website. Also runs the Uk Theatre Availability System (**www.uktheatreavailability.co.uk**) which allows touring companies to check the availability and suitability of theatre spaces.

Casting procedures

Uses freelance casting directors and does not welcome casting enquiries and submissions from actors.

Adam Spiegel Productions

2nd Floor, 20-22 Stukeley Street, London WC2B 5LR
tel 020-7438 4565 *fax* 020-7438 9577
email enquiries@adamspiegel.com
Director Adam Spiegel *Managing Director* Bob Eady
General Manager Amanda Riley

Production details

Founded in 1996, the company has been responsible for staging *Fame* and *Saturday Night Fever* in London's West End and on tour. In general 25-30 actors are involved in each production, and both have played in more than 40 different venues across the country.

Casting procedures

Uses freelance casting directors. Sometimes holds general auditions as well. Casting breakdowns are available via *PCR* or *SBS*. Welcomes letters (with CVs and photographs) but not email submissions. Offers SOLT/Equity contracts.

Barrie Stacey UK Productions Ltd

Flat 8, 132 Charing Cross Road, London WC2H OLA
tel 020-7836 6220/4128 *fax* 020-7836 2949
email hopkinstacey@aol.com
Director Barrie Stacey *Stage Director* Tony Joseph

Production details

Founded in 1966. Specialises in children's musicals and songbook concerts. Stages 24 productions annually and gives 100 performances during the course of the year. Tours to 8 different theatres in Southern England, including the London area. In general 8 actors are involved in each production. Recent productions include: *West End to Broadway* and *Movie Memories.*

Casting procedures

All casting is done in-house. Holds general auditions. Casting breakdowns are available on request. Welcomes letters (with CVs and photographs) but not email submissions. Advises actors: "Don't be grand when just starting."

Stage Further Productions Ltd

Westgate, Stansted Road, Eastbourne BN22 8LG
tel (01323) 739478 *fax* (01323) 736127
email info@stagefurther.co.uk
Director Garth Harrison *Producer* David Nott *Artistic Director* Keith Myers

Production details

Founded in 1985. Produces plays and pantomimes for its repertory seasons and national tours. Also provides entertainment and shows to the cruise industry. Stages 10 productions annually and performs in around 18 different venues, including arts centres and theatres nationwide and cruise vessels. In general 6 actors are involved in each production. Recent productions include: *Anybody for Murder* and *Dead of Night.*

Casting procedures

Holds general auditions. Casting breakdowns are available via *PCR, The Stage* and from agents. Welcomes letters (with CVs and photographs) but not email submissions. Invitations to view individual actors' websites are also accepted.

Stanhope Productions Ltd

The Penthouse, Charles House, 7 Leicester Place, London WC2H 7RJ
tel 020-7734 0710 *fax* 020-7734 7185
email office@stanhopeprod.com
Director Kim Poster *Production Coordinator* Chrissie Dugan

Production details

Founded in 2001. Theatrical producing company. Stages 4-5 productions annually and gives 576 performances during the course of the year. Tours to 2-4 different theatres, primarily in the West End and London area. In general 18 actors are involved in each production. Recent productions include: *A Woman of No Importance* and *Brand.*

Casting procedures

Uses freelance casting directors. Holds general auditions. Casting breakdowns are available via Equity Job Information Service.

Tenth Planet Productions

75 Woodland Gardens, London N10 3UD
tel 020-8442 2659 *fax* 020-8883 1708
email artdir@tenthplanetproductions.com
website www.10thplanetproductions.com
Artistic Director Alexander Holt *Literary Manager* Mark Underwood *Associate Directors* Susan Harriet, Alex Scrivenor

Production details

Founded in 1998, the company has produced more than 30 productions to date. Stages 4-6 productions annually and presents 100-150 performances during the course of the year. Tours to 2-6 different regional theatres in the UK; also tours internationally in association with Sh! Productions Co (its sister company), performing dinner theatre in the Emirates. Performs in site-specific locations such as the Rose Theatre in London. For the past few years the company has been resident Upstairs at the Gatehouse in London. In general 4-8 actors are involved in each production. 2004/05 productions included: *Trestle at Pope Lick Creek* (in association with Royal Exchange); *Deathtrap*; *Taking Steps*; *Rough Crossing.* Forthcoming productions include: *The Rise and Fall of Little Voice* in the West End.

Casting procedures

Holds general auditions. Actors should write in response to advertisements only, or consult the website for information on forthcoming productions. Casting breakdowns are available via *SBS, PCR,* CastNet and Castweb (see entry under *The Spotlight, casting directories and information services* on page 267). Showreels and invitations to view individual actors' websites are also accepted. Advises that the company principally casts NCDT-trained actors or well-established actors with demonstrable experience. As it is unable to retain submissions on file, actors should only write in when casting is advertised, or telephone first.

West End International

17 Leighton Place, London NW5 2QL
tel 020-7428 0555 *fax* 020-7428 0577

website www.westendinternational.com
Director Martin Yates *General Manager* Alison Price
Administrator Annie Rose

Production details

"West End International has been producing first-class entertainment throughout the world since its inception in 1995. Our unique practice of engaging artists of the highest calibre has resulted in unprecedented success and respect on a worldwide basis." Stages 50 productions each year and tours to about 30 theatres/outdoor venues around the world. The average cast size is 5. Recent productions include: *Fascinatin' Rhythm* (Symphony Hall, Birmingham); *The Best of West End* (Glasgow Royal Concert Hall); and *Beatlemania!*.

Casting procedures

Will accept casting enquiries and letters (with CVs and photographs) from actors previously unknown to the company provided that these are posted and not emailed. Does not welcome unsolicited showreels.

Kevin Wood Productions

5 Archery Square, Walmer, Deal, Kent CT14 7JA
Director Kevin Wood

Production details

Founded in 1980. Produces tours, pantomimes and plays. Stages 4-6 productions with 400 performances each year. Tours to 16 different UK theatres annually. In general 12 actors are involved in each production. Recent productions include: *Godspell.*

Casting procedures

Uses freelance casting directors. Sometimes holds general auditions. Actors should write requesting inclusion in response to advertisements. Casting breakdowns are available on Castweb (see entry under *The Spotlight, casting directories and information services* on page 267). "Unsolicited letters without an sae are not replied to."

Mounting a production without a base theatre

Graham Cowley

So. There's a play you're desperate to do, but you have no theatre. You're in one of two situations: either you are a funded company with good relationships with producing or touring theatres, or it's just you on your own.

Out of Joint started ten years ago. Max Stafford-Clark was about to leave the Royal Court after 13 years; he'd spent all his working life up until then producing new plays, and needed an environment in which that work could continue. As the former Artistic Director of The Traverse, Joint Stock and the Royal Court, and with an international reputation, he could have been forgiven for assuming that funding would be readily available for a new venture such as this. But the fledgling Out of Joint was in competition for the meagre Arts Council project funds along with everyone else, and its early years were as hand-to-mouth as those of any new company. There was no office, so Max and Sonia Friedman, the company's first producer, set up productions and booked tours from their front rooms; blind eyes were turned as small quantities of Royal Court stationery disappeared; and friends were persuaded to give help and advice for no payment.

Financially, the early years were a balancing act between Arts Council Touring grants, stretched as far as they would go, and co-production deals with producing theatres. For the first few shows this was the Royal Court, but since then Out of Joint has co-produced with other theatres as well: Hampstead, the Young Vic, the Soho Theatre, the National, the Liverpool Everyman and Playhouse, and the Abbey, Dublin. Out of Joint co-productions usually take a straightforward form. Both partners agree a pre-production budget, covering the rehearsal costs, wages and fees, building the set, acquiring costumes and props and generally assembling the show. They agree to split this cost in some fashion – either 50/50 or in a ratio reflecting how long each company will have use of the play. If Out of Joint is touring for eight weeks and the run at the Soho Theatre is four weeks, there is a case for an unequal split of the cost of mounting the play. Then, each partner takes full responsibility for the running costs and income while the show is under its management. In Out of Joint's case, this means we pay the wages and all other costs while the show is touring, and our co-producer does the same while it plays in London (or Liverpool, or Dublin).

This way of working has many virtues. For both parties, it represents an opportunity to get more value from a pre-production budget – either by saving money, or, more commonly, by enhancing the total budget available. For the company, it brings not only financial stability but also a temporary home. Having an office and a rehearsal room is all very well, but theatre people like to belong to a theatre. For the theatre, it means that their programme is enhanced by a play or project which would not otherwise have been available to them. And whoever was the initiator, both parties feel an ownership of the play. This is vital, although it involves a good deal of give and take on each side. Where will you rehearse? Who builds the set? Can the theatre contribute a stage manager? All these things are important in encouraging a feeling of joint ownership.

Now, happily, Out of Joint receives regular funding from the Arts Council, and has its own office and photocopier. But early habits of frugality remain: the company has tiny overhead costs, employs only five full-time staff and still enjoys co-producing. A touring company cannot run up substantial debts: with the only tangible assets being some lighting equipment and an ageing van, there is no security for an overdraft. So preserving financial security is crucial.

Financial security can seem like a pipe dream for those at the sharper end of producing. Together with some good friends, I have been putting on plays independently for several years, under the banner of Two's Company. This year we received a small Arts Council grant, for the first time. But by then we had established a way of working with some of London's small theatres which enabled us (just) to operate.

So – you have a play. The first thing is to secure the rights. For an existing play in a small theatre, all you'll get is a licence for your production dates. This may well mean that you need to have a theatre. The first question to ask is, where should it ideally go? It's by no means unknown for plays with epic themes and huge casts to be seen in tiny pub theatres, but perhaps this one needs more space, more facilities? Or is this three-hander capable of filling 250 seats? Maybe we should keep it to 70 ... *Time Out* and *Contacts*, between them, have the most complete lists of the theatres available. How many do you know? It's easier to have a view about a theatre if you've seen a show there. If you don't think your play will fit the policies and criteria of the Bush, Hampstead, the Almeida or the Royal Court, or you don't want to wait (sometimes) a long time for them to tell you that, you can approach one of the fringe theatres. If you've thought carefully about the match between your play and the theatre, you'll have a better chance of securing a suitable venue.

Most theatres are unfunded, so if they show interest, and have a production slot that fits your dates, they will charge you a weekly rent. At this point you'll need to finalise your budget. You know how many actors you need and how much you can pay them. The budget for a set, costumes and props – well, how long is a piece of string? Priorities are all-important. If your play needs army uniforms, you'll almost certainly have to hire them, so allow enough for that. On the other hand, to secure a clever designer, it's often worth sacrificing some money from the physical budget to add to his/her fee – inventiveness can add huge value to your budget.

Clarity about exactly what you can expect from the theatre in return for your rent is important to establish. What hours can you use it for? Can you work all night on the get-in, or are there neighbours who object? What staff, if any, will work with you, and what will they do? How long does it take to move the seating, and who knows how it all works? And almost most important of all, what marketing support will the theatre provide? There might be a season brochure, but how many are produced and where do they go? How does the box office operate, and what figures will you get? And so on. Theatres vary enormously in what they can offer, how much they will support you and how welcoming they are.

Even the smallest show needs some sort of funds to operate with. Even though the box office receipts will be an important source of income (you hope), you can't expect the theatre to pay the takings over until they are very sure you've paid everything that you owe them, so you'll need enough money to keep cash flowing. Nothing demoralises a cast of actors more than being told you can't pay them yet. And while a lot can be done with the beg/borrow/steal method, there are some things you just have to pay for. So you apply to the Arts Council, charitable trusts, businesses, ask friends and relations to give you money. This all takes a long time, so start as soon as you can. Please don't remortgage your house.

In London, particularly, press reviews can be of enormous importance as to whether or not your production is a success. It's really worth engaging a press rep who knows his/her stuff. That, by the way, is a very difficult judgement to make until you've worked with somebody, so see if you can get some informed opinions about the person you're contemplating hiring. If s/he can get you advance press publicity, that's wonderful, but what you really need is for the critics to come, and to come early – it's no use their appearing after the run is over. Some shows take off like a rocket; some burn slowly for a bit before catching alight; and lots more need an audience to be laboriously reached and persuaded to come. Sometimes, it seems, one by one. But whichever it is, your job isn't over until every seat is sold.

So why do it? Because there is a play you believe in, a director of genius, stunningly talented actors – or at least, some of those things. I firmly believe that if you're going to produce a play, you've got to love it. The response of the critics and the audience is personal, and therefore unpredictable – so it's important to be able to say at the end, "Well, I liked it." And, of course, there is nothing like the feeling you get when you look round the theatre bar, or the dressing room, or indeed the auditorium, and think, "All these people are here because I brought them together." Good luck!

Graham Cowley is Producer with Out of Joint, and also Two's Company. He was previously with the Theatre of Comedy Company, the Royal Court Theatre (on whose behalf he transferred a string of hit plays to the West End), the Half Moon Theatre, and Joint Stock Theatre Group.

Middle and smaller-scale companies

This section covers a huge range of companies: from the very prestigious, often subsidised (like Out of Joint), which usually only perform in theatres with around 500 seats (or more), to the very small, which frequently have little or no public subsidy and perform wherever they can find a paying audience. The bigger companies operate much like the commercial 'big boys' in the previous section – except they tend to have longer rehearsal periods. The smaller companies rarely use casting directors, tend to do only one or two performances in each venue, and often pay below Equity rates – and it's probable that you'll have to help with get-ins and get-outs. It's very hard work and you have to rise to the peak of performance every time in spite of travelling in cramped vans, sharing unsatisfactory digs and rarely, if ever, being seen by anyone who could advance your career. However, some very prestigious companies have grown from such very small beginnings – and a number of now highly respected directors, playwrights and actors have started this way. It is important to assess the potential quality of the product (as well as the pay, and terms and conditions) before accepting such a job.

As such companies tend to come and go with great rapidity, the listings only contain companies that have been in existence for three years or more.

Note Some of the companies listed are members of the Independent Theatre Council (ITC) – **www.itc-arts.org**.

Actors of Dionysus (AOD)

14 Cuthbert Road, Brighton BN2 0EN
tel/fax (01273) 692604
email info@actorsofdionysus.com
website www.actorsofdionysus.com
Artistic Director Tamsin Shasha *Development Officer* Alice Booth

Production details

National and international touring company founded in 1993. A member of the ITC and Arts & Business, it currently receives no regular funding. Specialises in performing new adaptations of Ancient Greek drama through a fusion of poetry, music and movement. Has a strong educational focus and runs international summer schools. Stages 1-2 productions each year with an average annual total of 120-150 performances. Venues include arts centres, theatres (including Greek and Turkish theatres), and educational venues across the UK, Eire and Turkey. Also performs on cruise ships. In general 4-6 actors work on each production. Recent productions include: *Trojan Women* (2005), *Hippolytus* (2004), and *Oedipus* (2003 & 2006).

Casting procedures

Does not use freelance casting directors. Holds general auditions; actors should write to request inclusion in August and December. Casting

breakdowns are available through the website and *PCR*. Does not welcome general submissions from actors but will accept invitations to view individual actors' websites. Offers non-Equity contracts. Actively encourages applications from disabled actors and promotes the use of inclusive casting.

Actors Touring Company (ATC)

Malvern House, 15-16 Nassau Street, London W1W 7AB
tel 020-7580 7723 *fax* 020-7580 7324
website www.atc.online.com
Artistic Director Gordon Anderson *Executive Producer* Emma Dunton

Production details

Established in 1979. 2 productions are staged annually, touring to arts centres and theatres and employing roughly 4-6 actors. Offers ITC/Equity approved contracts. Recent productions include: *A Brief History of Helen of Troy* (UK tour).

Casting procedures

Encourages applications from disabled actors and promotes the use of inclusive casting. Unsolicited approaches from actors are discouraged.

Admiration

PO Box 50255, London EC3A 5WA
tel 0870-765 1584 *fax* 0870-765 1594

email enquiries@admirationtheatre.co.uk
website www.admirationtheatre.co.uk
Director Jon Hewitt

Production details

Founded in 2001, the company stages 3-4 productions each year with an average annual total of 30 performances across theatres in London. Cast size varies from 2-8 actors. Recent productions include: *Ubu Roi* (Courtyard Theatre, London – Summer 04); *Seasons of Purity* (Theatro Technis, London – Dec 04).

Casting procedures

Uses freelance casting directors but sometimes holds general auditions. Welcomes letters and emails (with CVs and photographs) from actors previously unknown to the company. Will also accept showreels and invitations to view actors' websites.

Attic Theatre Company

New Wimbledon Theatre, The Broadway, London SW19 1QG
tel/fax 020-8543 7838
email info@attictheatre.com
website www.attictheatre.com
Artistic Director Jenny Lee *Associate Director* Merhdad Seyf *Administrator* Teun Timmers *Booking & Finance Manager* Victoria Hibbs *Production Manager* Kate Reynolds

The company was formed in 1987 to produce high-quality theatre and develop audiences for new plays, musicals, reworked clasics and contemporary plays with a cutting edge. Work is presented at Wimbledon Studio Theatre and other venues, and the company tours on average 1 production each year. Tours up to 15 venues across the UK annually; these include arts centres, theatres, educational venues and community venues. Cast size varies from 1-6 actors. Recent productions include: the premiere of *Jessie Kesson – A Good Crack at Life* by Jenny Lee (RSC Stratford Summerhouse, Edinburgh Festival and Scottish tour 2002-03); *Hamlet* (Cannizaro Park Open Air Theatre Festival 2002); *The Member of the Wedding* by Carson McCullers (2002); and the premiere of *Wigs and Wide Boys and The Rulers of The World* by Jane James (2002). In 2003 the company mounted the first UK tour of *Knives in Hens* by David Harrower. This was followed in 2004 by the world premiere of *Markings* by Dominic Francis – an ATTIC commission.

Community work is an integral part of the company's vision. In the past 3 years it has developed *Ma Kelly's Doorstep*, an entertaining show with a serious message on the topic of bogus callers, which tours to day centres and lunch clubs in London boroughs. The sequel is a show on home safety – *Ma Kelly Plays it Safe*. In 2004 the company produced a show celebrating age, with music, dance and drama – *It's the Ritz!*; in 2005, it collaborated with Croydon

Clocktower on *Dancing in The Dark* – a celebration of the lives of Croydon people during World War II.

Attic Theatre Young People's Company holds workshops for 11-15 year-olds who meet every Wednesday evening in term time.

Casting procedures

Uses freelance casting directors. Does not hold general auditions and does not welcome casting enquiries or submissions from actors.

Badapple Theatre Company

Crimple Brow, York Road, Green Hammerton, York YO26 8BN
tel (01423) 339168
email office@badapple.freeserve.co.uk
website www.badapple.freeserve.co.uk
Director Kate Bramley

Production details

Founded in 1998, the company specialises in small-scale tours of new biography drama. Stages 1-2 productions each year with an average annual total of 60 performances. Venues include arts centres and theatres across Scotland, Wales and England. In general 3-4 actors work on each production. Recent productions include: *Still Marilyn,* which played to 35 arts centres in spring 2003.

Casting procedures

Does not use freelance casting directors. Casting breakdowns are available through Equity Job Information Service, *PCR* and advertisements in *The Stage.* Actors should write (with CVs and photographs) in response to casting breakdowns only. Does not welcome email submissions. Invitations to view individual actors' websites are accepted.

Benchtours Productions Ltd

Bonnington Mill, 72 Newhaven Road, Edinburgh EH6 5QG
tel 0131-555 3585
email info@benchtours.com
website www.benchtours.com
Co-directors Peter Clerke, Catherine Gillard *General Manager* Ben Walmsley

Production details

Founded in 1991, Benchtours is Scotland's leading international touring ensemble. The company seeks to extend the boundaries of theatre and open it up to new and diverse audiences, and is committed to new writing, highly visual theatre, rural touring and disability work. Normally stages 2 productions each year with an average annual total of 40 performances. Tours to approximately 25-30 theatres, arts centres, educational venues and community venues across

Scotland (including islands and Highlands) and Northern England each year. Benchtours also tours internationally – recently, to Poland and the USA. Recent national tours include: *The Emperor's Opera* and *Crowhurst*.

Casting procedures

Holds casting workshops in December each year, which the artistic directors invite selected actors to attend. Actors are advised to email CVs and cover letters in October/November. Benchtours offers Equity ITC contracts to all performers and actively encourages applications from disabled actors as part of its integrated casting policy.

Big Telly Theatre Company

Town Hall, The Crescent, Portstewart, Londonderry BT55 7AB
tel 028-7083 6473 *fax* 028-7083 2588
email info@big-telly.com
website www.big-telly.com
Director Zoë Seaton

Production details

Big Telly Theatre Company is Northern Ireland's longest established professional not-for-profit theatre company, formed in 1987 and based in Portstewart on the North Coast. The company produces theatre, interactive workshop programmes and community creativity projects, which mainly tour throughout Northern and Southern Ireland and international markets. It concentrates on the visual potential of theatre through fusion with other art forms such as dance, music, circus, magic and film to create a unique sense of spectacle. "Big Telly's work is driven by a determination to offer audiences entertainment that surprises, stimulates and ignites the imagination."

Casting procedures

Does not use freelance casting directors. Casting breakdowns are available through the website and Equity Job Information Service, and are also released to agents. Welcomes submissions (with CVs and photographs) from actors previously unknown to the company sent by post or email. Invitations to view individual actors' websites are also accepted. Offers ITC/Equity contracts, and endeavours to employ disabled actors when casting for disabled characters.

Boilerhouse

Gateway Theatre, The Arts Quarter, 40-44 Elm Row, Edinburgh EH7 4AH
tel/fax 0131-556 5644
email paul@boilerhouse.org.uk
website www.boilerhouse.org.uk
Director Paul Pinson *Producer* Chloe Dear *General Manager* Jon Clarke

Production details

Founded in 1992, Boilerhouse is an Edinburgh-based performance company which has developed a reputation as a leading creator of exciting, high-quality work in non-theatre spaces. Over the last 12 years, work has been produced in clubs, car parks, warehouses, Pacific ocean-front wharves, London's Docklands, derelict buildings, churches and under a motorway bridge. Boilerhouse aims to create performance events of spectacle and meaning. We work with artists from an extensive range of disciplines in the development of medium- to large-scale outdoor and street-theatre productions. Work has involved collaborations with award-winning novelists (including Irvine Welsh, Alan Warner and Duncan McLean), poets, playwrights, dancers, performers, composers, designers, choreographers, musicians, metal sculptors, pyro-technicians, DJs, trapeze artists and car mechanics.

The company normally stages 2 productions each year totalling approximately 15-30 performances, and tours to a variety of venues across the UK, Europe and New Zealand. The cast size can be anything from 2 to 12 actors. Recent productions include: *The Bridge* (large-scale outdoor show, with aerial choreography, live and pre-recorded film, pyrotechnics and performed in Scotland and France – with audiences of up to 10,000 per show); and *Running Girl* (large-scale indoor promenade production with a cast of 8, including a performer running throughout the show, moving film-screens and live music).

Casting procedures

Does not use freelance casting directors; actors may write requesting inclusion in the next round of auditions at any time. Will accept letters, emails, showreels, CVs and photographs from actors previously unknown to the company, but advises all applicants to do their research first and only to send details if they are sure that they are right for Boilerhouse's style of work.

Border Crossings

Chocolate Factory II, 4 Coburg Road, London N22 6RJ
tel 020-8829 8928 *fax* 020-8361 2308
email info@bordercrossings.org.uk
website www.bordercrossings.org.uk
Director Michael Walling

Production details

Established in 1995. International company working in theatre and combined arts that creates dynamic performances by fusing many forms of world theatre, dance and music. Stages 1 or 2 productions per year touring to up to 15 venues including arts centres and theatres. Roughly 4-9 actors used in each production.

Recent credits include: *Bullie's House* (Riverside Studios); *Orientations* (Oval House); and *Double Tongue* (UK tour).

Casting procedures

Casting breakdowns available via postal application with an sae. Welcomes letters (with CVs and photographs) from actors previously unknown to the company if sent by post, but not by email. Invitations to view individual actors' websites and showreels are accepted. Actively encourages applications from disabled actors and promotes the use of inclusive casting.

Borderline Theatre Co.

North Harbour Street, Ayr KA8 8AA
tel (01292) 281010 *fax* (01292) 263825
email enquiries@bordertheatre.co.uk
website www.bordertheatre.co.uk
Producer Edward Jackson

Production details

Founded in 1974, the company stages 2-3 productions each year with an average annual total of 60-90 performances. Each tour normally runs for 31 performances across 13 different venues. Venues include arts centres and theatres across Scotland. In general 4 actors work on each production. Recent productions include: *Tally's Blood*, *Women on the Verge of HRT* and *Angel's Share*.

Casting procedures

Does not use freelance casting directors. Currently releases casting breakdowns to agents, but may publish these on the website in future. Welcomes submissions (with CVs and photographs) from actors previously unknown to the company sent by post or email. Also accepts showreels.

Cahoots Theatre Company

11-15 Betterton Street, London WC2H 9BP
tel 020-7470 8812 *fax* 020-7379 0801
email denise@cahootstheatre.co.uk
Artistic Director Denise Silvey

Production details

Founded in 1999. Produces theatre, cabaret and CD recordings, as well as acting as a general management and press agent. (See also Denise Silvey Associates' entry under Agents). Stages 3-4 productions a year, with 100 performances over 15 venues (arts centres, theatres and cabaret venues) in London, Edinburgh and New York. Productions may have from 1 to 17 performers involved. Does not offer Equity-approved contracts. Recent credits include: *A Clockwork Orange*, *Rain Pryor in Concert*, and *The Translucent Frogs of Quuup*.

Casting procedures

Uses freelance casting directors. Also publishes casting breakdowns on the Equity JIS and *PCR*. Welcomes letters (but not emails) with CVs and photographs from individuals previously unknown to the company. Does not welcome showreels, but is happy to receive invitations to view actors' websites. Will consider applications from disabled actors to play characters with disabilities.

Cavalcade Theatre Company

57 Pelham Road, London SW19 1NW
tel 020-8540 3513 *fax* 020-8540 2243
Directors Graham Ashe, Kim Joyce, Carol Crowther
Touring Manager Colin Agate

Production details

Founded in 1972. Stages an average of 5 productions each year – an annual total of around 200 performances. Tours approximately 20 venues per year, including arts centres, theatres, and outdoor, educational and community venues throughout the UK and Ireland. Also performs at conferences and exhibitions and covers publicity and PR events. In general 8 actors work on each production. Recent productions include: *Alice in Wonderland*, *The Adventures of Brer Rabbit*, pantomimes, musicals and some small-scale plays.

Casting procedures

Does not use freelance casting directors. Sometimes holds general auditions; actors may write at any time to request inclusion. Casting breakdowns are available in *PCR*, *The Stage* and through agents. Welcomes submissions (with CVs and photographs) from actors previously unknown to the company if sent by post, but does not welcome email enquiries. Also accepts invitations to view individual actors' websites.

Channel Theatre Company & Chalkfoot Theatre Arts

36 Park Place, Margate CT9 1LE
tel (01843) 280077 *fax* (01843) 280088
email info@channel-theatre.co.uk
website www.channel-theatre.co.uk or www.chalkfoot.org.uk
Director Philip Dart *Outreach Director* Claudia Leaf
Administrator Eddie de Souza

Production details

Founded in 1980, Channel works in Theatre in Education, Health in Education and produces commissioned pieces on various scales. Stages 3-4 productions each year, averaging an annual total of about 150 performances. Tours to schools and community venues in the South East and South West of England. In general 3-4 actors work on each production. Recent productions include: 3 drug education programmes and a domestic violence project for young people aged 5-14.

The company's touring and outreach arm, Chalkfoot Theatre Arts, was founded in 2003. Funded by the Arts Council of England, it is committed to touring non-theatre venues and specialises in rural theatre. 2-3 productions are staged each year, totalling 75 performances at 60 venues. 3-5 actors are involved in each production; recent productions include: a new adaptation of Jane Austen's *Emma*; and *Life Rites!* (celebrating cultural diversity).

Casting procedures

Both companies cast in-house and neither holds general auditions. Casting breakdowns are available by postal application with sae. Will only accept invitations to view individual actors' websites when casting. Offers ITC/Equity approved contracts. Actively encouragees applications from disabled actors and promotes the use of inclusive casting.

Cherub Company London

9 Park Hill, London W5 2JS
tel 020-8723 4358 *fax* 020-8248 0318
email mgieleta@cherub.org.uk
website www.cherub.org.uk
Director Michael Gieleta *Producer* Rebecca Miller

Production details

Founded in 1973, Cherub stages an average of 3 productions a year, with 40 performances across 5 theatre venues in the South East region. Roughly 10 actors are employed for each production. Offers Equity approved contracts.

Casting procedures

Uses freelance casting directors; also holds general auditions from time to time. Casting breakdowns are available by sending the company an sae. Welcomes letters (with CVs and photographs) from actors previously unknown to the company, but does not welcome these by email. Happy to receive both showreels and invitations to view actors' websites. Actively encourages applications from disabled actors and promotes the use of inclusive casting.

Clean Break

2 Patshull Road, London NW5 2LB
tel 020-7482 8600 *fax* 020-7482 8611
email general@cleanbreak.org.uk
website www.cleanbreak.org.uk
Executive Director Lucy Perman *Administrative Producer* Helen Pringle

Production details

Clean Break was founded in 1979 by 2 women prisoners at HMP Askham Grange. The company commissions professional writers to produce new work looking at issues faced by women with experience of the criminal justice system. The company generally stages 1 production, presenting 35 performances each year. Tours to around 5 theatres and prisons across England and Scotland annually. The average cast size is 3-4. Recent productions include: *Compact Failure* by Jennifer Farmer (including Contact Theatre, Manchester; York Theatre Royal; the Arcola, London; Traverse 2, Edinburgh); and *Didn't Die* by Annie Caulfield (similar venues).

Casting procedures

Uses freelance casting directors but also holds general auditions in May/June. Casting breakdowns are available via the website, Equity Job Information Service, *PCR* and *The Stage*. Welcomes letters, CVs and photographs from actors, but prefers not to be contacted by email and does not accept unsolicited showreels. "Clean Break only employs women (section 5(2)(a) of the Race Relations Act and section 7(2)(a) of the Sex Discrimination Act apply). We also actively seek to work with artists with an offending background."

Close for Comfort Theatre Company

34 Boleyn Walk, Leatherhead, Surrey KT22 7HU
tel (01372) 378613
email close4comf@aol.com
website www.hometown.aol.com/close4comf
Director Janet Gill *Co-director* Glenn Johnson

Production details

Founded in 2001. "Takes theatre to living rooms across the country." Stages 3-4 productions each year, averaging an annual total of 30-40 performances in the same number of private homes in the South East, South West and the Midlands. 2 actors work on each production. Recent productions include: *Dossier: Ronald Ackerman in a House in Bristol*.

Casting procedures

Does not use freelance casting directors or hold general auditions.

Complicite

14 Anglers Lane, Kentish Town, London NW5 3DG
tel 020-7485 7700 *fax* 020-7485 7701
email email@complicite.org
website www.complicite.org
Artistic Director Simon McBurney *Producer* Judith Dimant *Education & Marketing* Natasha Freedman

Production details

Award-winning theatre company founded in 1983. Constantly evolving its ensemble of performers and collaborators. Work ranges from entirely devised pieces to theatrical adaptations and revivals of classic texts. On average presents 2 productions annually, and gives 50-100 performances during the course of the year. The average cast size is 7 but can be up to 18. Recent productions include: *The Elephant Vanishes* and *Measure for Measure*.

Casting procedures

Occasionally uses freelance casting directors. Welcomes letters (with CVs and photographs) sent by post rather than email. "We are always more inclined to meet actors previously unknown to us if they are familiar with our work (i.e. if they have seen a Complicite show or participated in an Open Workshop). Complicite's Education Department programmes up to 2 Open Workshop seasons for actors each year. Contact us to join the Open Workshop mailing list." Actively encourages applications from disabled actors and promotes the use of inclusive casting. Contracts vary: some are TMA/Equity approved; some (as in for *The Elephant Vanishes*) are non-Equity.

Comyns Carr and Tyger's Heart

18 St Ann's Terrace, London NW8 6PJ
tel 020-7586 5252 *fax* 020-7722 1945
email tygersheart@comynscarr.fsnet.co.uk
website www.comynscarr.co.uk
Artistic Director Melissa Holston *Associate Producer* Victoria Walker

Production details

Originally founded in 1995, Comyns Carr now includes a new division, Tyger's Hart, founded in 2003. Stages 1-4 productions each year, averaging an annual total of 40-70 performances. Tours up to 22 venues per year, including arts centres, theatres, and outdoor, educational and community venues throughout London and the South East. In general 5-8 actors work on each production. Recent productions include: *Fair Maid of the West* and *The Way of the World*.

Casting procedures

Uses freelance casting directors. Actors should only write to request inclusion when auditions have been announced. Casting breakdowns are available through Equity Job Information Service and *PCR*. Welcomes letters (with CVs and photographs) from actors previously unknown to the company, but not email submissions. Also accepts invitations to view individual actors' websites.

Concordance

Finborough Theatre, 118 Finborough Road, London SW10 9ED
tel 020-7244 7439 *fax* 020-7385 1853
email admin@concordance.org.uk
website www.concordance.org.uk

Production details

Concordance is a theatrical production company, founded by Neil McPherson in 1981, and is resident at the Finborough Theatre, London – see entry under *Fringe theatres* on page 173. The company presents new writing, revivals of neglected work and music theatre. Sometimes offers ITC/Equity contracts. Actively encourages applications from disabled actors and promotes the use of inclusive casting.

Cragrats Theatre

Cragrats Mill, Dunford Road, Holmfirth, West Yorkshire HD9 2AR
tel (01484) 686451 *fax* (01484) 686212
email info@cragrats.com
website www.cragrats.com
Director Mark Greenop *Head of Casting* Emma Adamson

Production details

Established in 1989. Cragrats is a theatrical communications company that use performance to inspire learning. It is a values-driven creative organisation, offering an immense variety of work in TIE, corporate training and in its in-house venue. 300+ productions per year are performed in educational venues, touring in the UK, France and the Middle East. Offers Equity approved contracts. Roughly 4 actors are used in each production.

Casting procedures

Casting breakdowns are available on the website, and in *PCR* and *The Stage*. Welcomes letters (with CVs and photographs) from actors previously unknown to the company, sent by post and email. Accepts invitations to view individual actors' websites and showreels. Actively encourages applications from disabled actors.

Creation Theatre Company

2nd Floor, Kennett House, 108-110 London Road, Headington, Oxford OX3 9AW
tel (01865) 761393 or *fax* (01865) 245745 (Box Office)
email enquiry@creationtheatre.co.uk
website www.creationtheatre.co.uk
Director David Parrish

Production details

Produces site-specific Shakespeare. Stages 2-5 productions annually in unusual, non-traditional theatre venues (e.g. open air shows in parks, factory spaces, and a spiegletent) and gives approximately 150 performances per year, mostly in Oxford. 8 actors work on each production. Recent productions include: *The Snow Queen* and *King Lear*

Casting procedures

Does not use freelance casting directors or hold general auditions. Casting breakdowns are available by postal application (with sae) and via *PCR* and *Castfax*. Welcomes letters and emails (with CVs and photographs) from actors previously unknown to the company at any time of year.

Dead Earnest Theatre

The Quadrant, 99 Parkway Avenue, Sheffield S9 4WG
tel 0114-227 0085 *fax* 0114-227 0089
email info@deadearnest.co.uk
website www.deadearnest.co.uk
Director Ashley Barnes *Drama Project Leader* Rachel Scott *Administrator* Daniel Ramsden

Production details

Founded in 1993, the company creates theatre pieces of varying length and for various audiences. Original productions tour regionally and nationally, with shorter performances being created for training or community empowerment. Characteristically, live music is used in these productions, which focus on social issues. 1 touring show and 4 shorter forum pieces are staged per year, with an average annual total of 12 touring and 20 forum productions. Touring productions perform to arts centres and theatres, while forum pieces are staged in educational and community venues. Tours mainly to Yorkshire and the North West, and less frequently to the East Midlands and South West. In general 3-5 actors work on each production. Recent productions include: *Stalingrad*, *Comfort*, and *The Puzzle Women*.

Casting procedures

Uses freelance casting directors. Sometimes holds general auditions. Welcomes postal or email submissions (with CVs and photographs) from actors previously unknown to the company. Applicants should live locally or aim to have a local base, since company resources do not extend to assistance with accommodation. Also accepts invitations to view individual actors' websites. The company often employs new actors for its short forum pieces. Those with musical skills are particularly favoured.

Eastern Angles Theatre Company

Sir John Mills Theatre, Gatacre Road, Ipswich IP1 2LQ
tel (01473) 218202 *fax* (01473) 384999
email info@easternangles.co.uk
website www.easternangles.co.uk
Director Ivan Cutting *General Manager* Jill Streatfield

Production details

Founded in 1982, the company tours theatre productions around East Anglia. New writing and a flavour of the region colour all of its original work. Stages 4-5 pieces each year, with an average annual total of 200 performances at 80 different venues. These include arts centres and theatres, educational and community venues, and site-specific locations. Tours mainly to East England but also nationally on occasion. In general 6 actors work on each production. Recent productions include: *Margaret Down Under, Another Three Sisters, The Edge of the Land* and *East Anglian Psychos*.

Casting procedures

Does not use freelance casting directors or hold general auditions. Casting breakdowns are not currently publicly available but may, in future, be posted on the website. Welcomes letters (with CVs and photographs but not saes); no email submissions please. Advises applicants to consult the website to get an idea of the sort of work the company produces. Applicants should only write once and should specify in their letter if they are local or native to the region.

English Touring Theatre

25 Short Street, London SE1 8LJ
tel 020-7450 1990 *fax* 020-7450 1991
email admin@englishtouringtheatre.co.uk
website www.englishtouringtheatre.co.uk
Director Stephen Unwin *Executive Director* Tim Highman *Marketing and Press Manager* Drew Cowerd

Production details

Founded in 1993. "An artistically led national touring company that aims to achieve the highest artistic standards in acting, directing, lighting and music." Stages 3 productions annually and gives approximately 120 performances per year in arts centres and theatres throughout England and Scotland. 4-15 actors are involved in each production. Recent productions include: *Romeo and Juliet*.

Casting procedures

Uses freelance casting directors. Welcomes submissions (with CVs and photographs) sent by post or email.

European Theatre Company

39 Oxford Avenue, London SW20 8LS
tel 020-8544 1994 *fax* 020-8544 1999
email admin@europeantheatre.co.uk
website www.europeantheatre.co.uk
Directors Adam Roberts, Jennie Graham

Production details

Founded in 1992, the company produces French-language theatre which tours the UK. Stages 3 or more productions a year, with around 250 performances in arts centres, theatres, schools and community venues. Normally employs 5 actors for each production.

Casting procedures

Casts in-house, and publishes its casting breakdowns via *PCR* and *SBS*. Welcomes letters (not emails) with CVs and photographs from French-speaking actors previously unknown to the company.

Forbidden Theatre Company

18 Rupert Street, London W1D 6DE
tel 0845-009 3084
email info@forbidden.org.uk
website www.forbidden.org.uk
Director Pilar Ortí

Production details

Physical and visual theatre company. Produces small-scale productions of adaptations of classics and devised work. Stages 1 production annually and gives approximately 40 performances per year. Tours 2 venues on average and performs in arts centres and theatre venues in London and Scotland. In general, 4-6 actors work on each production. Recent productions include: *Spell*, *Alice in Wonderland*, *Antigone* and *Freestyle Performances*.

Casting procedures

Does not use freelance casting directors. Sometimes holds general auditions. Actors can write at any time requesting inclusion. Welcomes letters (with CVs and photographs) but not email submissions. Advises that the company will only reply to actors if inviting them to audition. CVs are kept on file.

Forced Entertainment

The Workstation, 46 Shoreham Street, Sheffield S1 4SP
tel 0114-279 8977 *fax* 0114-221 2170
email fe@forcedentertainment.co.uk
website www.forced.co.uk
Artistic Director Tim Etchells *General Manager* Matt Burman *Administration/Education* Eileen Evans

Production details

Forced Entertainment comprises a group of artists who have been working together since 1984, producing new works in theatre and performance as well as projects in digital media, video and installation. Projects frequently explore and experiment with the 'rules' of theatre and with audience expectations. Tours across the UK and mainland Europe to mid-scale theatres, arts centres, studios and site-specific projects. A member of the ITC, it is regularly funded by the Arts Council England and Sheffield City Council. In general a

company of 6 actors works on each production. Aside from the permanent ensemble, the company involves artists from other disciplines, introducing fresh skills and ideas to support and develop their work. Recent productions include: *Bloody Mess*, *Erasure*, *Imaginary Evidence* and *So Small*.

Forkbeard Fantasy

PO Box 1241, Bristol BS99 2TG

Production details

Founded in 1974; an artist-led, multimedia film and performance company. Stages 1-2 productions and performs about 50 times per year. Tours to 10 venues both nationally and internationally on an annual basis. As this is an artist-led company, actors are only occasionally involved in productions. Performed recently at the Blackpool Puppet Festival, Warwick Arts Centre and The Lowry, Salford.

Casting procedures

Never holds general auditions. Advises actors that the company usually performs with artists who are already in the core team.

Foursight Theatre

Newhampton Arts Centre, Dunkley Street, Wolverhampton WV1 4AN
tel (01902) 714257 *fax* (01902) 428413
email foursight.theatre@boltblue.com
website www.foursight.theatre.boltblue.net
Artistic Director Naomi Cooke *Special Projects Coordinator* Frances Land *Administrator* Emma Beale

Production details

National touring theatre company. Emphasises the need for "total theatre" combining word, movement and music. Specialises in biographical plays about women in history and runs a strong Education programme. Stages 1 production annually in addition to its regional and education work. Performs at about 20 different venues during its national tour, including arts centres, theatres and educational venues. Cast size varies according to production needs. Recent productions include: *Hecuba*, *Agamemnon*, *Six Dead Queens & An Inflatable Henry*, and *Thatcher: The Musical*.

Casting procedures

Casting breakdowns are not publicly available. Actors are advised to keep an eye on the website for information posted prior to productions. Welcomes submissions (with CVs and photographs) by post and email. Invitations to view individual actors' websites are also accepted. Offers ITC/Equity approved contracts. Actively encourages applications from disabled actors and promotes the use of inclusive casting.

Frantic Theatre Company

32 Wood Lane, Falmouth TR11 4RF
tel (01326) 312985 *fax* (01326) 312985
email info@frantictheatre.com
website www.frantictheatre.com

Production details

Founded in 1990. Stages 2 productions annually with around 1500 performances in 1500 venues throughout the UK and Ireland every year. Venues include arts centres, village halls, theatres, outdoor venues, educational and community venues, private homes and hospitals. On average 4 actors work on each production. Recent productions include: *Can I Do You Now, Sir?* and *Don't Dilly Dally*.

Casting procedures

Holds general auditions. Actors should write in May and November to request inclusion. Casting breakdowns are available by postal application (with sae), Equity Job Information Service, *PCR* and advertisements in *The Stage*. Welcomes submissions (with CVs and photographs) by post or email. Showreels and invitations to view individual actors' websites are also accepted. Actors are advised not to telephone, and to send their details only when they have researched the company's very specific work and can explain their suitability.

Full Body & The Voice

Lawrence Batley Theatre, Queen's Street, Huddersfield HD1 2SP
tel (01484) 484441 *fax* (01484) 484443
email fullbody@lbt-uk.org
website www.fullbody.org.uk
Key contact Jon Palmer

Production details

Established in 2000. Production company exploring a range of projects that include actors with learning disabilities and promote inclusive working practices. Approximately 1 production per year tours to 10-15 venues, including arts centres and theatres in Yorkshire, the North West and internationally. Roughly 5-8 actors are used in each production.

Casting procedures

Occasionally uses freelance casting directors. Does not welcome unsolicited CVs. Actively encourages applications from disabled actors and promotes the use of inclusive casting. Offers Equity approved contracts.

Gagged Theatre

11 Wheatsheaf Court, Off Kendall Road, Colchester, Essex CO1 2BU
tel (01206) 525712
email gag@fsmail.net

website www.gaggedtheatre.com
Director Lucy Traube

Production details

A new writing company established in 2002 and funded by Arts Council England. The company stages 1-2 productions with approximately 35 performances each year. Has toured to theatres and arts centres across the Eastern region, London and the Edinburgh Festival. Cast sizes are normally somewhere between 1 and 6 actors. Recent productions include: *Shot* (Colchester Arts Centre, Hemel Old Town Hall and Ipswich's Pulse Festival); and *Again* (Mercury Theatre, Colchester, Edinburgh Festival and Upstairs at the Gatehouse, London).

Casting procedures

Uses freelance casting directors, but actors may write with CVs and photographs and their details will be kept on file until the company is next auditioning. Will also accept showreels, emails and invitations to view websites. The company runs a comprehensive workshop programme and therefore particularly welcomes actors with this kind of experience.

Galleon Theatre Company Ltd

Greenwich Playhouse, Greenwich Station Forecourt, 189 Greenwich High Road, London SE10 8JA
tel 020-8858 9256
email boxoffice@galleontheatre.co.uk
website www.galleontheatre.co.uk
Artistic Director Alice de Sousa *Theatre Director* Bruce Jamieson

Production details

Founded in 1990. Stages 12-14 productions annually and presents 282 performances at its own venue, Greenwich Playhouse. Has toured throughout Britain in previous years. On average 15 actors work on each production. Productions include: *A Doll's House*. See website for most recent information.

Casting procedures

Uses in-house casting director. Holds general auditions; actors should write to request inclusion when the company is casting for a specific project. Casting breakdowns are available via the website and through *PCR* and advertisements in *The Stage*. Welcomes letters (with CVs and photographs) but not email submissions. Showreels and invitations to view individual actors' websites are also accepted.

David Glass Ensemble

59 Brewer Street, Soho, London W1F 9UN
tel 020-7734 6030 *fax* 020-7734 0365
email matthew@davidglassensemble.com
website www.davidglassensemble.com

Production details

Founded in 1990, the company tours nationally and internationally, especially in South East Asia – recent productions have toured to Cambodia, Vietnam and Korea, as well as performing at the Portsmouth New Theatre Royal and the Battersea Arts Centre in London. Stages 2 productions a year, and tours to roughly 10 theatre venues, with a company of around 5 actors. Offers ITC/Equity approved contracts.

Casting procedures

Does not issue casting breakdowns. Welcomes CVs and photographs from actors whose work is not known to the company, and also welcomes showreels and invitations to view actors' websites. The company actively encourages applications from disabled actors and promotes the use of inclusive casting.

Graeae Theatre Company

LVS Resource Centre, 356 Holloway Road, London N7 6PA
tel 020-7700 2455 *fax* 020-7609 7324
email info@graeae.org
website www.graeae.org
Artistic Director Jenny Sealey

Production details

Founded in 1980. Produces theatre made by disabled people (actors, directors and other theatre practitioners) with physical and sensory impairments. Stages 3 productions annually and gives 70 performances at 50 venues each year. Venues include arts centres and theatres in England, Scotland, Wales and Ireland. 3-6 actors are involved in each production. Recent productions include: *On Blindness* (co-production with Frantic Assembly and Paines Plough); *George Dandin*; and *Bent*.

Also trains up to 12 disabled actors a year through its Missing Piece programme, in partnership with the London Metropolitan University. Lasting 9 months, and culminating in a London showcase, this aims to give a thorough grounding in performance training, with the expectation that most participants will go on either to further training or education in performing arts, or directly to work in the performing arts. While not yet a substitute for a 3-year drama school course, it is building links with drama schools such as ALRA, Arts Ed, and Rose Bruford.

Casting procedures

Sometimes holds general auditions. Welcomes postal or email submissions (with CVs and photographs) from actors with physical and sensory impairments. Also accepts showreels and invitations to view individual actors' websites. Offers ITC/Equity approved contracts.

Grassmarket Project

1 Harley Street, London W1G 9QD
tel 020-7307 8734
email info@grassmarketproject.org
website www.grassmarketproject.org
Artistic Director Jeremy Weller

Production details

Founded in 1989. Independent theatre company producing new work in theatres across Europe, USA and the UK. Stages 2 productions annually and gives 30-40 performances every year. On average, 5-6 actors work on each production. Recent productions include: *De Andre (The Others)*; *Fathers & Sons* (Betty Nansen Theatre, Copenhagen); *Bus Stops* (Glasgow); and *The Foolish Young Man* (Roundhouse Theatre, London).

Casting procedures

Productions are cast by freelance casting directors or the company's artistic director. Sometimes holds general auditions. Employs a mixture of trained and untrained actors. Welcomes letters (with CVs and photographs) by post or email. Showreels and invitations to view individual actors' websites are also accepted. Offers non-Equity contracts. Will consider applications from disabled actors to play characters with disabilities.

Grid Iron Theatre Company

85 East Claremont Street, Edinburgh EH7 4HU
Director Ben Harrison *Producer* Judith Doherty
General Manager Claire Robb

Production details

Founded in 1995. Produces new writing and site-specific theatre. Stages 1-3 productions annually and gives 20-50 performances every year. Performs in theatres, outdoor and site-specific venues in Scotland, England and Northern and Southern Ireland. 2-8 actors work on each production. Recent productions include: *Variety, Decky Does A Bronco* and *Those Eyes, That Mouth*.

Casting procedures

Sometimes holds general auditions. Actors may write requesting inclusion at any time throughout the year. Welcomes submissions (with CVs and photographs) sent by post and email. Showreels and invitations to view individual actors' websites are also accepted.

Handstand Productions

13 Hope Street, Liverpool L1 9BH
tel 0151-708 7441 *fax* 0151-709 3515
email info@handstand-uk.com
website www.handstand-uk.com
Director Han Duijvendak *Producer* Nicholas Stanley
Co-producer Lucy Dossor

Production details

Founded in 1993. Works across a broad range of artforms from live theatre to film and television projects. Theatre work has a strong actor-musician and international bias. Stages 1 production every 2 years with up to 140 performances each year at 1-15 venues. Venues include arts centres, theatres, and community venues in the UK, Netherlands and Greece. On average 5-15 actors work on each production. Recent productions include: *Sweet Charity* and *The Sofa*.

Casting procedures

Never holds general auditions. Casting breakdowns are available via the website, Equity Job Information Service, *PCR* and agents. Requests that actors do not submit anything to the company unless a specific casting requirement has been made available on the website and via the usual industry channels.

Highly Sprung Performance Company

49 Abercorn Road, Chapelfields, Coventry CV5 8EE
tel 020-7667 0141
email mail@sprunghq.fsnet.co.uk
website www.highlysprungperformance.co.uk
Artistic Director Sarah Hunt *Company Director* Mark Worth

Production details

Founded in 1999. Aims to create original and innovative performances exploring the relationship between dance, text and physical theatre. Also runs community and educational activities alongside productions. Stages 1 production annually with 25 performances every year. Tours 10-15 venues annually: these include arts centres, theatres, outdoor and educational venues in the West Midlands, London, Manchester and Edinburgh. On average 2-8 actors work on each production. Recent productions include: *Pretend I'm Not Here* and *More Than Kisses*.

Casting procedures

Holds general auditions. Actors should send CVs and photographs by post or email. These will be kept on file for future auditions. Casting breakdowns are available on the website, by postal application and via Equity Job information Service and advertisements in *The Stage*. Showreels and invitations to view individual actors' websites are also accepted.

Hijinx Theatre

Wales Millennium Centre, Bute Place, Cardiff CF10 5AL
tel 029-2030 0331 *fax* 029-2030 0332
email info@hijinx.org.uk
website www.hijinx.org.uk
Artistic Director Gaynor Lougher *Associate Director* Chris Morgan *Administrative Director* Val Hill

Production details

Founded in 1981, the company stages 2 productions on one-night stands across Wales and England, with an annual total of around 100 performances. In general, 1 show is aimed at the general public and 1 targets adults with learning disabilities. Writers are commissioned by the company, and all shows include a high level of music. On average 4 actors work on each production. Recent productions include: *Paul Robeson Knew My Father* (Sherman Theatre, Cardiff; Theatr Clwyd, Mold; some community venues); and *Into My Own* (touring day centres, gateway clubs and colleges).

Casting procedures

Shows are cast by the artistic director and/or associate director. Holds general auditions in December and April and welcomes letters, CVs and photographs from actors previously unknown to the company. Does not accept emails or showreels.

Historia Theatre Co.

8 Cloudesley Square, London N1 0HT
tel 020-7837 8005 *fax* 020-7278 4733
email kateprice@lineone.net
website www.historiatheatre.com
Artistic Director Catherine Price

Production details

Established in 1997. "Historia presents plays that have their source or inspiration in history." 1 production annually with 20-30 performances. Touring productions visit theatres, arts venues, National Trust houses and village halls around London and Warwickshire. (2005 was the company's first year of touring.) Roughly 10 actors are used in each production. Recent productions include: *Five Eleven or The Powder Treason* (tour); and *Evalina* (Pentameters Theatre). Offers non-Equity contracts although is a member of ITC.

Casting procedures

Does not use freelance casting directors or hold general auditions. Breakdowns are published via *PCR*, *SBS* and Equity's Job Information Service. Unsolicited approaches from actors are discouraged. "Watch *PCR/SBS/JIS* and apply accordingly." Will consider applications from disabled actors when casting for characters with disabilities.

Hoipolloi Theatre

Office F, Dale's Brewery, Gwydir Street, Cambridge CB1 2LJ
tel/fax (01223) 322748
email info@hoipolloi.org.uk
website www.hoipolloi.org.uk
Director Shôn Dale-Jones *Associate Director* Stephanie Müller *Production Manager* Richard Couldrey

Production details

Founded in 1994, the company creates visually and physically dynamic, imaginative and comic work which tours to small- and middle-scale theatres and arts centres throughout the UK. In 2005 the company worked in overseas locations such as the USA and Europe; it is also involved in educational work. Stages 1-2 productions annually, presenting 100 performances every year at 60-70 venues. On average 4-5 actors work on each production. Recent productions include: *My Uncle Arly*.

Casting procedures

Sometimes holds general auditions. Actors may write at any time requesting inclusion. Welcomes letters (with CVs and photographs) but not email submissions. Invitations to view individual actors' websites are also accepted. Advises actors approaching the company to have some knowledge of its work.

Horse and Bamboo Theatre

The Horse and Bamboo Centre, Waterfoot, Rossendale, Lancashire BB4 7HQ
tel (01706) 220241 *fax* (01706) 831166
email horse.bamboo@zen.co.uk
website www.horseandbamboo.org
Key personnel George Harris, Alison Duddle

Production details

Established in 1978. A visual touring theatre using masks, puppetry, video and movement in theatre. Produces approximately 3 productions per year, touring to 60 venues including arts centres and outdoor venues in the UK, Europe and the USA. Performers must have mask/puppetry or dance experience to a professional level.

Casting procedures

Welcomes letters (with CVs and photographs) from actors previously unknown to the company if sent by post, but not by email. Invitations to view individual actors' websites are also accepted. Will consider applications from disabled actors to play characters with disabilities.

Indigo Entertainments

Tynymynydd, Bryneglwys, Corwen, Denbighshire LL21 9NP
tel (01978) 790211 *fax* (01978) 790626
email info@indigoentertainments.com
website www.indigoentertainments.com
Director Emma Hands

Production details

Founded in 2000. Takes existing small-scale theatre productions, usually with a literary theme, and tours them around the UK and internationally. Stages 5-10

productions annually and gives 50 performances in 50 venues every year. These include arts centres, theatres, outdoor and educational venues, community venues and hotels all over the UK and in the Middle East and Far East. On average 1-3 actors work on each production. Recent productions include: *The Tale of Beatrix Potter, Dear Liar, Turn of the Screw, Testament of Youth*, and *Hic! The Entire History of Wine (Abridged)*.

Casting procedures

Does not welcome unsolicited CVs. Will accept showreels if they demonstrate productions of interest and are not just an actor's general showreel. Advises that the shows presented are usually intelligent, light, witty commercial pieces rather than experimental work. Offers non-Equity contracts.

Jasperian Theatre Company

29 Harvard Court, Honeybourne Road, London NW6 1HL
tel 020-7435 4246
email tony.jasper@blueyonder.co.uk
Artistic Director Tony Jasper *Production Directors* Ken Pickering, Peter Moreton, Harry Gostelow, Clare Davidson

Production details

Founded in 1992, JTC specialises in straight plays and revues that have a religious underpinning and/or deal with the human condition. The company is a member of ITC and casts all shows on artistic ability – not on any religious affiliation. Normally stages 3-5 productions each year with a total of around 100 performances. Tours to a variety of different venues including theatres, churches and private houses across the UK. In general 3-7 actors work on each production. Recent productions include: *John Wesley* (a fast-paced romp playing to more than 60 venues); *Goodnight Twentieth Century Goodnight* (dealing with suffrage, Nelson Mandela, and the Arms Race, among other things); and *Catherine Booth* (a study of the woman who founded the Salvation Army, but was also involved in women's rights and child protection).

Casting procedures

Uses freelance casting directors. Actors may write requesting inclusion in the next round of auditions at any time, but the beginning of February, June and September are normally good times. Casting breakdowns are available through *SBS* and CastNet. Prefers actors to send in their details by post but will accept the occasional email. Showreels are also accepted. Advises actors to read audition notices carefully and only come if suitable and available over the time period specified. A member of ITC, offers non-Equity contracts; however: "I also offer all accommodation and meals paid, and in some instances this is better than a basic Equity contract. I attempt to cast only Equity members. In 14 years, no-one has been owed money [by me]." Actively encourages applications from disabled actors and promotes the use of inclusive casting.

Kabosh

The Old Museum Arts Centre, 7 College Square North, Belfast BT1 6AR
tel 028-9024 3343 *fax* 028-9023 1130
email kabosh@dircon.co.uk/info@kabosh.net
website www.kabosh.net
Artistic Director Karl Wallace *Company Touring Manager* Azucena Avila

Production details

Founded in 1994. Produces innovative physical and visual theatre for local, national and international touring and site-specific work. Stages 2-4 productions annually and gives 56 performances during the course of the year. Tours to around 30 venues annually, including arts centres and theatres, and site-specific locations. In general 2-6 actors are involved in each production. Countries covered include Northern Ireland, Republic of Ireland, England (including London), Scotland, Wales, parts of Europe and North America. Recent productions include: *Rhinoceros* and *Todd*.

Casting procedures

Auditions are by invitation only. Actors should write requesting inclusion in July (for autumn productions) and November (for spring productions). Welcomes applications (with CVs and photographs) sent by post and email. Also accepts invitations to view individual actors' websites. Any actor known to the company is welcome to send a CV and headshot (which will be kept on file), and to notify the director of performances where their work may be seen. The director will endeavour to see new actors. Any unseen actor who has sent a CV will be notified of open auditions, should they arise.

Kaos Theatre

39-41 North Road, Islington, London N7 9DP
tel 020-7700 3885 *fax* 020-7700 3885
email admin@kaostheatre.com
website www.kaostheatre.com
Director Xavier Leret

Production details

Founded in 1994. Working ensemble of actors, musicians, designers and artists working with text-based theatre. Stages both new writing and contemporary adaptations of existing work (classic and modern). Receives funding from Arts Council England. Stages 1-2 productions annually and gives 80 performances during the course of the year. The company tours on average to 30 different venues

across the UK (excluding the Highlands and Islands) each year. Recent productions include: *Titus Andronicus* and *The Kaos Importance of Being Earnest*.

Casting procedures

In-house casting. Does not hold general auditions. Casting breakdowns are publicly available via the website, postal application (with sae), Equity Job Information Service, *PCR* and advertisements in *The Stage*. Sometimes welcomes letters (with CVs and photographs) but not email submissions. Accepts invitations to view individual actors' websites. Advises that the company mainly works with a regular ensemble of performers and only occasionally meets or auditions newcomers. Members of the ensemble come from a diverse training background (rarely straight from drama school). Does not welcome over-persistent enquiries; the company will make contact if interested in an applicant.

Kneehigh Theatre

14 Walsingham Place, Truro, Cornwall TR1 2RP
Artistic Director Emma Rice

Production details

Stages 3 productions annually and gives 130 performances during the course of the year. On average tours 15 venues annually. Performs in arts centres, theatres, outdoor and "out of the ordinary" indoor venues across the UK and internationally. Recent productions include: *The Bacchae*, *The Wooden Frock*, and *Tristan and Yseult*.

Casting procedures

Does not hold general auditions. Advises that the company works with a pool of performers, but is interested in meeting new actors – either by personal recommendation or by seeing their work. Offers ITC/Equity approved contracts. Actively encourages applications from disabled actors and promotes the use of inclusive casting.

Lip Service

The Comedy Suite, 116 Longford Road, Manchester M21 9NP
tel 0161-881 0061 *fax* 0161-881 0061
email info@lip-service.net
website www.lip-service.net
Joint Artistic Directors Sue Ryding, Maggie Fox

Production details

Founded in 1985. National touring company specialising in comedy and funded by Arts Council England. The company's artistic directors write and perform the majority of the work, which is co-produced with other theatres. Stages 1 production annually and gives 60 performances during the course of the year. 3 actors (including the artistic directors) are normally involved in each production. Tours have covered the North West, Manchester, Yorkshire, Scotland and East Anglia. Recent productions include: *Horror for Wimps*, *Very Little Women*, *The Importance of Being Earnest*, *Withering Looks* and *Hector's House*.

Casting procedures

Uses casting directors of co-producing venue. Does not hold general auditions. Actors should write requesting inclusion when extra performers are needed for a new production. Casting breakdowns are available direct from the co-producing theatre; details of these are available via the website. Welcomes invitations from actors to view their work, and information from actors familiar with the company's work. Offers TMA/Equity approved contracts. Rarely (or never) has the opportunity to cast disabled actors.

London Actors Theatre Co.

Unit 5a, Spaces Business Centre, Ingate Place, London SW8 3NS
tel 020-7978 2620 *fax* 020-7978 2631
email latchmere@fishers.org.uk

Production details

Founded in 1987 and normally stages 1-2 productions annually, employing 6-8 actors on non-Equity contracts. However, no productions have been staged in the past 3 years.

Casting procedures

Casting breakdowns are published in *PCR* or *The Stage*. Any approaches not relating to a specific breakdown are discouraged.

Mad Dogs and Englishmen

The Old Post Office, Green Lane, Quidenham, Norfolk NR16 2AP
tel (01953) 888499 *fax* (01953) 888499
email info@mad-dogs.org.uk
website www.mad-dogs.org.uk
Director Ann Courtney *Administration* Jacqui Merryweather

Production details

Founded in 1995. Theatre company based in Norfolk, whose policy is to provide well-balanced, entertaining and educational drama. Main areas of work are new writing, adaptations and classical work. Stages 2 productions annually with 70 performances during the course of the year, plus 30 workshops for schools. Tours to rural venues (churches, public houses) as well as arts centres, theatres, outdoor venues, educational venues, and community venues. On average 4-9 actors are involved in each production.

Recent productions include: *As You Like It* and *Outrageous Nonsense*.

Casting procedures

Sometimes holds general auditions. Audition criteria are published in *PCR* at the appropriate times of the year. Welcomes letters (with CVs and photographs) but not email submissions.

Magnetic North Theatre Productions

18 Brandon Terrace, Edinburgh EH3 5DZ
tel 0131-556 3299 *fax* 0131-556 3299
email mail@magneticnorth.org.uk
website www.magneticnorth.org.uk
Director Nicholas Bone

Production details

Founded in 1999. Commissions and produces new plays: 2 full productions and 1 film have been produced so far. Stages 1 production annually and gives 12 performances during the course of the year. Tours on average to 8 different venues in Scotland annually. About 5 actors are involved in each production. Recent productions include: *Word for Word* and *The Dream Train*.

Casting procedures

Sometimes holds general auditions. Actors should write to request inclusion when productions are announced on the website. Casting breakdowns are publicly available through the website, postal application (with sae) and *PCR*. Welcomes submissions (with CVs and photographs) sent by post or email. Also accepts invitations to view individual actors' websites. Advises that the company has a low turnover of productions and a small staff, and finds it difficult to respond to general enquiries about available work.

Guy Masterson Productions

The Bull Theatre, 68 High Street, Barnet EN5 5SJ
Director Guy Masterson

Production details

10-year-old producer of small- to mid-scale work. Stages 4-6 productions annually and gives 400 performances during the course of the year. Tours on average to 350 different national and international venues, including arts centres, theatres, and outdoor, educational and community venues. Recent productions include: *Twelve Angry Men*, *Animal Farm* and *Under Milk Wood*.

Casting procedures

Sometimes holds general auditions. Only works with actors seen on a previous occasion, and then only by invitation.

Meeting Ground Theatre Co.

4 Shirley Road, Nottingham NG3 5DA
tel 0115-962 3009
website www.meetingground.org.uk
Director Tanya Myers

Production details

At the heart of the company's artistic policy and vision is the theatrical exploration of what the company calls "the politics of the imagination". The controls on our imagination shape all our destinies. Their work is based on the belief that, by taking artistic work across barriers and frontiers, whether they be national, psychological, intellectual, cultural, spiritual or disciplinary, new sources of energy and creativity can be engendered.

Since 1985 Meeting Ground has been celebrating the meeting of artists from different disciplines and cultures. Building a strong international reputation for new production work of the highest innovative standards and qualities, the company has toured extensively throughout Germany, Poland, Italy and the UK also appearing at numerous festivals.

Drawing together people into extensive and intensive programmes of workshops and performances the company focuses on new work and uses developmental research as a central inspirational force.

Midland Actors Theatre (MAT)

25 Merrishaw Road, Northfield, Birmingham B31 3SL
tel 0121-608 7144 *fax* 0121-608 7144
email news@midlandactorstheatre.co.uk
website www.midlandactorstheatre.co.uk
Director David Allen *Secretary* Judith Aston

Production details

Founded in 1999. Produces classics and new work inspired by stories and legends from different cultures. Stages 3 productions annually and gives 90 performances during the course of the year. Tours on average to 75 different theatres, schools, and other venues in the West Midlands, East Midlands, and nationally each year. Around 4-5 actors are involved in each production. Recent productions include: *Macbeth*, *Prospero's Island*, and *The Children*.

Casting procedures

Sometimes holds general auditions. Actors should write requesting inclusion when auditions are advertised. Casting breakdowns are publicly available via Equity Job Information Service and *PCR*. Welcomes letters (with CVs and photographs) but does not welcome email enquiries. Advises that the company is primarily interested in actors who are Midlands-based. Offers ITC/Equity approved contracts. Actively encourages applications from disabled actors and promotes the use of inclusive casting.

Mu-Lan Theatre Company

The Albany, Douglas Way, London SE8 4AG
tel 020-8694 0557 *fax* 020-8694 0618
email mailbox@mu-lan.org
website www.mu-lan.org
Director Paul Courtenay

Production details

Founded in 1988. Stages 1 production annually and gives 30 performances during the course of the year. Tours have covered the North West, South and South West England. About 8 actors are involved in each production. Recent productions include: *Sun is Shining, Romeo and Juliet* and *Takeaway*.

Casting procedures

Uses freelance casting directors. Does not hold general auditions. Casting breakdowns are publicly available via *PCR*. Welcomes submissions (with CVs and photographs) sent by post or email. Also accepts invitations to view individual actors' websites.

Muzikansky

The Forum, Fonthill, The Common, Tunbridge Wells TN4 8YU
tel 01892 542 260 *fax* 01892 542 260
email admin@mzky.co.uk
website www.mzky.co.uk
Artistic Director Nicolette Kay

Production details

Established 1992. One production staged annually, with 20 to 30 performances in arts centres, theatres and fringe venues, mainly in South East and London. Recent productions include *Seed* which toured to Margate Theatre Royal, Oxford's Old Fire Station and The Finborough, London. "Productions occur infrequently."

Casting procedures

Casting breakdown available via Equity Job Information Service and *PCR*. Welcomes letters but not showreels or invitations to view individual websites. The company will consider applications from disabled actors and promotes the use of inclusive casting.

NITRO

6 Brewery Road, London N7 9NH
tel 020-7609 1331 *fax* 020-7609 1221
email info@nitro.co.uk
Artistic Director Felix Cross *Executive Producer* Matthew Jones *Administrator* Neena Agarwal

Production details

Founded in 1978; formerly known as Black Theatre Co-operative Ltd. National touring theatre company that generates and produces contemporary black musical theatre. First established to provide training for black writers, directors and artists. Aims to explore ways of using black music as a means of attracting new audiences to theatre. Stages 1-2 productions annually and gives 1-2 performances during the course of the year. Recent productions include: *Nitrobeat* and *A Nitro at the Opera*.

Casting procedures

Sometimes uses agents when casting. Also holds general auditions; actors should write at the start of the year to request inclusion. Welcomes submissions (with CVs and photographs) sent by post or email. Accepts invitations to view individual actors' websites. Advises that the company keeps an up-to-date catalogue of black actors and would particularly welcome CVs from actors of different ethnic backgrounds. Offers TMA/Equity approved contracts. Actively encourages applications from disabled actors and promotes the use of inclusive casting.

No Limits Theatre

Dundas Street, Monkwearmouth, Sunderland SR6 0AY
tel (0191) 565 3013 *fax* (0191) 565 3015
email info@nolimitstheatre.org.uk
website www.nolimitstheatre.org.uk
Artistic Director/Chief Executive Janet Nettleton
Technical Director Alan Parker

Production details

Founded in 1995, No Limits is a touring theatre company that works with adults with and without learning disabilities. Aims to produce high-quality, devised work that challenges traditional perceptions of theatre and disability, staging 1 production in 20 different venues across the UK each year. It also has a strong commitment to outreach and development work. In general 5-8 actors work on each production. Recent productions include: *I Catch Your Breath* (The Lowry, Manchester); *Silver Street* (The Maltings, Berwick); *Wall of Whispers* (Blackfriars, Boston).

Casting procedures

Welcomes letters, CVs and photographs from actors previously unknown to the company, but does not accept emails or unsolicited showreels. Advises that the company already has a core acting team but often takes on new actors in workshop training sessions.

NTC Touring Theatre Company

The Playhouse, Bondgate Without, Alnwick, Northumberland NE66 1PQ
tel (01665) 602586 *fax* (01665) 605837
email admin@ntc-touringtheatre.co.uk
website www.ntc-touringtheatre.co.uk
Director Gillian Hambleton *General Manager* Anna Flood *Tour Administrator* Hilary Burns

Production details

Founded in 1978 as Northumberland Theatre Company. Small-scale touring theatre company performing at village halls, small theatres and community venues in predominantly rural areas. Main areas of work are new writing and ensemble physical theatre pieces. Stages 3-4 productions annually and gives more than 120 performances during the course of the year. Tours on average to 120 different venues nationally. 5 actors are usually involved in each production. Recent productions include: *Bedazzled*, *Great Expectations* and *Alex, The Warrior & The Winter Star*.

Casting procedures

Sometimes holds general auditions for locally based actors (best time to write is early June or September), but most casting is done through agents via *SBS*. Casting breakdowns are available on request via postal application (with sae) and on the website. Welcomes submissions (with CVs and photographs) sent by post. Also accepts invitations to view individual actors' performances and will always reply to individual actors. Particularly interested in locally based actors or actors with local origins, and will keep details on file for future reference unless requested to do otherwise. Offers ITC/Equity approved contracts. Actively encourages applications from disabled actors and promotes the use of inclusive casting.

The Okai Collier Company

103 Lexington Building, The Bow Quarter, Fairfield Road, London E3 2UH
tel 020-8983 4858 *fax* 020-8983 0858
email info@okaicollier.co.uk
website www.okaicollier.co.uk
Artistic Director Omar F Okai

Production details

The Okai Collier Company was formed in 1994 by artistic director Omar F Okai and producer Simon James Collier to explore and push the boundaries of everyday ideas, opinions and opportunities in the creative arts: music, theatre, dance, painting and the written word. Using a variety of media including IT, the company aims to break down contemporary social barriers and encourage new talent by developing a range of projects in this field. These projects include award-winning theatrical productions, opera, creative writing with young people, exhibitions for new artists and community arts projects, as well as its innovative publishing division. Okai Collier is committed to maintaining a balanced portfolio of work, divided between the commercial and charitable spheres and drawing on a diverse range of people and disciplines.

Out of Joint

7 Thane Works, Thane Villas, London N7 7PH
tel 020-7609 0207 *fax* 020-7609 0203
email ojo@outofjoint.co.uk
website www.outofjoint.co.uk
Director Max Stafford-Clark *Administrator and Education Manager* Natasha Ockrent *Producer* Graham Cowley

Production details

Stages 2 productions annually with approximately 230 performances during the course of the year. Tours both nationally and internationally playing to around 12-15 arts centres and theatres each year. Recent productions include: *Duck, The Permanent Way, Macbeth* and *Talking to Terrorists.*

Casting procedures

Welcomes letters (with CVs and photographs) but not email submissions. Also accepts performance notices from individual actors. Offers Equity approved contracts. Will consider applications from disabled actors to play characters with disabilities.

Ovation Productions

Upstairs at The Gatehouse, Highgate, London N6 4BD
tel 020-8340 4256
website www.ovationtheatres.com
Director John Plews *Casting Director* Katie Plews

Production details

Founded in 1985. Owns and operates Upstairs at the Gatehouse, a fringe theatre in North London (see entry under *Fringe theatres* on page 172). Recent productions include: *Little Shop of Horrors, Jeffrey Bernard is Unwell* and *Rough Crossing.*

Casting details

Casting breakdowns are publicly available via *PCR* and advertisements in *The Stage.* Welcomes letters (with CVs and photographs) but not email submissions. "We are always looking for actor-musicians. Always check to see whether there is a casting coming up." Offers non-Equity contracts. Will consider applications from disabled actors to play characters with disabilities.

The Oxford Shakespeare Company

3 Gunter Grove, London SW10 0UN
tel 020-7351 5417
email info@oxfordshakespearecompany.co.uk
website www.oxfordshakespeare.company.co.uk
Directors Kevin Hosier, Charlotte Windmill, Nick Green

Production details

Founded in 2001. Took over from Bold and Saucy (established in 1992), staging Shakespeare plays in Wadham College Gardens, Oxford. Also has a residency at North Garden, Lincoln's Inn, London. Stages 3 productions with 90-100 performances during the course of the year. 9-10 actors are involved in each production. Tours have reached Oxford, London and Basingstoke. Recent productions include: *Merry Wives of Windsor* and *Macbeth.*

Casting procedures

Actors requesting inclusion should write in March or April. Casting breakdowns are released to agents and are available via *PCR.* Welcomes letters (with CVs and photographs) but not email submissions. Actors applying should be able to demonstrate experience of Shakespeare and the rigours of open-air performing.

Oxford Stage Company

Chertsey Chambers, 12 Mercer Street, London WC2H 9QD
tel 020-7438 9940 *fax* 020-7438 9941
email info@oxfordststage.co.uk
website www.oxfordstage.co.uk
Artistic Director Rupert Goold *Key contact* Henny Finch

Production details

Established in 1974. National touring theatre company dedicated to new ways of making theatre by exploring revolutionary writers and practitioners of the past, present and future. Stages 4-6 annually performing 24-32 weeks of the year. Touring nationally to Arts Centres and Theatres. Recent productions include *The Quare Fellow* (Tricycle), *Rookery Nook* (UK Tour) and *Men Should Weep* (UK Tour).

Casting procedures

Accepts submissions (with CVs and photographs) from actors previously unknown to them if sent by post and email. Invitations to view individual actor's website and showreels are also accepted. Offers TMA/Equity approved contracts. Actively encourages applications from disabled actors and promotes the use of inclusive casting.

Oxfordshire Touring Theatre Co

The Annex, SS Mary & John School, Meadow Lane, Oxford
tel 01865-249444
website www.ottc.org.uk
Artistic Director Brendan Murray *General Manager* Jenny Roberts

Production details

Rural touring theatre company established in 1980, taking "big theatre to small spaces". Mounts three productions a year, with 120 performances over 80 venues – arts centres, theatres and community venues. Tours Oxfordshire, Leicestershire, Nottinghamshire, Worcestershire, Buckinghamshire and Berkshire. An average of 4 actors are involved in each production, and the company offers Equity approved contracts. Recent productions include *Beauty & The Beast, People are Living There, Housewives' Choice* (tour of residential homes and day centres), and a bi-lingual (English and British Sign Language) production of *Under Milk Wood*.

Casting procedures

Casts in-house and only occasionally holds general auditions. Casting breakdowns are published in *PCR* and *SBS*. The company does not welcome unsolicited submissions from individuals at other times. Actively encourages applications from disabled actors and promotes the use of inclusive casting.

Paines Plough

4th Floor, 43 Aldwych, London WC2B 4DN
tel 020-7240 4533 *fax* 020-7240 4534
email office@painesplough.com
website www.painesplough.com
Artistic Director Roxanna Silbert *Associate Director* Indhu Rubasingham *Assistant Director* George Perrin *Projects Manager* Susannah Matthews *Administrative Assistant* Helen Poole

Production details

Founded in 1974, the company is dedicated to producing new writing. Stages 3-4 productions annually and gives 100 performances during the course of the year. Tours to 25 different arts centres and theatres in London, the South Coast, Yorkshire, Scotland, and the North annually. Recent productions include: *The Drowned World* and *The Straits*.

Casting procedures

Sometimes holds general auditions. Advises that the company cannot accept unsolicited CVs or photographs as it has no facility to store such information.

Pentabus

Bromfield, Ludlow, Shropshire SY8 2JU
tel (01584) 856564 *fax* (01584) 856254
email john@pentabus.co.uk
website www.pentabus.co.uk
Development Director John Moreton *Artistic Director* Theresa Heskins (until Dec 2006)

Production details

Founded in 1974, Pentabus is a national touring company focused on the development and production of new writing. Stages 1-2 productions

annually and gives 20-60 performances during the course of the year. In general 5 actors are involved in each production. Tours annually to about 10 different arts centres, theatres and outdoor venues. Recent productions include: *Silent Engine* by Julian Garner; *Precious Bane* by Bryony Lavery. Actors are also used in writing development workshops as well as in productions.

Casting procedures

Occasionally uses freelance casting directors. Casting breakdowns are available via Equity Job Information Service, *PCR* and the website. Welcomes letters (with CVs and photographs) but not email submissions.

Playbox Theatre (Generator)

The Dream Factory, Shelly Avenue, Warwick CV34 6LE
tel 01926-419 555 *fax* 01926-411 429
email stewart@playboxtheatre.com
website www.playboxtheatre.com
Artistic Director Stewart McGill *Directors* Emily Quash, Mary King

Production details

Established in 1986, Generator is the professional acting company of Playbox Theatre, reworking classic drama for contemporary audiences. 2 productions staged annually touring nationally to arts centres, theatres, outdoor venues and educational venues. Based in Warwick. Up to 12 actors used in each production. Offers Equity approved contracts. Recent productions include *A Doll's House, Henry VI – The Wars of the Roses*.

Casting procedures

Accepts submissions (with CVs and photographs) from actors previously unknown to them if sent by post or by email. Actively encourages applications from disabled actors and promotes the use of inclusive casting.

Prime Productions

54 Hermiston Village, Currie, Midlothian EH14 4AQ
tel/fax 0131-449 4055
email mheller@primeproductions.co.uk
website www.primeproductions.co.uk
Artistic Director Martin Heller

Production details

Founded in 1985, operates small-scale touring of mainstream drama throughout Scotland, project funded by Scottish Arts Council. One production is staged each year, touring around 30 venues – arts centres, theatres, educational and community venues. Between 4 and 10 actors are involved in each production. Recent credits include *Further than the Furthest Thing, Romeo & Juliet, Mary Queen of Scots Got Her Head Chopped Off, Sunset Song*.

Casting procedures

Casts in-house. Casting breakdowns are not publicly available, and the company does not welcome unsolicited approaches from actors, although they are happy to receive invitations to view individuals' websites. "We stage productions with very specific casting requirements which we seek at the time."

Primecut Productions

285a Ormerth Road, Belfast BT7 3GG
tel 028-90645101 *fax* 028-90645101
email info@primecutproductions.co.uk
website www.primecutproductions.co.uk

Production details

'Primecut is an independent touring company based in Belfast bringing the best of contemporary international playwrights to Irish audiences'. Recent productions include a double bill of *The Mercy Seat* and *Ashes to Ashes* at the Belfast Lyric, and touring productions of Caryl Churchill's *A Number* and Owen McCaffery's *Cold Comfort*. The company stages 2-3 productions per year and tour to 10-15 venues across Northern and Southern Ireland.

Casting procedures

The company does not publish casting breakdowns, but welcomes CVs and photographs from individual actors whose work is previously unknown to them and welcomes invitations to view actor's websites. The company will consider applications from disabled actors when casting for characters with disabilities. Offers ITC/Equity approved contracts.

Proteus Theatre Co

Queen Mary's College, Cliddesden Road, Basingstoke, Hants RG21 3HF
tel 01256-354 541 *fax* 01256-350 186
email info@proteustheatre.com
website www.proteustheatre.com
Artistic Director Mary Swan

Production details

Established in 1981. Touring theatre company operating in the South. Stages 2-3 productions annually touring to 80 venues including arts centres, theatres, outdoor venues, educational and community venues and churches. Recent credits include *Peter Pan* and *Whatever Happened to Bette and Joan?*

Casting procedures

Casting breakdowns available via the website, Equity Job Information service and *PCR*. Does not welcome unsolicited CVs. Actively encourage applications from disabled actors and promote the use of inclusive casting. Offers ITC/Equity approved contracts.

Purple Fish Productions

197 Goldhawk Road, London W12 8EP
tel (07976) 809693
email info@purplefishproductions.co.uk
website www.purplefishproductions.co.uk
Directors Michelle Seton, Luan de Burgh

Production details

Founded in 2001. Aims to produce both established work and exciting devised pieces for adults and children. Michelle Seton and Luan de Burgh both trained in London and at Le Coq in Paris. Stages 3 productions with 75 performances during the course of the year. Tours to 20 different arts centres, theatres, educational and community venues annually. Tours have covered Greater London, Ireland and Canada. In general 2 actors are involved in each production. Recent productions include: *Told by a Dodo* and *The Two of Us*.

Casting procedures

Casting breakdowns are available via *PCR* and the website. Welcomes letters (with CVs and photographs) but not email submissions. Actors should write only when the company advertises. Invitations to view individual actors' websites are also accepted.

Pursued by a Bear

The Maltings, Bridge Square, Farnham, Surrey GU9 7QR
email pbab@pbab.org
Director Stuart Mullins

Production details

Theatre company touring new writing across the UK. Stages 2 productions annually and gives 60 performances during the course of the year. Tours to around 10 different arts centres, theatres, educational and community venues each year. Tours have covered the East, North East, South East, South West and London. In general 2 actors are involved in each production. Recent productions include: *Double Helix*, *You Don't Kiss* and *All Fall Away*.

Casting procedures

Welcomes submissions (with CVs and photographs) sent by post or email.

Raised Eyebrow Theatre Company

Low Hall Cottage, Carr Lane, Brompton, Scarborough YO13 9DH
tel/fax (01723) 850538
email admin@raisedeyebrow.co.uk
website www.raisedeyebrow.co.uk
Artistic Director Lizi Patch *Associate Director* Jon Stokes

Production details

A community and TIE company staging 2-3 productions each year and presenting approximately 220 performances in schools and community venues across England. The company also runs youth theatres and workshops. In general 5 actors work on each production. Recent productions include: *Strings* (which has toured to more than 70 schools each year since 2000); *Best Before* (Etcetera Theatre, London); *Lab Rats* (Memorial Hall, Pickering Youth Theatre).

Casting procedures

Casting is done in-house and with the help of freelance casting directors. Casting breakdowns are available by postal application (with sae), and in *PCR* and *The Stage*. Welcomes letters and emails (with professional CVs and proper 10x8 photographs) from actors previously unknown to the company. Will also accept showreels and emails. Advises that professional applications will be given priority over photocopies, passport photos and holiday snaps.

The Red Room

Cabin E, Clarendon Buildings, Ronalds Road, London N5 1XJ
email info@theredroom.org.uk
website www.theredroom.org.uk
Director Lisa Goldman *Administrator* Claire Stanley

Production details

Founded in 1995. Produces new work which 'frees the imagination against the status quo'. Develops new plays from concept to production. Engages in cultural activism, and established Artists against the War in 2001. Stages 1-2 productions annually and gives 25-50 performances during the course of the year. Tours to 12 different theatres in international and national locations. In general, fewer than 5 actors are involved in each production. Recent productions include: *Animal*, *The Bogus Woman*, *Stitching*, *Going Public* and *Hoxton Story*.

Casting procedures

Accepts letters (with CVs and photographs) but 'we are too small and busy to respond to other forms of enquiry' such as telephone calls and emails. Offers ITC/Equity approved contracts. Actively encourages applications from disabled actors and promotes the use of inclusive casting.

Rejects Revenge Theatre Company

The Annexe, 15 Hope Street, Liverpool L1 9BH
tel 0151-708 8480 *fax* 0151-708 8480
email rejects.revenge@virgin.net
website www.rejectsrevenge.com
Director Ann Farrar *Administrator* Adrian Watts

Production details

Founded in 1990. Tours physical comedy to small- and mid-scale venues in the UK and abroad. Stages 1-3 productions annually with 60-90 performances during the course of the year. Tours to 50-70 different arts centres, theatres, educational and community venues across the UK each year. In general 3-4 actors are involved in each production. Recent productions include: *Peasouper* and *Bicycle Bridge*.

Casting procedures

Uses freelance casting directors. Sometimes holds general auditions. Casting breakdowns are available via Equity Job Information Service and the website. Welcomes letters (with CVs and photographs) but not email submissions. Invitations to view individual actors' websites are also accepted.

Richmond Productions

47 Moor Mead Road, St Margaret's, Twickenham TW1 1JS
Director Alister Cameron

Production details

Founded in 1993. International touring company producing small-cast comedies. Stages 2 productions annually. Tours to hotels in the Middle East and Eastern Europe. Offers non-Equity contracts. Rarely (or never) has the opportunity to cast disabled actors.

Casting procedures

Advises that the company only uses actors already known to them.

Rocket Theatre

9a Niederwald Road, Sydenham, London SE26 4AD
tel 020-8291 5545 *mobile* (07788) 723570
email martin@rockettheatre.co.uk
website www.rockettheatre.co.uk
Director Martin Harris

Production details

Founded in 1995, the company began life in Manchester, touring predominantly in the North with regional premières of work recently staged by some of London's new-writing venues (particularly the Royal Court and the Bush). Has also produced some completely new plays. Having recently relocated to London, the company is now looking at several projects for the future, including: *National Theatre of Shorts* – due to launch throughout the UK in 2007. Past productions include: *I Licked a Slag's Deodorant* by Jim Cartwright (Contact Theatre, Manchester; Chester Gateway; Dukes, Lancaster; Bolton Octagon); and *Howie the Rookie* by Mark O'Rowe (Library Theatre, Manchester; Stamwix Arts Theatre, Carlisle).

Casting procedures

Casting breakdowns are usually available on the Rocket website and through various industry casting resources. Welcomes letters, CVs and photographs at any time, which will be kept on file and looked at when casting. Applications by email will not be accepted.

SCAMP

44 Church Lane, Arlesey, Bedfordshire SG15 6UX
tel 01462-734 843
email admin@scamptheatre.com
website www.scamptheatre.com
Directors Jennifer Sutherland, Louise Callow

Production details

Established in 2003. 2/3 productions staged annually. 150 performances per year. Touring to 75 venues including arts centres and theatres. 1 to 4 actors involved in each production. Offers Equity approved contracts negotiated through the ITC. Recent productions include *Private Peaceful* (UK Tour), *Screw Machine/Eye Candy* (Edinburgh Fringe)

Casting procedures

Casting breakdowns available via website and *PCR*. Accepts submissions (with CVs and photographs) from actors previously unknown to them if sent by post, but not by email. Actively encourages applications from disabled actors and promotes the use of inclusive casting.

Scarlet Theatre

Studio 4, The Bull, 68 High Street, Barnet EN5 5SJ
tel 020-8441 9779 *fax* 020-8447 0075
email admin@scarlettheatre.co.uk
website www.scarlettheatre.co.uk
Director Grainne Byrne

Production details

A touring theatre company founded in 1982 which stages between 2 and 6 productions each year. On average the company tours to 10 venues across the UK, Ireland and the rest of Europe annually, with anywhere between 2-10 actors working on each production. Recent productions include: *The Chair Women* (Riverside Studios and Traverse Theatre); *The Wedding* (Southwark Playhouse).

Casting procedures

Casting is done in-house and actors are welcome to write or email with their CVs and photographs. The company prefers not to receive showreels unless it has requested them.

Sgript Cymru

Chapter, Market Road, Canton, Cardiff CF5 1QE
tel 029-2023 6650

email sgriptcymru@sgriptcymru.com
website www.sgriptcymru.com
Director Simon Harris *Administrative Director* Mai Jones

Production details

Founded in 2000 and funded by the Arts Council of Wales, Sgript Cymru is a strategic new writing theatre company. Stages 3 productions annually and gives 75 performances during the course of the year. Tours to 25 different arts centres, theatres, and community venues in Wales, Scotland, London and the North West. In general 5 actors are involved in each production. Recent productions include: *Crossings* by Clare Duffy; *The Life of Ryan... and Ronnie* by Meic Povey.

Casting procedures

Uses freelance casting directors. Welcomes letters (with CVs and photographs) but not email submissions. Offers ITC/Equity approved contracts. Will consider applications from disabled actors to play characters with disabilities.

Shakespeare at The Tobacco Factory

Raleigh Road, Southville, Bristol BS3 1TF
tel 0117-936 3054
email office@sattf.org.uk
website www.sattf.ogr.uk
Artistic Director Andrew Hilton *Administrator* Alix Sherman

Production details

Established in 2000. 2 productions staged annually giving 80 performances. Up to 18 actors used in each production. Performances in Bristol and London. Recent productions include *Macbeth* and *The Changeling* performed at The Pit, Barbican.

Casting procedures

Casting breakdowns available via the website. Accepts submissions (with CVs and photographs) from actors previously unknown to them if sent by post and via email. Invitations to view individual actors' websites are also accepted. Actors writing to request inclusion should make contact in Oct/Nov. Rarely has the opportunity to cast disabled actors.

Shared Experience

The Soho Laundry, 9 Dufour's Place, London W1F 7SJ
tel 020-7434 9248 *fax* 020-7287 8763
email admin@sharedexperience.org.uk
website www.sharedexperience.org.uk
Joint Artistic Directors Nancy Meckler, Polly Teale
Administrative Producer Jon Harris

Production details

An award-winning theatre company founded during the 1970s, Shared Experience stages 2-3 productions annually and tours to different arts centres and theatres in the UK and abroad. In general 6-10 actors are involved in each production. Recent productions include: *After Mrs Rochester, Madame Bovary: Breakfast with Emma* and *A Passage to India.*

Casting procedures

Uses freelance casting directors. Advises that actors should contact Liz Holmes by phone to enquire about the current casting director. "Please do not send unsolicited mail." Offers TMA/Equity approved contracts. Actively encourages applications from disabled actors and promotes the use of inclusive casting.

Sphinx Theatre Company

25 Short Street, London SE1 8LJ
tel 020-7401 9993 *fax* 020-7401 9995
email admin@sphinxtheatre.co.uk
website www.sphinxtheatre.co.uk
Director Sue Parrish *Administrator* Bonnie Mitchell
General Manager Susannah Kraft-Levene

Production details

Established 30 years ago, the company specialises in writing and directing by women. Stages 1-2 productions annually and gives 40 performances in the course of the year. Recent productions include: *The Little Mermaid, As You Like It* and *Wedding Story.*

Casting procedures

Occasionally employs a casting director. Casting breakdowns are available via email, postal application, *SBS* and *PCR*. Welcomes letters (with CVs and photographs). Offers Equity approved contracts. Will consider applications from disabled actors to play characters with disabilities.

Suspect Culture

CCA, 350 Sauchiehall Street, Glasgow G2 3TD
tel (0141) 332 9775 *fax* (0141) 332 8823
email info@suspectculture.com
website www.suspectculture.com
Director Graham Eatough *Administrative Producer* Purni Morell

Production details

Suspect Culture was formed in 1990 by Graham Eatough, David Greig and Nick Powell. Early productions include *One Way Street* (1995), *Airport* (1996), *Timeless* (1997) and *Mainstream* (1999). The company is based in Glasgow and tours 1-2 productions throughout Scotland and internationally each year. Generally uses 2-6 actors on each production. Recent productions include: *8000m* (Tramway, Glasgow); *One-Two* (Traverse, Edinburgh; Contact Theatre, Manchester; MAC, Birmingham; Tron, Glasgow; Byre Theatre, St

Andrews; Lemon Tree, Northampton; Tolbooth, Stirling and Paisley Arts Centres).

Casting procedures

Suspect Culture does not hold formal auditions, but rather open workshops which are by invitation. This gives the company a chance to meet practitioners it hasn't worked with before (and vice versa). The company welcomes letters, emails, showreels, invitations to view actors' websites, CVs and photographs from actors – but asks all applicants to gain a full understanding of Suspect's particular working methods before writing. Only rarely employs actors who have not seen at least some of Suspect's work.

TABS Productions

57 Chamberlain Place, London E17 6AZ
tel 020-8527 9266
email adrianmljames@aol.com
website www.tabsproductions.co.uk
Directors Adrian Lloyd-James, Karen Henson

Production details

Founded 15 years ago, the company stages approximately 6 productions each year totalling around 300 performances. It has produced No 1 and middle-scale tours and has co-produced with repertory theatre companies. Generally tours to about 45 different arts centres, theatres and outdoor venues across the UK annually. The average cast size is 4-8 actors.

Casting procedures

Welcomes letters, CVs and photographs from actors previously unknown to the company, but does not accept emails or showreels. Actors should only write when a job has been advertised to agents through *SBS*. Occasionally offers Equity approved contracts. Rarely (or never) has the opportunity to cast disabled actors.

Talawa Theatre Co Ltd

3rd Floor, 23-25 Great Sutton Street, London EC1V ODN
tel 020-7251 6644 *fax* 020-7251 5956
email hq@talawa.com
website www.talawa.com
Director Patricia Cumper *Interim CEO* Nadia Stern

Production details

Founded in 1986, the company aims to use black political experience and culture to further inform, enrich and enlighten modern British theatre. Stages up to 4 productions annually with an average of 3 or more actors involved in each production. Seeks to develop new writing and runs a summer programme for 16-25 year-olds annually. Recent productions include: *Urban Afro Saxons, Blest Be The Tie, Blues for Mr Charlie* and *High Heel Parrotfish*.

Casting procedures

Welcomes submissions (with CVs and photographs) sent by post or email. Offers ITC/Equity contracts. Actively encourages applications from disabled actors and promotes the use of inclusive casting.

Tamasha Theatre Company

Unit 220 Great Guildford Business Square, 30 Great Guildford Street, London SE1 0HS
tel 020-7633 2270 *fax* 020-7021 0421
email info@tamasha.org.uk
website www.tamasha.org.uk
Artistic Directors Kristine Landon-Smith, Sudha Bhuchar *Executive Director* Alex Darbyshire

Production details

Founded in 1989. Produces "untold stories" in mainstream theatre venues. Stages 1-2 productions annually and gives approximately 50 performances during the course of the year. Tours annually to about 6 small- and mid-scale theatre venues in London, Yorkshire, Newcastle, the Midlands, the South West and Cornwall. In general 2-15 actors are involved in each production. Recent productions include: *A Fine Balance, The Trouble with Asian Men, Strictly Dandia, Ryman and the Sheikh*.

Casting procedures

Actors requesting inclusion should write in the run-up to productions – suggests 3 months in advance. Welcomes submissions (with CVs and photographs) sent by post or email. Offers ITC/Equity approved contracts. Actively encourages applications from disabled actors and promotes the use of inclusive casting.

theatre-rites

The Warehouse, 12 Ravensbury Terrace, London SW18 4RL
tel 020-8946 2236 *fax* 020-8946 0965
email info@theatre-rites.co.uk
website www.theatre-rites.co.uk
Artistic Director Sue Buckmaster *Associate Artist* Sophia Clist *General Manager* Natalie Highwood

Production details

Founded in 1995, theatre-rites is versatile in its approach, creating theatre shows which tour the UK and abroad and pieces set in unusual spaces such as an old tidal mill, a disused corner shop and an empty ward of a real working hospital. Theatre-rites also creates interactive exhibitions and installations in galleries, museums and other public spaces. Drawing on a rich fusion of performance, installation art, puppetry, video and sound, theatre-rites creates

work, which stirs the imagination of children and adults alike. Recent productions include *Hospitalworks, The Thought that Counts* (part of the Young Genius season at the Barbican) and a national re-tour of *In One Ear*.

Casting procedures

Welcomes letters (with CVs and photographs) from actors previously unknown to the company. "Multi-disciplined performers are always very welcome." Offers ITC/Equity approved contracts.

Theatre Absolute

57-61 Corporation Street, Coventry CV1 1GQ
tel 024-7625 7380
email info@theatreabsolute.co.uk
website www.theatreabsolute.co.uk
Artistic Director Chris O'Connell *Producer* Julia Negus

Production details

Founded in 1992, the company develops, produces and tours new plays. Its development arm, the Writing House, works with writers, actors and directors on new scripts. Stages 1 production annually and gives 30-40 performances during the course of the year. Tours to around 20 arts centres and theatres in the North West, West Midlands, East Midlands, London and the South East. In general 6 actors are involved in each production. Recent productions include: *Car, Raw* and *Kid*.

Casting procedures

Actors should consult the website for details of the next project and for casting breakdowns and information. In addition to its annual production, the company works with actors in writing workshops throughout the year. Welcomes letters (with CVs and up-to-date photographs) but not email submissions. Advises actors not to send blanket letters and CVs. "Find out about our work first – we always see actors who have seen our work if they're suitable for the role offered." Also happy to give advice to new/emerging actors.

Theatre Alibi

Northcott Studio Theatre, Emmanuel Road, Exeter EX4 1EJ
tel/fax 01392-217315
email alibi@eclipse.co.uk
website www.theatrealibi.co.uk
Artistic Director Nikki Sved *Marketing Director* Annemarie Macdonald *Administrative Director* Jenny Lawrence

Production details

Founded in 1982, the company works with existing and commissioned stories to create work that is physically and visually inventive and often enriched by other art forms – original music, film, puppetry, dance and photography, for instance. Stages two productions a year, with a total of around 130 performances. Tours 20 theatres and arts centres as well as schools and community venues, although the nature of the venues depends on the individual show. There are generally five actors in each show, and the company offers ITC/Equity approved contracts.

Past work includes *Birthday* (based on the work of Marc and Bella Chagall, which was nominated for a Fringe First), *Little White Lies* (Time Out Critics' Choice) and *Shelf Life*. Recent productions: *The Crowstarver* (mid-scale national tour for 8-13 year-olds), *Bonjour Bob* (tour of South West for 5-10 year-olds and their families), and *One in a Million* (national tour of small-scale venues aimed at adults).

Casting procedures

Casts in-house. Does not publish casting breakdowns, but welcomes letters (not emails) with CVs and photographs from individuals previously unknown to the company at any time of year. Does not welcome showreels or invitations to view individuals' websites. Actively encourages applications from disabled actors and promotes the use of inclusive casting.

Theatre Babel

11 Sandyford Place, Glasgow G3 7NB
tel (0141) 226 8806 *fax* (0141) 249 9900
email admin@theatrebabel.co.uk
website www.theatrebabel.co.uk
Director Graham McLaren *General Manager* Kate Bowden *Producer and Casting Director* Rebecca Rodgers

Production details

Founded in 1994, the company stages 1-2 classical theatre productions each year which tour to 10 venues across the UK and internationally. Normally presents approximately 60 performances annually with an average of 8 actors working on each production. Recent productions include: *Macbeth, A Doll's House, Thebans* and *Uncle Vanya*.

Casting procedures

Welcomes letters, CVs and photographs from actors previously unknown to the company, but does not accept email applications or showreels.

Théâtre Sans Frontières

Queen's Hall, Beaumont Street, Hexham, Northumberland NE46 3LS
tel (01434) 652484 *fax* (01434) 607206
email admin@tsfront.co.uk
website www.tsf.org.uk
Directors Sarah Kemp, John Cobb *General Manager* Helen Green *Marketing* Michelle van den Berg

Production details

Founded in 1991. Set up by former students of Philippe Gaulier and Monika Pagneux. Specialises in physical theatre and stages texts in different languages for adults and children using international performers. Stages 2-3 productions annually and gives 60-100 performances during the course of the year. Tours to 30 different venues annually, including arts centres and theatres in all regions of the UK. Also tours to schools. In general 3-6 actors are involved in each production. Recent productions include: *Aladin et la Lampe Enchantée, El Sombrero De Tre Picos, Le Petit Chaperon Rouge* and *Le Tour de France*.

Casting procedures

Sometimes holds general auditions. Actors may write at any time requesting inclusion. Casting breakdowns are available on request. Welcomes submissions (with CVs and photographs) sent by post or email. Invitations to view individual actors' websites are also accepted. "We are usually looking for actors who have languages other than English (especially French, Spanish or German), and who have a clear physical theatre training (i.e. Le Coq, Gaulier, Pagneux or Complicite)."

Theatre Set-up

12 Fairlawn Close, Southgate, London N14 4JX
website www.ts-u.co.uk
Charitable Director Wendy Macphee

Production details

Founded in 1976. Presents Shakespeare productions in historic and beautiful sites. Stages 1 production annually with 55 performances over the course of the year. Tours to 38 different outdoor venues annually in the UK, Norway, the Netherlands and Belgium. In general 8 actors are involved in each production. Recent productions include: *The Merry Wives of Windsor*.

Casting procedures

Sometimes holds general auditions. Actors should write in February requesting inclusion. Welcomes letters (with CVs and photographs) but not email submissions. Advises actors that "the tour is rigorous and not for the faint-hearted".

Theatre Workshop

34 Hamilton Place, Edinburgh EH3 5AX
tel 0131-225 7942 *fax* 0131-220 0112
email afleming@twe.org.uk
website www.theatre-workshop.com
Artistic Director Robert Rae *Company Manager* Anne Fleming

Production details

Founded in 1965; stages 4 productions a year with around 60 performances across 2 theatre venues.

Occasionally tours internationally. Employs an average of 5 actors on each production, using ITC/Equity approved contracts. Recent productions include: *The Jasmine Road* (No Limits International Theatre Festival, Berlin); and *The Threepenny Opera* (Edinburgh Festival Theatre & Tramway, Glasgow).

Casting procedures

Casting breakdowns are available from the website and Equity Job Information Service. Welcomes letters and emails (with CVs and photographs) from individuals previously unknown to the company. Also happy to receive showreels and invitations to view individuals' websites. Encourages applications from disabled actors and promotes the use of inclusive casting. "Theatre Workshop casts both disabled and non-disabled actors in all our productions."

Tinderbox Theatre Company

Imperial Buildings, 22 High Street, Belfast BT1 2BE
tel 028-9043 9313 *fax* 028-9032 9420
email info@tinderbox.org.uk
website www.tinderbox.org.uk
Artistic Director Michael Duke *General Manager* Kerry Woods

Production details

Founded in 1988. Produces, develops and stages new work which interrogates life in Northern Ireland. Stages 2-3 productions and tours to 12 different venues annually, including arts centres, theatres and site-specific locations in Ireland, England and Scotland. In general 6 actors are involved in each production. Recent productions include: *Revenge* and *Family Plot*.

Casting procedures

Sometimes holds general auditions. Welcomes letters (with CVs and photographs) but not email submissions. Invitations to view individual actors' websites are also accepted. Offers ITC/Equity approved contracts. Encourages applications from disabled actors and promotes the use of inclusive casting.

Told by an Idiot

c/o BAC, Lavender Hill, London SW11 5TF
tel 020-7978 4200 *fax* 020-7978 5200
email ggranger@dial.pipex.com
website www.toldby.dircon.co.uk
Directors Hayley Carmichael, Paul Hunter, John Wright *General Manager* Ghislaine Granger *Associate Producer* Nick Sweeting

Production details

Founded in 1992, the company tours to arts centres and theatres throughout England.

Casting procedures

Sometimes holds general auditions. Actors may write at any time throughout the year. The company will make contact if and when a relevant project arises. Welcomes submissions (with CVs and photographs) sent by post or email. Invitations to view individual actors' websites are also accepted. Offers ITC/Equity contracts. Actively encourages applications from disabled actors and promotes the use of inclusive casting.

TOSG Gaelic Theatre Company

Sabhal Mor Ostaig, Sleat, Isle of Skye IV44 8RQ
tel (01471) 888542 *fax* (01471) 888542
email tosg@tosg.org
website www.tosg.org.uk
Artistic Director Simon Mackenzie *General Manager* Janet Ward

Production details

Founded in 1996. Professional Gaelic Theatre Company producing theatre for both adults and children. Also runs a new writing scheme. All productions are performed in Gaelic. Stages 2 productions annually and gives 50 performances per year. Tours to 30 different venues annually, including arts centres, theatres, educational and community venues in Scotland. In general 5 actors are involved in each production.

Casting procedures

Sometimes holds general auditions. Gaelic-speaking actors can write in May requesting inclusion. Welcomes letters (with CVs and photographs) but not email submissions. Invitations to view individual actors' websites are also accepted.

Trading Faces

28 Brick Meadow, Bishops Castle, Shropshire SY9 5DH
tel 01588-630 555
email admin@tradingfaces.org.uk
website www.tradingfaces.org.uk
Director Tony Davis *Key Personnel* Thomasina Carlyle

Production details

Established in 1987. Trading Faces specialises in creating original theatre using masks. The company employs actors with a genuine interest in mask theatre and with strong physical and devising skills. One production staged annually touring to 40 venues including arts centres and community venues in the West Midlands and the South East. Offers ITC/Equity approved contracts. Recent productions include *Creaking Shadows*, *The Little Prince*, *Jungle Book*, *The Wife of Bath* and *The Man Who Woke Up in the Dark*.

Casting procedures

Casting breakdowns available via website. Accepts submissions (with CVs and photographs) from actors previously unknown to them if sent by post, but not by email. Actively encourages applications from disabled actors and promotes the use of inclusive casting.

Trestle Theatre Company

Trestle Arts Base, Russet Drive, St Albans AL4 0JQ
tel (01727) 850950 *fax* (01727) 855558
email admin@trestle.org.uk
website www.trestle.org.uk
Artistic Director Emily Gray *Administrative Director* Valerie Evans

Production details

Founded in 1981. Small- to mid-scale theatre company touring new, devised or commissioned work. Principal medium is the full mask, but also uses text, puppets and live music. Stages 2-3 productions annually and gives more than 100 performances. Tours to 50 different venues each year, including arts centres and theatres in Britain, Europe and other international locations. In general 5 actors are involved in each production. Recent productions include: *The Smallest Person, Tonight We Fly, Island* and *The Adventures of the Stoneheads.*

Casting procedures

Rarely holds general auditions. Does not welcome 'on spec' CVs. Will consider invitations to see actors in shows if the performance style is relevant to the way in which Trestle works. If looking for suggestions, casting breakdowns will be put on the website. Usually casts actors with strong mask/physical/visual theatre acting training or experience.

UK Arts International

2nd Floor, 6 Shaw Street, Worcester WR1 3QQ

Production details

Stages 1 production annually which tours to approximately 70 different venues, including arts centres, theatres, education and community venues across the UK.

Casting procedures

Does not hold general auditions and does not welcome submissions from actors previously unknown to the company.

Unlimited Theatre

Studio 11, Aire Street Workshops, 30-34 Aire Street, Leeds LS1 4HT
tel 0113-234 5400
email unlimited@unlimited.org.uk
website www.unlimited.org.uk
Artistic Director Jon Spooner *Development Director* Liz Margree

Production details

Founded in 1997. Creates work intended to "explore how personal experience can illuminate political debate, and which puts marginalised voices centre-stage". Stages 1-2 productions annually, and gives 50-100 performances. Tours to 10-20 different venues each year including arts centres and theatres throughout the UK (including Glasgow, Edinburgh and Belfast) and overseas. In general 4-6 actors are involved in each production. Recent productions include: *Safety, Neutrino,* and *Zero Degrees and Drifting.*

Casting procedures

Sometimes holds general auditions. Welcomes letters (with CVs and photographs) but not email submissions. Invitations to view individual actors' websites are also accepted. "We are a small- to middle-scale organisation and only occasionally employ freelance actors. We are always interested in hearing from potential new collaborators." Offers ITC/Equity approved contracts. Actively encourages applications from disabled actors and promotes the use of inclusive casting.

Volcano Theatre Company

Swansea Institute, Townhill Road, Swansea SA2 0UT
tel (01792) 281280
email volcano.tc@virgin.net
website www.volcanotheatre.co.uk
Directors Paul Davies, Fern Smith *General Manager* Katie Keeler

Production details

Founded in 1987. Small-scale national and international touring company based in Wales. Specialises in physical theatre, new writing, devised and collaborative work and adaptations/ deconstructions of classics. Stages 2-4 productions and gives 50 performances each year. Tours to 35 different venues annually. Venues have included arts centres and theatres in Wales, England, Ireland, Scotland, Europe, Central Asia, South America, Canada and Sri Lanka. In general 2-5 actors are involved in each production. Recent productions include: *The Imaginary Woman* and *Talk Sex Show.*

Casting procedures

Casting breakdowns are available by postal application (with sae). Welcomes letters (with CVs and photographs) but not email submissions. Invitations to view individual actors' websites are also accepted. The company also runs workshops that can sometimes lead to casting invitations.

Keith Whitall

10 Woodlands Avenue, West Byfleet, Surrey KT14 6AT
tel (01932) 343655
Director Keith Whitall

Production details

Founded in 2000. Produces revues, small-scale musicals and occasionally plays and one-person shows. Stages 2-3 productions annually and gives 20 or more performances in theatres in Brighton and the South East. So far has only toured to 1 arts centre. In general 9-10 actors are involved in each production. Recent productions include: *Broadway Calling*.

Casting procedures

Sometimes holds general auditions. Actors may write at any time requesting inclusion. Casting breakdowns are usually made available to casting directors or actors seen in a production. Welcomes letters (with CVs and photographs) but not email submissions. The company's director, Keith Whitall, is also a freelance casting director. "In my revues I usually use 3-4 experienced artistes plus new young artistes in whom I am especially interested." Musical theatre experience is preferable.

The Wrestling School

42 Durlston Road, London E5 8RR
tel 020-8442 4229
website www.thewrestlingschool.co.uk
Director Howard Barker

Production details

Founded in 1988. "Develops ways of presenting complex ideas in the theatre through the work of Howard Barker." Stages 1 production annually and gives 35 performances. Tours to 6 different venues each year including arts centres and theatres. In general 5-7 actors are involved in each production.

Casting procedures

Sometimes holds auditions. Welcomes letters when casting (with CVs and photographs) but not email submissions. Actors should telephone in late July to find out if the company is casting.

Y Touring Theatre Co

8-10 Lennox Road, Finsbury Park, London N4 3JQ
020-7272 5755 020-7272 8413
email m.ball@ytouring.org.uk
website www.ytouring.org.uk
Artistic Director Nigel Townsend *Administrator* Martin Ball *General Manager* Michael White

Production details

Y Touring is central YMCA's Awards winning professional touring theatre company for young people and adults. Stages 2-4 productions per year giving 100 performances at around 50 venues. Offers ITC/Equity approved contracts.

Casting procedures

Uses freelance casting directors and also holds general auditions. Casting breakdowns are available on the website, PCR and Equity Job information service. The company welcomes CVs and photographs (by letter, not email) from actors whose work was previously unknown to them. Does not welcome showreels or invitations to view individuals' websites. Will consider applications from disabled actors to play characters with disabilities.

Starting your own theatre company

Pilar Ortí

The first question you should ask yourself before starting a theatre company is – do you really need to set up a company, or do you just want to put on a show? In order to put on a show you don't need to go through all the hassle of setting up a company. If you *do* want to set up a company – why? In some cases this might be as difficult a question to answer as, "Why do you want to act?", but it's worth having an idea of why you want to invest so much time and energy in setting up and running an organisation rather than looking for acting work. Whatever your answer, be honest with yourself. And the clearer you can be, the better, as this will affect the kind of organisation you end up creating.

Of course, many companies emerge after a group of actors produce a show together: at some point, someone decides that as a company of people, you are worth keeping together. If this is the case, then you are ready to run a company of your own. But there are many ways of making theatre, as you well know, and the range of theatre produced is also vast. What kind of work do you want to do? At this point it is worth bearing in mind your 'artistic policy', and coming up with a couple of sentences that escribe the work you do. I know that 'policy' sounds dry, but if you end up constituting yourself as a non-commercial organisation and applying to public funds (or trusts and foundations), you will need to learn a whole new vocabulary which seems to have little to do with your art. You should never lose sight of your artistic dreams and ambitions – but you may need to talk about them in terms of policy, objectives, qualitative evaluation, benefits, management structure, cultural diversity, contingency ... the list goes on and on. This article is meant to inspire you, not send you off to sleep, so don't despair: learn the language and then use it in a creative way that makes sense to you.

Allow yourself to dream

Long-term plans are necessary – so learn to dream. (Okay, give it a try in the first instance by putting on a show. Then, if you enjoy it, carry on!) Plans, of course, can change along the way: I suggest that you have an absolutely ambitious dream plan and a let's-try-and-see-what's-possible-now plan. Opportunities arise when you least expect them, and if you know where you are heading, you can grab them without letting them throw you off-course.

I view running a theatre company rather like directing a show: the more theatre you watch, the stronger the idea you will have of what *you* want the show to be, what is unique about it, and what you can realistically achieve. So, if you, like me, trained as an actor or actress and suddenly find yourself running a company, seek advice and look at how others operate. If you consider how other people do things, you will be able to adapt the bits you like and which make sense to you. In a sector such as ours, it is not difficult to find those pleased to help – and the freshness of people just starting out reminds us all of how much can be achieved when we don't know our limitations.

Seek help

There is an awful lot of free/cheap advice out there. During the year in which we focused on building the administrative foundations for our company, my colleague and I talked to as many consultants, local authority officers, venue managers, etc. as we could. Some of these conversations came about through informal meetings; others, by taking part in official programmes. We found out what funders were really looking for, and what other companies were doing in our area; we learnt to draw up business plans with budgets covering three and five years; and we discovered what our strengths and weaknesses were, and what threats and opportunities exist 'out there'.

A word of warning: take *all* advice (including that which I am giving you now) with a pinch of salt, especially from those who hardly know you and your work. Follow your gut instinct. When we were in pre-production for *Antigone*, a business consultant suggested that we invite Funeral Services to advertise in our programme, "seeing as how they all die in the end". Mmm.

The best consultancies are those which have been carefully structured so that the consultant spends time with you, getting to know you and your plans, and then helps you find your own answers by providing their expertise. Arts & Business's 'Business in the Arts' programme is worth checking out, although you need to have a very definite idea of what you need help with. (To see what else Arts & Business do, check out their webiste, **www.aandb.org.uk**.)

Making it 'proper'

Once you have decided on the work you want to do and how you want to go about producing it, you will need to find a legal structure for your company. This shows outsiders that you are serious, and it also makes monetary transactions easy.

Forbidden's first show was produced in Edinburgh: the only 'proper' thing the company had was a bank account (and a name!). We then registered the name and became a limited company, and after our first London show, became a registered charity. This was a good idea as our income mainly comes from trusts and foundations (most of which require you to be a charity to receive their grants, for tax purposes); it also allows us to claim Gift Aid when we receive donations from individuals. (Gift Aid is great: the donor claims their donation as tax-deductible, and you receive an extra 23 per cent from the Inland Revenue.)

Setting up a charity still allows you to pursue your own artistic programme: making theatre for the public is considered to 'advance education', which is a charitable objective. So you can still run your company as a business, drawing salaries, etc. and making sure that any annual profits stay within the company.

Just like a limited company, a registered charity is governed by a Board. The main difference between the two set-ups is that those who sit on a charity's Board (the Trustees) do so on a voluntary basis. It therefore would make no sense for *you* to be part of the Board (although there is talk of a possible change in the law to allow Trustees to be remunerated for their work). This means that, in theory at least, you are putting the fate of your company in the hands of other people. So choose your Trustees very carefully – and try to include people who have some knowledge of legal matters and accountancy.

This set-up has worked for Forbidden, as we have been extremely lucky: we have managed to find experienced individuals with integrity and a passion for what we do. You might prefer a different kind of set-up which gives you more legal control: banks and Business Links offer free advice on the different options. If you want some focused advice and have a bit of cash to spare, you might attend the Independent Theatre Council's (ITC) seminar on 'Starting a Theatre Company' ... and when you have a bit more cash, you might want to join the ITC – membership is bound to come in handy when questions on legal matters start to arise. (Have a look at the website, **www.itc-arts.org.uk**.)

Learn as you go along

Know your strengths and weaknesses. Setting up a theatre company will involve doing ten thousand things you might never have done before; however, a lot of it can be learnt along the way, and much of it is common sense. It won't take you long to discover those things you are useless at, and those that you absolutely hate. You then have two choices: do them anyway, or find someone else to do them for you/with you.

If there are more than two of you running the company, decide who will be in charge of what. Certain things like fundraising might be too daunting for one person to do on their own, but you can break it down into more manageable pieces: someone might have a clearer head for numbers and can prepare the budget, and someone else can write the description of the show and why it will make a huge contribution to theatre in this country.

Let's talk about money

And seeing as I've come to fundraising, I shall dwell on it. You can't escape it. No matter how much your company grows, no matter how successful you are, no matter how large your staff is – if you are in charge, you will worry about it, so learn to enjoy it. I know that this sounds perverse ... but fundraising applications are your chance to enthuse someone else about what you do. To tell them about your plans – about what you want to do and why you want to do it. Tell them how you want to make a difference; about *why* you think it's different; about how it will help you, and others, grow. And yes, you will need to learn some new vocabulary and be able to distinguish between qualitative and quantitative evaluation, but it helps if you see this as a game with which you have to keep up. (At the last ITC annual general meeting, I found out that 'well-being' is a new way of convincing funders that theatre is necessary to people's lives!) What's really important is to convince funders that you really want to do the work, and that you want to do it well. (When I talk about funders, I am referring to anyone who might want to donate to or invest in your company. I have no experience of commercial deals, but I imagine that these work in a similar way: you find out what it is that people want in return for their money, and then convince them that you can provide it – as well as putting on a really good show.)

This is also where having long-term plans comes in handy: funding applications usually take between six weeks and three months to be assessed. Sometimes, even more: our first successful application for an Education Officer took more than one year from the date on which I sent it to the day the letter of acceptance came through. While I'm on the subject of those who will give you money – *nurture your relationships with them*. We have found that those trusts, foundations and individuals who are willing to help us out once, are likely to do so again.

I have also discovered that funding applications help you plan in detail how you are going to realise a production or a project. Good funding applications might come in useful even if you don't get the money – they will probably provide a good description of your plans which you can then show others interested in your work. (For books and directories on Fundraising, check out the Directory of Social Change's website, **www.dsc.org.uk**. They also have a small bookshop in Stephenson Way, near Euston Square in London NW1.)

Final words

I have left the most important thing until last. *Treat those working with you well, especially your actors.* Make working with you an enjoyable experience. If you hold auditions, make them worthwhile for those attending. When you are able to pay your personnel, pay them on time. Treat them like the professionals that they are. And when things go wrong, as they inevitably will, take responsibility for your company and make up for the hassle with a gesture, however small – custard creams work for me!

When I first started running Forbidden, I kept hearing that I should treat it like running a business. What I have discovered is that it is an exercise in people management. Forbidden exists because people have believed in our work and are willing to invest their time and money in what we do. Different organisations work in different ways: I hope these words have helped you find one that will work for you.

Pilar Ortí is currently Artistic Director of Forbidden Theatre Company (**www.forbidden.org.uk**), an artist-led organisation dedicated to creating, and inspiring the creation of, highly theatrical work. She also freelances as a workshop leader and voice-over artist, and teaches vocational acting to the sixth-form students at Arts Educational Schools.

English-language European theatre companies

This small section seems to be populated by companies set up by enthusiasts who have kept on going with very little subsidy – and sometimes with none at all. Although living away from home and isolated from auditions, it can be fun working for such companies. It is important to note that the work often involves educational projects and/or touring.

ACT Company
25 Avenue du Marechal Leclerc, 92240 Malakoff, France
tel (33) 1 4656 2050
email andrew.wilson@wanadoo.fr
Artistic Director Andrew Wilson *Administrator* Anne Wilson

Founded in 1981. An English-language theatre company focusing on research and development to create high-quality productions. Aims to make theatrical experiences in English accessible to a non-native-speaking public. Runs Theatre in Education projects, performing English theatre for young French native speakers. Recent productions include: *Robinson Crusoe*, *Sir Gawain and the Green Knight*, *Animal Farm*, and *The Canterville Ghost*.

Dear Conjunction Theatre Company
6 Rue Arthur Rozier, 75019 Paris, France
tel (33) 1 4241 6965
email dearconjunction@wanadoo.fr
Artistic Directors Leslie Clack, Patricia Kessler

Founded in 1991, this bilingual company is composed of professional actors, directors and writers who are resident in Paris and who present productions in both French and English. Past productions include: Pinter's *Ashes to Ashes* and *The Hothouse*; and *Someone Who'll Watch Over Me* by Frank McGuinness. Welcomes letters and emails (with CVs and photographs) from actors previously unknown to the company. Contact Leslie Clack for more information.

The English Speaking Theatre Oslo (TESTO)
Jacob Aalls Gate 30, 0364 Oslo, Norway
tel (47) 22 466248
email testo-no@online.no
website home.tiscali.no/testo.no
Artistic Director Simon Lay *Director* Kristin Zachariassen

Founded in 1996 by actors Simon Lay and Kristin Zachariassen. Main focus of work is Theatre in Education. Produces theatre adaptations targeted at Norwegian students but also appealing to the general Norwegian public. Recent productions include: *How High Is Up?*, *Too Much for Punch and Judy*, *Pygmalion* and *The Woman in Black*.

The English Theatre Company Ltd
Nybrogatan 35, 114 39 Stockholm, Sweden
tel (46) 8 662 4133 *fax* (46) 8 660 1159
email etc.ltd@telia.com
website www.englishtheatre.se
Artistic Director Christer Berg

Founded in 1981. Stages 2 productions annually. Recent productions include: *Shirley Valentine* and *A Christmas Carol*. Uses freelance casting directors. Holds general auditions; actors requesting inclusion should write between August and September. Casting breakdowns are not publicly available. Welcomes postal enquiries from actors previously unknown to the company.

English Theatre Frankfurt
Kaiserstrasse 34, D-60329 Frankfurt, Germany
tel (49) 69 242 31615 *fax* (49) 69 242 31614
email mail@english-theatre.org
website www.english-theatre.org
Artistic Adviser Clive Paget *Managing Director* Daniel Nicolai

Founded in 1979. Presents contemporary plays, musicals and classics. 5 productions performed in the main house each year, totalling 260 performances. Uses London-based freelance casting directors. Does not hold general auditions. Actors should write requesting inclusion in the company in April. Casting breakdowns are only available via Spotlight.

The English Theatre of Copenhagen
The London Toast Theatre, Kochsvej 18, 1812 Fred C, Copenhagen, Denmark
tel (45) 3322 8686
email mail@londontoast.dk
website www.londontoast.dk
Artistic Director Vivienne McKee *Administrator* Soren Hall

Founded in 1982. The largest English-speaking theatre company in Northern Europe. Presents theatre productions and provides corporate entertainment, stand-up comedy and Murder Mystery shows in Scandinavia and abroad. The company's voice-over bureau, 'Speaker's Corner', provides English and American voices for films and commercials. Recent productions include: *Dracula – A Pain in the Neck!* and *The Importance of Being Earnest.*

The English Theatre of Hamburg

Lerchenfeld 14, 22081 Hamburg, Germany
tel (49) 40 227 7089 *fax* (49) 40 229 5040
email ETHamburg@onlinehome.de
website www.englishtheatre.de
Contact Robert Rumpf, Clifford Dean

Founded in 1976 by 2 Americans, Robert Rumpf and Clifford Dean, who originally trained and worked professionally in the USA. They share general management responsibilities, plan the artistic programme and direct productions. Since 1981 the theatre has occupied its present premises at Mundsburg in 22081 Hamburg. Performs 8 times per week from September to June. A typical season at the English Theatre includes a classic American or British drama, a comedy and a thriller. Recent productions include: *Over the River and Through the Woods, I Ought To Be in Pictures, Educating Rita* and *When the Reaper Calls*. Also runs Education programmes.

Light Nights – The Summer Theatre

Baldursgata 37, IS-101 Reykjavik, Iceland
tel (354) 551 9181 *fax* (354) 551 5015
website www.lightnights.com
Artistic Director Kristín G Magnús

Production details

Runs a summer theatre show at the Idnó Theatre in Reykjavik. Previous productions have included: *Light Nights* and *On The Way to Heaven.*

Casting procedures

Sometimes holds general auditions. The best time to write requesting inclusion is February/March. Casting breakdowns are not publicly available. Welcomes letters (with CVs and photographs) from actors previously unknown to the company, but not via email. Does not welcome showreels, but is happy to receive invitations to view actors' websites. Offers non-Equity contracts; rarely (or never) has the opportunity to cast disabled actors.

Merlin International Theatre

1052 Budapest, Gerloczy Utca 4, Hungary
tel (36) 1 317 9338 *fax* (36) 1 266 0904
email angol@merlinszinhaz.hu
website www.szinhaz.hu/merlin/english
Director Laszlo Magacs *Associate Director* Emma Vidovsky

Founded in 1991; Hungary's first and currently its only international theatre. Recent productions

include: *The Importance of Being Earnest, Don't Drink the Water, Stones in His Pockets* and *Twelfth Night.* Resident companies at the Merlin Theatre are the Atlantis Company, Junion Group and Madhouse.

Onatti Theatre Company

9 Field Close, Warwick, Warwickshire CV34 4QD
tel (01926) 495220 *fax* 0870-164 3629
email info@onatti.co.uk
website www.onatti.co.uk
Artistic Director Andrew Bardwell *Company Manager* Seanna Hardaker-Jones

Presents foreign-language productions for schools, touring productions, theatre in museums, and theatre function entertainments. Contact Alan Hamlet, Educational Adviser (**tie@onatti.co.uk**) for details of Theatre in Education programmes. Recent productions include: *The Way of the World, Premier Amour, Greensleeves* and *The Child King.*

Theatre From Oxford

69-71 Oxford Street, Woodstock, Oxford OX20 1TJ
tel/fax (33) 47 7662 0420
email theatre.oxford@virgin.net
Artistic Director Robert Southam

Founded in 1984, the main aim for the past 20 years has been to introduce audiences on the continent to the best of theatre in English. The company has toured plays by Shakespeare, Shaw, Wilde, Willy Russell, Tennessee Williams and Arthur Miller, among others. Touring for 3 months from September to Christmas in 7 European countries, the company plays in anything from the best theatres to school gyms – but nearly always to full houses. Tours again in the spring to many of the same venues, providing theatre workshops. Half of the spectators are students; the other half, adult theatre-goers.

Actors are advised that the tours are enjoyable but demanding, and that the company seldom accepts anyone straight from drama school. Casts often include actors with RSC and RNT experience. Recently has been working with African, Asian and Latin American actors and writers, which has meant less work for British and American actors. Casting breakdowns are available by postal application (with sae) and actors are welcome to write letters or emails with their CVs and photographs. Showreels, however, are not welcomed. Offers non-Equity contracts. Will consider applications from disabled actors to play characters with disabilities.

Vienna's English Theatre

UK address: VM Theatre Productions Ltd, 16 The Street, Ash, Canterbury CT3 2HJ
tel (01304) 813330 *fax* (01304) 813330
email office@englishtheatre.at
Theatre address: Josefsgasse 12, A-1080 Vienna, Austria
tel (43) 1 4021 2600 *fax* (43) 1 4021 26042

website www.englishtheatre.at

Founded in 1963; the oldest English-language theatre in continental Europe. Originally intended as a summer theatre for English-speaking tourists, it has now developed a year-round programme staging 5 shows each year in the Main House and sending 4 Theatre-in-Education tours around the schools of Austria. The season runs from September to July each year; casting breakdowns are posted on the website and actors may write to the UK address above with their CV and photograph at anytime. Emails and showreels, however, are not accepted. "All contracts are especially written for us by Equity."

White Horse Theatre

Bördenstrasse 17, 59494 Soest-Müllingsen, Germany
tel (49) 2921 339339 *fax* (49) 2921 339336
email theatre@whitehorse.de
website www.whitehorse.de
Artistic Director Peter Griffith *Casting Director* Michael Dray

Founded in 1978. Tours schools in Germany with occasional visits to neighbouring countries. Contracts are for 10-11 months. 6 companies of 4 actors each perform 3 plays. Recent productions include: *The Glass Menagerie*, *Oliver Twist*, *A Midsummer Night's Dream* and numerous plays for 10-13 year-olds and for 14-16 year-olds.

Does not use freelance casting directors. Holds general auditions; actors should write in April requesting inclusion. Casting breakdowns are available through the website, postal application (with sae), Equity Job Information Service, *PCR* and advertisements in *The Stage*. Welcomes postal and email enquiries from actors previously unknown to the company. Invitations to view individual actors' websites are also accepted. Contracts are approved by GDBA (the German equivalent of Equity). Rarely has the opportunity to cast disabled actors since "all our actors must take part in 3 different plays, and they must also cope with the rigours of touring".

A touring actor's survival guide

Maev Alexander

Touring is more tiring, harder work, more all-consuming and more relentless than playing in one house. In order to give your best to it and get the best from it, you need to be thoroughly organised and disciplined. The main differences are, of course, the travelling and the accommodation. If you arrange these well in advance, you're on your way to having a happy and rewarding experience and saving yourself angst and money.

Getting there

At the beginning of rehearsals, or even before, you'll be given a schedule of dates and venues and a sheaf of digs lists. Work out as early as you can how you will travel and where you will stay.

If you have your own transport you can plan your journeys on a week-by-week basis, pulling maps and route finders and estimated journey times off the Internet – if you have access – both to digs and to theatres. A good company manager will supply maps of town centres with the venue clearly marked. If you don't have your own transport, ask around the company and find out if anyone lives close enough to you, and is willing, to give you lifts. Make it clear that you will contribute to petrol costs, be punctual and not bring too much luggage. If you are using public transport, book as far in advance as you can: Apex (or the equivalent) on trains and low-budget airlines will save you huge amounts of money. The touring company will expect you to do this, and will calculate the amount they give you in fares as economically as possible. Be aware that fares are worked out from venue to venue, and not to your home and out again. Remember also that you may get stuck on a Saturday night if your show comes down after the last train, which is more likely than not; this may add to your accommodation expenses. It also eats into your only day off; most No. 1 tours play Monday to Saturday, running for a week in each venue.

The rule for fares and touring allowance is: outwith 15 miles of your permanent base to qualify for fares only, and 25 miles to qualify for touring allowance. This is calculated from postcode to postcode – not by the most convenient or quickest route. Equity has negotiated sharp rises in the level of touring allowance over the last few years, and it is now reasonable. It's meant to cover accommodation and living expenses – and if you're frugal and careful, it can. You have to balance the level of comfort and convenience with which you need to live happily with the budget on which you have to do it.

Finding the right digs

Digs lists cover hotels, guesthouses, self-contained flats, houses for sharing, B&Bs and rooms in private houses. They normally tell you the price (per night or per week), the type of accommodation, the facilities, the prohibitions (i.e. no smoking, no pets), the extras (TV, kettle in room) and the distance from the theatre. The headliners can probably afford to stay in hotels (and many hotels do deals for touring actors), but other ranks will have to juggle their priorities. If you can feel comfortable in a room in a private house, sharing a bathroom and having access to a kitchen, you can do so remarkably cheaply. If you can't do without an en suite or need to be self-contained, it will obviously be more expensive, and so on up the scale; but read the list carefully and you will find something that will tick most of your boxes without too much compromise. The people who do the letting are generally friends of the theatre in some way, and the standard of accommodation is usually pretty high.

Start ringing the most promising-sounding digs as soon as possible, before everyone else does. Good options are places within a 15-minute walk (obviating cabs or long, lonely walks or parking problems) or a house or cottage that is further out, possibly in countryside, to share with fellow company members both in terms of rent and transport. Beware of landlady-speak for 'a 15- to 20-minute walk' – some landladies clearly have seven-league boots! The level of rates varies from place to place: locations like Bath and Malvern tend to be more expensive across the board than, say, Southampton and Coventry. In big centres like Glasgow, Manchester, Birmingham and Leeds you will probably have to travel to the outskirts unless you can afford hotels.

When you've agreed terms with a landlord/lady, write to confirm the booking and the dates, and arrange to ring a couple of days in advance of the stay to negotiate a mutually convenient time to arrive (leave half an hour's leeway so you don't panic about getting lost). It's wise at least to drop off your luggage before the show so that you know you know where the place is, have keys and don't disturb anyone at a late hour – especially on the first night when there are likely to be drinks front-of-house afterwards. Sorting out digs gets easier the more you tour and the more contacts you acquire. Do ask experienced tourers if you're new to it – most actors are very generous about sharing the secrets of top digs. For future reference, keep records of where you've stayed and what it was like. Pay up front and remember to leave keys when you leave; get a receipt and behave well enough for the landlord/lady to wish to stay on the digs list. You represent future tourers.

What to take

It's important to pack well. Travel as light as you can, and have as much of your luggage on wheels as possible. You need enough clothes for a week, or longer if you need to go straight to the next venue; keep it simple, remembering to have something warm and something cool (because this is Britain) and something smart for the first-night drinks often provided by the host management or friends of the theatre. A towelling robe doubles as a dressing gown and post-shower gear. Take comfortable, reasonably weatherproof shoes, since you'll spend a lot of time walking. Remember your phone charger (it's worth having a spare for touring), and a toothbrush charger and adapter in case there are no shaving points. It's also worth having an emergency kit containing plasters and painkillers and cold remedies. In most places towels are provided, but pack a hand towel just in case. Travel with a hottie in winter: the only miserable digs I've had were very smart but *freezing*. I complained – do complain; you're not paying to freeze. A pocket torch is useful for unfamiliar, unlit keyholes. Don't forget comforts like books or a radio or iPod.

If you have to be away from your base for extended periods, negotiate doing your laundry with the wardrobe department. If you're home on Sunday, it saves time and hassle if you've put what needs washing into a separate bag in your case so that repacking is straightforward and quick. I was told early in my career that no proper actor has less than three weeks' worth of underwear!

You can generally travel with your make-up and other dressing-room necessities, comforts and amusements in a bag or box on the truck transporting the set and props, etc. This is not an automatic right, though, so check with your company manager. Some reasonably rigid receptacle is optimum to avoid breakage; label it clearly with the name of the production and your own name and do not expect anyone else to lug it to or from your dressing room week by week. Pack it as soon as you can on Saturday night and check where you can leave it so it's not in the way of the get-out.

Eating and drinking

It's easy to be lazy about eating sensibly on tour – financially and nutritionally. Even if there are cooking facilities in your digs, it's not always convenient to be there and it's tempting to eat out all the time or grab burgers. You're going to need all your energy, so make a point of eating healthily.

In most theatres you'll have access to a microwave and possibly a fridge: ring the stage door and check. They're often in the crew room, so ask if you may use them and be considerate about clearing up after yourself. Making an interesting dressing-room picnic is a worthy challenge even if everything has to be cold. Supermarkets do better and better ranges of salads and sushi. Invest in a mini kettle for your touring box and pack a plate, a mug and cutlery. Set yourself a daily budget for food and then you'll know if you can splash out on a restaurant meal.

It's also tempting to do a great deal more after-show drinking when you're away from home: it can feel as if you're living in a bubble, out of the real world. Ask yourself if you're getting jaded/broke, and limit alcohol to within sensible limits. (The same sense of not being quite in the real world can lead too to the most unlikely affairs: be discreet, whether it involves other people or yourself.)

Bonding and recreation

After-show company meals, weekly or fortnightly, are good bonding exercises providing you all get on. Remember that it's not only part of your job to get on, but also in your best interests. It's even more important in the living-in-each-others'-pockets world of touring to be a good company member; leave your troubles firmly at the stage door and don't moan or gossip. If there's someone you find tricky, keep out of their way. In my experience, touring companies bond well and form even more of a parallel family than usual.

That said, getting away by yourself for a time is restoring. Find the local Tourist Information Office and find out about places of interest and specialist shopping. There's bound to be something that appeals to you ,even if you're not a galleries/museums/castles/cathedrals person (the ABC of touring is famously, "another bloody cathedral"). I am lucky – and not alone – in regarding touring as being paid to go sightseeing. Stage door, or your company manager, can tell you of gym and leisure facilities and often arrange temporary membership; they can also point you in the direction of the nearest supermarkets and best-value restaurants.

Sussing out the theatre

One of the interesting and rewarding things about touring is playing the same show in lots of different theatres – from 900-seaters to 2000-seaters, from raked stages to flat stages, from Victorian to modern, from those with acres (seemingly) of orchestra pit to those where the front row is looking up your nose. You'll be called early on in the first day of each new venue, generally at about 5 or 6pm, to walk the stage, get to know the backstage layout and take note of significant differences. The presence or lack of a rake may mean more or fewer steps on a staircase, for instance; furniture may be closer together or further apart; wing space may be tight; prop tables may be in different places; dressing rooms will be varying distances away and you may be sharing in one venue and by yourself in another. Take time to absorb these differences, test the acoustic and plan how you're going to accommodate any changes you personally will have to make. Discuss these changes too with anyone else they may affect. Bear in mind that the audiences are always different, as well: it's amazing that what makes people laugh or weep in Cardiff is not the same as what makes people laugh or weep in Hull.

Find out when stage door opens; most theatres allow you access to your dressing room from quite early in the day, which is useful for dumping shopping or 'nesting' when it's tipping with rain. A few don't open until much later on, though, which is a great bore and makes it good to have digs close by.

Money matters

On a business level, keep a work diary and note down all your expenses (and mileages if you're driving). Have an envelope or plastic wallet in which to file all your receipts and payslips: it's much easier to lose track of these when you're away from home.

Tax offices vary in what they will allow you to claim on tour. Travel and accommodation expenses above your allowances are OK, but some accept claims for all eating expenses (again over and above), some for restaurant/cafe receipts only, and some – including my own – clearly expect you not to eat at all.

Research a mobile phone tariff that will let you keep in touch with family and friends, and your agent, as cheaply as possible.

Finally ...

More and more of the available work involves touring at some level. You might just as well maximise your chances of having a good time and making a decent profit. Regard it as an adventure.

Maev Alexander trained at the Royal Scottish Academy of Music and Drama and has been working in theatre, television and radio for 40 years. She has performed in Rep all over the country, playing everything from Cleopatra to a French poodle, been a member of the RSC, and holds the record as the longest-serving Mollie in *The Mousetrap*. She has starred in two TV series and guested in many others, presented the Newsdesk on *That's Life*, and played in dozens of radio dramas. She's just completed her 5th No. 1 tour in as many years, transferring with the latest – *A Man for All Seasons* – to the Theatre Royal Haymarket in January 2006.

Editors' note There are a number of websites that can help you plan your journeys to and from the locations on your tour; they may also save you money. Here are some of the major ones:

● *Maps*: **www.streetmap.co.uk**, **www.multimap.com**, and **maps.google.co.uk**.

● *Driving*: **www.theaa.com** and **www.rac.co.uk** both offer route-planning and maps, as does Google maps (above).

● *Trains*: **www.nationalrail.co.uk** for timetables and **www.thetrainline.com** for booking the cheapest tickets available. Also worth looking at **www.megatrain.com** to check for promotional fares. In addition to these, **www.jplanner.org.uk** and **www.traveline.org.uk** are good ways of exploring options (train, coach, plane, etc.) for getting to a location.

● *Coaches*: **www.nationalexpress.co.uk**, **www.citylink.co.uk** (Scotland), **www.megabus.com/uk** (which often has promotional fares), and **www.eurolines.com** (destinations around Europe). In addition there are some local companies offering low-cost services to major cities such as London, which a little research should uncover.

- *Tube*: **journeyplanner.tfl.gov.uk** or, from your mobile, text 60835 (60TFL) with 'a to b' (where 'a' and 'b' are stations, stops or postcodes in London) to find out the best way – tube, train or bus – of getting to where you're going. For example: 'Clapham Junction to The Old Vic'. Common sense and some knowledge of the geography of London may need to be applied to the directions given: in this example the text service recommends a bus journey from Waterloo Station to The Old Vic – a walk of three minutes at most.
- *Flying*: **www.deckchair.com** (lists all available flights; when you see a cheap fare listed, go to the website of the airline concerned to see if you can get it more cheaply by going direct).

'Vanning it': the golden rules

Andrew Piper

Maev Alexander's article covers pretty much all you need to know about large-scale touring, and many of these principles carry over into small-scale touring too. However, the major difference between the two levels of touring is … The Van.

On a large-scale (or No. 1) tour you are generally responsible for getting to the venue yourself, since these are often in large towns with good transport links. By contrast, much of the work of mid- and small-scale companies is done in venues rather more 'off the beaten track' (a.k.a. The Middle of Nowhere), and often with only one performance in each venue. Most of these companies, then, will transport their actors around the country in a mini-bus, coach or van, which may also contain the set and lighting rig. Whereas the large-scale companies employ stage crew to do the get-ins and get-outs, on such productions it's often up to the actors and the stage manager to do everything.

'Vanning it' presents an additional set of challenges for the actor. If you don't get on with a fellow actor in a large-scale show, then you may be able to limit the amount of contact you have with them, other than your interaction on stage. If you're on a small-scale tour you will spend most of your waking hours in their company, so it's important that all company members work hard to keep a harmonious atmosphere. Van etiquette is similar to dressing-room etiquette – balancing your needs with the cast's collective needs, and the individual needs of cast members. You can never legislate for a happy company, but here are some of the 'Golden Rules' that will help enormously in that direction:

● *Pull your weight.* This kind of touring is very hard work – you may be travelling, doing a get-in, a show, and a get-out every day for several weeks or months, and slacking off is the one thing guaranteed to make you as popular as herpes. Don't dawdle in the get-out, either; being the cause of not getting to the pub in time for last orders will also not endear you to your colleagues.

● *Be punctual.* The call time is when the van *leaves*, not the time you start to leave your accommodation. Be sitting in your seat, bag stowed, ready to leave at least 5 minutes before the call time. As with almost anything in this business, you're wasting several people's time by keeping them waiting, so respect your fellow actors by being on time.

● *Music.* Bring a personal stereo or MP3 player; don't expect everyone in the van to like your taste in music. One stage manager I know resorted to telling the cast that the stereo had broken rather than sit through yet another argument about whose music to listen to. You might also want to consider a portable DVD player, either for the journeys (unless you're susceptible to travel sickness) or for something to do when you get to your accommodation. Check whether these would be covered by the company's insurance in case anything happened to them, and remember that very few pieces of electronic equipment are built to withstand the rigours of touring.

● *Mobile phones.* Keep conversations short, even (perhaps especially) with loved ones. There are few more irritating things to be forced to listen to than someone cooing to their lover for hours on end. If you're someone who gets a lot of calls, consider setting your phone to silent vibrate; there are only so many times one can listen to the Nokia tune before being overwhelmed by the urge to throw the offending phone out of the window.

- *Smoking. Never* smoke in the van, even if the windows are rolled down – it's inconsiderate, and most companies operate a no-smoking policy anyway. (Since the van is considered your workplace, it may also be covered by recent anti-smoking legislation.) Remember, too, that if you're puffing away seconds before climbing aboard then you will carry a strong smell of smoke with you into the van. Be considerate, too, about smelly food – curry, chips, fish, etc. – unless you're all tucking in.
- *Personal hygiene.* Important at all times in this business, but especially so when you're stuck in a confined space with the rest of the cast for what may be hours at a time, perhaps after a particularly physical show and/or get-out. Your fellow actors may be upfront enough to tell you if you're pongy – but don't rely on it. If someone else in the company is niffing, don't gossip behind their back: just tell them, in as direct and as kind a way as possible. Don't let it fester (in more senses than one!).
- *Games.* It's worth bringing a few travel games for when the conversation runs out, even if it's just a pack of playing cards – although not everyone will want to play at any given moment. A good book can help while away the time, too, although not everyone can read in a van without getting travelsick.
- *Sweets.* The 'tub of love'. It does wonders for morale if someone takes it upon themself to buy a big tub of sweets for the van.
- *Alcohol.* Check the company's policy. If it's permitted, then it's probably best that you either buy your own (sharing around if you desire) or join up with one or two other members of the cast. It's generally preferable not to have a kitty for the whole cast, because not everyone will want to drink the same stuff or the same quantities. If you are getting merry in the back of a van, be considerate to the driver: don't distract them (dangerous!) or be unreasonably raucous. S/he will have had a hard evening too, and tunelessly drunken renditions of football chants will hardly make the journey more pleasant. Remember too that requests for toilet stops when everyone's tired and wants to get home may not be popular.
- *Make the most of solo time.* When you do get some time to yourself, make the most of it. Go for a walk, listen to music, read, exercise, meditate, call friends or just sit in a coffee shop and watch the world go by. Camaraderie and team spirit are important in this kind of work, but don't be afraid to take time for yourself when you need it.
- *Plan your meals.* You may be performing in some village hall miles from the nearest source of food, so be prepared. Sometimes – in village halls, especially – sandwiches are provided by the locals, but not always, so stock up before heading off for the day's performance, and keep an emergency supply of biscuits/fruit/pot noodles in your bag just in case. Make the most of the hotel or B&B breakfast.
- *Travel light.* Remember that you will be probably be checking into several different hotels or B&Bs a week, so only take with you what you can comfortably carry by yourself in one go. For ease of access when you want to find that one pair of socks or pants, wheeled suitcases or large hold-alls are preferable to rucksacks. While you may want to have more stuff back at your base, when you're on the road stick to one large bag and a day bag.
- *Finally, keep a sense of humour and a sense of perspective.* Not always the easiest thing to do on some jobs, but you're all in this together so have a good laugh at the absurdity of it all – it may just save your sanity.

Andrew Piper trained at Bristol Old Vic Theatre School. This piece was written in the van belonging to Northumberland Theatre Company (NTC) while he was playing Herbert Pocket, Uncle Pumblechook and Orlick in their production of *Great Expectations.*

Fringe theatres

Essentially, the idea of 'fringe theatre' began at the Edinburgh Festival more than half a century ago. It really started taking off (especially in London) in the late 1960s as an arena for 'alternative' and 'experimental' theatre. The 1990s saw a huge expansion in the number of venues being used, and a downturn in the exploration of theatre forms: the 'fringe' became more commercial and much more competitive – and not just in London and Edinburgh. Today, the terms 'alternative' and 'experimental' are far less frequently used, and the Fringe is now largely seen as a way for actors, directors and writers to showcase their work.

Casting for Fringe productions is usually advertised by one or more of the casting information services, and agents and casting directors do scout for new talent in them. However, it's highly unlikely that you will make any money from participating in such a production – you might end up with a net loss after deducting your expenses. Also agents and casting directors get blitzed with so many invitations that the chances of getting one of them to see you are not high. The only reasons for being in a Fringe production are (a) you might be 'seen'; (b) you fundamentally believe in the production's potential; and (c) it could help keep your acting-juices flowing – you might find classes less time-consuming and possibly more beneficial.

Although it is generally regarded as 'professional' work, there is a tendency in Fringe productions for professional standards (and facilities) to be somewhat lacking – and that is sometimes an understatement. Poor technical back-up, indifferent front-of-house arrangements and general unreliability are too often the case, almost inevitably damaging the quality of the final product.

Some potential problems to watch out for

● *The ego trip.* A number of productions are set up by individuals wanting a starring vehicle for themselves – much like the old actor-managers. It is generally better to avoid such enterprises unless you can be fairly sure that the central 'ego' will not be damaging to your contribution. Ask around for objective advice before accepting a part in such a production.

● *What else will you have to do?* Will you have to do other things – like paint the set, distribute posters, help with the get-in, and so on? You may think that you can make time to do things like this, but are you sure you want to be thus distracted in the last few days before opening night?

● *Is the script good enough?* There really is no point in doing a production that's flawed before it leaves the page.

● *Can you work well with the director?* This is a highly subjective judgement, but since you are not being properly paid, it is important that you feel as sure as you can be that it'll be a worthwhile experience.

● *Can you actually afford to do it?* There is no point in taking time out from paid work in order to rehearse and perform a Fringe production unless you really think that you'll get something out of the experience. (It can be worth asking if your rehearsal-calls can be arranged around your work commitments.) Also, check whether your participation will affect your benefits in any way.

- *Your agent.* If you have one, will s/he be happy for you to do the production?
- *Contracts.* In 2005, Equity published a set of guidelines (working hours, etc.) and a suggested contract for Fringe producers. This is not intended as an alternative to Equity's other agreements; rather, it is designed to help Fringe companies develop good employment practices. Some companies issue their own contracts; it is important to read these carefully and check with Equity if you have any doubts.
- *Will the production get reviews?* A good review equals good publicity – important for any production. Some productions in the most prestigious venues get reviewed in national newspapers. However, because there are so many productions at any one time, the press has strict rules (length of run, for instance) about what they will send reviewers to. It is important to note that the perceptiveness of some of the latter is somewhat shallow (that's not sour grapes; it's a fact).
- *Will the publicity and marketing be sufficient?* After the cost of hiring the venue, publicity and marketing represent the next major cost of a Fringe production. Too many productions try to skimp on these. In such a competitive environment, they are very, very important.
- *Does the venue have a good reputation?* It is much, much harder to get people into less prestigious ones.
- *Promises.* While enthusiasm for a project is wonderful, beware of promises when they seem over-the-top. Too much optimism can blind people to important practical realities.
- *Is it going to be properly organised?* There is far more to putting on a production than most actors realise (see below). Ask questions based on the above and, if you don't feel sufficiently satisfied, politely back away. There is no point in being miserable, as well as unpaid, for several weeks.
- *If I'm not being paid, can I not just pull out if something better comes along?* Legally, you can; morally and professionally it's an extremely dubious thing to do without the full understanding of your fellow participants – and you never know who, among them, might gain 'casting clout' in the future.

Setting up your own production

Too many people think that mounting a production is just a matter of getting a few friends together, borrowing some props and costumes, and getting on with it. What about the costs of hiring a venue, a rehearsal space, the publicity and marketing, the author's royalties (if still in copyright), and so on?

You may be lucky enough to get some, or even all, of these for free, or you might find a rich auntie. But however you fund the above essentials, you have got to do a lot of careful planning before rehearsals start. Will the playwright (and/or translator) allow you to do a production of the play in the first place? Just because a play is in print, it doesn't mean that anyone can perform it. Is the rehearsal room available enough of the time? What is the deadline for getting the poster design to the printers, so that they can get the result back to you in time for the distributors to get them displayed in good time before opening night? And so on, and so on, and so on ... Oh, and it is essential to plan and budget with contingency in both time and money – there are always several things that take more time than you'd thought, and several things that cost more than you'd thought (or forgotten to budget for in the first place).

Doing it yourself is far more complex than most people realise, but can be incredibly satisfying if you succeed. For a technically simple production you probably need to find at least £5000 – and that's without paying any of the participants. The chances of recouping this through the box office are very low; the average audience on the Fringe is about 30 per cent. A recent report stated that: "Theatres are among the most over-regulated businesses in the UK." Legal requirements like Health & Safety, VAT and performance rights cannot be neglected.

The Edinburgh Fringe Festival

There is a real sense that every actor should try this 'Carnival of theatre' experience – 'the biggest theatrical lottery in the world' – at least once. You'll meet lots of new people, make contacts and it's a great few weeks, even if your own production doesn't hit the heights.

Good advice on mounting a production on the Edinburgh Fringe is available from the Festival Office (details below).

The listings that follow are restricted to the more 'established' venues, with performance spaces for hire. Some Fringe theatres only programme-in work known to them.

Note If you are thinking of mounting a Fringe production and/or starting your own theatre company, start researching and planning well in advance. It is well worth consulting the Independent Theatre Council (ITC) – **www.itc-arts.org**.

UMBRELLA ORGANISATIONS

Edinburgh Festival Fringe

The Fringe Office, 180 High Street, Edinburgh EH1 1QS
tel 0131-226 0026 *fax* 0131-226 0016
email admin@edfringe.com
website www.edfringe.com

The Fringe Society was formed in 1959 to coordinate publicity and ticket sales, and offer a comprehensive information service both to performers and to audiences. It compiles information about venues, press and suppliers, and produces a series of publications designed to answer frequently asked questions. Its brochure contains details for 183 Fringe venues in Edinburgh. The office is open all year round and the staff are available to help by phone, email or personal appointment.

Fringe Theatre Network (FTN)

c/o Old Red Lion, 418 St John Street, London EC1V 4QE
tel 020-7833 3053
email helenoldredlion@yahoo.co.uk
website www.fringetheatre.org.uk
Coordinator Helen Devine

The FTN provides services, support and a network of contacts for venues, producing companies and individuals working on the London Fringe with the aim of increasing the level of professionalism in Fringe theatre. Acting as an umbrella organisation, the FTN puts forward the interests of Fringe theatre

in its dealings with statutory authorities, funding bodies, policy-makers and other arts organisations.

LONDON FRINGE VENUES

BAC (Battersea Arts Centre)

Lavender Hill, London SW11 5TN
tel 020-7326 8219
email lydias@bac.org.uk
website www.bac.org.uk
Programme Administrator Lydia Spry

BAC aims to help create and promote exciting, high-quality, collaborative arts activity. The emphasis is on devised rather than script-based work, and especially on the collaboration between different artforms. On the first Sunday of every month, *Scratch Nights* are held at which artists present no more than 10 minutes of material at a very early stage in its development – sometimes stopping in the middle for advice. The audience pays what it can to watch 3-4 of these projects and has a chance to offer feedback to the artists in the bar afterwards. Often presented as part of BAC's Opera Festival or OctoberFest are 2- or 3-night runs of *Scratch Performances*; these are rough show drafts and usually last between 40 minutes and 1 hour. Again, the audience is invited to the bar to give feedback after the show.

The next stage of development comprises 2- or 3-night runs of *Showcase Performances*, at which work is marketed to wider audiences, and is usually presented in the context of one of BAC's annual festivals. Following this, artists may be offered 3- to 6-week runs of *Showcase Performances* for which national reviews will be actively sought.

Artists can get on the BAC ladder of development at different stages and can progress at different rates as appropriate. Work is rarely programmed on the strength of a proposal alone, and the theatre's staff do not have time to read unsolicited scripts. Instead they prefer to build up a relationship with artists over time, viewing their work outside of BAC initially.

At certain times of year the theatre-spaces are hired out to drama schools for showcase events, but all theatre companies must go through the programming process. The BAC has 3 flexible black-box theatre spaces: Studio 1 and Studio 2 (average capacity 43/56) and the Main House (average capacity 150). For all programming enquiries, contact Lydia Spry.

Barons Court Theatre

The Curtain's Up, 28A Comeragh Rd, West Kensington, London W14 9RH
tel 020-7602 0235 *fax* 020-7603 8935
email baronstheatre@hotmail.com
Artistic Director Ron Phillips

A central London 55-seat theatre in the basement of the Curtain's Up public house and restaurant. Offers 1- to 5-week runs and can be booked up to 7 months in advance at a moderate rental. Also available for 1-day actors' showcases.

The Bridewell Theatre

Bride Lane, Fleet Street, London EC4Y 8EQ
tel 020-7353 3331
website www.stbrideinstitute.org/theatre.html

The Bridewell Theatre is a versatile space, which provides both an atmospheric entertainment venue and an unique conference facility in the heart of the City. In addition to a 12x8m performance space, there is a modular tiered seating system that in standard configuration can accommodate a raked audience of 134 people. The theatre also offers dressing rooms with en suite amenities, as well as a box-office/reception area and a fully equipped bar. All areas of the theatre are accessible to disabled users via lift.

Camden People's Theatre

58-60 Hampstead Road, London NW1 2PY
tel 020-7419 4841 or (08700) 600 100 (Box Office) *fax* 020-7813 3889
email admin@cptheatre.co.uk
website www.cptheatre.co.uk

A 60-seat flexible performance space, available for single nights as well as full runs. Also has rehearsal studio.

Canal Café Theatre

The Bridge House, Delamere Terrace, Little Venice, London W2 6ND

tel 020-7289 6056 *fax* 020-7266 1717
email newsrevue@mail.com
website www.newsrevue.com

A 60-seat café theatre situated above the Bridge House pub next to the canal in Little Venice. Welcomes comedy.

Chelsea Centre Theatre

World's End Place, King's Road, London SWI0 0DR
tel 020-7352 1967 *fax* 020-7352 2024

A 110-seat theatre which can be booked-up 6 months in advance. Particularly welcomes new writing.

Cockpit Theatre

Gateforth Street, London NW8 8EH
tel 020-7258 2920 *fax* 020-7258 2921
email dave.wybrow@awc.ac.uk

Theatre seats 180 (60 seats on 3 sides) and should be booked 6 months in advance. Welcomes classics, foreign-language theatre and other niche market work.

The Courtyard Theatre

10 York Way, King's Cross, London Nl 9AA
tel 020-7833 0870
email info@thecourtyard.org.uk
website www.thecourtyard.org.uk

Flexible seating arrangements for up to 70 with separate rehearsal rooms, foyer and gallery. Normally offers 4-week runs; can be booked up to a year in advance.

Diorama Studio Theatre

34 Osnaburgh Street, London NW1 3ND
tel 020-7916 5467 *fax* 020-7916 5282

As we go to press this venue is scheduled for demolition.

Etcetera Theatre

Oxford Arms, 265 Camden High Street, London NW1 7BU
tel 020-7482 4857 *fax* 020-7482 0378
email etc@etceteratheatre.com
website www.etceteratheatre.com

A black-box studio space with 42 raked seats, the theatre particularly welcomes new writing and comedy. Presents an early and a late show Tuesday to Sunday (usually running for 3 weeks or more), with one-off performances on Monday nights.

Finborough Theatre

The Finborough, 118 Finborough Road, London SW10 9ED
tel 020-7244 7439 *fax* 020-7835 1853
email admin@finboroughtheatre.co.uk
website www.finboroughtheatre.co.uk
Artistic Director Neil McPherson

Founded in 1980, the Finborough is "one of London's leading new writing venues" (*Time Out*). It also presents rediscoveries of neglected work from 1850 onwards, music theatre and UK premières of foreign work, particularly from the US and Canada. The 50-seat theatre is available for hire for 4-week runs and 1-night performances: more information is available on the website.

See entry for Concordance, its resident company, under *Middle and smaller-scale companies* on page 134.

Greenwich Playhouse

Greenwich Station Forecourt, 189 Greenwich High Road, London SE10 8JA
tel 020-8858 9256 *fax* 020-8310 7276
email alice@galleontheatre.co.uk
Artistic Director Alice de Sousa

Theatre seats 84 and boasts state-of the art facilities. Available for hire for short seasons at very affordable weekly rates. Visiting productions benefit free of charge from the advice and support of the resident Artistic Director – see entry for Galleon Theatre Company Ltd, under *Middle and smaller-scale companies* on page 129.

Hen & Chickens Theatre

Above Hen & Chickens Theatre Bar, 109 St Paul's Road, Islington, London N1 2NA
tel 020-7704 2001

A 60-seat theatre welcoming new writing. Directly opposite station. Offers 3- to 4-week runs with Monday nights available separately.

Jacksons Lane Theatre

269A Archway Road, London N6 5AA
tel 020-8340 5226
email mail@jacksonslane.org.uk
website www.jacksonslane.org.uk

Rooms are available for hire on a daily or hourly basis for private parties, rehearsals and performances. The Lavender Room seats up to 40; the Primrose Room seats up to 40; a multipurpose space seats up to 80; the Youth Space seats up to 25; and the Main Theatre seats 125-163.

King's Head Theatre

115 Upper Street, Islington, London N1 1QN
tel 020-7226 8561
website www.kingsheadtheatre.org

Famous for helping to launch the careers of many new writers, directors and actors including Stephen Berkoff, Anthony Sher and Victoria Wood. The theatre is situated above a public house with flexible seating for up to 105.

The Landor Theatre

70 Landor Road, London SW9 9PH
tel 020-7737 7276 *fax* 020-8480 8536
email info@landortheatre.co.uk

website www.landortheatre.co.uk

A 60-seat theatre situated above a public house.

Menier Chocolate Factory

51/53 Southwark Street, London SE1 1RU
tel 020-7907 7060
email info@menierchocolatefactory.com

2900sq ft of highly versatile and atmospheric theatre space, with lighting rig, sound, and video projection. Capacity 200. Recently transferred its production of Sondheim's musical *Sunday in the Park with George* (starring Daniel Evans and Jenna Russell) to the Wyndhams Theatre in the West End.

New End Theatre

27 New End, Hampstead, London NW3 1JD
tel 020-7472 5800 *fax* 020-7472 5808
email mail@newendtheatre.co.uk
website www.newendtheatre.co.uk

Theatre seats 84 and has a strong tradition of presenting new plays and musicals, as well as reviving works from the classical canon. Recent productions include: Sondheim's *Assassins*; *A Dangerous Woman* (starring Fenella Fielding); and *Weill & Lenya* (directed by Ken Russell).

Old Red Lion

418 St John Street, Islington, London EC1V 4NJ
tel 020-7833 3053 *fax* 020-7833 3053
website www.oldredliontheatre.co.uk
Theatre Manager Helen Devine

Founded in 1979, the Old Red Lion Theatre is a 60-seater Fringe theatre primarily dedicated to new writing. Companies wishing to hire the venue should post a script, some company information and a production proposal to the Artistic Director. Normally programmes 3 months ahead.

Oval House Theatre

52-54 Kennington Oval, London SE11 5SW
tel 020-7582 0080
email Karena.Johnson@OvalHouse.com
website www.ovalhouse.com
Programmer Karena Johnson

Comprises 2 spaces; the upstairs theatre seats 50 and the downstairs theatre seats 100. Presents a diverse programme of work.

Pleasance Theatre London

Carpenters Mews, North Road, London N7 9EF
tel 020-7619 6868 *fax* 020-7700 7366
email info@pleasance.co.uk
website www.pleasance.co.uk/LONDON

The Pleasance now has 2 spaces: the Main Theatre, seating just under 300; and the Pleasance Stage Space, a new venue created to nurture the best in new theatre writing and emerging comedy talent, seating 54.

Riverside Studios

Crisp Road, London W6 9RL
tel 020-8237 1000
website www.riversidestudios.co.uk

Riverside has a varied programme of both domestic and international performance, theatre, dance and other events. Considers work – either hires or co-productions – within the context of the building's artistic policy.

Studio Two is a medium-sized black-box space with a comprehensive motorised grid, suited to all types of production: flexible configurations seating up to 400. Selected recent shows include: Graeae Theatre's *Mother Courage and Her Children*; Complicite's *Mnemonic*. Studio Three is a small black-box studio, opening off the foyer; raked theatre-style seating available – 156 seats installed as standard. Studio Four is a high-quality general-purpose room on the second floor, particularly suited to rehearsals, auditions, workshops and small-scale filming. No permanent seating; capacity up to 100 (not currently accessible by wheelchair). Other spaces available for hire include many smaller office spaces, a cinema auditorium and a television studio.

Rosemary Branch Theatre

2 Shepperton Road, London N1 3DT
tel 020-7704 6665
email cecilia@rosemarybranch.co.uk

Under the same management since 1996, the theatre has recently been expanded to hold a maximum of 65 seats. Presents a diverse programme including opera, classics, new writing, musicals and cabaret. A rehearsal space is also available. Normally books 3-week runs but this is negotiable. The theatre offers all visiting companies lots of support and goodwill.

Soho Theatre

21 Dean Street, London W1V 6NE
tel 020-7478 0117 *fax* 020-7287 5061
email hires@sohotheatre.com
website www.sohotheatre.com

Soho Theatre + Writers' Centre aims to discover and develop new playwrights, produce a year-round programme of new plays, and attract new audiences. Founded in 1972, the company premiered the early work of such playwrights as Caryl Churchill, David Edgar, Hanif Kureishi, Tanika Gupta, and Timberlake Wertenbaker; more recently it has presented new plays by Laura Wade, Will Eno, Adriano Shaplin, Debbie Tucker Green, Matt Charman, Rebecca Lenkiewicz and Toby Whithouse.

Soho Theatre + Writers' Centre is now a key producing venue of new plays and comedy. Offering the nation's most extensive unsolicited script-reading service, the Writers' Centre provides a range of developmental schemes including: the Writers' Attachment Programme; Launch Pad Workshops;

The Verity Bargate Award; The Westminster Prize; a thriving Young Writers' Programme; commissions and seed bursaries; Writers' Rooms; and an extensive Research & Development programme of readings, workshops, script surgeries, seminars and initiatives, all of which "enable us to attract and nurture the most outstanding writers from our local community and throughout the country".

Three writers' rooms are available free of charge, complete with computer, printer and access to a growing script library. They are available to writers free of charge from 10am – 6pm, Monday to Friday and can be booked for as little as an hour or up to a month; priority will be given to writers whose work is being developed by STC.

Soho Theatre + Writers' Centre includes a flexible 144-seat theatre, a large self-contained Studio space with 85-seat capacity, theatre bar, restaurant, offices, rehearsal, writing and meeting rooms. All spaces are accessible and available for hire. For bookings and general information, please visit **www.sohotheatre.com**.

There are 4 spaces to hire at Soho Theatre. Each is air-conditioned, has full disabled access and can be set up to specific requirements. The theatre seats 144 and has a maximum stage area of 11m wide x 6m deep. The studio measures 9m x 11m and is a self-contained and sound-proofed space with an acoustic wall dividing the room into 2. The studio is equipped with a PA system and mini disc; seating is flexible with a capacity of 85. The writers' seminar room measures 7m x 3.5m; it is a light, airy room with a balcony looking over Dean Street. The terrace measures 4m x 3m and has a glass-fronted balcony. It includes a separate waiting area and is suitable for castings and small meetings. For more information, please visit the website, or telephone.

See also entry under *Producing theatres* on page 112.

Southwark Playhouse

5 Playhouse Court, 62 Southwark Bridge Rd, London SE1 0AS
tel 020-7652 2224 *fax* 020-7261 1271
email admin@southwarkplayhouse.co.uk
website www.southwarkplayhouse.co.uk

Formed in 1993, this studio theatre has been nominated 3 times for the Empty Space Peter Brook Award. Alongside its own productions, the theatre presents and supports the work of talented young companies with a mixed programme of classic and new plays. Maximum seating capacity is 90. In general the theatre is booked-up 3-4 months in advance, but this can vary. Proposals should be sent by post or email to the Playhouse with a 1-page synopsis of the production and all the relevant details.

Tabard Theatre

2 Bath Road, Turnham Green, London W4 1LW
tel 020-8994 5985

Artistic Director Fred Perry

Situated above the Tabard pub, close to Turnham Green tube. Offers 3- to 4-week runs which are programmed 4-5 months ahead.

Theatre 503

The Latchmere, 503 Battersea Park Road, London SW11 3BW
tel 020-7229 8530 *fax* 020-7229 8140
email mail@theatre503.com
website www.theatre503.com

Situated above a public house, Theatre 503 aims to provide a venue for new playwrights, comedians and directors to develop their shows. It has a working relationship with television commissioners and producers, literary managers of established theatres and literary agents, and tries to offer a stepping-stone from Fringe to 'big' theatres.

Theatro Technis

26 Crowndale Road, London NW1 1TT
tel 020-7387 6617 *fax* 020-7383 2545
email info@theatrotechnis.com
website www.theatrotechnis.co.uk

Theatro Technis' ideas and policies are realised for anyone who is interested in the development of individuals and communities. The theatre maintains a balance between classic and contemporary work, and serves to embrace a variety of diverse artforms ranging from theatre and dance to art, photography, music and film.

Union Theatre

204 Union Street, Southwark, London SE1 0LX
tel 020-7261 9876 *fax* 020-7261 9876
email sasha@uniontheatre.freeserve.co.uk
website www.uniontheatre.freeserve.co.uk

Primarily a new writing venue, the theatre aims to present a diverse programme featuring the best new talent. Guest performances are supplemented by regular in-house productions. Normally offers 3-week runs.

Upstairs at the Gatehouse

The Gatehouse Pub, North Road, London N6 4BD
tel 020-8340 3477
email events@ovationproductions.com
website www.upstairsatthegatehouse.com

Seats 132 (140 in cabaret style). A rehearsal room is also available. See entry for Ovation Productions under Middle and smaller-scale companies.

V&A Theatre Museum Studio

1E Tavistock Street, London, WC2E 7PR
tel 020-7943 4717 *fax* 020-7943 4777
email r.fraser@vam.ac.uk
website www.theatremuseum.org.uk
Commercial Activities Manager Roddy Fraser

Located in Covent Garden, at the heart of the V&A Theatre Museum (also known as the National Museum of Performing Arts), it seats 81 people when using the normal ¾-thrust configuration. The usual run duration for a show in this space is 4-6 weeks, although this can vary. Hire rates are currently £200 per day or £1050 per week, and the space is accessible for performers with disabilities. Bookings are not usually possible during the month of December. Does not currently produce any in-house shows. Selected recent visiting shows include: *Much Ado About Nothing*, *The Trial of Sir Henry Irving*, *Amy Evans' Strike*, *The Suicided Man*, and *Titus Andronicus*.

Note The Studio (along with the rest of the Theatre Museum building) is threatened with closure at the end of 2006. While it is hoped that a home will be found for the Museum's exhibitions, the fate of the Studio is, as we go to press, unclear. Contact the Museum for the latest information, or see its main entry on page 319.

White Bear Theatre

138 Kennington Park Road, London SE11 4DJ
tel 020-7793 9193

An L-shaped studio space with seating for up to 50. Generally prefers new writing but occasionally accepts revivals.

Wimbledon Studio Theatre

In Wimbledon Theatre, 103 The Broadway, London SW19 1QG
tel 020-8543 4549 *fax* 020-8543 6637
email live@wimbledontheatre.demon.co.uk

A recently refurbished theatre with seating for up to 80. Normally offers 3- to 4-week runs which are programmed 6 months ahead.

EDINBURGH FRINGE VENUES

Many of these venues are only available for hire during the Edinburgh Festival Fringe in August. For a full list of venues, contact the Fringe Society (see above).

Assembly Rooms

Assembly Theatre, 250 George Street, Edinburgh EH2 2LE
tel 0131-624 2442 *fax* 0131-624 7131
email info@assemblyrooms.com
website www.assemblyrooms.com

The Assembly Rooms have presented more than 1000 productions featuring most of the major names in British comedy – as well as a huge array of theatre, dance and music events which have been seen by more than 1.5 million people over the last 20 years of the Edinburgh Festival Fringe. The daily programme runs from 11.00am to 3.30am with exhibitions, a café, 2 public bars and a club bar. Aims to programme a balance of theatre, comedy and new work.

Augustine's

Augustine United Church, 41 George IV Bridge, Edinburgh EH1 1EL
tel 0131-220 1677

During the rest of the year this venue is known as Augustine United Church. It is adapted during the Festival to house 2 performance spaces (the upper venue seats 110; the lower venue seats approximately 105). Programmes theatre, musicals, dance and children's theatre from the UK and elsewhere.

Bedlam Theatre

11B Bristo Place, Edinburgh EH1 1EZ
tel 0131-225 9873
email bedlam.theatre@ed.ac.uk
website www.bedlamtheatre.co.uk

A 90-seat black-box theatre in central Edinburgh housed in a neo-gothic church. The theatre is available for hire when not in use by the Edinburgh University Theatre Company.

C venues

Administration Office: C Venues Limited, 5 Alexandra Mansions, Chichele Road, London NW2 3AS
email info@cvenues.com
website www.cvenues.com

Comprises 4 theatre venues in Edinburgh: C; C too; C central; C cubed. Presents drama, physical theatre, comedy, music, musicals, dance, opera, children's shows and visual arts with an emphasis on new and dynamic work. C's 4 locations include a 203-seat thrust space, 2 end-on black-box studios seating 95 and 144, and a permanent 160-seat proscenium-arch auditorium in the basement. There is also a platform stage in the bar and extensive exhibition space on each foyer level. In total there are 10 spaces including a new basement cabaret bar and 3 intimate black-box theatres at C central.

Gilded Balloon

25 Greenside Place, Edinburgh EH1 3AA
tel 0131-226 6550 or 0131-622 6555

Has a very strong comedy programme; also presents live music.

Greyfriars (Studios 1 and 2)

Greyfriars Kirk House, 86 Candlemaker Row, Edinburgh EH1 2QA

Studio 1 (upstairs, seats 60) and Studio 2 (seats around 40) are intimate spaces suited to 1- to 3-handers, storytelling or poetry. Applications should be made by February for hire during the Festival Fringe.

Hill Street Theatre

Hill Street Theatre, Universal Arts, Gateway Theatre, Elm Row, Edinburgh EH7 4AH
tel 0131-478 0195 *fax* 0131-478 0185
email hillstreet@universal-arts.com

Presents a programme of well-known works alongside new writing, musicals, dance, mime and physical theatre. Theatrical production includes comic writing but not stand-up comedy. The main theatre seats 120 while the studio theatre is a more intimate space, seating a maximum of 73. Suited to 1-handers, the studio can accommodate up to 8 performers comfortably.

The Netherbow

43-45 High Street, Edinburgh EH1 1SR
tel 0131-556 9579
website www.scottishstorytellingcentre.co.uk

Intimate 100-seat theatre presenting drama, poetry, storytelling and puppetry events. Offers a strong programme of family shows. The whole building, being new-build from 2005, is very wheelchair-friendly both for the public and for actors.

The Pleasance

The Pleasance Courtyard: 60 The Pleasance, Edinburgh EH8 9TJ
tel 020-7619 6868
The Pleasance Dome: 1 Bristo Square, Edinburgh EH8 9AL
The Pleasance Administration Office: Carpenters Mews, North Road, London N7 9EF
website www.pleasance.co.uk

The Pleasance presents more than 160 shows across its 16 venues during the 4 weeks of the Festival Fringe. With more than 190,000 visitors, it remains one of the most popular venues of the Fringe, offering a mix of comedy, theatre, dance and music.

The Underbelly

Off Cowgate, Edinburgh Permanent Office: 25 Greenside Place, Edinburgh EH1 3AA
tel 0131-622 6566 *fax* 0131-622 6576
email ed@smirnoffunderbelly.co.uk
website www.theunderbelly.co.uk
Venue Manager Ed Bartlam

Comprises 6 spaces over 4 floors with 3 bars. Venues cater for audiences of 60-200 with different seating configurations available. Programmes new writing, theatre, dance and comedy.

Traverse Theatre

10 Cambridge Street, Edinburgh EH1 2ED
email mike@traverse.co.uk
website www.traverse.co.uk
Administrative Director Mike Griffiths

Centre for new playwriting. All-year-round venue in underground purpose-built theatre with 2 auditoria. Has staged premières of plays by Rona Munro and David Greig, and productions by Paines Plough. Also presents late-night comedy.

OTHER FRINGE LOCATIONS

Komedia

44-47 Gardner Street, Brighton BN1 1UN
tel (01273) 647101 *fax* (01273) 647102
email info@komedia.co.uk
website www.komedia.co.uk

An upstairs and downstairs cabaret bar serving hot food and drinks, each with a capacity of 230 seated around tables, and a 160-seat theatre. Komedia presents a programme of theatre, world music, cabaret, comedy and children's shows. Has been host to names such as Graham Norton, Mel & Sue, League of Gentlemen and The Right Size.

Sevenoaks Stag Theatre

London Road, Sevenoaks, Kent TN13 1ZZ
tel (01732) 451548
email julian.woolford@stagtheatre.co.uk

The theatre can seat up to 453 and has provision for wheelchair-users. Companies should book the space up to 6 months in advance. Programmes a wide range of theatre and dance events.

Watermans Arts Centre

40 High Street, Brentford, Middlesex TW8 0DS
tel 020-8847 5651 *fax* 020-8569 8592
email enquiries@watermans.org.uk
website www.watermans.org.uk

An arts venue comprising 239-seat theatre, 125-seat cinema, studio 1 (large), studio 2 (small), gallery, restaurant and bar, and river views of the Thames. Programmes across a range of different artforms including Asian arts, new media, children's theatre, cinema and participative arts. The studios have a nominal capacity of 80 and 30 seats respectively, but these spaces are mostly used for workshops, meetings and rehearsals.

Children's, young people's and Theatre in Education companies

Paul Harman

Work in this very large sector of employment for actors in the UK varies greatly – both in the style of theatre created and presented, and in the wages and conditions offered by employers. Anyone taking work in the field should always be clear about the aims and status of their prospective employer.

Most producing theatres offer plays for young audiences as part of a season, and Christmas shows and pantomimes are mounted by a large number of receiving theatres and commercial touring companies. Some 200 independent touring companies regularly present original theatre productions, usually in schools, reaching a total audience of at least five million annually. Smaller touring companies may operate for profit, or as profit-share partnerships. Companies which are members of ITC (Independent Theatre Council) offer pay and conditions agreed with the performers' trade union, Equity.

Reality check

There is no official agency that collects reliable statistics or regulates the quality of what is offered. Your work may never be publicly reviewed – and it can be hard and demanding. Casts are often small, and living conditions on the road are sometimes difficult. The work may involve a lot of driving (if you are over 25 and insurable) as well as humping sets in and out of vans. However, the rewards for good-quality work conscientiously presented lie in the warmth of welcome from audiences and bookers alike, and a directness and openness of audience response which is often less evident at more formal, adult-orientated theatre events. In schools, you will perform in daylight, very close to children – so it helps if you like them. They can see every blemish on you, and you can see every reaction on a hundred faces.

You will need physical stamina; the ability to play many parts convincingly; and the facility to hit a peak of performance two or more times in a day, six days a week. You may need skill in playing a musical instrument. In addition, other aptitudes may be called upon. A play may be preceded or followed by workshop activity with young people – from 'hot-seating' in character to involving children in a performance. An understanding of drama education techniques is therefore an advantage, and experience of Youth Theatre useful.

What shows?

For good economic and marketing reasons, most theatre for children presented in larger houses is based on well-known stories by established authors, or on characters from TV shows. Companies may receive financial support from official agencies to present plays on health and social issues. Plays related to the National Curriculum, such as science topics, are in great demand from schools.

Theatre in Education (TIE) is a term commonly used to mean many kinds of theatre in schools. In the strict sense, TIE implies an extended theatre event, combining performance and participatory elements and designed to engage pupils in exploring their own knowledge, feelings and attitudes. This is quite a different process from explaining how magnets work or presenting an account of an historical event. Very few companies nowadays can afford the time and staffing needed to support real TIE, but there are many opportunities to create and present challenging educational plays on a wide variety of subjects.

Independent touring companies receiving public subsidy from Arts Councils in England, Wales, Scotland and Northern Ireland generally aim to present original, commissioned drama. A small group of writers specialises in this field, addressing personal and social topics, from fear of the dark or the break-up of families to genetics and migration. This group of companies – whose aims are primarily artistic, rather than just to entertain or deliver educational messages – find like-minded companies in 70 countries through ASSITEJ (International Association of Theatre for Children and Young People). Overseas tours and international collaborations are increasing.

Above all, don't look upon this field as an easy step towards something else. Your first experiences may well be tough, but an apprenticeship served with a supportive company will open an area of work you can return to with growing enjoyment and professional satisfaction.

Paul Harman has worked as an actor and director in professional theatre since 1963. He joined Belgrade Theatre in Education team in 1966, headed Education work at Liverpool Everyman from 1970, and founded Merseyside Young People's Theatre Company in 1978. Since 1994 he has been Artistic Director of CTC Theatre, Darlington. He is the current Chair of ASSITEJ UK.

Note Some of the companies listed are members of the Independent Theatre Council (ITC) – **www.itc-arts.org.uk**.

6.15 Theatre Company
22 Brookfield Mansions, Highgate, London N6 6AS
tel 020-8342 8239 *fax* 020-8340 5696
email six15@dircon.co.uk
website www.six15.co.uk
Artistic Director James Tillitt *Associate Director* Nicola Cussons

Production details
Founded in 1984. Tours to schools, trade exhibitions and conference venues across the UK. Singing ability, proficiency with a musical instrument and a driving licence are required. Actors may be expected to lead workshops. Recent productions include: *Wise Up!*, an interactive drug education project for the Mentor Foundation; and *CR7*, a musical presentation on cancer prevention for Cancer Research UK.

Casting procedures
Does not hold general auditions, but casting breakdowns are available through the website, Equity Job Information Service and *PCR*.

Applause Productions
Beechwood House, 13 Beechwood Road, West Moors, Dorset BH22 0BN
tel (01202) 887439 *fax* (01202) 849493
email admin@derekgrant.co.uk
website www.derekgrant.co.uk
Artistic Director Derek Grant *Administrative Director* Michael Jones

Production details
Founded in 1989. "We present traditional children's/family shows and pantomimes. A strong storyline features in every show, along with colourful costumes and scenery, bright musical numbers and lots of joining in!" Normally tours 2 projects each year, with an average annual total of 200 performances and 200 different venues. Venues include arts centres and theatres across the UK, including Northern Ireland, Channel Islands and the Isle of Man. In general 5 actors go on tour and play to audiences aged 3-93. Singing ability, dance/physical theatre skills and a driving licence are required. Recent productions include: *Goldilocks and the Three Bears, Pinocchio* and Hans Anderson's *The Snow Queen*.

Casting procedures
Sometimes holds general auditions; actors can write at any time requesting inclusion. Accepts submissions (with CVs and photographs) from actors previously unknown to the company sent by post or email. Will also accept showreels and invitations to view individual actors' websites.

Big Wheel Theatre in Education

The Institute, PO Box 18221, London EC1R 4WJ
tel 020-7689 8670 fax 020-7689 8670
email info@bigwheel.org.uk
website www.bigwheel.org.uk
Artistic Directors Roland Allen, Jeni Williams

Production details

Since 1984 has developed interactive theatre for use in education and training in the UK and abroad. Normally tours 10 projects each year, with an average annual total of 400 performances and 200 different venues. Venues include schools and conference centres across the UK, Europe, Japan, Kenya and South Africa. In general 2 actors go on tour and play to audiences aged 7 upwards. Actors are required to hold a driving licence and to lead workshops. Experience in teaching or training is also useful. Recent productions include: *Introduction to Shakespeare*, a game-show-based interactive workshop; *Breakfast with Big Wheel*, a show to teach English in European schools; and a variety of workshops for the NHS about communication, partnerships and peripatetic working.

Casting procedures

Sometimes holds general auditions; actors may write at any time requesting inclusion. "It's quite specialist work. Best to have a good look at the website and only send us your stuff if you think it really is your cup of tea."

Bitesize Theatre Company

8 Green Meadows, New Broughton, Wrexham LL11 GSG
tel (01978) 358320 fax (01978) 358315
email admin@bitesizetheatre.co.uk
website www.bitesizetheatre.co.uk
Artistic Director Linda Griffiths Administrator Bill Robertson

Production details

Founded in 1992, the company strives to provide high-quality, entertaining theatrical productions for young people – from children's classics to Shakespeare and pantomime to new works. Also runs Theatre in Education projects and bespoke workshops. In general the company stages 11 productions each year, totalling approximately 910 performances in schools and community venues across the UK. Rehearsals take place in North Wales. Between 3-6 actors work on each show and play to audiences aged 3-19 years. Actors are required to be able to sing, dance and drive and may also be expected to participate in workshops. Recent productions include: *Romeo and Juliet*, *Macbeth*, *Jack and the Beanstalk*, *Cinderella* and *Peter and the Wolf*.

Casting procedures

The company holds general auditions; actors requesting inclusion in these should write in May. Casting breakdowns are available in *PCR*, *The Stage*, *Castcall* and *SBS*. Although actors are welcome to write with their CVs and photographs, the company prefers not to receive emails or showreels. Mainly takes actors from recognised drama schools; actors aged over 25 years are preferred for jobs requiring driving. All employees must pass a CRB (Criminal Records Bureau) check for work with children. Offers non-Equity contracts. Actively encourages applications from disabled actors and promotes the use of inclusive casting.

Bournemouth Theatre in Education

BCCA, 93 Haviland Road, Bournemouth BH7 6HJ
tel (01202) 395759 fax (01202) 399597
email tie@bournemouth.gov.uk
Artistic Directors Tony Horitz, Sharon Muiruri
Administrator Shaz Watkins

Production details

Founded in 1967. "Theatre in Education service within a lifelong learning framework." Works in schools, presenting theatrical performances and facilitating drama; is also actively involved in the field of social inclusion. Normally tours 10-15 projects each year to schools, arts centres, outdoor venues, community venues, prisons and hospitals in the South of England. In general 3-4 actors go on tour and play to audiences of all ages. Actors are required to have good workshop skills and the ability to relate well to people. Recent productions include: *My Name Is Savitri*, an anti-racism play for Year 4 children; *Angel*, with a disabled actors theatre company; and *Sleeping Beauty*, with Tops (actors with learning difficulties).

Casting procedures

Sometimes holds general auditions; actors may write at any time requesting inclusion. Accepts submissions (with CVs and photographs) from actors previously unknown to the company sent by post or email. Will also accept showreels and invitations to view individual actors' websites. "We do use professional actors on a fairly regular basis, but prefer to use those living in or around the Bournemouth area."

Box Clever Theatre Company

12 G1 The Leathermarket, Weston Street, London SE1 3ER
tel 020-7357 0550 fax 020-7357 8188
email admin@boxclevertheatre.com
website www.boxclevertheatre.com
Artistic Director Michael Wicherek
Administrator Zareen Graves

Production details

Founded in 1996, the company produces contemporary theatre for young people: new plays, contemporary adaptations of classic texts, and issue-based and educational work. 6 major national tours are staged each year with an average annual total of approximately 600 performances in 500 different venues. The company performs to more than 60,000 young people every year. Venues include arts centres, theatres, and educational and community venues nationwide. Approximately 3 actors are involved in each production. Recent productions include: *Time for the Good Looking Boy* (for theatres); *The Buzz, Driving Ms Daisy, The Hate Plays* and *Boxed Macbeth* (for secondary schools); and *Car Story* for primary schools.

Casting procedures

Does not use freelance casting directors. Casting breakdowns are available via Equity Job Information Service, the website (normally June/July and October/November), and *PCR*. Welcomes submissions (with CVs and photographs) from actors previously unknown to the company if sent by post and if in response to casting breakdowns only. Advises actors that the company receives a huge response to advertisements placed in *PCR*, and is therefore unable to return photographs or respond in writing to applicants not invited to audition. Non-Equity contracts "in line with ITC". Considers applications from disabled actors to play characters with disabilities.

C&T

University College Worcester, Henwick Grove, Worcester WR2 6AJ
tel (01905) 855436
email info@candt.org
website www.candt.org
Artistic Director Paul Sutton

Production details

Founded in 1988. A theatre company incorporating performance, learning and digital media. Works in schools, colleges and universities in the UK and across Europe. Normally tours 2-3 projects each year with an average annual total of 50-100 performances at 50-100 different venues. In general 2-3 actors go on tour and play to audiences aged 5-65. Dance/physical theatre skills, proficiency with computers and digital media, and a driving licence are required. Actors are also expected to lead workshops. Recent productions include: *Living Newspaper.com*, a docu-drama project online for schools.

Casting procedures

Sometimes holds general auditions; actors should write in September requesting inclusion. Accepts submissions (with CVs and photographs) from actors previously unknown to the company sent by post or email. Will also accept showreels and invitations to view individual actors' websites.

Channel Theatre

See entry under Channel Theatre Company & Chalkfoot Theatre Arts under *Middle and smaller-scale companies* on page 132.

Cwmni Theatr Arad Goch

Stryd Y Baddon, Aberystwyth, Ceredigion SY23 2NN
tel (01970) 617998 *fax* (01970) 611223
email post@aradgoch.org
Artistic Director Jeremy Turner *Administrative Manager* Nia Wyn Evans

Production details

Founded in 1989. Main focus of work is Theatre in Education. Normally tours 6 projects each year with an average annual total of 150 performances and more than 100 different venues. Venues include schools, theatres and community venues across Wales and occasionally abroad. In general 3-6 actors go on tour and play to audiences aged 4 upwards. Singing ability, proficiency with a musical instrument, fluency in Welsh and a driving licence are required. Actors may also be expected to lead workshops. Recent productions include: *Llew Lletchwith* for 7-11 year-olds; and *Riff*, a community theatre piece for young people.

Casting procedures

Sometimes holds general auditions; actors requesting inclusion should write before the start of the academic year. Accepts submissions (with CVs and photographs) from actors previously unknown to the company sent by post or email. Will also accept showreels and invitations to view individual actors' websites. Offers ITC/Equity approved contracts. Rarely (or never) has the opportunity to cast disabled actors.

Daylight Theatre

66 Middle Street, Stroud, Gloucestershire GL5 1EA
tel (01453) 763808
Artistic Director Hugh Young *Key personnel* Roger Burfield

Production details

Founded in 1977. Tours educational theatre into schools. Topics have included drugs, HIV/AIDS, Shakespeare, history and mythology, and have been linked to the National Curriculum. Normally tours 7 projects each year with an average annual total of 200 performances and 150 different venues. Venues include schools (mainly primary but some secondary), arts centres and theatres across the UK,

Germany and Luxembourg. In general 2-3 actors go on tour and play to audiences aged 4-18. Actors are required to hold a driving licence and may also be expected to lead workshops. Recent productions include: *Can You Take It?* – drugs, alcohol and tobacco education for 9-11 year-olds; *A Midsummer Night's Dream* and *Macbeth* for Key Stage 2 level; and *Ghostcliff Grange*, a World War II drama, also for Key Stage 2.

Casting procedures

Advises that the company rarely needs new female actors.

Gazebo Theatre in Education Company

37 Imex House, Imex Business Park, Upper Villiers Street, Wolverhampton WV2 4XE
tel (01902) 313009 *fax* (01902) 313229
email gazebotie@tiscali.co.uk
website www.gazebotie.co.uk
Artistic Project Leaders Pamela Cole-Hudson, Michael O'Hara

Production details

Founded in 1979. Normally tours 3-5 projects each year plus workshops, with an average annual total of 300 performances and 250 different venues; these include schools and community venues in the West Midlands and South Shropshire. In general 5 actors go on tour and play to audiences aged 4-25. Musical ability and movement skills are sometimes required, as is a driving licence. Actors may also be expected to lead workshops. Recent productions include: *Macbeth* (Key Stage 3); *Home* (KS2); *Spaceman Sid* (Early Years); and *Going It Alone* (KS3).

Casting procedures

Casting breakdowns are sometimes available by postal application (with sae) or through Equity Job Information Service. The company website will also show details of auditions and artists' opportunities. Accepts submissions (with CVs and photographs) from actors previously unknown to the company if sent by post. Open auditions take place over the summer months. Does not welcome unsolicited emails. Will also accept invitations to view individual actors' websites. Non-Equity contracts. Actively encourages applications from disabled actors and promotes the use of inclusive casting.

Greenwich & Lewisham Young People's Theatre (GLYPT)

Building 18, Royal Arsenal West, Woolwich, London SE18 6ST
tel 020-8854 1316
email info@gypt.co.uk
website www.gypt.co.uk
Artistic Director Jeremy James *Education Officer* Caroline Edwards

Production details

GLYPT creates theatre for, with and by young people. It runs Youth Theatre workshops for 8-21 year-olds, and specialist programmes for young people with learning difficulties. The company also runs a comprehensive programme of workshops for young refugees and new arrivals. Tours 2 productions a year to young audiences across South East London and beyond; these visit schools as Theatre in Education programmes, and also play at community and arts centres and at theatres. The work explores current and provoking issues that affect the lives of young audiences, and offers a platform for aesthetic and educational debate. Recent productions have included: *Red, White, Black & Blue*, *Who R U Talkin' 2?* and *Master Juba*.

Casting procedures

Operates the ITC/Equity contract and works with actors committed to the young people's theatre sector. "We actively encourage applications from disabled actors and promote the use of inclusive casting." Welcomes letters and emails (with CVs) from actors and skilled workshop facilitators.

Gwent Theatre

The Drama Centre, Pen-y-Pound, Abergavenny NP7 5UD
tel (01873) 853167 *fax* (01873) 853910
email gwenttie@aol.com
website www.gwenttie.co.uk
Artistic Director Gary Meredith *Administrator* Julia Davies

Production details

Founded in 1976. Tours at least 4 projects each year with an average annual total of 180 performances. Venues include schools, theatres, outdoor venues and community venues in Gwent and across Wales. In general 3-5 actors go on tour and play to audiences aged 6 upwards. Singing ability, proficiency with a musical instrument and dance/physical theatre skills are required. Actors may also be expected to lead workshops. Recent productions include: *Pa Mor Uchel Yw Fyny?*, *Home Front*, *The Watching* and *Shadow Seeker* (all for schools).

Casting procedures

Sometimes holds general auditions and actors can write at any time requesting inclusion. Accepts submissions (with CVs and photographs) from actors previously unknown to the company if sent by post. Does not welcome unsolicited emails. Will also accept invitations to view individual actors' websites.

Half Moon Young People's Theatre

43 Whitehorse Road, London E1 0ND
tel 020-7265 8138 *fax* 020-7709 8914

email admin@halfmoon.org.uk
website www.halfmoon.org.uk
Artistic Director Chris Elwell *Administrative Director* Jackie Eley

Production details

Founded in 1989. "Young people's theatre touring in London and nationally with a reputation for high-quality work. Also a receiving venue for young people's work." Normally tours 2 projects with an average annual total of 170 performances and 45 different venues. Venues include schools, arts centres, theatres and community venues. In general 2-3 actors go on tour and play to audiences aged under 17. Singing ability and physical theatre skills are required; actors may also be expected to lead workshops.

Casting procedures

Casting breakdowns are available through the website, postal application (with sae) and Equity Job Information Service. Sometimes holds general auditions; actors can write at any time requesting inclusion. Accepts submissions (with CVs and photographs) from actors previously unknown to the company sent by post or email. Will also accept invitations to view individual actors' websites.

Hopscotch Theatre Company

2nd Floor, 7 Water Row, Glasgow G51 3UW
tel 0141-440 2025 *fax* 0141-440 2025
email info@hopscotchtheatre.com
website www.hopscotchtheatre.com
Artistic Director Grant Smeaton *General Manager* Susan McGregor

Production details

Founded in 1988. A Theatre in Education company touring 4 productions each year to primary schools with an average annual total of 520 performances. Venues include schools, arts centres, theatres and community venues across Scotland. In general 4 actors go on tour and play to audiences aged 5-12 years. Singing ability and some proficiency with a musical instrument are required. Recent productions include: *The Romans in Scotland*, *Mary Queen of Scots* and *Tam O' Shanter*.

Casting procedures

Holds general auditions; actors requesting inclusion should write in May or June. Accepts submissions (with CVs and photographs) from actors previously unknown to the company sent by post or email. Will also accept showreels. Offers non-Equity contracts. Rarely (or never) has the opportunity to cast disabled actors.

Jack Drum Arts

Enterprise House, Harmire Park, Barnard Castle, Co. Durham DL12 8XT

email info@jackdrum.co.uk
Artistic Director Julie Ward *Administrator* Jill Cole

Production details

Founded in 1986. "Delivers a strong programme of participatory arts for all sectors of the community." Normally tours 3 projects each year with an average annual total of 60 performances and 60 different venues. Venues include schools, arts centres, theatres, outdoor venues and community venues across the UK and abroad, with a focus on rural touring. In general 3-4 actors go on tour and play to audiences of pre-school age and upwards. Singing ability, proficiency with a musical instrument and a driving licence are required for some shows. Actors may also be expected to lead workshops. Recent productions include: *Red Riding Hood and Her Amazing Grandmother*.

Casting procedures

Accepts submissions (with CVs and photographs) from actors in the North East area only. "We like to know who is around in the North East, especially if based in County Durham. Can help access local networks and professional development." Offers non-Equity contracts. Rarely (or never) has the opportunity to cast disabled actors.

Kinetic Theatre Co.

Suite H, The Jubilee Centre, Lombard Road, London SW19 3TZ
tel 020-8286 2613 *fax* 020-8286 2645
Director Graham Scott *Company Manager* Sarah Toner

Production details

Founded in 1989, Kinetic tours science-based plays to schools, theatres and arts centres across the UK. On average it produces 4 shows a year, with 2 actors in each – each show staging around 300 performances. Singing and dancing skills are important, as is a clean driving licence. Actors are not expected to lead workshops. The age range of the audience is 8-12 years. Previous productions have included: *Lamps in the Circuit*, *The Bunsen Towers Mystery*, *The Light Fantastic* and *More Tea Vicar*.

Casting procedures

Casting breakdowns are issued through *PCR* and CastWeb. Welcomes letters (but not emails), with CVs and photographs, from actors previously unknown to the company. Does not welcome showreels or invitations to view actors' websites. Offers actors TMA/Equity approved contracts. Rarely (or never) has the opportunity to cast disabled actors.

Krazy Kat Theatre Company

173 Hartington Road, Brighton BN2 3PA
tel (01273) 692552 *fax* (01273) 692552

email krazykattheatre@ntlworld.com
website www.krazykattheatre.co.uk
Artistic Director Kinny Gardner

Production details

A children's theatre company founded in 1972, specialising in highly visual forms of theatre that are accessible to deaf children. Normally tours 4-6 projects each year with an average annual total of 150 performances and 75 venues. Venues include schools, arts centres, theatres, outdoor venues and community centres in Essex, Sussex, Kent and London. In general 2 actors go on tour and play to audiences aged 3-7. Singing ability, physical theatre skills, sign language and a driving licence are required. Actors may also be expected to lead workshops. Recent productions include: *Three Pigs*, *Jack & The Beanstalk*, and *The Very Magic Flute*.

Casting procedures

Sometimes holds general auditions; actors can write at any time requesting inclusion. Accepts submissions (with CVs and photographs) from actors previously unknown to the company if sent by post. Does not welcome unsolicited emails. Will also accept invitations to view individual actors' websites. Offers non-Equity contracts. Actively encourages applications from disabled actors and promotes the use of inclusive casting.

M6 Theatre Company

Studio Theatre, Hamer County Primary School, Albert Royds Street, Rochdale OL16 2SU
tel (01706) 355898 *fax* (01706) 712601
email info@m6theatre.co.uk
website www.m6theatre.co.uk
Artistic Producer Dorothy Wood *General Manager* Deborah Palmer

Production details

Theatre in Education company founded in 1977. Normally tours 3 productions each year, with an average annual total of 150 performances and 70 different venues. Venues include schools, arts centres, theatres, festivals, prisons and community centres mainly in the North West. In general 3-4 actors go on tour and play to audiences aged 3-18. Actors may also be expected to participate in workshops. M6 creates a range of high quality, accessible theatre projects for young people. Recent projects include: *Sonya's Garden* (an Early Years production using child-sized puppets to tell a story of sharing and friendship); *All Talk* (a series of single-voice, short contemporary monologues for ages 13+); *Danny, King of the Basement* (a play for ages 9+ celebrating the power of imagination to deal with personal challenges); and *Homeward Bound* (exploring the impact of imprisonment on partners and children – toured to secondary schools and prisons). The company also runs a range of participatory drama workshops.

Casting procedures

Accepts submissions (with CVs and photographs) from actors previously unknown to the company. The company is unable to return photos. Offers ITC/ Equity approved contracts. Will consider applications from disabled actors to play characters with disabilities.

Monster Productions

Buddle Arts Centre, 258B Station Road, Wallsend, Tyne and Wear NE28 8RH
Artistic Directors Chris Speyer, Ievan Einion *Youth Theatre Director* Laura Lindon *Administrator* Doreen Ford

Production details

Set up in 2000 to continue the work for children under 7 begun by the directors at Northern Stage. Creates new music theatre for young children and runs a youth theatre programme for North Tyneside. Normally tours 2 projects each year with an average annual total of 150 performances and 30 different venues. Venues include schools, arts centres, theatres and community venues across the UK, Wales and Ireland. In general 3-5 actors go on tour and play mainly to audiences under 7 years old. Actors may also be expected to lead workshops. Recent productions include: *The Terrible Grump* and *Trouble Under Foot* (both for under-7s); and *Street of Strangers* for young people and adults.

Casting procedures

Sometimes holds general auditions; actors should write requesting inclusion when advertised in *PCR*. Accepts submissions (with CVs and photographs) from actors previously unknown to the company if sent by post. Does not welcome unsolicited emails. Will also accept invitations to view individual actors' websites. "Due to our scale of work we only employ a small number of actors each year. We favour multiracial casts to reflect our audiences. Musical and movement skills are a great advantage."

Oily Cart Company

Smallwood School Annexe, Smallwood Road, London SW17 0TW
tel 020-8672 6329 *fax* 020-8672 0792
email oilies@oilycart.org.uk
website www.oilycart.org.uk
Artistic Director Tim Webb *General Manager* Tracy Brunt *Administrator* Toma Dim

Production details

"Oily Cart makes gentle, interactive theatre for carers and babies as young as 6 months old, and elaborate multisensory pieces transcending the most complex sensory and intellectual impairments." Tours to schools, arts centres, theatres and special needs schools across the UK. In general 4 actors go on tour and play to infant audiences. Singing ability, proficiency with a musical instrument, dance/physical theatre skills, puppeteering ability and a driving licence are required. Recent productions include: *Moving Pictures*, an interactive, highly personal piece for children and young people with profound and multiple learning disabilities; and *Jumpin' Beans*, a show for children aged between 6 months and 6 years.

Casting procedures

Casting breakdowns are available through Equity Job Information Service and advertisements in *The Stage*. Offers ITC/Equity approved contracts. Actively encourages applications from disabled actors and promotes the use of inclusive casting.

Passe-Partout

13 Stanford Avenue, Brighton BN1 6AD
tel (01273) 557595 *fax* (01273) 701694
email office@passe-partout.demon.co.uk
Artistic Director Michele Young *Manager* Richard Crane

Production details

Founded in 1986. "Theatre for social change – assisting people to have a voice about an issue which concerns them." Normally tours 3 projects each year, with an average annual total of 20 performances and 20 different venues including schools, outdoor centres, community venues and office spaces in the UK and abroad. In general 4 actors go on tour and play to audiences of all ages. Any additional skills that actors may have will be put to use. Actors may also be expected to lead workshops. Recent projects include: anti-bullying strategy development (prisons, UK); *Social Capital* (various schools, Europe); *Street Children* (Nairobi, Kenya).

Casting procedures

"We cast from the group of people who have proposed an issue they want to take forward. We sometimes build-in 1 or 2 people from outside that group who have interest and energy."

Pied Piper Theatre Company in association with the Yvonne Arnaud Theatre

1 Lilian Place, Coxcombe Lane, Chiddingfold GU8 4QA
tel (01428) 684022 *fax* (01428) 684022
email twpiedpiper@aol.com
website www.yvonne-arnaud.co.uk
Artistic Director Tina Williams

Production details

Founded in 1984, and joined with Yvonne Arnaud in 1994. Has had 5 national tours funded by Arts Council England. Normally tours 2 projects each year with an average annual total of 140 performances. In general 3-8 actors tour to schools in Surrey playing to audiences aged 3 and upwards. Work is also taken to arts centres and theatres accross the UK every year. Singing ability, proficiency with a musical instrument, dance/physical theatre skills and a driving licence are required. Recent productions include: a national tour of Anne Fine's *The Diary of a Killer Cat*, and Klaus Baumgart's *Laura's Star*.

Casting procedures

Holds general auditions; actors requesting inclusion should write during the summer. Casting breakdowns are available through Equity Job Information Service. "Actors must be happy to tour. Most music is live. Must have a passion for children/young people's theatre." Offers TMA/Equity approved contracts. Rarely (or never) has the opportunity to cast disabled actors "due to work load and get-ins, etc.".

Playtime Theatre Company

18 Bennell's Avenue, Whitstable, Kent CT5 2HP
tel (01227) 266272 *fax* (01227) 266648
email Playtime@dircon.co.uk
website www.playtime.dircon.co.uk
Artistic Director Nicholas Champion *Administrator* Sara Kettlewell

Production details

Established in 1983 with the aim of bringing imaginative and innovative professional theatre to children and young people. Has grown to become "one of the leading children's theatre companies in the South East", and tours both nationally and internationally. Normally tours 2-4 projects each year with an average annual total of 200 performances and 190 venues. Venues include schools, arts centres, theatres, community venues and festivals. Tours have covered the South East, Yorkshire and Humberside and various countries in Europe. In general 2-4 actors go on tour and play to targeted audiences of 5-7, 4-11, 7-11 and 9-13. Actors are expected to offer 1-2 additional skills. Singing ability, proficiency with a musical instrument, physical theatre, puppetry and mime skills and a driving licence are all useful. Actors may also be expected to lead workshops. Recent productions include: *A Tale O' Two*, an adaptation of *The Canterbury Tales*; *Secrets*, a fairy-tale; and *The Happy Prince*, a co-production with a Hungarian theatre company.

Casting procedures

Holds general auditions; actors should write in August requesting inclusion. Casting breakdowns are available through the website, postal application (with sae), Equity Job Information Service, *PCR*, *The Stage* and Castcall (see entry under *The Spotlight*, casting directories and information services on page 267). Welcomes submissions (with CVs and photographs) from actors previously unknown to the company sent by post or email. Also accepts showreels and invitations to view individual actors' websites (if actor is shown performing). Advises actors to: "Be truthful. Tell us about the things that make you stand out. Tell us briefly why you want to work in children's theatre and why you like touring. Seriously consider the implications of living away from your base for months on end!" Offers non-Equity contracts. Will consider applications from disabled actors to play characters with disabilities.

Polka Theatre for Children

240 The Broadway, Wimbledon, London SW19 1SB
tel 020-8545 8320 *fax* 020-8545 8365
email info@polkatheatre.com,
casting@polkatheatre.com
website www.polkatheatre.com
Artistic Director Annie Wood *Associate Director* Roman Stefanski

Production details

Established in 1979. A theatre for children and young people. 7 productions staged annually with 700-800 performances per year. Average age of audience 3-18 but often 1-91. The following skills are required from actors: singing, musical instruments, dance, puppetry and physical theatre. Offers TMA/Equity contracts.

Casting procedures

Casting breakdowns available via *SBS*. Actors are invited for specific shows. Accepts submissions (with CVs and photographs) from actors previously unknown to the company if sent by post, but not by email. Showreels and invitations to view individual actors' websites are also accepted. Actively encourages applications from disabled actors and promotes the use of inclusive casting. "Find out in advance what we're doing, come and visit Polka and see the work."

Pop-Up Theatre

27A Brewery Road, London N7 9PU
tel 020-7609 3339 *fax* 020-7609 2284
email admin@pop-up.net
website www.pop-up.net
Artistic Director Michael Dalton *Theatre Co-ordinator* John Johnston

Production details

Founded in 1982. Produces and tours theatre for young people to an annual audience of more than 25,000 across theatres, arts centres, schools and nurseries both in the UK and overseas. Normally tours 3 projects each year with an average annual total of 150 performances and 75 different venues. Venues include schools, arts centres, theatres and community venues across the UK. In general 2-4 actors go on tour and play to audiences aged under 11.

Casting procedures

Accepts submissions (with CVs and photographs) from actors previously unknown to the company sent by post or email. Will also accept invitations to view individual actors' websites. Offers ITC/Equity approved contracts. Actively encourages applications from disabled actors and promotes the use of inclusive casting.

Q20 Theatre

19 Wellington Crescent, Shipley, West Yorks BD18 3PH
Artistic Director John Lambert *Administrators* David Smith, Gillie Kerrod

Production details

Normally tours 10 projects each year with an average annual total of 350 performances. Venues include outdoor venues, corporate workspaces and shopping centres in the North East, Yorkshire and Cambridge. In general 2 actors go on tour and play to audiences of all ages. Singing ability and dance/physical theatre skills are required. Recent productions include: *Pirate Pranks* at Wakefield Shopping Centre; *Metro Gnomes* at Metrocentre.

Casting procedures

Sometimes holds general auditions; actors should write in May or October to request inclusion. Accepts submissions (with CVs and photographs) from actors previously unknown to the company only if sent by post. Does not welcome unsolicited emails. Will also accept invitations to view individual actors' websites.

Quantum Theatre

The Old Button Factory, 1-11 Bannockburn Road, Plumstead SE18 1ET
tel/fax 020-8317 9000
email office@quantumtheatre.co.uk
website www.quantumtheatre.co.uk
Artistic Directors Michael Whitmore, Jessica Selous *Administrator* Gideon Escott *Production Manager* Rachel Hogden

Established in 1993. 15 productions performed annually. National touring productions visit schools, arts centres, theatres and outdoor venues. Casting breakdowns available. Holds general auditions. Accepts submissions (with CVs and photographs) from actors previously unknown to the company if sent by post, but not by email. Showreels, voice tapes and invitations to view individual actors' websites are also accepted. Offers TMA/Equity approved contracts.

Quicksilver Theatre

The Glasshouse, 4 Enfield Road, London N1 5AZ
tel 020-7241 2942 *fax* 020-7254 3119

email talktous@quicksilvertheatre.org
website www.quicksilvertheatre.org
Artistic Directors Guy Holland, Carey English

Production details

Founded in 1977. Normally tours 3 plays each year with an average annual total of 180 performances. Venues include schools and small- to mid-scale arts centres and theatres across the UK. Up to 5 actors go on tour and play to audiences of all ages. Singing ability, proficiency with a musical instrument, dance skills and a driving licence are an advantage. Actors may also be expected to lead workshops. Recent productions include: *Little Victories* (for 8 years upwards); *Sea of Silence* (for 7-11 years); *Upstairs in the Sky* (for 3-5 years).

Casting procedures

Casting breakdowns are available though the website, postal application (with sae), *PCR* and advertisements in *The Stage*. Accepts submissions (with CVs and photographs) from actors previously unknown to the company sent by post or email. Will also accept showreels and invitations to view individual actors' websites.

Replay Productions

Old Museum Arts Centre, 7 College Square North, Belfast BT1 6AR
tel 028-9032 2773 *fax* 028-9032 2724
email replay@dircon.co.uk
website www.replayproductions.org
Artistic Director Richard Croxford *Administrator* Ali Fitzgibbon

Production details

"Founded in 1988, Replay aims to produce high-quality theatre and related activities that entertain, educate and stimulate children and young people." Normally tours 3 projects each year with an average annual total of 100 performances. Venues include schools, arts centres, theatres and community venues in Northern Ireland and occasionally the Republic of Ireland. In general 4 actors go on tour and play to audiences aged 3-18. Recent productions include: *Striking Distance* by Raymond Scannell (for 14 years upwards); *Little Lou Tells a Story* by Sarah Fitzgibbon (for 3-6 years).

Casting procedures

Sometimes holds general auditions; actors should write during June or July requesting inclusion. Casting breakdowns are available through the news section of the website. Accepts submissions (with CVs and photographs) from actors previously unknown to the company sent by post or email. Will also accept invitations to view individual actors' websites.

Scat Theatre Company

The Old School House, Bedhampton Arts Centre, Bedhampton Road, Havant, Hampshire PO9 3ET
tel 023-9236 6829 *fax* 023-9236 3241
Artistic Directors Paul Hayles, Geraldene Owen

Production details

Founded in 1982. A children's theatre company producing original shows and workshops for schools. Normally tours 3 projects each year (not including workshops) with an average annual total of 180 performances. Although most work is geared towards schools, the company also tours to arts centres, theatres and community venues in Hampshire and local counties. In general 3 actors go on tour between December and February and play to audiences aged 4-11. Actors holding a driving licence will be at an advantage. Recent productions include: *Stowaway!*, *Old Macdonald Has a Cold*, and *Mouse in the House*.

Casting procedures

Holds auditions/workshops; actors should write between July and September to request inclusion. Accepts postal submissions (with CVs and photographs) from actors previously unknown to the company but does not welcome unsolicited emails. Usually employs actors with professional experience of performing to children aged 4-11. As the company has no technician, actors are also responsible for get-ins. Offers non-Equity contracts. Rarely (or never) has the opportunity to cast disabled actors.

Shakespeare 4 Kidz

42 Station Road East, Oxted, Surrey RH8 OPG
tel (01883) 723444 *fax* (01883) 730384
email office@shakespeare4kidz.com
website www.shakespeare4kidz.com
Producer & Director Julian Chenery *Producer* Carolyn Chenery *Company Manager* Paul Reynolds

Production details

Founded in 1997. "Recognised as the national Shakespeare company for children and young people, it has pioneered its Music Theatre & Shakespeare and Creative Shakespeare Education Programme both in the UK and abroad." Normally tours 2 projects each year with an average annual total of 230 performances across 60 different theatres. In general 13 actors go on tour and play to audiences aged 8 upwards. Singing ability and dance/physical theatre skills are required; marketing skills are also advantageous. Recent productions include: *Shakespeare 4 Kidz Macbeth* and *Shakespeare 4 Kidz Twelfth Night*.

Casting procedures

Holds general auditions; actors should write in March requesting inclusion. Casting breakdowns are available through the website, *PCR* and *The Stage*. Accepts submissions (with CVs and photographs) from actors previously unknown to the company sent by post or email. Will also accept showreels and invitations to view individual actors' websites.

Sixth Sense

The Burkhardt Hall, Swindon College, Regent Circus, Swindon SN1 1PT
tel (01793) 614864 *fax* (01793) 616715
email sstc@dircon.co.uk
website www.sixthsensetheatrecompany.co.uk
Artistic Director Benedict Eccles *General Managers* Fiona Da Silva-Adams, Marvyn Heard

Production details

Founded in 1986. Tours to schools and small-scale venues in the South and South West. Receives funding from Swindon Borough Council and Arts Council England, South West and has an "excellent reputation in the region". Normally tours 3 projects each year with an average annual total of 150 performances across 90 venues. Venues include schools, arts centres and community venues. In general 3 actors go on tour and play to audiences aged 5-18. Singing ability, proficiency with a musical instrument, dance skills and a driving licence may be required. Actors are usually expected to lead workshops. Recent productions include: *Aesop's Fables* (for 5-11 years); *The Secret Garden* (for 11-18 years).

Casting procedures

Sometimes holds general auditions; actors should write in September requesting inclusion. Accepts submissions (with CVs and photographs) from actors previously unknown to the company sent by post or email. Will also accept invitations to view individual actors' websites. Issues ITC/Equity contracts for 5- to 10-week tours. "Happy to receive actors' details but can't always respond. Please don't chase us; if we're interested we'll contact you."

Spare Tyre Theatre Company

Hampstead Town Hall, 213 Haverstock Hill, London NW3 4QP
tel/fax 020-7419 7007
email sttc@sparetyretheatrecompany.co.uk
website www.sparetyretheatrecompany.co.uk
Joint Artistic Directors Arti Prashar, Clair Chapwell
Administrator Paul Margrave

Production details

The company has 3 principal strands of work:
• Work with elders: weekly workshops in resource centres in North London; summer production; training for public sector workers using theatre created and performed by elder participants.
• Work with people with learning disabilities: the 'inc.Theatre' course is a full-time, OCN (Open

College Network) approved partnership with Redbridge College for people of all ages with learning disabilities. The 'incSpots' programme provides further opportunities for development and performance for previous students on the inc.Theatre course.
• Work with schools: professional TIE productions for school pupils tackling homophobia in schools. Also: 'Dealing with Difference', a workshop for school staff looking at approaches to tackling homophobia within schools.

Each strand of work has 1 major production a year, touring to roughly 100 venues – from schools, theatres and community venues to hospitals, GP surgeries, residential homes, special needs schools and public sector venues. Primarily covers the London area, but also Yorkshire, Manchester, Kent and Wales. Skills required from actors include (ideally) a driving licence, but also workshop-leading and facilitation skills, experience working with community groups, and a sensitivity to and understanding of relevant issues.

Casting procedures

Casting breakdowns are published in *The Stage* and on the website. Unsolicited approaches – including CVs, showreels and invitations to view individuals' websites – at other times are discouraged. Offers ITC/Equity approved contracts. Actively encourages applications from disabled actors and promotes the use of inclusive casting.

Theatr Iolo

The Old School Building, Cefn Road, Cardiff CF14 3HS
tel 029-2061 3782 *fax* 029-2052 2225
email admin@theatriolo.com
website www.theatriolo.com
Artistic Director Kevin Lewis *Administrative Director* Wendy York

Production details

"Formed in 1987, Theatr Iolo aims to produce and programme the best of live theatre, making it widely accessible to children and young people in Cardiff and the Vale of Glamorgan to stir the imagination, inspire the heart and challenge the mind. Theatr Iolo works alongside teachers and advisers to enhance teaching and learning across the curriculum." Normally tours 5 projects each year with an average annual total of 150 performances across 120 venues. Venues include schools, arts centres and theatres in Wales and occasionally England. Cast sizes vary, playing to audiences aged 3-18. Singing ability, proficiency with a musical instrument, dance/physical theatre skills and a driving licence are frequently required. Actors may also be expected to lead workshops. Recent productions include: *Warrior Square* by Nick Wood (for 9+ years); and *Whose Shoes* by Mike Kenny (5-7 years).

Casting procedures

Sometimes holds general auditions; actors should write in June requesting inclusion. Casting breakdowns are available through Equity Job Information Service. Accepts submissions (with CVs and photographs) from actors previously unknown to the company if sent by post. Emails are also welcome, as long as the file is not too big. Offers ITC/Equity approved contracts. Actively encourages applications from disabled actors and promotes the use of inclusive casting.

Theatr Na N'Og

Unit 3, Millands Road Industrial Estate, Neath SA11 1NJ
tel (01639) 641771 *fax* (01639) 647941
email cwmni@theatr-nanog.co.uk
website www.theatr-nanog.co.uk
Artistic Director Geinor Jones *Administrator* Janet Huxtable

Production details

"Formerly Theatre West & Glamorgan, the company has been producing high-quality original theatre for young people for more than 20 years. We provide a first-class Theatre in Education service to schools in 3 county boroughs, and tour to general audiences in venues across the UK." Normally tours 3 projects each year with an average annual total of 200 performances. In general 3 actors go on tour. Singing ability is required and actors may also be expected to lead workshops.

Casting procedures

Holds general auditions; actors may write at any time requesting inclusion. Casting breakdowns are available through the website. Accepts submissions (with CVs and photographs) from actors previously unknown to the company sent by post or email. Will also accept invitations to view individual actors' websites. "Please learn to spell the names of the company's personnel properly!"

Theatr Powys

The Drama Centre, Tremont Road, Llandrinod Wells, Powys LD1 5EB
tel (01597) 824444 *fax* (01597) 824381
email theatr.powys@powys.gov.uk
website www.theatrpowys.co.uk
Artistic Director Ian Yeoman *General Manager* Nikki Leopold

Production details

Founded in 1976. Has an average annual total of 250 performances across 150 different venues. Venues include schools, arts centres, theatres and community venues across Wales. In general 4 actors go on tour and play to audiences aged 4 upwards. Recent

productions include: *The King, The Crow & The Girl*, and *Grey Seal Cut Stone*.

Casting procedures

Holds general auditions; actors may write at any time requesting inclusion. Casting breakdowns are available through postal application (with sae), Equity Job Information Service, *PCR* and advertisements in *The Stage*. Accepts submissions (with CVs and photographs) from actors previously unknown to the company sent by post or email. Will also accept invitations to view individual actors' websites. Offers TMA/Equity contracts. Actively encourages applications from disabled actors and promotes the use of inclusive casting.

Theatre Centre

Shoreditch Town Hall, 380 Old Street, London EC1V 9LT
tel 020-7729 3066 *fax* 020-7739 9741
email admin@theatre-centre.co.uk
website www.theatre-centre.co.uk
Artistic Director Rosamunde Hutt *Administrator* Thomas Kell

Production details

Founded in 1953. A new writing company commissioning, developing and producing new plays which are toured nationally and internationally to schools, arts centres and theatres. Normally tours 3 projects each year with an average annual total of 180 performances across 100 different venues. In general 3-4 actors go on tour and play to targeted groups aged 4-18. Singing ability, proficiency with a musical instrument and dance/physical theatre skills may be required. An affinity with new writing and touring audiences is an advantage.

Casting procedures

Casting breakdowns are available through the website, postal application (with sae), Equity Job Information Service, *PCR* and advertisements in *The Stage*. Accepts submissions (with CVs and photographs) from actors previously unknown to the company sent by post or email; actors should write around New Year or Easter. "We keep all unsolicited CVs on file and do consult them when casting – therefore do send refreshed CVs! Get to know us and our work; there are regular free open day/showcase performances to which people on the mailing list are always invited." Offers TMA/Equity approved contracts. Actively encourages applications from disabled actors and promotes the use of inclusive casting.

Theatre Company Blah Blah Blah!

East Leeds Family Learning Centre, Brooklands View, Leeds LS14 6SA
tel 0113-224 3171 *fax* 0113-224 3172

email admin@blahs.co.uk
website www.blahs.co.uk
Artistic Director Anthony Haddon *General Manager* Kate Rose *Project Director* Ruth Cooper

Production details

A Leeds-based Theatre in Education company founded in 1985; also produces theatre for young people with integrated workshops. Normally tours 2-3 projects each year with an average annual total of 100 performances across 60 different venues. Venues include schools, arts centres, community venues and youth centres in Yorkshire. In general 3-4 actors go on tour and play to audiences aged 5 upwards. Singing ability, proficiency with a musical instrument, dance/physical theatre skills and a driving licence are all potentially useful. Experience of TIE work is also helpful, as actors are generally expected to lead workshops. Recent productions include: *Barkin'*, a play for teenagers based on the novel *Lady – My Life as a Bitch* by Melvin Burgess, which toured youth centres; *Hansel and Gretel*, a series of workshops for Primary schools; *Silas Marner*, touring to rural community venues and schools with related workshops.

Casting procedures

Sometimes holds general auditions; actors may write at any time requesting inclusion, as CVs are kept on file for 1 year. Accepts submissions (with CVs and photographs) from actors previously unknown to the company only if sent by post. Does not welcome unsolicited emails. Will also accept invitations to view individual actors' websites. "We are particularly interested in hearing from people with both acting and facilitation skills."

Theatre Exchange Ltd

The Old NAAFI, Weston Drive, Caterham, Surrey CR3 5XY
tel (01883) 331545
email info@theatre-exchange.org.uk
website www.theatre-exchange.org.uk
Artistic Director Katy Potter *Education Director* Stephen Cordwent

Production details

An educational theatre company focusing on the creative exchange between young people, artists and those who work with young people. Works on up to 21 projects each year, with an average annual total of 650 performances across 400 different venues. Venues include schools, arts centres, theatres and community venues across the South East of England. In general 6 actors go on tour and play to audiences aged 4-13. Interest in and some experience of working with young people is necessary; a driving licence is also useful. Actors are also expected to lead workshops. Recent productions include: *Monsters, Myths & Legends*, *Luverly Jubilee* and *The Greeks*.

Casting procedures

Holds general auditions; actors requesting inclusion should write between May and July. Casting breakdowns are available by postal application (with sae), on Equity Job Information Service and through advertisements in *The Stage*. Accepts submissions (with CVs and photographs) from actors previously unknown to the company sent by post or email. Will also accept invitations to view individual actors' websites. "Please send a letter detailing why you are interested in working with young people, along with your CV."

Tiebreak Theatre Company

42-58 St George's Street, Norwich NR3 1AB
tel (01603) 665899 *fax* (01603) 666096
email info@tiebreak-theatre.com
website www.tiebreak-theatre.com
Artistic Director David Farmer *Administrator* Kaja Holloway

Production details

Founded in 1981, Tiebreak tours new writing and adaptations to schools in East Anglia, and does a national circuit of arts centres and theatres. 3 full-time staff work together with freelance actors, writers, composers and designers to produce original, accessible and stimulating theatre for young people and families. On average the company stages 2-3 shows each year totalling approximately 120 performances. 3-5 actors work on each production and play to audiences aged 3-11. The ability to sing, play a musical instrument, dance and perform physical theatre are all useful. Actors may also be needed to lead workshops. Recent productions include: *Jack and the Beanstalk*, *The Nightingale*, *Frog in Love* and *My Uncle Arly*.

Casting procedures

Casting breakdowns are available through the website, Equity Job Information Service and *PCR*. The company welcomes submissions (with CVs and photographs) from performers with a range of musical and physical skills, and who have a genuine commitment to children's theatre. Prefers not to receive emails, showreels or invitations to view actors' websites.

Travelling Light Theatre Company

13 West Street, Old Market, Bristol BS2 0DF
tel 0117-377 3166 *fax* 0117-377 3167
email info@travlight.co.uk
website www.travlight.co.uk
Producer Jude Merrill *General Manager* Cath Creig

Production details

"Since 1984 the company has produced innovative and inspiring work for young audiences. Uses live music, visual and physical performance in its work." Normally tours 2 projects each year with an average annual total of 200 performances across 25 different venues. Venues include schools, arts centres, theatres, community venues and festivals across England, Northern Ireland, Scotland, Wales, North America and the Republic of Ireland. In general 2-3 actors go on tour and play to audiences aged 3-18. Singing ability, proficiency with a musical instrument and physical theatre skills are required. Actors may also be expected to lead workshops. Recent productions include: *Cloudland* (for 3-6 years); *The Stones* (for 12 years upwards).

Casting procedures

Casting breakdowns are available through Equity Job Information Service, *PCR* and Castweb (see entry under *The Spotlight, casting directories and information services* on page 267). Accepts submissions (with CVs and photographs) from actors previously unknown to the company only if sent by post. Does not welcome unsolicited emails. Will also accept invitations to view individual actors' websites.

Twisting Yarn Theatre

The Alhambra Theatre, Morley Street, Bradford BD7 1AJ
tel (01274) 437490
email twisting-yarn@bradford.gov.uk
website www.bradford-theatres.co.uk
Artistic Director Keith Robinson *Administrator* Su Holgate

Production details

Founded in 1996, Twisting Yarn is the producing arm of the Alhambra Theatre. It creates innovative, high-quality shows (that are not 'issue-based') for children and young people of school age and older. It tours schools and community venues as well as performing in the Alhambra Studio. Twisting Yarn also provides the Education and Outreach work for Bradford Theatres.

Produces 3-4 shows a year, with around 270 performances at (on average) 140 venues of all kinds, including outdoors. Predominantly, these venues are in West Yorkshire, but occasionally will tour further afield across Britain and Northern Ireland. 5-6 actors tour with each production, and applications are particularly welcome from actors with experience of physical theatre. Actors are occasionally asked to lead workshops.

Recent shows have included: *The Calif of Córdoba* (Spain under Islamic rule); *The Queen Who Would Be King* (Hatschepsut in ancient Egypt); and *Life of Pi* (a national tour, adapted from the novel of the same name).

Casting procedures

Holds general auditions; casting breakdowns are available via the Equity Job Information Service and

The Stage. Welcomes letters (but not emails), with CVs and photographs, from actors previously unknown to the company. Does not welcome showreels or invitations to view actors' websites. Offers Equity approved contracts.

Unicorn Theatre for Children

147 Tooley Street, More London, London SE1 2HZ
tel 020-7645 0500 *fax* 020-7645 0550
email stagedoor@unicorntheatre.com
website www.unicorntheatre.com
Artistic Director Tony Graham *Associate Director* Rebecca Gatward *Associate Director & Literary Manager* Carl Miller *Education Director* Alison Barry

Production details

Founded in 1947. "The UK's premier professional children's theatre company has just opened, near London Bridge, the first purpose-designed theatre for children in the UK." Performed 9 projects in 2005/06 with a total of 460 performances. Has produced site-specific works across England and in Cardiff, Glasgow and Edinburgh. In general 7-8 actors are involved in each production and play to audiences aged 4-11. Singing ability, proficiency with a musical instrument and dance/physical theatre skills are required. Recent productions include: *Clockwork*, an opera of Philip Pullman's novel of the same name, for the Linbury Studio, Royal Opera House and touring; *Rama and Sita: Path of Flames*, a storytelling piece at the Pleasance Theatre, London; and Ken Campbell's *Old King Cole*, a slapstick comedy.

Casting procedures

Accepts CVs and photographs from actors previously unknown to the company only if sent by email. Advises actors to send an interesting covering note detailing why they are interested in working with Unicorn in particular. Offers TMA and ITC/Equity approved contracts. Actively encourages applications from disabled actors and promotes the use of inclusive casting.

Whirligig Theatre

14 Belvedere Drive, Wimbledon, London SW19 7BY
tel 020-8947 1732 *fax* 020-8879 7648
email whirligig.theatre@virgin.net or davidwoodplays@virgin.net
Artistic Director David Wood

Production details

Founded in 1979, for many years Whirligig toured a musical play for children to major UK theatres, including a London season at Sadler's Wells Theatre. The company ceased regular activity in 2004, but still considers one-off projects at home and abroad. Tours, when they happen, are usually to around 15 theatre venues across the UK, playing mostly to primary-school-age children and their families. 8-10 actors, with skills such as singing, musical instruments, dance and physical theatre, would make up the company, and they would sometimes be asked to lead workshops. Recent productions include: *The Gingerbread Man*, *Save the Human*, and *Babe, the Sheep Pig*.

Casting procedures

Holds general auditions, although advises actors to check whether or not a production is imminent. Casting breakdowns are issued through *SBS*. Welcomes letters (but not emails), with CVs and photographs, from actors previously unknown to the company. Does not welcome showreels or invitations to view actors' websites. Offers TMA/Equity approved contracts.

Whirlwind Theatre Productions with Whirlwind Children's Theatre Company

54 High Road, Halton, Lancaster LA2 6PS
tel (01524) 812851
email enquiries@whirlwindtheatre.org.uk
website www.whirlwindtheatre.org.uk
Artistic Directors Myette Godwyn, Mike Whalley
Associate Artistic Director Alistair Ganley *Patron* David Wood OBE

Production details

Formed in 2000 to produce a community play for the Museum of Cannock Chase in association with Illyria Theatre Company, and a South of England tour of a music-based show for 5-10 year-olds – *Goldie Locks and the Three Bears*. The company has close ties with the Palm Court Theatre Orchestra, and productions are period-music-based with physical and visual performance aimed at the 4-10 year age-group. Whirlwind runs a performance summer school; also has a Saturday youth theatre club and a programme of workshops.

Normally undertakes 2-3 projects each year with a total of around 150 performances. Venues include churches, arts centres, fields, schools, theatres, outdoor and community venues across England. In general 3 actors go on tour and play to audiences aged 4 upwards. Actors must be proficient in workshop-leading for this age-group; will also need singing, dance/physical theatre skills and preferably the ability to play an instrument to a high standard. A driving licence is also required and actors must be prepared to help with get-ins and get-outs. Whirlwind Theatre has a strong Christian ethos, and most rehearsals and community work are carried out at King's Community Church in Lancaster. Although the company welcomes applications from actors of all different beliefs and backgrounds, they should feel at ease with this when applying. Recent productions include: *King's New Clothes* (TIE); *Hamish Bear and Storytelling Magpie* (TIE); *Toad of Toad Hall* (summer-school production in Ryelands Park, Lancaster).

Casting procedures

Sometimes holds general auditions; these are always held in Lancaster. Casting breakdowns are advertised in *PCR*. Welcomes letters and emails (with CVs and photographs) from actors previously unknown to the company. All actors are required to be CRB (Criminal Records Bureau) checked.

Zip Theatre

Newhampton Arts Centre, Dunkley Street, Wolverhampton WV1 4AN
tel (01902) 572250 *fax* (01902) 572251
email admin@ziptheatre.co.uk
website www.ziptheatre.co.uk
Artistic Director Jon Lingard-Lane *Administrator* Alyson Lanning

Production details

Founded in 1980. Normally tours 6 projects each year with an average annual total of 300 performances. Venues include schools, arts centres, theatres, outdoor venues and community venues mainly in the West Midlands area. In general 7 actors go on tour and play to audiences aged 5 upwards. Singing ability and dance skills are required. Actors are also expected to lead workshops. Recent productions include: *Behind a Smile* – Theatre in Education pieces based on sexual exploitation; and *Wind Dragons* – an outdoor summer show.

Casting procedures

Sometimes holds general auditions; actors may write at any time requesting inclusion any time. Accepts submissions (with CVs and photographs) from actors previously unknown to the company only if sent by post. Does not welcome unsolicited emails.

Casting calendar

Many companies are happy to receive CVs and photographs from actors at any time of the year, but some – such as those listed below – have a regular, annual schedule of casting and as such are most receptive to approaches in certain months. The table below shows the best time to approach companies, and gives information about whether their casting breakdowns are published on their website; whether they will send out breakdowns on receipt of an sae; where they publish their breakdowns (other than via the Spotlight Link); and in what section of this book their details may be found. ('JIS' is the Equity Job Information Service. Details for most of the casting breakdown services can be found under *The Spotlight, casting directories and information services* on page 267.)

Read the company's entry carefully before contacting them, to ensure that you are not wasting either their time or yours by making an inappropriate submission. The letters in brackets after the company name indicate the section in which their details may be found.

PT = *Producing theatres* (page 99)
IM = *Independent managements/theatre producers* (page 117)
MSS = *Middle and smaller-scale companies* (page 129)
Euro = *English-language European theatre companies* (page 160)
YP = *Children's, young people's and Theatre in Education companies* (page 179)

Companies are invited to notify us of corrections or omissions at **actorsyb@acblack.com**.

Month	Company	Web?	SAE?	Breakdowns published
Jan	Nick Brook Ltd (IM)	Yes	Yes	
Jan	Coliseum, Oldham (PT)		Yes	
Jan	Shakespeare's Globe (PT)			
Jan	Traverse, Edinburgh (PT)			
Jan/Feb	Open Air, Regents Park (PT)			
Jan-April	Sheringham (PT)			JIS
Feb	Jasperian Theatre Co. (MSS)			*SBS*/Castnet
Feb	Theatre Set-up (MSS)			
Feb	Manor Pavilion, Sidmouth (PT)			
March	Creation Theatre Co. (MSS)		Yes	*PCR*/Castfax
March	Hijinx Theatre Co. (MSS)			
March	Shakespeare 4 Kidz (YP)	Yes		*PCR/ The Stage*
March/April	Oxford Shakespeare Co. (MSS)			*PCR*
March/April	Library Theatre, Manchester (PT)			
April	English Theatre, Frankfurt (Euro)			
April	White Horse Theatre (Euro)	Yes	Yes	*PCR/ The Stage*
April	Citizens, Glasgow (PT)			
April	Ladbroke Productions (Radio)			
April/May	Clean Break (MSS)	Yes		JIS/*PCR/ The Stage*
April/May	Queens Theatre, Hornchurch (PT)			
May	Salisbury Playhouse (PT)		Yes	
May	Nick Brook Ltd (IM)			
May	Frantic Theatre Co. (MSS)		Yes	JIS/*PCR/ The Stage*
May	TOSG Gaelic Theatre Co. (MSS)			
May	Haymarket Theatre, Basingstoke (PT)		Yes	

Month	Company	Web?	SAE?	Breakdowns published
May	Bitesize (YP)			*PCR/The Stage/* Castcall/*SBS*
May	Q20 (YP)			
May/June	Hopscotch Theatre Co. (YP)			
May-July	Theatre Exchange (YP)		Yes	JIS/*The Stage*
June	Benchtours Productions (MSS)	Yes		
June	Jasperian Theatre Co. (MSS)			*SBS*/Castnet
June	Crucible, Sheffield (PT)		Yes	
June	Orange Tree, Richmond (PT)		Yes	
June	Traverse, Edinburgh (PT)			
June	Torch Theatre (PT)		Yes	JIS
June	Theatr Iolo (YP)			JIS
June/July	Box Clever Theatre Co. (YP)	Yes		JIS
June/July	Replay Productions (YP)	Yes		
July	Kabosh (MSS)			
July	Wrestling School (MSS)			Phone
June/July	The Theatre, Chipping Norton (PT)			
July-Sept	Scat Theatre Co. (YP)			
August	Actors of Dionysus (AOD) (MSS)	Yes		*PCR*
Aug/Sept	English Theatre Co., Stockholm (Euro)			
Sept	Jasperian Theatre Co. (MSS)			*SBS*/Castnet
Sept	Traverse, Edinburgh (PT)			
Sept	Ladbroke Prods (Radio)			
Sept	C&T (YP)			
Sept	Sixth Sense (TY)			
Sept/Oct	Pitlochry Festival Theatre (PT)		Yes	
Oct	Creation Theatre Co. (MSS)		Yes	*PCR*/Castfax
Oct	Crucible, Sheffield (PT)		Yes	
Oct	Q20 (YP)			
Oct	Salisbury Playhouse (PT)		Yes	
Oct/Nov	Box Clever Theatre Co. (YP)	Yes		JIS
Oct/Nov	Benchtours Productions (MSS)	Yes		
Nov	Frantic Theatre Co. (MSS)		Yes	JIS/*PCR/The Stage*
Nov	Hijinx Theatre Co. (MSS)			
Nov	Kabosh (MSS)			
Nov	Southwold & Aldeburgh (PT)			Phone
Dec	Actors of Dionysus (AOD) (MSS)	Yes		*PCR*
Dec/Jan	Chichester Festival Theatre (PT)			

Festivals

These are populated by all kinds of companies listed in previous sections. Some are hired-in by a festival's organisers; others 'hire' space in order to participate – the latter predominate at the most famous festival of all, in Edinburgh. Participation in a festival can be enormous fun, and a great opportunity to meet other actors and see other productions. However, the chances of such a production transferring, let alone making money, are limited.

UMBRELLA ORGANISATIONS

British Arts Festivals Association (BAFA)
3rd Floor, The Library, 77 Whitechapel High Street, London E1 7QX
tel 020-7247 4667 *fax* 020-7247 5010
email info@artsfestivals.co.uk
website www.artsfestivals.co.uk

Provides information and a professional network for the festivals movement in the UK, working to promote the profile and status of arts festivals. As well as the arts festivals website, which catalogues festivals in the UK and provides links to festivals in Europe, BAFA also publishes a free Calendar and Directory of the 105 festival members in print, and produces an advance festivals press pack each January. Members have the opportunity to attend BAFA conferences, training courses and focus meetings. Membership is open to all arts festivals in the UK and associate membership to other arts organisations. Does not promote individual artists, companies or tours.

British Federation of Festivals for Music, Drama and Speech
Festivals House, 198 Park Lane, Macclesfield, Cheshire SK11 6UD
tel 0870-7744 290 *fax* 0870-7744 292
email julia@festivals.demon.co.uk
website www.festivals.demon.co.uk

Provides information and a network for amateur and competitive festivals in the UK. The Federation includes more than 300 festivals.

The European Festivals Association
General Secretariat, Kleine Gentstraat 46, B-9051 Gent, Belgium
email info@efa-aef.org
website www.efa-aef.org

Represents more than 90 high-quality festivals and 11 national festivals in 35 European countries. The website offers a general overview of these festivals, together with a detailed list of thousands of events and performances in its annual calendar.

UK ARTS FESTIVALS

Arundel Festival
tel (01903) 883474
email arundelfestival@btopenworld.com
website www.arundelfestival.co.uk

For 10 days each August, the market town of Arundel is host to a multi-arts festival which began in 1977. Street theatre and a festival Fringe are regular features, as are concerts, exhibitions, fireworks and jazz. The festival culminates in an open-air production of a Shakespeare play in the grounds of Arundel Castle. Each production is led by a cast of experienced professional actors, and extended with members of the local community who work with the professionals throughout the 6-week rehearsal period.

Barbican International Theatre Event (BITE)
Barbican Centre, Silk Street, London EC2Y 8DS
tel 020-7638 4141
email theatre@barbican.org.uk
website www.barbican.org.uk/bite

Since its first programme in 1998, BITE has sought to create a venue in London dedicated to presenting some of the most significant and innovative artists around the world. The Spring 2005 season featured music, theatre and dance pieces from many different countries. Events included: Theatre O's *Astronaut*; Peter Brook's *Ta Main dans la Mienne*; and Fabulous Beast Dance Theatre's production of *Giselle*.

Bath Shakespeare Festival
Theatre Royal, Sawclose, Bath BA1 1ET
tel (01225) 448844
website www.bathshakespeare.org.uk

Presenting premières, international productions and new commissions, the Bath Shakespeare Festival takes place over 2 weeks in March. In addition to full-scale Shakespeare productions there are workshops, film screenings and education events.

Belfast Festival at Queens

25 College Gardens, Belfast BT9 6BS
tel 028-9027 2600
email a.mcGrath@qub.ac.uk
website www.belfastfestival.com

Founded in 1963, the Belfast Festival is an annual 3-week international arts festival held in October and November each year. The largest festival of its kind in Ireland, it covers all artforms including theatre, dance, classical music, literature, jazz, comedy, visual arts, folk music and popular music, attracting more than 50,000 visitors. Theatre performances in 2004 included: the Belfast Theatre Company's production of *A Most Notorious Woman*; Theatre Royal Bath's production of *Blithe Spirit* with Penelope Keith. Artists wishing to participate in the festival should submit a written proposal to the address listed above.

Birmingham ArtsFest

tel 0121-685 2605
email mail@artsfest.org.uk
website www.artsfest.org.uk

ArtsFest is one of the UK's largest free arts festivals and is held in venues across Birmingham for 2 days in September. It programmes a range of free performances including theatre, jazz, opera and dance events. Street theatre also features heavily, with musicians, jugglers, visual artists and stand-up comedians all presenting their work outside. There are also a variety of workshops on offer, ranging from screenwriting to Bollywood dancing.

Bradford International Festival Ltd

Business Innovation Centre, Angel Way, Listerhills, Bradford BD7 1BX
tel (01274) 722272 *fax* (01274) 736600
email info@bethere2003.com

The Bradford Festival has been established for 14 years and continues to grow each summer. For 2 weeks in July the festival celebrates a creative fusion of cultures from across the District and West Yorkshire. The main events are the Mela, which is the largest event of its kind in Europe; the Lord Mayor's Carnival Procession; and the Street Theatre Festival.

Brighton Festival

email info@brighton-festival.org.uk
website www.brighton-festival.org.uk

Founded in 1967. For 3 weeks in May, there are more than 300,000 attendances at 800 separate arts events taking place in venues across Brighton and Hove. Artists from a number of different countries are represented in theatre, dance, music, opera, books, events and outdoor spectaculars.

Running alongside Brighton Festival, Brighton Festival Fringe (previously called 'the Open') has been in existence for 37 years and is the biggest in England, showcasing a variety of artforms and activities. Applicants for the Fringe should first read the 'How to be in Brighton Festival Fringe' document available on the website, and then register online.

Cambridge Hotbed Festival

Junction CDC, Clifton Road, Cambridge CB1 7GX
tel (01223) 578000
email cat@junction.co.uk
website www.hotbedfest.co.uk

Following the success of the original Hotbed 2002, Menagerie Theatre Company (**www.menagerie.uk.com**) and Junction CDC (**www.junction.co.uk**) joined forces to present Hotbed 2004, the second Cambridge New Writing Theatre Festival. Over 3 weeks in July, venues around Cambridge – including CB2, Cambridge Drama Centre and Cambridge Arts Theatre's Playroom – hosted a variety of new plays by a selection of regional and national writers. Productions ranged from 15-minute lunchtime shorts to full evening performances, with a selection of workshops, talks, masterclasses and seminars also included in the programme.

The festival presents opportunities both for writers and for actors to get involved. Any writer may submit a complete play for 2 actors lasting 15-20 minutes. Successful writers will see their production professionally developed and performed at various central Cambridge venues throughout the 3-week festival. A repertory company based around the members of Menagerie Theatre Company supports the festival, and actors are welcome to audition for the company a few months in advance. For further information about the next Hotbed and how to get involved, contact Cat Moore by phone, email or post.

Canterbury Festival

Christ Church Gate, The Precincts, Canterbury, Kent CT1 2EE
tel (01227) 452853
email info@canterburyfestival.co.uk
website www.canterburyfestival.co.uk

Founded in 1929, the Canterbury Festival takes place over 2 weeks in October. The festival features music, dance, drama, opera, film, community events, talks, walks and visual arts.

The Marlowe and Gulbenkian Theatres in Canterbury and the Theatre Royal in Margate are host to major dance, drama and opera companies. Many small professional and amateur companies perform in the smaller venues and present a wide variety of drama and dance during the 2 weeks of the festival. These have included local companies as well as small foreign companies such as the Brazilian company Teatro Sao Paulo Fabrica, and Hungarian children's theatre Kolibri Theatre.

Other drama companies that have appeared at the festival include the Royal Shakespeare Company, the

National Theatre Company, Actors Touring Company, Trestle Theatre, Compass Theatre, Shared Experience and Yellow Earth Theatre.

Chichester Festivities

Box Office, 45 East Street, Chichester, West Sussex PO19 1HX
tel (01243) 780192
email info@chifest.org.uk
website www.chifest.org.uk

The Box Office is open for making reservations a month in advance of the festival. At other times consult the website or make contact by email.

Chichester Festivities are programmed over 2 weeks in July and have included performances of classical, jazz and world music, talks, contemporary sculpture in the Cathedral Cloisters, fireworks at Glorious Goodwood Racecourse and outdoor theatre productions. Founded in 1975, the festival celebrated its 30th anniversary in 2005.

The event has attracted performers such as Dame Judi Dench, Jools Holland, Fay Weldon and Nigel Kennedy.

Dumfries and Galloway Arts Festival Ltd

Gracefield Arts Centre, 28 Edinburgh Road, Dumfries DG1 1JQ
tel (01387) 260447 *fax* (01387) 260447
email info@dgartsfestival.org.uk
website www.dgartsfestival.org.uk

An annual 10-day festival at the end of May, established in 1979. Founded with the aim of bringing high-quality international events to community audiences that would not otherwise have the opportunity to experience such talent, the festival now also presents local talent of international standing.

The festival programmes a wide range of events covering music – including classical, jazz and folk – dance, theatre, literary, children's and the visual arts. Events take place in a range of venues throughout the region.

The Ealing Comedy Festival

Festivals and Events, Room 3.03, Ealing Town Hall, New Broadway, Ealing, London W5 2BY
tel 020-8825 6064 *fax* 020-8825 6069
email events@ealing.gov.uk
website www.ealing.gov.uk/services/ealing+summer/comedy+festival

The Ealing Comedy Festival takes place in Walpole Park over 1 week in July and reaches audiences of over 1000 each night. The festival has played host to some of the leading names in modern British comedy – including Ricky Gervais, Harry Hill, Al Murray, Rob Brydon and Jimmy Carr– and generally features around 25 comedians each year.

Edinburgh Festival Fringe

The Fringe Office, 180 High Street, Edinburgh EH1 1QS
tel 0131-226 0026 *fax* 0131-226 0016
email admin@edfringe.com
website www.edfringe.com

The Fringe was started in 1947 to complement the first Edinburgh International Festival. It now breaks its own record every year as the largest arts festival on the planet, bringing thousands of performances of hundreds of shows in more than 200 venues across Edinburgh each August.

The Fringe Society was formed in 1959 to coordinate publicity and ticket sales and offer a comprehensive information service both to performers and to audiences. It compiles information about venues, press and suppliers and produces a series of publications designed to answer frequently asked questions. The office is open all year round and the staff are available to help by phone, email or personal appointment.

Edinburgh International Festival

The Hub, Castlehill, Edinburgh EH1 2NE
tel 0131-473 2001 *fax* 0131-473 2003
email eif@eif.co.uk
website www.eif.co.uk

Founded in 1947, the Edinburgh International Festival is an annual event held over 3 weeks in August, using all the major concert and theatre venues in the city. With music, opera, theatre, film, dance, and the Military Tattoo at the Castle, the festival is now recognised as one of the world's most important celebrations of the arts.

Also offers a programme of year-round activities, with courses and workshops on diverse subjects from playwriting to the use of digital video, and one-off projects for school children, students and adults collaborating with actors, directors, choreographers and musicians involved in the festival. Performance at the Edinburgh International Festival is by invitation only, issued by the Festival Director.

Exeter Summer Festival

Exeter City Council, Civic Centre, Paris Street, Exeter EX1 1JJ
tel (01392) 265205 *fax* (01392) 265366
email general.festivals@exeter.gov.uk
website www.exeter.gov.uk/residents/arts/exeter_festival

The city's celebration of contemporary and classical music, theatre, dance, comedy and visual arts.

Over 2 weeks in June/July, Exeter Summer Festival programmes diverse arts events, exhibitions and firework displays. Artists interested in performing should contact **artist.enquiries@exeter.gov.uk**.

Fierce!

608B The Big Reg, 120 Vyse Street, Birmingham B18 6NF
tel 0121-244 8080 *fax* 0121-244 8081
email fierce@fierceearth.com
website www.fierce.info

Annual festival of performances and events in theatres, bars, clubs, galleries and public spaces across the West Midlands; now in its 8th year. The festival takes place over 1 month in May/June.

Grassington Festival

The Festival Office, Grassington Festival, Grassington, North Yorkshire BD23 5AU
tel (01756) 752691
email arts@grassington-festival.org.uk
website www.grassington-festival.org.uk

A multi-disciplinary festival featuring contemporary and classical music, theatre, poetry and film, and taking place over 2 weeks in June/July.

Greenwich and Docklands Festivals (GDF)

6 College Approach, London SE10 9HY
tel 020-8305 1818 *fax* 020-8305 1188
email info@festival.org
website www.festival.org

Taking place over the 4 weekends of July, the Greenwich and Docklands Festival programmes multi-disciplinary arts events around East London each summer. As well as programming large-scale, visually impressive work, the festival places emphasis on educational projects and participatory arts.

The International Festival of Musical Theatre in Cardiff

Market Chambers, 5/7 St Mary Street, Cardiff CF10 1AT
tel 029-2034 6999 *fax* 029-2037 2011
email enquiries@CardiffMusicals.com
website www.CardiffMusicals.com

The 2nd International Festival of Musical Theatre was held in March 2005. The festival aims to present the best of musical theatre, old and new, large and small. Its new-writing programme, 'The Global Search for New Musicals', showcases new musicals selected from a year-long search; many of the musicals showcased in 2002 Global Search have gone on to enjoy success around the world. In addition there are masterclasses enhancing the work being shown in the festival programme; in 2005 these included a Cole Porter Day, a Stephen Sondheim Symposium and a performance masterclass from Broadway musical director, Don Pippin. Also presented as part of the festival is the BBC Radio 2 Voice of Musical Theatre, where young professional singers from around the world compete for a substantial cash prize and BBC broadcast engagements.

International Playwriting Festival

Warehouse Theatre, Dingwall Road, Croydon CR0 2NF
website www.warehousetheatre.co.uk
Festival Administrator Rose Marie Vernon *Casting* Sally Vaughan

The International Playwriting Festival has been in operation since 1986 and has consolidated the Warehouse Theatre Company's role in discovering and developing new writing talent. Launching the career of many successful playwrights, the festival has seen many of its plays transferred to the West End, the Royal Court, Hampstead Theatre and Stratford-upon-Avon.

Taking place over a few days in November, the festival is held in 2 parts. The first is a competition (for which entries must be received by June) which is judged by a panel of distinguished theatre practitioners; the second is a showcase of the selected plays in November.

The festival has received applications from writers in the USA, Hong Kong, Croatia, Holland, Australia, Estonia, Sierra Leone, Italy and New Zealand, as well as from the UK.

Lichfield International Arts Festival

7 The Close, Lichfield, Staffordshire WS13 7LD
tel (01543) 306270
email lichfield.fest@lichfield-arts.org.uk
website www.lichfieldfestival.org.uk
Administrator Peter Bacon

Annual 10-day event held in early July and featuring music, theatre, lectures, exhibitions, workshops, community events and education projects.

London Comedy Festival

20 Chancellors Street, Hammersmith, London W6 9RN
tel 0870-119 611
email info@londoncomedyfestival.com
website www.londoncomedyfestival.com

The London Comedy Festival is a celebration of London's established comedy scene, with many of the capital's top clubs hosting stand-up events, a programme of humour literature events across London's libraries and bookshops including workshops, readings, competitions and debates, and major events at some of London's landmarks, along with other comedy activities. It takes place over 10 days in May.

Highlights in previous years have included the first ever open-air cinema event in Trafalgar Square; the creation of the world's largest cartoon strip; 'Wit Lit' – London's largest ever humour literature event; and the GOSH Gala, a star-studded fundraiser hosted by Graham Norton and Suggs.

Anyone can put on a show as part of the London Comedy Festival. Over the past 3 years the event has encompassed not just comedy clubs but pubs, theatres, galleries and libraries. Registration begins in January with a deadline for inclusion in the Festival Guide of mid-March.

London International Festival of Theatre (LIFT)

19/20 Great Sutton Street, London EC1V 0DR
email info@liftfest.org
website www.liftfest.org
Directors Rose Fenton, Lucy Neal

Started in 1981, LIFT is a biennial summer festival introducing some of the world's most exciting artists and theatre-makers to London. LIFT events have been staged in more than 30 London venues as well as in a number of site-specific venues such as streets, disused buildings, the river, parks and open spaces.

Also runs developmental and educational programmes exploring the nature of exchange and creativity for a range of audiences including schoolchildren and industry leaders.

London International Mime Festival

35 Little Russell Street, London WC1A 2HH
tel 020-7637 5661 *fax* 020-7323 1151
email mimefest@easynet.co.uk
website www.mimefest.co.uk
Directors Joseph Seelig, Helen Lannaghan

Founded in 1977, the London International Mime Festival presents innovative visual theatre. Events are non-text-based and can include animation theatre, circus skills, mask, mime, clown and visual theatre. Most of the work programmed will not have been performed in London before.

The festival takes place over 15 days in January with the deadline for submissions in mid-July. Participation is by invitation only. To be considered, send a VHS video to Helen Lannaghan and Joseph Seelig at the address above with an sae enclosed for the return of material.

Ludlow Festival

email info@ludlowfestival.co.uk
website www.ludlowfestival.co.uk

Running for more than 45 years, the Ludlow Festival takes places over 2-3 weeks in June/July with a range of music, theatre and exhibitions on offer. Each year it features open-air Shakespeare productions which are staged in the grounds of Ludlow Castle. The 2005 production was *Richard II* directed by Steven Berkoff.

The Mayor's Thames Festival

website www.thamesfestival.org

The Mayor's Thames Festival is a free annual event that takes place on and around the River Thames between Westminster and Southwark Bridges, using the river as a powerful unifying symbol for the whole of London. One of the festival's main aims is to

enable more collaborations between artists and community groups. Over 1 weekend in September it programmes events such as night carnivals, fireworks spectaculars, mass choirs, music stages, a range of participatory activities, and both artist-led and river-orientated events.

Merseyside International Street Festival

tel 0151-709 3334 *fax* 0151-709 4994
email info@brouhaha.uk.com
website www.brouhaha.uk.com

Established in 1990, the Merseyside International Street Festival brings a mix of dance, drama, acrobatics, music, comedy, puppetry and street theatre to around 30,000 spectators in Liverpool each July/August.

Minack Theatre Summer Festival

Porthcurno, Penzance, Cornwall TR19 6JU
tel (01736) 810694 *fax* (01736) 810779
email minack@dial.pipex.com
website www.minack.com

Founded in 1932. An annual, 17-week summer season of plays, musicals and opera held at Minack's unique open-air theatre carved into the Cornish cliffside. Created in 1929 by Rowena Cade and her gardener Billy Rawlings, the Minack lends itself to large-cast plays. Most companies involved are amateur, although approximately 3 each year are professional.

National Student Drama Festival (NSDF)

D14, The Foxhole Centre, Dartington, Totnes, Devon TQ9 6EB
tel (01803) 864836 *fax* (01803) 840693
email admin@nsdf.org.uk
website www.nsdf.org.uk
General Manager (For tickets, administration and sponsorship) Rachel Williams *Director (For general artistic enquiries)* Andrew Loretto *Assistant to Director (To enter a production and request an information pack)* Ian Abbott

The National Student Drama Festival is a week-long event bringing together students and leading theatre and media professionals. Taking place in the Easter holidays, it celebrated its 50th year in 2005. The festival showcases and nurtures innovative theatre by young people and offers masterclasses, workshops and forums for debate and discussion. A panel of 3 eminent judges awards the prestigious NSDF Prizes, Awards and Bursaries at the end of the festival.

NSDF is open to colleges, youth theatres, community organisations and universities, and takes place each spring in Scarborough. Professionals who have attended include Mike Leigh, Willy Russell, Mark Ravenhill, Sir Alan Ayckbourn and Michael Billington.

The NSDF Ensemble is a company of talented young theatre practitioners from all over the UK. Supported by professional artists, Ensemble members take part in a one-off training/residency. On the recommendation of the NSDF selection team, members are invited to audition each year from the wide range of shows entered for the festival.

National Theatre's Watch This Space Festival

Royal National Theatre, South Bank, London SE1 9PX
tel 020-7452 3328
email wts@nationaltheatre.org.uk
website www.nationaltheatre.org.uk/wts
Platforms Producer Angus MacKechnie

Takes place outside the National Theatre over the summer. The festival features theatre, music, dance, variety, film and circus from Britain and abroad. All events are free and run for about 8 weeks from late June to early September.

Pride of Place ('Upstix') Theatre Festival

c/o NTC Touring Theatre, The Playhouse, Bondgate Without, Alnwick, Northumberland NE66 1PQ
website www.prideofplace.org.uk

Festival held every 2 years to celebrate the work of theatre companies involved in rural touring, and to debate the role of theatre in rural communities. Features seminars, discussions and performances from many of the major rural touring companies, including Chalkfoot, Eastern Angles, Farnham Maltings, Forest Forge, New Perspectives, Northumberland Theatre Company (NTC), Oxfordshire Touring, Pentabus and Proteus. In March 2006 the festival was hosted by Eastern Angles in Ipswich and Woodbridge; in 2008 the festival will be hosted in Alnwick, Northumberland by NTC Touring Theatre. See NTC's entry under *Middle and smaller-scale companies* on page 144 for contact information.

Push

Almeida Theatre, Almeida Street, London N1 1TA
tel 020-7288 4938
website www.pushherenow.com

As part of a new artistic collaboration, Push has been based at the Almeida since January 2003. Push develops cross-artform productions and television comedy with the aim of creating high-quality artistic partnerships between black artists and mainstream arts organisations.

Royal Court Young Writers Festival

Young Writers Festival, The Site, Royal Court Theatre, Sloane Square, London SW1W 8AS
website www.royalcourttheatre.com/ywp

A biennial festival, the Royal Court Young Writers Programme presents full professional productions of work by the most promising young playwrights aged 13-25. It is the world's largest festival of new playwriting by young people, attracting critical acclaim and the support of leading theatre practitioners including Kathy Burke, Max Stafford-Clark, Hanif Kureishi, Meera Syal and Richard Wilson. The festival has launched the careers of playwrights such as Leo Butler, Lucy Prebble, Christopher Shinn, Simon Stephens, and Laura Wade.

Selected scripts are acted and directed by professionals from October to November. For information or application details for the next festival, consult the website or send an sae to the address above. For casting procedures, see entry for the Royal Court under *Producing theatres* on page 99. The theatre is wheelchair-friendly.

Salisbury Festival

87 Crane Street, Salisbury, SP1 2PU
tel (01722) 332977 *fax* (01722) 410552
email info@salisburyfestival.co.uk
website www.salisburyfestival.co.uk

Established in 1973, for 20 years the festival consisted mostly of classical music events. It is now multi-disciplinary and combines prestigious Cathedral concerts with family street entertainment, circus, theatre and other arts events. There are normally between 30-50 different programmes and projects and a total of some 100 different events which take place at the end of May and beginning of June.

Shrewsbury Summer Season

tel (07709) 685156
website www.shrewsburysummer.co.uk

The first Shrewsbury Summer Season took place in June, July and August 2004 with a programme of visual arts, music, drama, dance, spoken word and comedy events.

Soho Writers' Festival

Soho Theatre and Writers' Centre, 21 Dean Street, London W1D 3NE
tel 020-7287 5060 *fax* 020-7287 5061
email mail@sohotheatre.com
website www.sohotheatre.com

Established in 2000, Soho Theatre's Writers Festival takes place over 3 weeks in October/November with a programme of masterclasses, workshops, seminars, talks, rehearsed readings and performances led by some of the UK's leading writers, directors and industry professionals. Panel discussions have covered a range of topics from the latest revolutions happening in the theatre world to TV sitcom writing, with a line-up of Perrier-Award-winning comedy to end each day.

The Stratford-upon-Avon Poetry Festival

Shakespeare Birthplace Trust, Shakespeare Centre, Henley Street, Stratford-upon-Avon, Warwickshire CV37 6QW
tel (01789) 204016 *fax* (01789) 296083
email reception@shakespeare.org.uk (general enquiries only)
website www.shakespeare.org.uk

Established in 1954 by the Shakespeare Birthplace Trust, the festival presents recitals of poetry held over 9 successive Sundays in the summer. Nearly every major British poet from *Beowulf* onwards has featured somewhere in the festival, along with other poetry written or translated into English.

Over the last 50 years, many leading actors have been involved in the readings, including Judi Dench, Ralph Fiennes, John Gielgud, Ian Holm, Anthony Hopkins, Jeremy Irons, Derek Jacobi, Ben Kingsley, Ian McKellen, Helen Mirren, Vanessa Redgrave, Ian Richardson, Diana Rigg and Robert Stephens. In addition to the 9 traditional recitals, the festival now also includes a Local Poets evening, activities for children and a Poetry Mass. Most venues are wheelchair-friendly – contact the festival organisers for specific details.

Professional role-playing

Robbie Swales

In 1992 an actor rang me and asked if I would do a job with him, which he had been offered through another actor. The job was to do a role-play with some accountants. I said, "What's role-play?" My friend explained that I had to role-play a demotivated worker, and that the purpose of the role-play was to help the accountants learn how to motivate members of their team. I did the job and enjoyed it. Since then – my first experience of role-play – this area of work for actors has expanded enormously. Although there are still networks of individual actors gaining role-play assignments, the bulk of the work for actors is provided by drama-based training companies, which provide organisations with role-players and actor/facilitators.

So why has this sector grown, and why is there a need for drama-based training companies, rather than individual actors applying directly to the end-user to offer their acting skills?

Trainers and developers within organisations have discovered that when they deliver behavioural skills training, an experiential interactive session provides better learning opportunities for the participants than the traditional talk-and-chalk approach. Because actors can put different behaviours on and take them off like a coat, they have become a valuable resource to the trainers; they make the sessions lively, interesting, interactive and memorable. Participants remember the learning and then go and use the skills in the workplace. Training and development in the workplace is only carried out if a company or organisation believes that it will improve efficiency, and therefore productivity. The use of actors for training is no exception: they help to make the behaviour of people in organisations more effective.

Drama-based training companies are what one might call one-stop shops. If an organisation, such as a high street bank, wants to employ actors to role-play on a series of development centres, the training department in the bank will find it easier to approach a role-play company. The trainer from the bank can explain their needs, check how that role-play company guarantees the quality of their actors, and then negotiate a fee. The role-play company can book the actors, brief them appropriately and arrange for them to be in the right place at the right time.

The field of drama-based training is growing more and more sophisticated, and some of these companies are becoming more like consultancies, with entire interactive theatre programmes being researched, designed, written, rehearsed and delivered by the drama-based company. For such companies to be effective at this type of work, they need a core team of full-time staff, while maintaining a freelance team of actors trained in the appropriate skills whom they can employ on a project-by-project basis.

There are, very broadly, two types of role-play work: role-playing one-to-one with a participant; and role-playing with another actor in front of an audience, with whom the actors then interact. Most role-play work is improvised; however, there are some types of interactive theatre which kick off the session with a scripted scene, before the actors then start improvising the suggestions of the audience.

One-to-one role-play

The range of work performing one-to-one role-play with a participant requires different levels of skill from the actor. An example of the simplest type of role-play is improvising a patient for an assessment centre, where no feedback is required from the actor to the participant. The Royal College of Anaesthetists requires candidates for their anaesthetist qualifying exams to role-play with a simulated patient (an actor), so that the communications and empathetic skills of the candidate can be assessed. The role-play lasts about five minutes and is not complex.

An example of a one-to-one role-play at the more challenging end of the scale would be role-playing a Senior Tax Manager being interviewed for a job. It is important to remember that an actor is used, primarily, to display different types of behaviour (e.g. being nervous, arrogant, aggressive, etc.). However, for the actor to be a convincing Senior Tax Manager for a behavioural role-play, they need to have an overall grasp of what the job entails, and they may need to throw in a few technical phrases to add reality to the situation. This kind of role-play requires a day of training for the actor so that they can learn about the role of the Tax Manager, memorise a few key technical words and phrases and rehearse the role-play encounter.

Actors are also required to give each participant with whom they role-play some high-quality feedback about their performance. At this highly sophisticated level of role-play, being able to deliver such feedback is an essential skill. Remember to frame the feedback with affirmative and supportive language.

The skills required to be a good one-to-one role-player are: the ability to go into character instantly; the ability to improvise well; the ability to understand and interpret the brief; the ability to memorise some technical terms; the ability to adjust your performance in relation to the quality of the input from the participant; and the ability to give feedback that is communicated sensitively and is useful to the participant.

Delivering an interactive theatre session

This technique has been used in schools by Theatre in Education companies for many years, and is now being used increasingly in the workplace. There are many different variations in the way that interactive theatre, or forum theatre, is delivered, but the principle is quite simple. Actors playing a scene will break out from that scene and talk to the audience, in character, asking for advice. This advice is then taken back into the scene by the actor and played out to see if it is effective.

Many aspects of development and learning can be addressed via interactive theatre: managing difficult conversations; feedback skills; diversity awareness; assertiveness skills; customer service; influencing skills; leadership; performance management; coaching; recruitment; employment law awareness.

The skills necessary for performing high-quality forum theatre are: good improvisational skills; the ability to gain a thorough understanding of the objectives of the programme; being an able facilitator in order to confidently handle the responses from the audience; and the ability to hang onto a character while improvising and facilitating.

Applying for work

There are many different types of role-play/drama-based training companies. When we created Steps in 1992, we were one of only a handful of role-play companies; I have now lost count of the number of similar organisations! They all have different cultures and different ways of approaching the work, and each individual company's style probably reflects the personalities of their creators. Some companies may only provide actors to do one-to-one role-play, while others may concentrate on providing interactive theatre. Companies may have a large database of actors; others may have a small pool of actors who work on a fairly regular basis.

My advice would be to browse through the websites of the companies listed and get a feel of what they all claim to be offering. Find out from other actors who have worked in this area about their experiences. Ask them what they think of the company who employed them. At Steps we look at all actor CVs that we receive and run audition workshops as, and when, we need to select new actors onto our team.

Role-playing for learning is no less a professional activity than professional acting. Punctuality, wearing the appropriate business/work clothes, maintaining confidentiality, interacting in an exemplary way with clients and participants, and working effectively as a member of a high-performance team with fellow role-players, are all behaviours that are required during a role-play assignment.

Being a role-player is a fascinating way for an actor to use their skills in between acting assignments while maintaining an income. Also, from the feedback I have received from role-players, the benefits are not only one-way: actors can learn a great deal from the organisations in which they role-play. The work they do can build their confidence and help them to discover new ways of managing their own careers.

Robbie Swales attended the Bristol Old Vic Theatre School from 1968 to 1970. During the 1970s he acted in Rep, toured and appeared in the West End; during the 1980s he made the most of his income from TV commercials. In 1994 Robbie joined Steps – Drama Learning Development and is now one of six directors who manage the company. In 2002 and 2003 Steps was one of the hundred fastest-growing inner-city companies in the UK, appearing on the HM Treasury-sponsored Inner City 100 Index.

Role-play companies

Actors have long used their craft in promotional areas like selling products and services over the phone and in department stores; work opportunities in these fields are advertised in *The Stage*. More recently, the idea of using theatre skills deeper inside the world of business (and the service professions, like medicine) has grown considerably. Essentially, the high level of co-operation ('interactivity') and the excitement, creativity and inspirational power of good theatre is being grasped by hierarchies 'outside the proscenium arch'. Role-play practitioners today are using techniques evolved by the Theatre in Education movement in the 1960s and 70s – but with far better-paying 'customers'.

The established companies – mostly created by actors – have built up a great deal of expertise in this new world and do not take on new 'role-players' lightly. It is therefore especially important to research each individual company's *modus operandi* before spending time and money in contacting them. However, this is a world well worth exploring as an exciting and lucrative alternative area of work.

Activation

Riverside House, Feltham Avenue, Hampton Court, Surrey KT8 9BJ
tel 020-8783 9494 *fax* 020-8783 9345
email info@activation.co.uk
website www.activation.co.uk
Director Paul Gilmore

A leading provider of bespoke interactive training. Services include forum theatre, role-play, scriptwriting and performance, and the design and delivery of training programmes. Incoming actors are trained by the company, according to the requirements of the project. Strong acting and listening skills are required of all the actors. Recent clients include: Diageo, Barclays, and Lloyds TSB.

Periodically extends its actor-base, often by word-of-mouth but also using the Internet. Welcomes letters (with CVs and photographs) from actors previously unknown to the company if sent by post, but not by email. Does not welcome showreels, but is happy to receive invitations to view individuals' websites. Will consider applications from disabled actors to play characters with disabilities.

Barking Productions Ltd

PO Box 597, Bristol BS99 2BB
tel 0117-939 3171 *fax* 0117-939 3625
email info@barkingproductions.co.uk
website www.barkingproductions.co.uk
Key personnel Christopher Grimes, Neil Bett, Stephanie Weston

Company's work

Creative development and corporate entertainment company run by professional actors and specialising in drama-based training. The company's comedy show, *Instant Wit*, is regularly performed at corporate events. Provides incoming actors with some training in the form of familiarisation with company style and approach. Clients include: Marks & Spencer, Microsoft, Aardman Animations and Orange.

Recruitment procedures

Periodically extends its actor-base. Welcomes letters (with CVs and photographs) and always consults them when recruiting actors. Requires actors to be highly experienced with a businesslike manner (particularly for corporate work), and living in Bristol or London. Advises actors to visit the website and get a good idea of "who we are and what we do" before approaching the company.

Cragrats

The Cragrats Mill, Dunford Road, Huddersfield HD9 2AR
tel (01484) 686451 *fax* (01484) 686212
email jill@cragrats.com
website www.cragrats.com
Creative Director Mark Greenop *Business Director* David Bradley

Company's work

A theatrical communications company founded in 1989; specialises in corporate training, TIE and issue-based theatre nationwide. Employs 500 actors per year. Project managers and facilitators are trained in-house. Clients include: ASDA, NHS, Learning & Skills Councils, and the Royal Bank of Scotland.

Recruitment procedures

Extends its actor-base each month. Recruits actors through the website and through agents, Equity Job

Information Service and advertisements in *The Stage*. Welcomes submissions (with CVs and photographs) by post or email from actors with at least 3 years of training at an approved drama school. "We regularly recruit actors aged 21-60. Please contact us. All rehearsals are Yorkshire-based, though work can be anywhere in the UK."

Interact

Bowden House, 14 Bowden Street, London SE11 4DS
tel 020-7793 7744 *fax* 020-7793 7755
email info@interact.eu.com
website www.interact.eu.com
Directors Derek Hollis, Ian Jessup *Company Administrator* Jamie Wright

Company's work

Founded in 1996, the company aims to bring theatre skills to business using the abilities of professional actors, writers, directors and facilitators. Role-play constitutes just 30% of output. Provides incoming actors with some training in the form of a briefing for basic role-play, rehearsal and guidance for complex work. Offers facilitators specific training in project management. Clients include: ACAS, the Foreign & Commonwealth Office, the BBC, and Royal and Sun Alliance.

Recruitment procedures

Periodically extends its actor-base. Recruits actors through the website and through agents, Equity Job Information Service, *PCR* and direct contact. Fluency, confidence and strong acting and improvisation skills are required. Business and forum theatre experience can also be an advantage. Welcomes letters (with CVs and photographs) but not email submissions. Invitations to view individual actors' websites are also accepted. Advises actors that: "Those with previous experience are most likely to be interviewed. We are unable to reply to submissions. If you are of interest to us, you will be contacted."

Maynard Leigh Associates (MLA)

Marvic House, Bishops Road, London SW6 7AD
email michaelm@maynardleigh.co.uk
website www.maynardleigh.co.uk

Company's work

MLA is essentially a community of about 25 people who share common values, are committed to their own and other people's personal growth, and are passionate about their work affecting an increasing number of individuals and organisations. They are required to be expert workshop leaders with an interest in the psychological aspects of human potential development. Clients include: Hewlett

Packard, Halifax plc, Ernst & Young, BBC TV, Vodafone, Barclay, Virgin and FT.com.

Recruitment procedures

All new consultants and leaders go through a rigorous and lengthy training process regardless of their professional experience. It can take up to 18 months of participation in MLA activities before an actor is allowed to represent the consultancy with clients. There are regular personal development sessions in which people explore how they are doing in MLA and how they need to develop and grow further. As MLA invests heavily in its existing Associates, its pace of growth is limited and it is unable to extend its actor-base regularly. Professional actors with a good working knowledge of business and corporate life should submit their details by email.

Steps Drama Learning Development

Unit 4.1.1 The Leathermarket, Weston Street, London SE1 3ER
tel 020-7403 9000 *fax* 020-7403 0909
email mail@stepsdrama.com
website www.stepsdrama.com
Account Directors Robbie Swales, Richard Wilkes, Janet Rawson, Simon Thomson, Mark Shillabeer, Angela McHale

Company's work

Founded in 1990, the company supplies training to a wide variety of corporate companies through the use of drama. The work includes role-play, forum workshops and drama facilitation. Incoming actors receive training in the areas of feedback skills, forum workshops, coordinator workshops, facilitation skills and 'train the trainer'. Clients include: JP Morgan, NHS, AXA PPP, Disney, and the BBC.

Recruitment procedures

Extends its actor-base once or twice a year, selecting 2-3 people in each round. Welcomes letters (with CVs and photographs) but not email submissions; consults submitted CVs when recruiting. Actors should have excellent improvisation skills and be able to present themselves realistically as part of the business world in both their dress and language. Requires actors to behave in a professional manner both in their dealings with Steps and with their clients. Must be organised, reliable and good team players.

Turning Point Theatre Company

20 Couper Meadows, Exeter EX2 7TF
tel (01392) 446818 *fax* (01392) 446279
email turningpoint@eclipse.co.uk
website www.turningpointtheatre.co.uk
Director Lyn Ferrand *Administrator* Anne Williams

Company's work

Founded in 1990, the company aims to raise awareness of specific health and social issues using theatre and theatre-related techniques. Gained Pavilion Award for innovations in training (2000). Works in partnership with the corporate, voluntary and statutory sectors. Creates training courses and videos for health and social service professionals; other activities include national and regional tours, residencies, workshops and conferences. Provides incoming actors with some training in forum theatre techniques if required. Clients include: Devon County Council, the Princess Royal Trust for Carers, and Rethink (NSF).

Recruitment procedures

Periodically extends its actor-base in accordance with the demands of specific projects. Actors are recruited via agents and *PCR*. Welcomes submissions (with CVs and photographs) sent by post or email. Showreels and invitations to view individual actors' websites are also accepted.

Recorded media
Introduction

The last decade has seen incredibly rapid advancements in recording technology, computers, digital media and the Internet. There has also been an enormous growth in the principal broadcasting companies contracting-out much of their output; this in turn has led to an increase in the number of independent companies employing actors. (There are also companies whose output does not include drama – these have not been included in the listings.)

Most film and television companies use casting directors, and it's usually a waste of time and money writing to anyone else unless you have a personal contact. It is worth remembering that many companies do work for businesses – training and promotional films, for instance.

Student films may be a somewhat poor relation to Hollywood blockbusters, in terms of pay (if any) and exposure, but they can provide useful experiences, be a good addition to your CV, and have the potential to lead onto something that is properly paid and much more prestigious. Extracts from such a film could also be useful for your showreel.

Casting for radio is much more akin to that for theatre, although often without the use of a casting director.

Countdown to 'Action!'

Edward Hicks

The shooting process will vary slightly from production to production, and will present different challenges. But the one element that is certain – be it multi-camera studio or single-camera location – is the waiting. It's hardly surprising that actors have a reputation for story-swapping; it helps to pass the time! However, as actors spend the day unable to fully relax, in a permanent state of standby ready for 'Action', the waiting can be strangely tiring.

The average shooting day is long, and even though a finished shot lasts seconds on-screen, setting up a shot and lighting takes hours. If the sequence involves stunts, special-effects, animals or supporting artistes, it can take several days. For the actor, this means intense moments of concentrated activity (lasting minutes) followed by long periods of waiting (lasting hours). This balance between being relaxed, yet at the same time remaining focused and energised, can be difficult to achieve. Then, when things fall behind schedule (which inevitably they do), the pressure to get it right intensifies – making it even harder to relax.

A small role in an episode of a long-running television programme can frequently be far more nerve-racking than a larger part. I've often seen actors sitting around all day waiting to do a few lines, only to discover that their little scene is to be covered in one shot … which is to be the last shot of the day. The director knows that the crew (who have worked flat-out all day) must finish on time, as there's no money in the budget for overtime; a good 1st AD won't be shy about reminding the director of this. So with only ten minutes to get the scene in the can, you're frantically called to the set (not a good moment to leave a jacket or prop in your dressing room!); you're introduced to the 1st AD (the person responsible for keeping the director on schedule); you do a rough block with the director, followed by final make-up and wardrobe checks; then someone screams "turn over", the board is read out and the director yells "Action!" Suddenly, with all eyes on you (not to mention a camera), the pressure to get it right first time is enormous. This kind of scenario may sound extreme, but every actor will experience it.

Every production will be slightly different, but the countdown to a standard shoot (if such a thing exists) will probably be as follows.

Firstly, the audition. Remember that getting one is an achievement in itself – so make the most of it. It's hard to get seen for TV and films, and even if you don't land this job, the audition may lead to others. Nearly all castings are handled by a casting director who liaises with the agents and assembles various actors to meet the director. These castings are more like an interview than an audition, involving a brief chat followed by a reading. Arrive early, as you may find a couple of pages waiting for you at reception. Don't be surprised if you only get to read the scene a couple of times; that's quite normal and the casting director usually reads the other roles. It will probably be filmed and may only last ten minutes or so.

Having been cast, you'll be sent a script (possibly a revised draft) and a schedule. Read them both carefully. The schedule is an important document and should help to answer a lot of your questions. At the very least, it will contain a call sheet with details of where you need to be and when; most are far more detailed than that, and include cast lists, crew lists, phone numbers, maps, directions to locations, travel arrangements, health and safety regulations, etc. Check that your contact details are correct and that the dates on the schedule are the dates you were booked for. It's rare for them to be wrong, but it's always best to check as you may start work before your contract arrives. Your agent would have the original booking dates from when the company first checked your availability.

Next you'll receive several phone calls. Firstly, one from the 2nd AD or a production assistant confirming your call. If you have any questions that the schedule can't answer, this is the time to ask. For instance, if by this stage you've not received a script, mention it. They listed me as the wrong character on a schedule once and when I mentioned it to the 2nd AD, it turned out that some of the lines and my character's name had been changed. Nobody had told me and I had learnt the wrong role. Luckily, I still had time to learn the right one! Then, you'll probably get calls from someone in the Costume and Make-up departments. Depending on the scale of the production they may arrange fittings and make-up tests. Either way, make sure you know all your measurements for Costume, including hat and glove sizes. (Incidentally, it's not uncommon in TV for you not to try on your costume until you arrive for the shoot – so give them your real sizes, not the sizes you wish to be!) Also, if your hair is different from your Spotlight photo, tell them, as they might be making decisions based on it.

While waiting for your shooting day to come around, work on your script; familiarise yourself with the lines and characters. Any work you do at home that better prepares you before the shoot could prove useful, especially as less and less time is allocated for rehearsing on set. Don't forget to work on the standby scenes too; these are scenes that are held in reserve in case the schedule is changed at the last minute. They'll be on the call sheet listed as standby scenes or wet weather scenes. You'll probably then hear nothing until a day or two before you start, when they'll ring to confirm your call.

When you arrive at the unit base, the first person you'll meet will most likely be the 2nd AD who, among other things, is responsible for your whereabouts during the shoot. Make sure that they or someone else knows where you are at all times: 2nd ADs are full of stories about wandering actors bringing shoots to a grinding halt because they decided to look around a location. Remember, you'll end up looking foolish – but the 2nd AD gets the blame.

Having arrived at the unit base or the studios, and provided the shoot is running to schedule, you'll be shown to a dressing room or green room. If the schedule has been changed (it often is), you'll be taken straight to Costume and Make-up. If on location, the unit base will either be a building or various trailers and trucks. You'll probably be left on your own as most people will be shooting somewhere else, but there may be other actors around (and if on location, catering people and various drivers). However, at some point you'll be collected and taken to Costume and Make-up. First thing in the morning these places are a hive of activity, so look out for the other actors in your first scene that day. The chances are that some of them will be in make-up at the same time as you.

Depending on the size of the production, you may have your own make-up artist and your own dresser who will be responsible for your costumes. As you will end up spending a lot of time with these people, they'll be a large factor towards your enjoyment of the shoot. I know one director who judges the mood of his cast and crew by the atmosphere in the Wardrobe, Make-up and Catering trailers.

Once you are in costume and have been to Make-up, you'll probably get sent back to your dressing room or trailer. How long you spend waiting to be called will depend on how well they are sticking to the schedule ... and how you pass the time is up to you. Every actor I've met has their own way (I know of one actor who used to spend his time trying to write sitcom scripts, and ended up becoming a very successful writer). Some actors (but not all!) like to get together and run lines, which is great if you are inexperienced as it can help calm the nerves. However, the important thing to remember is that you have to be ready, so that whenever you are called to the set, you are able to do the best you can when the director yells, "Action!"

Every actor knows that work generates work. So no matter how small your role is, never forget that you've been given an opportunity many other actors would relish. I can't think of a more exciting place than a film set full of talented technicians and actors, who are all pulling together to create something. So make the most of it and enjoy it, because if you're lucky, you can work in some amazing places with some incredibly talented people.

Edward Hicks has worked as an actor under the name Edward Rawle-Hicks since the age of ten, and has appeared in numerous TV, film and theatre productions. He has also worked behind the camera, having trained as a director at the London Film School, shooting several films and promos. Between acting and directing jobs, he currently works at East 15 Acting School where he heads up the Media department and runs a specialist Postgraduate course for actors looking to gain more TV and radio training.

Television companies

These almost always use casting directors who, in turn, will circulate casting breakdowns to agents they trust. However, a carefully timed (and crafted) submission from an individual can occasionally excite interest.

BBC network television

For more information, visit the BBC website – **www.bbc.co.uk**.

The new structure

Major restructuring, introduced by the former Director-General, Greg Dyke, resulted in the creation of five programming divisions:

- Radio and Music
- Drama, Entertainment and CBBC (Children)
- Factual and Learning
- Sport
- News

BBC Broadcast and BBC Production have been abolished. In the areas of sport, children's and education, commissioning and programme-making are now integrated. A New Media division is developing the BBC's interactive television online activities.

Television genre commissioners in drama, entertainment and features now work with the television channel controllers to strengthen the BBC's output in these areas.

The disbanding of the Independent Commissioning Group has not diminished the value the BBC now places on the contribution of independents. However, in future they will take the same commissioning routes as in-house producers.

The restructuring also gives output guarantees for in-house departments, including Nations and English Regions, and longer-term commissions to enable better planning and a greater focus on creativity.

Casting information

The BBC no longer has a central casting department. Casting advisers are appointed to each specific programme as required. Output includes: *Casualty, Holby City, Doctors, EastEnders, Born and Bred, The Inspector Lynley Mysteries, Waking the Dead, Judge John Deed, Dalziel and Pascoe, Silent Witness* and *Spooks*. The various programmes' casting departments will accept letters from actors previously unknown to them (with CVs, photographs and performance notices); however, actors are advised that while casting personnel are on the lookout for new talent and do attend shows, they are extremely busy and tend to use agents when casting.

The recently launched BBC Talent initiative is designed to offer 'raw talent' (actors without formal qualifications or experience) the opportunity to act their way onto a major drama. In 2003, several of the actors cast for the BBC1 drama, *The Canterbury Tales*, were winners of BBC Talent auditions. For the latest information on BBC Talent's projects, see the website – **www.bbc.co.uk/talent**.

Drama

Drama has departments in London, Birmingham and Manchester and produces a broad range of plays, serials, series and readings for TV, film, BBC Radio 3, BBC Radio 4 and BBC World service.

London

BBC Television, Wood Lane, London W12 7RJ
020-8743 8000
BBC Elstree, Neptune House, Clarendon Road, Borehamwood WD6 1JF
website www.bbc.co.uk/drama
Controller, Drama Commissioning Jane Tranter
Controller, Continuing Drama Series & Head of Independent Drama John Yorke *Head of Drama Serials & Series* TBC *Joint Head Independent Drama* Lucy Richer *Head of Casting, Drama Series* Julia Crampsie *Head of Radio Drama, Bush House* Alison Hindell *Head of Films & Single Drama* David Thompson *Head of Development Films* Tracey Scoffield *Head of Development, Drama Serials* Sarah Brown *Head of Interactive Drama & Entertainment* Sophie Walpole
Note that while most of these senior programme makers are based at Wood Lane, many BBC casting directors are based at the Elstree site. See the Casting Directors section on page 82 for more information.

Birmingham

BBC Birmingham TV Drama Village, Archibald House, 1059 Bristol Road, Selly Oak, Birmingham B29 6LT
tel 0121-432 8888
website www.bbc.co.uk/birmingham
Executive Producer Birmingham Drama Will Trotter

Manchester

New Broadcasting House, Oxford Road, Manchester M60 1SJ
tel 0161-200 2020
website www.bbc.co.uk/manchester
Executive Producer Manchester Drama Anne Mensah
Executive Producer, Radio Drama, Manchester Sue Roberts

The New Writing Initiative

BBC Writersroom, 1 Mortimer Street, London W1T 3JA
tel 020-7765 2703
email writersroom@bbc.co.uk
website www.bbc.co.uk/writersroom
Creative Director Kate Rowland *Development Manager* Paul Ashton

Entertainment

BBC Television Centre, Wood Lane, London W12 7RJ
tel 020-8743 8000
website www.bbc.co.uk/entertainment
Head of Comedy Sophie Clark-Jervoise *Head of Comedy Entertainment* Jon Plowman

Entertainment welcomes new half-hour TV situation comedy scripts, and material is reviewed by its Comedy Script Unit. Radio is also a good entry-point for new comedy writers, performers and ground-breaking innovative series such as sketch shows and panel games.

CBBC (Children)

BBC Television Centre, Wood Lane, London W12 7RJ
tel 020-8743 8000
Head of Drama Elaine Sperber *Head of Entertainment* Anne Gilchrist

There are opportunities for new writers in this highly competitive area. Unsolicited material is read by the department, preferably in the form of synopses of ideas. The preferred genres are contemporary comedy and drama.

Entertainment and Features, Manchester

BBC New Broadcasting House, PO Box 27, Oxford Road, Manchester M60 1SJ
tel 0161-200 2020

A bi-media department which makes programmes for both radio and TV. It is responsible for a wide range of factual, entertainment and music programming, and specialises in spotting new comedy talent; aims to see all new stand-up performers/writers in the North West. Write with details of events to Comedy Entertainment, Room 4033.

Network Production, Birmingham

BBC Birmingham, Pebble Mill Road, Birmingham B5 7QQ
tel 0121-432 8888
Editor, Radio Drama, The Archers Vanessa Whitburn

A vast range of radio and TV programming which encompasses Asian, consumer affairs, leisure, lifestyle, motoring, music and rural affairs.

BBC Northern Ireland

BBC Broadcasting House, Ormeau Avenue, Belfast BT2 8HQ
tel 028-9033 8000
website www.bbc.co.uk/ni
Entertainment and Events Mike Edgar *Head of Drama* Patrick Spence

BBC Northern Ireland produces a broad spectrum of radio and TV programmes, both for the BBC's networks and for its home audience. Output includes news and current affairs, documentaries, education, entertainment, sport, music, Irish language and religious programmes. It also has a thriving drama department which reads unsolicited scripts across all genres, i.e. single, serials, series, feature films and the short-film scheme Northern Lights, which is aimed at new talent from within Northern Ireland.

In addition to making network radio programmes, broadcasting on BBC Radio 1, 2, 3, 4, and 5 Live and BBC World Service, BBC Northern Ireland also makes programmes for its local radiolisteners.

BBC Scotland

BBC Broadcasting House, Queen Margaret Drive, Glasgow G12 8DG
tel 0141-339 8844
website www.bbc.co.uk/scotland
Head of Drama Barbara McKissack

BBC Scotland is the BBC's most varied production centre outside London, providing BBC TV and radio networks and BBC World Service with pivotal drama, comedy, entertainment, children's, leisure, documentaries, religion, education, arts, music, special events news, current affairs and political coverage. Internet development is also a key element of production activity.

Its drama department, along with Scottish Screen, is responsible for the highly successful initiative, *Tartan Shorts*, which promotes film-making in the nation and provides a platform for emerging Scottish creative talent, including actors, writers, directors and producers.

In addition to making network output, more than 850 hours of TV programming per year is transmitted on BBC1 Scotland and BBC2 Scotland. BBC Radio Scotland is the country's only national radio station, and is on air 18 hours a day, 7 days a week. Local programmes are also broadcast on Radio Scotland's FM frequency in the Northern Isles, and there are daily local bulletins for listeners in the Highlands, Grampian, Borders, and the southwest. BBC Radio Nan Gaidheal provides a Gaelic service on a separate FM frequency for around 40 hours a week.

BBC Wales

BBC Broadcasting House, Llandaff, Cardiff CF5 2YQ
tel 029-2032 2000
website www.bbc.co.uk/wales
Head of Drama Julie Gardner

BBC Wales provides a wide range of services in Welsh and in English, on radio, TV and online. This includes more than 20 hours a week of programmes on BBC1 Wales and BBC2 Wales, as well as the new BBC Wales digital services. Regular output includes the flagship news programme *Wales Today*, the current affairs strand *Week In Week Out*, and the rugby magazine *Scrum V*. A further 10 hours are shown on the Welsh-language channel S4C, including the news programme *Newyddion*, the nightly drama serial *Pobol y Cwm* plus a range of programmes for schools. Its two radio stations – BBC Radio Wales, broadcasting in English, and BBC Radio Cymru, broadcasting in Welsh – each provide 18 hours a day of news, entertainment, music and sports output. Political coverage on all services has expanded as a result of the creation of the National Assembly for Wales.

BBC Wales also makes popular drama, documentaries, education and music programmes for audiences throughout the UK, including the biennial Cardiff Singer of the World competition, accompanied by the BBC National Orchestra of Wales.

Casting for television

Janie Frazer

There are now many casting directors working in television, and each will have their own way of working. This is my own viewpoint and may not be shared by others, but I hope it may be helpful.

I came into casting by way of the theatre. When I was a schoolgirl I fell in love with the theatre and, being good at English, thought perhaps I could become a drama critic. However, some wise person suggested that before writing about the theatre I should work within it, and so I managed to get a job – at first unpaid, sweeping the stage and as a dresser, and subsequently as an ASM and then handling publicity for the Citizens Theatre Glasgow. I had also been involved in the big auditions held at the start of each season for the Citizens, and had come to realise that the actors were the thing that interested me most about the theatre. Subsequently I moved to London and incessantly badgered LWT for a job as a casting assistant, which finally transpired. I have worked there, through several mergers which have resulted in the company currently known as ITV, for many years. I have cast for all types of television productions; mainly drama, comedy drama and situation comedy, but also sketch comedy, factual drama, hidden camera, animation (voice-over), and various others programmes which defy definition.

Each production has its own specificity, but there are basic requirements that apply to all.

The script

This is the first principle and the foundation for everything else, even though the script may change beyond recognition during the process of getting the production to the screen. The script contains the characters, their descriptions, and the dialogue; from this, in consultation with the director and producer, I will put together a list of suggested actors for the roles.

Casting for television carries with it certain commercial considerations. The casting of the main characters is often crucial to a programme getting commissioned in the first place, since in commercial television the advertisers need to be assured of getting a specific audience for the programmes around and within which they buy advertising space. This is the reason for the often-heard grumble that the same well-known faces crop up again and again, and the reason for it is that they have good form – i.e., the programmes they appear in produce good viewing figures, which is what both ITV and the BBC are striving to maintain.

Beyond the 'name' casting, the casting for other roles involves interpreting the director's vision, style, ideas and the tone of the piece to come up with suggestions that will best express the way in which the director wants to portray the material. Therefore, the same script may elicit different suggestions from me, according to the individual director.

Suggestions for actors

How do I arrive at these? I have many lists, and many files, sorted in an idiosyncratic fashion over the years and added to constantly after seeing actors' work on stage and screen. Also there is *Spotlight*, which is the casting director's invaluable and indispensable tool. If there was only one piece of advice I could offer to an actor, it would be to appear in *Spotlight*, and to keep one's entry accurate and up to date. I now use *Spotlight* almost exclusively via the Internet, as the information contained on the website is wonderfully comprehensive and well organised, and allows me to do cross-reference searching (e.g. for a 30-year-old Punjabi speaker with a Manchester accent) which is extremely swift and useful. The information contained on the site does however rely entirely on the input of the actors who subscribe to *Spotlight*, and it is therefore very important that actors keep their credits and personal details current.

Also and most importantly, their photographs. To state the crashingly obvious, television is a visual medium. It's vital that an actor's photograph is up to date and actually looks like them. Vanity should not be the issue, as television requires all types and ages to be portrayed; moreover, an inaccurate photograph can be misleading and time-wasting. The Spotlight's website has now progressed to offer audio and video clips of each actor, and I have found that these can be really useful to play to a director when discussing casting. Therefore, I would strongly recommend that actors make full use of all the opportunities offered by *Spotlight* to show their wares.

Via the Spotlight Link I am also able to send out a breakdown of characters to the agents, who then relay back their suggestions, which I can order, prioritise and follow up. I will discuss with the director and producer the various suggestions we have made between us, and those that have come from agents; I will then arrange casting sessions for the various roles.

Getting in touch

I would love to be able to say that receiving letters with photos and CVs, or emails with all those attachments, is always a boon – but I'm afraid it's not usually the case. More useful is to be notified of actors' forthcoming performances: even if it's not always possible to cover these, it's good to know what work you are doing, and one may ask other casting directors if they have seen you in the piece.

Showreels on VHS/CD can be useful to view as examples of an actor's work, but tend not to be so significant if they arrive unsolicited – there are simply not enough hours in the day to watch everything that is sent in. I find I am most likely to watch them if they are directly relevant to a current project (for instance, if I am looking for young Northern actors, or working on a sketch comedy show, I will select to watch those that might fall into the relevant categories).

When you are called for audition

Almost invariably now, casting sessions for television dramas and comedy are video-taped. This allows for greater scrutiny of the actor, and assessment of their presence on screen away from the social context of the audition. It does not mean that the actor has had to produce a flawless reading, but many things emerge from watching an actor on screen which may have been missed during the live reading. The camera is sensitive to minute changes in thought-processes and expression as the actor is being filmed in close-up; this is something the actor needs to bear in mind during a television casting audition – that the performance will be watched at close hand, and therefore a loud voice and large expressions will convey considerable impact which may need to be scaled down.

Whatever an actor's looks, the most important feature on screen is the eyes. The people casting the programme need to see yours. Therefore, it will help enormously if you are able to absorb, familiarise yourself with, or best of all learn the scene so that you are able to raise your eyes from the script. Almost all 'sides' or scenes for reading will have been emailed to your agent or yourself prior to audition. Make sure you have an email address. Acquaint yourself with script formats such as Final Draft (at the time of writing, a free download for viewing scripts in Final Draft format is available from the website **www.finaldraft.com**). If you wear glasses, print the scene in a large font so that you can still read it if at the casting they would prefer to see you without glasses.

Other basic things to bear in mind are to arrive on time; make sure you know the specific whereabouts of the casting venue, and how long it is likely to take you to get there. You may be unavoidably kept waiting, in which case make sure you let the casting director know if you have another appointment you need to get to. If you can, do some prior research, both about the project, and also about the producer and director of the programme. You can find out about their previous work via the IMDb website, **www.imdb.com** – and since they will after all be looking at your CV, they may be impressed and flattered if you also know something about theirs.

Spend some time thinking about the material you've seen, so you have something to say about it. Many actors would be surprised at how much their observations have contributed to the final version of the script. In television as in film, time is money. Pre-production periods have been reduced to the minimum, which means that there is often very little time for rehearsal once shooting begins. Directors often therefore use the casting process to try out ways in which they would like to scenes to play – this can be rewarding for the actor, and useful even if they do not finally land the part; often directors keep their interview lists and bear actors in mind whom they've liked but who haven't been quite right for the part in question.

If you look good, I look good

Sometimes actors view casting interviews as an exam, or as some sort of test they have to pass. However, there is at least one person in the room who is completely on your side – the casting director. The casting director's reputation relies on the calibre of the actors invited for interview, and if the actors aren't up to it then the casting director is the one who's on the line. Therefore, by getting you in for audition, the casting director is demonstrating faith in your ability and rightness for the part.

Know your value

Everyone has their own USP – their unique selling point. Even if you are Mr/s Ordinary, then that's it. It's valuable. Get to know what it is that is most intriguing about you, and play to your strengths. Ask your colleagues for constructive criticism and listen to it. Emphasise your strengths and don't pretend to be what you are not. Whereas the theatre can thrive on disguise and artifice, the camera takes no hostages and is ruthless in its exposure.

Did you get it?

If you got the part, then congratulations! But an actor is often confused as well as disappointed about not getting a part. They will ask: should I have done it like this, dressed like that, what did I do wrong? It's hard to explain to an actor that the choice is not dependent on something they did or didn't do, but often is the result of someone else being more right for the part than they are. This is a nebulous assessment which I can appreciate is very unsatisfactory to hear, but it is nevertheless the truth. Those actors who have ever been on the other side of the casting process often remark how they now understand what this means, but it doesn't help much with the feeling of frustration. One can only suggest that by the law of averages, eventually the part will come up for which you are the most right; that you've done pretty well to get the interview in the first place; that the director may well have clocked you for the future – and that the whole experience stands you in good stead.

Janie Frazer worked for the Citizens Theatre Glasgow and the Bristol Old Vic before joining LWT's Casting Department, where she worked as a casting assistant before becoming a casting director in her own right in 1994. She has cast single dramas, drama series, continuing drama, factual drama, comedy drama, situation comedy, single comedy, sketch comedy and animation series. She is also currently the London-based casting director for *Coronation Street*.

Independent television

ITV (**www.itv.com**) is the biggest commercial television network in the UK. It is made up of a network of 15 different regional licences, each with its own set of obligations and conditions designed to reflect the particular character of their region and the interests of their viewers. ITV plc (**www.itvplc.com**) owns 12 of the ITV licences; the remainder are owned by SMG, Ulster, and Channel.

ITV1 is the most popular commercial television channel in Britain. Watched on average by 45 million people every week, it has the largest programme budget of any commercial channel in Europe. Network programmes are commissioned by the ITV network controllers purely on merit. At least 25 per cent of programmes shown on ITV1 each year come from independent producers. Regional programmes are commissioned by each regional company.

Note Neither Channel 4 nor Channel 5 make any of their own programmes, so do not have casting departments.

Channel Television
The Television Centre, St Helier, Jersey JE1 3ZD
tel (01534) 816816 *fax* (01534) 816777
website www.channelonline.tv

Provides programmes for the Channel Islands during the whole week, relating mainly to Channel Islands news, events and current affairs. Does not produce any in-house drama.

Grampian Television
Television Centre, Craigshaw Business Park, West Tullos, Aberdeen AB12 3QH
tel (01224) 848848
Harbour Chambers, Dock Street, Dundee DD1 3HW
tel (01382) 591000 *fax* (01382) 591010
23-25 Huntly Street, Inverness IV3 5PR
tel (01463) 242624
website www.grampiantv.co.uk

Provides programmes for North Scotland during the whole week.

ITV Anglia
Anglia House, Norwich NR1 3JG
tel (01603) 615151 *fax* (01603) 631032
website www.itvregions.com/Anglia

Provides programmes for the East of England, daytime discussion programmes, documentaries and factual programmes for UK and international broadcasters. Does not produce any in-house drama.

ITV Border
The Television Centre, Carlisle CA1 3NT
website www.itvregions.com/Border

Provides programmes for Cumbria, the Borders and the Isle of Man during the whole week.

ITV Central
Gas Street, Birmingham B1 2JT
tel 0121-643 9898 *fax* 0121-643 4897
website www.itvregions.com/Central

Provides ITV programmes for the East, West and South Midlands every day.

ITV Granada
Granada Television Centre, Manchester M60 9EA
tel 0161-832 7211
email casting@itv.com
website www.itvregions.com/Granada
Casting Director, Coronation Street Gennie Radcliffe
Casting Director June West

The ITV franchise-holder for the North West of England. Produces programmes across a broad range for both its region and the ITV network.

Welcomes submissions (with CVs and photographs) from actors previously unknown to the company sent by post or email. As the Casting Department is extremely busy, it cannot guarantee to respond to all submissions. Advises actors to call to find out what projects are being cast, and to send in their details as and when appropriate.

ITV London
South Bank, London SE1 9LT
tel 020-7620 1620
email casting@itv.com
website www.itvregions.com/London
Casting Director Janie Frazer *Assistant Casting Director* Stephanie Dawes

The ITV franchise-holder for the London area. Produces programmes across a broad range for both London and the ITV Network.

Welcomes submissions (with CVs and photographs) from actors previously unknown to the company sent by post or email. As the Casting Department is extremely busy, it cannot guarantee to respond to all submissions. Advises actors to call to find out what projects are being cast, and to send in their details as and when appropriate.

ITV Meridian

Forum One, Solent Business Park, Whiteley, Hants PO15 7PA
tel (01489) 442000
website www.itvregions.com/Meridian

The ITV franchise-holder for the South and South East coast of England. Does not produce any in-house drama.

ITV Tyne Tees

Television House, The Watermark, Gateshead, Tyne and Wear NE11 9SZ
tel 0191-404 8700
website www.itvregions.com/Tyne_Tees

Broadcasts to the North of England 7 days a week, 24 hours a day.

ITV Wales

ITV Wales, The Television Centre, Culverhouse Cross, Cardiff CF5 6XJ
tel 029-2059 0590
website www.itvregions.com/Wales

Provides programmes for Wales during the whole week. Produces programmes for home and international sales.

ITV West

Television Centre, Bath Road, Bristol BS4 3HG
tel 0117-972 2722 *fax* 0117-971 7685
website www.itvregions.com/west

Produces programmes for the West of England and for use across the ITV network. Also runs the ITV West Television Workshop, aimed at young people (up to 26) to offer experience in the performance and production skills required for TV, film, theatre and radio. See **www.itvworkshop.co.uk** for more information.

ITV Westcountry

Langage Science Park, Plymouth PL7 5BQ
tel (01752) 333333 *fax* (01752) 333444
website www.itvregions.com/Westcountry

Provides programmes for South West England throughout the week. In-house production is mainly news, sport, and regional current affairs; other regional features are commissioned from independent producers.

ITV Yorkshire (YTV)

The Television Centre, Leeds LS3 1JS
tel 0113-243 8283 *fax* 0113-244 5107
website www.itvregions.com/Yorkshire
Casting Director Sue Jackson *Assistant Casting Director* Faye Styring

Established in 1968, YTV is one of the biggest ITV companies. Following the new Communications Act and the merger of Granada and Carlton, it is part of the new single ITV plc which began life on 2nd February 2004.

YTV continues to produce a range of drama and light entertainment programmes, including: *A Touch of Frost*; *Emmerdale* (shown on the network every weekday night); and *Heartbeat* – ITV1's most popular long-running drama series. In 2003 a new sister programme, *The Royal*, attracted 11.3 million viewers and a 41.3% share of the television audience. In addition to its drama series, YTV has made a number of one-off dramas for the ITV network, including: *Booze Cruise* and *Brides in the Bath*. With an audience of 9.7 million viewers and a 44% audience share, *Booze Cruise* ranked as the best performing Single Drama from any channel for the whole of 2003.

The Casting Department generally works through agents, but will accept submissions (with CVs and photographs) from actors previously unknown to the company if sent by post. As the Department is very busy it cannot guarantee to acknowledge all submissions, but advises actors to enclose an sae for a quicker response. Prefers not to be contacted by telephone or email.

London Weekend Television (LWT)

See entry for ITV London on page 221.

SMG TV Productions Ltd (formerly Scottish Television)

100 Govan Road, Glasgow GS1 1JL
tel 0141-300 3000
website www.smgproductions.tv or www.scottishtv.co.uk
Drama Coordinator Angela Morton

Network television production arm of SMG plc, incorporating London-based Ginger Television. Its client list includes all UK terrestrial networks and major satellite and cable channels. Output includes drama, factual/factual entertainment, entertainment and children's programming.

The Drama Department has more than 20 years' experience of producing network drama for ITV1. Its current Head is Eric Coulter, who is supported by Roz Kidd, Head of Development. Credits include: *Taggart* (now in its 22nd year); *Dr Finlay*; *Rebus*; and *Goodbye Mr Chips*. The Drama team is based at the SMG TV Productions offices in Glasgow. Casting procedures differ from project to project; generally uses independent casting directors, but also accepts letters from actors 'on spec' (with CVs and photographs). Where appropriate these will be passed on to a relevant programme or project. The Drama

Coordinator, Angela Morton, is happy to act as a point of contact for actors' enquiries.

UTV

Havelock House, Ormeau Road, Belfast, Northern Ireland BT7 1EB

tel 028-9032 8122 *fax* 028-9024 6695
email info@u.tv
website www.u.tv/television

Provides programmes for Northern Ireland. All drama is produced by the ITV network.

Independent film, video and TV production companies

Companies in this field start up and close down all the time, and it is very important to have a proper contract if offered work with an independent. If in doubt, check with Equity.

Absolutely Productions

Alhambra House, 27-31 Charing Cross Road, London WC2H 0AU
tel 020-7930 3113 *fax* 020-7930 4114
email info@absolutely-uk.com
website www.absolutely-uk.com
Managing Director Miles Bullough

Founded in 1988. Produces drama and comedy for cinema and TV, and TV entertainment programmes. Recent credits include: *Dead Air* (C4), and *Skin and Blister* (short film).

Actaeon Films Ltd

49 Blenheim Gardens, London, NW2 4NR
tel 020-8830 7990 *fax* 0870-134 7980
email info@actaeonfilms.com
website www.actaeonfilms.com
Company Director/Producer Daniel Cormack *Producer* Matt Gunner *Head of Development* Becky Connell

Production details

Actaeon Films is a London-based production company established in 2004 to develop and produce theatrical motion pictures, both drama and comedy. Recent productions include: *Nightwalking* (HD, 2006; produced by BAFTA-winning producer, Natasha Carlish); and *Amelia and Michael* (35mm, 2006; starring Anthony Head – *Buffy*, *Little Britain*).

Casting procedures

Uses freelance casting directors and publishes casting breakdowns in *PCR*. Offers Equity approved contracts. Actively encourages applications from disabled actors and promotes the use of inclusive casting. "We welcome invitations to showcases, screenings and theatrical productions and will view showreels, but we don't advise sending CVs/headshots unless in relevant response to a current casting call."

Anglo-Fortunato Films Ltd

170 Popes Lane, London W5 4NJ
tel 020-8932 7676 *fax* 020-8932 7491
Contact Luciano Celentino (Managing Director)

APT Films

225A Brecknock Road, London N19 5AA
tel 020-7284 1695 *fax* 020-7482 1587
email admin@aptfilms.com
website www.aptfilms.com
Managing Director Jonny Persey *Director* Paul Morrison *Producer* Stewart Le Marechal

Young enterprise dedicated to development and production of feature films for national and international audiences. Also produces short films. Recent credits include: *Wondrous Oblivion* and *Solomon and Gaenor*. Upcoming work includes *Deep Water*; the company has 3 micro-budget films in development.

Avalon Television Ltd

4A Exmoor Street, London W10 6BD
tel 020-7598 7280 *fax* 020-7598 7300
website www.avalonuk.com
Directors Jon Thoday, Richard Allen-Turner, Sally Debonnaire

Production details

TV, film and radio company producing drama, comedy and documentaries. Recent credits include: *The Frank Skinner Show*, *Shane*, *Harry Hill's TV Burp*, and *The Sketch Show*.

Casting procedures

Always casts through freelance casting directors and does not issue public casting breakdowns. Does not welcome unsolicited contact of any kind from actors previously unknown to the company. Offers Equity approved contracts.

Big Red Button Ltd

91 Brick Lane, London E1 6QL
email hello@bigredbutton.tv
website www.bigredbutton.tv
Key personnel John Burns, Pier Van Tijn, Sagar Shah

Production details

Established in 2002. Specialises in short films and music videos. Works in live action, puppetry and animation. Also employs actors in drama, comedy and commercials.

Casting procedures

Holds general auditions and actors can write to request inclusion at anytime. Casting breakdowns are available on the website and in *PCR*. Welcomes letters (with CVs and photographs) from actors previously unknown to the company if sent by post, but not by email. Invitations to view individual actors' websites are not accepted, but showreels are welcome. Does not offer Equity approved contracts. Rarely has the opportunity to cast disabled actors.

Blue Wand Productions Ltd

2nd Floor, 12 Weltje Road, London W6 9TG
tel 020-8741 2038 or (07885) 528743 *fax* 020-8741 2038
email lino@bluewand.co.uk
Managing Director Lino Omoboni *Executive Producer* Paola Omobomi

Established in 1990, the production company works exclusively in feature film production. Recent credits include: *Camelot*.

The company employs freelance casting directors and does not welcome enquiries and submissions from actors.

Carlton Television Productions

35-38 Portman Square, London W1H 0NU
tel 020-7486 6688 *fax* 020-7486 1132
Director of Programmes Steve Hewlett

Comprises Carlton Television Productions, Planet 24 and Action Time. Makes drama programmes for all UK major broadcasters (ITV, BBC, Channel 4, Channel 5 and Sky) and regional programmes for Carlton Central, Carlton London and Carlton Westcountry.

Carnival (Films & Theatre) Ltd

12 Raddington Road, Ladbroke Grove, London W10 5TG
tel 020-8968 0968 *fax* 020-8968 0177
email info@carnival-films.co.uk
website www.carnival-films.co.uk
Chairman Brian Eastman *Assistant* Claire Phillips

Founded in 1978. Works mainly in TV production, creating drama with a popular and international feel. Employs actors for drama. Commissioned by major UK broadcasters including BBC, Channel 4 and ITV. Has received various prestigious awards/nominations, including Oscars and BAFTAs. Recent credits include: *Poirot*, *BUGS*, *Traffik*, *The Grid*, *Hotel Babylon*, and *Rosemary and Thyme*.

Uses freelance casting directors; does not deal directly with actors. Offers PACT/Equity contracts. Will consider casting disabled actors to play characters with disabilities.

Celador Productions Ltd

39 Long Acre, London WC2E 9LG
tel 020-7240 8101 *fax* 020-7845 9541
website www.celador.co.uk
Joint Managing Directors Christian Colson (films), Danielle Lux (TV)

Works also in television and radio. TV output is mostly non-fiction and light entertainment – e.g. *Who Wants to be a Millionaire?* and *You Are What You Eat* – although the company produced the sitcom, *All About Me*, starring Jasper Carrott and Meera Syal.

"The company is developing a number of other projects, including a further Neil Marshall project for production in 2006/7; BAFTA-winner Adrian Hodges' adaptation of Claire Tomalin's Whitbread Award-winning biography of Samuel Pepys, *The Unequalled Self*; *Farang*, a low-budget road movie set in Thailand – a collaboration with writer Richard Cottan and director Peter Webber; an original screenplay from Paul Webb, based on events following the accession of Lyndon Baines Johnson to the United States presidency in the aftermath of Kennedy's assassination; and *Big Deal*, a comedy about a hapless English journalist attempting to navigate the shark-infested waters of the international poker circuit."

Celtic Films

31 Sackville Street, London W1S 4DZ
tel 020-7734 4434 *fax* 020-7734 4744
email info@celticfilms.co.uk
website www.celticfilms.co.uk

Production details

Established in 1986, Celtic Films has acted as a co-producer for 15 feature-length episodes of *Sharpe* for ITV, and for the award-winning *The Girl from Rio*.

Casting procedures

Accepts submissions (with CVs and photographs) from actors previously unknown to the company if sent by post or by email. Showreels, voice tapes and invitations to view individual actors' websites are also accepted. Offers Equity approved contracts. Will consider applications from disabled actors to play characters with disabilities.

Chatsworth Television Ltd

97-99 Dean Street, London W1D 3TE
tel 020-7734 4302 *fax* 020-7437 3301
email television@chatsworth-tv.co.uk
website www.chatsworth-tv.co.uk
Managing Director Malcolm Heyworth

Founded in 1980, the company produces entertainment, factual programmes and drama. Has sister companies in TV distribution and licensing.

Children's Film and Television Foundation Ltd

Elstree Film and Television Studios, Borehamwood, Herts WD6 1JG
tel 020-8953 0844 *fax* 020-8207 0860

Involved in the development and co-production of films for children and the family, both for the theatrical market and for television.

Collingwood O'Hare Entertainment and Convergence Productions

10-14 Crown Street, London W3 8SB
tel 020-8993 3666 *fax* 020-8993 9595
email info@crownstreet.co.uk
Head of Development Helen Stroud

Founded in 1988. Animation series for children (COE), documentary series, and drama films and series (Convergence). Does not deal directly with actors; prefers to deal with agents.

Company Pictures

Suffolk House, Whitfield Place, London W1T 5JU
tel 020-7380 3900 *fax* 020-7380 1166
email enquiries@companypictures.co.uk
website www.companypictures.co.uk
Managing Directors George Faber, Charlie Pattinson

Founded in 1998. Works mainly in film and TV production and employs actors for dramas. Recent credits include: *P.O.W.*, *White Teeth*, *The Life and Death of Peter Sellers*, and *Morvern Callar*.

Uses freelance casting directors and does not deal directly with actors.

Cowboy Films

2nd Floor, 87 Notting Hill Gate, London W11 3JZ
tel 020-7792 5400 *fax* 020-7792 0592
email info@cowboyfilms.co.uk or charles@cowboyfilms.co.uk
website www.cowboyfilms.co.uk
Co-founder Charles Steele

Until recently, Cowboy Films represented a range of top-quality commercials and music video directors, and also worked on feature films such as *The Hole* and *Goodbye Charlie Bright*. Sister company Crossroads Films in the US has taken over the roster of music video and commercial projects, while Cowboy continues to work on features. Kevin Macdonald's *The Last King of Scotland* is the company's most recent project.

Create Media Ventures (formerly Create TV & Film)

52 New Concordia Wharf, Mill Street, London SE12 2BB
tel 020-7154 6960
email assistant@cmventures.co.uk
website www.cmventures.co.uk
Key personnel Vanessa Chapman, David Kerney

Production details

Originally established in 2000 (as Create TV & Film) and relaunched in 2005 as Create Media Ventures.

Specialises in TV and film in the areas of drama, children and animation. Recent credits include: *Little Robots* and *Bionicle* (employing voice cast).

Casting procedures

Casting breakdowns can be obtained via the casting director. General auditions are held, and actors are advised to apply in January and September for inclusion.

Welcomes letters (with CVs and photographs) from actors previously unknown to the company if sent by post, but not by email. Invitations to view individual actors' websites are also accepted. Actively encourages applications from disabled actors and promotes the use of inclusive casting.

Don Productions Ltd

26 Shacklewell Lane, London E8 2EZ
tel 020-7690 0108 *fax* 020-7690 4333
email info@donproductions.com
website www.donproductions.com
Director Donald Harding

Japanese/English bilingual TV and media production company based in London. Produces TV drama, documentaries, news and sports programmes. Clients include: Japan Broadcasting Corporation, Nippon Television and Channel 4. Recent work includes: *The Life of Charles Darwin*.

Provides a casting service and will accept submissions from actors previously unknown to the company. Showreels are also accepted but unsolicited emails will not be opened.

The Drama House

Coach Road Cottages, Little Saxham, Bury St Edmunds, Suffolk IP29 5LE
tel (01284) 810521 *fax* (01284) 811425
email jack@dramahouse.co.uk
website www.dramahouse.co.uk
Chairman/Chief Executive Jack Emery

Produces drama and drama-documentaries for film and TV. Recent credits include: *Breaking the Code*, *Witness Against Hitler*, *Little White Lies* and *Suffer the Little Children*. Commissioned by major broadcasters including BBC and Channel 4. Hopes that high-profile work will encourage writers and other professionals to come to the Drama House.

Ecosse Films Ltd

Brigade House, 8 Parsons Green, London SW6 4TN
tel 020-7371 0290 *fax* 020-7736 3436
email info@ecossefilms.co.uk
website www.ecossefilms.com
Director Douglas Rae *Head of Drama* Robert Bernstein

Founded in 1988. Works mainly in TV and feature film production and employs actors in dramas and comedies. Recent credits include: *Mrs Brown*,

Charlotte Gray, *Monarch of the Glen* and *Amnesia*. Uses freelance casting directors and does not deal directly with actors.

Elstree Film and Television Studios

Borehamwood, Hertfordshire WD6 1JG
tel 020-8953 0844 *fax* 020-8207 0860
email annahome@cftf.onyxnet.co.uk

Involved in the development and co-production of films for children and the family, both for the theatrical market and for television.

Eye Film and Television

Chamberlain House, 2 Dove Street, Norwich, Norfolk NR2 1DE
tel (01603) 762551 *fax* (01603) 762420
email production@eyefilmandtv.co.uk
website www.eyefilmandtv.co.uk
Managing Director Charlie Gauvain

Independent producers of film and TV drama and documentaries. Also produces corporate, commercial, education and training material. Clients include: BBC, ITV1/Anglia, Channel 4, Five, and First Take Films. Recent credits include: *The Secret of Eel Island* and *POV*.

Offers PACT/Equity contracts. "Although there has been limited opportunity to employ disabled actors in the past, we hope that this will change as we do more drama."

The Farnham Film Company

34 Burnt Hill Road, Lower Bourne, Farnham GU10 3LZ
tel (01252) 710313 *fax* (01252) 725855
email info@farnfilm.com
website www.farnfilm.com
Key personnel Ian Lewis, Melloney Roffe

Production details

Areas of work include film, TV, video, documentaries and corporate. Recent productions include: *The Chef's Apprentice*, and *Mona the Vampire*.

Casting procedures

Casting breakdowns are available via the website and in *PCR*. Offers Equity contracts. Does not welcome unsolicited CVs. Actively encourages applications from disabled actors and promotes the use of inclusive casting.

Feelgood Fiction Ltd

49 Goldhawk Road, London W12 8QP
tel 020-8746 2535 *fax* 020-8740 6177
email feelgood@feelgoodfiction.co.uk
Managing Director Philip Clarke *Drama Producer* Laurence Bowen

Producers of film and TV drama.

Film & General Productions Ltd

4 Bradbrook House, Studio Place, London SW1X 8EL
tel 020-7235 4495 *fax* 020-7245 9853
email cparsons@filmgen.co.uk
Directors Clive Parsons, Davina Belling

Founded in 1971, the company produces a wide range of feature films, television drama and children's drama. Work includes: *I am David, Tea with Mussolini*, *The Queen's Nose* and *Green-Eyed Monster*. Upcoming productions include: *Children of Glory*.

Uses freelance casting directors and does not, therefore, welcome casting enquiries and submissions from actors. Producers may send short synopsis by email to Clive Parsons, but the company only accepts showreels from agents.

Flashback Television Ltd

9-11 Bowling Green Lane, London EC1R 0BG
tel 020-7490 8996 *fax* 020-7490 5610
email mailbox@flashbacktv.co.uk
website www.flashbacktelevision.com
Managing Director & Executive Producer Taylor Downing *Creative Director & Executive Producer* David Edgar *Director of Production* Tim Ball

Founded in 1982. Produces factual entertainment programmes, which include documentaries, historical drama-documentaries, and full-length drama. Recent credits include: *Pacific: The Lost Evidence*, *Superhomes*, *Top Tens* and *Married to the Prime Minister*. Offers PACT/Equity approved contracts. Rarely has the opportunity to employ disabled actors.

Focus Films Ltd.

The Rotunda Studios, rear of 116-118 Finchley Road, London NW3 5HT
tel 020-7435 9004 *fax* 020-7431 3562
email focus@focusfilms.co.uk
website www.focusfilms.co.uk
Director David Pupkewitz *Head of Production* Lucinda Van Rie

Feature-film production company founded in 1982. Recent credits include: *51st State* with Robert Carlyle and Samuel L Jackson; *Book of Eve* with Claire Bloom and Julian Glover; *Crimetime* with Stephen Baldwin and Pete Postlethwaite.

Uses freelance casting directors and does not welcome enquiries or submissions from actors. Any approaches should be timed to coincide with a production. After the leads have been secured, the rest of the casting is done – usually 2 months before official preparation.

Focus Productions Ltd

58 Shelley Road, Stratford-upon-Avon, Warwickshire CV37 7JS
tel 01789-298 948 *fax* 01789-294 845
email maddern@focusproductions.co.uk, martinweitz@focusproductions.co.uk

website www.focusproductions.co.uk
Directors Ralph Maddern, Martin Weitz

Production details

Established 1993. Specialising in TV features and documentaries. Employs actors in TV, radio and film. Also for presentation and voice-overs. Recent credits include *The Real Rain Man* (C5), *Painting the Mind* (C4), *The Piano Player* (C5) and *Vivaldi's Fantasia* (film)

Casting procedures

Holds general auditions. Actors are advised to apply requesting inclusion at any time. Casting breakdowns are available by telephone. Welcomes letters (with CVs and photograph) from actors previously unknown to them if sent by post, but not by email. Also accepts invitations to view individual's websites. Offers Equity approved contracts. Rarely has the opportunity to cast disabled actors.

Mark Forstater Productions Ltd

27 Lonsdale Road, London NW6 6RA
tel 020-7624 1123 *fax* 020-7624 1124

Works in film and TV production. Does not deal directly with actors.

Green Umbrella

4 The Links, Old Woking Road, Old Woking, Surrey GU22 8BF
tel (01483) 726969 *fax* (01483) 721188
email jules@greenumbrella.co.uk
website www.greenumbrella.co.uk
Producers/Directors Steve Gammond, Mont Tombleson, Bruce Vigar *Managing Director* Jules Gammond

Founded in 1990. Works mainly in video and DVD production; employs actors to do voice-overs for sports and special-interest programmes. Recent credits include: *The Story of Football*, *Britain in the 50s* and *Fight the Fat*. Does not use freelance casting directors. Welcomes voice demos.

Greenwich Village Productions

Greenwich Village Productions, 14 Greenwich Church St, London SE10 9BJ
tel 020-8853 5100 *fax* 020-8293 3001
email info@greenwichvillage.tv
website www.fictionfactory.co.uk/gvtv
Producer/Director John Taylor

An established producer of documentaries for the BBC World Service and BBC Radio 4, Greenwich Village Productions has recently undertaken a number of film projects for broadcast, for sale to the public and for educational purposes. It specialises in "intelligent entertainment". Recent credits include: *An Arundel Tomb* (first in a short film series, *Poems in the Picture*); and *Pluckley – England's Haunted*

Village (documentary/dramatic reconstruction of ghost narratives).

Hasan Shah Films Ltd

153 Burnham Towers, Adelaide Road, London NW3 3JN
tel 020-7722 7789 *fax* 020-7483 0662
email hsfilms@blueyonder.co.uk

Production details

Established 1985. Produces feature films, music videos, documentaries and short films. Recent productions include: *Rough Cut and Ready Dubbed*, *Art of the Critic* and *11th Dimension*.

Casting procedures

Welcomes letters (with CVs and photographs) from actors previously unknown to the company sent by post or email. Showreels, voice tapes and invitations to view individual actors' websites are also accepted. Offers Equity approved contracts. "We rarely have the opportunity to cast disabled actors."

Hat Trick Productions Ltd

10 Livonia Street, London W1F 8AF
tel 020-7434 2451 *fax* 020-7287 9791
email info@hattrick.com
website www.hattrick.com
Joint Managing Directors Denise O'Donoghue, Jimmy Mulville

Founded in 1986, Hat Trick Productions is one of the UK's most successful independent production companies working in situation and drama comedy series and light entertainment shows. Recent credits include: *The Kumars at No. 42*, *Worst Week of my Life*, *Have I Got News for You* and *Room 101*.

Uses freelance casting directors and does not deal directly with actors.

Heavy Entertainment Ltd

222 Kensal Road, London W10 5BN
tel 020-8960 9001/2 *fax* 020-8960 9003
email info@heavy-entertainment.com
website www.heavy-entertainment.com
Director David Roper

Established in 1992. Audio and video producers. Areas of work include drama, corporate, commercials and audiobooks. Offers Equity approved contracts. Welcomes showreels, voice tapes and invitations to view individual actors' websites.

Hurricane Films Ltd

19 Hope Street, Liverpool L1 9BQ
tel 0151-707 9700 *fax* 0151-707 9149
email sol@hurricanefilms.co.uk
website www.hurricanefilms.net
Managing Director Solon Papadopoulos *Head of Development* Julie Currie

Founded in 2000. Development and production of creative content. Produces single films and documentary series from original ideas. Recent credits include: *Warship* (in association with Granada TV); *Comm-Raid on the Potemkin* (FilmFour); and *Wrecked* (BBC2).

Kelpie Films

227 St Andrews Road, Glasgow G41 1PD
tel 0141-429 3565 *fax* 0141-429 8438
email info@kelpiefilms.com
website www.kelpiefilms.com

Independent production company. Main area of work is corporate. Has a number of commissioned projects, ranging from short films for cinema distribution to drama and documentary for television release. Recent short film/feature credits include: *Out to Lunch* and *Don't Ask*. Email **fiction.films@kelpiefilms.com** for information on films in production.

LWT and United Productions

London TV Centre, Upper Ground, London SE1 9LT
tel 020-7620 1620
Controller of Drama Michele Buck

Founded in 1996. Producers of TV and film.

Manic Television and Film

24 Tannery House, 6 Deal Street, Spitalfields, London E1 5AG
tel 020-7377 8473
email info@themanicgroup.co.uk
website www.themanicgroup.co.uk
Directors Andrew Bains, David Donigue, Ian Zachary Whittingham *Casting Director* Ian Zachary Whittingham

Founded in 2002. Works mainly in TV production and employs actors for dramas and comedies. Recent credits include: *Rules of the Game*.

Uses freelance casting directors. Accepts submissions (with CVs and photographs) from actors previously unknown to the company only if sent by post. Will also accept showreels. "We welcome actors to become researchers here while they're resting."

Maverick Television

Units 1-4 Progress Works, Heath Mill Lane, Birmingham B9 4AL
tel 0121-771 1812 *fax* 0121-771 1550
website www.mavericktv.co.uk
Casting Director Alexandra Fraser *Executive Producer* Jim Sayer

Production details

Established in 1994. Television production company producing broadcast and non-broadcast content to all terrestrial and specialist channels. Recent productions include: *10 Years Younger*, *The Property Chain*, *VEETV*, *Born Too Soon* and *The Comedy Lab*.

Casting procedures

Accepts submissions (with CVs and photographs) from actors previously unknown to the company, sent by post only – no emails please. Welcomes invitations to view individual actors' websites; does not accept showreels. Offers Equity approved contracts. Actively encourages applications from disabled actors.

Maya Vision International Ltd

6 Kinghorn Street, London EC1A 7HW
tel 020-7796 4842 *fax* 020-7796 4580
email info@mayavisionint.com
website www.mayavisionint.com
Producer/Director Rebecca Dobbs *Producer* Sally Thomas *Writer* Michael Wood

Founded in 1982. Film and TV production company. Produces features, TV dramas and documentaries, and arts programmes. Recent credits include: *Alexander the Great*, *In Search of Shakespeare* and *Conquistadors* (BBC); *Caught Looking* (Channel 4); and *The World Turned Upside Down* (BBC2/Arts Council).

OVC Media Ltd

88 Berkeley Court, Baker Street, London NW1 5ND
tel 020-7402 9111 *fax* 020-7723 3044
email eliot@ovcmedia.com
website www.ovcmedia.com
Director Joanne Goldring

Production details

Established in 1982. Areas of work include TV, film, video and documentary production. Recent credits include: *History of the World Cup*, *African Odyssey*, *My Matisse*.

Casting procedures

Accepts submissions (with CVs and photographs) from actors previously unknown to the company if sent by post, but not by email. Showreels, voice tapes and invitations to view individual actors' websites are also accepted. Offers Equity approved contracts.

Penumbra Productions Ltd

80 Brondesbury Road, London NW6 6RX
tel 020-7328 4550 *fax* 020-7328 3844
email nazpenumbra@aol.com
Contact H O Nazareth

Founded in 1981. Independent film and TV producer. Makes contemporary social-issue drama and documentaries. Also produces non-broadcast videos when commissioned.

Picture Palace Films Ltd

13 Egbert Street, London NW1 8LJ
tel 020-7586 8763 *fax* 020-7586 9048
email info@picturepalace.com

website www.picturepalace.com
Producer & Chief Executive Malcom Craddock *Head of Development* Katherine Hedderly

Founded in 1972. Works mainly in feature films and TV drama production. Recent credits include: *Rebel Heart* (BBC); *Extremely Dangerous* (ITV); *A Life for a Life* (*The True Story of Stefan Kizko*); and the *Sharpe* series.

Uses freelance casting directors and does not deal directly with actors.

The Reel Thing Ltd
20 The Chase, Coulsden, Surrey CR5 2EG
tel 020-8668 8188
email info@reelthing.tv
website www.reelthing.tv
Key personnel Frazer Ashford, Chris Day

Established in 2001. Specialising in corporate and business TV production. Workin the UK and worldwide for small, local clients and large multinationals. Recent credits include: *Fire Safety* (Homebase Ltd) and *Lake Avalon* (US). Does not welcome unsolicited CVs. Actively encourages applications from disabled actors and promotes the use of inclusive casting.

September Films
22 Glenthorne Road, London W6 ONG
tel 020-8563 9393 *fax* 020-8741 7214
email september@septemberfilms.com
website www.septemberfilms.com
Chairman David Green *CEO* Marcus Plantin *Director of Production* Elaine Day

Founded in 1992. Has offices in London and Hollywood and works mainly in TV production. Specialises in factual entertainment, reality programmes and entertainment formats. Also produces feature films and TV movies. Uses freelance casting directors and does not deal directly with actors.

Seven Stones Media Ltd
The Old Butcher's shop, High Street, St. Briavels, Gloucester GL15 6TA
tel (01594) 530708 *fax* (01594) 530094
email info@sevenstonesmedia.com
website www.sevenstonesmedia.com
Directors Adam Alexander, Mike Cunliffe *Managing Director* Peter Edwards *Creative Director* Jeremy Gibson

Established in 2005. Recent productions include: *Return to Tuscany* and *Urban Chef*. Does not welcome unsolicited CVs.

Sightline
Dylan House, Town End Street, Godalming, Surrey GU7 IBQ
tel (01483) 861555 *fax* (01483) 861516

email alex@sightline.co.uk
website www.sightline.co.uk
Director Keith Thomas *PA to Director* Alex Hayes

Production details
Established in 1985. Complete in house multimedia production company specialising in corporate videos, CD Roms, DVDs and websites. Employs actors in corporate and commercials. Recent credits include: Edexcel, BAA, and London and Quadrant HT.

Casting procedures
Welcomes letters (with CVs and photographs) from actors previously unknown to the company – please send by email, not by post. Invitations to view individual actors' websites are welcome. Does not offer Equity approved contracts. Rarely has the opportunity to cast disabled actors.

Sixteen Films
2nd Floor, 187 Wardour Street, London W2 5SH
tel 020-7734 0168 *fax* 020-7439 4196
email info@sixteenfilms.co.uk
website www.sixteenfilms.co.uk
Director Ken Loach, *Producer* Rebecca O'Brien

Founded in 2002, Ken Loach's production company works exclusively in feature film production. Recent films include: *Ae Fond Kiss*, *Sweet Sixteen* and *The Navigators*.

The company uses freelance casting directors and does not generally deal directly with actors. Casting is usually region-specific and actors (or preferably their agents) should only get in contact when news of the next project is out. Details of forthcoming projects will be printed in *Screen International*. Will accept letters (with CVs and photographs) from actors but they will just get filed; realistically, this is unlikely to be an efficient use of actors' resources. Emails and showreels are not welcomed.

Spellbound Productions Ltd
90 Cowdenbeath Path, Islington, London N1 0LG
tel 020-7713 8066 *fax* 020-7713 8066
email phspellbound@hotmail.com
Producer Paul Harris

Small independent production company specialising in feature films and drama for television. Current projects include: *Twist of Fate*, a romantic comedy in development with Columbia Pictures (LA); and *Chicane*, a NY crime thriller in development.

Uses freelance casting directors; *Twist of Fate* was cast by Hubbard Casting. Accepts letters (with CVs and photographs) from actors previously unknown to the company sent by post and email. Will also accept showreels and invitations to view individual actors' websites. However, advises actors to establish and maintain contact with casting directors.

Stagescreen Productions

12 Upper St Martin's Lane, London WC2H 9JY
tel 020-7497 2510 *fax* 020-7497 2208
Director Jeffrey Taylor *Development Executive* John
Segal

Founded in 1986, Stagescreen is a film and TV
production company with offices in London and Los
Angeles. Recent credits include: *What's Cooking*,
directed by Gurinder Chadha (Lionsgate); *Foreign
Affairs*, directed by Jim O'Brien (Turner); *Handful of
Dust*, directed by Chris Sturridge (Newline).
Forthcoming work includes: *Young Wushu Warrior*.

Uses freelance casting directors; therefore, all casting
enquiries should be addressed to the appointed
casting director. Will accept letters (with CVs,
photographs and showreels) from actors previously
unknown to the company, but does not welcome
emails. Does not accept unsolicited script
submissions.

Table Top Productions

1 The Orchard, Chiswick, London W4 1JZ
tel 020-8994 1269 *fax* 020-8742 0507
email berry@tabletopproductions.com
website www.tabletopproductions.com
Director Alvin Rakoff *Production Manager* Ben Berry

Production details

Established in 1967. Credits include: *A Voyage Round
My Father*, *Romeo and Juliet*, *Liberty Tree*, *Don
Quixote*, *Dance to the Music of Time* (C4), and
Separate Tables (Mill at Sonning Theatre).

Casting procedures

Casting breakdowns are available via the website;
apply only when in production. Offers Equity
approved contracts. Does not welcome unsolicited
CVs. Rarely has the opportunity to cast disabled
actors.

TalkBack Productions

20-21 Newman Street, London W1T 1PG
tel 020-7861 8000 *fax* 020-7861 8001
website www.talkback.co.uk

Founded in 1981. Produces TV situation comedies
and comedy dramas, features, and straight drama.
Credits include: *Property Ladder*, *Jamie's Kitchen*,
Smack the Pony, *The 11 O' Clock Show* and *Da Ali G
Show*. TalkBack is part of the Fremantle Media
Group.

Tiger Aspect Productions

Drama address: 5 Soho Square, London W1V 5DE
tel 020-7434 0672 *fax* 020-7544 1665
email general@tigeraspect.co.uk
Comedy address: 7 Soho Street, London W1D 3DQ
tel 020-7434 0700 *fax* 020-7434 1798

website www.tigeraspect.co.uk
Head of Drama Greg Brenman

Founded in 1993. Produces TV drama, comedy and
sitcoms. "Investing in and working with the leading
writers, performers and programme-makers to
produce original, creative and successful
programming." Strives to produce entertaining,
challenging and varied drama. Credits include:
Teachers (C4), *My Fragile Heart* (ITV), and *Playing
the Field* (BBC1).

Twenty Twenty Television

20 Kentish Town Road, London NW1 9NX
tel 020-7284 2020 *fax* 020-7284 1810
email mail@twentytwentytv.co.uk
website www.twentytwenty.tv
Managing Director Peter Casely-Hayford *Executive
Producer* Claudia Milne *Head of Development* George
Kay

Founded in 1982. Produces current affairs,
documentaries, science and educational programmes,
and reality TV. Began producing TV drama in 2000
and has been commissioned by the BBC and ITV
networks. Credits include: *Lad's Army* and *Second
Sight*.

TwoFour Productions Ltd

TwoFour Studios, Estover, Plymouth PL6 7RG
tel (01752) 727400 *fax* (01752) 727450
email eng@twofour.co.uk
website www.twofour.co.uk
Director of Broadcast Melanie Leach *Press & Publicity*
Amanda Wood

Production details

Established in 1987. Independent television
production company specialising in factual, lifestyle
and documentary programming. Recent credits
include: *Accidents Can Happen* (BBC1); *Cruise with
Stelios* (Sky); *The Hotel Inspector* (C5); *Why Men
Wear Frocks* (Channel 4); and *Life Begins Again* (C4).

Casting procedures

Welcomes actors' showreels. Offers Equity approved
contracts. Will consider applications from disabled
actors to play characters with disabilities.

Video Enterprises

12 Barbers Wood Road, High Wycombe, Bucks HP12
4EP
tel (01494) 534144
email videoenterprises@ntlworld.com
website www.videoenterprises.co.uk
Director Maurice R Fleisher

Uses freelance casting directors but will accept letters
(with CVs, photographs and showreels) from actors
previously unknown to the company. Does not offer
Equity approved contracts. Rarely (or never) has the
opportunity to cast disabled actors.

Videotel Productions

84 Newman Street, London W1T 3EU
tel 020-7299 1800 *fax* 020-7299 1818
email mail@videotelmail,com
website www.videotel.co.uk
Casting Directors Stephen Bond, Peter Wilde,
Kathrein Guenther

Production details

Established in 1975, Award-winning Videotel is "the
world leader for the production of DVD/video,
multimedia and web-deliverable training material for
the maritime industry".

Casting procedures

Hold general auditions; casting information available
via the website, Spotlight, Talent Circle, Casting Call
Pro and CastNet UK. Offers Equity approved
contracts. Accepts submissions (with CVs and
photographs) from actors previously unknown to the
company sent by post or email. Showreels, voice
tapes and invitations to view individual actors'
websites are also accepted. Rarely has the opportunity
to cast disabled actors due to the fact that most of the
company's work is filmed aboard ships.

Walsh Bros Ltd

24 Redding House, Harlinger Street, King Henry's
Wharf, London SE18 5SR
tel 020-8858 6870 *fax* 020-8858 6870
email walshbros@mail.com
website www.walshbros.co.uk
Director John Walsh *Casting Director* Maura Walsh
Producer David Walsh

Founded in 1994, Walsh Bros Ltd is an award-
winning production company of documentaries and
feature films. Recent credits include: *Monarch*
(feature film); *Headhunting the Homeless* (for the
BBC and nominated for the Grierson Award); and
Trex, Boyz & Girlz, Cowboyz & Cowgirlz (for Channel
4).

Will accept submissions (with CVs and photographs)
from actors previously unknown to the company sent
by post or email. Will also accept showreels but asks
actors to check first before sending in any items.

Michael Winner Ltd/Scimitar Films

219 Kensington High Street, London W8 6BD
tel 020-7603 7272 *fax* 020-7602 9217
email winner@ftech.co.uk
Directors Michael Winner, John Fraser

Production details

Established in 1956. Specialises in film and television
commercial production. Employs actors in drama,
comedy and commercials.

Casting procedures

Welcomes letters (with CVs and photographs) from
actors previously unknown to the company if sent by
post, but not by email. Offers Equity approved
contracts.

Working Title Films

76 Oxford Street, London W1N 9FD
tel 020-7307 3000 *fax* 020-7307 3003
email dan.shepherd@unistudios.com
website www.workingtitlefilms.com
Chairmen Tim Bevan, Eric Fellner *President* Liza
Chasin, *President UK Production* Debra Hayward

A film production company founded in 1982. Has
produced more than 70 films and won BAFTAs,
Academy Awards, and prizes at the Cannes and
Berlin Film Festivals. Recent credits include: the
popular romantic comedies *Four Weddings and a
Funeral, Notting Hill, Bridget Jones's Diary* and *Love
Actually*; and novel adaptations *Captain Corelli's
Mandolin* and *High Fidelity*.

World Productions Ltd

Eagle House, 50 Marshall Street, London W1F 9BQ
tel 020-7734 3536 *fax* 020-7758 7000
email firstname@world-productions.com
website www.world-productions.com
Executive Producer Tony Garnett *Executive Producer/
Head of Development* Simon Heath *PA & Office
Manager* Helen Saunders

Produces TV drama features, series and serials.
Recent credits include: *Between the Lines,
Ballykissangel*, and *Love Again* – a film about Philip
Larkin (BBC). Currently developing more "unique"
drama projects. Uses freelance casting directors and
does not deal directly with actors.

Zenith Productions Ltd

43-45 Dorset Street, London W1U 7NA
tel 020-7224 2440 *fax* 020-7224 3194
email general@zenith-entertainment.co.uk
website www.zenith.tv.co.uk
Managing Director Ivan Rendall *Casting Director* Matt
Western *Head of Drama* Adrian Bate

Founded in 1984. Part of the Zenith group, which
comprises Zenith North and Zenith Productions.
Works mainly in producing a wide range of
programmes for terrestrial, satellite and cable
television, and feature films for worldwide theatrical
distribution. Employs actors for dramas, comedies,
documentaries and make-over shows. Recent credits
include: *Byker Grove, Two Thousand Acres of Sky,
Murder Most Foul, Inspector Morse* and *Garden Rivals*.
Uses freelance casting directors and does not deal
directly with actors.

Film schools

Although the work is minimally paid (if at all), it is well worth contacting film schools for casting consideration. Despite the fact that you'll often find yourself in the hands of a director with no idea about actors and acting, the potential of gaining something from the experience is possibly greater than that of participating in a Fringe theatre production – and the end result could contain material worthy of use in a showreel. Some schools keep files of actors' CVs and photographs for students to refer to when casting.

Castings for many low- or non-paid films are advertised on *Shooting People* (**www.shootingpeople.org**) – see entry on page 311.

The Arts Institute at Bournemouth
Wallisdown, Poole, Dorset BG12 5HH
tel (01292) 533011
Key contact/Lecturer Mike Fisher
Students do not only consider local actors for their short films. Actors are generally offered their expenses and a VHS copy. Welcomes enquiries (containing CV, photograph and covering letter) from new actors; actors' details are kept on file.

ARTTS International (Advanced Residential Theatre and Television Skillcentre)
Highfield Grange, Bubwith, North Yorkshire YO8 7DP
tel (01757) 288088 *fax* (01757) 288253
email admin@artts.co.uk
website www.artts.co.uk
Key contact Geoffrey Bicker

The basis of ARTTS' training is multi-skilling, offering fast-track, intensive training in a single year. Every aspect of the training gears students practically towards a career in the entertainment industry. All our trainers are people who have already worked at high levels within the fields of film, television, theatre and radio, and who understand the demands and realities of the marketplace.

100% practical 'on-the-job' training results in students working at the very highest standards, both technically and personally – making them far better equipped to walk into a paid job in the media industry anywhere in the world. ARTTS has an impressive 94% graduate employment record. Using broadcast-standard, state-of-the-art technology, students have the opportunity to work on external corporate videos under the guidance of professional directors and producers. ARTTS Skillcentre houses a dedicated production company with a satellite office based in London, developing material for the corporate and broadcast market.

Actors interested in working on student short films should submit their details to Geoffrey Bicker at the address above.

Brighton Film School
Administration, 13 Tudor Close, Dean Court Road, Rottingdean BN2 7DF
tel (01273) 302166 *fax* (01273) 302163
email info@brightonfilmschool.org.uk
website www.brightonfilmschool.org.uk
Key contact Franz von Habsburg

Film-industry-recognised. Provides training in all aspects of motion pictures production: screenwriting, directing, cinematography, editing and production management. More than 30 student short films are made each year; students generally recruit actors through *Shooting People* (**www.shootingpeople.org**). There is no formal agreement with Equity. Students do not only consider local actors. Actors are generally offered their expenses and a VHS copy. Welcomes enquiries (containing photograph and 1-page CV) from new actors if sent by post.

International Film School Wales
University of Wales College, Caerleon Campus, PO Box 179, Newport NP18 3YG
tel (01633) 432677 *fax* (01633) 432680
email post.ifsw@newport.ac.uk
website www.ifsw.newport.ac.uk
Head of School Humphry Trevelyan

A recognised Welsh national institution for the production and development of the audiovisual culture of Wales, through training, education and postgraduate research. On average 60-80 student short films are made each year. Students generally recruit actors through agents, casting directors, Equity Job Information Service and public notices at the Royal Welsh College of Music & Drama. There is no formal agreement with Equity. Actors' details are held on file. Welcomes enquiries (with CV, photograph and covering letter) from new actors. Students at BA and MA level increasingly work in production groupings and cast professionally. "As the main centre for film education and training in Wales, we seek, encourage and support the casting of professional actors wherever possible. We also require actors to teach part-time on our BA Hons in Performance course."

The London Film School

24 Shelton Street, London WC2H 9UB
tel 020-7836 9642 *fax* 020-7497 3718
email c.bright@lfs.org.uk
website www.lfs.org.uk
Librarian/Casting Chrissy Bright

London Film School offers a 2-year MA course in the art and technique of filmmaking, with approximately 120-130 student short films being made each year. Students generally recruit actors through *Spotlight, PCR, Star Now* and *Shooting People*. Expenses and a VHS copy of the film are normally offered to actors cast in student films. The school welcomes enquiries from actors (with CVs and photographs) and will be happy to keep their details on file for future productions.

National Film and Television School

Beaconsfield Studios, Station Road, Beaconsfield HP9 1LG
tel (01494) 671234 *fax* (01494) 674042
email admin@nftsfilm-tv.ac.uk
website www.nftsfilm.ac.uk
Key personnel Lindsey Moore

Offers 2-year MA courses including fiction direction, cinematography, production design, editing, sound, animation, and documentary. Students generally recruit actors through casting directors, *Spotlight, Shooting People* (**www.shootingpeople.org**), and from actors' files kept by Lindsey Moore. Has a formal agreement with Equity. Students do not only consider local actors. Actors are generally offered their expenses. Welcomes enquiries (with CVs and photographs) from new actors which should be marked for the attention of Lindsey Moore. Actors'

details are held on file. Actors are also required throughout the year for workshops, and files are kept for this purpose. Graduation projects are cast by external casting directors.

UCCA Farnham (Surrey Institute of Art and Design)

Falkner Road, Farnham GU9 7DS
tel (01252) 722441 *fax* (01252) 892787
email sjeans@ucreative.co.uk
website www.ucreative.ac.uk
Director of Studies (Media) Sarah Jeans

The course, accredited by the British Kinematograph, Sound & Television Society, offers a broad grounding in film and video practice. Students work on both 16mm productions and video. The course emphasises film as social practice, and the study of issue-based work is a dominant theme. An average of 40-50 student short films are made each year. Actors are recruited through *Spotlight, PCR* and Shooting People. Only local actors are considered. Travel expenses and a copy of the film are offered, although it is not always possible to provide transfers of 16mm projects. Welcomes CVs and photographs (sent by post, not email) from actors.

University of Westminster

University of Westminster, Watford Road, Northwick Park, Harrow, Middlesex HA1 3TP
email hunninj@westminster.co.uk
website www.westminster.ac.uk/mad
Key personnel Joost Hunningher, Peter Hort, Malcolm Mowbray

40 short films made per year. Equity student guidelines used. Offers expenses and copy of film to actors involved. Accepts submissions (with CVs, photographs and contact details) from actors previously unknown to the company.

Acting for radio

Gordon House

I remember once, in a burst of evangelical enthusiasm at having decided never to touch a cigarette again, upbraiding a distinguished member of the Radio Drama Company for her constant disappearances to the Green Room to light up. (Nowadays, of course, all BBC Green rooms are smoke-free, and your poor cigarette-smoking actor has to shiver in the car park.) "My dear man," she wheezed grandly. "The only reason you employ me on the wireless is because of my nicotine-nourished, port-soaked larynx. Living badly has made me the radio actress I am today!"

Well – it's a point of view. Just as the camera relishes certain skin textures, so the microphone may embellish the actor or actress who has lived a little – resulting in, shall we say, an idiosyncratic oesophagus. But as a way of getting a radio part, it's not a course of action I'd recommend. Radio simply doesn't pay enough to sustain a life of alcoholic debauchery.

So how do you get into radio? "It's a closed shop," moaned one actor to me the other day. "You hear the same names, time and again – and there's no way of breaking into this magic circle." I personally have worked with well over 800 actors, so it can't be that much of a closed shop … though it's true that given the ruthless time constraints of the medium (a 60-minute play will be rehearsed and recorded in two days), there's a natural tendency for producers to work with those actors whom they know can 'deliver' quickly. There's no joy to be had in the seventh take of a difficult scene when your nervous newcomer is finally coming to grips with the ambiguities of his or her character, as well as the technical demands of this strange new medium, while everyone else's performances have long-since peaked and are now beginning to sound tired and lacklustre.

But that said, new writers and new actors are the lifeblood of the medium. And what do you need to be a good actor on radio? It's simple. You need to be a good actor. If you're successful in the theatre, in film, on TV – then of course you can be successful on radio. A good actor is a good actor. It obviously helps if your voice doesn't sound like a creaking door (given that creaking doors are a staple diet of many a radio play), and the medium has no place for prima donnas. With every producer sparingly counting his or her loose change, there's no such happy luxury as a radio 'extra'; so if you're cast as Hamlet, you can also expect to do your fair share of off-mic mumbling in Claudius' court. And if that doesn't appeal, don't do radio.

You also have to be prepared to work fast and make almost instant decisions. Over the years I've worked with a few actors whom I admire hugely; whom I've seen – in other media – give performances of rare charm and intelligence; but who in radio have simply been unable to 'come off the page' – make the character they're playing sound truthful and real. Of course this may simply be attributed to the crass inadequacy of the director. But for some actors the sheer speed at which they have to make decisions about character, motivation, sub-text and so forth is incredibly daunting. And then there's the physical absurdity of much of what they have to do: "How the xxx do you expect me to be 'truthful' when I'm carrying a xxxing great script in my left hand, a glass of water, masquerading as gin, in my right, and you want me to walk through a carpet of scrunched-up audio tape and pretend it's a meadow," shrieked one despairing actor to me a couple of years ago.

And yet that's exactly what we expect – truth. There's no medium as unforgiving for exposing over-acting or over-emoting (or worse – simple 'reading'). A radio play – and particularly a contemporary, naturalistic play – should make listeners feel that they are eavesdropping on real conversation. It's a medium that may owe much to theatre for providing it with great writing and acting talent (though the reverse is equally true), but the technique of radio acting is far closer to that of film than of theatre. "Less is more! Less is more!" as my erstwhile colleague, Martin Jenkins, one of Radio Drama's finest practitioners, used to impress on his casts. (It was Martin, incidentally, who uttered the memorable phrase: "Good Luck – Please!" before the umpteenth take of one particularly stressful scene.)

How do you bring yourself to the attention of radio producers? Well – there's no denying the fact that a lovingly crafted CD arriving on your desk just as you're in the process of casting your next play, and can't for the life of you think who you can get to play the embittered Glaswegian ex-shipbuilder who's contemplating a sex change, can make all the difference. But choose the pieces you record with care – and keep them short. There's no point in doing all sorts of varied accents, if varied accents are not a speciality. Obviously, it's a great asset to be master – or mistress – of many different voices, this being a medium where 'doubling' and 'trebling' is done with impunity. But a CD where the truthfulness of most of your extracts is undone by your game but doomed attempt to do a passable Geordie, won't help anyone. Many years ago I remember auditioning Jeremy Sinden for a part. "What accents do you do?" I asked him. "I do two actually," he said. "I do posh. And I do very posh." Well a mere two accents didn't stop Jeremy getting a load of work in every medium – including radio – in his all-too-brief, but exhilarating, career.

Having recorded your tape or (preferably) CD, you can, of course, circulate it to every producer who's ever made a radio play. But my advice would be to be a little more discerning. Listen to some radio plays (a great way of determining for yourself what works and what doesn't) and note the names of the producers whose productions particularly appeal to you. You can then write a personal note to them – you know the kind: "I must say, Mr House, I really enjoyed your fascinating and unusual interpretation of *Hedda Gabler* on Radio 3 last night, and incidentally Hedda is a part I've always yearned to play myself,"(etc.). I'm not saying it will get you a part, but producers are as vain as the next person (I should know) and it may well make them more inclined to slip your CD into the CD player, on the basis that anyone with such discerning judgement as yours must be worth hearing.

Radio is a fantastic, and hugely under-rated medium, and actors, by and large, love working for it. It can also be the stepping-stone to fame and fortune. For many years we've been running our own radio bursary scheme for accredited drama schools – the Carleton Hobbs Competition (named after one of the great 20th century radio actors) – and the role-call of actors who have been winners, from Richard Griffiths to Stephen Tompkinson, from Nerys Hughes to Emma Fielding, is hugely impressive. Our new bursary scheme, the Norman Beaton Fellowship, for actors who didn't go to an accredited drama school, is also providing us with some excellent new talent. Details of both these schemes can be found on the BBC website.

And of course we producers don't simply wait to receive your CDs, but are constantly on the lookout for new and exciting talent from wherever we can find it. You may not need to approach us – we may approach you! As World Service Drama producers, Hilary Norrish and myself gave a young actor called Ewan MacGregor his first two professional jobs, having seen him in a drama school showcase. And Ewan – if you ever get to read this – where are the invitations to those glamorous film previews you promised you'd send us when you were famous? Remember – it was radio that gave you your first break!

Gordon House is the former Head of the BBC Radio Drama Department. He joined the BBC as a studio manager in 1972, working in Children's Television and Radio Sport before becoming a drama director. For 14 years he headed the small BBC World Service Drama team, during which time the Unit won more than 30 national and international awards. In 1998 Gordon won the Writers' Guild Special Prize for services for his work with new writers, and has twice won the Sony Drama Award. He is a founder member of The Worldplay Group, a radio association of drama directors from broadcasting stations around the world, which initiates a yearly season of international radios dramas broadcast on BBC World Service, ABC, CBC, RTE, Radio New Zealand and Radio Television Hong Kong.

Radio companies and other 'voice-work' opportunities

Unlike in the visual media, many radio directors have their roots in theatre and will go to stage productions to inform their future casting. And, unlike their visual media counterparts, they have a far greater understanding of actors and acting, and are far more open to casting against obvious physical type.

The BBC has by far and away the biggest radio drama output, and it also uses actors to read poetry, narrations and stories. Some of this 'output' is made in-house; a good proportion is contracted-out to independent companies. This is one area of work that doesn't very often use casting directors. It is a good idea to listen to radio drama to become aware of its ways – you won't hear much swearing, for instance. Also see 'Voice-over agents' (page 75) and 'Showreel and voice-demo companies' (page 287); some of the latter have excellent advice on making a voice demo on their websites.

BBC Radio Drama

Bush House, The Strand, London WC2B 4PH
tel 020-7557 1013
website www.bbc.co.uk/drama/radio
Head of Radio Drama Alison Hindell *Coordinator, Drama Company* Cynthia Fagan *Production Executive, Radio Drama* Rebecca Wilmshurst

BBC Radio Drama Department is the biggest producer of drama on radio in the world. It provides more than 700 hours of drama a year for Radio 3, Radio 4, BBC World Service, BBC7, and the BBC Asian Network. Plays are broadcast every day of the week and can be heard at any time, either on air or on the website. An audience of about half a million people is listening every time a play is aired. Output includes: *Westway* (drama set in a London health centre); *The Archers* (countryside soap opera); the Friday and Saturday plays (thrillers, mysteries and love stories); afternoon plays, classic serials, Woman's Hour Drama (weekday drama serial); play of the week (from around the world); book of the week (non-fiction); book at bedtime (fiction, including modern classics).

The Radio Drama Company was founded in 1940 as the BBC Repertory Company, and is still frequently referred to as The Rep. The company's focus allows new acting talent to work alongside established actors in a variety of radio productions. Actors joining the RDC have already worked with many eminent artists such as Julia Mackenzie, Derek Jacobi, Richard Griffiths, Cheryl Campbell, Anna Massey and Daniel Day-Lewis.

Past members of the company have included Stephen Tompkinson, Alex Jennings, Adjoa Andoh, Norman Bird, Emma Fielding, Anthony Daniels, Ben Onwukwe, Joanna Monro, Ann Beach, Janet Maw, Suzanna Hamilton and Carolyn Pickles.

The RDC does not use freelance casting directors and casting breakdowns are not publicly available. Sometimes holds general auditions and actors can write at any time requesting inclusion. Welcomes postal submissions from individual actors previously unknown to the company, but does not accept email enquiries. Voice demos and invitations to view individual actors' websites are also accepted.

The Norman Beaton Fellowship is part of BBC Radio Drama's commitment to place integrated casting at the heart of its output. The NBF aims to provide access to BBC Radio Drama for talented actors from non-traditional training backgrounds, and particularly those from minority ethnic backgrounds who are currently under-represented in radio drama.

The Radio Drama Company will also be forging links with theatre companies all over Britain to help develop and nurture new talent for both radio and the stage and to find new NBF bursary winners. Consult the website for information about the next Norman Beaton Fellowship and for details of eligibility requirements.

The Carleton Hobbs Bursary is aimed at students graduating from accredited drama courses across the country. Looks for distinctive, versatile radio voices to form the next season's Radio Drama Company. It aims to recruit 4-6 winners annually. Students will be seen through an audition process, from which an equal mix of men and women will be selected. Winners receive a 6-month binding contract as members of the Radio Drama Company. Up to 4 runners-up will be engaged as freelance actors in one-off productions.

BBC Radio Drama (Belfast)

Room 3.07 Blackstaff House, Great Victoria Street, Belfast BT2 7BB
tel 028-9033 8476 *fax* 028-9033 8462
email heather.larmour@bbc.co.uk
website www.bbc.co.uk/ni/drama
Producers Gemma McMullan, Eoin O'Callaghan, Lawrence Jackson *Executive Producer* Anne Simpson
Key contact Heather Larmour

Production details

Produces drama (29 plays last year) and readings for Radio Ulster, Radio 3, Radio 4 and BBC 7; particularly welcomes enquiries from actors with regional dialects and singing ability.

Casting procedures

Casts in-house; does not issue casting breakdowns. Happy to receive approaches from actors unknown to the company, either by post (with a CD voice reel, preferably with no commercials) or by email to Heather Larmour. Offers Equity approved contracts. Rarely has the opportunity to cast disabled actors.

World Service

Bush House, Strand, London WC2B 4PH
tel 020-7557 2941
website www.bbc.co.uk/worldservice

BBC World Service provides radio services in English and 42 other languages, via short wave and, in an increasing number of cities around the world, on MW and FM. The English service is also available 24 hours a day in real audio on the Internet. Classic contemporary drama, novels, short stories, soap operas and poetry are all a feature of its English service, plus a wide range of arts, documentaries, education, features, music, religious affairs, science, sports and youth programmes. In addition, BBC World Service provides on-the-spot coverage of world news, giving a global perspective of international events.

INDEPENDENT RADIO COMPANIES

Above the Title Productions

Level 2, 10-11 St George's Mews, London NW1 8XE
tel 020-7916 1984 *fax* 020-7722 5706
email mail@abovethetitle.com
website www.abovethetitle.com
CEO Bruce Hyman *Managing Director* Helen Chattwell

Founded in 1998, Above the Title Productions has made over 500 hours of radio programming covering a range of genres, from comedy to factual programmes, drama, discussion programmes, and music and the arts. See the website for detailed programme credits.

All casting is done through agents; direct contact with actors is not welcomed. Is no longer able to accept voice demos and CVs, as the company has received such a large number of applications in the past.

Bona Broadcasting Ltd

19 Dalgleish House, Scrimgeour Place, Dundee DO3 6TU
tel (01382) 225403 *fax* (01382) 229300
email enquiries@bonabroadcasting.com
website www.bonabroadcasting.com
Key personnel Turan Ali

Founded in 1994. Staffed by former BBC producers and directors, the company has been a registered supplier to the BBC since 1994. Areas of work include drama, documentaries and light entertainment. Recent drama credits include: *The Confessions of Nostradamus*, *The Flood* and *Existence*. Casting is through agents only: "Get a good agent."

The Comedy Unit Ltd

Glasgow TV and Film Studio, Craigmont Street, Glasgow G20 9BT
tel 0141-305 6666 *fax* 0141-305 6600
email general@comedy unit.co.uk
website www.comedyunit.co.uk
Producers/Directors Colin Gilbert, Niall Clark, Rab Christie

Founded in 1996. Works in TV and radio productions – has produced approximately 30 hours of TV and 25 hours of radio. Areas of work include drama, sitcoms, comedy and other light entertainment. Recent drama credits include: *Ronan the Amphibian* and *Coming Home*.

Sometimes holds general auditions. Actors can write at any time requesting inclusion. Submissions from actors previously unknown to the company are accepted, sent by post or email. Voice demos and invitations to view individual actors' websites are also accepted.

CSA Word

6a Archway Mews, 241a Putney Bridge Road, London SW15 2PE
tel 020-8871 0220 *fax* 020-8877 0712
email info@csaword.co.uk
website www.csaword.co.uk
Key personnel Victoria Williams, Clive Stanhope

Founded in 1991. Producer of audiobooks, drama, readings, feature programmes and documentaries for BBC Radios 4, 2 and BBC World Service.

Does not hold general auditions, as the company tends to use agents for casting. Invitations to view individual actors' websites are accepted. Equity contracts are not used, "but we usually pay above Equity minimum". Happy to consider actors with disabilities: "We work mainly in speech, audio and radio work, so rarely an issue with regard to physical disability."

Culture Wise

1 Chiswick Staithe, London W4 3TP
Key personnel Mukti Jain Campion, Chris Eldon Lee

Founded in 1988. Areas of work include TV and radio documentaries. Does not hold general auditions. Invitations to view individual actors' websites are accepted. The company rarely employs actors, as the primary focus is on factual output: actors are generally used for short readings only within a feature programme.

Devlin Morris Productions Ltd

97b West Bow, Edinburgh EH1 2JP
Key personnel Morris Paton

Producers of theatre, radio and cultural tourism projects. Areas of work include drama and light entertainment. Recent drama credits include: features for BBC Scotland, Radios 4 and 3, and the World Service. Does not hold general auditions. Actors can write at any time requesting inclusion. Submissions from actors previously unknown to the company are accepted if sent by post. Voice demos and invitations to view individual actors' websites are also accepted. Does not accept email enquiries.

Falling Tree Productions (formerly Alan Hall Associates)

13 Cliffview Road, London SE13 7DD
tel 020-8305 6936
email alan.hall@easynet.co.uk
website www.fallingtree.co.uk
Executive Director Alan Hall

Founded in 1998, Falling Tree Productions is an independent supplier to BBC Network Radio (3 and 4 principally) and foreign broadcasters, crafting documentaries and music feature productions. Winner of the Sony Gold in 2004 feature category, and previously, in the music feature category too. Has also been awarded the Prix Italia (twice) and the Prix Bohemia. The company has employed actors in documentaries, music features, anthology programmes and museum guides. Recent credits include: *Song on the Death of Children, Brahms' Beard* and *Something Understood.*

Will accept submissions (written or emailed) and voice tapes from actors previously unknown to the company. Welcomes invitations to view an actor's website. Advises that actors are used mainly for readings in radio productions, but also in the production of numerous voice-overs for museum and art gallery audioguides.

The Fiction Factory

14 Greenwich Church Street, London SE10 9BJ
tel 020-8853 5100 *fax* 020-8293 3001
email info@fictionfactory.co.uk
website www.fictionfactory.co.uk
Key personnel John Taylor, Celia de Wolff, Joanna Green, Roland Jaquarello

Founded in 1993. Makes radio drama and features for the BBC and has recently expanded into video production. Areas of work include drama, documentaries, light entertainment and voice-overs. Recent drama credits include: *Wild Ride to Dublin, A Nursery in the Nineties* and *What Maisie Knew* (Radio 4).

Does not hold general auditions. Submissions from actors previously unknown to the company are accepted if sent by post. Voice demos are also accepted. Does not welcome email submissions or invitations to view individual actors' websites. "It is helpful if showreels contain material appropriate to the kind of work sought; for example, corporate voice-overs or radio advertisements don't necessarily show off acting skills."

First Writes

Lime Kiln Cottage, High Starlings, Banham, Norwich NR16 2BS
tel (01953) 888525 *fax* (01953) 888974
email ellen@firstwrites.fsnet.c.uk
website www.firstwrites.co.uk
Key personnel Ellen Dryden, Richard Blake, Jonathan Dryden Taylor

Established in 1992. Areas of work include BBC Radio Drama, Radio 3, and World Service. Produces 6 audiobooks per year. Recent credits include: *The Franchise Affair, I Was Born There* and *The Eliza Stories.* Offers Equity approved contracts. Accepts submissions from actors previously unknown to the company if sent by post, but not by email. Welcomes voice demos and invitations to view actors' websites.

Heavy Entertainment Ltd

222 Kensal Road, London W10 5BN
tel 020-8960 9001/2 *fax* 020-8960 9003
email info@heavy-entertainment.com
website www.heavy-entertainment.com
Director David Roper

Established in 1992. Audio and video producers. Areas of work include drama, corporate, commercials and audiobooks. Offers Equity approved contracts. Welcomes showreels, voice tapes and invitations to view individual actors' websites.

Ladbroke Productions

Essex House, 29 Foley Street, London W1W 7JW
tel 020-7323 2770 *fax* 020-7079 2080
email info@electricairwaves.com
website www.electricairwaves.com
Producers/Directors Neil Gardner, Richard Bannerman, Paul Kent, Andy Jordan *Assistant Producer* Anna Van Dieken

Founded in 1975, Ladbroke Productions produces for all BBC networks in many genres, including drama, documentaries, music, light entertainment and features. Its studio and production facilities are also used by BBC Drama, BBC Readings and BBC Factual

Learning. Actors are mainly employed by the company in its drama and documentary production. Recent credits include: *Sitting in Limbo* (BBC World Service) and *In the Company of Men* (BBC Radio 3).

Will accept unsolicited submissions (written or emailed), voice demos and invitations to view actors' websites. April and September are generally better months to write.

L'Ocean Ltd
5 Darling Road, London SE4 1YQ
tel/fax 020-8692 0145
email roj@l-ocean.org
website www.l-ocean.org
Producers/Directors Roger Elsgood, Willi Richards

L'Ocean Ltd is a production company specialising in making high-production-value, location-recorded long-form drama for BBC Radio 3 and 4 with international casts and directors. Recent work includes: *The Mrichhakatikaa* for Radio 3, recorded entirely on location in India; *To the Wedding* for Radio 3 in collaboration with Complicite; *Shooting Stars*, for Radio 3 (directed by Mike Hodges and starring Michael Gambon, Michael Sheen and Clive Owen); *King Trash*, the second play in Mike Hodges' radio trilogy; and *Inferno* with Corin Redgrave, Alex Jennings and Laurie Anderson.

The company is always happy to receive submissions and voice demos from actors (preferably as hard copy), and auditions as necessary. It sometimes offers Equity contracts. Actively encourages applications from disabled actors and promotes the use of inclusive casting.

Pennine Productions
2 Grimeford Lane, Anderton, Chorley PR6 9HL
tel (01257) 482559 *fax* 0870-131 8291
email mike@pennine-biz
website www.penine.biz
Producers Janet Graves, Mike Hally, Clare Jenkins, Mark Whitaker

Founded in 2000. Has made documentaries and features for BBC Radio 4 since 2001, and programmes for BBC Radio 3 since 2004. Has produced book readings for Radio 4 since 2005. Broadcasts northern, national and international stories. Main areas of work include documentaries and readings. Recent credits include: *Israel in East Africa*, *When Jesus Rode into Bristol* and *Land of the Oval Ball* (all Radio 4, 2003).

"We only welcome unsolicited approaches from actors with significant broadcast experience, particularly of book readings – or other audiobook productions. We are too small to be useful to actors trying to break into the network radio or TV."

Pier Productions
Lower Ground Floor, 1 Marlborough Place, Brighton BN1 1TU
tel (01273) 691401 *fax* (01273) 693658
Managing Director Peter Hoare

Founded in 1993, Pier is an award-winning Brighton-based company and is a significant supplier of factual and drama productions to BBC Radio 4. The company employs actors for drama productions and is keen to work with talent located in Brighton and the surrounding area. Recent productions include: a production of JM Barrie's *Little White Bird*, and dramatisations of *Scenes from Married Life* and *The Nutcracker*.

The company does not hold general auditions. Submissions from actors are accepted by post and email, but we do not welcome invitations to view individual actors' websites. It must be emphasised that opportunities in radio drama are limited and that the company does not use the services of voice-over artists.

So Radio Ltd
18 Hatfields, London SE1 8GN
tel 020-7960 2000 *fax* 020-7960 2095
email info@sotelevision.co.uk
website www.sotelevision.co.uk
Producer/Director Graham Stuart

Founded in 2003 as the radio arm of So Television Ltd. Recent credits include: *The Storyman with Andrew Clover* and *It's that Jo Caulfield Again* for BBC Radio 4. The company has employed actors mainly for light entertainment productions.

Will accept unsolicited written submissions and voice demos from actors, but advises them to email beforehand. As the company is small it cannot promise to reply to all enquiries. Offers Equity approved contracts (where applicable). Actively encourages applications from disabled actors and promotes the use of inclusive casting.

Lou Stein Associates Ltd
14a Tavistock Place, London WC1H 9RD
email info@loustein.co.uk
Producer/Director Lou Stein *Co-Director* Deirdre Gribbin

Lou Stein founded the Gate Theatre, Notting Hill, and was Artistic Director of the Palace Theatre, Watford. Lou Stein Associates was formed to continue Lou's interest in new work, adaptations, music theatre and media. Employs actors for drama programmes. Recent drama credits include: *Fear and Loathing in Las Vegas* (adapted and directed by Lou Stein, starring Harry Dean Stanton); *My Month with Carmen* (starring Miriam Colon and Julian Glover); *Grace Notes* by Lou Stein (based on the Bernard MacLaverty novel, starring Amanda Burton); and *Embers* (adapted by Lou Stein from the novel by Sandor Marai and starring Patrick Stewart).

Voice demos and invitations to view individual actors' websites are accepted, but actors are requested to email in the first instance. Please note that although unsolicited letters, CDs and CVs will be retained for possible future casting, no reply will be given unless the actor is suitable for immediate casting. Offers Equity approved contracts. Actively encourages applications from disabled actors and promotes the use of inclusive casting.

Tintinna Productions

Summerfield, Bristol Road, Bristol BS40 8UB
tel (01275) 333128 *fax* (01275) 332316
email tintinna@aol.com
Producers Ian Bell *Research & Production* Sandy Bell

Founded in 1998. Specialises in factual documentaries including history, lifestyle and human interest. Main area of work is documentaries. Does not hold general auditions. Submissions from actors previously unknown to the company are accepted if sent by post. Voice demos are also accepted. Does not welcome email submissions or invitations to view individual actors' websites.

Unique the Production Company

Unit 1B, 50 Lisson Street, London NW1 5DF
Producer Frank Stirling *Editor, Speech Programmes* Laura Parfitt

Produces drama, documentaries, comedy and light entertainment for radio. Recent drama credits include: *Dramascape* (BBC World Service); *Something Understood* (poetry and prose readings for BBC Radio 4).

Submissions from actors previously unknown to the company are accepted sent by post or email. Voice demos are also accepted. Does not welcome invitations to view individual actors' websites. Advises actors to "include radio work on demo".

Whistledown Productions

66 Southwark Bridge Road, London SE1 0AS
tel 020-7922 1120
email davidprest@whistledown.net
website www.whistledown.net
Producers/Directors David Prest, Sarah Cuddon

Founded in 1993. One of the largest independent suppliers to BBC Radio, with a background in features and documentaries. Main area of work is documentaries. Recent credits include: *The Child Migrants* and *Headstrong and Proud*. Does not hold general auditions. Accepts submissions from actors previously unknown to the company; voice demos are also accepted.

AUDIOBOOKS

Barefoot Audio Books Ltd

123 Walcot Street, Bath BA1 5BG
Director Tessa Strickland *Group Project Manager* Emma Parkin

Recent titles include: *Mrs Moon, Animal Boogie* and *Tales of Wisdom and Wonder*. Does not use freelance casting directors. Accepts submissions from actors previously unknown to the company if sent by post, but does not welcome email enquiries. Voice demos and invitations to view individual actors' websites are also accepted. Singing ability is required from actors, and Caribbean and African voices are needed in particular.

HarperCollins Audio

77-85 Fulham Palace Road, London W6 8JB
tel 020-8307 4630 *fax* 020-8307 4517
email rosalie.george@harpercollins.co.uk
website www.harpercollins.co.uk
Director Rosalie George *Editorial/Production Manager* Nicola Townsend

Has produced more than 1000 titles for both children and adults over the last 15 years. Work spans all genres including crime, comedy, literary fiction, mass market fiction, non-fiction, poetry and classics. Recent titles include: *Brick Lane* by Monica Ali; *Sharpe's Havoc* by Bernard Cornwell; and *Lovers and Liars* by Josephine Cox.

Foreign languages and regional dialect skills are required from actors. Does not use freelance casting directors. Advises actors to make contact by email or telephone, or preferably through an agent. Also accepts invitations to view individual actors' websites.

Isis Audio Books

7 Centremead, Osney Mead, Oxford OX2 0ES
tel (01865) 250333 *fax* (01865) 790358
email sales@isis-publishing.co.uk
website www.isis-publishing.co.uk
Audio Production Manager Catherine Thompson

Founded in 1975. Publishes unabridged audiobooks. Recent titles include: *Going Postal* by Terry Pratchett; *The Jump* by Martina Cole; and *Red Queen* by Margaret Drabble.

Does not use freelance casting directors. Accepts submissions from actors previously unknown to the company if sent by post or email, but does not welcome telephone enquiries. Voice demos are also accepted. Actors should have a range of voices and good sight-reading ability. Offers non-Equity contracts. Actively encourages applications from disabled actors and promotes the use of inclusive casting.

Macmillan Audio Books

20 New Wharf Road, London N1 9RR
Audio Publisher Alison Muirden *Audio Editorial Coordinator* Zoe Howes

Has recently published titles by Agatha Christie, Wilbur Smith and Colin Dexter. Does not use freelance casting directors. Accepts submissions from actors previously unknown to the company if sent by post, but does not welcome email enquiries. Voice demos are also accepted.

Naxos Audio Books

18 High Street, Welwyn, Herts AL6 9EQ
tel (01438) 717808 *fax* (01438) 717809
email naxos_audiobooks@compuserve.com
Producer/Director Nicolas Soames

Founded in 1984. Produces classic fiction, modern fiction, drama, poetry and children's classics on CD and tape. Recent titles include: *The Canterbury Tales*, *Heidi* and *King Lear*. Regional dialect skills are required from actors. Accepts voice demos.

Random House Audio Books

20 Vauxhall Bridge Road, London SW1V 2SA
tel 020-7840 8400 *fax* 020-7834 2509
email gmarnham@randomhouse.co.uk
website www.randomhouse.co.uk
Editor Zoe Howes *Audio Books Assistant* Louisa Gibbs

Created in 1991, the Audiobooks division of Random House acquired the Reed List in 1997. Has recently published titles by Kathy Reich, Chris Ryan, Ruth Rendell and John Grisham.

Regional dialects are required from actors and should be stated in any covering letter. Does not use freelance casting directors. Accepts submissions from actors previously unknown to the company sent by post or email. Voice demos (not advertisements) and invitations to view individual actors' websites are also accepted.

Soundings Audiobooks Ltd

Isis House, Kings Drive, Whitley Bay, Tyne & Wear NE26 2JT
tel 0191-253 4155 *fax* 0191-251 0662
website www.isispublishing.co.uk
General Manager Gillian Bell

Founded in 1984, the company records around 190 audiobooks a year. Recent productions include: Robert Ludlum's *The Ambler Warning*; Anna Jacobs' *Seasons of Love*; and Alexandra Connor's *The Tailor's Wife*.

Casts in-house and does not issue casting breakdowns. Welcomes letters (not emails) with voice demos or invitations to view individuals' websites. Prefers voice demos without commercials. Uses non-Equity contracts. "We rarely (or never) have the opportunity to cast disabled actors."

Media festivals

These are geared towards showcasing directors, rather than actors. However, they can be useful places to network, learn and (if your film is short-listed) gain extra exposure.

Belfast Film Festival

The Exchange Place, 23 Donegal Street, Belfast BT1 2FF
tel 028-9032 5913 *fax* 028-9032 5911
email info@belfastfilmfestival.org
website www.belfastfilmfestival.org

Normally held in March/April each year, the Belfast Film Festival brings the best of independent, world, local and classic cinema to screens across Belfast. In addition there are panel discussions, workshops, music events and a series of related club events in venues across the city.

Candidates may submit features, shorts, animation and documentaries for inclusion in the festival. The deadline for submissions is normally early December. While all categories will be considered for screening, the only competitive category is the Irish short film. To be eligible for the £1000 Kodak Short Film Prize, films must have been shot in Ireland during the previous year and last no longer than 20 minutes.

BFM International Film Festival

tel 020-8527 9582 *fax* 0870-132 2249
email festival@bfmmedia.com
website www.blackfilmmakermag.com/festival

Presenting the UK's premier black film event each September across venues in London, the BFM promotes the range and diversity of black cinema and television around the world. Showcasing an array of award-winning features, documentaries, animation and short films by established international talent alongside black British film-makers, the BFM also screens a substantial amount of high-quality work from up-and-coming filmmakers. In addition there are exclusive preview screenings, seminars, workshops and masterclasses on offer. Awards are presented to winners in the following categories: best actor, best actress, best film, best cinematography, and best screenplay.

Birmingham Screen Festival

9 Margaret Street, Birmingham B3 3BS
tel 0121-643 0631
email info@birminghamscreenfestival.com
website www.birminghamscreenfestival.com
Director Barbara Chapman

A 6-day event in March celebrating the best of film, television and interactive software at venues across Birmingham. The programme features UK premières, previews, retrospective work, experimental work, shorts, documentaries, animation, international cinema, masterclasses and community events. Awards include: the Norman Beaton Award for Film and TV Drama; the Samuelson Award for Achievement in Drama; Birmingham Screen Festival Best Newcomer Award; Birmingham Screen Festival Special Award for Lifetime Achievement.

Applications are by invitation only; contact the festival for further details.

Bite the Mango

National Museum of Photography, Film & Television, Bradford BD1 1NQ
tel (01274) 203326 *fax* (01274) 203387
email adeni.rutter@nmsi.ac.uk
website www.bitethemango.org.uk

Founded in 1994, Bite the Mango aims to promote the best in world cinema with an eclectic mix of features, shorts and documentaries from many countries around the world. The festival runs for 1 week in September and features premières, previews, retrospectives, masterclasses and seminars by leading figures in world cinema.

Bradford Film Festival

National Museum of Photography, Film & Television, Bradford BD1 1NQ
tel (01274) 203308 *fax* (01274) 770217
email ben.eagle@nmsi.ac.uk
website www.bradfordfilmfestival.org.uk
Director Tony Earnshaw *Contact* Ben Eagle

Held each year in March, the Bradford Film Festival presents a number of special guests, tributes, screentalk interviews, masterclasses, spotlights, the Crash symposium and the Widescreen weekend over a 15-day period.

Features, shorts, documentaries and experimental work submitted for competition must have been completed during the previous 2 years.

Brief Encounters Festival

Watershed Media Centre, 1 Canon's Road, Harbourside, Bristol BS1 5TX
tel 0117-915 0186 *fax* 0117-930 9967
email info@brief-encounters.org.uk
website www.brief-encounters.org.uk

Brief Encounters is an international short film festival which runs for 1 week in November and promotes new talent in the film industry. With more than 20 screenings of diverse new shorts from around the world, special guests and events, parties, awards, seminars, masterclasses, surgeries and focus sessions, the festival offers insights and advice from industry professionals about every aspect of film. For advice about funding and submitting your work, visit the website.

Cambridge Film Festival

Arts Picture House, 38-39 St Andrew's Street, Cambridge CB2 3AR
tel (01223) 500082 *fax* (01223) 462555
email cff@picturehouses.co.uk
website www.cambridgefilmfestival.org.uk

Established in 1977, the festival was relaunched in 2001 after a 5-year hiatus and now runs for 10 days in July. Aiming to screen the best of current international cinema and to rediscover neglected films of the past, it also runs a programme for children supported by events and workshops, and organises free outdoor screenings and touring events across the Eastern region. The festival is attended by many actors and directors and is complemented by parties, receptions, drive-in movies and educational events. Recent visitors include Cate Blanchett, Richard Harris, Timothy Spall and Joel Schumacher.

Directors such as Peter Greenaway, Patrice Chereau, Philip Kaufman and Francesco Rosi have also presented work at the festival, and many acclaimed films – including *Reservoir Dogs*, *Intimacy*, *Bowling for Columbine*, *Goodbye Lenin!* and *La Haine* – received their UK première in Cambridge.

Cardiff Screen Festival

10 Mount Stuart Square, Cardiff CF10 5EE
tel 029-2033 3324 *fax* 029-2033 3320
email enq@iffw.co.uk
website www.iffw.co.uk
Festival Manager Sarah Howells

Celebrating film, TV and new media from Wales and further afield, the festival offers a wide selection of screenings, special guest appearances, debates and programmed industry events for 10 days each November.

The DM Davies award is open to any short-film director who is of Welsh origin or has been a native of Wales for 2 or more years. It is one of the largest short-film prizes in Europe; previous winners have included Justin Kerrigan (*Human Traffic*) and Sara Sugarman (*Very Annie Mary*). Entries are screened towards the end of the festival, with many of the directors in attendance. The winner receives a comprehensive package of funding, facilities and assistance to shoot a 10-minute film in Wales.

Celtic Film & Television Festival

249 West George Street, Glasgow G2 4QE
tel 0141-302 1737
email mail@celticfilm.co.uk
website www.celticfilm.co.uk

The Celtic Film Festival celebrates the cultures and languages of Cornwall, Brittany, Ireland, Scotland and Wales in film and in television broadcasting. Awards include: Short Drama Award, Drama Feature Award and Drama Series Award. The festival is attended by producers, directors, commissioning editors, film executives, media students, distributors and schedulers.

The Seaward Chichester Film Festival

Chichester Cinema at New Park, New Park Road, Chichester PO19 1XN
tel (01243) 786650 *fax* (01243) 790235
email info@chichestercinema.org
website www.chichestercinema.org
Director Roger Gibson

An 18-day festival in August/September presenting more than 70 feature films, Q&As with visiting directors, and related talks. More than half the films shown are previews and premières; the remainder form retrospectives on important contributors to the film world.

The Commonwealth Film Festival

Unit 9, Greenheys Business Centre, Manchester Science Park, 10 Pencroft Way, Manchester M15 6JJ
tel 0161-342 0044 *fax* 0161-342 0055
email info@commonwealthfilm.com
website www.commonwealthfilm.com
Director Mathieu Ravier

The festival promotes filmmaking talent in the Commonwealth and seeks to develop new audiences for their work. Committed to inclusivity and excellence, it also aims to promote respect for human rights, equality, freedom and sustainable economic development. Founded in 2001, the festival presents documentaries, short films, seminars, workshops, industry networking events and parties during its 10-day run across April/May, and is the largest festival showcase for Indian, Canadian and South African cinema in Europe. Submissions must be made in or co-produced with one of the 72 nations of the Commonwealth.

Disability Film Festival

London Disability Arts Forum, 20-22 Waterson Street, London E2 8HE
tel 020-7749 4352 *fax* 020-7749 4363
email caglar@disabilityfilm.org
website www.disabilityfilm.co.uk
Festival Coordinator Caglar Kimyoncu

Showcasing the talent of disabled filmmakers, the Disability Film Festival takes place over 4 days in December, and is hosted by the National Film Theatre. The festival offers filmmakers, film-goers and industry professionals the opportunity to meet, exchange feedback, network and socialise. It has also become a forum for debate, challenging the exclusion of disabled people either on screen or as filmmakers.

Submission forms and guidelines are available to download from the website.

Edinburgh International Film Festival

Filmhouse, 88 Lothian Road, Edinburgh EH3 9BZ
tel 0131-228 4051 *fax* 0131-229 5501
email info@edfilmfest.org.uk
website www.edfilmfest.org.uk
Artistic Director Shane Danielsen *Managing Director* Ginnie Atkinson

Celebrating cinema for nearly 60 years, the festival aims to entertain, challenge and inspire audiences for 10 days each August. The programme covers a range of different areas such as British Cinema, red carpet gala events, live interviews with cinema greats, retrospectives, debuts and second films from new filmmaking talent, short films and special events. Previous events have included the National 48 Hour Film Challenge, Script Factory masterclasses and performed readings, a BAFTA-sponsored interview with Terence Davies, and a Skillset event on Careers in Film.

Submissions should be received by April; all the forms, rules and regulations can be downloaded from the website. Films submitted from outside the UK must have been produced during the 2 years previous to the festival, and British films during the year beforehand.

Foyle Film Festival

The Nerve Centre, 7-8 Magazine Street, Derry, BT48 6HU Northern Ireland
tel 028-7126 7432 *fax* 028-7137 1738
email competition@nerve-centre.org.uk
website www.foylefilmfestival.com
Director Shauna Kelpie *Programmer* Brónagh Corr

Established in 1987, the Foyle Film Festival runs for 10 days each November, screening more than 200 films and featuring a number of special guests, events, presentations, workshops and seminars.

Awards are available for the Best Irish Short, Best International Short, Best Animation, Best Feature and Best Documentary. The application forms and rules and regulations for the competition can be downloaded from the Foyle Film Festival website. Send an email or call the office to request a hard copy.

Hull International Short Film Festival

Hull Film, Danish Buildings, 44-46 High Street, Hull HU1 1PS
tel (01482) 381512 *fax* (01482) 381517
email office@hullfilm.co.uk
website www.hullfilm.co.uk
Director Esther Johnson

Held over 5 days in late September, the festival shows short narrative, documentary, animated and experimental films. The aim is to show international

and local short films as an innovative and exciting artform, as well as to provide training opportunities in the region. The festival also includes outdoor screenings, music and film events, international speakers and archive events.

Leeds International Film Festival

PO Box 596, Leeds LS2 8YQ
tel 0113-247 7952 *fax* 0113-247 8397
email filmfestival@leeds.gov.uk
website www.leedsfilm.com
Director Chris Fell

Leeds International Film Festival has been presenting extensive programmes of new and unseen cinema from around the world since 1987, supported by a number of events and workshops for those wanting to get into film and TV. The Yorkshire Short Film Competition highlights emerging new filmmaking talents in the Yorkshire region, while the Louis Le Prince International Short Film Competition promotes some of the best fiction completed in the last year around the world. The key features of the festival include UK Film Week, an annual showcase of emerging talent; Film Festival Fringe, where the bars and clubs of Leeds host human rights films, music documentaries and special events; the Main Programme; Unique Retrospectives.

The festival is complemented by the Leeds Children's and Young People's Film Festival held in April each year, with an award for National Young Filmmaker of the Year.

London Film Festival

National Film Theatre, South Bank, London SE1 8XT
tel 020-7815 1322 or 020-7815 1323 *fax* 020-7633 0786
website www.lff.org.uk

The Times bfi London Film Festival is Europe's largest public film event, screening an average of 280 films from 60 countries in October/November each year. Leading figures in the film industry present their work at the festival, and the programme is supported by a number of interviews, industry and public forums, lectures, education events, Gala films and special screenings promoting the best in cinema across the world.

London Lesbian & Gay Film Festival

c/o National Film Theatre, Belvedere Road, South Bank, Waterloo, London SE1 8XT
tel 020-7928 3535 or 020-7928 3232 (Box Office)
website www.llgff.org.uk
Senior Programmer Jonathan Keane *Head of Festivals (bfi)* Sandra Hebron *Festival Producer* Helen de Witt

Running since 1986, this annual festival showcases the best of British and international Queer Cinema in all its forms – mainstream and avant garde. Features and shorts are complemented by discussions and interviews with writers and filmmakers. The London run of the festival is based at the National Film Theatre (NFT), with other screenings taking place at the Tate Modern and Odeon Leicester Square. Following this run in March and April, it continues on tour around the UK until the autumn. See the website for programme details, including the tour schedule, or contact the NFT box office for a brochure of the London run.

Manchester International Short Film Festival

Kinofilm, 42 Edge Street, Manchester M4 1HN
tel 0161-288 2494 *fax* 0161-281 1374
email john.kino@good.co.uk
website www.kinofilm.org.uk
Director John Wojowski

British New Wave and an International Panorama of film provide the main focus to the festival, with a regional showcase, 'Made up North', aimed at promoting films from local and regional filmmakers. Education and Professional Development events are also hosted by the festival and are presented by external curators and organisations.

The festival is open for film submissions each year from January to June, with shortlisted entries being screened at the festival itself in October. Short films on any theme, subject or category and made on any format are eligible, as long as they run no longer than 20 minutes and have been made within the 18 months prior to the festival. The Kinofilm Awards acknowledge outstanding achievements in short film, with awards in many categories. Rules, regulations and application forms are available on the website.

Raindance Film Festival Ltd

81 Berwick Street, London W1F 8TW
tel 020-7287 3833 *fax* 020-7439 2243
email info@raindance.co.uk
website www.raindance.co.uk/festival
Producer Oli Harbottle

Running for 2 weeks in October, Raindance is the UK's largest independent film festival and is committed to screening the boldest, most innovative and challenging films from the UK and around the world. Weighted heavily towards new talent, the festival offers more than 100 features (many of which are directorial debuts), 20 shorts programmes and a wide range of events, workshops, parties and the British Independent Film Awards.

Rushes Soho Shorts Festival

PO Box 2868, London W1A 5QL
tel 020-7851 6207 *fax* 020-7851 6369
email info@sohoshorts.com
website www.sohoshorts.com

Taking place for 1 week in July/August, shortlisted films are screened free of charge throughout Soho's cafes, bars and cinemas, as well as other special events and screenings being held. In addition, Vue cinemas around the country will also be holding screenings throughout that week. The festival culminates in an awards cremony with winners being announced in the following categories: Short Film, Newcomer, Animation, Music Video, and Title Sequence & Idents. Patrons of the festival include BAFTA and the Directors' Guild of Great Britain.

Films for submission should be no longer than 12 minutes, and should have been produced in the 12 months prior to the deadline.

UK Jewish Film Festival

PO Box 3217, Brighton BN1 6QA
tel (01273) 735522 *fax* (01753) 327766
website www.ukjewishfilmfestival.org.uk

Established in 1997, the festival is committed to showing a wide variety of films which celebrate the diversity of Jewish cultures and identity, and which reach both Jewish and wider audiences. In addition to film screenings there are education projects and talks with directors. The UK Jewish Film Festival Short Film Fund offers a grant of up to £15,000 for the production of a short film or video (drama, animation or factual) of a Jewish theme and with a significance to Jewish and general public audiences. For application details, consult the website.

Actors with disabilities
Introduction

This section brings together companies and organisations of specific interest to disabled actors. It should also be noted that (a) some agents and companies now welcome enquiries from disabled actors (see listings), and (b) the Conference of Drama Schools (CDS) states that, "All members of the Conference of Drama Schools are committed to a policy of widening access, to reflect the social and cultural diversity of society." Some drama schools have more detail on their disability admissions policies on their websites.

A number of television companies want to increase the representation of disabled performers, contributors and production crew in their programme-making. To this end they have set up databases of disabled people with interests and/or skills in acting, reporting, and other aspects of film, television and radio production. The contact details are as follows:

- *BBC Diversity Database* – Contact David Pain, Room DG20, BBC Centre House, Wood Lane, London W12 8SB (send CV and photograph), or email **diversity.database@bbc.co.uk**.
- *Channel 4* – Contact Alison Walsh (**awalsh@channel4.com**) or 020-7306 8125; **www.channel4.com/4disabledtalent**.
- *ITV* – Contact Janie Frazer (performers only) on 020-7261 3848. More contact details are in the casting directors section. Her details are on page 86.

In addition, Equity members with disabilities can add their details to the Disability Register, which is published by Spotlight. Casting directors looking for actors with disabilities can search this register via the Spotlight website.

Note The UK Government recognised BSL as an official language in March 2003, and the editors acknowledge that many deaf people consider themselves to be members of a linguistic and cultural minority – Deaf with a capital 'D' – rather than disabled people. For the sake of simplicity, however, this book generally uses a broad definition of disability, similar to that of the 1995 Disability Discrimination Act (DDA), to encompass those with hearing impairments (although an individual entry will retain the distinction if such is used in the material provided to us by that company).

The editors would like to thank Silvie Fisch (of The National Disability Arts Forum) and the staff of Graeae Theatre Company for their help in compiling this section.

TRAINING

Apart from the training offered by drama schools, a number of theatre companies and organisations operate training schemes or courses for actors with disabilities. Many of these schemes are relatively short – a few days or weeks – but Graeae's Missing Piece, Lawnmower's Liberdade, Chicken Shed's BTEC National Diploma, Mind the Gap's Staging Change, and Shysters' Shyster-Shadows operate over a longer term. Shorter courses are run by (among others) Birds of Paradise, Blue Eyed Soul, CandoCo, and Oily Cart. These are often advertised through the NDAF's email newsletter, EtCetera – **www.ndaf.org** has more information about how to subscribe – or contact the company concerned for more information. (Details for all the theatre companies listed here can be found in the *Sources of work* section below.)

Share Music

email jaci@sharemusic.org.uk
website www.sharemusic.org.uk

Share Music runs an annual programme of week-long residential courses at specialised centres throughout the UK and in Sweden.

The courses incorporate music, dance and theatre and culminate in a final public performance. None of the work produced on the week is pre-planned and courses provide a fully integrated atmosphere, where disabled and non-disabled people work alongside each other as artistic equals.

While the courses attract many musicians and other artists, participants are not required to have any former experience. Workshops are designed so that people of all skill levels are able to get involved in the creative process; this includes the use of state-of-the-art technology so that those with more severe forms of physical disability are not excluded.

Touchdown Dance

Waterside Arts Centre, Sale M33 7ZF
tel 0161-912 5760 *fax* 0161-912 5783
email info@touchdowndance.co.uk
website www.touchdowndance.co.uk
Director Katy Dymoke

Touchdown Dance provides dance workshops for visually impaired and sighted people of all ages and ability, ranging from 'jam' weekends to more intensive courses.

SOURCES OF WORK

Amici Dance Theatre Company

Turtle Key Arts, Ladbroke Hall, 79 Barlby Road, London W10 6AZ
tel 020-8964 5060 *fax* 020-8964 4080
email info@amicidance.org
website www.amicidance.org
Artistic Director Wolfgang Stange

Dance theatre company integrating able-bodied and disabled artists and performers.

Anjali Dance Company

The Mill Arts Centre, Spiceball Park, Banbury, Oxfordshire OX16 8QE
tel/fax 01295-251909
email info@anjali.co.uk or education@anjali.co.uk
website www.anjali.co.uk
Artistic Director Nicole Thomson *Admin Officer* Adrienn Szabo

Production details

Anjali Dance Company is a professional contemporary dance company. All Anjali's dancers have a learning disability. The company produces and tours performances, and undertakes Educational and Outreach work: it is one of the first of its kind in the world. Anjali aims to show that disability is no barrier to creativity. Stages 1-2 productions a year with up to 10 performances over 6-8 venues around the country, such as the Mill Arts Centre (Banbury), Stratford Circus (London), and the Pegasus Theatre (Oxford).

Casting procedures

Casts in-house, does not issue casting breakdowns, and welcomes letters (but not emails) from individuals previously unknown to the company. Welcomes invitations to view individuals' websites, but not showreels.

art+power

St Werburghs Community Centre, Horley Road, Bristol BS2 9TJ
tel 0117-908 9859 *fax* 0117-9089861 *minicom* 0117-908 9860
email info@artandpower.com
website www.artandpower.com

A group of disabled people working together in Bristol in the media of visual arts, theatre, creative writing and music, to challenge attitudes to disability. art+power's theatre company, the Portway Players, performs regularly at the Bristol New Vic Studio and occasionally at other venues around the country.

Birds of Paradise Theatre Company

333 Woodlands Road, Glasgow G3 6NG
tel 0141-339 1155 *fax* 0141-339 1177
email all@birdsofparadisetheatre.co.uk
website www.birdsofparadise.co.uk
Artistic Director Morven Gregor *'Agent for Change'* Robert Softley

Birds of Paradise is a professional touring theatre company which produces adventurous and challenging work that places disability in the public arena. The company has toured throughout Scotland for 12 years with inventive programmes of performances and workshops, both for traditional theatre-going audiences and people who have difficulty experiencing theatre due to disability or geographical isolation.

Birds of Paradise shares its knowledge of good practice across the arts and disability sector with a clear objective: to increase the number of disabled professional theatre practitioners working in Scotland.

The company recognises that in order to reverse hundreds of years of discrimination against people with physical disabilities, it needs to present high-quality work and positive role models for contemporary Scottish Theatre, its audiences and practitioners. These role models are also engaged to support the company's work with physically disabled young people, who continue to be excluded from participating and engaging in the arts.

Since 1995, the company has intensively trained 150 people over 22 acting courses and technical skills. 400 general Outreach and Taster Workshops have been run, involving approximately 4800 people, and there have been 7 inclusive touring productions with disabled and non-disabled performers and stage workers. 23 disabled actors have been employed; 12 non-disabled actors have also been employed. 4 disabled people were employed in technical jobs.

Previous productions include: *The Farce of Circumstance* by Tom Lannon (1995); *The Resistible Rise of Arturo Ui* by Bertolt Brecht (1996); *Tongues* by Sam Shephard and Joseph Chaikin (1997); *Working Legs* by Alistair Gray (1998 commission); *Playing for Keeps* by Archie Hind (1998 commission); *Merman* by Susan McClymont and Dave Buchanan (2000 commission); *Twelve Black Candles* by Des Dillon (2001); and *The Irish Giant* by Garry Robson (2003).

Blue Eyed Soul Dance Company

Pimley Barns, Sundorne Road, Shrewsbury, Shropshire SY4 4SA
tel (01743) 271900 *fax* (01743) 271516
email admin@blueeyedsouldance.com
website www.blueeyedsouldance.com
Director Rachel Freeman

Production details

Founded in 1994, Blue Eyed Soul is a successful inclusive dance company, which offers a dance repertoire, and education and training programmes. It embraces difference, and actively seeks out creative partnerships between disabled and non-disabled people. It stages 1 production a year, with an average of 20 performances in a wide range of locations including arts centres, theatres, outdoor venues, educational and community venues. Areas covered have included the West Midlands, London, North West and the South East.

Casting procedures

Uses freelance casting directors, and holds general auditions. Casting breakdowns are available by postal application (with sae). Does not welcome unsolicited CVs, showreels or invitations to view individuals' websites from dancers unknown to the company. Offers non-Equity contracts.

CandoCo Dance Company

2T Leroy House, 436 Essex Road, London N1 3QP
tel 020-7704 6845 *fax* 020-7704 1645
email info@candoco.co.uk
website www.candoco.co.uk

Artistic Director Celeste Dandeker *Assistant Artistic Director* Claire Russ *Education Officer* Sarah Howard *Administrator* Verity Golding

CandoCo is a contemporary dance company and a leading training and education provider of integrated dance practice.

The company was founded in 1991 by Celeste Dandeker and Adam Benjamin with the aim of providing a professional environment in which disabled and non-disabled dance artists and performers could work together.

The company commissions artists to create new dance work that tours throughout the UK and abroad. It also runs a year-round programme of integrated dance education and training projects, ranging from open workshops, INSET, schools work, international summer schools and professional development programmes, to running an integrated youth dance company from its base in London, named Cando II.

Chicken Shed

Chase Side, Southgate, London N14 4PE
tel 020-8351 6161 *minicom* 020-8350 0676
website www.chickenshed.org.uk

Children and young people's theatre company producing shows that are inclusive and accessible to all. Performs a wide range of works, spanning experimental pieces to full-scale productions; original works to Shakespeare. In addition the company runs:
• An inclusive theatre education workshop programme for nearly 700 members from the ages of 5 to 24 (550 up to the age of 18)
• The only inclusive BTEC National Diploma in Performing Arts in the country
• Special interactive performances to pre-school children and their parents and carers
• Training and work experience in performance and all aspects of theatre production to young people
• Training in inclusive practice through workshops and seminars to a range of professionals from the fields of education, social services and health
• A community facility that is completely accessible physically and has a warm and welcoming ambience
• A national training and development programme with mainstream and special educational needs schools; this has already established 15 new inclusive children's and youth theatre companies across the country, with more on the way

Common Ground Sign Dance Theatre

32-36 Hanover Street, Gostin's Building (4th Floor), Hanover Street, Liverpool L1 4LN
tel/fax 0151-707 8033
textphone 0151-707 8380
email info@signdance.com
website www.signdance.com
Artistic Director & Choreographer Denise Armstrong
Administrative Director Simeon Hart

Founded in 1986, Common Ground is a dance theatre company creating unique performances (through the fusion of sign language, dance and physical theatre) which are accessible to all audiences.

Deafinitely Theatre

Office 11, Beethoven Centre, Third Avenue, London W10 4JT
minicom 020-8968 1589
textphone 020-8968 1589
email paula@deafinitelytheatre.co.uk
website www.deafinitelytheatre.co.uk

Artistic Director Paula Garfield *Development Director* Steven R Webb *Community & Education Director* Kate Furby

Founded in 2002 to produce performance ideas by deaf people. All the company's work is Deaf-led, but is accessible to hearing people as well. The company also runs projects and workshops for youth theatres, community groups, colleges and schools. Recent productions include: *Children of a Greater God* (Jackson Lane Theatre); *Dysfunction* (Oval House); *Motherland* (Jackson Lane); and *Two Chairs* (Oval House).

Full Body & The Voice

Lawrence Batley Theatre, Queen's Street, Huddersfield HD1 2SP
tel (01484) 484441 *fax* (01484) 484443
email fullbody@lbt-uk.org
website www.fullbody.org.uk
Key contact Jon Palmer

Production details

Established in 2000. Production company exploring a range of projects that include actors with learning disabilities and promote inclusive working practices. Approximately 1 production per year tours to 10-15 venues, including arts centres and theatres in Yorkshire, the North West and internationally. Roughly 5-8 actors are used in each production.

Casting procedures

Occasionally uses freelance casting directors. Does not welcome unsolicited CVs. Actively encourages applications from disabled actors and promotes the use of inclusive casting. Offers Equity approved contracts.

Graeae Theatre Company

LVS Resource Centre, 356 Holloway Road, London N7 6PA
tel 020-7700 2455 *fax* 020-7609 7324
email info@graeae.org
website www.graeae.org
Artistic Director Jenny Sealey

Production details

Founded in 1980. Produces theatre made by disabled people (actors, directors and other theatre practitioners) with physical and sensory impairments. Stages 3 productions annually and gives 70 performances at 50 venues each year. Venues include arts centres and theatres in England, Scotland, Wales and Ireland. 3-6 actors are involved in each production. Recent productions include: *On Blindness* (co-production with Frantic Assembly and Paines Plough); *George Dandin*; and *Bent*.

Also trains up to 12 disabled actors a year through its Missing Piece programme, in partnership with the London Metropolitan University. Lasting 9 months, and culminating in a London showcase, this aims to give a thorough grounding in performance training, with the expectation that most participants will go on either to further training or education in performing arts, or directly to work in the performing arts. While not yet a substitute for a 3-year drama school course, it is building links with drama schools such as ALRA, Arts Ed, and Rose Bruford.

Casting procedures

Sometimes holds general auditions. Welcomes postal or email submissions (with CVs and photographs) from actors with physical and sensory impairments. Also accepts showreels and invitations to view individual actors' websites. Offers ITC/Equity approved contracts.

Hijinx Theatre

Wales Millennium Centre, Bute Place, Cardiff CF10 5AL
tel 029-2030 0331 *fax* 029-2030 0332
email info@hijinx.org.uk
website www.hijinx.org.uk
Artistic Director Gaynor Lougher *Associate Director* Chris Morgan *Administrative Director* Val Hill

Production details

Founded in 1981, the company stages 2 productions on one-night stands across Wales and England, with an annual total of around 100 performances. In general, 1 show is aimed at the general public and 1 targets adults with learning disabilities. Writers are commissioned by the company, and all shows include a high level of music. On average 4 actors work on each production. Recent productions include: *Paul Robeson Knew My Father* (Sherman Theatre, Cardiff; Theatr Clwyd, Mold; some community venues); and *Into My Own* (touring day centres, gateway clubs and colleges).

Casting procedures

Shows are cast by the artistic director and/or associate director. Holds general auditions in December and April and welcomes letters, CVs and photographs from actors previously unknown to the company. Does not accept emails or showreels.

Krazy Kat Theatre Company

173 Hartington Road, Brighton BN2 3PA
tel (01273) 692552 *fax* (01273) 692552
email krazykattheatre@ntlworld.com
website www.krazykattheatre.co.uk
Artistic Director Kinny Gardner

Production details

A children's theatre company founded in 1972,
specialising in highly visual forms of theatre that are
accessible to deaf children. Normally tours 4-6
projects each year with an average annual total of 150
performances and 75 venues. Venues include schools,
arts centres, theatres, outdoor venues and community
centres in Essex, Sussex, Kent and London. In general
2 actors go on tour and play to audiences aged 3-7.
Singing ability, physical theatre skills, sign language
and a driving licence are required. Actors may also be
expected to lead workshops. Recent productions
include: *Three Pigs*, *Jack & The Beanstalk*, and *The
Very Magic Flute*.

Casting procedures

Sometimes holds general auditions; actors can write
at any time requesting inclusion. Accepts submissions
(with CVs and photographs) from actors previously
unknown to the company if sent by post. Does not
welcome unsolicited emails. Will also accept
invitations to view individual actors' websites. Offers
non-Equity contracts. Actively encourages
applications from disabled actors and promotes the
use of inclusive casting.

Lawnmowers Independent Theatre Company & Liberdade

Swinburn House, Swinburn Street, Gateshead NE8
1AX
tel/fax 0191-478 9200
email thelawnmowers@onetel.net.uk
website www.thelawnmowers.co.uk
Artistic Director Geraldine Ling *Apprenticeship
Coordinator* Rob Huggins

Theatre company addressing issues of concern for
people with learning difficulties, often with an
international dimension. Uses theatre and drama as a
means for people with learning difficulties to explore
and develop ideas, and help plan and take control of
their futures.

Also runs the Liberdade Apprenticeship Scheme, a 3-
year physical theatre apprenticeship scheme for
young adults with learning difficulties who aim to
form their own theatre company.

Magpie Dance

tel 020-8509 1288
email info@magpiedance.wanadoo.co.uk
website www.magpiedance.org.uk
Artistic Director Avril Hitman *General Manager*
Emma McFarland

Magpie is an inclusive community dance company
for adults with and without learning disabilities; has
been based in Bromley since 1993. Also runs a
mentoring project to support learning-disabled
choreographers.

Mind the Gap

Queens House, Queens Road, Bradford BD8 7BS
tel (01274) 544683 *fax* (01274) 544501
email arts@mind-the-gap.org.uk
website www.mind-the-gap.org.uk
Artistic Director Tim Wheeler *Administrative Director*
Julia Skelton *Outreach Director* Emma Gee *Project
Manager* Rachel Porter

Production details

Founded in 1988, Mind the Gap is a theatre company
with a belief in quality, equality and inclusion, and a
mission to dismantle barriers to artistic excellence so
that learning disabled and non-disabled actors can
appear as equals. The company has 5 main areas of
activity:
• National Touring: in 2000, Mind the Gap
progressed from devised work to adaptations of well-
known texts. In recent years the company has
produced: *Of Mice and Men* (2000 and 2005); *Dr
Jekyll and Mr Hyde* (2001); *Pygmalion* (2002); *Don
Quixote* (2003 – collaboration with Northern Stage);
and *Cyrano* (2004). Total audiences for the 2005 tour
were approximately 6700.
• Learning & Skills: each year Mind the Gap runs a
full-time accredited training course for people with
learning disabilities. In addition, as part of the DaDA
awards scheme, the company runs Staging Change –
a residential, nationally recruited training course for
people with learning disabilities, working in
partnership with 5 of the country's leading
mainstream drama schools.
• Acting Company: comprising 7 learning-disabled
graduates of Mind the Gap's training courses who
work on National Touring productions and their
own programme of local and regional performance
work and workshops.
• Outreach: each year, Mind the Gap's Outreach
programme works with 300 young learning-disabled
people from West Yorkshire on short-term drama
training and performance projects.
• Advocacy: Mind the Gap advocates for people who
are traditionally excluded or marginalised from
mainstream practices. Mind the Gap is also
commissioned to do a variety of performance
projects: e.g. *Finding their Feet* – a production
commissioned by Bradford School of Health Studies;
and *Inside Knowledge* – commissioned by Tonic as
part of a consultation to provide guidance for the
design of a new cancer care centre in Leeds.

Stages 1 or 2 national tours annually (25-30
performances each), 1 large-scale regional
performance project (3-6 performances), and 1 or 2

regional schools tours (12 performances). The national tour visits 15-20 venues: in 2005 these included West Yorkshire Playhouse; The Theatre, Chipping Norton; Ustinov Studio, Bath; Norwich Playhouse; Rose Theatre, Ormskirk; New Vic, Newcastle-under-Lyme; and Jackson's Lane Theatre, London. 3-5 actors are involved in the national tour, up to 7 actors in the schools tour, and over 20 performers in the regional performance project.

Casting procedures

Casts in-house. When the company is seeking to recruit an actor outside of the core company, it contacts agents, and advertises in *The Stage* and on its website. Casting breakdowns are available "on request". Welcomes letters (with CVs and photographs) as well as showreels and invitations to view individuals' websites, "... although we do not often employ actors who are not known to us. For national touring work we rarely cast outside our core Acting Company, but we do keep on record, details which have been sent to us. We are particularly interested in hearing from artists with disabilities." Offers TMA/Equity approved contracts.

Nasty Girls

email info@nasty-girls.co.uk
website www.nasty-girls.co.uk

Disabled/Deaf women who devise, write and perform their own material specialising in cardboard characters, overblown egos, cheap laughs and slapstick.

Oily Cart Company

Smallwood School Annexe, Smallwood Road, London SW17 OTW
tel 020-8672 6329 *fax* 020-8672 0792
email oilies@oilycart.org.uk
website www.oilycart.org.uk
Artistic Director Tim Webb *General Manager* Tracy Brunt *Administrator* Toma Dim

Production details

"Oily Cart makes gentle, interactive theatre for carers and babies as young as 6 months old, and elaborate multisensory pieces transcending the most complex sensory and intellectual impairments." Tours to schools, arts centres, theatres and special needs schools across the UK. In general 4 actors go on tour and play to infant audiences. Singing ability, proficiency with a musical instrument, dance/physical theatre skills, puppeteering ability and a driving licence are required. Recent productions include: *Moving Pictures*, an interactive, highly personal piece for children and young people with profound and multiple learning disabilities; and *Jumpin' Beans*, a show for children aged between 6 months and 6 years.

Casting procedures

Casting breakdowns are available through Equity Job Information Service and advertisements in *The Stage*. Offers ITC/Equity approved contracts. Actively encourages applications from disabled actors and promotes the use of inclusive casting.

Salamanda Tandem

38 Laurie Avenue, Forest Fields, Nottingham NG7 6PN
tel/fax 0115-942 0706
email info@salamanda-tandem.org
website www.salamanda-tandem.org
Artistic Director Isabel Jones *Company Manager* Lisa Craddock *Dance Development* Julie Hood

Works with a wide spectrum of people to create dance, music and visual artworks.

Shed MK (part of Inter-action MK)

The Old Rectory, Waterside, Peartree Bridge, Milton Keynes MK6 3EJ
tel (01908) 678514
email mandy@interaction.clara.co.uk
website www.interactionmk.org.uk/shedmk.html
Project Manager Hannah Kitchen

Inspired by the work of Chicken Shed Theatre Company (see page 251), Shed MK runs various inclusive performance projects – among them, youth theatre projects for 7-11 and 12-16 year-olds.

Shoot Your Mouth Off

10 Brigandine Close, Seaton Carew, Hartlepool TS25 1ES
tel (01429) 42349 *mobile* (07960) 532554
email karensheader@aol.com
Director Karen Sheader

Shoot Your Mouth Off is a film company run by a disabled producer/actor, Karen Sheader. SYMO began making films with a local professional video production company, Carpet Films, in 2001; Carpet Films has since become part of SYMO. The company has made 12 films to date, many of which have been screened at both disability and mainstream festivals in the UK and internationally, including San Francisco and Moscow. An award-winning production company based in the North-East of England, it works with actors who consider themselves to be disabled – "all our films explore some aspect of the experience of being a person with impairments in a disabling society". Makes comedies, dramas, documentaries and interactive digital media.

Spare Tyre Theatre Company

Hampstead Town Hall, 213 Haverstock Hill, London NW3 4QP
tel/fax 020-7419 7007
email sttc@sparetyretheatrecompany.co.uk
website www.sparetyretheatrecompany.co.uk

Joint Artistic Directors Arti Prashar, Clair Chapwell
Administrator Paul Margrave

Production details

The company has 3 principal strands of work:
• Work with elders: weekly workshops in resource
centres in North London; summer production;
training for public sector workers using theatre
created and performed by elder participants.
• Work with people with learning disabilities: the
'inc.Theatre' course is a full-time, OCN (Open
College Network) approved partnership with
Redbridge College for people of all ages with learning
disabilities. The 'incSpots' programme provides
further opportunities for development and
performance for previous students on the inc.Theatre
course.
• Work with schools: professional TIE productions
for school pupils tackling homophobia in schools.
Also: 'Dealing with Difference', a workshop for
school staff looking at approaches to tackling
homophobia within schools.

Each strand of work has 1 major production a year,
touring to roughly 100 venues – from schools,
theatres and community venues to hospitals, GP
surgeries, residential homes, special needs schools
and public sector venues. Primarily covers the
London area, but also Yorkshire, Manchester, Kent
and Wales. Skills required from actors include
(ideally) a driving licence, but also workshop-leading
and facilitation skills, experience working with
community groups, and a sensitivity to and
understanding of relevant issues.

Casting procedures

Casting breakdowns are published in *The Stage* and
on the website. Unsolicited approaches – including
CVs, showreels and invitations to view individuals'
websites – at other times are discouraged. Offers ITC/
Equity approved contracts. Actively encourages
applications from disabled actors and promotes the
use of inclusive casting.

Spiral

See entry for First Movement on page 257.

Stalking Histories

St Thomas Centre, Ardwick Green North,
Manchester M12 6FZ
tel 0161-273 4664
email stalkinghistories@supanet.com
website www.stalkinghistories.com
Artistic Director Ruth Collett *Administrator* Will
Ward

Stalking Histories is an independent disability arts
project exploring lost or hidden stories from
disability history and culture. It uses a number of
artforms to do this, including theatre, puppetry and
multimedia.

Starfish Theatre Company (formerly Jumpstart)

See entry for Prism Arts on page 258.

StopGAP Dance Company

Farnham Maltings, Bridge Square, Farnham, Surrey
GU9 7QR
tel (01252) 718664
email vicki@stopgap.uk.com
website www.stopgap.uk.com
Artistic Director Vicki Balaam

A vibrant integrated dance company that includes
dancers with and without disabilities. It challenges
traditional notions about dance by using each
dancer's physical and intellectual potential as a
starting point for creating new work. "We work from
a philosophy of physical, psychological and social
integration. In so doing, we recognise and celebrate
individuality and the differences between people,
while continually seeking artistic and technical
excellence in all that we do."

The Shysters (part of Open Theatre Company)

AUEW Building, 57-61 Corporation Street, Coventry
CV1 1GX
tel/fax (02476) 239186
email shysters@opentheatre.co.uk
website www.theshysters.co.uk
Artistic Director Richard Hayhow *Associate Director*
Kathy Joyce *Company Manager* Sue Walker

The Shysters Theatre Company was set up by Open
Theatre Company (OTC) in partnership with the
Belgrade Theatre, Coventry in 1997, but is now
incorporated fully into the work of OTC. The
company uses an ensemble way of working to
develop ways of "making theatre that reflects our
unique characteristics (which we call 'Shysterness')
and which has its roots in learning disability". It is
keen to collaborate with others, discover new ways of
making theatre, and involve as many people as
possible in its work.

Currently developing a 3-year rolling programme of
professional development for artists, working with
Arts & Media Training; in 2002 set up
ShysterShadows to train young people with learning
disabilities in performing arts skills and 'Shysterness'.

Theatre Workshop

34 Hamilton Place, Edinburgh EH3 5AX
tel 0131-225 7942 *fax* 0131-220 0112
email afleming@twe.org.uk
website www.theatre-workshop.com
Artistic Director Robert Rae *Company Manager* Anne
Fleming

Production details

Founded in 1965; stages 4 productions a year with
around 60 performances across 2 theatre venues.

Occasionally tours internationally. Employs an average of 5 actors on each production, using ITC/Equity approved contracts. Recent productions include: *The Jasmine Road* (No Limits International Theatre Festival, Berlin); and *The Threepenny Opera* (Edinburgh Festival Theatre & Tramway, Glasgow).

Casting procedures

Casting breakdowns are available from the website and Equity Job Information Service. Welcomes letters and emails (with CVs and photographs) from individuals previously unknown to the company. Also happy to receive showreels and invitations to view individuals' websites. Encourages applications from disabled actors and promotes the use of inclusive casting. "Theatre Workshop casts both disabled and non-disabled actors in all our productions."

VisABLE People

PO Box 80, Droitwich WR9 0ZE
tel (01905) 776631
email louise@visablepeople.com
website www.visablepeople.com
Agent Louise Dyson

Founded in 1996, VisABLE is the UK's first agency representing only people with disabilities for professional engagements. It represents artistes with a wide range of impairments and in every age group, including children. 1 agent represents around 50 artistes in all areas of acting, including presenting.

Does not welcome performance notices: "Sorry, no time to get out and see them usually; existing clients only." Happy to receive other enquiries (with CVs and photographs) from disabled actors via email only. Showreels should always be accompanied by an sae for return. Also happy to receive invitations to view individual actors' websites. Recommends the photographer Derek Lee. *Commission*: 10-17%

Wolf + Water

The Plough, 9-11 Fore Street, Torrington, Devon EX38 8HQ
tel (01805) 625533
email w+w@eclipse.co.uk
website www.wolfandwater.org
Co-founders Steve Newton, Philip Robinson
Administrator Peter Smith

Since establishing itself independently in 1991 after 3 years as the Beaford Centre's 'Common Sense Project', Wolf + Water Arts Company has brought its creative and therapeutic approaches to a wide variety of groups locally, nationally and internationally. These groups have included people with learning difficulties, people with mental health issues, people in conflict situations, offenders, communities, young people at risk, children with life-threatening illnesses and their families, and staff groups working with all the above. The company produces original topical performances for conferences and for tour, and provides a wide range of training courses for those wishing to use drama and arts techniques in special needs situations. Work has taken the company throughout the UK, Eire, Scandinavia, the Middle East and the Balkans.

FESTIVALS

Disability Film Festival

London Disability Arts Forum, 20-22 Waterson Street, London E2 8HE
tel 020-7749 4352 *fax* 020-7749 4363
email caglar@disabilityfilm.org
website www.disabilityfilm.co.uk
Festival Coordinator Caglar Kimyoncu

Showcasing the talent of disabled filmmakers, the Disability Film Festival takes place over 4 days in December, and is hosted by the National Film Theatre. The festival offers filmmakers, film-goers and industry professionals the opportunity to meet, exchange feedback, network and socialise. It has also become a forum for debate, challenging the exclusion of disabled people either on screen or as filmmakers. Submission forms and guidelines are available to download from the website.

ARTS ORGANISATIONS

Acadea (formerly Northern Disability Arts Forum)

MEA House, Ellison Place, Newcastle upon Tyne NE1 8XS
tel/fax 0191-222 0708
minicom 0191-261 2238
email info@arcadea.org
website www.arcadea.org

Arcadea aims to promote the artistic and cultural equality of disabled people in the North East region, serving Co. Durham, Northumberland, Tees Valley and Tyne & Wear.

Articulate

Cleveland Arts, 3rd Floor, Melrose House, Melrose Street, Middlesbrough TS1 2HZ
tel (01642) 264651 *fax* (01642) 264955
email feedback@articulate.org.uk
website www.articulate.org.uk

Articulate is a programme run by Cleveland Arts which aims to develop cutting-edge arts projects inspired by, involving and relating to disabled people.

Artlink Central

Cowane Centre, Cowane Street , Stirling FK8 1JP
tel (01786) 450971 *fax* (01786) 465958
email info@artlinkcentral.org

website www.artlinkcentral.org

Established in February 1988, Artlink Central is a registered charity founded in the belief that involvement in the arts is life-enhancing and should be available to all. It enables a wide range of marginalised and special needs groups to work with experienced professional artists on high-quality arts projects in the Stirling, Falkirk and Clackmannanshire areas of Central Scotland.

Artlink Edinburgh
13a Spittal Street, Edinburgh
tel 0131-229 3555 *fax* 0131-228 5257
website www.artlinkedinburgh.co.uk

As Artlink Central, but based in Edinburgh and the Lothians.

Artsline
54 Chalton Street, London NW1 1HS
tel 020-7388 2227 *fax* 020-7383 2653 *minicom* 020-7388 2227
email access@artsline.org.uk
website www.artsline.org.uk

Founded in 1981 with the aim of increasing disabled people's participation in the arts, and to provide them with accurate information about access to arts and cultural events in London. In collaboration with the London Disability Arts Forum, it began producing *Disability Arts in London (DAIL)* magazine in 1986, and now provides a newly launched access database with details for arts and entertainment venues across London, including: theatres, cinemas, museums, art centres, tourist attractions, comedy, music venues and selected restaurants. For details of other publications, projects and services available, consult the website.

Carousel
Community Base, 113 Queens Road, Brighton BN1 3XG
tel (01273) 234734 *fax* (01273) 234735
Artistic Director Mark Richardson *Administrator* Mark Tidmarsh *General Manager* Liz Hall

Carousel was founded in 1982, and operates primarily in the South East of England. It is a Brighton-based arts organisation that works with people who have learning disabilities. Among its projects are the High Spin Dance Company and the Oskabright Film Festival.

Disability Arts Cymru
Sbectrwm, Bwlch Road, Fairwater, Cardiff CF5 3EF
tel 029-2055 1040 *textphone* 029-2055 1040
fax 029-2055 1036
email post@dacymru.com
website www.dacymru.com

Disability Arts Cymru is the only organisation in Wales providing Disability Equality Training (DET)

specifically for arts providers; it lists among its clients the Arts Council of Wales and the Royal Welsh College of Music and Drama. A number of documents are available from its excellent website, which offer advice on a range of subjects including access issues for touring companies. In June 2006 the company ran 'The Unusual Stage School', a free 11-day course aimed at would-be actors with disabilities living in Wales.

First Movement
PO Box 6447, Matlock DE4 3ZP
tel (01629) 57687
email fmt@first-movement.org.uk
website www.first-movement.org.uk

First Movement is an experimental arts organisation developing projects which uniquely reflect the experiences, choices and abilities of groups of people with severe and profound learning disabilities. Runs a performance company called Spiral.

Ithaca
The Annexe, SS Mary and John School, Meadow Lane, Oxford OX4 1TJ
tel (01865) 791668 *fax* (01865) 791668
email admin@ithaca.org.uk
website ithaca.org.uk
Director Alison Leverett-Morris *Arts Project Worker* Julie Walters

Arts organisation working in Oxfordshire and Berkshire with people with disabilities – including those with identified mental health needs, learning difficulties or physical and sensory impairments, and older people.

London Disability Arts Forum (LDAF)
20-22 Waterson Street, London E2 8HE
tel 020-7739 1133
email info@ldaf.org
website www.ldaf.org

London Disability Arts Forum (LDAF) is a disability-led organisation focused on promoting Disability Arts and the work of disabled artists.

LDAF was founded in 1986 by a group of disabled artists and activists frustrated by the lack of provision for disabled people in the arts world. Access to mainstream arts was very limited, and the arts in no way reflected the experience of disabled people, who comprise at least 17% of the population.

Registered as a charity in 1992, LDAF receives core funding from Arts Council England and project funding from trusts or local bodies. In all it does, LDAF seeks to strengthen and develop the image of disability arts and culture.

LDAF also runs the Disability Film Festival (see entry under *Festivals*) and publishes *Disability Arts in London (DAIL) Magazine*, edited by Jamie Beddard (**jamie@ldaf.org**).

National Disability Arts Forum (NDAF)
59 Lime Street, Newcastle upon Tyne NE1 2PQ
tel 0191-261 1628 *minicom* 0191-261 2237
fax 0191-222 0573
email ndaf@ndaf.org
website www.ndaf.org

The National Disability Arts Forum aims to create equality of opportunity for disabled people in all aspects of the arts. It does this by:
• Supporting the development of Disability Arts Agencies, both regional and local, throughout the UK
• Maintaining and developing a network through which these Agencies can support and assist each others' development
• Establishing favourable conditions within which disabled people can explore and express the condition of disability through the arts
• Promoting the value of art by disabled people

It also:
• Promotes and supports examples of good and/or innovative practice that encourages the participation of disabled people in the arts
• Assists organisations in developing good and/or innovative practice that encourages the participation of disabled people in the arts

The members of the Forum believe that it should be disabled people themselves who determine where and with whom responsibility for decision-making and advocacy on their behalf should lie. Hence, the organisation is accountable to, and controlled and managed by, disabled people.

Like other 'self-led' disability organisations in the UK, NDAF is committed to promoting equal opportunities and prioritises the employment of disabled people, as well as operating an ethical fundraising programme to finance its projects. It works to promote similar practices throughout the arts community, and supports other arts organisations with corresponding policies.

The Forum's main strategy for delivering its mission is to support and work with others whose work involves making their products or services more accessible or attractive to disabled people, those who are engaged in producing and promoting Disability Arts, and those who provide specialist arts services to disabled people, such as workshops or exhibitions.

NDAF aims to undertake at least 1 major arts project a year that is targeted directly at disabled people. Usually these are 'model' projects, or projects that are designed to break new ground.

Note Visit the website to sign up to *EtCetera*, NDAF's email newsletter, which contains (among other things) job opportunities, training and workshops, and a Pick-of-the-Week for television and radio. Also on the website you can listen and subscribe to its Disability Arts podcast.

North West Disability Arts Forum
MPAC Building, 1-27 Bridport Street, Liverpool L3 5QF
tel 0151-707 1733 *minicom* 0151-706 0365
fax 0151-708 9355
email nwdaf@nwdaf.co.uk
website www.nwdaf.co.uk

North West Disability Arts Forum is a disabled and deaf people's arts organisation run by and for disabled and deaf people. It aims to facilitate the active participation of disabled and deaf people in all aspects of the arts and creative industries, and both promote and celebrate disability and deaf arts and culture. Based in Liverpool City Centre, the Forum covers Merseyside, Cheshire, and work throughout the UK.

Northern Ireland Arts & Disability Forum
109-113 Royal Avenue, Belfast BT1 1FF
tel 028-9024 7770
email info@adf.ie
website www.adf.ie
Information Officer Louise Stevenson

A non-profit-making voluntary organisation that aims to provide:
• Information to people with disabilities and organisations – both inside and outside of the arts sector
• A body that advocates on behalf of people with disabilities in the arts sector
• A networking, developmental and coordinating body
• A body that identifies and fills gaps in training provisions for people with disabilities working in the arts
• A focus for campaigning

Also runs a gallery to exhibit the work of disabled artists.

Prism Arts
Unit 1, Brampton Business Centre, Union Lane, Brampton CA8 1BX
tel (01697) 745011 *fax* (01697) 745006
email office@prismarts.fsnet.co.uk
website www.prismarts.co.uk

Promotes disabled peoples' access to creative arts activities in Cumbria. Runs Starfish Theatre Company, a group of learning-disabled performers.

Shape
LVS Resource Centre, 356 Holloway Road, London N7 6PA
tel 020-7619 6160 *minicom* 020-7619 6161
fax 020-7619 6162
email info@shapearts.org.uk
website www.shapearts.org.uk

Shape is based in North London with offices in Hammersmith and Fulham, Wandsworth and Islington. It is a charity that opens up access to the arts, enabling greater participation by disabled and older people.

West Midlands Disability Arts Forum (WMDAF)

116 Greenhouse, Gibb Street, Birmingham B9 4AA
tel 0121-224 7881 *fax* 0121-224 7882
email info@wmdaf.org
website www.wmdaf.org

WMDAF's objective is to create a sustainable network for disability arts in the region.

RIGHTS, ADVICE AND SUPPORT

Broadcasting & Creative Industries Disability Network (BCIDN) – see Employers' Forum on Disability.

Directgov

website www.direct.gov.uk/disability

The government's Public Services portal, with links to information and advice on employment, home and housing options, financial support, health, education and training, rights and obligations, transport, travel and holidays, leisure and recreation, and caring for someone.

Disability Rights Commission

DRC Helpline, FREEPOST MID02164, Stratford upon Avon CV37 9BR
tel (08457) 622633 *textphone* (08457) 622644
(You can speak to an operator at any time between 8am and 8pm, Monday to Friday) *fax* (08457) 778878

The Disability Rights Commission (DRC) is an independent body established in April 2000 by Act of Parliament to stop discrimination, and to romote equality of opportunity for disabled people.

The DRC:
• Gives advice and information to disabled people, employers and service providers – its Helpline has taken more than half a million calls
• Supports disabled people in getting their rights under the DDA
• Helps solve problems, often without going to a court or employment tribunal
• Supports legal cases to test the limits of the law: it funded 84 legal cases in 2002/3
• Provides an independent Disability Conciliation Service for disabled people and service providers through Mediation UK
• Campaigns to strengthen the law
• Organises campaigns, such as the Open 4 All campaign, to change policy, practice and awareness
• Produces policy statements and research on disability issues, and publications on rights and good practice for disabled people, employers and service providers

Employers' Forum on Disability

Nutmeg House, 60 Gainsford Street, London SE1 2NY
tel 020-7403 3020 *fax* 020-7403 0404 *minicom* 020-7403 0040
email jenny.stevens@employers-forum.co.uk
website www.employers-forum.co.uk
BCIDN Network Manager Jenny Stevens

The leading employers' organisation focused on disability as it affects business. Funded and managed by more than 400 members, the Forum works to make it easier for companies to recruit and retain disabled employees and to serve disabled customers. Umbrella organisation for the Broadcasting & Creative Industries Disability Network (BCIDN), a forum for the UK's major broadcasters to explore and address disability as it relates to the media industry. It is advised by a panel of associates – 14 disabled people with considerable media experience who work in different areas of broadcasting and the media in general.

FASED

website fased.org

Freelance and self-employed disabled people in the arts. East Midlands-based organisation, primarily aimed at visual artists, but with some good general advice for freelancers on their Documents page.

Ouch!

website www.bbc.co.uk/ouch

The BBC's online disability magazine, including weblogs, message board, and a monthly podcast.

Skill: National Bureau for Students with Disabilities

Chapter House, 18-20 Crucifix Lane, London SE1 3JW
tel 020-7450 0620 *fax* 020-7450 0650 *minicom* 020-7450 0620
email info@skill.org.uk
website www.skill.org.uk

An independent charity that promotes opportunities for people with any kind of disability in learning and employment. Since 1974 has been helping young people and adults over 16 years of age with any kind of disability, including physical and sensory disabilities, learning and mental health difficulties, throughout the UK. Skill believes that for many disabled people, education is the key to leading a fulfilling and independent life. Information Service: open Tuesdays: 11.30am – 1.30pm; Thursdays: 1.30 – 3.30pm; *tel* 0800-328 5050 (freephone)and 020-7657 2337. "Ringing us on the second phone number saves us money – thanks!"

Provides a free information and advice service for individual disabled people and the professionals who work with them, via a freephone helpline, email and the website. This information and advice helps disabled people to overcome financial and physical barriers, ignorance and discrimination so that they can study, train or find work.

Informs and influences key policy-makers to improve legal rights and support for disabled people in post-16 education and training. Skill works together with individual disabled people, professionals working in education, training and careers, employers and disability organisations to influence government. We listen to the people who contact our Information service so that we know what the real issues are.

Promotes best practice through:
• Skill membership: keeping professionals up to date and informed about policy changes, providing the opportunity for exchanging information and ideas and to be more closely involved with Skill's work
• Running topical conferences and seminars
• Producing informative and practical publications
• Providing consultancy and staff training for colleges, universities and other organisations

Conducts research and develops projects on education and disability issues to address gaps in provision and to take forward new ideas.

Opportunities for disabled actors

Jamie Beddard

The plethora of journeys and experiences of disabled performers over the past 30 years has ranged from the lonely, demoralising, and depressing to the downright bizarre. The barriers encountered far outreach the regular obstacles preventing non-disabled actors from learning, and plying their trade. Performance attributes of technique, voice, improvisation and movement seem distant concepts when you cannot get through the doors of drama school, producers baulk at the idea of employing disabled performers, and most training and employment opportunities are based around strict notions of 'the classical actor'. This is altogether surprising in the creative industries, which should surely celebrate uniqueness, individuality and diversity. However, where once black actors were denied access to stage and screen, so those with different bodies have fought similar battles for opportunity, acknowledgement and representation. This, against a backdrop in which esteemed, non-disabled actors regularly pick up Oscars for their touching portrayal of characters with disability; Daniel Day Lewis in *My Left Foot*; Jamie Foxx in *Ray*; John Voight in *Coming Home*; Tom Hanks in *Forrest Gump* – the list is endless. One-dimensional replication of impediments, far outweighing any considerations around full and meaningful characterisations. Authenticity has been a label seldom attached to the portrayal of disability in the mainstream.

Personal anecdotes are perhaps best served in exploring the issues faced by disabled performers, as until recently, there have been no formal routes of progression into the industry. Those few who have made the periphery have tended to have random and short-lived paths based around such indeterminates as maverick directors, word of mouth or, as in my particular case, luck. The groundbreaking film *Skalligrigg* – a road movie in which a rag tag of disabled characters take to the road on a mythical quest – in the early 1990s, threw my staid career path into chaos, and levered a window (previously boarded up!) into performance. In the absence of disabled actors, many first-timers, with no experience, were suddenly thrust onto a film set; I thought the sound-boom was a cheap prop! 'Rough diamonds' probably most accurately described those of us fortunate enough to get such a break, and for me, the film opened up a completely new, and exciting, world. A mixture of bluff, wide-eyed enthusiasm and no little begging had to suffice in the absence of any formal training.

This 'new and exciting world' was also populated by baffling and disheartening prejudices, and initial enthusiasm soon became tinged with disappointment and anger. A casting director for *Eastenders* once informed me that a disabled character – played by a disabled actor, heaven forbid! – would place the programme in the realm of freak show. So much for diverse communities and gritty realism! This attitude is unfortunately still painfully prevalent and theatre directors are worried that their audiences will be put off by seeing a disabled person on stage.

I contacted Graeae Theatre Company – a company that had been going since the early 1980s, and was run by, and for, actors with sensory and physical disabilities. Graeae had become accustomed to (and was hardened by) irksome battles against prevalent prejudices and barriers. I found a group of like-minded individuals who were challenging these ridiculous, outdated and offensive attitudes, and determined to pursue careers considered impractical and unrealistic. They were developing, writing and performing theatre as does any small-scale company; sometimes very good, and sometimes not so good. However, the normal critical faculties brought to bear on other companies seemed strangely absent from assessment of Graeae's work, with emphasis on the 'oh so strange impairments' rather than art. The *Independent*, when reviewing Graeae's 2002 production – *Peeling* – came up with such helpful insights as, "Beaty is four feet tall; Coral has tiny limbs and a torso about the same size as her head." Apart from gross inaccuracies, the obvious offence to the individual actors involved and the banality of such revelations, what relevance has this to the art? Hopefully, the paying public didn't recoil in shock at this assembled collection of bizarre physical specimens!

I always yearned for a bad – rather than ignorant, ill informed and avoiding – review, because this would suggest a considered judgement based on the same criteria as any other performer. Undoubtedly, I have been involved in a few 'turkeys', and they should be recognised as such! However, fascination with individual impediment always seems the central tenet of any assessment of performance. Perhaps it would be interesting to apply such criteria to the wider acting fraternity – solely judging Woody Allen on his glasses, Tom Hanks on his stature, or Kenneth Williams on his nasal inflection.

Over the years the profile of Graeae, and of disabled performers in general, has grown, and there has been a gradual acceptance that it is no longer acceptable to marginalise their talents, aspirations and contributions. In many ways the Arts have lagged behind society in taking the first steps towards embracing and committing to diversity. Although, there has, in many quarters, been a genuine will to broaden participation, the stick of the Disability Discrimination Act has been instrumental in initiating fundamental appraisal and change. The possibility of legal challenges has shaken many organisations, venues and makers from their comfy inertia. Even tokenism is preferable to apartheid!

Drama schools, in particular, have found the concept of students with disability difficult to grasp, but the introduction of the (Dance & Drama Awards) has started the process of drama schools thinking not only about the physical access to their buildings, but also the attitudinal access and ways to promote inclusive teaching. This is very exciting and will no doubt pave the way for young disabled people to go through mainstream training rather than be reliant on Graeae.

While the process of change will take time (especially the attitudinal aspect), Graeae has had to respond to the obvious demand by setting up the training course in conjunction with London Metropolitan University. The course offers all the elements found in drama schools, and provides the skills, disciplines and training that were denied people of my age. Lack of sufficiently trained and experienced disabled actors has long been an excuse for the 'cripping up' of non-disabled actors, while training providers continually stress the unlikelihood of disabled graduates sustaining careers in the industry. A classic chicken-and-egg situation, in which aspirant disabled performers are denied entrance at all levels. However, the percentage of those who have graduated through Missing Piece, and gone into the industry, compares favourably with other drama schools, and Graeae is frequently approached by casting directors looking for disabled talent. So, young people with disabilities do share the same aspirations as any others; there is an increasing demand for such actors; and the institutions are failing to shoulder responsibility.

Missing Piece is fulfilling this vacuum, and has now been running since 2000. The nine-month (September to May) intensive training allows disabled students to work with a wide range of theatre practitioners – both specialist and mainstream. The course can act as a foundation course to further education or drama school – access- and will-permitting! – or, as is often the case, a direct gateway into the industry. Academic and practical elements of performance are covered, and opportunities for showcasing and touring afforded. The last two years have culminated in professional touring productions of *Mother Courage* and *George Dandin*, and many relationships have been brokered between our performers and directors, producers and casting directors. There is a crossover with the Performing Arts degree at London Metropolitan, with our disabled performers working alongside and in collaboration with tutors and students at the University. As well as the main Missing Piece course, Graeae run a series of taster workshops throughout the year for prospective actors.

So strides are being made by Graeae, and by other companies; the excuses and barriers preventing inclusion are slowly being dismantled. There are viable careers for those with the talent, determination and thick skin when necessary.

BBC has set up a talent fund for disabled actors to try and address dated attitudes, and to encourage writers to write storylines which are not always hospital-based or about the whole 'disability thing' !

However the failure of mainstream films such as *Inside I'm Dancing*, which continue to propagate stereotypes and exclusion – with all the main disabled characters played by non-disabled actors – will hopefully mark a sea-change in attitudes and imaginations among creators. The existing, and perspective, body of talent out there no longer allows for petty excuses or wilful misrepresentation. Disabled people, like any others, can make good, bad or indifferent performers, and should be judged as such. However, we have a right to expect the same opportunities, treatments and prospects as all. Banging the door down has become boring – just let us in. It's not rocket science!

Jamie Beddard is an actor, writer and director. Involved with Graeae since 1991, he was Associate Director of the company for some years. He is currently working as a freelance director and co-editor of *DAIL* magazine. Graeae productions 2006/7 include *Blasted* by Sarah Kane, touring March to May; *Once Beyond These Walls, A Girl* by Richard Cameron, touring October to November; and *Whiter Than Snow* by Mike Kenny – a co-production with Birmingham Rep, touring February to April 2007. For full details, visit the website **www.graeae.org**. For information on Missing Piece, contact: **ellie@graeae.org**.

Resources
Introduction

This section covers those practical items (and sources of more detailed help and advice) that are, to the actor, what tools and a first-aid kit are to a carpenter. Some may be irrelevant to you – for instance, you may feel as though you could never have the organisational skills to set up your own company. Others are essential to all actors: good photographs, for example. Whatever your needs, time taken clearly to formulate your requirements before approaching any of the contacts listed below will be time well spent.

Equity

Louise Grainger

Equity is the only Trade Union to represent performers and people working creatively across the entire spectrum of arts and entertainment, both live and recorded. The main function of Equity is to negotiate minimum terms and conditions of employment throughout the entire world of entertainment, and to endeavour to ensure that these take account of social and economic changes. We look to the future as well, negotiating agreements to embrace the new and emerging technologies which affect performers – so satellite, digital television, new media and so on are all covered, as are the more traditional areas. We also work at national level by lobbying government and other bodies on issues of paramount importance to the membership. In addition we operate at an international level through the Federation of International Artists which Equity helped to establish, the International Committee for Artistic Freedom, and through agreements with sister unions overseas.

As well as these core activities, Equity strives to provide a wide range of services for members so that they are eligible for a whole host of benefits which are continually being revised and developed. These include helplines, job information, insurance cover, members' pension scheme, charities and others. (For more information, visit the Equity website **www.equity.org.uk**. For details of Equity's Job Information Service, see entry under The Spotlight, casting directories and information services.)

Louise Grainger is a Marketing & Membership Services Officer for Equity.

Equity

Head Office, Guild House, Upper St Martins Lane, London WC2H 9EG
tel 020-7379 6000 *fax* 020-7379 7001
email info@equity.org.uk
website www.equity.org.uk
• Job Information Service: 0870-901 0900
• Theatre, Variety, Opera & Dance Helpline: 020-7670 0237
• Film, Television, Radio & Audiovisual Helpline: 020-7670 0247
• Tax & Benefits Helpline (Tuesdays & Thursdays only): 020-7670 0223
• Bullying Reporting Line: 020-7670 0268
• Subscription Enquiries: 020-7670 0219

Regional offices:

Midlands
PO Box 1221, Warwick, CV34 5EF
tel 01926-408 638
email tjohnson@midlands-equity.org.uk

North East
The Workstation, 15 Paternoster Row, Sheffield, S1 2BX
tel 0114-275 9746
email njones@sheffield.equity.org.uk

North West
Conavon Court, 12 Blackfriars Street, Salford M3 5BQ
tel 0161-832 3183 *fax* 0161-839 3133
email info@manchester-equity.org.uk

Scotland, Northern Ireland and Isle of Man
114 Union Street, Glasgow G1 3QQ
tel 0141-248 2472 *fax* 0141-248 2473
email igilcrist@glasgow.equity.org.uk

South East
Guild House, Upper St Martins Lane, London WC2H 9EG
tel 020 7670 0229 *fax* 020 7379 7001
email jainslie@equity.org.uk

Wales and South West
Transport House, 1 Cathedral Road, Cardiff CF1 9SD
tel 029-2039 7971 *fax* 029-2023 0754
email info@cardiff-equity.org.uk

The Spotlight, casting directories and information services

Spotlight is a fundamental part of the fabric of the acting profession, and it is essential to have an entry. (It is a false economy not to have one.) The growth of the Internet has seen a rise in companies offering similar services – usually, for a lower subscription. Once again it is important thoroughly to research the value to you of investing in one of these. As well as trying to assess whether such an investment will really enhance your visibility to employers, an essential part of that research is to read the 'small print' properly.

With some exceptions (major musicals, for instance), many employers do not openly advertise the properly paid acting work they have to offer. It's simpler to contact agents whom they know and trust for casting suggestions. This limits the number of submissions, largely prevents (time-wasting) unsuitable applicants, and goes some way towards ensuring that those suggested for consideration are really suitable for the parts available. Consequently, the time required to consider all the CVs and photographs submitted is contained within reasonable limits. It can take a day's work to go through a thousand submissions to select whom to interview; it can take another day's work to interview just 30 of these.

Casting information services – often allied to Internet casting directories – glean their information from all kinds of sources. The important thing to remember is that some of the information about 'properly paid acting work' is of a second-hand nature – that is, it was not sent directly to them in the first instance. Consequently, it is important to research reputations for accuracy (and 'up-to-dateness') before committing your funds to such companies. However, many Fringe production and student film opportunities are directly advertised in such publications, and such opportunities might lead on to 'properly paid acting work'.

The Spotlight

Head Office, 7 Leicester Place, London WC2H 7RJ
tel 020-7437 7631 *fax* 020-7437 5881
email info@spotlight.com
website www.spotlight.com

The Spotlight was founded in 1927 and has since become world-famous for its casting directories. Today more than 30,000 performers appear in the book and Internet versions of *Spotlight*, including actors and actresses, child artists, presenters, dancers and stunt artists. As the industry's leading casting resource, *Spotlight* is used by TV, film, radio and theatrical companies throughout the UK, and many worldwide. Its Internet casting services have become an essential communication tool, uniting actors, agents and production professionals more quickly and easily than ever before.

Membership of The Spotlight means that a performer is promoted to casting opportunities in a number of ways. Firstly, each artist has a photo and contact details in the *Spotlight Directories*, which are printed once per year. Their details are also held on an Artists' Records telephone database, so that casting/production professionals know immediately where to call when they want to get in touch.

Additionally, every performer is promoted on *Spotlight Interactive* (**www.spotlight.com**) – the online version of *Spotlight*. Here, casting professionals can search performers' details according to very specific criteria. For example: "Show me all actors with black hair, aged 35-40, who can speak French and play the guitar."

Performers can upload showreels, voice-clips and additional photos to enhance their online CVs, which is a far quicker and more cost-effective way of promoting themselves than sending out endless copies to casting directors and agents in the post. Artists are also issued with a pair of unique PIN numbers which allow them respectively to access their CV whenever they wish – keeping credits and skills up-to-date – or to email to others, a link to their *Spotlight* CV.

Spotlight is also used on a daily basis by production professionals sending out casting briefs to agents. In 2005, a weekly average of 130 casting breakdowns was sent out via The Spotlight Link, with more than 26,000 artists submitted weekly for an average of 400 individual roles, spanning a wide variety of TV, film, theatre, radio and commercial work. This makes The Spotlight by far the busiest casting service in the UK. The Spotlight is also due to launch a job information service which goes directly to artists themselves: see the website for the latest details.

The Spotlight also publishes *Contacts* every November. This is a directory of companies and invidiuals working across TV, film, stage and radio and costs £11.50.

To join The Spotlight, visit the website **www.spotlight.com**, call 020-7437 7631, or email **info@spotlight.com** for application forms. Entry is strictly limited to professionally trained and/or professionally experienced performers, and applications are always vetted.

Actors Inc.

FREEPOST NATW1128, Bracknell RG12 9BR
tel (01344) 449314
email info@actors-inc.co.uk
website www.actors-inc.co.uk

Casting breakdowns are delivered instantly via email, in addition to a weekly jobs newsletter which is sent every Friday afternoon. Members can search the website for information, advice and details of workshops and events, as well as the Jobs Notice Board which is updated daily. Actors' details are included in a fully searchable database which is accessible to casting professionals. Voice samples can also be incorporated. Actors Inc. also posts job advertisements for casual temporary work geared towards resting actors.

The monthly membership fee is £5 with an option of a 5-week free trial period. Recent auditions posted on the website have included Phoenix Dance Theatre Company, a UK tour of *Starlight Express*, and a singer for a funk group.

Castcall

106 Wilsden Avenue, Luton LU1 5HR
tel (01582) 456213 *fax* (01582) 480736
email info@castcall.co.uk
website www.castcall.co.uk

Details of casting information services

Established in 1986. Information service is available by email or fax, with regular updates throughout the week. Actors should be professionally trained or experienced to be included. Charges £34 for 12 weeks. Allows actors to put subscriptions on hold if required and to resume when appropriate. Also offers general advice and free image scanning.

Sources of casting breakdowns have included: Crocodile Casting, Casting Unlimited, Panto People, Layton & Norcliffe, Pippa Ailion, Jayne Collins, Vital Productions, the BBC, Greenwich Films, Nina Gold and many repertory theatres.

Casting Call Pro

website uk.castingcallpro.com

Casting Call Pro offers free standard membership to all professional actors. Actors fill in a registration form to join a central database and be alerted to acting jobs which match their skills.

To join Casting Call you must either have graduated from an NCDT-accredited drama course, be a current member of Equity, or have performed in at least 3 professional shows (extra work and non-speaking parts do not count) and have a professional, b&w headshot. If you don't meet one of these criteria your profile will be automatically removed from the site. Casting Call is not an agency; its standard service is entirely free and it does not take commission.

Casting People Ltd

PO Box 26736, London SW17 7FW
fax 020-8672 9738
email info@castingpeople.com
website www.castingpeople.com

Details of casting information services

Established in 2000. Information service is only available online, with emails circulated to subscribers on a daily basis. Charges £7.50 per week, £35 for 6 months and £55 for a year. Also produces a free CV for members.

Sources of casting breakdowns have included: film schools, TIE and profit-share companies.

CastNet Ltd

20 Sparrows Herne, Bushey, Hertfordshire WD23 1FU
tel 020-8420 4209 *fax* 020-8421 9666
email admin@castingnetwork.co.uk
website www.castingnetwork.co.uk
Key contact Alyson Sharron

Details of casting information services

Established in 1997. The information service is only available online, with information circulated to members by email every day. Casting information is tailored to the exact requirements of the actor; if an actor is not interested in working in certain areas, such as student films or TIE, they will not be sent details of those projects. Information is also filtered according to the skills and physical characteristics of actors. When suitable casting opportunities do arise, CastNet will send actors free text messages and emails. Actors may make a submission for any project via the website or by telephone; CastNet will then send their CV, headshot and a covering letter to the casting director.

All reproductions of photos and postage costs are included in the subscription charge. Sends a weekly summary report by email, detailing every production for which actors have been submitted. CastNet receives casting breakdowns from a range of clients including Fringe theatre, mainstream films and TV.

Details of actors' Internet directories

All actors must meet the following criteria to be included: have graduated from an NCDT-accredited course; have a minimum of 3 professional theatre, film or acting credits (does not include extra or drama school work); be able to use 1 UK-based accent to a 'native' standard; have full membership of Equity (or be eligible); have a professionally taken b&w publicity photograph; and be at least 18 years old at the time of application.

Admits new members every week. The CastNet Directory is distributed to more than 1500 casting directors and production companies. Actors' CVs are included on the website, with instant messaging facility for casting directors to contact them by email or text message. Will also include up to 4 photos, showreel and voice demo at no extra charge. Registers personal domain name for each actor and points it directly to their online CV. Anyone can access online directory, but printed directory is only available to industry professionals. Members' online details are updated daily and the book is updated on a quarterly basis. For details of current clients (both actors and casting professionals), consult the website.

The weekly subscription rate is £6.50 and includes all the services listed above.

Castweb

7 St Luke's Avenue, London SW4 7LG
tel 020-7720 9002 *fax* 020-7720 3097
email castweb@netcomuk.co.uk
website www.castweb.co.uk
Key contact Rodney Watney

Details of casting information services

Established in 1999. Information service is available online only, with emails being circulated to subscribers every day. The monthly subscription rate is £15.95. Has received casting breakdowns from approximately 150 casting directors and more than 600 production companies. The service is designed for The Spotlight members only; new applicants are entitled to a 7-day free trial with no further obligation.

Equity Job Information Service (JIS)

Guild House, Upper St Martin's Lane, London WC2H 9EG
tel 0870-901 0900

website www.equity.org.uk

Launched in 1999, this service is now available 24 hours a day via the Equity website in addition to the low-cost telephone service. It is available free of charge to all members. The service provides details of job opportunities in the wide range of fields in which Equity members work. Users of the service can search for jobs in acting, singing, dance, variety, light entertainment and circus, and in non-performance work such as stage management. All the work listed is at least reasonably paid (although not necessarily at full Equity-agreed rates), thoroughly checked for accuracy, and the job-providers checked for their record of fair treatment of employees.

The effectiveness of this service relies on members only submitting themselves for suitable roles. Too many unwanted applications will make employers reluctant to advertise on JIS in the future, and reduce the number of opportunities for actors.

Mandy.com

website www.mandy.com

Posts casting calls for actors for film. See entry under *Publications, libraries, references and booksellers* on page 309.

Performers Directory

PO Box 29942, London SW6 1FL
tel 020-7610 6699 *fax* 020-7736 6088
email admin@performersdirectory.co.uk
website www.performersdirectory.co.uk
Directors Antonia Stratton, Clive Stevens

Details of casting information services

Established in 1995. Information is available online only, with emails being circulated to subscribers every day.

Details of actors' Internet directories

Includes actors' CVs, photos and voice samples in the online directory, which is accessible only to casting professionals. Members' details are updated as and when requested. Clients have included: Disney, the BBC, Bollywood producers, Universal, the National Theatre and the Royal Shakespeare Company. Has also suggested actors for *The Bill*, *Jonathan Creek*, *Jerry Springer the Opera* (West End), Walkers Crisps commercials, Selfridges' Fashion Show and various club events.

Annual subscription rate is £37 and includes all services listed above.

Production & Casting Report (PCR)

PO Box 100, Broadstairs, Kent CT10 1UJ
tel (01843) 860885 *fax* (01843) 860899
website www.pcrnewsletter.com

Details of casting information services

Established in 1968. Available in print and online, *PCR* is a weekly newsletter which carries details of casting and crew opportunities in film, television and theatre. Information is checked carefully by staff and always comes directly from the production company or casting director – *PCR* never prints second-hand information. A free telephone information line is also available to help subscribers track down casting leads. Every week, dozens of opportunities are featured from such sources as Hubbard Casting, David Grindrod, Lucinda Syson, Birmingham Stage, Red Shift and Jeremy Zimmermann, among others. Low-budget film, voice-over, pop promo, commercial, corporate video and Fringe casting calls are also featured.

The subscription rate is £29.00 for 5 weeks, but other rates are available for varying time periods – for example, £260 for a year.

Other publications include:
• *Filmlog*: lists feature films in pre-production and development, with details of studios, locations, key people and addresses (£11.50 for 3 months, £40 for 12)
• *Theatre REPort*: covers the regional repertory scene and other selected venues with a 'Fringe Focus' section (£11.50 for 3 months, £40 for 12)
• *Who's Where*: an A-Z of contacts (free to new subscribers, £8 to other subscribers)
• *Who's Where of Casting Directors*: a quick reference to UK casting directors (£2)
• *Who's Where USA*: A-Z listing of casting directors in America (£7)
• *Castingdex*: A-Z names and addresses of advertising agencies, voice-over specialists, freelance casting directors and production houses (£18)

SBS (Script Breakdown Services)
16 Sidmouth Road, London NW2 5JX
tel 020-8451 2852

SBS is a publication giving casting breakdown information. It is circulated to agents *only*. It is not available to individuals.

Shooting People
email contact@shootingpeople.org
website www.shootingpeople.org
Co-founders Cath LeCouteur, Jess Search *Casting Editor* Andrew Robertson

Shooting People allows thousands of people working in independent film to exchange information via a range of daily email bulletins, including a daily UK Casting Bulletin. This allows actors to discuss their craft and receive casting calls from directors, producers and casting directors. Shooting People's overall membership is currently more than 34,000. Actors can create a public casting profile as well as

getting significant discounts off key film products and services.

Part-membership allows subscribers to receive email bulletins only, and is free. Full membership costs £20 per year and entitles users to a range of other services. See entry under *Publications, libraries, references and booksellers* on page 311 for further details.

The Stage
47 Bermondsey Street, London SE1 3XT
tel 020-7403 1818 *subscriptions tel* (01858) 438895
email newsdesk@thestage.co.uk
website www.thestage.co.uk
Managing Director Catherine Comerford *Editor* Brian Attwood

Established in 1880. A weekly newspaper for professionals in the entertainment industry, with some job advertisements for actors.

Talent Circle
website www.talentcircle.co.uk

Details of casting information services
Established in 2003. Provides a free online casting information service and resource where emails are circulated to members on a daily basis.

Details of actors' Internet directories
Directory is open to all actors free of charge and is publicly accessible. Casting directors can select level of experience required at sign-up, as no minimum criteria are demanded of members. Members can update their own entry (to include photograph, voice sample and CV) at any time.

Talent Spot UK
1 Colindale Avenue, Edgware Road, London NW9 5DS
tel 0845-045 4111
email info@talentspotuk.com
website www.talentspotuk.com
Key contact (for new members) Dean Ezekiel

Details of casting information services
Established in 2002. Casting bulletins are posted online each week and can be accessed for £6.99 per month at the time of writing. Produces a montly newsletter and circulates related special offers to members.

Details of actors' Internet directories
Admits new members on a daily basis at a charge of £6.99 per month, or £59.99 per year at the time of writing. Actors' CVs, photos and voice samples are posted on the website. "Specialises in providing networking and lifestyle services for the talent and entertainment industry."

UK Theatre Network

PO Box 3009, Glasgow G60 5ET
tel 0870-760 6033 *fax* 0870-760 6033
email editor@uktheatre.net
website www.uktheatre.net

Details of casting information services

Established 2001. Casting information is circulated to members daily, by email. In addition the company offers webmail, website hosting, reviews, contacts and listings of what's on. All services are provided free of charge. New members should contact **uktheatre-daily@getresponse.com**.

Details of actors' Internet directories

This service is available free of charge to all active performers aged 16 upwards. Members' details are available publicly and can be updated by the actor at any time. Actors can include their CV, photograph and voice sample on the directory.

Getting the most from your photographs

Angus Deuchar

When searching for actors, most casting directors or directors start with a pile of photographs. Their time is limited, so they really only want to see the people who stand a chance of being right for a part – and the picture will be a vital part of their decision-making process. It's important therefore, to ensure that the photographs you use are as good as they can possibly be.

Have a flick through *Spotlight*. As well as being compulsive entertainment for any actor, it can be a great way to decide what works and what doesn't. If *you* were the casting director, who would (and wouldn't) you see? Try it for different types of production: a musical, a Shakespeare play, a TV drama. You may be surprised at the assumptions you make based on the photographs.

I'm going to look at what makes a good actor's photograph; help you think through how to choose a photographer; and discuss how you can get the best results from a photo session. Here is a list of, in my opinion, some important qualities to look for in a good headshot. It should be:

● **Honest.** This to me is the key to a good actor's photograph. Decisions at interviews are often largely made in the first few seconds, so it's important that the person who walks through the door is the person they saw in the photograph. If an actor looks different in some way, the interviewer's first reaction may well be disappointment. Which can't be a good start!

● **Well lit.** The face and hair should be well lit. If there are excessively bright areas or shadows on the face, the photo is probably not doing the actor any favours.

● **In focus.**

● **A good connection with the eyes.** These are possibly the most important feature, as these are what we generally look at first. We make a connection with the eyes. They should be well lit, in focus, looking *at* the camera and not squinting. They should also be 'alive' and not glazed over.

● **Well framed.** Ideally just head and shoulders. Not too close up, as it can look a bit overbearing. Likewise, not too far away as the face becomes too small.

● **Nothing 'tricksy'.** No fake hand-gestures, and certainly no props!

Can't I just get my friend to take some pictures in the back garden? Well, you could (in fact, some do). But what kind of image of yourself would that portray? You can always see such pictures in *Spotlight* – the actor looking awkward, squinting into the sunlight or the picture out of focus. Again, if you were the casting director, would you consider that actor to be serious? There's no point in cutting costs here. Decent photographs can more than pay for themselves.

Finding a photographer

Assuming you've decided to employ a photographer, how do you find the right one? Professional photographers are not all alike. Some who may be fantastic at, say, press or fashion, may not be good at actors' portraits. It's important that the photographer knows the business of Acting. There are countless listings of specialist actors' photographers – in publications like this one; as adverts in *Contacts*; or on posters in Actors Centres; but the style of photographs, and the ability of the photographers, are as varied as the prices and packages. It is therefore essential to check out their work for yourself. Have a look at their website if they have one, or at least try to see several different examples of their work.

Don't make a choice based solely on price. The amount a photographer charges is not necessarily an indication of how good (or bad) they are. Wherever possible, make your decision about a photographer based mostly on the *work* they produce, rather than how much they charge. It's important ultimately that you get the best possible photographs.

Find out the following:

● **Studio or natural light?** Studio light is easier to standardise and can be used at any time of the day or night and during any weather. It can be made to flatter someone, but won't necessarily show what they will look like in 'real life'. I prefer natural light, as I believe it to be generally more honest. Good natural light can still show someone at their best, but it won't deceive. It can also be more relaxing for the subject to be outside for the session. Casting directors often prefer natural light as it gives a better indication of who is actually going to walk through the door.

● **Film or digital?** Digital technology has moved on to such an extent that the quality of either format is comparable. Digital tends to produce a cleaner, less grainy image *and* you can check the results as you go along. It is essential however, that whoever is preparing the final photograph knows how to convert the image into a good-quality black and white print, with decent contrast and without loss of detail. This takes a reasonable amount of skill and know-how.

● **How much do they charge?** Does that include VAT? If relevant, you may want to ask about concessions for students.

● **How many photos do I get?** Find out how many photos will actually be taken at the session and how many different, finished 8x10 prints you can choose.

● **How will I view my proofs?** Some photographers will put your proofs onto a website enabling you to view them blown up on the screen. You may prefer a paper contact sheet, which, although much smaller to view, is more portable. If you want both, you may need to pay extra – so ask.

● **How long until I see my proofs?** Websites can often be published the same day as the session, while a paper contact will usually need to be produced and posted, so will take a few days. Some photographers will show you pictures on a computer straight away. This can be useful as a guide, but you probably shouldn't try to make final decisions without a bit of time to think.

● **How long will it take until I get my finished prints?** Try to get an indication of how long you should expect to wait after placing your final order. Hopefully, no more than a few days.

● **Do I get a CD?** As well as the prints, a few electronic versions of the final photos are extremely useful. They can be used on a website, to send a submission via email, to send to The Spotlight, to print out yourself, or to act as the master-copy for your 'repros'. Find out if the photographer will provide you with a few different versions on a CD, and if it's included in the price.

The session itself

Here are some important things to prepare before – or think about during – your photo session.

- **Your 'look'.** Do you want to appear neutral or as a particular 'type'? For instance, earrings (on men especially) or other piercings, may limit you to modern or even 'alternative' characters. A formal jacket might suggest a business person or MP. Any of these looks may be fine, as they can make you 'ideal' for a particular type of role – but it's likely that that's all you'll ever be seen for while using that photograph! You decide – it really depends upon how you are marketing yourself.
- **Make-up and hair.** Preferably little or no make-up, but certainly no more than you would wear normally, day to day. Some photographers provide a 'hair and make-up' service but I would strongly discourage actors from using this. Don't confuse actors' portraits with having a glamorous photo to stick on top of the piano! If someone else prepares you, you're unlikely to look like the 'normal' you and it may be difficult to recreate that look in the future. Likewise, if you're planning to get a new hairstyle before your session, do so several days in advance to give you a chance to get used to it.
- **What to wear.** Concentrate on the neckline. Wear something you feel comfortable in, but avoid distracting patterns or logos. Most colours are fine, and black often works well. Bright white can affect the exposure so is less helpful. A jacket of some sort for some of the photos can often work well. Jewellery can be distracting so is usually best avoided.
- **Facial expression.** A big smile is often great for musicals or front-of-house pictures, but for other casting purposes it can seem a little over the top. Any kind of 'emoting' can seem over-earnest or, worse, corny. I tend to favour a good neutral expression with 'spark' behind the eyes. A kind of a relaxed, open look with the smallest hint of a smile.

Ultimately, photographs play an important part in helping you get a foot in the door. But once you've been called for the interview, it's over to you ...

Angus Deuchar trained as an actor, during which time he subsidised his grant by taking photographs of his fellow students. When he left drama school in 1987 he soon realised that this was an ideal way to make a living between jobs! He pursued both careers for the first seven years, but has continued with just the photography since then. A website showing examples of his work can be seen at **www.actorsphotos.co.uk**.

Photographers and repro companies

Good photographs (and quality reproductions of same) are an essential part of an actor's professional armoury and there is absolutely no point in trying to scrimp on them. ('A picture is worth a thousand words.')

Your photograph is a silent, static, two-dimensional representation of vocal, mobile, three-dimensional you. It should be of your head down to your shoulders, reasonably stylish and well produced without necessarily being too glamorous. It should look natural and have life, energy and personality – especially in the eyes, the most important part of your face. Your photo should say, 'Here I am; I know who I am; I'm OK with who I am.' Also, it is very important that your photograph really looks like you when you arrive for interview.

Crucial to the final result is finding a good photographer (a) who understands the world that the end result is intended for and (b) with whom you can work well. In the listings that follow, you'll find a wide range of prices and deals. It is important to research as many of these as possible, without making cost your prime consideration. Ask friends, teachers and your agent (if you have one) for recommendations, and check through *Spotlight* and websites to see samples of work. Read the details under each listing to get a 'feel' for who might produce the 'goods' for you. Once you have a shortlist of possibilities, phone each with appropriate questions (what to wear, studio or natural light, and so forth) in order to get a sense of how well you might be able to work with him/her. Only *after* you've done all this research should cost be a consideration. Even then, a cheap deal could mean that the photographer will spend much less time, and take fewer photographs, than a more expensive one. You might be lucky with the former, but you'll enhance your chances of getting really good results with the latter.

Note Allow plenty of time for this research. Also, bear in mind that as the deadline for *Spotlight* gets nearer, photographers become increasingly busy and it becomes more difficult to book a session.

Copyright

Under the Copyright, Designs & Patents Act 1988, the photographer owns the copyright on any new photograph, even though you've already paid for the original. That means that you have to obtain his/her permission to have new photographs reproduced in *Spotlight* or anywhere else. Your photographer may be happy to approve such reproduction, but may not be so happy about any cropping or other alterations: you must get permission if you intend to do this. The other important new legal requirement is that your photographer must be credited on any reproduction of the original. Some of the repro companies are now doing this as a matter of course.

Repros

You could get subsequent, high-quality reproductions done by your photographer or by someone else nominated by him/her. However, these will be expensive. The specialist repro companies can do this significantly more cheaply with minimal loss of quality. Once again, check with others about the quality (and service and reliability) of individual companies before taking costs into consideration. It is also useful to overestimate the number of copies you might need over the lifetime (generally, about two years) of your chosen photograph – because (a) you'll almost always find that you underestimate that number in the first place, and (b) you can take advantage of cheaper unit costs.

Note It is often preferable to send a 10x8in (25x20cm) photograph for submissions; however, good-quality 'jpegs' (around 400 pixels wide) inserted into your CV are becoming increasingly acceptable. If you're planning to email a CV containing your photograph, make sure that the total document size is not more than about 200kb, or you'll end up clogging up the casting director's mailbox. (Most image editing software will have a menu option to allow you to reduce the image size if required.)

10 out of 10 Photography

Forest Hill Business Centre, Clyde Vale, London SE23 3JF
tel 0845-123 5664
email pauljneed@hotmail.com
website www.pauljneed.co.uk
Photographer Paul J Need

Charges £80 for a photo shoot. Photographer has a background in theatre, film, concert and television lighting, as well as teaching lighting design at RADA. Offers digital photography.

Abacus Photography

156 Kingshill Road, Swindon SN1 4LN
tel (01793) 537257 *mobile* (07966) 551909
fax (01793) 344208
email nickabacus@fsdial.co.uk
website www.abacus-photography.co.uk

Services & rates

Charges £50 for a photo shoot which includes photographer's fee and studio and equipment costs. This does not include the cost of any 10x8in (25x20cm) prints which are priced at £5 each. A variety of packages is also available. Offers discounts for group bookings. Digital photography is also available at a charge of £50 for 24 images. Always advises clients to bring a change of clothing and discuss their requirements before the shoot.

Work portfolio

Established in 1992. Photographs can be viewed on the website. Has taken publicity shots for around 20-30 actors.

The Actor's One-Stop Shop

54 Belsize Avenue, Palmers Green, London N13 4TJ
tel 020-8888 7006 *fax* 020-8888 9666
email info@actorsone-stopshop.com
website www.actorsone-stopshop.com

Services & rates

Charges £195 for a photo shoot which includes photographer's fee, studio and equipment costs, processing of 1 b&w 36exps, contact sheet and 4 10x8in (25x20cm) prints. Offers 10% discount for group (2 or more) bookings. Offers both pre-shoot and post-shoot consultancy, advising clients on clothing, image projection and selection of photos, as well as general advice on how best to promote themselves within the acting industry.

Work portfolio

Established in 1997. Photographs can be viewed on the website or in person by visiting the studio. Has taken publicity shots for around 250 actors. Recent clients include: Tagforce (an actor register), Omar Khan, Samuel L Jackson, Anna Friel and Rachel Watkins.

Ric Bacon

30 Fortis Green Road, Muswell Hill, London N10 3HN
mobile (07970) 970799
website www.ricbacon.co.uk

Services & rates

Charges £280 for a photo shoot which includes photographer's fee, processing of 2 b&w 36exps, 6x4in print of every shot (rather than a contact sheet) and all negatives. Offers reduced rates to students. Shoots in a very relaxed manner, in natural light or studio, and offers advice on all aspects including clothing and make-up. Prints are ready to view in 1 hour and will be reviewed with the client, offering advice on selection of images for self-promotion if needed. Happy to look at old photographs of the client that they particularly like or dislike. Works with film or digital.

Work portfolio

Established in 1999. Photographs can be viewed on the website and has a comprehensive portfolio at The Spotlight offices. Has taken publicity shots for around 500 actors.

Chris Baker

tel 020-8441 3851
email chrisbaker@photos2000.demon.co.uk
website www.chrisbakerphotographer.com

Service & rates

A photographer since 1974, charges £245 for a photo shoot including 2 b&w 36exps, contact sheets and 5 10x8in prints. Student rate is £210 for the same service. Also offers a digital service at the same rates for around 60 digital images and 5 retouched photos on disk. Shoot takes place in a studio or outdoor location – only the outdoor location is wheelchair-accessible.

Work portfolio

Examples of work can be seen on the website or at The Spotlight offices. Has taken photographs for several thousand actors, among them Sally Anne Triplett, Julia Sawalha, Kim Medcalf, Todd Carty, and David Griffin. "Informality and relaxation are the secret to a successful photo session. Clients get 2 hours, giving us time to have a cup of tea and discuss their requirements.

I recommend that clients look as natural as possible, and discourage the use of make-up artists as it's far more important that my subjects look 'like themselves'! Tops should be unfussy and typical of the wearer. If in doubt, a simple black shirt is hard to beat.

I shoot digital or film, depending on the preference of my client, and am happy to advise on which will work best for you. I retouch the final selected images whether they're prints or on disc, eliminating stray hairs, spots or anything else that distracts from the real you.

I've been doing this for 30 years and am a full-time professional – not someone just dabbling as a sideline! My work is of the highest technical quality, but more importantly reflects the personality and potential of my clients; that's why so many of them come back."

A Beautiful Image Photography & Design (Debal Bagachi)

31 Church Walk, Brentford, Middlesex TW8 8DB
tel 020-8568 2122 *mobile* (07956) 861698
email debal@abeautifulimage.com
website www.abeautifulimage.com

Services & rates

Charges £150 for a photo shoot which includes photographer's fee, studio and equipment costs, processing of 2 b&w 36exps, contact sheets and 2 10x8in (25x20cm) prints (either hand- or digitally printed). Occasionally offers 10% discount for clients sharing a shoot. Digital photography is also available

at the same rate; images can be supplied on CD Rom. Also able to provide website and print publicity. Advises actors to keep make-up simple for b&w photography and wear unfussy, unpatterned tops with simple necklines.

Work portfolio

Established in 1994. Photographs can be viewed on the website and at The Spotlight offices. Has taken publicity shots for around 50 actors. Recent clients include: Elizabeth Alexander, Patrick Regis, Fiona Marchant and Diane Cracknell.

Sheila Burnett

email sheilab33@ntlworld.net
website www.sheilaburnett-photography.com

Charges £200 + VAT (£180 + VAT for students) for a photo shoot. Includes 4 10x8in prints. Offers digital photography. Photos taken in studio. Works with 170 actors per year, including Imelda Staunton, Catherine Tate, David Soul, Paul Freeman, Simon Pegg, Anita Harris and Jackie Clune.

"I always chat on the phone to give advice if it is needed. When my client arrives, I always have a chat with a cup of tea to see what he or she would like – that's if they are not sure."

Robert Carpenter Turner Photography

The Studio, 62 Hemstal Road, London NW6 2AD
tel 020-7624 2225
email robert@carpenterturner.co.uk
website www.carpenterturner.co.uk

Services & rates

Charges £225 for a photo shoot which includes all costs and at which at least 70 high-quality digital photographs are taken. These are then displayed on the web with a private code for only the customer and agent to view. From these are ordered 6 pictures, which are corrected and improved as required, or changed to high-quality b&w images before being written to CD Rom. 2 10x8in prints are included. Time allowed for photoshoot is 2 hours.

Work portfolio

Established in 1960. Portfolio of photographs, latest rates and other information can be viewed on the website. He has taken publicity pictures for many hundreds of actors and performers over the past 40 years. Studio contains a grand piano for use by musicians.

Charlie Carter

tel/fax 020-8222 8742
email charlie@charliecarter.com

Established in 1998. Charges £375 for photo shoot including 3 x 36exps films and 4 x 10x8in prints. Starting to work with digital, but still mostly film.

Sessions are in a home studio on the second floor, so not wheelchair-accessible. Examples of work can be viewed at The Spotlight offices. Clients include: Kenneth Branagh, Tom Hollander, Roger Allam, Emily Blunt, Isla Blair, Eve Best, Harry Enfield, Eleanor Bron, Martin Shaw, Kerry Condon, Paul McEwan, Serena Evans and Charlie Condou – as well as agents Ken McReddie Ltd, Rebecca Blond Associates, Conway van Gelder, ICM, PFD, Hamilton Andrews, Elinor Hilton, and Billboard.

Advises clients to start preparing several days beforehand – timing haircuts so that there's time for it to grow out a little, cutting out alcohol, drinking lots of water, taking exercise – so that skin and eyes will look their best. Advises women to check their diaries to make sure that menstrual hormones are not likely to interfere with their mood or appearance on the day. Don't just turn up without thinking about how you're going to look your best. "By the time you add together the cost of photographs, repros and *Spotlight*, it's a lot of money – so protect your investment by doing everything you can to feel as good about yourself as possible. The session will take as long as it takes."

Andrew Chapman

198 Western Road, Sheffield S10 1LF
tel 0114-266 3579 *mobile* (07779) 861921
email andrew@chapmanphotographer.co.uk

Services & rates

Charges from £125 for a photo shoot, which includes all photography and computer labour charges, studio and equipment costs. The session includes 40-70 photos, b&w and/or colour) which are transferred to the computer; you may select any or all images and these are written to a CD for you to take away for immediate use. Prints and contacts are available (e.g. a 10x8in is £12) if required, but in most cases images are emailed directly to *Spotlight* and for repros. Also gives clients a 'release note' so that photos can be used for PR, repros, agents, *Spotlight*, etc.

Black and bright colours work well in b&w, and higher necklines are usually better than low: "I always advise people on an individual basis. Ideally, allow about 2 hours for the session."

Work portfolio

Has more than 2500 actors on database as well as singers, dancers, models, martial artists and others. Clients are from agents across the country; they include: Philippa Howell, Sharron Ashcroft, Jane Hollowood, Liberty Management, David Daly, Direct Line, and Act One. "Qualified member of BIPP, SWPP, BPPA with over 20 years' experience."

John Clark Photo Digital

tel 020-8854 4069
email clarkdigital@btopenworld.com

website www.johnclarkphotography.com

Services & rates

Charges £145 per hour for digital photography.

Work portfolio

Established in 1982. Photographs and advice can be found on the website. Has taken publicity shots for around 500-600 actors. Recent clients include: actors represented by Roger Carey & Associates, Collis Management, Crawfords, Rossmore and Langford Associates.

Grant David Photography

34a Manor Park Road, London N2 0SJ
tel 020-8815 9789
email grantdavidphotos@tiscali.co.uk
website www.grantdavid.co.uk

Services & rates

Charges £100 for a photo shoot: this includes all fees and studio costs, processing of 2 b&w 36 exps, contact sheets and 2 10x8in prints. Offers the same package to students at the reduced rate of £60. Digital photography is also available at the same rates and will enable the client to leave the session with all the shots on CD. Advises clients to use very little make-up and to bring 3 tops, keeping patterns and jewellery to a minimum. Post-production includes air-brushing on blemishes/spots for free.

Work portfolio

Established in 1992. Photographs can be viewed on the website and at The Spotlight offices. Has photographed around 600 actors, with recent clients including: Janine Smith, Amanda Fulton and Luke Long.

Angus Deuchar

PO Box 25799, London SW19 1WQ
tel 020-8286 3303 *mobile* (07973) 600728
email angus@actorsphotos.co.uk
website www.actorsphotos.co.uk

Services & rates

Charges £225 for a photo shoot taken in natural light. Price includes approximately 120 shots to choose from, a website or contact sheets to view the proofs, 4 finished b&w 10x8in prints and a CD for best-quality repros. Student deals available. Telephone or email for further information.

Work portfolio

Photographs and "advice to actors seeking photographs" can be viewed on the website. Has more than 15 years' experience of taking actors' portraits, and used to be an actor himself. Recent clients include: Neil and Adrian Rayment (*The*

Matrix Reloaded), Anne Reid, James Bolam, John Alderton, Richard Lumsden.

DF: Photographer

Studio 29-31, Stafford Road, Brighton BN1 5PE
tel (01273) 549967 *mobile* (07958) 272333
email info@image2film.com
website www.image2film.com
Photographer David Fernandes

Has worked as a photographer since 1995, and has taken photographs for roughly 500 actors. Charges £85 for a photo shoot including 2 10x8in prints, using either film or digital. Special 'shared sitting' rates are available to students. Works in a studio, outdoors or in the client's home. The studio is not wheelchair-accessible. Advises clients to "bring a selection of tops with different necklines. Not too 'fussy'. A black top always works well".

Elliott Franks Photography Services

PO Box 29801, London SW19 1WW
tel 020-8544 0156 *mobile* (07802) 537220
email frankse@aol.com
website www.elliottfranks.com

Services & rates

Charges £85 (reduced from £160 for *Actors' Yearbook* readers) for a 2-hour photo shoot in Wimbledon studio with 5 changes of tops, 3 rolls of medium-format film (high quality) with 12 shots per roll, and 3 contact sheets. Usually shoots a fourth roll for fun which is supplied on CD Rom. One-off 10x8in (25x20cm) prints are priced at £11.31 each; repros of 12 10x8in prints are priced at £1.85 each.

Work portfolio

Established in 1997. Photographs can be viewed on the website and at The Spotlight offices. Has taken publicity shots for more than 300 actors. Recent clients include: actors represented by ICM and Wendy Lee Management Ltd.

James Gill

6 Hanover Gardens, London SE11 5TL
tel 020-7735 5632

Services & rates

Charges £85 for a photo shoot which includes photographer's fee, studio and equipment costs, processing of 1 b&w 36exps, contact sheet and 2 10x8in (25x20cm) prints. Increases to £130 for 2 rolls and 4 10x8in prints. Extra 10x8in prints are priced at £12.50 each. Advises actors to keep it simple. Will take photos of actors as they wish to be presented, and will take all the time necessary.

Work portfolio

Established in 1992. Photographs can be viewed at The Spotlight offices. Has taken publicity shots for around 500 actors and in addition has more than 40 years' experience of working in theatres, both in casting and as company manager.

Charles Griffin Photography

PO Box 36, Deeside, Chester CH5 3WP
tel (01244) 535252
email studio@charlesgriffinphotography.co.uk
website www.charlesgriffinphotography.co.uk

Services & rates

Photographer since 1993. Charges £149 for photo shoot, which includes processing of 2 x 12exps medium-format (high-quality) rolls, contact sheets and 2 10x8in prints. (Offers this service at £92.83 if client mentions *Actors' Yearbook* when booking a 2-hour session. Student rates are also available – telephone or email for information.) Digital service also available at the same rates, although an extra charge is made to provide the images on CD. Uses studio and outdoor location (both wheelchair-accessible).

Work portfolio

Examples of work can be seen on the website. Has taken photographs for around 250 actors, among them Raquel Lee, Gemma Gray, Sam Gratton, Paul Draw. "Sessions are conducted in a relaxed atmosphere: I will shoot images of actors as they wish. Clients should bring a variety of plain tops: those with high neckline or v-neck in red, grey or black are most useful."

Claire Grogan

12 Calverley Grove, London N19 3LG
tel 020-7272 1845
email claire@clairegrogan.co.uk
website www.clairegrogan.co.uk

Services & rates

Charges £180 for a photo shoot which includes photographer's fee, studio and equipment costs, processing of 2 b&w 36exps, contact sheets and 4 10x8in (25x20cm) prints. Special packages offered to actors are: 1 36exps plus 2 10x8in prints for £90; and 2 36exps plus 4 10x8in prints for £140. Offers full advice on clothing and make-up when a booking is made. Sessions last 90 minutes in a relaxed atmosphere. Aims to take photographs reflecting the actor's personality.

Work portfolio

Established in 1991. Photographs can be viewed on the website and at The Spotlight offices. Takes around 300 publicity shots for actors each year. Recent clients include: Zehra Naqvi, Steve McFadden, Stephen Tompkinson, Jonathan Kydd and Heather Pearce.

Jamie Hughes Photography

mobile (07850) 122977
website www.jamiehughesphotography.com/
headshots

Charges £250 for a digital photo shoot (including fee,
approx. 100 images supplied on CD Rom, and
retouching and processing of 3 10x8in prints).
Additional prints (including retouching) are available
for £10 each. Uses a studio and outdoor location,
both of which are wheelchair-accessible. Examples of
his work – featuring some very famous faces – can be
seen on the website.

Remy Hunter

Flat 2, 9 Belsize Park, London NW3 4ES
tel 020-7431 8055 *mobile* (07766) 760724
email remy_hunter@hotmail.com
website www.remyhunter.co.uk

Established in 2003. Charges £180 for a photo shoot
including 2 36exps films, contacts sheets and 4 10x8in
prints. Offers a student rate of £140 and shared
sessions are available, splitting the cost (and the
number of rolls/prints) between 2 people. Also offers
digital photography sessions at £140 (£100 for
students). Uses a studio that is not accessible to
wheelchair users. Has taken photographs for roughly
500 actors, including (with Spotlight View PIN in
brackets): Freya Dominic (2211-8979-4470), Gemma
Harvey (0615-5643-5877), Julie Pollin (0459-1206-
3661), Jonathan Grace (aka James Dillinger – 2517-
8940-4373). Advises clients to "bring a range of tops
with varying necklines. Black tends to come out best,
so a couple of black tops are a good idea. For make-
up, bring what you'd wear from day-to-day".

Neil Kendall Photography

19 Oakfield Court, Haslemere Road, London N8 9RA
tel 020-8340 4214 *mobile* (07776) 198332
email mondo.nez@virgin.net
website www.neilkendallphotography.com

Services & rates

Charges £135 for a photo shoot which includes
photographer's fee, studio and equipment costs,
processing of 3 b&w 36exps, contact sheets and 2
10x8in (25x20cm) prints. Uses both studio and
natural light.

Work portfolio

Photographs can be viewed on the website. Has taken
publicity shots for around 30-35 actors. Recent clients
include: Vanessa Earl, Peter Ackyroyd, Graham
Norton and Liberty X.

L B Photography

36 Nutley Lane, Reigate, Surrey RH2 9HS
tel (01737) 224578 *mobile* (07885) 966192
email labowerman@hotmail.com

Services & rates

Charges £95 for a photo shoot which includes
photographer's fee, studio and equipment costs,
processing of 1 b&w 36exps and poster-sized contact
sheet. Price increases to £140 for 2 sheets. All photos
are taken in natural light. 10x8in (25x20cm) prints
are priced at £7 each. A discounted rate of £90 for 1
roll is available to students. Advises simple make-up
(none for men) and plain tops. The photographer
herself is a working actress and is happy to provide
guidance on the phone.

Work portfolio

Photographs may be viewed at The Spotlight offices
or in *Contacts*. Has taken publicity shots for over
3000 actors. More than 50 agencies send clients on a
regular basis, including Narrow Road, Evans & Reiss,
Brown and Simcocks, Hatton & McEwan and CAM.

Steve Lawton

134 Randolph Avenue, Maida Vale, London W9 1PG
mobile (07973) 307487
email stevelawton2@msn.com
website www.stevelawton.com

Services & rates

Charges £200 for a photo shoot. This includes all fees
and studio costs, processing of 2 b&w 36exps and A3-
sized contact sheets. This package is offered to
students at the reduced price of £170. 10x8in prints
are priced at £5.50 each and digital photography is
also available. Advises clients not to bring patterned
tops; fitted t-shirts and v-necks in blue, grey or black
are most effective.

Work portfolio

Established in 2001. Has taken photographs for more
than 700 actors and is recommended by Curtis
Brown, International Artistes, Vincent Shaw
Associate, AIM, Janice Tildsley Associates, CAM and
Shane Collins. A full portfolio and price information
is available on the website.

Murray Lenton

5 Brief Street, Camberwell, London SE5 9RD
tel 020-7733 6769 *mobile* (07941) 427458
email murray@theatrephotography.co.uk
website www.theatrephotography.co.uk

Services & rates

Charges £150 for a photo shoot; this includes all fees
and studio costs, processing of 2 b&w 36exps and
enprints. 10x8in prints are priced at £12 each. Will
offer a discount to students, negotiable at the time of
booking. Also offers digital photography at the same
rates, but advises against this unless prints are needed
instantly. With film it is possible to have both a low-
resolution CD for viewing and email use, and a high-

resolution CD (for an extra fee). Advises clients to bring in previous headshots and any examples of preferred style.

Work portfolio

Established as a general photographer in 1983, and as a theatre photographer in 1997. Recent clients include: Tamsin Greig, Simon Dormandy, Luke Sorba and Wild Girls.

MAD Photography

200 Gladbeck Way, Enfield EN2 7HS
tel 020-8363 4182
email mad.photography@ukonline.co.uk
website www.mad-photography.co.uk

Services & rates

Charges £110 for a photo shoot which includes photographer's fee, studio and equipment costs, processing of 1 b&w 36exps, contact sheet and 2 10x8in (25x20cm) prints. Offers discounted rate of £55 to students (no prints, 36 contact sheet only). Extra 10x8in prints are priced at £11.75 each. "Hair and make-up should be natural. Bring 4 tops in any colours: one v-neck, one collar, one t-shirt and one jacket. No white!"

Work portfolio

Established in 1998. Photographs can be viewed on the website and in *Contacts*. Has taken publicity shots for 3000-4000 actors. Recent clients include: Shane Richie, Michael Knowles and Jessica Wallace.

Casey Moore Photography

125 Hartington Road, Vauxhall, London SW8 2HB
tel 020-7498 0461
email casey@caseymoore.com
website www.caseymoore.com

Services & rates

Charges £195 for a photo shoot to include all fees and studio costs, processing of 4 medium-format b&w 15exps films, contact sheets and 2 10x8in prints. Offers a 30% discount to students. Digital photography is also available at the same rates.

Work portfolio

Established in 2001. Photographs can be viewed on the website at The Spotlight's offices and advertisements in *Contacts*. Has taken photos of around 25 actors.

Adam Parker

1 Hoxton House, 34 Hoxton Street, London N1 6LR
mobile (07710) 787708
email portraits@apfolio.com
website www.apfolio.com

Established in 1996. £150 for a photo shoot; includes 4 10x8in prints. Offers special rates for students. Photos taken outdoors, in clients' homes and in the studio. Offers digital photography. Works with 150 actors per year.

"I provide a service using high-end digital equipment in which great care is taken over lighting to ensure the highest quality. Make-up artists, hair and fashion stylists can be arranged."

Michael Pollard Photographer

Manchester-based
tel 0161-456 7470
email info@michaelpollard.co.uk
website www.michaelpollard.co.uk

Services & rates

Charges £75 for 20 frames or £110 for 40 frames indoors or outdoors. Shoots medium format, not 35mm. 10x8in (25x20cm) prints are priced at £8.50 each; student rates are available. A 10x8in print is included in the sitting price for 2 or more actors booking and arriving together. Digital photography is also available. Uses studio, outdoor locations and client's home (different rates apply). The studio is not wheelchair-accessible. Encourages actors to bring 2-3 tops, ranging from lighter to darker tones. "Tops should be simple and comfortable with either a round or v-neck. Hair needs to be tidy, but do not go to the hairdresser the day before to have it cut. Make-up should be simple and sparing — men can use a simple foundation or cover stick if needed. Women should not use lip liner or lipstick that is too dark or too red. The main thing is to be positive and be prepared. Think how you want to look and how you don't want to look. Enjoy it and be yourself!"

Work portfolio

Established in 1982 (1993 for actors). Photographs can be viewed on the website and at the Northern Actors Centre, Manchester. Has taken publicity shots for around 2500 actors. Recent clients include: Sarah Jayne Dunn (*Hollyoaks*), Peter Ash (*Fooballers' Wives*), Georgina Mellor (*Coronation Street*) and Jody Latham (*Shameless*).

David Price Photography

69 Pevensy Road, London SW17 0HT
mobile (07950) 542494
email info@davidpricephotography.co.uk
website www.davidpricephotography.co.uk

Charges £120 for 1 roll of 36exps, or £160 for 2 rolls. This includes processing of 2 or 4 10x8in prints (respectively). Offers a digital photography package for £120. Offers student rate of £100 for digital or 1 roll of film, and £140 for 2 rolls. Uses studio and outdoor locations, and is also able to visit the client's home with a portable studio. Examples of work can be seen on the website. Recent clients include: graduates from Bristol Old Vic Theatre School, LAMDA and RAM; clients from VocalWorks International; and commissions from The Actors Workshop Youth Theatre.

"Your headshots should be a fair and flattering portrait of the professional that you are. I aim to achieve this in every sitting. Professional make-up is available and I'm always happy to give advice on all aspects of your publicity shots. A showreel service is available for all actors with limited TV experience through business partners, November Films. Prices are subject to change – see website for current package prices."

Howard Sayer Photography
Kingston-on-Thames
mobile (07860) 559891
email howardsayer@btconnect.com
website www.howardsayer.co.uk

Services & rates

Charges £125 for a photo shoot which includes photographer's fee, studio and equipment costs, processing of 2 b&w 36exps and contact sheets. 10x8in (25x20cm) prints are priced at £6 each. Also offers digital photography at the same rates. Actors can preview images during the photo shoot. Includes a CD containing 10 best images as part of a student package. Images can be reproduced in either colour or b&w.

Work portfolio

Established in 1987. Photographs can be viewed on the website. Has taken publicity shots for around 1000 actors. Recent clients include: actors working for the BBC, Teddington Studios and Benedict Productions.

Catherine Shakespeare Lane
The Monsell Stores, 43 Monsell Road, London N4 2EF
tel 020-7226 7694
email bankual@madasafish.com

Services & rates

Charges £380 for a photo shoot which includes photographer's fee, studio and equipment costs, processing of 2 b&w 36exps, contact sheets and 4 10x8in prints. Offers a student package for £250 (1 roll of 36 and 2 10x8in prints). In special circumstances this package is also available to non-students for £270. Uses natural light inside and favours a natural look. "My aim is to show my clients at their most interesting."

Work portfolio

Established in 1975. Photographs can be viewed at The Spotlight offices and in *Contacts*. Has taken publicity shots for more than 2000 actors.

Peter Simpkin
17 Grove Avenue, London N10 2AS
tel 020-8883 2727
email petersimpkin@aol.com
website www.petersimpkin.co.uk

Services & rates

Charges £305.50 (inclusive of VAT) for a photo shoot which includes photographer's fee, studio and equipment costs, processing of 3 b&w 36exps, contact sheets and 6 10x8in (25x20cm) prints. Student price is £246.75 inclusive of VAT.

Work portfolio

Established in 1973. Photographs can be viewed on the website. Has taken publicity shots for thousands of actors. Recent clients include: actors represented by ARG, Curtis Brown, Christina Shepherd Associates; students from Webber Douglas, LAMDA, Mountview and Bristol Old Vic.

ToShoot.Com (formerly 7LA Studios)
42b Medina Road, London N7 7LA
tel/fax 020-7686 2324
mobile (07960) 726957
email hi@toshoot.com
website www.toshoot.com
Photographer Carlos Cicchelli

Services & rates

Established in 2003. "Actors' and models' headshots and portfolios done on digital of film. Prices vary depending on the job. Email for quotation."

Steve Ullathorne
39c Tavistock Road, London W11 1AR
tel 020-7985 0810
email steve@ullapix.com
website www.ullapix.com

Services & rates

Charges £150 for a digital photo shoot; this covers all fees and studio costs, contact sheets and 5 10x8in prints. Will offer a discount to students, negotiable at the time of booking. All clients receive an online contact sheet with a web address that they can pass on to their agent. Prior to the shoot, clothing and locations will be discussed with the client on the telephone. All photos are retouched in Photoshop to remove any blemishes plus any other light retouching required by the actor. Email proofs are sent of each chosen image. Rather than specifying a number of images, prices are dictated by duration of the shoot, which is 1.5 hours. Actors usually end up with more than 100 shots to choose from.

Work portfolio

Established in 2001. Photographs can be viewed on the website and at The Spotlight offices. Has taken photographs of 70-100 actors with recent clients including: Barry Cryer, Amelia Warner, Ed Byrne, Shazia Mizra, Annette Ekblom and Ronnie Golden. Agency recommendations include: Brown and Simcocks, Sally Hope Associates, Conway van Gelder and Jonathan Altaras.

Robin Watson
tel 020-7833 1982
email robin@robinwatson.biz
website www.robinwatson.biz

Services & rates
Charges £180 for a photo shoot. This includes all fees and studio costs, processing of 2 b&w 36exps, contact sheets and 2 10x8in prints. Digital photography is also available and costs an additional £10 for transferring images to CD. Advises clients to keep clothing simple with unfussy necklines and mid-tone single colours, not black and white. Make-up should also be simple, perhaps a little eye-liner and some foundation powder if the complexion is shiny.

Work portfolio
Established in 1994. Photographs can be viewed on the website or in *Spotlight*. Has taken photographs of hundreds of actors, with recent clients including: Rula Lenska, Christopher Timothy and Finty Williams.

Robert Workman
32 West Kensington Mansions, Beaumont Crescent, London W14 9PF
tel 020-7385 5442
email bob@robertworkman.demon.co.uk
Studio address: Studio 103B, The Business Village, Broomhill Road, London SW18 4JQ
website www.robertworkman.demon.co.uk

Services & rates
Charges £250 plus VAT for a photo shoot which includes photographer's fee, studio and equipment costs, processing of 2 b&w 36exps, contact sheets, 5 10x8in (25x20cm) prints and a CD for digital submissions to casting directors and *Spotlight* online. Special student portrait session costs £150 plus VAT.

Work portfolio
Photographs can be viewed on the website. Has been taking around 200 publicity shots for actors every year for 20 years. Recent clients include: Caroline Quentin, Jude Law and Philip Middlemiss.

REPRO COMPANIES

Denbry Repros Ltd
27 John Adam Street, London WC2N 6HX
tel 020-7930 1372 *fax* 020-7925 0183
email denbrys@vfree.com

Charges £7.20 plus VAT for the initial copy of a b&w negative. Can also reproduce from a digital image.

Repros of a b&w 10x8in (25x20cm) are priced as follows:
£26 for 25, £47.05 for 50, £89.05 for 100, £178.10 for 200, £200.40 for 250 and £393.75 for 500.

Repros of a b&w postcard print are priced as follows:
£19.50 for 25, £36.30 for 50, £66.05 for 100, £132.10 for 200, £133.75 for 250 and £234.95 for 500.

All prices exclude VAT. Colour repros are also available at an increased price.

Other services include a studio for casting photography, downloading images from the Internet and supplying images on CD in colour or b&w.

Denman Repros
Burgess House, Main Street, Farnsfield, Nottinghamshire NG22 8EFF
tel (01623) 882272 *fax* (01623) 882272

Initial scan of a 10x8in (25x20cm) print is free. Can also work with CDs, negatives and transparencies.

Repros of a b&w 10x8in are priced as follows:
£28 for 25, £39 for 50, £48 for 100, £64 for 250 and £88 for 500.

Repros of a b&w postcard print are priced as follows:
£24 for 25, £31 for 50, £34 for 100, £39 for 250 and £64 for 500.

Offers additional 20% free to actors including students.

Note Please ring for latest prices.

Faces Prints
10 Avondale Road, Carlton, Nottingham NG4 1AF
tel (0115-847 5640 *fax* 0115-847 5640
email facesprints@ntlworld.com

Initial scan is free.

Repros of b&w 10x8in are priced as follows:
£28 for 25, £43 for 50, £56 for 100, £73 for 200, £85 for 250 and £99 for 500.

Repros of a b&w postcard print are priced as follows:
£22 for 25, £32 for 50, £37 for 100, £49 for 200, £59 for 250 and £85 for 500.

Will also provide a free gloss on quantity of 25, free photo retouch, free design on 'z-cards', and email proofing and free name/caption insertion.

Moorfields Photographic Ltd
2 Old Hall Street, Liverpool L2 2NY
tel 0151-236 1611 *fax* 0151-236 1677
email kev@moorfieldsphoto.com
website www.moorfieldsphoto.com

Charges £10 for initial scan of 10x8in print.

Repros of b&w 10x8in are priced as follows:
£25 for 25, £45 for 50, £80 for 100, £150 for 200, £180 for 250 and £300 for 500.

Repros of a b&w postcard print are priced as follows: £8.75 for 25, £14 for 50, £22 for 100, £38 for 200, £45 for 250 and £81.75 for 500.

Will dispatch prints the next day when working from disc, email or negative, and 2 days later when working from print. Special delivery costs from £6.50.

Profile Prints

Courtwood Film Service Ltd, FREEPOST TO55, Penzance, Cornwall TR18 2BF
tel (01736) 365222 *fax* (01736) 350203
email people@courtwood.co.uk
website www.courtwood.co.uk

Charges £2.75 for initial scan of a 10x8in (25x20cm) print. Can also work with negatives in colour or b&w, slides or digital images.

Repros of a b&w 10x8in are priced as follows: £29.75 for 24, £49.25 for 50, £89.25 for 100 and £187.25 for 250.

Repros of a b&w postcard print are priced as follows: £19 for 50, £32.50 for 100 and £72.50 for 250.

Specialises in smaller self-adhesive photos suitable for CVs.

Visualeyes Ltd

11 West Street, Covent Garden, London WC2H 9NE
tel 020-7836 3004 *fax* 020-7836 8780
website www.visphoto.co.uk

Charges £5 plus VAT for the initial scan of a b&w 10x8in (25x20cm) print.

Repros of a b&w 10x8in (25x20cm) are priced as follows:
£22 for 25, £39 for 50, £70 for 100, £140 for 200, £165 for 250 and £300 for 500.

Repros of a b&w postcard print are priced as follows:
£15 for 25, £27 for 50, £50 for 100, £100 for 200, £120 for 250 and £225 for 500.

All prices exclude VAT. A 10% discount is available to members of Equity and/or The Spotlight, and to students.

Other services include free transmission of the image to *Spotlight* and free blemish clean-up.

Voice-overs

Bernard Shaw

'Voice-overs' are very buoyant, with more available work than ever before and more opportunities for 'newcomers' to find their place in this exciting world. The voice business is strictly that – business! Learn how it works and learn how to earn your place within it. Focused and targeted effort will be rewarded; a business-like approach might well open lucrative doors for you.

You are unlikely to make any professional progress without a 'demo' CD showing the quality and range of your natural voice. Newcomers are more likely to be booked for their 'own' voice than for their ability to perform a multitude of doubtful regional accents and unrecognisable impressions. Given that very few employers actively seek a 'versatile voice', there is little point in marketing yourself under this rather old-fashioned banner. Identify your natural strengths and market them in places where they might be in demand. Demonstrate, briefly, what you can do well.

Historically, actors had interminable voice-demo cassettes designed to be all things to all listeners, with many of them containing up to 20 tracks ranging from Shakespeare to coffee ads. These are no longer acceptable: anyone sending out such a thing will be regarded as out of touch with current reality and will not be taken seriously. The medium of choice is now CD and the preferred running length is three minutes! The BBC and other companies producing Radio Drama will tolerate eight or nine minutes. Voice Actors (the cool way to describe yourself) should have a master CD containing a range of material which can be 'picked and mixed' to suit a variety of recipients. Home computers make it very easy to create a different content and running order for each CD produced.

This master CD ought to be produced and recorded by one of the few reputable studios specialising in this work and should contain only genuine material. Do not write your own scripts or rely on 'spoofs'. Your recordings need to sound as professional as the real thing and should be complete with music and sound effects. For work voicing ads you should have three or four 30-second commercial scripts such as hard sell, soft sell, real person, and 'character' voice. For documentary work, you could have a two-minute 'wildlife' read together with a contrasting piece 'explaining' a concept or process. This material is easily found as there are thousands of scripts available on the Internet.

If you have specialised knowledge (perhaps from a former profession or hobby), you should include a recording demonstrating this. Computer games are now bigger business than Hollywood films so it would be wise to record some material for this market. You might be possessed of the deep tones of a Super Hero or discover the ability to voice cutesy cuddly toys – or both! The voices required for these games are similar in range and extremes to those heard in cartoon films and children's stories. Games companies do not normally cast on the strength of a 'demo' CD, but professionally produced recordings might well get you a place on their audition list.

Radio Drama producers expect to receive a CD containing four pieces no longer than two minutes each. The material should be one 'classical', one 'contemporary', one 'comic' and a poem. The ideal is to produce a balanced listen which gives an overall glimpse of your range and abilities, but without straying into the trap of attempting to demonstrate your skill (or lack thereof) in producing large numbers of accents and characters. Be yourself!

Your CDs should be well and imaginatively labelled and packaged. Ideally they should be as impressive, interesting and memorable as anything bought in a high street shop. Full-time Voice Actors spend much time, effort and money on designing their packaging. It should be memorable enough for the CD to be found from within a pile of 100 others long after the name of the artist has faded from memory. Use a memorable 'catch phrase' with a coordinated picture or design. You cannot rely solely on the quality of your voice, nor on the open-mindedness of employers and agents, to get you a hearing. High-quality, imaginative packaging is essential. The software which helps you produce it is to be found in most modern computers; if it is not resident on your desktop, it can be bought for only £10.

There are two ways to find work. You can either ask an agent to put you on their books, or you can contact the employers yourself. Before a voice-over agent agrees to represent you, it will be necessary for you to demonstrate that you can provide them with a new income stream. The primary function of any agent is to make money for themselves; it is a waste of time and effort to approach agents who already represent someone who sounds the same as you. Agents have Internet sites where their clients' voices can be heard; visit these sites, and if you hear someone sounding like you, don't waste your time and energy on a pointless phone call. When you find someone who does not already represent what you have to offer you will be able to call them from a position of strength and confidence.

Many successful Voice Actors choose to represent themselves. They enjoy the challenge of running what is essentially a 'Small Business' from home. Their core reference book is Mr Osborne's *Voice-Over Contacts*, which is a most useful and reasonably priced publication containing details of a large number of employers and other important contacts within the voice business. Full details can be found at **www.voiceovercontacts.co.uk**. Newcomers may be surprised to find their phone calls meeting with a much warmer response from the advertising agents than from the voice agents.

Treat the voice world in a professional and business-like manner, and it will, at the very least, listen to what you have to offer. Always present yourself as a 'solution' rather than a 'problem' and, above all, try to match your strengths to their needs. Good luck!

Bernard Shaw is the author of *Voice-Overs: A Practical Guide* – a popular training manual on both sides of the Atlantic. He runs regular Voice-Over and Radio Acting workshops at the Actors Centres in London, Birmingham, Manchester and Newcastle. He works full time in the voice business and is one of the most experienced producers of voice demos in the world. His website, **www.bernardshaw.co.uk**, contains further advice and interesting links.

Showreel and voice demo companies

The rapid growth in recording technology has seen an explosion of such companies over the last decade. There has also been a significant increase in the amount of (sometimes contradictory) advice offered on content, length, and so on. Much of this 'advice' is available on individual companies' websites, where you can sometimes also find samples of their work.

Voice demos have been around for several decades, and a good one could attract the attention of a voice agent. However, the world of voice-overs is hard to break into and so a quality-produced demo is very important. Showreels are a more recent innovation and are not yet the 'norm' – some agents and casting directors won't watch them. However, a good one might just tip the balance in your favour.

If you intend to travel down these routes, check the details (including pricing) of each possible company and the quality of their work. You should also assess whether the financial investment(s) involved could produce sufficient return. These additional 'calling cards' need to be of broadcast quality and professionally packaged to have any impact. As with photographers, it is very important to research as thoroughly as possible before committing your meagre funds. Is there a real possibility that one (or both) will enhance your chances of acting work?

Note It is very important that you have permission from the copyright-holders of any material that you intend to use. Some companies will help with this.

The Actor's One-Stop Shop

First Floor, Above the Gate Pub, Station Road, London N22 7SS
tel 020-8888 7006 *fax* 020-8888 9666
email info@actorsone-stopshop.com
website www.actorsone-stopshop.com
established 1997

Showreel services

Offers broadcast-quality, professionally packaged reels. Scenes are crafted like film/TV excerpts rather than being 'audition pieces'. Actors can choose either monologue or dialogue scenes, in any combination they wish. A single scene (monologue) reel costs £175 (including final copy in box DVD presentation).

Also edits reels from past work at a cost of £60 per hour; clients sit-in on the edit and receive the finished product the same day. A typical edit lasts 2.5 hours and includes full archiving of material so that the reel can be easily and affordably updated in the future. Actors can order DVD, CD Rom or VHS copies. The company also supplies 'streamed' copies for agency and The Spotlight websites.

Recommended by several agents, The Spotlight, CastNet and CastingCall Pro. See website for reel samples.

Crying Out Loud

Covent Garden, London
tel 020-7379 0177 *mobile* (07796) 266265
email simon@cryingoutloud.co.uk
website www.cryingoutloud.co.uk
Key contact Simon Cryer
established 1999

Voice-demo services

Supplies scripts for actors to use if desired. Charges £210 to produce a voice demo from scratch; this includes studio and equipment costs, recording and editing of new material, scripts and 1 CD copy – there are no hidden extras. CDs usually last around 12 minutes and consist of commercials (5 minutes); narrative (2 minutes); documentary (1 minute); drama (4 minutes). Charges £40 per hour to produce a voice CD from existing material only – this includes editing existing recordings and encoding them for use on CD. Additional CDs are priced at £4 each.

A special package is available to students at a cost of £150. This covers the pre-selection of material, 1.5 hours of recording time, up to 2 hours of editing and 1 master CD with full-colour artwork and case.

Each client (excluding students) meets with the director, Marina Caldarone, or with Simon Cryer for an hour-long consultation to select the best material for their voice. Clients should aim to leave 7 days between their consultation and their recording so that they have sufficient time to prepare.

Recent clients have included: Simon Day (PFD), Beth Cordingly (PFD), Elizabeth Norman (voice of BT 1571), Evan Roberts (CAM), Andrew Castle, Annabel Croft, Jonathan Edwards CBE and Sally Gunnell OBE.

Opus Productions Ltd

9a Coverdale Road, London W12 8JJ
tel 020-8743 3910 *fax* 020-8749 4537
email into@opusproductions.com
website www.opusproductions.co.uk
Key personnel Claire Bidwell, Neil Wilkes

Established in 1999. Working mainly in computer media production. Specialising in video and audio encoding, DVD authoring, video editing, graphic design and website design. Will edit, produce and encode video and DVD showreels for actors.

The Reel Deal Showreel Co.

6 Charlotte Road, Wallington, Surrey SM6 9AX
tel 020-8647 1235 *fax* 020-8395 8091
email info@thereel-deal.co.uk
website www.thereel-deal.co.uk
established 2003

Showreel services

Charges £185 to produce a showreel from existing material only; this includes 2 VHS copies. Average duration of showreel is 5-6 minutes. DVD authoring is £40 and includes design of on-screen menu, packaging and 1 DVD. Extra copies are priced at £2.20 per VHS and £4 per DVD. Will offer a reduced rate of £30 per hour for actors who do not have a lot of material.

Recent clients include: James McAvoy (PFD), Aden Gillett (Conway van Gelder) and Matt Berry (KAL Management).

Replay Film & New Media

199 Piccadilly, London W1J 9HA
tel 020-7287 5334
email showreels@replayfilms.co.uk
website www.replayfilms.com
established 1991

Showreel services

Although Replay can record presentations and performances from scratch, for most clients the task is to produce a carefully constructed compilation of highlights from existing TV and film performances. Advises that the correct selection and juxtaposition of these clips is essential, and it is therefore vital that clients sit-in on the editing process to ensure that they are happy with the final result. Most showreels last 4-7 minutes. Will supply scripts if requested, but does not organise for copyright clearance.

As most showreels take around 4 hours to edit, Replay has put together the following package for a fixed fee: up to 4 hours in the edit studio with the editor (digitising existing clips from VHS, capturing digitised clips onto an Avid editing suite, editing the captured clips and inserting titles where required); and 3 VHS copies. The digital master tape will be archived at 2 sites. Exact prices are available on application only. Discounted rates are available to actors, presenters, students and non-commercial theatre companies. Overtime (anything over 4 hours) is charged at approximately 50% of the commercial editing rate.

Recent clients include: Donald Standen, Julian Hanshaw, Justine Waddel, Michael Mears, Patsy Kensit, Shared Experience Theatre Company and Vicky Johnson.

Bernard Shaw

Horton Manor, Canterbury CT4 7LG
tel (01227) 730843
email bernard@bernardshaw.co.uk
website www.bernardshaw.co.uk
established 1980

Voice-demo services

Supplies scripts for actors to use if desired. Charges £350 to produce a voice demo from scratch. This includes the company fee, studio and equipment costs, recording and editing of new material and 1 CD copy. Normally produces voice demos lasting 6-15 minutes but this varies according to the wishes and ability of the client. Charges £60 per hour to produce a voice demo from existing material only. Advises actors to reproduce CDs with a specialist duplicator for a cheaper price.

Material is selected in consultation with the client, either from their resources or from an extensive in-house library. Does not organise for the copyright clearance of material chosen. Recent clients include: actors from major agencies and broadcasting organisations such as BBC Radio Drama. Has also provided services for actors at the Royal Shakespeare Company, the Royal National Theatre and various drama schools. Work can be heard on The Spotlight online casting directory or on **www.excellentvoice.co.uk** (select Casting Couch and then Lyndham Gregory or Dian Perry).

Bernard Shaw is a voice-over tutor at the Actors Centres in London, Birmingham, Manchester and Newcastle (see entries under *Short-term and part-time courses* on page 24) and is the author of *Voice-Overs, a Practical Guide* published by A & C Black Publishers Ltd. He specialises in directing and producing tapes for BBC Radio acting.

Advises actors to attend classes at the Actors Centres (see entries under *Short-term and part-time courses*), research voice-over websites, talk to people working

in the field and study *Voice-Overs*. Also see
www.voiceovercontacts.co.uk for a recommended
publication.

Showreelz

1 Thornhill Court, Crescent Road, London N8 8AY
mobile (07885) 253477
email brad@showreelz.com
website www.showreelz.com
established 1998

Showreel services

Supplies scripts for actors to use if desired. Charges
approximately £250 to produce a showreel from
scratch. This includes the company fee, studio and
equipment costs, recording and editing of new
material and 2 VHS copies. Rates are set at £50 per
hour of filming and £30 per hour of editing.
Normally produces showreels lasting 5 minutes.
Charges £30 per hour to produce a showreel from
existing material only. Sends clients to Stanley
Productions for duplicate VHS copies. Will offer 10%
discount to actors quoting *Actors' Yearbook*.

Offers free consultation to actors, ascertaining the
roles they are most likely to be cast in and selecting
pieces accordingly. Does not organise for copyright
clearance of material used.

Recent clients include: Marjie Campie (*Brookside*),
Rosemary Ashe (*Les Miserables, Phantom of the
Opera*), Alex Ferns (*Eastenders*) and Chris Gascoyne
(*Coronation Street*).

Advises clients to do the edit on paper before arriving
– i.e. rewind tapes, reset the video counter and make
a note of minutes and seconds as each clip starts. This
saves the client a lot of time and money. Clients with
a good range of clips can opt for a montage sequence
at the beginning, consisting of 10 2-second clips of
extreme close-ups, big gestures, etc. These would be
put together, sound-stripped and a music soundtrack
overlaid. This is often an effective strategy because,
even if a viewer does not watch the tape through, they
have at least a glimpse of the range on offer.

Voice-demo services

Supplies scripts for actors to use if desired. Charges
approximately £150 to produce a voice demo from
scratch. This includes the company fee, studio and
equipment costs, recording and editing of new
material and 2 CD copies. Rates are set at £30 per
hour. Normally produces voice demos lasting 3
minutes. Will offer 10% discount to actors quoting
Actors' Yearbook.

Offers free consultation suggesting different scripts
and looking at any pieces brought by the client.
Advises on the suitability of all pieces chosen. Recent
clients include: Helen Bang and Siobhan McGill.

Silver-Tongued Productions

Sidcup, Kent
tel 0870-240 7408 *fax* 0871-242 7288
email contact-us@silver-tongued.co.uk
website www.silver-tongued.co.uk
established 1996

Voice-demo services

Charges £25 per hour for studio time plus £75 for
editing, mixing and producing the CD.

The company supplies commercials which are
selected in consultation with the actor, and which
take into consideration the age and style of the voice
while showing as much variety as possible. Readings
are chosen by the actor and can be taken from plays,
books, poetry or prose, but should allow for variety.

Silver-Tongued Productions always retains the master
of the CD voice reel and will produce copies as
needed. A better rate is given for bigger orders: 1 CD
is £5; 2-5 CDs are £4.50 each; 6-10 CDs are £4 each;
and 11 or more CDs are £3.50 each. Publicity photos
can be included on the front cover for an extra charge
of 50p per CD.

Recent clients include: Philip Glenister, Robert
Duncan, Judi Shekoni, Pip Torrens, Guy Masterton
and Jeremy Edwards. Agency recommendations
include: Ken McReddie Ltd, Hobson's Voices and
Foreign Voices.

Take Five

37 Beak Street, London W1F
tel 020-7287 2120 *fax* 020-7287 3035
email info@takefivestudio.co.uk
website www.takefivestudio.co.uk
Key contact Charlie Lort-Phillips
established 1995

Showreel services

Charges £70 per hour for filming and £45 per hour
for editing (this includes all studio and equipment
costs). VHS copies are priced at £6 each, DVDs at £13
each and CDs at £6 each. Discounts are offered for
bigger quantities.

A script consultation is held with each actor,
preferably 7 days prior to filming. Scenes can be shot
in the studio or on location and benefit from
professional direction, lighting and cameramen. Most
showreels last around 5 minutes. The company
advises actors who are sending in existing material
only to cue scenes on the tape or to have the
timecodes written down to speed up the capturing
process.

Recent clients include: Siobhan Hewlett (Hamilton
Hodell), Harry Eden (ICM), Lee Ingleby (Conway
van Gelder) and Tim Barlow (Paul Becker).

Between engagements
or 'How to survive until the next job'
Andrew Piper

All the articles in this publication are one person's perspective, and as such need to be tested against your own judgement and experience. None more so than this article, because like you I'm just another actor. Unless you are extremely lucky (or have only just graduated from drama school), you will have experienced periods of unemployment, and will have come up with your own strategies for coping with this. What follows is a collection of thoughts on what seems *to me* to be good advice for any actor finding themself temporarily out of work. I don't always follow this advice, but it does seem to help when I do. Not everything here will be right for you, but I hope that some of it will make it easier for you get to your next acting job with body and soul intact.

I've grouped the suggestions in this article under four headings: stay solvent, stay employable, stay visible, and stay sane. Do all these things, and acting work should never be too far away.

Stay solvent

It might surprise you that I start with this, but money problems can make all the other suggestions in this article so much more difficult to do. Your first priority as an actor, therefore, is to make sure that you can keep a roof over your head, food in your fridge, and your creditors (if any) off your back. Without these things it becomes next to impossible to present a confident face to the world, to maintain the self-esteem and self-belief that one needs to survive as an actor, and to plan any strategies for finding acting work. So with this in mind – and recognising that this is the least interesting bit – here are my tips for staying solvent:

• Save money when you are working. That's not easy if you're on the sort of wages that are common in theatre, but the more money you can save now, the more you'll have in reserve for the lean times ahead. Even if you have another job to go onto after this one, the chances are that there will be a few weeks between finishing one and starting the next, and that's time that potentially no one will be paying you for. Remember too that your wages will rarely have tax deducted from them, which means you will need something in reserve for when the tax bill is due. If you're doing a long theatre job, then consider setting up a standing order to a savings account – even if you only manage to save a few pounds a week, you may be glad of it further down the line.

• Live as cheaply as you can. The lower your overheads, the more you can save and the longer you can ride out a period of reduced income.

• Make your extravagances count. If you've been frugal during the week, then you can treat yourself at the weekend. Something as simple as making your own sandwiches may save you enough to pay for a meal out in as little as a few days. Skipping two or three nights of drinking and clubbing could even save you enough for a weekend in Paris or Prague.

• Probably the largest single expense you'll have is your rent or mortgage. This is generally unavoidable – unless of course you're still living with your parents – but if you're someone who does a lot of touring then it can be frustrating to be paying some exorbitant London rent for a room that you're hardly using. (Mortgages are different, of course, because at least you'll own something at the end of it.) However, for most people, having a place you can call home and look forward to returning to is immensely important. Whether or not you feel there are savings that can be made – by subletting while away, say, or moving to a cheaper area – don't leave it out of the equation when looking at keeping your costs down.

● Get a second phone. That might seem perverse, but if you don't have access to a landline (for example, if you're away from home) and you have an 'anytime minutes' contract with one of the operators, get yourself an old mobile phone (eBay is quite good for this) and put a pay-as-you-go SIM card in it for making all your off-peak calls. That way, all your long off-peak chats to your mum/partner/best mate won't eat up your valuable 'anytime' minutes. Shop around, and see what will work out best for you.

● Have a look at **www.moneysavingexpert.com**. Run by the journalist Martin Lewis, this website has all sorts of tips and tricks for making your money go further.

● Get a 'day job'. Even Kenneth Tynan's actor mistress once observed that "the worse thing about not working is having to work". And ain't that the truth! Sooner or later most of us – especially those who work mostly in theatre – have to knuckle down to something unrelated to acting in order to pay the bills. What form this takes will depend on your particular skills – it doesn't hurt to get some IT and typing skills under your belt when you get the chance – but consider office temping, waiting and bar work, call centres (one company, RSVP – **www.rsvp.co.uk** – is even run by actors), and shop work, for starters. If you have a teaching qualification, then you could make some slightly better money by doing 'supply teaching', covering for full-time teachers in case of illness. Many of the photographers listed in this book are (or were) also working actors – although this shouldn't be regarded as a way to a quick buck: those guys have worked long and hard at perfecting their skills. One of the most popular ways of earning cash between jobs is promotions work. Have a look at these sites for more information: **www.stuckforstaff.com**, **www.turns.net**, **www.ays.co.uk** and **www.promojobspro.com** (this last one is run by the same people as CastingCall Pro). I've even turned my hand (if that's the right expression) to artists' life-modelling, although I've never managed to earn more than beer money for it. One friend of mine took a course in massage in order to have another string to his bow – although I'm generally cautious about diverting money, time and energy into training that won't actually improve your employment prospects as an actor. One job I wouldn't recommend is 'extras' work, unless what you aspire to be is a background artiste. Never did a job so eloquently encapsulate the meaning of the phrase, 'so near, and yet so far'. (*Note* This point doesn't really belong in the 'stay solvent' section, but while we're on the subject of day jobs: Never take a job that you couldn't in good conscience drop at short notice to go to an audition or accept acting work, unless you want to be stuck doing that job for the rest of your life. Alas, almost any job that one could describe as 'interesting' or 'stimulating' also requires a degree of commitment. For this reason, most 'day jobs' that are suitable for actors are tedium incarnate. I wish it were otherwise. I really *really* wish it were otherwise.)

● Don't sit around waiting for the money to run out. If you have managed to bring in a good chunk of money, paid off your debts, set aside enough for your tax bill, had a holiday, and still have enough left not to need to work for a while ... get a part-time job. Your savings will last you longer, and instead of turning into a couch potato (which can happen frighteningly quickly) you will retain a sense of yourself as a working, earning person. By all means do the other things you never had time to do before – take classes, see films, visit galleries, meet friends – but do these on your days off.

● Know what State Benefits you're entitled to, and claim them (and if you're not entitled, then don't). I loathe and detest signing on – Jobcentres are rarely beacons of hope and optimism – and will do almost any kind of work rather than do so, but if you do find yourself without work then it is worth taking the time to fill in the forms. Talk to Equity if the Jobcentre is sniffy about you signing on as an actor.

● Act quickly if you do get into financial trouble. If you find yourself borrowing money for your day-to-day living expenses (including using credit cards) or to make payments on existing debts, then you have a problem, and one that must be dealt with as soon as possible. This is too big an issue for me to tackle here, but you can get advice on dealing with unmanageable debts from your local Citizens' Advice Bureau, **www.citizensadvice.org.uk** (in Scotland this is **www.cas.org.uk**); from National Debtline, **www.nationaldebtline.co.uk** or *tel* 0808-808 4000; and from Consumer Credit Counselling Service, **www.cccs.co.uk** or *tel* 0800-138 1111. Whatever you do, don't be tempted to take out another credit card (even a zero interest one) or another loan unless this will allow you to cancel your existing credit cards, because you'll spiral even further into debt. Never *ever* touch those 'debt consolidation', 'one-easy-payment' companies that advertise on daytime TV – they just want to make money out of you and will make matters worse. It doesn't have to be scary – you have more power than you might think. The banks want their money back, of course, but would much prefer to accept a repayment plan which fits your budget, than go through the expense of legal proceedings when they know you can't pay.

Stay employable

This is perhaps the easiest section for me to write, because, well, we all know it all already. But do we do it? No, neither do I. Time and money are big factors, of course, but so are simple inertia and laziness. "Chance," said Louis Pasteur, "favours the prepared mind," so here's my list of best practices, given in the knowledge that I rarely get around to more than a handful of them when I'm between jobs.

● Brush up your skills – voice, dance, singing, stage combat, Shakespeare, Alexander Technique, etc. – and learn new ones. There are various places in London and around the country that offer professional-grade courses in these, such as the London and Manchester Actors Centres, The City Lit, and the drama schools and universities listed in the Short Courses section of this book. Get a driving licence if you don't already have one.

● Keep fit, whatever your preferred means is. Sport, gym, dance, swimming, walking, martial arts – even regular bouts of acrobatic sex would do it, I suppose, as long as afterwards you didn't light up or order pizza. Aerobic fitness is most important as this provides both the stamina to get through an evening's performance (I'm talking theatre now, not sex) and the twinkle in the eye that says 'energy and vitality' to an auditioning director. (A twinkle that says 'regular, acrobatic sex' is probably quite effective too, in certain circumstances.)

- Brush up on your audition speeches and songs. How would you feel if, at short notice, you got an audition for a great job, and you fluffed it because your speeches or songs were rusty or tired? It's happened to me; don't let it happen to you.
- Read plays. Not because you *should* (because if that's your reason then you won't) but because they're *fun*. A lot of us came into this business because we loved plays – it's odd that once we got here we read so few of them. (Keep an eye open for good audition speeches while you're reading.)
- Keep in touch with what's going on in the business. Read *The Stage*, talk to your agent and your actor friends, keep your finger on the pulse. Know which theatres have new artistic directors, which casting directors are working on which projects, and so on. Remind yourself that you're an actor – not always easy after the umpteenth week of photocopying and filing in some awful temp job.
- Watch TV. And no, I don't mean *Trisha* or *Cash in the Attic* – watch drama on TV, and go to the theatre and cinema. Remind yourself of how it's done, and make a note of the performers, directors, casting directors and production companies whose work you most admire.
- Visit your dentist. That smile of yours is important, so look after it. You don't have to go getting expensive cosmetic work done (unless your gnashers are particularly hideous, or unless you're up for a lot of romantic leads in film and television), but get a check-up with your regular dentist and make sure any problems are spotted early. I had an abscess while on tour once, and was in agony for several days. This pain was as nothing, though, compared to the shock of the bill I had for a (private) emergency dentist to perform root canal surgery. Don't let it happen to you: get them sorted before you go away.
- Lastly, but perhaps most importantly: keep yourself **available**. Remember what your real job is. As I mentioned in the previous section, it's a sad fact that almost any job that's interesting will require a degree of commitment, but if you are so committed to your 'day job' that you can't drop everything for an audition or acting work then you are putting yourself and your acting career at a real disadvantage. Talk to your agent (if you have one) when you're planning a holiday – he or she must know your every movement, even if it's only a long weekend, because both you and your agent will look stupid if an audition is arranged for a time when you're actually going to be sunning yourself on some Mediterranean beach, or giving the Best Man's speech at your brother's wedding. Talk to your agent, too, if you're considering applying for Fringe work. In some circumstances this can be a good showcase for your talents, but this must be offset against the fact that it will put you out of the running for any paid work – talk it through with your agent and discuss what you hope to get out of it. Keep your mobile phone switched on whenever possible, and return calls from your agent immediately.

Stay visible

All the preparation in the world won't count for much if nobody knows you're there. There are thousands of us out there, all chasing too few jobs, and it can be hard enough to get noticed even when you're doing everything right. That means that being a wallflower just isn't an option, however much you might hate the idea of marketing yourself. So here are a few (relatively painless) suggestions for keeping your name and face in employers' minds.

- Keep your *Spotlight* CV up to date. An entry in *Spotlight* is essential for film, television and increasingly also theatre jobs. Unless your CV is up to date then (a) the casting director's picture of you is incomplete and (b) it will look like you haven't worked for the last x years.

• Keep your photo up to date. Angus Deuchar's excellent article on page 272 will tell you why, and what to do if it's not. It's significant that all the casting directors who have written for this book have stressed how important it is that your photograph actually looks like you.

• Keep in touch with past employers. Unless you've disgraced yourself while working for them, these people represent your best chance for further work. Send a friendly email or postcard to let them know what you've been doing, with perhaps a mention that you'd love to work with them again and would appreciate a call next time they're casting.

• The best time to write to other potential employers and casting directors is when you're working and can invite them to see you. Of course there's a pretty slim chance that any London-based employers will travel up to Pitlochry to see your Stanley Kowalski or Blanche Dubois, but that's not the point: they will see that you are working – not 'just finished' working (the meaning of which can be curiously flexible) – but actually working, right now.

• Keep covering letters brief, but as individual as possible. Most companies get stacks of CVs from actors with nothing but the baldest of covering notes, so a sentence along the lines of "I'm hoping to see your *Macbeth* when it comes to Leeds" or "My friend John Smith is having a great time working for you at the moment" may make yours stand out from the rest.

• Think about your marketing materials: photo, CV, covering letter. Are they well presented? They represent you: do they do a good job? Are the CV and letter on good-quality paper or the nasty, cheap stuff you get in photocopiers? Get someone who knows what they're talking about to give constructive criticism about them. There are differing opinions about this, but I think it's always worth printing your photo onto the CV itself. If it's well printed then many theatre companies are quite happy with this instead of a full 10x8. If you're sending out a lot of letters and CVs, then it might be worth asking your local printer to quote for some headed notepaper with your photo at the top. Don't get him to print the whole CV – it will go out of date long before you get round to mailing them all. (I should say that my agent completely disagrees with this idea – he reckons you should always send 10x8s, and leave printing your photo on your CV for when you've run out of photos. As I said, opinion is divided.)

• Additional marketing tools. Websites can be quite a good way of getting someone to spend time finding out about you, and of putting across a particular image. The cost of commissioning one from scratch can vary wildly, but someone with only a modicum of computer know-how should be able to knock together something quite presentable using a site like **www.moonfruit.com** or **www.easily.co.uk** (this latter also allows you to register quite cheaply your own domain name – e.g. andrew-piper.com). Don't fret if you haven't got one – your *Spotlight* web page already carries all the important information. Personal websites are currently a 'nice-to-have' not a 'need-to-have'.

• Postcards and business cards. Not a substitute for the CV and photo, but quite a useful additional tool – something to give or send someone who has met you, as a reminder of who you are. Postcards can also make quite good performance notices – something a casting director can read easily while eating breakfast. Have a look at **www.vistaprint.co.uk**

(and there are many others) for business cards, including ones with your photo on. There are a number of companies which can produce postcards quite cheaply: **www.justpostcards.co.uk** and **www.goodprint.co.uk** are two but there are others if you hunt around.

● Apply for jobs. Sounds obvious, but plenty of actors wait for their agent to submit them for everything. Even if the agent is doing their job, in practice this will mean that your CV arrives with a pile of others, with little or nothing to indicate why you are (a) particularly good for this job or (b) interested in working for this company. Find out what's casting – the listings in this book will tell you how best to do that for each company, and your agent may also be happy to tell you – and make your own applications. Tell your agent who you're writing to, and make sure that the CV your agent sends out on your behalf is accurate and up to date.

● On the subject of agents, stay visible to yours. Quite a number of agents have far too large a client list (30 to 35 per agent is about right, I reckon) so it's easy for them to forget about those they haven't heard from in a while. Some form of contact – phone or email, say – every week or two isn't unreasonable when you're not working. Make it a constructive call – not just "have you got me any auditions?" – and talk about what you can be doing to generate work: what's casting, who to write to, ideas for people to approach for general auditions (especially if you're travelling), and so on. Remember that they work for you, so make the most of their skills.

● Write to directors, producers and casting directors whose work you have seen, and tell them how much you enjoyed or admired it.

● Network. Go to see friends in plays, especially first nights, and get yourself invited to the party or pub afterwards. No need to be pushy – just be sociable. When you meet the director don't be tempted to 'do an audition' – casting is almost certainly the last thing on his or her mind right now, and you'll just alienate them. Conversely, don't *not* talk to them just because they're the director – that can be just as irritating. Remember that they're human beings. You won't be able to forget that they're the director, but try to see them as just someone you're meeting at a party. Then follow it up with a CV or showreel in the post. (Have one to hand in case they ask for one.)

● Showcase your talents. The Actors Centres run showcase evenings to which casting professionals are invited, and there are various others around – although be careful, before you stump up too much cash, that they are reputable. One recent addition to the collection is London Bites, which is monthly at Madame Jo-Jo's in Soho (**www.standupdrama.com**) and at the time of writing doesn't charge performers a fee. Also worth considering is Fringe theatre. It is a huge commitment in terms of time and money (in lost earnings alone) to embark on a Fringe production, so make sure you'll get something out of it. If you want to work on *Holby City*, ask yourself if a Fringe production of *Godspell* is really the best showcase for you. Also, if you want casting directors to travel to see you, is it going to be worth your while doing something dark and disturbing in some tiny, God-forsaken flea-pit in the middle of nowhere? More problematic is the question, 'Is it likely to be any good?' – and for that you'll have to do your homework. Find out what the director (and writer if it's a new play) has done before, because you may not want to give up several weeks' earnings to work with a first-time director straight out of college. Everyone has to start somewhere, but you've a right to be able to make an informed judgement if you're working for next to nothing. Google, Whatsonstage.com and Theatre Record may be helpful here. (See the introduction to the Fringe theatre section for more pitfalls to watch out for.)

● Do a short film. These can be useful camera experience, and occasionally provide material for a showreel. Some of these are paid (often badly); a great many are not. These days every kid with a media studies degree wants to be the next Guy Ritchie, so again if you're working for nothing, make sure you have confidence in your director and producer before committing yourself. You're not a charity, and you're not an amateur who just does it for fun.

Stay sane

Being an actor should carry a mental health warning – working away from home, unemployment, rejection, failure, insecurity, poverty: all of these can take their toll on your psychological health and on your relationships. And the worse thing about that is that it makes it even harder to find and get acting jobs – few things kill your chances in an audition quicker than the smell of desperation. After all, if *you* don't have confidence in yourself, why should they? So look after yourself, and take responsibility for your own wellbeing. Here are my suggestions for psychological pick-me-ups …

● Be sociable, even if you don't feel like it. It can be a lonely business when you're out of work – and often even when you're working – so make the most of the time to see as much of friends and family as possible. This is particularly important with partners, especially if the kind of work you tend to get means being away from home. Throw parties or invite your friends to dinner when you're feeling up, and call your actor friends for an understanding shoulder to cry on when you're not.

● Make time for things you enjoy, that make you feel good about yourself. Perhaps this may mean setting yourself challenges – do the garden, DIY around the home, learn French, run a marathon – or may just mean setting aside 'me' time. Yoga and meditation are particularly good for this, and some people draw great strength from religious observance.

● If (like me) you are a naturally anxious person, and meditation or yoga don't appeal, then consider getting some relaxation tapes and spend some time every day listening to them. If anxiety and self-image are your problem, don't go buying some motivational 'You too can be rich and famous' hypnosis tape or you could make things worse: deal with the problem in hand. Have a look at **www.relax-uk.com** or **www.relaxaudio.com** for some examples.

● Get out in the fresh air. Remember when you were younger, one or other of your parents urging you to switch off the telly and get outdoors? Well, they were right – exercise and sunlight are vitally important for both your physical and mental health, particularly in the winter months when daylight is in short supply. Even when we're working, often much of our time is spent in windowless boxes, so make the most of a nice day and go for a walk.

● Take a holiday. That's really not easy to do, especially at the start of one's career. A week away from the 'day job' is a week not earning money, which can be expensive if you've already used up your holiday pay subsidising those days or weeks of involuntary unemployment that often occur just before or just after an acting job. But everyone needs to recharge their batteries from time to time, even if it's just a long weekend visiting old friends.

● Detox. Most actors drink – I think it was Gene Hackman who once observed that all actors eventually become either directors or drunks – but if your last job involved a lot of boozing (or if you're currently waking up with one or more hangovers a week), then try a few weeks off the sauce. Drink two litres of water a day, get plenty of early nights, and try to make fruit and fresh veg a good 50 per cent of everything you eat. Some people also find it beneficial to give up bread or go veggie or vegan for a while. Go back to beer-and-burgers after that if you want, but notice the difference in your mood and concentration when you do.

● Keep a positive attitude. Remember, you're in this for the long term, so although six months or more can feel like a long time, compared with the 30- or 40-year career you have ahead of you, it's really not so long. Almost all actors are out of work for periods in their career – even very good ones – so don't panic.

● Don't give yourself a hard time about past failures: learn the lesson and move on. Make here and now your starting point, and plan for the future based on what *is* rather than what *might have been*.

● Silence your inner critic. Brendan Behan wrote that "Critics are like eunuchs in a harem: they know how it's done, they've seen it done every day, but they're unable to do it themselves." We all have a critic within us, but the less room we give it, the less we'll feel like eunuchs ourselves. Be generous to your fellow professionals, understanding of what they go through, and don't be threatened by their success. A friend of a friend of mine is doing very well for himself – very good-looking, great agent, lovely telly and film roles coming his way – and I so wanted to dislike him. But meeting him again at a party recently he was warm, relaxed, interested in what I was doing, remembered things I'd told him last time we met – in short, utterly charming. And I realised that that's actually what made him the star. Not just the looks or the talent – both of which he does have in spades – but also the generosity of spirit, the belief that 'I'm ok, you're ok'. It might be the acidic queen with the barbed tongue who gets the laughs at the party, but it's people like that actor who will in the end do well. So resist pressure to join in bashing reputations or impugning characters, and learn compassion for yourself and for others.

● Don't just wait for your agent to call. Be proactive. Take charge of your career. Keep doing the things listed above that will improve your chances of finding work.

● Finally – and you may be surprised that I give this advice in an actors' yearbook – if it really is getting too much for you, then it may be time to call it quits. Acting can be a very cruel business, and not everyone is built to withstand the emotional battering that visits most actors from time to time. If there is anything at all that you could be happy doing instead of acting, then do it: there is no shame at all in looking after your sanity. A very talented friend of mine who left the business after years of frustration described her new situation to me thus: "I'm doing a job that I hate and I'm happier than I've been in years." Many people who leave acting find related work – teaching, for example, or work in some aspect of production – but I know some who have found that proximity to what they've left behind to be too painful, and have opted for entirely unrelated occupations. In the end, it comes down to what makes you happy, where you feel at home, and what ultimately brings you peace. Enjoying acting is not the same as enjoying being an actor.

There's a 'prayer' that runs, 'Grant me the serenity to accept the things I cannot change, courage to change the things I can, and wisdom to know the difference.' This seems to me to be a good motto for any actor. A great many decisions affecting our lives as actors are out of our hands, but a great many more we *do* have control over. The trick to staying sane in this business seems to be knowing (and accepting) which are which.

Andrew Piper trained at the Bristol Old Vic Theatre School, and graduated in 2002 playing Shylock in *The Merchant of Venice*. Work since then has included Hamlet (in *Rosencrantz & Guildenstern are Dead*) for Jersey Opera House; Dr Detmold in the London premiere of Sondheim's *Anyone Can Whistle*; three tours for Northumberland Theatre Company; and John Terry in the two-hander, *Who Killed 'Agatha' Christie?* at Leeds Grand, Westcliff Palace and Eastbourne. He wrote and voiced the narration (in iambic pentameter) for a concert performance of Berlioz's *Béatrice et Bénédict* for the Cambridge Berlioz Festival, and playing World War Two pilot Tom Kirby-Green, he shares a Special Edition DVD with Steve McQueen. He is also editor of *Actors' Yearbook*.

Tax and National Insurance for actors

Philippe Carden

Actors enjoy a rare hybrid status. They are treated as self-employed for income tax purposes but as employees for National Insurance. This combination brings with it a number of advantages, but also certain complications. Many actors choose to instruct an accountant to benefit from those advantages, and to avoid the pitfalls created by the complications.

The income tax advantages include being able to claim a deduction for expenses against income in arriving at taxable net profit (or allowable loss), provided that those expenses are incurred "wholly and exclusively for the purposes of the trade". *The Equity Advice and Rights Guide*, available free of charge to its members, provides a very helpful list of usually allowable expenses, with suitable notes to restrain the enthusiasm of actors to stretch definitions to their limits. Self-imposed restraint in claiming for expenses is sensible in minimising the risk of being selected for an Inland Revenue enquiry. Some accountants produce their own list.

It is helpful to assess the types of expense according to the risk of being challenged by the Revenue. Here are some examples:

Low risk or No risk
- Commission paid to agent (including VAT)
- Annual subscription to Equity
- Travel and subsistence on tour
- Photographs and publicity (repros, *Spotlight* entry)
- Classes to maintain skills, e.g. voice, movement
- Business stationery and postage
- Fee paid to accountant

Medium risk
- Professional library – scripts, books, CDs
- Publications – *The Stage, Time Out*
- Travel and subsistence when not on tour
- Visits to theatre and cinema

High risk
- Wardrobe – renewal, dry cleaning and repair
- Hairdressing and make-up
- Gratuities to dressers and stage door-keepers
- Home as office

As the risk rises, so too must the care taken in deciding which to claim and which to discard. Engaging an accountant to use his or her experience, skill and judgement in carrying out a review of expenditure claims is a source of considerable reassurance to many actors. It is worth noting that entertaining, as in paying a meal for another person (even if a casting director), is never allowed.

An accountant's review may also be key in calculating the business proportions of motor car expenses, land-line and mobile telephone charges, and television and video hire and television licence. An accountant's help in computing capital allowances for expenditure on capital items (computer, motor car, musical instruments) is appreciated by all but the most self-confident.

The emphasis so far has been on the income tax advantages of being self-employed. Whilst many actors are happy to register themselves as self-employed within the three-month time limit, others enlist the help of an accountant even at that stage to provide a buffer-zone between themselves and the Inland Revenue. Once registration is done, a Unique Taxpayer Reference ('UTR') will be issued, often still referred to as a Schedule D number. Unless preventative action is taken at the time of registration, or very soon afterwards, a costly national insurance (NI) pitfall will trap the unwary actor.

If an actor is to be treated as an employee for NI, s/he certainly does not want to be seen as self-employed for NI as well. Such duplication is costly and usually brings no additional benefits. A common solution is to apply for small earnings exception (SEE) from the flat-rate weekly NI paid by 'normal' self-employed people – Class 2 – by completing and submitting form CF10.

For actors who do some work abroad and/or who write and direct as well as perform, the solution is more likely to involve paying Class 2 but applying for deferment of Class 4. That class of NI is the earnings-related charge borne by 'normal' self-employed people in addition to the flat-rate Class 2. It confers no benefits to the payer and is collected by the Inland Revenue as part of the self-assessment system.

The complexities of the NI regime, and especially the interaction of its different classes, encourage co-operation between actor and accountant at least as much as does the application of the criteria for acceptability of expenses for income tax purposes.

So, the basic bundle of services provided by an accountant includes the following:
- Annual income and expenditure account
- Capital allowances computations
- Advice on NI and the necessary form-filling
- Completion of the annual Tax Return
- Preparing a tax calculation and checking the Revenue's version

Additional services would include completing quarterly returns for actors successful enough to be registered for VAT, and advice on the tax and NI implications of performing abroad.

Most accountants charge according to time spent and the seniority and expertise of the persons doing the work. Here is an example of how this might work in practice for a young actor: he would need four hours of a book-keeper at £30 per hour (£120), plus an hour for a manager's review and tax return (£50); an hour of the manager's time to sort out the NI (£50); and finally half-an-hour of the principal's/partner's time for overall review and quality control (£50). With perhaps a few telephone calls or a shortish meeting, the annual fee would typically be £340 plus VAT, i.e. £399.50.

In my experience, as the cost of the initial meeting is rarely charged for, I make a loss in year 1 of a new client. I break even in year 2, and only make a profit in year 3 and subsequent years. It is not a surprise therefore that I see my relationship with a client as a long-term one, one which has time and effort invested in it by both actor and accountant.

To an actor in the early years of his career, the accountant's annual fee of about £400 represents a significant expense. The decision to instruct an accountant is a personal one. Some actors are much more comfortable and confident than others in dealing with money matters, taxation and National Insurance. Others shy away from such a course of action and choose to have an ally in the form of an accountant.

In general terms, for an actor with gross earnings of less than £15,000 but who still makes a profit, having an accountant is optional. For one with smaller earnings and who makes a loss, having an accountant could be worthwhile to use that loss effectively. For those with gross earnings in excess of £15,000, the choice is compelling.

Having made the decision to use an accountant, choose the firm carefully. The most desired method is word of mouth. A personal recommendation from another actor, from your drama school or indeed from the company manager works well. It is important that the accountant selected know about the taxation and NI of actors rather than being a general practitioner. It is also important that the accountant be a member of one of the professional bodies of accountants as an indication of quality – and just in case a dispute arises which cannot be resolved amicably. Most of the institutes have a system of arbitration for fee disputes, for example, which can be used as a last resort.

Another factor in the choice of accountant is the size of the firm. The range is huge: from a sole practitioner to a multinational firm employing thousands. The former will be suitable for an actor of modest means, while the latter might be a good match for a performer with very considerable earnings and royalties from several countries around the world. In between those extremes are smaller firms with one to five partners and which specialise in the tax affairs of those who work in theatre, television and film, and larger firms which have an entertainment and media department with a similar specialism. The smaller firms are likely to provide a more personal service and lower fees. The larger are likely to have access to a greater breadth of related expertise (such as film finance, production accounting) but fees will be correspondingly higher.

Each accountant will have his or her favoured way for actors to keep records. The most important point is that an actor must co-operate with his or her accountant to save time and maximise the return on effort. Here are some guidelines and handy hints:

- Keep all agent's remittance advices, payslips and invoices.
- Only claim expenses incurred "wholly and exclusively for the purposes of the trade".
- Use the Equity list of usually allowable expenses for guidance.
- Keep receipts for all expenses and write explanatory notes on them, e.g. for audition with ...
- File away carefully details of any interest or dividends received, jobseeker's allowance claimed, Gift Aid payments made and any other item which may be needed to complete your tax return.
- Deliver your accounts papers to your accountant as soon as you can after the end of the tax year – never leave it until close to the 31st January deadline!*

Philippe Carden is a chartered accountant specialising in the taxation of actors and other individuals working in theatre, film, television and dance, onstage and backstage, artistic and technical. He co-wrote *Investing in West End Theatrical Productions* (Robert Hale, 1992) and has written articles for *The Guardian*, *The Stage* and other publications.

* *Note* From 2008, all paper self-assessment returns must be received by 30th September. If you file online, you will have another two months until 30th November. Deadline for payment of any tax owing remains 31st January.

Accountants

M Barnfather & Co.
15 Birley St, Blackpool FY1 1DU
tel (01253) 622519 *fax* (01253) 294179
email mike@mikebarnfather.co.uk
Accountant Michael Barnfather

Founded in 1974. Charges between £150 and £250 for preparation of accounts and submission of tax return. Provides support by means of face-to-face meetings, phone and email (mostly phone and email). Provides Excel spreadsheets and Money Manager (cashbook accounting software, compatible with most PCs but not Mac or Linux) if necessary. 3 clients are actors, but other clients include circus artistes, magicians, singers and dancers. Offices are not wheelchair-accessible (2nd floor). "We encourage all clients to keep proper accounting records (we advise them on their specific requirements), and to forward tax correspondence (including Self-Assessment return forms) directly to us as soon as received."

P O'N Carden
56-58 High Street, Ewell, Surrey KT17 1RW
tel 020-8394 2957 *fax* 020-8394 2722
email philippe@poncarden.com
Accountants Philippe Carden, Manine Head

Founded in 1977. Charges £400 ("in the early years") for a complete set of accounts and tax return. "Time and complexity increase this – up to £2000 to include quarterly VAT returns. Tailor-made packages for really complex cases." Provides face-to-face meetings in central London. "My actor clients make clear how much support they feel they need, and the programme of work is tailored accordingly." Provides Excel spreadsheets appropriate to the client's needs. 40% of clients are actors; 45% are other entertainment-industry professionals. The offices are not wheelchair-accessible, but meetings can be held in wheelchair-accessible locations. Advises actors *not* to "just give your accountant bags of receipts. Provide information about why you are claiming particular expenses. Do be obsessive about keeping payslips and remittance advices".

Dub & Co.
7 Torriano Mews, Torriano Avenue, London NW5 2RZ
tel 020-7284 8686 *fax* 020-7284 8687
email office@dub.co.uk
Accountants George Dub, Joyce Davies

Chartered, certified accountants established in 1979. Charges from £400 + VAT for preparation of accounts for a tax return. Provides face-to-face meetings, phone and email support included in this fee. Does not provide software or spreadsheet templates to clients. Handles the tax and accountancy affairs of around 50 actors and 100 other entertainment industry professionals. The company's offices are wheelchair-accessible.

Dunbar & Co.
70 South Lambeth Road, London SW8 1RL
tel 020-7820 0082 *fax* 020-7820 0806
email mason@equitax.co.uk
Accountants Nick Mason (Senior Partner), Bob Long

Founded in 1896. Fees are on a time-cost basis, depending on the complexity of the client's tax affairs, but a typical fee range for an actor would be £330-£420 p.a. Support is provided via various means, including face-to-face meetings, phone and email. Provides spreadsheet templates for clients, which require Microsoft Excel. 50% of clients are actors, with a further 15%, other entertainment-industry professionals. Offices are wheelchair-accessible.

"We offer a full accountancy service, including bookkeeping, VAT, tax returns, tax advice, assistance with Revenue investigations, limited company accounts, personal and corporate tax planning. Our sister company, Sandford Dunbar, is authorised by the FSA as an independent financial adviser specialising in personal financial and pension planning."

Goldwins
75 Maygrove Road, London NW6 2EG
tel 020-7372 6494 *fax* 020-7624 0053
email aepton@goldwins.co.uk
website www.goldwins.co.uk
Accountant Anthony Epton

Established in 1987. Specialises in the entertainment industry, handling the tax and bookkeeping affairs of around 200 actors. Charges around £400 for preparation of an actor's tax return, although this can vary from £250 up to £1000 depending on the complexity of the job. Provides face-to-face meetings, phone and email support included in this price. Does not provide software or spreadsheet templates. The company's offices are wheelchair-accessible.

Goodman Jones LLP
29/30 Fitzroy Square, London W1P 6LQ
tel 020-7388 2444 *fax* 020-7388 6736
email jrf@goodmanjones.com
website www.goodmanjones.com
Partner Julian Flitter

Founded in 1934. "Each person is different and we tailor our support to the clients needs, so costs can range from £250 to £500 for more complex returns involving international aspects and multiple categories of income." This amount would include any support required in the form of face-to-face meetings, phone calls, letters and emails. "The range of services we offer includes tax compliance services from personal tax returns and VAT returns, advice on whether or not to incorporate as a limited company, when to register for VAT, how to deal with working abroad, bookkeeping services, preparation of financial accounts (limited company, sole trader, LLP or partnership) as well as full personal tax planning and company secretarial and payroll services." Can supply software templates to clients as required, but recommends "keeping it simple". Offices are wheelchair-accessible.

Hayles Farrar & Partners

39 Castle Street, Leicester LE1 5WN
tel 0116-233 8500 *fax* 0116-233 7288
email geoff.banks@hayles.co.uk
website www.hayles.co.uk
Accountants Geoff Banks, Amanda Jelley

Charges from £150 for preparation of a basic tax return. Provides face-to-face meetings, phone and email support. Initial consultation or advice is offered free of charge. Does not supply software or spreadsheet templates to clients. Advises actors to "open a separate business bank account and identify all receipts and payments, retaining all supporting documentation".

J Morris and Co.

17 St Ann's Square, Manchester M2 7PW
tel 0161-832 4841 *fax* 0161-835 2539
email johne@alexander.co.uk
website www.alexander.co.uk
Accountant John Evans

An accountant since 1969, John Evans merged the J Morris & Co. practice with Alexander & Co. in 2005. Charges for completion of accounts and submission of tax return start at £250 "dependent on complexity of case". Provides support by means of face-to-face meetings, phone, email and written correspondence, and can provide introduction to further specialist advice (e.g. legal) where required. Provides PC (Windows) compatible software or spreadsheets as required. Offices are not wheelchair-accessible. "We deal with a number of actors and entertainers, and we are on Equity's list."

Shaw Walker & Co.

31 Great Queen Street, London WC2B 5AE
tel 020-7242 1134 *fax* 020-7831 7232

email alison@shawwalker.co.uk
website www.shawwalker.co.uk
Accountants Mrs A McCarthy, Mr P Skinner, Mr T K Chong

Established in 1925, charges from £400 to prepare actors' accounts for the tax return, depending on the complexity of the accounts. Provides a face-to-face initial meeting; support thereafter is as convenient to the client, and this is included in the fee. Provides a complete range of accounting services – VAT, tax, PAYE, business support, book keeping *et al.* Software and/or spreadsheets are provided to the client as required. Offices are not easily wheelchair-accessible. Advice to actors: "Seek a *qualified* accountant."

Tax Watchdog Direct

Grosvenor House, St Thomas Place, Stockport SK1 3TZ
tel 0845-058 2223 *fax* 0845-059 2292
email bernard@taxrebates.com
website www.taxbuddies.com
Director Bernard Oster *Accountant (for actors)* Mike Parkes

Founded in 1996. A fixed-fee tax and accountancy service, charging £159 + VAT (£186.83) per year. Provides phone and email support to clients, as well as free bookkeeping software. Currently this is Entrax (which only runs on Windows 2000 or XP) but a web-based system is being developed which should be compatible with other operating systems (including Mac). 15% of clients are actors; 5% are other entertainment-industry professionals.

Wyatts

18 Highbury New Park, London N5 2DB
mobile (07710) 160442
fax 020-7226 0211
email wyatts@mail.com
Accountant Rachel Wyndham

Founded in 2000. Charges £250 for actors with turnover below £15,000 and £350 for those above £15,000 to prepare accounts for the annual tax return. Included in this price is support via face-to-face meetings, telephone and email. Provides software and/or templates to clients using Sage, Excel (& other MS Office software), Tas, QuickBooks and Money Manager, which are suitable for Windows and Apple computers. 50% of clients are actors, and 20% other entertainment-industry professionals. Offices are not wheelchair-accessible. "We provide a tax return checklist and two reminders. Our advice is to try to keep on top of it!"

Funding bodies

The competition for funding is so fierce that it is important to allow sufficient time for research, planning and proper presentation of your proposed project. It is well worth checking to see what information is available on the websites listed in this section. Many funding bodies are happy to advise on form-filling, what kind of projects stand a chance and what could constitute a realistic amount to ask for. It is also well worth going on one (or more) of the Independent Theatre Council's (ITC; see page 317) courses for assistance in the complex world of funding applications.

Bodies that offer individual funding should be approached with similar care and attention.

NATIONAL ARTS COUNCILS

Arts Council England
14 Great Peter Street, London SW1P 3NQ
tel 0845-300 6200 *fax* 020-7973 6590 *textphone* 020-7973 6564
email enquiries@artscouncil.org.uk
website www.artscouncil.org.uk

Arts Council England is the national development agency for the arts in England, promoting excellence, innovation and diversity within the arts. It awards grants to individuals, arts organisations and national touring projects using public money from government and the National Lottery.

Grants for individuals are generally between £200 and £30,000, while those for organisations range from £200 up to a maximum of £100,000. Most grants, however, will be under £30,000. National touring grants are available for individuals and organisations touring to 2 or more Arts Council England regions, and normally vary between £5000 and £200,000. Grants for individuals, organisations and national touring can cover activities lasting up to 3 years.

All applicants should apply to the region in which they are based. Application forms, guidance notes and information sheets can be downloaded from the website. A wide range of resources, publications, links and information about other funding sources is also accessible on the website.

Arts Council of Northern Ireland
MacNeice House, 77 Malone Road, Belfast BT9 6AQ
tel 028-9038 5200
email publicaffairs@artscouncil-ni.org
website www.artscouncil-ni.org

The prime distributor of public support for the arts, the Arts Council of Northern Ireland is committed to increasing opportunities for artists to develop challenging and innovative work. In addition to funding schemes for organisations and community groups, the council has developed a special programme of schemes to extend support for the individual artist. This programme includes the General Arts Award, which provides funding for specific projects, specialised research and personal artistic development; and the Major Individual Award, which supports established artists in the development of ambitious work.

Arts Council of Wales
9 Museum Place, Cardiff CF10 3NX
tel 029-2037 6500
email info@artswales.org.uk
website www.artswales.org.uk

Responsible for funding and developing the arts in Wales using money from Welsh Assembly Government and the National Lottery. Provides arts organisations and individuals in Wales with the opportunity to apply for funding towards clearly defined arts-related projects. Scheme Guidelines for the funding programmes are available on the website. Anyone applying for funding should speak to an Arts Development Officer in their local office to discuss how well the project aligns with national and regional priorities. Contact information for all local offices can be found on the website.

Scottish Arts Council
12 Manor Place, Edinburgh EH3 7DD
tel 0131-226 6051
email help.desk@scottisharts.org.uk
website www.scottisharts.org.uk

The Scottish Arts Council is the principal channel of public funding for the arts in Scotland, distributing money from the Scottish Executive and the National Lottery to those working at a professional level in the arts. Funding is available to individuals and organisations for arts projects, productions and presentation of work, research and development including short-term or one-off training courses, conference fees, master classes, mentoring, travel to see work, establishing contacts and partnerships and exploring opportunities for future projects.

REGIONAL ARTS COUNCIL OFFICES

Arts Council England, East
Eden House, 48-49 Bateman Street, Cambridge CB2 1LR
tel 0845-300 6200 *fax* 0870-242 1271
textphone (01223) 306893

Area covered: Bedfordshire, Cambridgeshire, Essex, Hertfordshire, Norfolk, Suffolk; and unitary authorities of Luton, Peterborough, Southend-on-Sea, Thurrock.

Arts Council England, East Midlands
St Nicholas Court, 25-27 Castle Gate, Nottingham NG1 7AR
tel 0845-300 6200 *fax* 0115-950 2467

Area covered: Derbyshire, Leicestershire, Lincolnshire (excluding North and North East Lincolnshire), Northamptonshire, Nottinghamshire; and unitary authorities of Derby, Leicester, Nottingham, Rutland.

Arts Council England, London
2 Pear Tree Court, London EC1R 0DS
tel 020-7608 6100 *fax* 020-7608 4100 *textphone* 020-7608 4101

Area covered: Greater London.

Arts Council England, North East
Central Square, Forth Street, Newcastle upon Tyne NE1 3PJ
tel 0845-300 6200 *fax* 0191-230 1020 *textphone* 0191-255 8585

Area covered: Durham, Northumberland; metropolitan authorities of Gateshead, Newcastle upon Tyne, North Tyneside, South Tyneside, Sunderland; and unitary authorities of Darlington, Hartlepool, Middlesbrough, Redcar and Cleveland, Stockton-on-Tees.

Arts Council England, North West
Manchester House, 22 Bridge Street, Manchester M3 3AB
tel 0845-300 6200 *fax* 0161-834 6969 *textphone* 0161-834 9131

Area covered: Cheshire, Cumbria, Lancashire; metropolitan authorities of Bolton, Bury, Knowsley, Liverpool, Manchester, Oldham, Rochdale, St Helens, Salford, Sefton, Stockport, Tameside, Trafford, Wigan, Wirral; and unitary authorities of Blackburn with Darwen, Blackpool, Halton, Warrington.

Arts Council England, South East
Sovereign House, Church Street, Brighton BN1 1RA
tel 0845-300 6200 *fax* 0870-242 1257
textphone (01273) 710659

Area covered: Buckinghamshire, East Sussex, Hampshire, Isle of Wight, Kent, Oxfordshire, Surrey, West Sussex; and unitary authorities of Bracknell Forest, Brighton & Hove, Medway Towns, Milton Keynes, Portsmouth, Reading, Slough, Southampton, West Berkshire, Windsor and Maidenhead, Wokingham.

Arts Council England, South West
Senate Court, Southernhay Gardens, Exeter EX1 1UG
tel 0845-300 6200 *fax* (01392) 229229
textphone (01392) 433503

Area covered: Cornwall, Devon, Dorset, Gloucestershire, Somerset, Wiltshire; unitary authorities of Bath and North East Somerset, Bournemouth, Bristol, North Somerset, Plymouth, Poole, South Gloucestershire, Swindon, Torbay.

Arts Council England, West Midlands
82 Granville Street, Birmingham B1 2LH
tel 0845-300 6200 *fax* 0121 643 7239 *textphone* 0121-643 2815
website www.artscouncil.org.uk
Literature Officer Adrian Johnson *Literature Assistant* Maeve Haughey

Area covered: Shropshire, Staffordshire, Warwickshire, Worcestershire; metropolitan authorities of Birmingham, Coventry, Dudley, Sandwell, Solihull, Walsall, Wolverhampton; and unitary authorities of Herefordshire, Stoke-on-Trent, Telford and Wrekin. Supports Ledbury Poetry Festival, *Poetry on Loan* in public libraries, and individual writers through grant aid which can be applied for by using the organisation's *Grants for the Arts* pack. Telephone for a full application pack.

Arts Council England, Yorkshire
21 Bond Street, Dewsbury, West Yorkshire WF13 1AX
tel 0845-300 6200 *fax* (01924) 466522
textphone (01924) 438585

Area covered: North Yorkshire; metropolitan authorities of Barnsley, Bradford, Calderdale, Doncaster, Kirklees, Leeds, Rotherham, Sheffield, Wakefield; and unitary authorities of East Riding of Yorkshire, Kingston upon Hull, North Lincolnshire, North East Lincolnshire, York.

NATIONAL AND REGIONAL FILM AGENCIES

UK Film Council
10 Little Portland Street, London W1W 7JG
tel 020-7861 7861
email info@filmcouncil.org.uk
website www.filmcouncil.org.uk

Established by the Government in 2000, the UK Film Council supports the development of the British film industry and film culture. Offers a variety of funding schemes to nurture new filmmaking talent and provides money to regional film agencies for distribution to local projects.

For general enquiries about any of the UK Film Council's short film schemes, and to be kept informed of future opportunities, contact **shorts@ukfilmcouncil.org.uk**.

Scottish Screen
249 West George Street, Glasgow G2 4QE
tel 0141-302 1700
email info@scottishscreen.com
website www.scottishscreen.com

Wales Screen Commission (formerly Sgrin Media Agency for Wales)
6G Parc Gwyddoniaeth, Cefn Llan, Aberystwyth, Ceredigion SY23 3AH
tel (01970) 627186/627831 *fax* (01970) 617942
email enquiry@walesscreencommission.co.uk
website www.walesscreencommission.co.uk

The Northern Ireland Film & Television Commission
3rd Floor, 21 Alfred House, Belfast BT2 8ED
tel 028-9023 2444
website www.niftc.co.uk

East Midlands Media
35-37 St Mary's Gate, Nottingham NG1 1PU
tel 0115-934 9090
email info@em-media.org.uk
website www.em-media.org.uk

Film London (formerly London Film & Video Development Agency)
Suite 6.10, The Tea Building, 56 Shoreditch High Street, London E1 6JJ
tel 020-7613 7676 *fax* 020-7613 7677
email info@filmlondon.org.uk
website www.filmlondon.org.uk

North West Vision
233 The Tea Factory, 82 Wood Street, Liverpool L1 4DQ
tel 0151-708 2967 *fax* 0151-708 2974
email info@northwestvision.co.uk
website www.northwestvision.co.uk

Northern Film & Media
Central Square, Forth Street, Newcastle upon Tyne NE1 3PJ
tel 0191-269 9200
email info@northernmedia.org
website www.northernmedia.org

Screen East
2 Millenium Plain, Norwich NR1 3JG
tel (01603) 776920
email info@screeneast.co.uk
website www.screeneast.co.uk

Screen South
Folkestone Enterprise Centre, Shearway Road, Folkestone, Kent CT19 4RH
tel (01303) 298222
email info@screensouth.org
website www.screensouth.org

Screen West Midlands
Screen West Midlands, 9 Regent Place, Birmingham B1 3NJ
tel 0121-265 7120 *fax* 0121-265 7180
email info@screenwm.co.uk
website www.screenwm.co.uk

Screen Yorkshire
Studio 22, 46 The Calls, Leeds LS2 7EY
tel 0113-294 4410
email info@screenyorkshire.co.uk
website www.screenyorkshire.co.uk

South West Screen
St Bartholomews Court, Lewins Mead, Bristol BS1 5BT
tel 0117-952 9977
email info@swscreen.co.uk
website www.swscreen.co.uk

OTHER SOURCES OF FUNDING

Actors' Benevolent Fund
6 Adam Street, London WC2N 6AD
tel 020-7836 6378 *fax* 020-7836 8978
email office@abf.org.uk
website www.actorsbenevolentfund.co.uk

For more than 120 years the Actors' Benevolent Fund has provided financial assistance to actors unable to work due to poor health, an accident or old age. To be eligible for assistance, applicants need several years of professional acting experience.

Calouste Gulbenkian Foundation
98 Portland Place, London W1B 1ET
tel 020-7636 5313 *fax* 020-7908 7580
email info@gulbenkian.org.uk
website www.gulbenkian.org.uk

Awards grants to professional organisations or professional artists, working in partnerships or groups, developing new art in any artform.

Department for Education and Skills (DfES)
tel 0870-000 2288
email info@dfes.gsi.gov.uk

website www.dfes.gov.uk

The Department for Education and Skills was established with the purpose of creating opportunity, releasing potential and achieving excellence for all.

On the website you can find information specifically about the Department, including departmental reports and strategy. You will also find information about the Ministerial team, a *Who's Who* chart, and details about how to contact individuals, user portals and gateways.

If you are looking for specific information or advice, you should visit one of the Department's portal websites. These sites bring together a wide range of education and skills information that is specific to different people's needs:
• For information on applying to university, life as a student or any other aspect of higher education not related to policy issues, please visit the Aimhigher website, **www.aimhigher.ac.uk**
• For specific information relating to student finance, consult the Student Support site, **www.dfes.gov.uk/studentsupport**
• For all of the public services you'll need as a student, visit Directgov, **www.direct.gov.uk/EducationAndLearning/UniversityAndHigherEducation**

Equity Trust Fund
222 Africa House, 64 Kingsway, London WC2B 6BD
tel 020-7404 6041 *fax* 020-7831 4953

The trust seeks to further education through support and development of the performing arts, and to provide for the welfare and health of professional performers, former performers, their relatives and dependants. Also offers free debt counselling and benefits advice.

The Esmée Fairbairn Foundation
11 Park Place, London SW1A 1LP
tel 020-7297 4700
website www.esmeefairbairn.org.uk

Offers Arts & Heritage grants with the aim of increasing provision of original and high-quality arts in areas of the UK less well served than others. Activities must take place outside London. See the website for further information.

First Light
Progress Works, Heath Mill Lane, Birmingham B9 4AL
tel 0121-693 2091 *fax* 0121-693 2096
website www.firstlightmovies.com

Supports short films which are made by or in collaboration with young people.

The Foyle Foundation
Rugby Chambers, 2 Rugby Street, London WC1N 3QU
tel 020-7430 9119 *fax* 020-7430 9830
email information@foylefoundation.org.uk
website www.foylefoundation.org.uk

The Foyle Foundation makes grants to registered charities in the UK whose core remit covers the arts, learning or health. It has supported tours, festivals and education projects, and helped to develop new work. It will also consider funding the building or updating of arts facilities. The average size of grant is between £5000 and £20,000. Application forms and guidelines are available to download from the website.

The Jerwood Charitable Foundation
22 Fitzroy Square, London W1T 6EN
tel 020-7388 6287
email info@jerwood.org
website www.jerwood.org.uk

Awards grants to young people, mainly aged 20 to 35, who have demonstrated achievement, commitment and excellence, particularly in the performing arts. Financial support has been offered to young actors, dancers, choreographers, playwrights, filmmakers, singers and musicians and others in the performing and visual arts. The charity seeks to make grants which will produce tangible and visible results and whose beneficial effects will extend beyond the immediate recipient of the grant.

NESTA (National Endowment for Science, Technology and the Arts)
Fishmongers' Chambers, 110 Upper Thames Street, London EC4R 3TW
tel 020-7645 9500
email nesta@nesta.org.uk
website www.nesta.org.uk

Offers a variety of funding schemes to promote innovation within the fields of science, technology and the arts.

The Oxford Samuel Beckett Theatre Trust Award
PO Box 2637, Ascot, Berks SL5 8ZN
email info@osbttrust.com
website www.osbttrust.com
Director Romilly Walton Masters

Aims to support experimental theatre by encouraging new generations of creative artists, whether dramatists, dancers, musicians, painters, sculptors or poets. Through this award, it is looking to help an artist, or a group, of high calibre to realise a fully resourced professional production. Innovation and quality weighs more heavily than potential commercial success or public appeal.

A grant of up to £30,000 and a 3-week run at the Riverside Studios (Studio 3) in November is offered each year. Further support is offered in the form of a mentor, administrative and artistic guidance from the team at Riverside Studios, a week of technical rehearsals in Studio 3 and help in finding a subsidised rehearsal space.

The Royal Theatrical Fund

11 Garrick Street, London WC2E 9AR
tel 020-7836 3322 *fax* 020-7379 8273
email admin@trtf.com
website www.trtf.com

Founded in 1839, the Royal Theatrical Fund makes grants which will alleviate the suffering, assist the recovery, or reduce the need, hardship or distress of theatrical artists or their families/dependants. To be eligible to receive a grant, a person must have professionally practised or contributed to the theatrical arts (on stage, radio, film or television) for a minimum of 7 years.

Sophie's Silver Lining Fund

17 Silver Street, Chacombe, Banbury, Oxon OX17 2JR
tel (01295) 711155
email TheLarges@aol.com
website www.silverlining.org.uk

Provides assistance to needy acting and singing students with the cost of their training.

The Wellcome Trust

UK Exhibitions and Science and Art Initiatives (SCIART), 210 Euston Road, London NW1 2BE
email sciart@wellcome.ac.uk
website www.wellcome.ac.uk

The Science and Arts Initiatives (SCIART) supports collaborations between art and science, providing 2 different kinds of award for projects in which visual art, music, digital media, film, creative writing or the performing arts interact with scientific research in an exciting way. Projects should aim to explore new modes of enquiry and stimulate fresh thinking and debate in both disciplines, while being accessible to diverse audiences.

Research Development Awards (up to £15,000) aim to support the further development of an idea in its formative stages. Production Awards (from £50,000 to £100,000) will be awarded to substantial projects likely to make a significant impact on the public's engagement with science. They can be used to fund major activities such as exhibitions, art projects, programmes for TV and radio, theatre, time-based media, public performance or events programmes.

Publications, libraries, references and booksellers

This section lists the major sources for scripts and sheet music – and routes to finding that elusive script or score. While Internet search engines can be extremely useful in such a quest, it sometimes requires some lateral thinking to find what you want. It is possible to find out-of-print plays via libraries or book-finding services and by combing second-hand book shops. Some publishers (even a few playwrights' agencies) will organise a photocopy – for a fee. Also, the British Library (in theory) has a copy of every play ever performed in this country, but there can be complications in actually getting hold of a copy. Start with your local library if you're determined to find a specific play; if they don't have it, they may well be able to get it from another library (via the inter-library loan system), but be prepared for it to take a long time. Another route is to try to find a theatre at which the play has been performed: they may be able to help.

AbeBooks.com

website www.abebooks.com

Excellent website which will search the catalogues of hundreds of secondhand booksellers in this country and around the world.

Amazon.co.uk & Amazon.com

website www.amazon.co.uk or www.amazon.com

UK and US sites (respectively) for books, DVDs, CDs and all sorts of other things. Secondhand items are listed alongside the new, so often a good place to find cheap scripts.

Barbican Library

Barbican Centre, London EC2Y 8DS
tel 020-7638 0569
website www.cityoflondon.gov.uk/barbicanlibrary

Situated on level 2 of the Barbican Centre, this is the largest lending library in the City of London. In addition to the general library, the strong arts and music sections reflect the Barbican Centre's emphasis on the arts. The library is fully accessible by wheelchair and has a number of other access facilities including hearing induction loops and a reading magnifier machine. Open Monday to Saturday.

BookBarn

Central Trading Estate, Bath Road, Bristol BS4 3EH
tel 0117-300 5400
White Cross, Somerset BS39 6EX
tel 01761-451777
website www.bookbarn.co.uk

"The UK's largest used book warehouse," with many thousands of cheap secondhand scripts and a searchable catalogue online.

The British Library

96 Euston Road, London NW1 2DB
tel 0870-444 1500 (Switchboard), 020-7412 7676 (Advance Reservations, St Pancras Reading Rooms and Humanities enquiries), 020-7412 7702 (Maps), 020-7412 7513 (Manuscripts), 020-7412 7772 (Music), 020-7412 7873 (Asia, Pacific & Africa Collections)
website www.bl.uk

The British Library is a marvellous institution which (in theory) contains (among many other things) copies of every play ever performed in the UK and Ireland, and some from other parts of the world. The sound archive also includes just about everything from the sound of Amazonian tree frogs to classic recordings of Shakespeare's plays. You'll need a Reader's Pass (details on how to acquire same is on the website) to access (and read) particular publications. The library will (for a fee) allow photocopying – subject to copyright legislation.

Chappell of Bond Street

50 New Bond Street, London W1S 1RD
tel 020-7491 2777 *fax* 020-7491 0133
email enquiries_bs@chappell-bond-st.co.uk
website www.chappellofbondstreet.co.uk

Stocks the largest range of printed music anywhere in Europe, covering everything from popular chart books to medieval instrumentals, exam pieces to orchestral scores. *Opening Hours*: Monday to Friday: 9.30am – 6pm; Saturday: 9.30am – 5pm.

Contacts

See separate section on The Spotlight.

Doollee.com
website www.doollee.com

An online guide to modern playwrights and theatre plays.

Dress Circle
57-59 Monmouth Street, Upper St Martin's Lane, London WC2H 9DG
tel 020-7240 2227 *fax* 020-7379 8540
email info@dresscircle.co.uk
website www.dresscircle.co.uk

Dress Circle was founded over 25 years ago to supply the widest possible selection of Musical Theatre and Cabaret-related products from around the world – CDs, cassettes, videos, DVDs, posters, cards, mugs, collectibles and more. Opening Hours: Monday to Saturday: 10.00am – 6.30pm. "If we can't get it – no one can!"

Samuel French Theatre Bookshop
52 Fitzroy Street, London W1T 5JR
tel 020-7255 4300 *fax* 020-7387 2161
website www.samuelfrench-london.co.uk

Samuel French has been publishing, selling and leasing plays for performance since 1830. Today it has more than 2000 playscripts available, covering all elements of performing theatre – from comedies to tragedies, sketches to full-scale musicals. In addition, the bookshop stocks a comprehensive range of playscripts and technical books on all aspects of theatre. Publishes *The Guide to Selecting Plays*, which lists plays according to genre and cast size.

Internet Movie Database
website uk.imdb.com

A comprehensive database and news round-up of film and television around the world.

The Knowledge
CMP Data & Information Services, CMP Information Ltd, Riverbank House, Angel Lane, Tonbridge, Kent TN9 1SE
tel (01732) 377041
email knowledge@cmpinformation.com
website www.theknowledgeonline.com

Covering all aspects of production, The Knowledge Online contains contacts and services for the UK film, television, video and commercial production industry. Its *Know-How* section contains studio and post-production charts, production guidelines, articles and maps, and in 2003 it introduced an overview of international co-production by the British Film Commission.

Limited access can be gained by registering online, but for full access to over 18,000 entries and to the *Know-How*, users must pay a £50 annual subscription.

London Arrangements
30 Maryland Square, London E15 1HE
tel 020-8221 2381 *fax* 020-8926 2724
email enquiries@londonarrangements.co.uk
website www.londonarrangements.co.uk
Director Stephen Robinson

The company started up in 2001 after it became clear that there was a lack of Internet companies specialising in bespoke sheet-music arrangements at affordable prices to performers (prices start at around £25 for a simple voice and piano arrangement). In 2002, it began backing-track production, and this is now the main business. Clips from the backing-tracks catalogue can be listened to on the website.

London Theatre
website www.londontheatre.co.uk

A website containing news, reviews, events, booking information and seating plans for London's theatre scene plus maps, hotels and general tourist information.

Mandy.com
website www.mandy.com

An online service providing a directory of 40,000 technicians, facilities and producers and a vacancy list for jobs in production, crew, art departments and post-production. Also posts casting calls for actors, classified ads and information about films for sale and distribution on its website.

National Theatre Bookshop
National Theatre, South Bank, London SE1 9PX
tel 020-7452 3456 *fax* 020-7452 3457
email bookshop@nationaltheatre.org.uk
website www.nationaltheatre.org.uk

Opening Hours: Monday to Saturday: 10am – 10.45pm (this varies on certain public holidays). David Hare once described it as "the most varied and complete performing arts bookshop in the English-speaking world".

Offstage Theatre and Film Bookshop
34 Tavistock Street, Covent Garden, London WC2E 7PB
tel 020-7240 3883 *fax* 020-7916 8046
email orders@offstagebooks.com
website www.offstagebooks.com

Offstage opened as London's only specialist theatre and film bookshop in 1982. Stocks an extensive range of technical and theoretical books in these fields. In addition to the Camden bookshop, offers a worldwide mail-order service. Offstage also provides offsite bookstalls at festivals and conferences for teachers and practitioners.

PlayDatabase.com
website www.playdatabase.com

US site that helps theatre-lovers find monologues and plays for production.

Production & Casting Report (PCR)

See entry under *The Spotlight, casting directories and information services* on page 267.

Project Gutenberg

website www.gutenberg.org

An online library of more than 18,000 books – and many classic plays – which have gone out of copyright in the US. Also a growing collection of music recordings and scores. Possibly the largest of its kind in the world.

Rogues and Vagabonds

13 Elm Road, London SW14 7JL
tel 020-8876 1175
email admin@roguesandvagabonds.co.uk
website www.roguesandvagabonds.co.uk

A subscription website for theatre-lovers and industry professionals providing news, amusement, information, interviews, reviews, quotes and profiles covering all aspects of theatre. With specific resources for actors, including free casting information, links to useful websites and information about a wide range of services offered to actors, the site also provides details of awards, plays, musicals, producers, theatres and directors.

While some areas are available to non-subscribers, the majority are only accessible to those who pay the annual subscription charge of £10.

Royal Court Theatre Bookshop

Sloane Square, London SW1W 8AS
tel 020-7565 5024
email bookshop@royalcourttheatre.com
website www.royalcourttheatre.com

Offers a diverse selection of contemporary plays and publications on the theory and practice of modern drama. The staff specialise in assisting with the selection of audition monologues and scenes. Royal Court playtexts from past and present productions cost £2. The Bookshop is situated in the downstairs Royal Court Bar & Food area. *Opening Hours*: Monday to Friday: 3pm – 10pm; Saturday: 2.30pm – 10pm.

Screen International

EMAP Media, 33-39 Bowling Green Lane, London EC1R 0DA
tel 020-7505 8080 *fax* 020-7505 8117
email ScreenInternational@compuserve.com
website www.screendaily.com
Editor Colin Brown

International news and features on the film business. Subscriptions cost £135 p.a. for 48 issues plus unlimited access to **ScreenDaily.com**.

Script Websites

Although subject to rules on copyright, a number of websites make the scripts for films and television shows, and suggestions for audition speeches, available online. These sites tend to come and go, but here are some that are current at the time of going to press:

- **www.script-o-rama.com**
- **www.playscripts.com**
- **www.simplyscripts.com**
- **www.whysanity.net/monos**
- **www.singlelane.com**
- **www.ubishops.ca/ccc/div/hum/dra/audition.htm**

Shooting People

27 Hedingham Close, London N1 8UA
email contact@shootingpeople.org
website www.shootingpeople.org

Shooting People allows thousands of people working in independent film to exchange information via a range of daily email bulletins. These include:
- Daily UK Filmmakers Bulletin – for directors, producers and crew to share information on the latest technologies, get advice, find crew, locations, production deals, events & screenings, training and more. Currently more than 22,000 members
- Daily UK Screenwriters Bulletin – writers all over the UK use this email network to discuss writing, share ideas and hear about competitions, opportunities and training. Currently more than 13,000 members
- Daily UK Casting Bulletin – for actors to discuss their craft and receive casting calls from directors, producers and casting directors. Currently more than 14,000 members
- Weekly UK Script Pitch Bulletin – a weekly collection of script pitches offered to producers and directors by the writers on the Screenwriters Network. Currently more than 11,000 members

Both part and full membership are available. Part membership allows subscribers to receive email bulletins only, and is free. Full membership costs £20 per year and entitles users to a range of other services. Full members can create an actors' personal profile with a photograph and be listed in the online directory, post to any bulletin and download guides on various confusing aspects of film-making such as actor contracts, health & safety and distribution. They are also entitled to create member cards and browse other member cards to find potential local collaborators.

Shooting People also organises a number of parties, screenings, workshops and other events for which full members receive advanced notice.

Skoob.com

website www.skoob.com

Excellent London-based secondhand bookshop. At the time of writing it is are searching for new premises, but is still operating an Internet mail-order service. See website for latest information.

The Spotlight

See *The Spotlight, casting directories and information services* on page 267.

The Stage

47 Bermondsey Street, London SE1 3XT
tel 020-7403 1818 *subscriptions* (01858) 438895
email newsdesk@thestage.co.uk
website www.thestage.co.uk
Managing Director Catherine Comerford *Editor* Brian Attwood

Established in 1880. A weekly newspaper for professionals in the entertainment industry, with reviews, comments and job advertisements.

Theatre Record

PO Box 445, Chichester, West Sussex PO19 3ZH
tel (01243) 539437 *fax* (01243) 539437
email (subscriptions) ruth@trsubs.demon.co.uk
website www.theatrerecord.com

Established in 1981 as *London Theatre Record*, the magazine was renamed in 1990 to cover work across the UK. *Theatre Record* publishes the complete, unabridged reviews of all new shows covered by national press and leading listing magazines. Fringe shows get extra attention from the critical teams of *Time Out* and *What's On*, while special supplements cover festivals and seasons such as Edinburgh (official and Fringe), LIFT and the London International Mime Festival.

As well as reviews, each show is represented by a full listing of cast, technical credits and, where possible, production photographs. Also lists opening nights for forthcoming productions. Issued fortnightly.

Virtual Library of Theatre & Drama

website www.vl-theatre.com

Lists online versions of plays and resources in more than 50 countries.

Westminster Reference Library

35 St Martin's Street, London WC2H 7HP
tel 020-7641 4638
website www.westminster.gov.uk/libraries/findalibrary/westref

General reference library with an extensive performing arts section. *Opening Hours*: Monday to Friday: 10.00am – 8.00pm; Saturday: 10.00am – 5.00pm.

Wikipedia

website en.wikipedia.org

A free, online encyclopedia with over one million articles. Originally created by an army of volunteers in 2001, it can be added to or edited by anyone at all – a very democratic publication. This democracy can sometimes mean that contentious or politically sensitive issues are not always presented in the most balanced way, although some measures are in place to prevent flagrant abuse of the system. Occasionally too, the editing process makes for some slightly disjointed articles. However, as a free source of information on just about any topic, it is unsurpassed. The theatre section can be accessed via the following link: **en.wikipedia.org/wiki/Portal:Theatre**.

The World of Musicals

website www.mtishows.com

A great resource for researching songs – some of which can be partially listened to and read about on this site.

The Writers' Guild of Great Britain

15 Britannia Street, London WC1X 9JN
tel 020-7833 0777 *fax* 020-7833 4777
email admin@writersguild.org.uk
website www.writersguild.org.uk

A Trade Union for all professional writers working in TV, radio, film, theatre, books and multimedia, it is affiliated to the Trades Union Congress (TUC) and has more than 2000 members. The Guild represents writers in matters such as terms of pay and credits for their work. The Minimum Terms Agreements and advice services aim to safeguard writers against exploitation. Also offered are professional, cultural and social activities to help provide writers with a sense of community, making writing a less isolated occupation. Further information and advice for writers working in theatre, film, radio or television can be found in *Writers' and Artists' Yearbook*, also published by A & C Black.

Organisations, associations and societies

This section contains details of all kinds of ways of getting involved, sourcing useful information, learning, finding interesting lectures, networking, and simply keeping in touch with what's going on. It is important for the 'jobbing' actor to keep up-to-date with developments within the industry, and getting involved in related activities can pay dividends in the future.

Actors' Benevolent Fund
See entry under *Funding bodies*.

Actors' Centre (London)
See entry under *Short-term and part-time courses*.

Actors Centre North East
See entry under *Short-term and part-time courses* on page 24.

The Agents' Association (GB)
54 Keyes House, Dolphin Square, London SW1V 3NA
tel 020-7834 0515 *fax* 020-7821 0261
email association@agents-uk.com
website www.agents-uk.com

Established in 1927 to represent and enhance the interests of entertainment agents in the United Kingdom and to standardise practice. Boasts a membership of more than 430 agencies, covering all fields of the entertainment industry.

Arts & Business
Nutmeg House, 60 Gainsford Street, Butlers Wharf, London SE1 2NY
tel 020-7378 8143 *fax* 020-7407 7527
email info@aandb.org.uk
website www.aandb.org.uk

With support from the Department for Culture, Media Sport and Arts Council England, Arts & Business delivers a range of services to arts organisations of all sizes across the UK promoting the effectiveness and creativity of business and arts partnerships.

Services include sponsoring seminar workshops, training courses, a resource centre, development forums, one-to-one advice sessions and a wide range of publications. Contact details for regional offices are available on the website.

Arts Councils (National and Regional)
See entries under *Funding Bodies*.

Arts Venues
website www.arts-venues.co.uk

Commissioned by the Arts Council England, this online guide brings together detailed information from venues, promoters and festivals across England.

The guide provides extensive information on each organisation, including contact details, artistic policy, programmes of work, artforms covered, spaces and stages available, facilities for companies, facilities for patrons, and details of public services available. Also provides each organisation's email address and website, plus a detailed location map. All material for the entries is supplied directly by the venues, promoters and festivals themselves.

British Academy of Dramatic Combat
3 Castle View, Helmsley, North Yorkshire YO62 5AU
email enquiries@badc.co.uk
website www.badc.co.uk

See entry under *Short-term and part-time courses* on page 26 for further details.

British Academy of Film and Television Arts (BAFTA)
195 Piccadilly, London W1J 9LN
tel 020-7734 0022 *fax* 020-7292 5868
email membership@bafta.org
website www.bafta.org

Founded in 1947, BAFTA provides facilities for screening and discussions, runs a popular and varied events programme coverings all aspects of film, television and interactive entertainment, encourages research and experimentation, and presents the annual Orange British Academy Film Awards.

Approximately 4 events are available to members each month. These range from major industry debates to pre-release screenings of film or television productions, followed by a question-and-answer session with the producer, director, writer and/or cast. A series of Networking Evenings was launched in 2001 to facilitate informal meetings and the exhange of ideas between industry professionals. One of the key events in the programme is the annual David Lean Lecture which has been given by such luminaries as Woody Allen, Ken Loach, John Boorman, Robert Altman and Sidney Pollack.

Applicants must have a minimum of 4 years' professional experience in the film, television or video games industries (or any combination of these) and must be able to demonstrate a significant professional contribution to the industry.

British Arts Festivals Association (BAFA)

3rd Floor, The Library, 77 Whitechapel High Street, London E1 7QX
tel 020-7247 4667 *fax* 020-7247 5010
email info@artsfestivals.co.uk
website www.artsfestivals.co.uk

Provides information and a professional network for the festivals movement in the UK, working to promote the profile and status of arts festivals. As well as the arts festivals website, which catalogues festivals in the UK and provides links to festivals in Europe, BAFA also publishes a free Calendar and Directory of the 105 festival members in print, and produces an advance festivals press pack each January.

Members have the opportunity to attend BAFA conferences, training courses and focus meetings. Membership is open to all arts festivals in the UK and associate membership to other arts organisations. Does not promote individual artists, companies or tours.

British Council

Arts Group, 10 Spring Gardens, London SW1A 2BN
tel 020-7389 3194 *fax* 020-7389 3199
email artweb@britishcouncil.org
Norwich Union House, 7 Fountain Street, Belfast BT1 5EG
tel 028-9024 8220 *fax* 028-9023 7592
email collette.norwood@britishcouncil.org
The Tun, 3rd Floor, 4 Jackson's Entry, Holyrood Road, Edinburgh EH8 8PJ
tel 0131-524 5714 *fax* 0131-524 5714
email art.scotland@britishcouncil.org
28 Park Place, Cardiff CF10 3QE
tel 029-2039 7346 *fax* 029-2023 7494
email chris.ricketts@britishcouncil.org
website www.britishcouncil.org/arts

The British Council is the UK's public diplomacy and cultural organisation and works in 100 countries, in arts, education, governance and science. The Arts Group supports around 2000 arts events every year encouraging international collaborations, performances and exchanges with some of the top UK artists. In addition they support arts-based workshops, seminars and online events.

The form of support which is offered varies according to the project. In most cases the Council acts as an advisory body and brokers partnerships with overseas contacts such as artistic programmers and producers, venues, choreographers and festival directors. Although most work is geared towards young people aged 16-35, this isn't an exclusive emphasis and classic or traditional work is supported, especially if it has a modern slant.

Resources available on the website include an annual directory of UK drama, dance, live art and street art companies that have work suitable for overseas touring; specialist information about drama/ performing arts education in the UK; and *Britfilms* (**www.britfilms.com**) – a portal site for the UK film industry with information about international film festivals, UK film directors and films, making a film in the UK, training and careers advice.

Not open to the public except by appointment. Write, phone or email to establish contact or get in touch with an artform specialist.

British Film Commission

See UK Film Council International.

British Film Institute (*bfi*)

bfi National Library, 21 Stephen Street, London W1T 1LN
tel 020-7255 1444
email library@bfi.org.uk
National Film Theatre, Belvedere Road, South Bank, Waterloo, London SE1 8XT
tel 020-7928 3535
email nft@bfi.org.uk
website www.bfi.org.uk

Established in 1933, the *bfi* strives to increase the level of understanding, appreciation and access to film and television culture. In addition to the *bfi* National Library which holds the largest film archive in the world, the organisation runs the National Film Theatre and London Film Festival (see entry under *Media festivals*), and the *bfi* IMAX Cinema. It also publishes books, releases films in cinemas, on video and DVD, runs educational programmes and has one of the largest collections of film stills and film posters in the world.

British Music Hall Society

82 Fernlea Road, London SW12 9RW
tel 020-8673 2175
website www.music-hall-society.com
Secretary Daphne Masterton

Founded in 1963 and with offices across England, the society aims to preserve the history of music hall and variety, to recall the artistes who created it and to support entertainers working today. Members receive copies of the society's quarterly magazine *The Call-Boy* containing news, views and information about the sector; they also have the opportunity to attend evening and weekend study group meetings. Arranges live theatre shows and it is possible for members to take part in such performances on these occasions.

Casting Directors Guild

website www.thecdg.co.uk

A professional organisation which represents casting directors working in film, television, theatre and commercials. The Casting Directors Guild aims to standardise professional working practice and to enable the exchange of information and ideas between members.

Election to the Guild is at the discretion of the Committee. Full members must have worked in 1 or more areas of the industry for at least 5 years and are entitled to use the initials CDG after their name. Probationary members must have worked as an assistant to a casting director for 3 years.

Members are listed on the website with information about their areas of work and recent credits.

Co-operative Personal Managers' Association

The Secretary, c/o 1 Mellor Road, Leicester LE3 6HN
tel 0116-233 8432 *fax* 0116-223 5537
email cpmauk@yahoo.co.uk

A professional organisation representing the interests of Co-operative Agencies.

Conference of Drama Schools (CDS)

PO Box 34252, London NW5 1XJ
email info@cds.drama.ac.uk
website www.drama.ac.uk

Founded in 1969 to strengthen the voice of member drama schools and encourage the highest standards of training, the CDS also helps students understand the range of courses on offer and how to apply for them. The CDS played a key role in the negotiations which led to the formation of the National Council for Drama Training (see entry below).

The 22 member schools offer courses in Acting, Musical Theatre, Directing and Technical Theatre training. CDS members offer courses that are professional, intensive and vocational. They are often mentally and physically demanding and, unlike most degree courses at universities and colleges, do not generally contain a high proportion of academic work.

Produces the *Guide to Professional Training in Drama and Technical Theatre* for careers officers, teachers and applicants, providing a description of each member school, its policy and the courses it offers together with information about funding. It also provides details of summer schools. The printed version is available free of charge from French's Theatre Bookshop (see entry on page 310). Alternatively it can be downloaded from the CDS website.

Conservatoire for Dance and Drama (CDD)

1-7 Woburn Walk, London WC1H 0JJ
tel 020-7387 5101 *fax* 020-7387 5103
email info@cdd.ac.uk
website www.cdd.ac.uk

The Conservatoire for Dance and Drama comprises a small number of small, specialist vocational schools committed to addressing the training needs of dance and drama professions. The Conservatoire aims to attract the most talented students who are selected irrespective of background and to sustain its affiliate schools' excellence in training and research.

The CDD was established in August 2001 in order to foster the development of conservatoire-style teaching in small schools of dance and drama in England which are of international standing. Its affiliate drama schools are Bristol Old Vic Theatre School, LAMDA and Royal Academy of Dramatic Art.

Council for Dance Education and Training (CDET)

Old Brewer's Yard, 17-19 Neal Street, Covent Garden, London WC2H 9UY
tel 020-7240 5703 *fax* 020-7240 2547
email info@cdet.org.uk
website www.cdet.org.uk

The Council for Dance Education and Training is the national standards body of the professional dance industry. It accredits programmes of training in vocational dance schools and holds the Register of Dance Awarding Bodies - the directory of teaching societies whose syllubuses have been inspected and approved by the Council. It is the body of advocacy of the dance education and training communities, and offeres a free and comprehensive information service, *Answers for Dancers*, on all aspects of vocational dance provision to students, parents, teachers, dance artists and employers.

Dance UK

Battersea Arts Centre, Lavender Hill, London SW11 5TN
tel 020-7728 4990 *fax* 020-7223 0074
email info@danceuk.org
website www.danceuk.org

Dance UK was founded in 1982 and works with and on behalf of dance, providing information, publications, networks, forums for debate and conferences and a unified voice for all its members. It has about 130 corporate members, including most of the major dance companies, venues, agencies, funders and educational institutions. Individual members include individual dance artists, choreographers, administrators, managers, technicians, teachers, students, writers and members of dance audiences.

The organisation is active in 3 main areas: Communication, Professional Development and Healthier Dance. As well as the website, Dance UK manages email groups for choreographers, dance managers and independent dance artists, and produces *Dance UK News* which is mailed quarterly to members. Has set up a number of practical initiatives to promote longer-lasting careers and professional development in dance including insurance schemes for teachers, the UK Choreographers Directory, and books and information sheets on floors, pensions, insurance and copyright.

Promoting the health and well-being of dancers, it also generates research, educational talks and events, posters, information sheets and books. The Practitioners Register is a telephone help-line providing contact information for local medical and complementary therapists with experience of working with dancers. For information about other dance organisations and performing companies, visit the links page on the website.

Department of Culture, Media and Sport (DCMS)

Information Centre, 2-4 Cockspur Street, London SW1Y 5DH
tel 020-7211 6200
email enquiries@culture.gov.uk
website www.culture.gov.uk

The DCMS is responsible for Government policy on the arts, sport, the National Lottery, tourism, libraries, museums and galleries, broadcasting, film, the music industry, press freedom and regulation, licensing, gambling and the historic environment.

Arts policies are carried out in partnership with Arts Council England and its Regional Arts Councils, other government departments such as the Department for Education and Skills, and with regional bodies such as local authorities.

Directors Guild of Great Britain

4 Windmill Street, London W1T 2HZ
tel 020-7580 9131 *fax* 020-7580 9132
email guild@dggb.org
website www.dggb.org

Founded in 1982, the Directors Guild of Great Britain represents directors in all media including film, television, theatre, radio, opera, commercials, corporate, multimedia and new technology. It is a trade union, offering help with contracts, a campaigning voice, policy to influence the future of the industry, and advice for members to meet and share their skills. It also organises many events with a focus on training such as masterclasses (topics have included working with actors, theatre for young people), panel events, careers advice sessions and short courses.

Actors can obtain information about the Guild's members and their career profile using the online searchable database. For information on directors who are not members of the Guild, the DGGB has a number of suggestions on their website. Actors may wish to consult the following websites for information on international directors:
• www.dga.org (Directors Guild of America)
• www.dgc.ca (Directors Guild of Canada)
• www.asdafilm.org.au (Australian Screen Directors Association)

Drama Association of Wales

The Old Library, Singleton Road, Splott, Cardiff CF24 2ET
tel 029-2045 2200 *fax* 029-2045 2277
website www.amdram.co.uk/daw1

Founded in 1934 and a registered charity since 1973, the Drama Association of Wales aims to increase opportunities for people in the community to be creatively involved in high-quality drama.

Its main activities are an extensive mail-order library service with more than 200,000 volumes of plays, biographies, critical works and technical theatre books, and training courses in all aspects of theatre, including a 7-day residential summer school and a winter school in the Mediterranean.

Also runs several new writing schemes offering a script-reading service, a playwriting competition, workshops and support for first productions, and organises the Welsh National Drama Festival from January to June, culminating in the Wales One Act Festival. Assists in founding and sustaining youth theatre companies and encourages cooperation between professional and amateur theatre.

UK membership costs just under £12 per year for individuals and £29 a year for Amateur Societies.

Dramaturgs' Network

69 Hounslow Road, Twickenham, Middlesex TW2 7HA
tel (07939) 270556
email info@dramaturgy.co.uk
website ee.dramaturgy.co.uk

The Dramaturgs' Network is a professional organisation which promotes the role of the dramaturg in the UK. Providing members with a network of support, the organisation brings dramaturgs, literary managers and script editors together to create opportunities for debate and sharing of information and experiences. In collaboration with other professional bodies such as the Directors Guild of Great Britain and Equity, the organisation seeks to standardise the definition and working practice of dramaturgs in the UK.

The website contains details of members, activities, a newletter archive and other information.

Equity

See entry on page 266.

Fringe Theatre Network (FTN)

c/o Old Red Lion, 418 St John Street, London EC1V 4QE
tel 020-7833 3053
email helenoldredlion@yahoo.co.uk
website www.fringetheatre.org.uk
Coordinator Helen Devine

The FTN provides services, support and a network of contacts for venues, producing companies and individuals working on the London Fringe with the aim of increasing the level of professionalism in Fringe theatre. Acting as an umbrella organisation, the FTN puts forward the interests of Fringe theatre in its dealings with statutory authorities, funding bodies, policy-makers and other arts organisations.

Independent Theatre Council (ITC)

12 The Leathermarket, Weston Street, London SE1 3ER
tel 020-7403 1727 *fax* 020-7403 1745
email admin@itc-arts.org
website www.itc-arts.org

Founded in 1974, the Independent Theatre Council negotiates contracts and has established standard agreements with Equity and other unions, on behalf of all professionals working in theatre. With more than 600 members, ITC provides management and legal advice, contractual negotiation and conciliation services, networking, advocacy, information exchange, and training and personal development services for performing arts organisations, individuals and venues.

Working across a variety of artforms including drama, dance, opera, music theatre, puppetry, mixed media, mime, physical theatre and circus, ITC members usually operate on the middle and small scale and are dedicated to producing innovative work, often in unconventional performance spaces.

ITC has commissioned a wide range of publications which offer guidance on potentially difficult aspects of working in the performing arts, advice on good practice and further sources of information. Courses and seminars, run by ITC and open to all, cover a similar range of topics and issues. Also offers in-house training and other services. For details of how to join and other benefits available to members, consult the website.

International Federation of Actors (FIA)

Guild House, Upper St Martin's Lane, London WC2H 9EG
tel 020-7379 0900 *fax* 020-7379 8260
email office@fia-actors.com
website www.fia-actors.com

The FIA currently represents 103 performers' unions and guilds in 73 countries around the world. Membership is limited to unions, guilds and professional associations - individual actors may not join. FIA works internationally to represent and co-ordinate the interests of performing artists and their professional organisations.

Services: Lobbying at European and international level on behalf of performers; defence of artists' freedom; trade union development; information exchange through conferences and meetings; networking.

Objectives: To promote a better understanding of performers' concerns and challenges around the world; the ensure that all main decision-making processes take due consideration of the specific needs of performers; to contribute to improve the social and professional conditions of performers worldwide; to facilitate the sharing of knowledge and experience on all issues of common interest between member organisations.

National Association of Youth Theatres (NAYT)

Arts Centre, Vane Terrace, Darlington DL3 7AX
tel (01325) 363330 *fax* (01325) 363313
email nayt@btconnect.com
website www.nayt.org.uk

Founded in 1982, the National Association of Youth Theatres is the leading development organisation for youth theatre practice in England and Wales. On behalf of registered groups it works with the Department for Education and Skills (DfES), Arts Council England, Regional Arts Councils and local authorities to achieve greater recognition and improved funding for the sector. Registration is open to any group or individual using theatre techniques in their work with young people, outside of formal education.

The NAYT provides a variety of resources, information and support for registered groups including training programmes, advice on a wide range of policy and strategy issues, an archive with project reports, surveys and case studies, and a monthly *Bulletin* containing the latest news on funding, training, performances and vacancies. With online information and contact details for more than 700 registered groups, the organisation also enables young people to contact youth theatres directly.

National Council for Drama Training (NCDT)

1-7 Woburn Walk, London WC1H 0JJ
tel 020-7387 3650 *fax* 020-7387 3860
email info@ncdt.co.uk
website www.ncdt.co.uk

The National Council for Drama Training is a partnership of employers in the theatre, broadcast and media industry, employee representatives and training providers who work together to increase support for professional drama training and education.

It seeks to maintain the highest standards and provides a credible process of quality assurance through accreditation for vocational drama, reassuring students that the courses they choose are recognised and respected by the drama profession.

National Operatic and Dramatic Association (NODA)

58-60 Lincoln Road, Peterborough PE1 2RZ
tel 0870-770 2480 *fax* 0870-770 2490
email everyone@noda.org.uk
website www.noda.org.uk
Patron Lord Lloyd-Webber

Founded in 1899, NODA is the main representative body for amateur theatre in the UK. It has a membership of around 2500 amateur/community theatre groups and 3000 individual enthusiasts throughout the UK, staging musicals, operas, plays, concerts and pantomimes in a variety of performing venues, ranging from professional theatres to village halls.

Produces a quarterly national magazine, *NODA National News*, containing advice and information for the amateur theatre sector, listings of performances in the National Theatre Diary and classified ads. Also holds area and national conferences, workshops and summer schools.

National Theatre Platforms

South Bank, London SE1 9PX
tel 020-7453 3000
email angus@nationaltheatre.org.uk
website www.nationaltheatre.org.uk/platforms
Platforms Producer Angus MacKechnie

An eclectic programme of pre-performance events celebrates all aspects of the arts, offering the chance to learn about the National's work and discover more about theatre in general. Platforms usually start at 6pm, lasting for 45 minutes - there are occasional afternoon events, usually starting at 2.30pm. Tickets: £3.50 (£2.50 concessions).

New Producers Alliance (NPA)

NPA Film Centre, Suite 1.07 The Tea Building, 56 Shoreditch High Street, London E1 6JJ
tel 020-7613 0440 *fax* 020-7729 1852
email queries@npa.org.uk
website www.npa.org.uk

The NPA is the UK's national membership and training organisation for independent new producers and filmmakers. It provides access to contacts, information and advice for more than 800 members, from film students to major production companies and industry affiliates. Individual membership costs £75 per year (£50 for students and the unemployed) and is open to producers, directors and writers.

North American Actors Association (NAAA)

tel 020-7938 4722
email americanactors@aol.com
website www.naaa.org.uk

The North American Actors Association is a network serving the entertainment industry by supporting North American actors with a base in Britain.

Membership is open to professional actors who can work on both sides of the Atlantic without restriction, are full members in good standing of at least one entertainment union, and have proof of professional contracts. To those involved in casting, we act as a resource of genuine North American actors, and are happy to provide agent and other contact details of our members.

Northern Actors Centre

See entry under *Short-term and part-time courses.*

PACT (Producers Alliance for Cinema & Television)

Procter House, 1 Procter Street, Holborn, London, WC1V 6DW
tel 020-7067 4367
website www.pact.co.uk

The UK trade association that represents the commercial interests of independent feature film, television, animation and interactive media companies.

PACT (Producers Alliance for Cinema and Television)

The Eye, 2nd Floor, 1 Proctor Street, London WC1V 6DW
tel 020-7067 4367 *fax* 020-7067 4377
email enquiries@pact.co.uk
Pact Scotland 249 West George Street, Glasgow G2 4QE
tel 0141-222 4880 *fax* 0141-222 4881
email margaret@pact.co.uk
website www.pact.co.uk
Chief Executive John McVay, *Information Manager* David Alan Mills
Head of Nations & Regions Margaret Scott

The main trade association for feature film and independent TV production companies. Represents the interests of over 1000 production companies throughout the UK: promotes and protects the commercial interests of its members; lobbies government and regulators on their behalf; negotiates terms of trade with broadcasters; provides a range of membership services including advice on business affairs, industrial relations and legal advice; operates a copyright registration service for members' proposals and treatments for films and TV programmes. Its representative office in Glasgow serves the interests of its regional members.

Personal Managers' Association

Rivercroft, 1 Summer Road, East Molesey, Surrey
KT8 9LX
tel 020-8398 9796 *fax* 020-8398 9796
email info@thepma.com

Founded in 1950, the PMA is an association of artists'
and dramatists' agents which provides members with
a forum to exchange ideas and information. The
association maintains a code of conduct and acts as a
lobby when necessary.

Royal Television Society (RTS)

Kildare House, 3 Dorset Rise, London EC4Y 8EN
tel 020-7822 2810 *fax* 020-7822 2811
email info@rts.org.uk
website www.rts.org.uk

Provides the leading forum for discussion and debate
on all aspects of the television industry, with
opportunities for networking and professional
development for people at all levels and across every
sector. The RTS has 14 national and regional centres
in the UK which draw up an annual programme to
suit the needs of their members.

Events organised by the RTS include dinners,
lectures, conventions, conferences and awards
ceremonies. In addition it produces a monthly
magazine, *Television*, outlining key industry debates
and developments.

The Royal Theatrical Fund

See entry under *Funding bodies*.

The Screenwriters' Workshop

Now part of the New Producers Alliance (NPA) - see
entry on page 318.

Society of London Theatre (SOLT)

32 Rose Street, London WC2E 9ET
tel 020-7557 6700 *fax* 020-7557 6799
email enquiries@solttma.co.uk
website www.officiallondontheatre.co.uk

Founded in 1908 by Sir Charles Wyndham, the
Society of London Theatre is the trade association
which represents the producers, theatre owners and
managers of the major commercial and grant-aided
theatres in central London.

Today the Society combines its long-standing roles in
such areas as industrial relations and legal advice for
members with a campaigning role for the industry,
together with a wide range of audience-development
programmes to promote theatre-going.

The Society of Teachers of Speech and Drama (STSD)

73 Berry Hill Road, Mansfield, Nottinghamshire
NG18 4RU
email stsd@stsd.org.uk

website www.stsd.org.uk

Protecting the professional interests of qualified,
specialist teachers of Speech & Drama, the STSD
encourages good standards of teaching and promotes
the study and knowledge of speech and dramatic art
in every form. Has established close links with drama
schools and examination boards and its publications
are read worldwide.

Members receive copies of its newsletters,
information sheets and the journal *Speech & Drama*.
They are entitled to free advice, to be included in a
register of members and to attend its summer
conference.

Students of Speech & Drama can search for suitable
teachers using the online database.

The Stephen Sondheim Society

265 Wollaton Vale, Wollaton, Nottingham NG8 2PX
email sondheimsociety@sondheim.org
website www.sondheim.org
Chair Mandy Dixon *Administrator* Lynne Chapman

Society to promote the works of the composer and
lyricist Stephen Sondheim. Keeps track of all
productions (professional and amateur) of
Sondheim's musicals, publishes a newsletter, arranges
theatre visits, and from time to time also sponsors
appropriate productions.

At the time of writing, membership is £15 (single),
£10 (concession) or £20 (joint) but please consult the
website for the latest rates.

The Theatre Museum

1e Tavistock Street, London WC2E 7PR
tel 020-7943 4700 *fax* 020-7943 4777
email tmenquiries@vam.ac.uk
website www.theatremuseum.org

The Theatre Museum is the National Museum of the
Performing Arts and a branch of the Victoria Albert
Museum (V&A). With a wide range of documents,
artefacts and works of art recording the history of the
performing arts in Britain from the 16th century to
the present, it holds the world's largest and most
important collections relating to the British stage.
Using costumes, designs, manuscripts, books, video
recordings (including the National Video Archive of
Stage Performance), posters and paintings, the
museum reconstructs details of past performances
and the lives of performers, past and contemporary.

All the live performing arts are represented, including
drama, dance, opera, musical theatre, circus,
puppetry, music hall and live art, and are made
available through exhibitions, educational
programmes, events, publications, study facilities and
the website. There is also a studio theatre, details of
which can be found on page 176. The museum is
wheelchair accessible and regularly hosts events for
and with theatre professionals with sensory

impairments. (Contact Sue Rolfe for more information - 020 7943 4740)

NB. As of April 2006, the museum building is threatened with closure, which would mean exhibits and events being moved to other V&A buildings in Kensington. Efforts to retain the exhibitions within theatreland are currently being supported by the Royal Opera House. Up-to-date information may be found on the website.

Theatre Royal Haymarket Masterclasses

Theatre Royal Haymarket, London SW1Y 4HT
tel 020-7389 9660 *fax* 020-7389 9697
email masterclass@trh.co.uk
website www.trh.co.uk/masterclass
Patrons Sir Peter Hall, Sir David Hare, Maureen Lipman CBE

Masterclass is an arts initiative which allows young people aged 17-30 to attend workshops and talks given by leading actors, directors, designers and writers working in theatre today. All events take place at the Theatre Royal Haymarket and are free of charge to young people aged 17-30. People over the age of 30 may also take part and contribute to the project by joining the Masterclass Friends scheme.

In addition to the masterclass events, the programme includes a longer-term new writing project and a series that gives career advice and support. Previous Masters have included Steven Berkoff, Simon Callow, Mike Leigh, Alan Rickman, Prunella Scales and Janet Suzman. For details of forthcoming events, consult the website.

Theatres Trust

22 Charing Cross Road, London WC2H 0QL
tel 020-7836 8591 *fax* 020-7836 3302
email info@theatrestrust.org.uk
website www.theatrestrust.org.uk

The Theatres Trust is an independent, advisory, non-departmental public body and a statutory consultee. Local authorities are required by Government Order to consult the Trust when considering planning applications affecting land on which there is a theatre. This applied to all theatre buildings, old or new, and regardless or whether or not they are still in use as theatres, in others uses or disused. The Trust's main objective is to safeguard theatre use of the potential for such use, but it also provides expert advice on design, conservation, property and planning matters to theatre operators, local authorities and official bodies, and also runs an information service. Its archives include records of over 3,500 theatre buildings and some 30,000 images, as well as plans and other documents. The Trust has a small professional staff supported by consultants and members of its Friends organisation, and works closely with other official bodies and voluntary groups.

Theatrical Management Association (TMA)

32 Rose Street, London WC2E 9ET
tel 020-7557 6700 *fax* 020-7557 6799
email enquiries@solttma.co.uk
website www.tmauk.org
Chief Executive Richard Pulford

TMA is the pre-eminent UK wide organisation dedicated to providing a professional support network for the performing arts industry. Founded in 1894 by Sir Henry Irving, it is now an association of people and throughout the UK professionally involved in the production and presentation of the performing arts. Its members include repertory and producing theatres, arts centres and touring venues, major national companies and independent producers, opera and dance companies, and associated individuals and businesses.

TMA is run by a Council elected from and by the membership. This Council represents all sectors of the business and employs the professional staff team who provide the services for members. Diverse as they are, TMA members share a common conviction that the professional and social advantages of membership increase their ability to run successful businesses. Member organisations are encouraged to follow best professional practice and are given advice to enable them to do so. Individuals can benefit from training and networking opportunities to help develop their careers.

TMA shares a common staff with the Society of London Theatre (SOLT).

UK Centre of the International Association of Theatre for Children & Young People

Arad Goch, Strydy Baddon, Aberystwyth, Dyfed SY23 2NN
tel (01970) 617998 *fax* (01970) 611223
email j.turner@apt.org.uk
website www.assitej.org
Contact Jeremy Turner

Supporting the provision of professional theatre for young people, APT encourages and enables the exchange of ideas, experience and advice between theatre companies in the UK and abroad. Information about member companies and their work is available on the website.

UK Film Council

See entry under *Funding bodies*.

Women in Film and Television (WFTV)

6 Langley Street, London WC2H 9JA
tel 020-7240 4875
email emily@wftv.org.uk
website www.wftv.org.uk

Membership & Events Manager Emily Compton

A membership association open to women with a minimum of 1 year's professional experience in the television, film or digital media industries. With more than 800 members including writers, actresses and directors, the WFTV promotes the interests and diversity of women working at all levels in these industries. Offers a network of national and international contacts with an online directory of members, and provides a number of social forums, workshops, seminars and preview screenings.

Youngblood

The Rag Factory, 16-18 Heneage St, London E1 5LJ
tel 020-7193 3207
email info@youngblood.co.uk
website www.youngblood.co.uk

A company of fight directors and stage-combat teachers. Runs ongoing classes for professional actors in various locations around London. Also provides fight directors and trainers for film, television and theatre projects, including low-budget productions.

An actor's guide to keeping sane
Tim Bentinck

This is not a flippant title. The psychological battle of being an actor/breadwinner is the war; doing the job is just the fighting.

If you're a good builder and you're not getting work, it's probably because you're being undercut by the East Europeans, but you still know you're a good builder.

If you're an actor, you have no such objective take on the matter. In order to be a professional actor, you *have* to believe you're bloody good, or you can't even get started, let alone continue. The problem is that your own estimation of your talent is inherently biased, because when a builder has finished a roof conversion that looks beautiful and doesn't leak, no one rings him to complain. When an actor has done a part on telly and no-one rings, is it because (a) they weren't watching? (b) they thought you were good but didn't bother to ring? (c) they thought you were crap? or (d) they didn't like you anyway and turned over the minute you appeared? Even when your best friends think you're crap, they almost never say.

Therefore, you have to rely on your own judgement, and as an actor it's extremely difficult to be objective, disinterested and honest about your own performance. On stage you get a good idea when your jokes fall flat and people talk about the set in the bar afterwards, but on screen and on radio, you really are not the best judge. Everyone, myself included, can believe they're being brilliant when they're not. When you start off as an actor you *have* to have at heart a naïve belief that your originality, eccentricity, new interpretation of a text, your life experience, your pain, your joy, your discovery of sex for the first time in history, your raw talent, or your chutzpah and charm will blow them all away.

This, dear actor, we all have. You can't *be* an actor without empathising with some part of the above.

The reality, *quelle malheur*, is mostly down to luck – the right place, the right time, and almost nothing more. Oh, and probably being unconventionally good-looking or sexy. Being good at it is an added bonus.

I'm 52. About 25 years ago someone I knew fairly well said to me drunkenly at a party, "Oh I saw you in that thing on telly last night, you were *awful*! Jeremy did you see it? Wasn't Tim dreadful?! Ha ha ha." At the time I was really hurt. I was shocked and rocked to the core. I had to find a way to deal with it, so I just decided she was a cow and mad and had no taste and didn't get it, and got on with life. About a year ago, when I watched the episode in question again on DVD, I realised she was painfully closer to the truth than I'd realised. I'd never done telly before and had just done nine months as a pirate in the West End and I was way OTT — lots of *acting* going on. I hadn't learned the 'do nothing' rule. In my defence I was fairly dishy and the swordfights were good. Yes she was a rude cow for saying it, but the point I'm circumlocutorily trying to reach is this: At the time, everyone said I was brilliant. No – I was *alright*. Beware the flatterers. Make people tell you the truth and then do something about it. Never be afraid of criticism; it's usually well founded, and sometimes well meant.

So in order to remain sane in this business, it is important that you have a very strong belief – backed up by some rigorous interrogation of your most trusted friends, your family, your loved ones and your fans – that you have what it takes, if given the chance, to be an astonishingly brilliant actor. Because unless you're very lucky, you are going to be hurt, rejected, abused, disrespected, talked down to, patronised, dismissed, ignored, not appreciated, paid badly, not paid at all, taken for granted and generally ground down for the rest of your life ... so if you can't face that, forget it.

From then on, one of three things is going to happen. The first is that you become a megastar. End of story, read a different book. The second is that you become a professional actor, earning some kind of living. The third is that it's a total bloody disaster. Here are some suggestions for how to remain sane with option two.

About five years ago, I spent a good six months of that year worrying about what things were going to be like five years in the future. Here I am today and everything's pretty fine. So I had effectively *wasted* all that time of my life worrying about something that didn't happen. Absurd. You have got to seize the day, or the night if that's your thing – *carpe noctem,* even!

Depression is a killer; it killed someone close to me, and I've been down that road too. But you can talk yourself out of it. You can bully yourself. Buy a bike and ride it, swim, have more sex, go to the pub and meet new people, get drunk with them and solve the problems of the world, sign up for a rally driving course, use the credit card to pamper yourself and don't worry about tomorrow (if that doesn't work, take Prozac but don't do the drinking thing – it's unhealthy, expensive and doesn't work). Do that until you've stopped being depressed, then you can worry about the debt with a more sanguine view – sanguine and proactive (dreadful word but can't think of an alternative).

You have *got* to treat it as a business. You're the product and if someone else isn't selling you (PR or agent), then it's down to you. My very first agent came from the world of PR and said to me that he knew nothing about acting, but aimed to get my name on the desks of everyone who mattered, every day of the week. He made me a lot of money. You're up against the PR might of comedians, footballers, models, weather-girls, body-builders, basketball players, TV presenters, extras, personal fitness coaches to the stars, drunks, reality-show winners, reality-show runners up, Pop Idols, and specifically Jade (insert adjective of choice, like 'talented', 'intelligent', 'thin', 'attractive') Goody.

Get a website, make a voice tape, make a video compilation, send them to Spotlight, send them to your agent, send a DVD to casting directors. Get yourself in the press, get yourself on radio, write plays, write songs, drive trucks, plant gardens, do classes, keep fit, look good, raise a family, change the nappies. Live a life, the experience of which you can bring to your acting. Be in trim and ready to grab the bits of luck that come your way with bold confidence.

Another thing: work on your memory, or carry a notebook. Remember the names of the casting directors; remember the directors you work for; be pleasant to the runner, because s/he'll be the producer/director in six year's time; remember what your agent looks like when you meet him/her at parties; remember the voice-overs you did and who directed them; also, get a copy of everything to add to your showreel. Remember to keep all your receipts and put money aside for tax; if you're VAT registered, you're being paid to be a tax collector, so do it yourself – keep the money and have a holiday.

If you're young – *do it now do it now*! Over 40? – you've learned the game, so play it; you're just a more mature version of you at 20. If you're over 50, this is the time to strike:

be bold, we've learned it all, we've got it all to give. Young filmmakers take heed: we are what you will be in 30 years' time, so we represent what you aspire to. You're pretty bright now, but don't you reckon that after 30 years you'll have learned a whole shed-load more? Well that's *us*. Welcome to Saga and the days of low insurance, paid-off mortgages and, finally, the bus pass, which I admit is still hard, at my age, to contemplate. It's eight years away though. Hmmm.

All the bloody pain and insecurity and rejection is mitigated, though, by this:

You could face a cavalry charge in the Crimea. You could star in a West End musical. You could fly an F3 Tornado simulator. You could fight duels and fire machine guns. You could sit on a rubber pad on the top of a mountain inside the Arctic circle in Norway for three days waiting for the fog to clear to shoot a commercial for beer and get frostbite. You could be protected at night from elephant and tiger by armed guards in the Masai Mara, filming an ad for ice cream – and get sunstroke. You could dice for the lead with Damon Hill in a Formula One Kart. You could re-voice Gerard Dèpardieu in a movie, be the voice of James Bond in a computer game and say "Mind The Gap" on the Piccadilly Line. You could be kissed by Kevin Kline or thrown overboard by Roger Moore. You could die in the arms of Sean Bean and snog loads of beautiful women. You could have Claudia Schiffer looking into your eyes saying, "Ich liebe dich, ich liebe dich...". You could dub the lucky guy who shags Sharon Stone in *Basic Instinct 2*. You could earn your living with an earring in your ear and a sword around your waist. You could star in sitcoms, television series and radio soaps. You could do live improvisation games on stage and be filmed on horseback, scuba diving, canyoning, parachuting and piloting a flying boat. You could time a kiss, on a beach on the Great Barrier Reef, so that the setting sun shines between your closing lips as the waves lap around your suntanned body.

Sorry, but look we're all bloody show-offs after all, and if after 30 years I couldn't give a list like the above, I'd have given it up.

It's a great, great adventure. It's a business and you have to run it. If it isn't working, give it up. I know plenty of ex-actors who are hugely successful at their new jobs. When I was training at Bristol, I remember thinking that *everybody* should do this course – not just actors, but everyone. If you've acted professionally for a while, it's a brilliant intro to everything else. Look at politicians – crap actors. Local government – the same. Most businessmen talking to their staff – abysmal. Actors can turn their hands to anything, so if you give it up, it wasn't wasted; it was part of your life-training.

Downer. What I mean is this: I've seen the highs and I've dived down deep with the lows. I know the reality but I'm still fired by the dream. That's what keeps us going.

Churchill said it most accurately, with all the power of the struggle of the war behind him: "Keep Buggering On."

See you on the green.

More about **Tim Bentinck** can be found at **www.bentinck.net**.

Bibliography

Books for aspiring, student and young actors

Margo Annett, *Actor's Guide to Auditions and Interviews* (3rd edition, A & C Black, 2004). A useful guide outlining some of the techniques needed for success.

Peter Barkworth, *The Complete About Acting* (Methuen, 1991). Another very good book about acting and getting work.

Simon Dunmore, *An Actor's Guide to Getting Work* (4th edition, A & C Black, 2004). A practical, comprehensive guide covering all aspects of marketing yourself as an actor.

Simon Dunmore, *Alternative Shakespeare Auditions for Women* (A & C Black, 1997). A collection of 50 less-well-known speeches for women.

Simon Dunmore, *MORE Alternative Shakespeare Auditions for Women* (A & C Black, 1999). Another collection of 50 less-well-known speeches for women.

Simon Dunmore, *Alternative Shakespeare Auditions for Men* (A & C Black, 1997). A collection of 50 less-well-known speeches for men.

Simon Dunmore, *MORE Alternative Shakespeare Auditions for Men* (A & C Black, 2002). Another collection of 50 less-well-known speeches for men.

Ellis Jones, *Teach Yourself Acting* (Hodder & Stoughton Ltd, 1998). A good overview of acting and the profession.

Anna Scher, *Desperate to Act* (Lions, 1988). Brilliant, basic advice for those so 'desperate', from a lady who should know.

William Shakespeare, *Hamlet, Prince of Denmark*. Especially Hamlet's advice to the players (Act 3, scene 2), which is some of the best advice on acting ever given.

Bernard Graham Shaw, *Voice-Overs, A Practical Guide* (A & C Black, 2000). A useful guide which explains and teaches the skills of voicing radio and television commercials.

Clive Swift, *The Job of Acting* (Harrap, revised 1984). Although some of it is out-of-date, this book is a wonderful read from an experienced and caring professional.

Malcolm Taylor, *The Actor and the Camera* (A & C Black, 1994). Another good 'primer' for the beginner.

Other career advice books for actors

Ed Hooks, *The Audition Book* (3rd edition, Back Stage Books, 2000). Excellent reading if you're thinking of trying your hand in the USA. It's also worth looking at Ed's website for his excellent 'Craft Notes' (**www.edhooks.com**).

Peter Messaline and Miriam Newhouse, *The Actor's Survival Kit* (3rd edition, Simon & Pierre, 1999). Well worth reading if you're thinking of trying your hand in Canada.

Books for any actor

Stephen Aaron, *Stage Fright: Its Role in Acting* (University of Chicago Press, 1986). Fascinating book, written by a psychotherapist who is also an experienced director and teacher.

Brian Bates, *The Way of the Actor* (Century Hutchinson, 1986). Very interesting insights into the inner workings of the actor's psyche.

Peter Brook, *The Empty Space* (Penguin, 1990). Written in the 1960s, but still essential reading.

Adrian Cairns, *The Making of the Professional Actor* (Peter Owen Publishers, 1996). A fascinating study of the history, and possible future, of the art of acting.

Simon Callow, *Being an Actor* (Penguin, 1995). Autobiographical books by famous actors are generally useless in terms of practical career advice. However, this one – part autobiography and part advice – has a great deal of down-to-earth common sense. His famous 'manifesto' on directors' theatre is spot on.

Nicholas Craig, *I, an Actor* (Pavilion Books, 1988). A very funny send-up of the starry actor's autobiography. A must.

Uta Hagen, *A Challenge for the Actor* (Macmillan, 1991). The best book on acting ever written.

Richard Hornby, *The End of Acting: a radical view* (Applause Books, 1992). Revelatory insights into the processes of acting.

David Mamet, *True and False* (Faber & Faber, 1998). This book cuts through much of the mythology that surrounds acting.

Kenneth Rea, *A Better Direction* (Calouste Gulbenkian Foundation, 1989). A very thorough inquiry into directors and the need for more training opportunities.

Patsy Rodenburg, *An Actor Speaks* (Methuen, 1997). An entirely practical guide with excellent advice and exercises to help develop the performer's voice.

Michael Sanderson, *From Irving to Olivier – A Social History of the Acting Profession* (Athlone Press, 1984). A very expensive, but nevertheless fascinating, study of the actor's world over the last century.

Michael Shurtleff, *Audition* (Walker & Company, 1984). An American book which should be read. It contains brilliant insights and thoughts to help any actor.

The Spotlight, *Contacts* (The Spotlight, annually in October). Contact details for everything you can think of (and more) that relates to the performing arts in general.

Webography

What follows is a selected collection of the most important websites for aspirants and professionals, and some others which the editors have found extremely useful, but don't quite fit elsewhere in this book.

Important websites for aspirants and professionals

www.actorscentre.co.uk – Actors Centre London
www.actorscentrene.co.uk – Actors Centre North East
www.agents-uk.com – Agents' Association of Great Britain
www.bbc.co.uk – BBC homepage
www.bbc.co.uk/drama/radio – BBC Radio Drama
www.thecdg.co.uk – Casting Directors Guild
www.drama.ac.uk – Conference of Drama Schools, with links to member schools' websites
www.dfes.gov.uk – Department for Education & Skills
www.eif.co.uk – Edinburgh International Festival
www.edfringe.com – Edinburgh Festival Fringe
www.equity.org.uk – Equity
www.fringetheatre.org.uk – Fringe theatre network, with listings of and links to London Fringe venues
www.itc-arts.org – Independent Theatre Council homepage with links to member companies' websites
www.imdb.com – Internet Movie Database; catalogues all sorts of information on more than 250,000 films and the 900,000 people who helped to make them
www.ncdt.co.uk – National Council for Drama Training
www.northernactorscentre.co.uk – Northern Actors Centre
www.spotlight.com – The Spotlight publishes the most important actors' directories
www.thestage.co.uk – *The Stage*, contains news, information and job advertisements which are updated each Thursday
www.art.ntu.ac.uk/scudd – Standing Conference of University Drama Departments
www.ucas.ac.uk – UCAS, the central organisation that processes applications for full-time undergraduate courses at UK universities and colleges

Other useful websites

www.artsline.org.uk – Arts-Line, provides access information on arts venues
www.bfi.org.uk/filmtvinfo/ftvdb – the British Film Institute's film and television database
www.britfilms.com – an extensive source of information on the UK film industry
www.britishtheatreguide.info – lots of articles, reviews and links about British theatre
www.companieshouse.gov.uk – Companies House: useful for checking background details (like date of foundation) of individual companies
www.edhooks.com – contains some interesting articles on acting
www.excellentvoice.co.uk – information and advice for voice-over artists with examples of good voice demos online
www.hiddenextra.com – a useful online guide for those looking to become supporting artistes

www.its-behind-you.com – seemingly a comprehensive list of pantomimes and their producers

www.ku.edu/~idea – the International Dialects of English Archive (IDEA) is a useful collection of English-language dialects and English spoken in the accents of other languages

www.officiallondontheatre.co.uk – Society of London Theatre website with news, reviews and booking information

www.royalist.info – a database that provides biographical details of thousands of individuals who have either belonged to, or been connected with, the royal family of England and Scotland during more than 1000 years of history

www.shakespeare-online.com – electronic copies of the plays and poems, along with other related material of interest. These copies of the texts should be checked against published editions before use in audition or performance, in order to gain the benefit of modern scholarship

www.simon.dunmore.btinternet.co.uk – advice on many aspects of the profession, including auditioning, marketing and good professional practice

www.sound.co.uk – information and advice for voice-over artists with links to many other sites

www.susan.croft.btinternet.co.uk/Supplements/Blackplays.htm – lists the work of those Afro-Caribbean and Asian playwrights whose work has been published, and in most cases produced, in Britain

www.theatredigz.com – a site aimed solely at touring professionals within the UK entertainment industry

www.theatrenet.com – news, events and special offers and links to agents, producers, theatre companies, venues and more

www.uksponsorship.com – an online database of UK sponsorship opportunities

www.uktw.co.uk – UK Theatre Web, with information, events and tickets for theatre in the UK

www.usefee.tv – a site which lets performers, their representatives and employers quickly calculate the appropriate use fee for featured players in TV commercials based on the established, industry-endorsed method approved by the Personal Managers' Association, the Association of Model Agents and Equity

www.visit4info.com – a site where you can see recent television and cinema commercials and get details of the companies who created them

www.vocalist.org.uk – a site for singers, vocalists, singing teachers and students of voice of all ages, standards and styles. The site contains useful information on aspects of singing, performance, plus free online singing lessons and articles for vocalists related to singing and getting into the music industry

www.voiceovers.co.uk – a forum for voice-over artists to advertise themselves

www.whatsonstage.com – a UK theatre listing service with search facilities, a ticket-ordering service, reviews, news and debate

Index